# CHOOSING BETWEEN POSSIBLE LIVES

To what extent should parents be able to choose the kind of child they have? The unfortunate phrase 'designer baby' has become familiar in debates surrounding reproduction. As a reference to current possibilities the term is misleading, but the phrase may indicate a societal concern of some kind about control and choice in the course of reproduction. Typically, people can choose whether to have a child. They may also have an interest in choosing, to some extent, the conditions under which they do so, such as whether they have a child with a serious disability or disease. The purpose of this book is to explore the difficult and controversial question of the appropriate ethical and legal extent of reproductive autonomy in this context.

The book examines ethical, legal and public policy issues in prenatal screening, prenatal diagnosis (PND), selective abortion and preimplantation genetic diagnosis (PGD). It explores the ethics of these selection practices and the ability of current ethical guidelines and legal mechanisms, including the law on selective abortion and wrongful birth, to deal with advances in genetic and other knowledge in these areas. Unlike in the United States, in England the relevant law is not inherently rights-based, but the impact of the Human Rights Act 1998 inevitably raises questions about the proper scope of reproductive autonomy in this context.

The implications of the analysis are considered for the development of relevant law, public policy and ethical guidelines and will be of interest to ethicists, lawyers, health professionals, academics, those working on public policy and students with an interest in these issues.

# Choosing Between Possible Lives

Law and Ethics of Prenatal and
Preimplantation Genetic Diagnosis

Rosamund Scott

·HART·
PUBLISHING

OXFORD AND PORTLAND, OREGON
2007

Published in North America (US and Canada) by
Hart Publishing
c/o International Specialized Book Services
920 NE 58th Avenue, Suite 300
Portland, OR 97213–3786
USA
Tel: +1 503 287 3093 or toll-free: (1) 800 944 6190
Fax: +1 503 280 8832
E-mail: orders@isbs.com
Website: http://www.isbs.com

© Rosamund Scott 2007

Rosamund Scott has asserted her right under the Copyright, Designs and Patents Act 1988, to be identified as the author of this work.

All rights reserved. No part of this publication may be reproduced, stored in a retrieval system, or transmitted, in any form or by any means, without the prior permission of Hart Publishing, or as expressly permitted by law or under the terms agreed with the appropriate reprographic rights organisation. Enquiries concerning reproduction which may not be covered by the above should be addressed to Hart Publishing at the address below.

Hart Publishing, 16C Worcester Place, OX1 2JW
Telephone: +44 (0)1865 517530 Fax: +44 (0)1865 510710
E-mail: mail@hartpub.co.uk
Website: http://www.hartpub.co.uk

British Library Cataloguing in Publication Data
Data Available

ISBN: 978-1-84113-718-6

Typeset by Columns Design Ltd, Reading
Printed and bound in Great Britain by
TJ International Ltd, Padstow, Cornwall

To Riccardo

and our newborn son

# *Acknowledgements*

I would like to thank the Arts and Humanities Research Council for its generous award of Research Leave. This enabled me to complete the book. I would also like to thank the School of Law, King's College London for its very helpful grant of sabbatical leave that preceded this. Without both of these, I would not yet have been able to finish this work. I would also like to thank my publisher, Richard Hart, for his decision to publish this book, Melanie Hamill for ensuring its production and Michael Bentley for his skilful copyediting of my text.

Several people have been kind enough to read and comment on earlier drafts of some of the chapters and I would particularly like to thank them. Roger Crisp read Chapters 1, 5 and 6; Jonathan Glover read Chapter 1 and work that formed the basis of Chapter 5; Stephen Wilkinson read Chapters 1 and 5 and also discussed issues relevant to Chapter 6. I am enormously grateful to each of them for their generosity in taking the time to comment in detail on the material they read and to discuss it so helpfully with me. I am also very grateful to two clinicians for reading and commenting on parts of the book. One is Susan Bewley, from the Department of Obstetrics/Maternal-Fetal Medicine, Guy's and St Thomas' Hospital, London. Until May 2007 she was the Chair of the Royal College of Obstetricians and Gynaecologists Ethics Committee. She read and commented on Chapter 2 and her insights were extremely valuable. The other is Peter Braude, from the Department of Women's Health/Centre for PGD, King's College London. He is the former Chair of the Scientific Advisory Committee of the Royal College of Obstetricians and Gynaecologists. He read and commented on an earlier version of Chapter 4 and his knowledge and experience have been very helpful indeed. I would also like to thank Bobbie Farsides, Kathryn Ehrich, Jane Sandall and Clare Williams, with whom I worked on a project entitled 'Facilitating Choice, Framing Choice: the Experience of Staff Working in PGD', funded by the Wellcome Trust. (Peter Braude was also a member of this research group.) I am very grateful to each of them for numerous discussions about PGD and for reading and commenting on an earlier version of Chapter 4. I have found working with them all hugely rewarding. I would particularly like to thank Bobbie Farsides also for broader discussions of relevance to the book as a whole. I would also very much like to thank the staff who kindly agreed to be interviewed as part of this project on PGD and to take part in ethics discussion groups.

I would also very much like to thank several people for support and encouragement that has made a great difference to me, namely Margot Brazier,

Roger Crisp, Jonathan Glover, John Harris, Sandy McCall Smith, Sally Sheldon and Stephen Wilkinson. And in this respect I would particularly like to thank Jonathan Glover.

Finally, I am very grateful to my friends and family for their encouragement and interest. And I thank specially my husband, Riccardo Rebonato, for all the talks we have had of relevance to this book and for his belief, love and support.

I am grateful to Oxford University Press for allowing me to make extensive use of material which originally appeared in the *Medical Law Review*, namely: Chapter 3, which originates in my 'Prenatal Screening, Autonomy and Reasons: the Relationship between the Law of Abortion and Wrongful Birth', (2003) 11/3 *Medical Law Review* 265–325, and Chapter 4 which originates in 'The Appropriate Extent of Preimplantation Genetic Diagnosis: Health Professionals' Views on the Requirement for a "Significant Risk of a Serious Genetic Condition"', (2007) 15/3 *Medical Law Review* 320–356, which I wrote with Clare Williams, Kathryn Ehrich and Bobbie Farsides.

# Contents

| | |
|---|---|
| Acknowledgements | vii |
| List of Abbreviations | xv |
| Table of Cases | xvii |
| Table of Legislation | xxi |

| | | |
|---|---|---|
| **Introduction — Purpose and Plan of the Book** | | **1** |
| **Chapter 1: Ethical Issues in Selection Practices — Whose Interests are at Stake?** | | **11** |
| I | Introduction | 11 |
| II | Reproductive Autonomy and the Embryo or Fetus | 12 |
| | A  Choosing Whether to Have a Child | 12 |
| | B  The Possibility of a Disabled Child | 14 |
| | C  Reproductive Autonomy and the Positive Duties Inherent in Child-raising | 15 |
| | D  The Moral Status of the Embryo and Fetus | 20 |
| | E  The Scope of Reproductive Autonomy: Interests, Reasons and Rights | 23 |
| III | Understandings of Disability | 26 |
| | A  Models of Disability | 27 |
| | B  Flourishing | 28 |
| | C  The Severity of a Condition | 29 |
| |    i  A life that someone may think is not worth living | 29 |
| |    ii  A life that someone will think is worth living | 30 |
| |    iii  Severity: whose interests? | 32 |
| IV | Birth and Harm | 34 |
| | A  A Life that Someone May Think is Not Worth Living | 34 |
| | B  A Life that Someone Will Think is Worth Living | 37 |
| | C  Person- and Non-person-affecting Principles | 38 |
| |    i  Moral requirements | 42 |
| |       a) The stage of development of the fetus | 44 |
| |       b) The difficulty of judging a disability to be serious | 45 |
| |       c) Costs or difficulties or loss of benefits for parents | 46 |
| |    ii  Moral permissibility | 47 |

x  *Contents*

| V | The Interests of People with Impairments | 48 |
|---|---|---|
| | A  Models of Disability and Discrimination Issues | 48 |
| | B  Information and Assumptions about Suffering or Difficulty | 50 |
| | C  The 'Expressivist Objection' | 54 |
| |    i  The fetus and personhood | 54 |
| |    ii  Devaluing impairments but equally valuing those with impairments | 57 |
| |    iii  The 'any/particular' distinction | 59 |
| |    iv  Interweaving parents' and children's interests | 62 |
| |    v  Opportunity — non-person-affecting principles again | 64 |
| VI | Eugenics | 65 |
| VII | Conclusions | 68 |

**Chapter 2: Selective Abortion — The Interpretation and Operation of the Law**     **71**

| I | Introduction | 71 |
|---|---|---|
| II | Exploring the Terms of the Disability Ground of the Abortion Act | 73 |
| | A  'Substantial Risk' | 73 |
| |    i  *Hansard* | 73 |
| |    ii  RCOG guidelines | 73 |
| | B  'Serious Handicap' | 76 |
| |    i  *Hansard* | 76 |
| |    ii  RCOG guidelines | 77 |
| |       a) The probability of effective treatment *in utero* or after birth | 78 |
| |       b) The probable degree of self-awareness and of ability to communicate with others | 81 |
| |       c) The suffering that would be experienced | 82 |
| |       d) The extent to which the actions essential for health that normal individuals perform unaided would have to be provided by others | 83 |
| |       e) The probability of being able to live alone and to be self-supporting as an adult | 85 |
| III | A Woman's or Couple's Moral and Legal Interests in Decisions Relating to Selective Abortion | 86 |
| | A  Parents' Moral Interests in Being Able to Choose Whether to Have a Disabled Child | 86 |
| | B  Legal Interests | 89 |
| |    i  Parents' possible legal interests in the interpretation of the disability ground of the Abortion Act | 89 |
| |    ii  Implications of the wrongful birth cases | 94 |
| IV | Cases Under the European Convention on Human Rights | 102 |

|   |   |   |   | 
|---|---|---|---|
|   | A | Article 8 | 102 |
|   | B | Article 2 | 103 |
|   | C | Legal Protection: Fetal Rights or Fetal Value? | 108 |
|   | D | Article 3 | 112 |
|   | E | Article 14 | 116 |
| V | Abortion for Fetal Anomaly After 24 Weeks | | 119 |
|   | A | The Pregnant Woman's Interests | 122 |
|   | B | The Fetus's Interests | 124 |
|   | C | Factors Overall | 134 |
| VI | Conclusions | | 137 |

## Chapter 3: Informational Duties — the Impact on Prenatal Screening, Diagnosis and Selective Abortion      143

|   |   |   |   |
|---|---|---|---|
| I | Introduction | | 143 |
| II | Consent to Screening and Diagnosis: Information and Counselling | | 144 |
|   | A | Capacity | 145 |
|   | B | Voluntariness: Offers of Screening and Testing | 145 |
|   | C | Information: Nature and Purpose, Not Results of Screening or Testing | 149 |
| III | The Effect of a Rights-Based Approach to Abortion on Prenatal Screening and Testing | | 153 |
|   | A | The Right to Abort For Any Reason | 153 |
|   | B | The Role of the Medical Profession | 155 |
|   | C | Autonomy — Information That Aids, Not Burdens | 157 |
| IV | The Role of Wrongful Birth Liability | | 160 |
|   | A | Tort's Concern to Protect Reproductive Autonomy, But Only So Far | 160 |
|   | B | Issues of Conscience for the Medical Profession | 162 |
|   | C | The Basis of the Wrongful Birth Action | 166 |
|   | D | The Standard of Care: Traditional Negligence or Negligent Non-disclosure | 169 |
|   |   | i   The risk of a given fetal condition | 172 |
| V | The Relationship Between the Seriousness of a Fetal Condition and the Reasons for Exercising Reproductive Autonomy | | 178 |
|   | A | Reasons: A Moral Framework | 178 |
|   | B | Reasons: The Law | 181 |
|   |   | i   Reasons in abortion law | 181 |
|   |   | ii  Reasons in wrongful birth case law | 182 |
|   |   | iii Defining seriousness in wrongful birth case law | 185 |

xii  *Contents*

        iv  Implications for the current and future scope of the wrongful birth action    187

VI  Conclusions    192

**Chapter 4: Preimplantation Genetic Diagnosis — The Interpretation and Operation of the Law    197**

I  Introduction    197

II  Background and Legal Context    199

III  The Recommendations on Risk and Seriousness    205
    A  'Significant Risk'    207
    B  'Serious Genetic Condition'    208
    C  The PGD Guidance    209

IV  Health Professionals' and Scientists' Views and Experience    211
    A  'Significant Risk'    212
    B  'Serious Genetic Condition'    213
        i  The view of those seeking treatment of the condition    214
        ii  The likely degree of suffering associated with the condition    220
            a  Very serious conditions    220
            b  Less serious conditions    225
                1  Cystic fibrosis    225
                2  Down's Syndrome    228
        iii  The extent of any intellectual impairment    237
        iv  The extent of social support available    237
        v  The family circumstances of the people seeking treatment    238
        vi  The availability of effective therapy or management now and in the future    239
        vii  The speed of degeneration in progressive disorders    240
        viii  Their previous reproductive experience    242

V  Conclusions    243

**Chapter Five: The Future Scope of Preimplantation Genetic Diagnosis    247**

I  Introduction    247

II  Fears of Trivial or Eugenic Use of Embryos    249

III  The Interests at Stake: The Reasons for Choosing Between Possible Lives    252
    A  The Moral and Legal Status of the Embryo and Fetus    253
    B  The Subject of Moral Concern    256

|     |     |     |                                                                                          |      |
| --- | --- | --- | ---------------------------------------------------------------------------------------- | ---- |
|     | C   |     | Selecting Against 'Serious' Genetic Anomalies                                            | 257  |
|     | D   |     | Selecting Against Or For Purely Aesthetic or Generally Trivial Features                  | 260  |
|     |     | i   | Parents' interests and attitudes: central versus marginal features                       | 261  |
|     |     | ii  | The child's interests: autonomy and flourishing                                          | 264  |
|     |     | iii | The claims of the embryo and the processes in PGD                                        | 270  |
|     |     | iv  | The professionals involved in IVF and PGD                                                | 274  |
|     |     | v   | The interests of those with impairments                                                  | 275  |
|     |     | vi  | The issue of legalisation                                                                | 277  |
|     | E   |     | Selecting in Favour of 'Serious' Features                                                | 279  |
|     |     | i   | Selecting for intelligence                                                               | 280  |
|     |     | ii  | Selecting for better health                                                              | 283  |
|     |     | iii | Selecting for specific aptitudes or abilities                                            | 285  |
| IV  | Conclusions |  |                                                                                  | 288  |

## Chapter Six: Uses of Preimplantation Genetic Diagnosis — Two Particular Cases .......... 297

|     |     |     |                                                                                          |      |
| --- | --- | --- | ---------------------------------------------------------------------------------------- | ---- |
| I   | Introduction |  |                                                                                 | 297  |
| II  | Selecting for Disability |  |                                                                     | 297  |
|     | A   |     | Person-affecting and Non-Person-Affecting Principles and Harm Revisited                  | 298  |
|     | B   |     | Choosing a Deaf Embryo Versus Failing to Cure a Deaf Child                               | 300  |
|     | C   |     | 'Sarah Can Hear, But I Can't'                                                            | 304  |
|     | D   |     | Parents' Possible Interests in Selecting for Disability and Implications for Third-Party Assistance | 307  |
|     | E   |     | Deafness and Opportunity                                                                 | 309  |
|     | F   |     | Selecting for Achondroplasia                                                             | 314  |
|     | G   |     | Selecting for Down's Syndrome or Cystic Fibrosis                                         | 315  |
|     | H   |     | Implications Overall                                                                     | 318  |
| III | Sex Selection |  |                                                                                | 319  |
|     | A   |     | Parents' and Children's Interests                                                        | 321  |
|     | B   |     | The Claims of the Embryo and the Processes in IVF and PGD                                | 323  |
|     | C   |     | The Views of Clinicians, Scientists and Those With Impairments                           | 326  |
|     | D   |     | The Views of the HFEA and Government: Is Legal Prohibition Justified?                    | 327  |
|     |     | i   | Analysis under Article 8(1) of the ECHR                                                  | 330  |
|     |     | ii  | Analysis under Article 8(2) of the ECHR                                                  | 332  |
|     |     |     | a) In accordance with law                                                                | 332  |
|     |     |     | b) Legitimate aim                                                                        | 333  |
|     |     |     | c) Necessary in a democratic society                                                     | 333  |
|     |     |     |     1  Pressing social need                                | 335  |
|     |     |     |     2  Proportionate to the legitimate aim pursued         | 335  |

|   |   |   |   |
|---|---|---|---|
|   | 3 | Relevant and sufficient reasons | 336 |
|   | 4 | Implications: justifiable interference? | 336 |
| IV | Conclusions |   | 345 |

**Bibliography**     **351**

**Index**     **359**

# List of Abbreviations

| | |
|---|---|
| ACOG | American College of Obstetricians and Gynecologists |
| AGCT | Advisory Committee on Genetic Testing |
| CFTR | Cystic Fibrosis Transmembrane Conductance Regulator |
| CMV | Cytomegalovirus |
| CPS | Crown Prosecution Service |
| CVS | Chorionic villus sampling |
| EB | Epidermolysis bullosa |
| ECHR | European Convention on Human Rights |
| ECtHR | European Court of Human Rights |
| EDG | Ethics discussion group |
| HFE Act | Human Fertilisation and Embryology Act 1990 |
| HFEA | Human Fertilisation and Embryology Authority |
| HGC | Human Genetics Commission |
| HLA | Human leukocyte antigen |
| HPRT | *hypoxanthine-guanine phosphoribosyltransferase* |
| IVF | *In vitro* fertilisation |
| JWP | Joint Working Party of the HFEA and HGC |
| LNS | Lesch-Nyhan syndrome |
| NHS | National Health Service |
| PGD | Preimplantation genetic diagnosis |
| PGS | Preimplantation genetic screening |
| PND | Prenatal diagnosis |
| PVS | Persistent vegetative state |
| RCOG | Royal College of Obstetricians and Gynaecologists |
| TSD | Tay-Sachs disease |

# Table of Cases

### NATIONAL

**Australia**

Rogers v Whittaker (1992) 67 ALJR 47................................................................. 168

**Canada**

Reibl v Hughes (1980) 114 DLR (3d) 1................................................................. 168

**United Kingdom**

A v Secretary of State for the Home Department [2004] UKHL 56.......................... 333
Alcock v Chief Constable of South Yorkshire Police [1991] 2 All ER 907................. 182
Allen v Bloomsbury HA [1993] 1 All ER 651.................................................. 96, 98
Attorney-General's Reference (No 3 of 1994) [1997] 3 All
  ER 936........................................................................ 106, 107, 111, 192
B, Re [1981] 1 WLR 1421............................................................................ 124
Bagley v North Herts Health Authority [1986] NLJ Rep 1014.................................. 167
Barr v Matthews (1999) 52 BMLR 217............................................................ 164
Bolam v Friern Hospital Management Committee [1957] 2 All ER 118.................... 171
Bolitho v City of Hackney HA [1997] 4 All ER 771 ............................................. 171
Bolton v Stone [1951] AC 850 ..................................................................... 173
C (Adult: Refusal of Medical Treatment), Re [1994] 1 FLR 31................................ 145
C, Re [1990] Fam 26........................................................................... 124, 151
C v S [1988] QB 135............................................................................ 71, 103
Chatterton v Gerson [1981] 1 All ER 257................................................... 144, 166
Chester v Afshar [2004] 4 All ER 587............................................................. 168
Deriche v Ealing Hospital NHS Trust [2003] EWHC 3104.................................... 169
Enright v Kwun [2003] EWHC 1000............................................................ 167
F, Re [1988] 2 All ER 193.......................................................................... 103
Groom v Selby [2002] 64 BMLR 47 ............................................................... 96
Hardman v Amin (2001) 59 BMLR 58........................................................... 96
Housecroft v Burnett [1986] 1 All ER 332....................................................... 96
J (a minor), Re [1991] Fam 33..................................................................... 124
J (a minor) (wardship: medical treatment), Re (1990) 6 BMLR 25.......................... 156
Jepson v The Chief Constable of West Mercia Police Constabulary [2003] EWHC
  3318 ............................................................ 71, 72, 77, 78, 80, 92, 112, 137, 140
JT (Adult: Refusal of Medical Treatment), Re [1998] 1 FLR 48.............................. 145
Latimer v AEC [1953] AC 643.................................................................... 175
Lee v Taunton and Somerset NHS Trust [2001] 1 FLR 419 .................................... 96
Lillywhite v University College London Hospitals NHS Trust [2005] EWCA Civ
  1466 ................................................................................................ 167
McFarlane v Tayside Health Board [2000] 2 AC 59 ...................... 95, 96, 97, 98, 99, 139
McKay v Essex AHA [1982] 2 WLR 890 ................................................... 118, 216

MB (Adult: Refusal of Medical Treatment), Re (1997) 8 Med
    LR 217 .................................................................................. 104, 145, 151, 254
P v Leeds Teaching Hospitals NHS Trust [2004] EWHC 1392 ................................ 167
Paris v Stepney Borough Council [1951] AC 367 ................................................ 184
Parkinson v St James and Seacroft University Hospital NHS Trust [2002]
    QB 266 ................................................................................ 95, 96, 97, 189
Paton v BPAS [1979] QB 276 ........................................................................ 71, 72
Pearce v United Bristol Healthcare NHS Trust [1999] PIQR 53 ................. 168, 185
Portsmouth Hospitals NHS Trust v Wyatt (2005) EWCA Civ 1181 ..................... 124
R (Carson) v Secretary of State for Work and Pensions [2006] 1 AC 173 ............. 117
R v Bourne (1938) 3 All ER 612 ................................................................... 122
R v Gibson and Sylveire [1991] 1 All ER 439 ................................................. 271
R v Smith (1974) 58 Cr App R 106 ................................................................ 72
Rance v Mid-Downs Health Authority [1991] 1 QB 587 ................... 94, 161, 189
Rand v East Dorset Health Authority [2000] 56
    BMLR 39 ................................................................. 33, 94, 95, 96, 97, 99, 139, 161
Rees v Darlington Memorial NHS Trust [2004] 1 AC 309 .......................... 98, 139
St George's Healthcare NHS Trust v S, R, Collins, ex parte S [1998] 3 All ER
    673 .................................................................................................. 111, 192
Sidaway v Board of Governors of the Bethlem Royal Hospital [1985] 1 AC 871 ...... 145,
                                                                                                151, 168
Smith v Barking, Havering and Brentwood HA [1994] 5 Med LR 285 ............ 101, 169
T (a minor) (Wardship: medical treatment), Re [1997] 1 All ER 906 ...................... 127
T, Re [1992] 4 All ER 649 ................................................................ 144, 146, 147
The Queen on the Application of Quintavalle v Human Fertilisation and
    Embryology Authority [2003] EWCA Civ 667 (CA), [2005] 2 All ER 555
    (HL) ................................................................. 200, 250, 251, 252, 268, 341
U v Centre for Reproductive Medicine [2002] 1 FLR 927 ...................................... 147

**United States**
Akron v Akron Centre for Reproductive Health, 35 L Ed 2d 147 (1973) .......... 153, 163
Arche v US Department of Army, 798 P2d 477 (Kansas 1990) ......................... 183, 184
Atlanta Obstetrics and Gynecology Group v Abelson, 398 SE 2d 557 (Ga 1990) ....... 183
Azzolino v Dingfelder, 337 SE2d 528 (NC 1985), cert denied, 479
    US 835 (1986) .................................................................................... 166, 183
Bardessono v Michels, 3 Cal 3d 780 (1970) ........................................................ 171
Berman v Allan, 404 A 2d 8 (1979) .............................................................. 160, 184
Canesi v Wilson, 158 NJ 490 (1999) ................................ 161, 166, 169, 170, 184, 186
Canterbury v Spence, 464 F2d 772 (DC 1972) ......................... 166, 168, 169, 173, 174
Colautti v Franklin, 58 L Ed 2d 596 (1979) ...................................................... 163
Dansby v Jefferson, 623 A2d 816 (PA Super 1993) .............................. 54, 94, 162, 170
Doe v Bolton, 35 L Ed 2d .............................................................................. 156, 163
Edmonds v W Pa Hosp Radiology Assoc, 621 A 2d 580 (Pa 1993), cert denied,
    114 SCt 63 (1993) ................................................................................ 166
Eisenstadt v Baird, 405 US 438 (1972) ............................................................... 158
Gonzales v Carhart (2007) 127 SCt 1610 .......................................................... 155
Griswold v Connecticut, 14 L Ed 2d 510 (1965) ........................................... 154, 158
Grubbs v Barbourville Family Health Centre, 120 SW 3d 682 (Ky 2003) ................ 183

Harris v McRae, 65 L Ed 2d 784 (1986) .................................................................. 158
Hickman v Group Health, 396 NW 2d 10 (Minn 1986) ................................. 164, 165
Karlsons v Guerinot, 394 NYS2d 933 (1977) .............................................................. 167
Largey v Rothman, 110 NJ 204............................................................................... 169
Maher v Roe, 53 L Ed 2d 484 (1977) ..................................................................... 158
Munro v Regents of University of California, 263 Cal Rptr 878 (Cal App 2 Dist
    1989) .............................................................................................................. 172
Planned Parenthood of Southeastern Pennsylvania v Casey, 120 LEd2d 674 (1992) .... 55,
    110, 154, 155, 156, 157, 163, 164, 165
Reed v Campagnolo, 630 A 2d 1145 (Md, 1993) ............................. 166, 169, 170, 171
Robak v US, 658 F2d 471 (1981)............................................................................ 165
Roe v Wade, 35 LEd2d 147 (1973) ..... 94, 110, 153, 154, 155, 156, 157, 160, 163, 165,
    169, 182, 183, 184, 185
Roe v Wade (1986) 95 Yale LJ 639 ........................................................................... 22
Schloss v Miriam Hospital, No CA 98–2076 (RI Super Ct, 11 January 1999) .... 94, 162
Seipal v Corson, 637 A 2d 289 (Pa 1993), cert denied, 115 SCt 60 (1994) ............... 166
Smith v Cote, 513 A 2d 341 (NH, 1986)................................ 160, 166, 171, 182, 184
Sojourner T v Edwards, 974 F 2d 27 (5th Cir 1992) ................................................ 155
Stenberg v Carhart, 530 US 914.............................................................................. 155
Thornburgh v American College of Obstetricians and Gynecologists, 76 L Ed
    2d 687 (1983).................................................................................................. 153
United States v Vuitch, 28 L Ed 2d 601 (1971)......................................................... 158
Verkennes v Corniea, 38 NW2d 838 (1949).............................................................. 167
Webster v Reproductive Health Services, 106 L Ed 2d 410 (1989).................... 155, 157
Wilson v Kuenzi, 751 SW2d 741 (Mo 1988), cert denied, 488 US 893 (1988)......... 166
Wisconsin v Yoder, 406 US 205 (1972)...................................................................... 262

### EUROPEAN COURT OF HUMAN RIGHTS

Abdulaziz, Cabales and Balkandali v UK (1985) 7 EHRR 471.................................. 116
Ahmut v Netherlands (1996) 24 EHRR 62............................................................... 332
Barthold v Germany (1985) 7 EHRR 383 ................................................................ 333
Botta v Italy (1998) 26 EHRR 241 .......................................................................... 116
Brüggemann and Scheuten v Germany (1981) 3 EHRR 244 ............ 102, 103, 105, 278
Costello-Roberts v United Kingdom (1995) 19 EHRR 112...................................... 331
Dudgeon v United Kingdom (1981) 4 EHRR 149 .................................................. 334
Evans v United Kingdom, Appl No 6339/05, Judgment of 10 April 2007. 104, 332, 342
Fredin v Sweden (1991) 13 EHRR 784 ................................................................... 117
Halford v United Kingdom (1997) 24 EHRR 423................................................... 332
Handyside v United Kingdom (1976) 1 EHRR 737 ................................. 333, 334, 335
Ireland v United Kingdom (1978) 2 EHRR 25......................................................... 113
Jersild v Denmark (1995) 19 EHRR 1 .................................................................... 336
Keegan v Ireland (1994) 18 EHRR 342................................................................... 334
Kroon v Netherlands (1994) 19 EHRR 263............................................................. 332
Laskey, Jaggard and Brown v United Kingdom (1997) 24 EHRR 39 ....................... 331
Lithgow v UK (1986) 8 EHRR 329 ........................................................................ 117

McMichael v United Kingdom (1995) 20 EHRR 205 .............................................. 335
National and Provincial Building Society v UK (1997) 25 EHRR 127 ..................... 117
Niemietz v Germany (1992) 16 EHRR 97 ........................................................... 331
Paton v UK (1981) 3 EHRR 408....................................................... 104, 105, 106, 107
Petrovic v Austria (2001) 33 EHRR 307 ................................................................ 116
Pretty v United Kingdom (1998) 26 EHRR 241 ..................................................... 330
Rees v United Kingdom (1987) 9 EHRR 56............................................................ 103
RH v Norway, Appl No 17004/90 (1992)................................................................ 104
Soering v United Kingdom (1989) 11 EHRR 439..................................................... 335
Stjerna v Finland (1994) 24 EHRR 194................................................................. 334
Sunday Times v United Kingdom (1979) 2 EHRR 245 ............................................. 334
Tyrer v United Kingdom (1978) 2 EHRR 1 ............................................................. 331
Tysiac v Poland, Appl No 5410/03 (2007) .............................................................. 103
Vo v France, Appl No 53924/00, Judgment of 8 July 2004........ 104, 107, 110, 116, 139,
                                                                                                                         342
X v United Kingdom (1980) 19 D & R 244............................................................ 104
X and Y v Netherlands (1986) 8 EHRR 235............................................................ 331

# Table of Legislation

**United Kingdom**

*Primary legislation*

Abortion Act 1967 ...... 3, 5, 34, 49, 72, 73, 89, 102, 108, 119, 151, 171, 176, 181, 186, 189, 193, 208, 212, 244, 246, 253, 256
   s 1(1) ................................................................ 3, 49, 109, 152, 206, 247, 254
     (a) ... 4, 72, 74, 75, 86, 88, 90, 92, 93, 96, 112, 135, 137, 139, 152, 182, 213, 217, 254, 324, 339
     (b) ......................................... 104, 116, 117, 118, 122, 124, 135, 141, 255
     (c) ................................................................................. 104, 116, 118
     (d) .. 3, 71, 78, 90, 91, 92, 93, 94, 95, 97, 102, 104, 123, 124, 140, 152, 161, 182, 195, 216, 217, 247, 255
   s 5(1) ............................................................................................. 109

Carers and Disabled Children Act 2000, ........................................................ 18
Carers (Equal Opportunities) Act 2004, ......................................................... 18
Children Act 1989, ...................................................................................... 189
   s 1 ................................................................................................ 303
   s 17(2) .......................................................................................... 189
Congenital Disabilities (Civil Liability) Act 1976, 108

Disability Discrimination Act 1995 .......................................................... 17, 117

Fatal Accidents Act 1976 ........................................................................... 167

Human Fertilisation and Embryology Act 1990 ............... 3, 49, 71, 104, 109, 128, 152, 200, 203, 206, 211, 247, 254, 255, 293, 297, 324, 327, 329, 332, 336, 347
   s 2(1) .................................................................................... 200, 201
   s 13(5) ................................................................ 201, 202, 238, 259, 312, 313
   Sched.2 ............................................................................... 197, 252, 343
     para 1 ............................................................................... 193, 251
       (1),
       (3) ....................................................... 200, 201, 211, 251, 288
       (d) ....................................................................... 200, 201
     para 1ZA ......................................................................... 193, 211, 252
       (a) ................................................................................ 201
       (b) ................................................................................ 201
       (c) ................................................................................ 201
     para 1ZB .............................................................................. 343
     para 3 .................................................................................. 271
   Sched.3 .................................................................................. 312
Human Rights Act 1998 ....................................... 5, 73, 102, 104, 270, 297, 334
   s 6,
     (1) ............................................................................................ 329
     (3) ............................................................................................ 330

## xxii  Table of Legislation

Infant Life (Preservation) Act 1929 ............ 109
  s 1(1) ............ 109

Mental Capacity Act 2005 ............ 145
  s 1 ............ 145
    (2) ............ 145
  s 2 ............ 145
    (1) ............ 145
  s 3(1) ............ 145

Obscene Publications Act 1950 ............ 333
Offences Against the Person Act 1861 ............ 99
  s 58 ............ 99, 109, 208
  s 59 ............ 99, 109, 208

*Secondary legislation*

Human Fertilisation and Embryology (Research Purposes) Regulations 2001, (SI 2001/188) ............ 271

NHS (General Medical Services) Regulations 1992, (SI 1992/635) ............ 164
  Sched.2,
    para 12 ............ 164

## United States

California Health and Safety Code,

s 151 ............ 161

Pa Senate Leg J 267, 17 September 1984 ............ 166
Partial-Birth Abortion Ban Act 2003 ............ 155
Pennsylvania Consolidated Statutes,

Title 42,
  s 8305 ............ 162

## International Treaties and Conventions

European Convention on Human Rights ............ 4, 5, 73
  Art 2 ............ 102, 103, 104, 105, 106, 107, 108, 110, 116, 118, 139, 332
    (1) ............ 103
  Art 3 ............ 102, 112, 113, 115, 139
  Art 8.. 9, 102, 103, 104, 139, 269, 278, 279, 290, 297, 320, 327, 328, 329, 330, 331, 332, 334, 335, 336, 339, 340, 341, 342, 347, 348
    (1) ............ 103, 270, 278, 328, 330, 332
    (2) ............ 102, 103, 270, 278, 279, 328, 332, 333, 341, 346
  Art 10 ............ 333
  Art 14 ............ 102, 104, 112, 116, 117, 118, 124, 139, 332
  Art 18 ............ 333

# Introduction—Purpose and Plan of the Book

HAVING A CHILD and becoming responsible for its upbringing significantly changes a person's life. The degree of this change may be considerably affected by the characteristics of the child. Generally, people can choose whether to have a child. In the light of developments in prenatal screening and diagnosis (PND) and preimplantation genetic diagnosis (PGD), to some degree people can also make choices about what kind of child they might have, particularly about whether they give birth to one with a serious impairment, disease or disorder. With advances in genetics, the range of possible choices will grow. However, to what extent any given choice would be morally acceptable and should be legally permissible, either in relation to selective abortion or when embryos are to be created and tested by PGD, is a sharply contested question. It is the one with which this book is concerned.

The analysis explores the appropriate moral and legal scope of reproductive autonomy in the context of prenatal screening, PND and PGD. It does this by considering the ethics of selection practices and the implications for the interpretation and operation of the current law and its future development. The book offers some arguments about the appropriate extent of prospective parents' reproductive autonomy in this context. Broadly speaking, these suggest that, either regarding the fetus in an established pregnancy or the embryos that would need to be created and tested by PGD, prospective parents do have a legitimate moral interest, within reason, in making certain kinds of choices in this context. In turn, this is an interest that should be recognised through the interpretation and operation of the relevant law. An unusual feature of the analysis is its combination of ethical and legal discussion.

In *Chapter 1* I discuss some of the key ethical questions and theoretical issues underlying debates about prenatal and preimplantation selection practices. This is intended as a foundation to the rest of the book. I consider the idea of reproductive autonomy and suggest some reasons why it might give rise to an interest, not just in deciding whether or not to have a child, but also in having some say about what kind of child that may be. However, the scope of this interest is highly contested due to the controversial question of the moral status of the embryo and fetus. PGD concerns embryos, particularly concurrent choices between them and the discard of those created but not chosen, while prenatal screening and PND, accompanied by selective abortion, concern the loss of a developing fetus, which may sometimes be quite advanced, and the thought that prospective parents may attempt to replace that fetus with another in a future pregnancy. In this light, unless we think that neither the embryo nor the fetus has any moral claims (and many people do think this), there will need to be some moral justification for embryo creation and discard on the one hand or selective abortion on the other.

I endorse a gradualist approach to this issue, which understands the embryo and then fetus to have growing moral claims, so that increasingly strong reasons are needed to try to justify the loss of fetal life. In this light, it may be that prospective parents will be most justified in exercising their reproductive autonomy when their interests in the kind of child they have will be seriously implicated, which could include the scenario in which their child is seriously impaired. Moreover, in such a case the ability to exercise their reproductive autonomy by making choices about whether to accept the birth of a disabled child is likely to be highly valuable to them. In turn, prospective parents' reproductive autonomy will be most deserving of protection in these circumstances. At the same time, the moral permissibility of selection between embryos on the basis, say, of less than serious features will require consideration of a number of ethical and other issues, including the question of to what extent society has the right to proscribe certain practices, a topic I address in different ways in Chapters 5 and 6, when I turn to consider different aspects of PGD. As will be seen, the moral status of the embryo and fetus may in turn be relevant to our interpretation of the law, where this leaves room for judgment, as it clearly does both in the contexts of PGD and of selective abortion. In addition, it will be important to recognise the widespread disagreement about the embryo's and fetus's moral status and to think about whether, and if so how, law and policy should accommodate this.

The discussion in Chapter 1 also considers two different models of disability ('medical' and 'social'), and the relevance of disability to people's lives, particularly the manner in which it may (but will not necessarily) impede their capacity to flourish.[1] Whether disability seriously affects someone's ability to flourish is likely to depend, in part, on how severe any given condition is. In this regard, we can roughly distinguish between conditions in which there is a serious risk[2] that someone will think her life not worth living (the case of so-called 'wrongful life') and those in which it is very likely that a person will not think this. Very severe conditions are in fact surprisingly rare. This means that most prenatal and preimplantation genetic diagnosis probably concerns the detection and possible avoidance of conditions which a future child would think compatible with his life being worth living.

Importantly, reflecting on this requires that we consider the justification for the majority of prenatal and preimplantation selection practices. On one approach, we can look to the other parties involved. If any given child would think her life worth living, we have to consider whether much of current practice is really concerned, though not overtly, with the fact that it may be in prospective parents'

---

[1] This analysis draws on J Glover, *Choosing Children: Genes, Disability and Design* (Oxford: OUP, 2006) 9, 51.
[2] *Ibid* 60.

interests to have a say about the kind of reproductive future they are able to take on. In this way, these selection practices are, in effect, focusing on the possible impact on other people of the birth of a disabled child, here the parents who have the primary moral and legal responsibility of care. In turn, recognition of this should affect the way the law is interpreted and applied, as discussed in later chapters.

Another approach to the ethics of selection practices would be to compare the choice of two possible different children. This is to think about two different states of affairs or possible worlds. In so doing, and other things being equal, we can think about whether one possible person has at least the potential for greater flourishing and well-being than another. This is to consider the application of non-person-affecting principles. Their relevance to selection practices is explored with particular reference to the implications of such practices for the moral requirements of prospective parents on the one hand, and the moral permissibility of their choices on the other. Whether non-person-affecting principles can have much weight against the claims of the developing fetus, and how much weight they might have against the much less developed and as yet not implanted embryo, is another question.

Importantly, Chapter 1 also discusses the interests of people with impairments in prenatal screening, PND and PGD. I focus on the important question of the information about disability that accompanies selection practices, which proves to be a central ethical issue in this context. I also consider the implications of the so-called 'expressivist objection', which asserts that these selection practices send a message that people with disabilities should not be, or have been, born. Whatever we might decide about the actual content of the message sent by selection practices, the way in which these practices are conducted has the potential to send unintended, unhelpful and potentially harmful messages to or about people with impairments. So this, too, is a central ethical issue in this context.

Lastly, the chapter briefly discusses the notion of 'eugenics', about whose meaning there is very little agreement, and considers what place, if any, concerns about eugenics might have in contemporary kinds of selection.

Having laid a foundation of ethical analysis in Chapter 1, on which I build further ethical analysis as well as interpretation of the law in subsequent chapters, in *Chapter 2* I turn to explore the law on selective abortion in England. Abortion is legal under section 1(1)(d) of the Abortion Act 1967 (as amended by the Human Fertilisation and Embryology Act 1990) if two doctors have formed an opinion in good faith that 'there is a substantial risk that if the child were born it would suffer from such physical or mental abnormalities as to be seriously handicapped'.[3] The terms of this section leave considerable scope for interpretation, particularly about the meaning of 'seriously handicapped'. This is a highly

---

[3] The relevant part of s 1(1) of the Abortion Act 1967 as amended by the HFE Act 1990 reads: 'Subject to the provisions of this section, a person shall not be guilty of an offence

contentious issue. As matters stand, the law entrusts the operation of the Abortion Act to doctors. Further, to date there has been no direct judicial interpretation of this section. However, several sources give some indication as to how the disability ground of the Act might be interpreted in the courts and, significantly, about whether prospective parents' interests and views about the seriousness of a disability in their future child can and should be taken into account in decision-making in this context.

Of considerable value are the guidelines of the Royal College of Obstetricians and Gynaecologists (RCOG), intended for clinicians, on the interpretation of this section of the Act. Although these have no legal status, they would probably be very influential in a court. One set of guidelines discusses a number of factors relevant to the decision to terminate a pregnancy in which the fetus has a serious anomaly; another focuses specifically on terminations after 24 weeks' gestation. The RCOG guidelines adopt a gradualist approach to the fetus's moral status.[4] Moreover, we will see that this is also reflected in the law, since the least stringent ground for abortion ceases to apply after 24 weeks.[5]

There are also two important sources of indirectly related law which can guide us in interpreting the disability ground of the Abortion Act. First, English law has an established body of 'wrongful birth' case law. The liability that is the subject of these cases stems from the duty of care of health professionals to advise a woman about the risk of disability in the future child she is carrying, so that she can decide (in consultation with her partner or husband if desired) whether she would like to continue the current pregnancy. In exploring these cases, I consider the extent to which judges have paid attention to the autonomy interests of parents in making decisions about the birth of a disabled child. I also consider whether there is scope, within reason, for parents' views about the seriousness of a given condition in a future child to be relevant to the legal interpretation of 'serious' disability under the relevant ground of the Act.

The second source of relevant law is in parts of the case law on abortion and fetal harm under the European Convention on Human Rights (ECHR), which

---

under the law relating to abortion when a pregnancy is terminated by a registered medical practitioner if two registered medical practitioners are of the opinion, formed in good faith… (d) that there is a substantial risk that if the child were born it would suffer from such physical or mental abnormalities as to be seriously handicapped'.

[4] RCOG, *Termination of Pregnancy for Fetal Abnormality in England, Wales and Scotland* (January 1996); RCOG Ethics Committee, *A Consideration of the Law and Ethics in Relation to Late Termination of Pregnancy for Fetal Abnormality* (RCOG Press, March 1998).

[5] This is s 1(1)(a) of the Abortion Act, which reads: 'Subject to the provisions of this section, a person shall not be guilty of an offence under the law relating to abortion when a pregnancy is terminated by a registered medical practitioner if two registered medical practitioners are of the opinion, formed in good faith — (a) that the pregnancy has not exceeded twenty-four weeks and that the continuance of the pregnancy would involve risk, greater than if the pregnancy were terminated, of injury to the physical or mental health of the pregnant woman or any existing children of her family'.

was directly incorporated into English law by means of the Human Rights Act 1998. The current state of this area of law gives some indication as to the legal position in relation to the Convention both for a pregnant woman and for the fetus. Since the existing body of law is limited, however, I also analyse the application of various possible articles of the ECHR to this context.

Finally, the chapter considers the particularly contentious area of terminations for fetal anomaly after 24 weeks, when only the more stringent grounds for abortion in English law remain. This analysis is aided by further consideration of the RCOG guidelines, the legal position on the treatment of neonates and important recent policy statements by the Nuffield Council on Bioethics.[6] Can a late termination for fetal anomaly ever be in the fetus's interests? If this is not true of any given case, could such a termination be justified with reference to the interests of a pregnant woman? The analysis of the various sources in this chapter is woven together with ethical argument building on that developed in Chapter 1.

In *Chapter 3*, I turn to consider the way the law shapes the practices of prenatal screening and PND. I start by looking at the legal elements for consent to these, particularly the important requirements of voluntariness and information as to the nature and purpose of screening or testing. Voluntariness has the potential to be compromised by the increasingly routine nature of prenatal screening, while information about screening and diagnosis may currently tend to concentrate on its nature, rather than its purpose, failing to give detailed and, particularly, what may fairly be seen as 'balanced' information about the prospect of life with a disability.

However, the majority of this chapter is concerned with the *content* of information about the developing fetus that might be revealed in prenatal screening and testing. In particular, I look at the way the jurisprudence on wrongful birth liability influences the scope of healthcare professionals' positive duties to provide information about anomalies in the fetus. This is particularly important given that genetic knowledge, and so the scope of genetic testing, is constantly increasing. In this light, one question that might arise is whether women or couples are legally entitled to greater — or even full — information about the genetic or other status of their fetus. In England, as Chapter 2 indicates, the terms of the disability ground of the Abortion Act play a large role in shaping the scope and standard of the duty upon health professionals to impart information. However, if ever Parliament were to consider modifying English abortion law to allow a legal right to abort (at least until a certain point in pregnancy), one concern might be that this would give women and couples the right to limitless genetic and other information about the fetus and that in some cases they might abort for relatively trivial reasons.

---

[6] Nuffield Council on Bioethics, *Critical Care Decisions in Fetal and Neonatal Medicine: Ethical Issues* (2006).

6  Introduction

We can explore this concern by looking at a jurisdiction in which there is a clear legal right to abort. This chapter therefore examines the law relevant to prenatal screening and diagnosis both in England and in the United States. In effect, this is to explore in detail the interrelationship of the law of abortion and that of wrongful birth. I consider the standard of care to which health professionals' duties to inform are subject, which in turn will determine the extent of information about the developing fetus that a woman (or couple) is told. In this way, the wrongful birth cases tell us for which kinds of reason a woman (or couple) will be able to choose to terminate a pregnancy and so reveal important information about the current legal scope of reproductive autonomy. The cases also tell us about the possible impact of the standard of care on developments in screening and testing that result from increasing genetic and other knowledge.

If a couple knows or fears that they are at risk of having a child with a genetic condition or disease before a woman becomes pregnant they may seek *in vitro* fertilisation (IVF) and PGD. In the second half of the book I turn to consider legal and ethical issues surrounding the use of this technique, which involves genetic testing of a cell extracted from a six-to-ten-cell (day three) embryo fertilised and grown *in vitro*. A key advantage of PGD is that, where successful, it may enable parents to avoid moral or other difficulties in the termination of an already-established pregnancy.

The purpose of *Chapter 4* is to analyse the interpretation and operation of the current legal criteria that govern the provision of PGD. This can be performed where there is a 'significant risk of a serious genetic condition being present in the embryo', the criteria established by the Human Fertilisation and Embryology Authority (HFEA) and the Human Genetics Commission (HGC).[7] In this way, these bodies adopted the 'precautionary principle' of broadly aligning the legal criteria for PGD with those for selective abortion.[8]

The key question on which this chapter focuses is what weight, if any, is and should be given to a pregnant woman's (or couple's) views on the issues of the degree of risk and the seriousness of a disability in a future child. I explore this question in two main ways: first, by analysing those recommendations of the HFEA and HGC that focus on the criteria of 'significant risk' and 'serious genetic condition'; second, by considering the views and experience of at least some health professionals and scientists, ones who provide PGD at a particular (unnamed) UK clinic. The latter analysis is structured with reference to the factors that the HFEA and HGC considered should be relevant in the decision to offer PGD, factors now incorporated into the HFEA's Code of Practice. These include, for example, 'the view of those seeking treatment of the condition' and 'the likely degree of suffering associated with the condition'. It is striking to compare the

---

[7] HFEA and HGC, *Outcome of the Public Consultation on Preimplantation Genetic Diagnosis*, 18 June 2001, rec 11.
[8] *Ibid* para 25.

apparent current scope of reproductive autonomy in PGD with that in selective abortion and the more overt attention, at least, given to prospective parents' views in the former context.

In *Chapter 5* I consider some moral arguments for and against expanding the current legal scope of PGD. As the HGC has recently noted, it is unlikely ever to be possible to test for multi-factoral genetic traits, such as intelligence.[9] However, expansion in the scope and power of PGD and related techniques will mean that it is possible to test for an increasing array of single-gene conditions or features.[10] Generally, as the entirely misleading and unhelpful term 'designer baby' indicates, there is a good deal of societal concern about the degree to which we should permit various kinds of testing in PGD. This has found expression in the consultation processes surrounding its use.[11]

Broadly speaking, PGD could occur in two main ways, either by selecting against certain features or conditions (what is sometimes called 'negative' selection), or by selecting in favour of other features or conditions (sometimes called 'positive' selection). In fact, in either case one is implicitly selecting both for and against a given aspect at the same time but the terms represent, to some extent, a useful shorthand way of describing any given kind of selection.

This chapter reflects on what are largely hypothetical choices (though this may change in some cases) and asks whether there are reasons why people should only be able to select against serious impairments or disorders, rather than against or in favour of relatively trivial features such as purely aesthetic ones (that is, ones not associated with any underlying genetic condition), or in favour of more serious features, such as ones associated with health or intelligence. I explore these issues with reference to six main questions. First, could such choices be important to parents and does the answer to this matter? Second, what harm, if any, could come to the resulting child? Third, is it acceptable to create and destroy embryos in order to carry out such testing? Fourth, given that the assistance of various medical and scientific parties will be required in this process, are their interests or concerns relevant? Fifth (referring back to the discussion in Chapter 1), what might people who have impairments think about this kind of selection and to what extent should we take their views into account? Sixth, whatever people might think about the moral permissibility of such practices, does society have the right to proscribe them or should they instead be legalised?

In the final chapter, *Chapter 6*, I consider two very specific and currently possible uses of PGD: to select a child with an impairment or disorder of some

---

[9] HGC, *Making Babies: Reproductive Decisions and Genetic Technologies* (2006) para 7.42.

[10] Note, eg, the development of preimplantation genetic haplotyping (PGH), discussed in P Renwick 'Proof of Principle and First Cases using Preimplantion Genetic Haplotyping — a Paradigm Shift for Embryo Diagnosis' (2006) 13/1 *Reproductive Biomedicine Online* 758.

[11] HFEA and AGCT, *Consultation Document on Preimplantation Genetic Diagnosis*, November 1999, para 26; HFEA and HGC, above n 7, para 25.

kind, and to select a child of a given sex. The first would be an unusual choice for parents to make, while the second is one that may be of interest to quite a number of prospective parents, at least in cases where they are already undergoing IVF.

It is often thought that to select an embryo that would come to be a child with an impairment would be to harm it, but it is not clear that we can say this, at least using a comparative sense of harm. Any given embryo can only come to exist as one possible child and, unless that child would not think his life worth living (and so perhaps have a 'wrongful life'), it may be that selecting a child who would have an impairment neither wrongs him nor harms him, though there are different views about this. In order to see what selection for deafness would actually entail, here it is useful to compare the idea of selecting, say, an embryo that will come to be a deaf child and failing to cure a deaf child.

Throughout the discussion, it is helpful to recall the distinction between person-affecting and non-person-affecting principles first discussed in Chapter 1 and the thought that, other things being equal, it seems right that we have reason to prefer to bring into the world people who will start life with as full capacities as possible and therefore with the most potential, at least, for flourishing. This gives us a *prima facie* starting point, at least in relation to the embryo, which on some views may have rather less moral status than the developing fetus. (In relation to the latter, as noted earlier, the application of non-person-affecting principles may be somewhat disingenuous, even if the fetus is arguably not a moral person.) How do prospective parents' interests in having an impaired child, such as a deaf child when they themselves are deaf, measure up against this *prima facie* position? This requires that we think about the possible loss of opportunity in a condition such as deafness, and also about the implications for third parties, and public resources, in assisting parents to select such a child at the embryonic stage. If the subsequently born child has some residual capacity for hearing, will the parents owe her the offer of some kind of hearing aid?

The case of selection for deafness can be usefully compared with that of selection for achondroplasia (or dwarfism), which is not capable of medical correction. It is also valuable to think about the idea of prospective parents *without* a given condition who nevertheless want a child *with* a condition such as cystic fibrosis or Down's syndrome. Alternatively, what if a couple with the latter condition wished to have a child with Down's syndrome?

When I turn to consider sex selection for non-medical reasons, I acknowledge but leave to one side some of the traditional concerns about this kind of selection, such as that it would discriminate against women, because the evidence in the United Kingdom at least is that prospective parents, taken as a group, do not have a preference for one sex or another. I briefly discuss the issue of sex selection with reference to the questions I identified in Chapter 5, when I considered the reasons for and against expanding the scope of PGD. These include whether parents have a serious interest in this kind of selection, whether we have enough reason to be concerned about harm to children through sex selection, the implications for the embryo where several are created but not all can be used, the views of third parties and the interests of people with impairments. However, the main focus of the discussion is upon the justification for the legal ban on the practice. I consider the HFEA's and the government's views on sex selection, which looks set to remain illegal,[12] and here I return to the highly important question, first introduced in Chapter 5, of whether as a society we have the right to proscribe this kind of practice. I now take the opportunity to consider this question in more detail, with particular reference to the possible application of the right to respect for private and family life within Article 8 of the ECHR in this context.

As observed at the start, the book's central concern is with the appropriate moral and legal scope of reproductive autonomy or liberty. Prospective parents' interests in the kind of child they have are likely to be seriously invoked where a child would have a serious impairment or disorder, so that they have an interest in being able to choose whether to continue an established pregnancy, or whether to engage in IVF and PGD so as to test their embryos when they know they are at risk of having such a child. In such cases, making a choice to avoid the birth of a disabled child may be both morally justifiable (as regards the embryo or fetus) and highly valuable (as regards their own interests). By contrast, their interest in reproductive autonomy is unlikely to be seriously invoked, and therefore as justifiably exercised or of as much value, where what is in issue is the colour of their future child's hair or eyes. However, this may not give us a reason, by itself, to proscribe such a choice (at least at the stage of embryo selection). At the same time, it is important to emphasise that it is unlikely that many prospective parents would put their emotional or physical energies into this kind of selection, or that where they did try to do so, they would ultimately risk their reproductive future (the live birth of a child) by attaching such importance to this kind of choice that they opted not to implant any embryos on the basis, say, that none would come to be a child with green eyes. Rather, particularly when faced with the existence of their own embryos or their fetus(es) in an established pregnancy, prospective parents' interests and concerns are likely to be very serious and increasingly reflective.

The point of noting, at the outset, the serious concerns that prospective parents are likely to have in this context is to encourage reflection on the ethical issues and interpretation of the law in a way that gives appropriate attention to the very real concerns and claims that prospective parents may sometimes reasonably have. At the same time, the thought that such concerns and claims may well be, and preferably should be, in some sense reasonable, acknowledges the need for an ethical and legal balance between, in particular, the interests of prospective parents and the claims of the embryo or fetus that is the subject of these selection

---

[12] Department of Health, *Review of the Human Fertilisation and Embryology Act: Proposals for Revised Legislation (including Establishment of the Regulatory Authority for Tissue and Embryos)*, December 2006, para 2.43.

practices. Prospective parents are the people centrally involved in choosing between possible lives. In so doing, they may also be choosing between different versions of their own lives.[13]

Overall, I have tried to identify many of the issues at stake, both ethical and legal and, in reflecting on these, clearly to offer my own reasoned thoughts and arguments. Since people will reasonably disagree about many of these issues, I have aimed to write honestly and openly and to present my ideas, not in any sense as certainties, but as a contribution to the ongoing debate.

---

[13] I am grateful here to Peter Oliver, who pointed out the latter meaning of 'choosing between lives' to me.

# 1

# *Ethical Issues in Selection Practices: Whose Interests are at Stake?*

## I INTRODUCTION

THIS CHAPTER IDENTIFIES some key ethical questions and theoretical issues underpinning debates about prenatal and preimplantation selection practices. It considers the possible justifications for such practices, including whose interests might actually be at stake in them. In part, this entails beginning to reflect on the appropriate scope of reproductive autonomy in selective abortion or when embryos need to be created for the purposes of preimplantation genetic diagnosis (PGD). For any one of us who is already born, it is unlikely to be in our interests to experience disease or to become disabled. Yet the degree to which such experiences are against someone's interests is a contentious issue. So is the question of whether it is against someone's interests to be born into a condition of disease or disability.

There are a number of ways we could begin to think about this question. For instance, we could start by posing the following related questions. First, what is it like to have a certain condition or disease and how should we understand the notion of 'disability'? Second, is any given condition or disease so severe that birth should be avoided in the interests of the person who would otherwise come to exist? This is a question about the moral requirements or duties of prospective parents, and potentially of doctors and regulators. Third, if there is no duty to avoid the birth of a given person, is it nevertheless acceptable to avoid the birth of that person for some other reason? This is a question about moral permissibility. For instance, someone else's interests, such as the parents', could be significantly affected in some way by the birth of a disabled child. Fourth, reflecting on the timing of the decision-making process, what are the implications of the fact that the subject of the decision is currently in embryonic or fetal form?

The people primarily involved in these reflections and this decision-making process are the parents. They are contemplating having a child. Moral reflection on this issue should therefore entail a consideration not just of the interests of a possible child but also of the prospective parents, as well as the relationship between the two. I begin this work in Section II, when I consider the nature of reproductive autonomy and whether it should extend to decisions about what kind of child someone has, rather than only the 'prior' question of whether he or she has a child. Where reproductive autonomy is to be exercised where a fetus already exists or where embryos need to be created for the purpose of testing them, we also need to consider the moral status of the embryo or fetus, the actual subject of selection processes. This will give some indications about the scope of reproductive autonomy in this context.

In Section III I turn to consider the 'medical' and 'social' models of disability and the possible impact of disability on someone's life, particularly in relation to a person's capacity for flourishing. I draw attention to the importance of reflecting on the severity of a given condition and endorse the distinction between a condition that leaves someone with a life he may not think worth living and one in which someone will, despite his disease or disability, nevertheless want to live his life. I relate this distinction to the question of whether selection decisions should only focus on the interests of the person who may be born, or whether prospective parents' interests may also carry some weight.

In Section IV, building on the distinction between conditions that do and do not leave someone with a life he thinks worth living, I reflect on birth, the idea of harm, and the possible implications for parents in either case. For instance, if a given future person might not think his life worth living, are parents morally obliged to avoid his birth? I also introduce the distinction between person- and non-person-affecting principles and consider their application in this context. For instance, comparing two possible lives, we might think it preferable, other things being equal, if the person is born who has at least greater potential for flourishing. But are such principles applicable when an embryo or fetus already exists, and what duties can they found for prospective parents?

I consider the interests of people with impairments in selection practices in Section V. I revisit models of disability in relation to the issue of discrimination; reflect on the question of information provision in prenatal screening, prenatal diagnosis (PND) and PGD and assumptions about suffering and difficulty; and consider the validity of the 'expressivist objection', which holds that prenatal and preimplantation selection practices send the message to people with impairments that they should not have been born and that their lives are in some sense worth less than other lives.

Finally, in Section VI I reflect briefly on the relevance, if any, of the notion of eugenics to contemporary selection practices.

## II REPRODUCTIVE AUTONOMY AND THE EMBRYO OR FETUS

### A Choosing Whether to Have a Child

Why do parents have children and what experiences do they seek in child-rearing? Not surprisingly, people have expressed a range of thoughts about this enterprise and it is hard to comment on it without sounding trite. Nevertheless, one important idea may be that of a genetic connection, though this will not always be the case. Another may be the idea of having a connection with future people.[1] For some people, the idea of something of themselves continuing in some form and to some degree has appeal. There are also certain experiences would-be parents seek. Nurturing is an obvious one and this will involve a host of feelings and aims, including loving, caring and teaching. Many people would probably agree that in raising a child a parent loves, cares for and hopes to teach that child in such a way that she develops capacities for autonomy and flourishing in her own life.

Ideally, parents take decisions and act in ways that are in the interests of the child and consistent with the desire that she should flourish. The scope of parental autonomy in child-rearing is wide and only subject to societal interference when a child is seriously harmed or at risk of such harm. Are the decisions made and the actions taken before a couple has any given child aspects of parental autonomy? Arguably, full-blown parental autonomy can only be exercised when the child is born. Before then, choices are either made before a pregnancy or in the course of one albeit, particularly in the latter case, with a view to the time when a child may or may not be born. Such choices may be exercises in what is typically called 'reproductive autonomy' or 'procreative liberty', a domain of autonomy or liberty that is sharply contested in scope.[2] What is reproductive autonomy and how far might it extend?

None of us has a moral or legal duty to reproduce, to have a child (though it might be argued that *collectively* we have a duty to reproduce so as to avoid the extinction of humanity). So, from a liberal perspective at least, we have a choice about whether we will have children, one which depends on access to contraception and, potentially, to abortion. Generally, then, people have a moral and legal interest, protected to different degrees according to the law, in choosing whether to take on or reject the birth of a child or of a certain number of children. In this light, we can say that we have autonomy in relation to whether or not we will try to become parents or how many children we will try to have.[3] It seems right to call this kind of autonomy 'reproductive'. What arguments have supported its recognition and development?

The main one is the moral interest in self-determination. Arguably, we have such an interest because of the various ways in which we might choose to live our lives and, one would hope, to flourish, including in projects and relationships with other people. Most of us wish to determine at least the rough shape and texture of

---

[1] C Strong, 'Overview: a Framework for Reproductive Ethics', in D Dickenson (ed), *Ethical Issues in Maternal-Fetal Medicine* (Cambridge: Cambridge University Press, 2002) 17, 20.

[2] A scholar using the term 'procreative liberty' is J Robertson. See, eg, J Robertson, 'Genetic Selection of Offspring Characteristics' (1996) 76 *Boston U Law Rev* 421. By contrast, English scholars tend to use the term 'reproductive autonomy'.

[3] The focus at this point is on a negative interest, the interest in being *permitted* to avoid. That is, I might value my autonomy *and* strongly want to have a child (so have no interest in avoiding). I am not concerned here with the extent to which the interest in having a child is protected, notably through positive assistance in the case of fertility problems.

our lives, including (and here typically with a partner) whether we have any or a particular number of children. The idea of self-determination is prominent in various defences of reproductive autonomy or procreative liberty, such as in the work of Ronald Dworkin and John Robertson.[4]

By contrast, there have been criticisms of the notion of reproductive autonomy. For instance, Onora O'Neill observes that whilst abortion concerns the avoidance of the birth of another, in reproduction it is the creation of another that is at stake.[5] So, although the autonomy at stake in abortion generally may have important connections with what she calls 'self-expression', since reproduction entails the creation of another person it is not appropriate 'primarily'[6] to construe it in this way. However, it is not clear that writers such as Ronald Dworkin, John Robertson and John Harris, whose work on reproductive autonomy or procreative liberty she critiques, in fact consider that these concepts are concerned with self-expression. Rather, as suggested above, the focus in their work appears to be on the idea of self-determination. O'Neill's repeated use of the term 'self-expression' is therefore somewhat puzzling. Despite this, the term 'self-expression', when applied to the wish actually to select the features of another, perhaps especially aesthetic ones, may capture something of relevance to which I return in Chapter 5 when I review the scope of PGD.

Does the concept of reproductive autonomy or procreative liberty only concern an interest in being able to choose whether to become a parent or does it also encompass something about what kind of child one will have?

## B  The Possibility of a Disabled Child

Since we can choose to have a child (or at least to try to do so), arguably before his or her birth we should have *some* say about what kind of child that may be. This line of thought is supported by a number of different writers, many from a broadly liberal perspective.[7] However, where selective termination is in issue, given that we are typically thinking particularly about planned pregnancies, it is an argument that will require considerable support.

Writing on reproduction in the context of disability, Allen Buchanan *et al* have broadly defended the notion of reproductive autonomy, identifying the interests

---

[4] See, eg, R Dworkin, *Life's Dominion: An Argument about Abortion and Euthanasia* (London: Harper Collins, 1993); J Robertson, *Children of Choice: Freedom and the New Reproductive Technologies* (Princeton, NJ: Princeton University Press, 1994).

[5] O O'Neill, *Autonomy and Trust in Bioethics* (Cambridge: Cambridge University Press, 2002) 61.

[6] *Ibid* 61.

[7] eg, A Buchanan, D Brock, N Daniels and D Wikler, *From Chance to Choice: Genetics and Justice* (Cambridge: Cambridge University Press, 2000); Robertson, above n 2; B Steinbock, 'Disability, Prenatal Testing and Selective Abortion', in E Parens and A Asch (eds), *Prenatal Testing and Disability Rights* (Washington, DC: Georgetown University Press, 2000) 108; J Botkin, 'Line Drawing: Developing Professional Standards for Prenatal Diagnostic Services' in Parens and Asch (eds), *ibid* 288.

and values that give moral importance to reproductive freedom as being self-determination, contribution to well-being and, potentially (where women care more for children than men) equality considerations.[8] The idea that parents should have some say about the kind of child who will be born appears also to find support in a writer from the disability critique of prenatal screening and selective abortion. Tom Shakespeare observes[9]:

> The role of prospective parents has largely been ignored by disabled radicals. Because these are predominantly non-disabled people, it is likely that they will hold some of the prejudicial attitudes to disability which are common in society. Yet the decision to terminate pregnancy is not one that the majority of people take lightly. Moreover, there are reasons to want to prevent the birth of a child affected by impairment which do not reflect discrimination against disabled people: for example, the desire to avoid the early death or suffering of a loved child, or a feeling that a family will be unable to cope with the strain of looking after a very impaired member.

Shakespeare's examples at the end of this passage capture an important part of what parents may be concerned about in having an impaired child. The experiences he describes are not ones that a couple would normally seek.[10] Of course, parents may well find themselves encountering disease or disability in their child for reasons which are not congenital. In this way, raising a child will inevitably entail a certain degree of difficulty. However, the focus at the preimplantation and prenatal stage is on the idea of possibly avoidable known difficulties. Should prospective parents have a say about such matters, at least if they have chosen to have a child?

## C Reproductive Autonomy and the Positive Duties Inherent in Child-raising

In my view there is a reason why such autonomy might extend in this way. For a start, one will be related to that child as a parent. More particularly, one will therefore have a moral duty to care for it. There is a great deal involved in this task and it lasts a very long time. Without prejudging many of the issues to be discussed, whether or not one's child is disabled or has a disease or disorder of some kind may have certain implications for what raising that child will entail and so for what it is like (such as how hard it may be) to fulfil that duty and how long it will take.[11]

---

[8] Buchanan *et al*, above n 7, 214 *ff*.

[9] T Shakespeare, '"Losing the Plot?" Medical and Activist Discourses of Contemporary Genetics and Disability' (1999) 21/5 *Sociology of Health and Illness* 669, 681.

[10] The exception is where parents have deliberately set out to have an impaired, such as a deaf, child. This is unusual and is discussed specifically in Ch 6, S II.

[11] See also D Heyd, *Genethics: Moral Issues in the Creation of People* (Berkeley: University of California Press, 1992) at 15: 'Not only is there a strong built-in impulse to have children, our own welfare is to a large extent dependent on theirs because each generation lives for quite a time with its dependants.' (footnote omitted) Heyd argues for the relevance

Now, the recognition of reproductive autonomy in its barest form — the freedom to avoid reproduction — also entails a recognition that without this freedom one would have the duties of a parent, preceded by pregnancy and birth for the woman. (Pregnancy therefore also invokes a woman's interest in bodily integrity.) In this light, I suggest that the freedom that may be at stake in what kind of child one will have and raise is not a completely different kind of freedom from that at stake in the choice of whether to have any child. Rather, in both cases reproductive autonomy is at stake and prospective parents may reflect on what the positive moral duties of parenthood may involve. The difference between the two scenarios may be that where they face the birth of a severely disabled or ill child they may have concerns, rightly or wrongly, about how hard the duties of parenting a *particular* child will be. Opinions will vary about what people feel is reasonable to take on, since the reasonableness of positive duties may legitimately be the subject of disagreement.[12]

There have been various studies about parents with disabled children. Some show that 'there is a level of agreement approaching consensus that the overall adaptational profile of families who have children with disabilities basically resembles the overall profile for families in general (including children with and without disabilities)'; they also show that 'family responses to disability are immensely variable'.[13] Further, Adrienne Asch notes that '[s]keptics about the [above] research findings and interpretations... suspect that the research reviewed does not tell the whole story and that a child with a disability poses substantial heartache, difficulty, and burden to families that far exceed in kind and degree the stresses modern parents typically face'.[14] In addition, the unknown variation in the severity of a condition may well affect decision-making in people who are risk-averse.[15] The uncertainty in the prognosis of a neonate, and therefore by implication also of a given fetus, is noted in the UK Nuffield Council on Bioethics' 2006 report, *Critical Care Decisions in Fetal and Neonatal Medicine: Ethical Issues* (the 'Nuffield Report')[16]:

---

only of a person-affecting approach to 'genethical' problems, 'anchoring all value in the actual decision-making party' (at 14). He therefore adds this point about interdependent welfare in order to mitigate some of the harsh implications of the approach, for instance in its potential egoism (at 15).

[12] Perhaps one of the earliest instances of an argument questioning the reasonableness of positive duties can be found in JJ Thomson 'A Defence of Abortion' (1971) 1 *Phil & Pub Aff* 47.

[13] P Ferguson, A Gartner and D Lipsky 'The Experience of Disability in Families: A Synthesis of Research and Parent Narratives' in Parens and Asch (eds), above n 7, 72, at 81 and 85 respectively.

[14] A Asch 'Why I Haven't Changed My Mind about Prenatal Diagnosis: Reflections and Refinements' in Parens and Asch (eds), above n 7, 234, 248, footnote omitted.

[15] M Baily 'Why I Had Amniocentesis' in Parens and Asch (eds), above n 7, 64, 70.

[16] Nuffield Council on Bioethics, *Critical Care Decisions in Fetal and Neonatal Medicine: Ethical Issues* (2006), para 3.6, referring further to paras 5.7–5.11.

One feature common to [the] developments in fetal and neonatal medicine is... the uncertainty of the initial prognosis for a particular baby. We shall see that in some cases doctors can give parents a reasonably certain account of whether their child is likely to survive, for how long and if he or she will have any disabilities. In many others, however, doctors may have to base their advice on statistical probabilities derived from studies such as EPICure... and will be unable to tell parents how their baby will fare, nor predict the extent of any disability that he or she may develop.

The quality of life of families with disabled children is in fact discussed in some detail in this report, which notes the 'substantial body of research on the quality of life experienced by families with young disabled children'.[17] The report uses the definition of disability in the Disability Discrimination Act 1995, such that 'a person has a disability if he has a physical or mental impairment which has a substantial and long-term adverse effect on his ability to carry out normal day-to-day activities'; further, the report observes[18]:

> This contemporary understanding of 'disability' means that discussions of disability in the specific context of the long-term future of severely ill babies must pay close attention to the relationships that will be available to that person, and broader social provision.

The report refers to a range of effects on families such as, on average, increased poverty: 'The average income for families with disabled children is 24% lower than the UK average; 22% have incomes that are less than half the UK average'.[19] Just 16% of mothers with disabled children work compared with 61% of mothers generally.[20] Further, 55% of disabled children in the United Kingdom grow up in or almost in poverty.[21] The report also discusses health problems amongst parents, citing a Department of Health study 'that found that 30% of those caring for a child had symptoms indicating a mental disorder'; 'in total, 76% felt that caring had affected their health in some way, 71% considered that their responsibilities caused them to worry, and 32% reported depression' and that '[p]roblems with mental health occurred more frequently when the person being cared for had

---

[17] *Ibid*, para 7.12, footnote omitted (which cites B Dobson, S Middleton, and A Beardsworth, *The Impact of Childhood Disability on Family Life* (York: YPS, 2001); Joseph Rowntree Foundation, *Supporting Disabled Children and their Families* (1999) available at: <http://www.jrf.org.uk /KNOWLEDGE/findings/foundations/N79.asp>, accessed 18 October 2007; Joseph Rowntree Foundation, *Minority Ethnic Families Caring for a Disabled Child* (1999) available at: <http://www.jrf.org.uk /knowledge/findings/socialcare/539.asp>, accessed 18 October 2007.

[18] *Ibid* para 3.29.

[19] *Ibid* text box 7.1, following para 7.11, citing Statistics from Contact a Family press releases, available at: <http://www.cafamily.org.uk/press.html>, accessed 18 October 2007.

[20] *Ibid*.

[21] *Ibid*.

18   *Ethical Issues in Selection Practices*

both physical and mental impairments'.[22] In addition, the report cites a survey conducted by Contact a Family that found[23]:

> 31% of parents reported that caring for their disabled child had caused some problems in their relationship and a further 13% reported that this had caused major problems. Nine per cent were separated and felt that having a disabled child had led to the separation. However, 23% of those surveyed felt that caring for their child had brought them closer.

Further, the report discusses the possible effects of a disabled child on siblings[24]:

> According to the 2001 Census, about 149,000 children and young people provide unpaid care in the UK, most of them probably for a member of their family, although the survey included care for others, such as neighbours or friends. Large-scale studies have not been undertaken in the UK, but evidence suggests that they could be at a higher risk of health problems, including back pain and mental health problems. Children may also experience bullying at school as a result of their family situation and their education and social lives may be affected. The role that these 'young carers' play has only recently been recognised by government.

Many of these problems highlight the increased need of families with a disabled child for social support, and the Nuffield Report further observes[25]:

> In 1999, the Government published its first national strategy for carers, which highlighted the need to 'care about carers'. Since then, a number of measures for carers, including new legislation (the Carers and Disabled Children Act 2000 and Carers (Equal Opportunities) Act 2004), have been introduced. It is hoped that these national policies and other initiatives will help families to cope with the pressures that result from caring for a disabled child.

I discuss the issue of social support in decisions about fetal anomaly further below (in the penultimate section of this chapter).

This picture of the possible negative effects of disability within a family is one that could give cause for concern to parents facing the birth of a disabled child, perhaps particularly where a child will have both physical and mental impairments. In my view, it is not clear that a concern with such issues would be unreasonable. Moreover, we do not have to understand the exercise of reproductive autonomy only negatively, as the avoidance of certain duties or degrees

---

[22]   *Ibid*, citing Office for National Statistics, *Mental Health of Carers* (London: The Stationery Office, 2002), available at <http://www.statistics.gov.uk/downloads/theme_health/Mental_Health_of_Carers_June02.pdf>, accessed 18 October 2007.

[23]   *Ibid*, citing Contact a Family (2004) *No Time for Us: Relationships between parents who have a disabled child.* Summary available at <http://www.cafamily.org.uk/relationshipsurvey.html>, accessed 18 October 2007.

[24]   *Ibid*.

[25]   *Ibid*, citing Department of Health, *Caring about Carers: A national strategy for carers* (London: The Stationery Office, 1999), available at <http://www.carers.gov.uk/supportingcarers.htm>, accessed 18 October 2007.

thereof. The reasons someone has for choosing to avoid assuming certain duties or seemingly more extensive versions of them do not just have to concern that person in themselves. We all have pre-existing commitments to other people, projects and concerns. Those other people may include relatives needing care, a partner needing particular support, work that contributes to society or, perhaps most strikingly, other children who need to be raised. As Erik Parens and Adrienne Asch have noted, the fact that many families cope well with stress does not mean that it is 'unreasonable or morally problematic' for parents to decide to avoid it where possible.[26]

The Nuffield Report also discusses the factors that might influence prospective parents' decisions in the light of a diagnosis of severe fetal anomaly, in fact observing that not much is known about this process[27]:

> The [British Medical Association] has observed that little is known about how parents make decisions following the diagnosis of severe fetal abnormality, including the kind of information and support they receive and how this affects their decision making. Available data suggest that parents experience difficulties in deciding how to proceed after such a diagnosis, with two factors reported as being important for decision making. These are first, the impact of the abnormality on the child, on themselves and on other immediate family members (including children they wish to have in the future), and secondly, their prior attitudes and beliefs about termination. It has been suggested that parents tend not to focus on levels of risk and the options available in an objective way, but rather on their perception of their own ability to cope. Decision making is made more complex when there is uncertainty over how seriously a child will be affected by any disability in the future.

Elsewhere (with respect to decisions about the treatment of neonates) the report observes[28]:

> If they have older children, parents might worry about the impact of having a new child who has disabilities. They may feel obliged to take the welfare of their other children into account in decision making.

So far, I have argued that prospective parents' interests in the kind of child who is born, particularly whether he or she is disabled or has a disorder of some kind and if so to what degree, can be understood as a legitimate aspect of their broader interest in reproductive autonomy. Just how serious a given disability or disorder may be is a highly contentious issue, one that I address below. It may well be

---

[26] E Parens and A Asch 'The Disability Rights Critique of Prenatal Genetic Testing: Reflections and Recommendations' in Parens and Asch (eds), above n 7, 3, 22.

[27] Nuffield Council, above n 16, para 4.17, footnotes omitted (citing British Medical Association 'Diagnosing Fetal Abnormality' in *Abortion Time Limits — A briefing paper from the BMA* (2005) available at <http://www.bma.org.uk/ap.nsf/Content/AbortionTimeLimits~Factors~Diagnosing>, accessed 18 October 2007; H Statham 'Prenatal Diagnosis of Fetal Abnormality: the Decision to Terminate the Pregnancy and the Psychological Consequences' (2002) 13 *Fetal Matern Med Rev* 213–47).

[28] *Ibid* para 3.16.

relevant to the question of how far reproductive autonomy should extend when a fetus already exists or embryos must be created for the purpose of testing them, unless of course one thinks — as many people do — that neither the embryo nor fetus has any moral claims.

I now turn to address the question of the moral status of the embryo and fetus.

## D  The Moral Status of the Embryo and Fetus

By way of introduction to this issue, we need to recognise the different ways in which the duties either of parenting any child or of parenting a particular child may be avoided. Ideally, and on some views without any need for moral justification (though many would disagree), the duties of child-raising inherent in giving birth to *any* child are avoided by means of contraception. (An alternative is (heterosexual) abstinence.) Less ideally, and with the need for moral justification unless one considers that the fetus has no moral claims, such duties may be avoided through abortion. In relation to avoiding the duties of parenting a *particular* child, since prospective parents will probably have sought a given pregnancy, contraception ceases to be relevant and the common method of avoidance is abortion. Whether abortion generally can be morally justified is a question I touch on below. Importantly, however, if it can be, it follows from the above argument about self-determination and the relevance of the avoidance of positive duties to the concept of reproductive autonomy, that it can also be morally justified in the 'particular' case, that is, where the avoidance of the birth of a particular child is in issue. Despite this, as discussed below, in both cases arguably abortion may not always be justifiable throughout a pregnancy.

Turning to the particular case of a disabled or otherwise affected child, parents may decide to avoid such a birth either by having IVF with PGD or by undertaking prenatal screening and PND, followed by selective abortion in the face of a positive test result.[29] Clearly, the latter is much more common. In either case, the decision may be made following reflection on what the life of a given possible child might be like. To some extent in some cases (subconsciously or otherwise), the decision may also be made after thinking about what it would be like for the parents themselves if a particular embryo were implanted or a certain pregnancy not terminated. However, at the time of the decision, the person whose life may be avoided is in embryonic or fetal form. That is, the decision to avoid the birth of a given child is made when that possible child is still an embryo or a fetus.

The subject of PGD, the embryo, is three to five days' old when tested and usually consists of six to ten cells.[30] However, these cells have enormous potential. For this reason, to describe the embryo as merely consisting of several cells would

---

[29] There are also limited pre-conceptual means, such as taking folic acid to prevent neural tube defects.

[30] F Flinter 'Preimplantation Genetic Diagnosis Needs to be Tightly Regulated' (2001) 322 *BMJ* 1008, 1008.

be reductive and misleading. The subject of prenatal screening, testing and potentially of selective abortion, is the fetus. Screening and testing for disability may begin as early as 11 or 12 weeks (by a nuchal translucency scan and chorionic villus sampling) and continue relatively late into pregnancy. This could be by means of a fetal anomaly scan at 20 weeks or scans for cardiac or other defects beyond this time. What moral claims, if any, does the embryo or fetus have and what bearing do these have on the decision-making processes at stake in these selection practices?

This is a highly controversial question and there are various answers to it that I have examined in more detail elsewhere.[31] For instance, the embryo has the moral status of a born child on a potentiality account.[32] On many other views, its status is either non-existent or very low when compared with that of a three- or six-month fetus, such that it lacks moral rights. On some moral views also the fetus lacks these, notably on the personhood argument which holds that the fetus, even a relatively advanced one, lacks the criteria for moral personhood.[33]

I take the intuitively appealing approach that the embryo's and fetus's moral status increases gradually. This is typically called a 'gradualist' account and is one I have explored in detail previously.[34] To some people, it will seem that the great weakness of this approach is that it entails no clear concepts, such as 'potentiality' or 'personhood'; nor can one point to any particular moment, such as conception or viability or the last week before birth, as deciding the embryo's or fetus's moral status. For my part, however, I think that the more one reflects on the moral status of the embryo or fetus, the less satisfactory the potentiality account at one end or the personhood account at the other, or the identification of some intermediate marker, such as the fetus's attainment of viability, can ever be. This may be because I think that, at least when we are thinking about reproductive autonomy, the question of the moral status of the embryo or fetus is necessarily, and primarily, a question about the relationship between the embryo or fetus and a woman (though to some degree also its father, arguably equally so where the embryo is *ex*

---

[31] For an elegant discussion of the possible views, see, eg, J Feinberg 'Abortion' (1979) in his *Freedom and Fulfillment* (Princeton: Princeton University Press, 1992) 37. I have discussed this issue in more detail in R Scott, *Rights, Duties and the Body: Law and Ethics of the Maternal-Fetal Conflict* (Oxford: Hart Publishing, 2002) Ch 1.

[32] For an adherent, see J Finnis 'The Rights and Wrongs of Abortion: A Reply to Judith Thomson' (1973) 2 *Phil & Pub Aff* 117. Reprinted in R Dworkin (ed), *The Philosophy of Law* (Oxford: OUP, 1977) 129.

[33] On fetuses, moral personhood and rights, see MA Warren 'On the Moral and Legal Status of Abortion' (1973) 57(1) *The Monist* 43. The possible criteria for personhood are consciousness, rationality and agency, but also the ability to communicate and self-consciousness.

[34] For other gradualist accounts, see Feinberg, above n 31; I Kennedy 'A Woman and her Unborn Child' in his *Treat Me Right* (Oxford: OUP, 1992) 364; Dworkin, above n 4.

*utero*). This is not to deny that others may also have a relationship with the embryo or fetus, such as health professionals. So what are the advantages of a gradualist approach?

On this approach, the longer a pregnancy has been allowed to develop, the greater must be the justification — or the more serious the reason — on the woman's (or prospective parents') part for terminating the life of the fetus. Another way of expressing this is to say that a woman's reasons for exercising her reproductive autonomy in this way must be that much more serious. The key to this approach is that it hinges on a simultaneous interplay of maternal (and, to some degree in this context, paternal) and fetal claims. Importantly, the approach avoids arguments about fetal rights by focusing instead on the imperfect obligations that may be owed the fetus. In my view, these features are some of its great merits.

A further considerable strength of this account is that in some ways it can be said to accommodate aspects of the ideas in other approaches to the question of the fetus's moral status. For instance, the gradualist approach can be said to be able to acknowledge both the ideas of potentiality and personhood, which are at the two extremes of the other moral accounts. On the one hand this is in the sense that a gradualist account (in my view at least) does not say that the embryo is 'nothing', so that there is some recognition of its huge potential. At the same time, however, that potential does not answer the question of its moral status. On the other hand, the gradualist account also recognises the developing embryo's, but particularly fetus's, progression towards being an independent person. But again the embryo's or fetus's *lack* of personhood (on the criteria of the personhood argument) does not decide the question of moral status.

Moreover, a gradualist account is also fully compatible with other moral accounts. For instance, it seems right that we should be able to acknowledge the fetus's development of sentience, and with it the capacity to feel pleasure and pain, as increasing the strength of its claims and as relevant to our treatment of it. At this point, we can also say that the fetus has interests. To have an interest is to have a stake in something, so that conscious awareness is a 'prerequisite' for the possession of interests.[35] Roughly speaking, the development of sentience may coincide with viability. Taking into account the current state of neonatal technology this probably occurs at around 24 weeks' gestation,[36] although the

---

[35] The idea of 'having a stake' in something is Joel Feinberg's, as outlined for instance in his *Harm to Others* (New York: OUP, 1984) at 34: 'In general, a person has a stake in X… when he stands to gain or lose depending on the nature or condition of X'. For a philosopher supporting the link between interests and sentience, see B Steinbock, *Life Before Birth* (New York: Oxford University Press, 1992) 24, n 24.

[36] On the idea of a distinction between 'technological' and 'natural' conceptions of viability see N Rhoden 'Trimesters and Technology: Revamping *Roe v Wade*' (1986) 95 *Yale LJ* 639, 671. The first is the idea of independence from the mother's body made possible by technological development, such that as a matter of fact fetuses may be viable at increasingly early dates. The second sense captures the moral or normative import of

relatively poor prospects for a fetus born at or near this time are discussed in the next chapter. The recognition of the fetus's acquisition of interests is compatible with the gradualist approach because, simply on the terms of that account, a fetus of 24 weeks has developed for some considerable time. However, it may be problematic to say that the fetus acquires rights with the development of sentience because of the ethical difficulties that would be created by the presence of two right-holder's in the woman's body (though we could more easily speak of *prima facie* rights).[37] Still, this is not a great moral stumbling block for the fetus because, as noted above, the gradualist account is itself concerned with the idea of imperfect duties that may be owed to the fetus, ones that are not correlated with rights. A gradualist account is also compatible with the idea that the moment of birth represents an important moral milestone when the fetus, as a neonate, becomes an independent being. This is so notwithstanding that at the very moment after birth the neonate will be no more developed than the fetus it was a few minutes before, although to survive on its own it will have had successfully to use its lungs.

Turning now to the case of selective abortion, the implication of a gradualist approach is that it may be morally justifiable to terminate a given pregnancy where a possible child would have a serious condition, because in such a case prospective parents may have a serious interest in avoiding its birth. However, the condition must reasonably be judged that much more serious as the pregnancy proceeds. Terminations beyond the stage of fetal viability require special consideration and are discussed in Chapter 2, when I turn to address the law on selective abortion. Overall, if the fetus has growing moral claims and if a decision to terminate is to be made, it is better if this is earlier rather than later. In this way, developments in screening techniques that result in earlier detection are to be welcomed. The implications of a gradualist approach to the moral permissibility of PGD are discussed in Chapters 4, 5 and 6.

## E   The Scope of Reproductive Autonomy: Interests, Reasons and Rights

Against this background of the relationship between reproductive autonomy and the possible moral claims of the embryo and fetus — and with a view to the analysis of different kinds of selection practices in various parts of the book — it is useful here to reflect on how we might understand the links between the concepts of reproductive autonomy, interests, reasons and, ultimately, rights.

Following Joseph Raz we might see autonomy as a value to which certain interests may be related and from which certain rights derived.[38] To elaborate

---

viability. It is fair to say that on this latter approach the moral significance of viability is assumed to depend upon its natural attainment.

[37] For further discussion see Scott, above n 31, Ch 1.

[38] J Raz 'Right-based Moralities' in J Waldron (ed), *Theories of Rights* (Oxford: OUP, 1984), 182, especially 186–95.

briefly here, Raz argues that to say that an individual has a right means, 'other things being equal, an aspect of *x's* well-being (his interest) is a sufficient reason for holding some other person(s) to be under a duty'.[39] Moreover, (simplifying a complex argument) he suggests that given that society at large is involved in facilitating the existence of the conditions that enable the pursuit of an autonomous life, it is unlikely that the interest of any one individual can justify imposing such an onerous duty on so many. It follows that there can be no right to personal autonomy as such, which means that personal autonomy is one example of an ideal or value at the heart of our morality.[40] On his view, there are 'derivative rights'[41] which protect and advance aspects of the individual's autonomy and contribute to making autonomy possible.[42]

To give an example of general relevance to medical law and ethics compatible with this analysis, autonomy is an important value in the medical treatment context. From it flow the interests in self-determination and bodily integrity, which in turn underpin the moral and legal right to consent to and refuse medical treatment. With regard to decisions in reproduction, the important value we are considering is that of reproductive autonomy. From it flows an interest in choosing to accept or avoid reproduction as well as an interest — which is of particular concern here — in having some say, either by prenatal screening, PND and selective abortion or, in a different way, PGD, in the kind of child who may be born. However, this latter interest and the moral (and legal) right that it might support is contested in scope: why?

As we have seen above, the reason lies in the controversial question of the moral (and legal) status of the embryo and fetus. As suggested earlier, unless one thinks that neither the embryo nor the fetus has any moral claims of any kind (as many people do), the exercise of reproductive autonomy either where a fetus exists as part of an established pregnancy or where embryos need to be created so as to test and choose between them will require some moral justification. By contrast, where someone simply exercises his or her interest in reproductive autonomy to avoid conception, no justification is required (unless one thinks, as I

---

[39] *Ibid* 183.
[40] *Ibid* especially 186–95. In addition to the sense of autonomy as a value, Raz distinguishes between two further senses of autonomy. The first refers to the life in which autonomy is achieved or realised, and is only found where an individual has been able to choose between various significant options in such a way as to shape his or her life. In the second sense, autonomy is seen as the capacity to achieve an autonomous life: whether the conditions of autonomy exist will depend both on the capacities of the individual as a rational agent and on the conditions of his life and the choices available to him. In this last sense, autonomy is only possible if various collective goods, such as that a society is a tolerant one, exist. *Ibid* 191.
[41] J Raz, *The Morality of Freedom* (Oxford: Clarendon Press, 1986) 247.
[42] Raz, above n 38, 195.

do not, that contraception is morally wrong). What are the implications of a gradualist approach to the embryo's and fetus's moral status for the link between autonomy, interests, reasons and rights?

In my view, when a fetus already exists or embryos would need to be created so as to test them before transfer, the exercise of reproductive autonomy will be most justifiable (as regards the embryo or fetus), valuable (as regards the parents' interests) and so worthy of protection when there are good or serious reasons for certain choices: these imply that the moral interests derived from the value of reproductive autonomy are seriously invoked. Importantly, this line of thought is fundamental to the analysis of a range of possible selection practices in this book. As we saw earlier, the key moral interest underpinning reproductive autonomy is that of self-determination. In the context of prenatal selection, of course, this may be something a couple wishes to exercise 'jointly'. On this understanding, prospective parents' interest in the kind of child they have will be seriously (or strongly) invoked where a child would have a serious impairment or disorder. In such a case, we might then say that they have a *prima facie* moral (and potentially legal) right to avoid the birth, subject to the stage of fetal development (as discussed above) and the degree of severity of the condition in the possible child (discussed below). Moreover, and importantly, on this analysis the question of how much weight should be given to their views about the seriousness of an impairment or disorder in a possible child, and so how broad their reproductive autonomy should be, can also be related to the question of how strong their interest is in what kind of child will be born. As I have suggested, this interest will be strongly invoked where a child would have a serious condition of some kind.

By contrast, selection against an embryo or fetus on the grounds of relatively trivial features will be less deserving of protection, since such a feature is unlikely seriously to affect prospective parents' lives. An important general aside should be made here about choices that will have greater or lesser impact on our lives. Arguably, whether someone has and becomes responsible for raising a child (including a disabled one) will have a highly significant impact on his or her life. By contrast, the colour that that person chooses to paint his or her bicycle will not do so. However, sometimes the *protection* of the right to choose the colour of one's bicycle may be particularly important, such as where civil liberties are generally curtailed. In this way, the right to paint one's bicycle yellow may have an element of an important symbolic freedom. Here having the choice or the right per se is highly important, even though the actual colour of one's bicycle will impact on one's life much less than whether one has and raises a child.[43]

Returning to prenatal and preimplantation choices, the question of selection for less serious or even trivial concerns is addressed in Chapter 3, when I consider the scope of the reasons for which selective abortion may be performed and the extent of the corresponding protection of abortion options in law. This protection

---

[43] I am grateful to Roger Crisp here.

occurs by means of the legal duty on health professionals to advise parents about a certain degree of fetal anomaly, encapsulated in the so-called 'wrongful birth' action that parents may bring where this duty has been breached. Further, in Chapter 5 I consider the idea of selection for less than serious or even trivial reasons when I discuss the future scope of PGD and whether we should allow selection for reasons other than against serious genetic conditions.

For now, how are we to understand the question of 'seriousness' in this context? Is a condition ever so serious that it might not be in the interests of a future child to be born? We now need to consider how the severity or seriousness of a condition is to be judged and to reflect more broadly on the notion of disability or disease.

### III UNDERSTANDINGS OF DISABILITY

Most likely, we have all experienced illness of some kind, particularly in an acute form. Quite a few of us have also experienced illness in chronic form, lasting months, years or perhaps ongoing. In this respect, we may have a condition that can be alleviated with drugs or other treatment, or our condition may be one for which medicine currently has no answers. A condition or impairment may result in physical pain or psychological suffering but will not necessarily do so, contrary to some presumptions.[44] Indeed, the Nuffield Report observes[45]:

> Many disabled people feel that portrayals by the media do not reflect the reality of their lives. This was demonstrated by a survey which analysed over 1,000 national and local press cuttings covering disability and disabled people over an eight week period in 1999. There were over 800 occurrences of pejorative terms. The terms used most frequently were 'suffer' and 'suffers', but these terms do not reflect accurately the perceptions of disabled people about themselves. It was also observed that the achievements of disabled people often went unreported.

A condition or impairment may (or may not) limit some of the things we can do. For instance, our lower limbs could be paralysed so that we cannot walk or run. If this were so, we would learn to use a wheelchair, though access to certain places would be difficult or impossible. Alternatively, we may be unable to hear or see. The loss of one of our senses is primarily associated with the inability to experience certain things.[46] Those of us who have experienced these senses all have our own thoughts about the things we enjoy and value — the sound of the wind in the leaves, music, the sight of the sun on water, paintings. The loss of one

---

[44] For warnings against such presumptions, see S Edwards 'Prevention of Disability on Grounds of Suffering' (2001) 27 *JME* 380.
[45] Nuffield Council, above n 16, para 3.32, citing Scope (1999) *Stop Press — an overview*.
[46] Typically, our experience of this is hopelessly limited — such as being unable to see because it is dark — and the thought of the permanent loss of one of these senses may well induce a sense of panic.

of our senses may also limit some of the things we can do and the opportunities open to us. However, adaptive techniques can be highly successful, such as the use of sign language and braille. Whether the use of sign language fully compensates for the inability to hear, particularly in terms of someone's relationship to others and society more broadly, is a strongly contested issue that I discuss further in Chapter 6 when I consider the idea of selecting for disability.[47] It is related to the question of whether disability should be understood as a medical or social condition.

## A  Models of Disability

Some of the key tensions about what it means to have a disability have been expressed in a debate about models of disability. Views of disability have been dominated by a medical conception of what it is to be disabled. A proponent is John Harris, although he prefers to call this a 'harmed condition' model. Harris defines disability as a 'physical or mental condition which we have a strong [rational] preference not to be in'.[48] By contrast the 'social model', as previously defended for instance by Shakespeare, distinguishes between impairment, as a medical condition of the body, and disability, as social prejudice and discrimination.[49] On this latter understanding, whether an impairment leads to a disability depends on the nature of the social environment the individual inhabits. The suggestion here is that while disability is social in nature, impairments are not. By contrast, on the medical model disability is situated within the individual.

Both models have been strongly defended. More recently, there has also been some accommodation of the alternative approach in either case. So Harris accepts that there may be 'social dimensions' to physical and mental conditions that affect the individual; and Shakespeare accepts that some impairments can result in significant problems in themselves and suggests that disabled people should debate 'the differential impact of impairments'.[50] (I discuss Tom Shakespeare's more recent work, in which he is quite critical of the social model, when I discuss the interests of people with disabilities in selection practices, in the penultimate section of this chapter.) The implication is that the problems of disability are not all due to inadequacies of social response.[51] So, while a significant contribution of

---

[47] See, eg, the debate in (2002) *BMJ* 325.
[48] J Harris 'Is There a Coherent Social Conception of Disability?' (2000) 26 *JME* 95, 97, citing S Reindal's interpretation of Harris in the former's 'Disability, Gene Therapy and Eugenics — a Challenge to John Harris' (2000) 26 *JME* 89.
[49] T Shakespeare 'Choices and Rights: Eugenics, Genetics and Disability Equality' (1998) 13/5 *Disability and Society* 665, 665 citing M Oliver, *The Politics of Disablement* (Basingstoke: Macmillan, 1990).
[50] Harris, above n 48, 95; Shakespeare, above n 49, 670.
[51] 'Not all problems of disability are socially created and, thus, theoretically remediable... The inability to move without mechanical aid, to see, to hear, or to learn is not inherently neutral. Disability itself limits some options.' Steinbock, above n 7, 115, citing A

the social model has been to draw attention to the important issue of discrimination against people with impairments and to their need for social support,[52] in itself the model appears limited. For instance, John Harris has suggested that if we were to reject the medical or 'harmed condition' model, we would have no way of explaining what is wrong in disabling someone or failing to cure, where possible, a disability.[53] Further, Sally Sheldon and Stephen Wilkinson (amongst others) have drawn attention to the inaccuracies of the failure to distinguish between disability and disadvantage that may occur with the social model.[54]

As Jonathan Glover has pointed out, it is now clear that some combination of the models is best placed to account for the significance of impairment and so the debate as to which is the better model should be dropped.[55] Because some combination of the two models is preferable to reliance on either one, I shall continue to refer to both 'impairments' and 'disabilities'. (From time to time I shall also refer to the notion of a disorder or disease, since in some cases it may not be appropriate to use the language of impairment or disability.)

## B  Flourishing

Moving beyond the debate about medical or social conceptions of disability, a key idea linking the significance of the potential losses — of experiences, activities or opportunities — involved in disease or disability may be that of the capacity to flourish. Jonathan Glover has written about disability in this way in a detailed account that pays particular attention to the views and experiences of people with disabilities. He suggests that disability is a 'functional limitation, which (either on its own or — more usually — in combination with social disadvantage) impairs the capacity for human flourishing'.[56] He recognises that this raises questions about what counts as 'normal human functioning' and suggests: 'The relevant concept of normality is a messy one. It is partly socially constructed. It is partly context dependent. And it combines elements of the numerical and the normative'.[57]

---

Asch 'Reproductive Technology and Disability' in S Cohen and N Taub (eds), *Reproductive Laws for the 1990s* (Clifton, NJ: Humana Press, 1989) 69, 73.

[52] Steinbock, above n 7, 115. It is understandable that if medicine has done all it can for one's impairments, then one can only look to social conditions further to redress these. John Harris suggests that there is a preference for the 'social model' in '[p]eople with irremediable disabilities... because the medical model is of no further use to them' Harris, above n 48, 99.

[53] Harris, above n 48, 99.

[54] S Sheldon and S Wilkinson 'Termination of Pregnancy for Reason of Foetal Disability: Are There Grounds for a Special Exception in Law?' (2001) 9 *Med Law Rev* 85, 103.

[55] J Glover, *Choosing Children: Genes, Disability and Design* (Oxford: OUP, 2006) 7–8.

[56] *Ibid* 9.

[57] *Ibid* 13.

A question that then arises, particularly when we ourselves may not have experienced any given condition, is whether and if so how we can make the judgment that it amounts to a disability. Glover suggests that strong weight should be given to the first-person accounts and views of those with disabilities. However, because people's identities are to some degree inherent in their disabilities, these need to be 'interpreted with alertness to possible biases'.[58] This seems right. He also notes that, in reflecting on whether a condition amounts to a disability, we have other sources upon which we can draw: on the one hand, ideas about human flourishing and the contribution that different aspects of our lives make to this; on the other, the knowledge that people who can see and hear, for instance, can give about the contribution of these senses to their lives.[59] On reflection Glover concludes that it is at least tenable to see deafness and blindness as disabilities and not just differences, even though not all would agree, although living without these senses is clearly fully compatible with having a life one thinks worth living.

Indeed, the question of the extent to which a disease or disability may impede flourishing is a question of degree. The 'differential impact of impairment', to use Shakespeare's phrase, or its severity, may well be critical to our understanding of many of the moral issues in the debate over reproductive autonomy and impairment in a possible child. We should now explore something of the range of possible severity and experience of disability.

## C  The Severity of a Condition

### i  A life that someone may think is not worth living

When born, a child may be or become so severely impaired that we might ask whether his or her life is overall good or bad for it, in terms of the well-being it contains. Part of this question entails reflection on the severity of the condition that a child would have. Tay-Sachs appears to be one example of a very serious condition[60]:

> The classical form of Tay-Sachs disease (TSD) is a fatal genetic disorder in children that causes progressive destruction of the central nervous system... By about two years of age, most children experience recurrent seizures and diminishing mental function. The infant gradually regresses, losing skills one by one, and is eventually unable to crawl, turn over, sit, or reach out. Other symptoms include increasing loss of coordination, progressive inability to swallow and breathing difficulties. Eventually, the child becomes blind, mentally retarded, paralyzed, and non-responsive to his or her environment. To date, there is no cure or effective treatment for TSD.

---

[58]  *Ibid* 22.
[59]  *Ibid* 15, 16 and 22, 23 respectively.
[60]  National Tay-Sachs and Allied Diseases Association, Inc <http://www.ntsad.org>, accessed 5 October 2007.

An example of what appears to be another very severe condition is Lesch-Nyhan syndrome[61]:

> Lesch-Nyhan syndrome (LNS) is a rare, inherited disorder caused by a deficiency of the enzyme *hypoxanthine-guanine phosphoribosyltransferase* (HPRT). LNS is an X-linked recessive disease — the gene is carried by the mother and passed on to her son. LNS is present at birth in baby boys. The lack of HPRT causes a build-up of uric acid in all body fluids, and leads to symptoms such as severe gout, poor muscle control, and moderate retardation, which appear in the first year of life. A striking feature of LNS is self-mutilating behaviors — characterized by lip and finger biting — that begin in the second year of life. Abnormally high uric acid levels can cause sodium urate crystals to form in the joints, kidneys, central nervous system, and other tissues of the body, leading to gout-like swelling in the joints and severe kidney problems. Neurological symptoms include facial grimacing, involuntary writhing, and repetitive movements of the arms and legs similar to those seen in Huntington's disease. Because a lack of HPRT causes the body to poorly utilize vitamin B12, some boys may develop a rare disorder called megaloblastic anemia.... The prognosis for individuals with LNS is poor. Death is usually due to renal failure in the first or second decade of life.

Judgments by third parties about the quality of life of possible others are obviously difficult and sensitive. As Jonathan Glover has suggested, rather than attempting to make clear-cut judgments about conditions that we have not experienced, it may be better to restrict ourselves to the question of whether there is a 'serious risk of a life not worth living', a life of very low quality.[62] It may be that this could fairly be said about life with the two conditions noted here. (On some views, it is possible that someone might be mistaken about whether or not his life is worth living. For instance, imagine a case in which someone is living a life of unadulterated agony, but believes it is very worthwhile, since he did something terrible in a former life and is now being punished for that. In this case, we may be inclined to think he is mistaken in thinking his current life worth living.[63])

### ii  *A life that someone will think is worth living*

When we move away from these extreme and rare conditions, judging the severity or seriousness of a condition becomes even more difficult and so controversial.[64] Parents, those with relevant conditions of some kind and the

---

[61] National Institute of Neurological Disorders and Stroke <http://www.ninds.nih.gov/disorders/lesch_nyhan/lesch_nyhan.htm>, accessed 5 October 2007.

[62] Glover, above n 55, 60.

[63] I am grateful to Roger Crisp here.

[64] For recognition of this difficulty in this context see, eg, HGC, *Response to the Human Fertilisation and Embryology Authority on the Consultation on Preimplantation Genetic Diagnosis*, para 6: 'It has proved impossible to define what "serious" should mean in this context. We have listed some factors that should be taken into account when considering seriousness, but perhaps the most important is that this technique should not be used for the purposes of trait selection or in a manner which could give rise to eugenic outcomes'. The HFEA and AGCT, in their *Consultation Document on Preimplantation Genetic Diagnosis* (November

medical profession may well have diverging views about this issue that have been informed, and so formed, in different ways. Conditions of debateable severity might be Down's syndrome or cystic fibrosis.[65]

The Down's Syndrome Association provides a mixture of information about the condition, some of the flavour of which is given by the following[66]:

> Children with Down's syndrome can and do grow up to live long and fulfilled lives. Provided they are allowed the opportunities they need to develop self-help skills and independence, people with Down's syndrome can thrive well into their fifties and beyond, facing many of the challenges we all encounter: school, further education, work and a home of one's own. Many children with Down's syndrome are now being integrated successfully into mainstream schools... People with Down's syndrome all have a certain degree of learning disability (mental handicap). The degree of disability varies from person to person and it is impossible to tell at birth what that degree will be... About one in three children born with Down's syndrome has a heart defect. Some heart defects are quite minor, such as murmurs; some defects are severe, requiring medication and/or surgery...

One of various possible heart conditions in Down's syndrome is an atrioventricular (septal) defect which 'can be corrected by major heart surgery in infancy, but for a few babies the operation is not medically advisable'.

In the case of cystic fibrosis[67]:

> [A] defective version of a protein called CFTR (Cystic Fibrosis Transmembrane Conductance Regulator) is produced. This is responsible for the transport of salts and water across the cell membranes. This means that in certain parts of the body, the secretions lack water, becoming thick and sticky. This means the lungs; pancreas (an internal organ which controls blood sugar and produces enzymes to break down food); intestines and other organs tend to get clogged up with thick, sticky mucus. Symptoms include poor weight gain, chest infections, coughs, abnormal stools and salty sweat. There have been improvements in the management of cystic fibrosis in recent years and with recent advances in treatment, most affected children now survive into adulthood. There is no cure for cystic fibrosis, but the faulty gene has been identified and further important medical advances are expected. The symptoms of cystic fibrosis vary... Cystic

---

1999), observe in para 31: 'individual judgments on seriousness will vary depending on personal and family circumstances and on the nature and severity of the condition and the likelihood of transmission'.

[65] For one view on such conditions, see A Asch 'Can Aborting "Imperfect" Children be Immoral?' in A Asch 'Real Moral Dilemmas' (1986) 46(10) *Christianity and Crisis*, 237. Reprinted in J Arras and B Steinbock, *Ethical Issues in Modern Medicine*, 5th edn, 384, 386: 'Down's syndrome, spina bifida, cystic fibrosis, or muscular dystrophy cause degrees of impairment ranging from mild to severe, the degree indeterminable at the time of prenatal diagnosis...'.

[66] Down's Syndrome Association, 'Your Baby has Down's Syndrome: a Guide for Parents', at 11, 4, 8, and 18 respectively <http://www.downs-syndrome.org.uk>, accessed 5 October 2007.

[67] NHS Direct Health Encylopaedia, 'cystic fibrosis' <http://www.nhsdirect.nhs.uk/articles/article.aspx?articleId=118>, accessed 5 October 2007.

fibrosis affects the enzyme secretion of the pancreas and the enzyme-secreting glands in the wall of the bowel. This causes defective absorption of important food constituents. Also recurrent upper respiratory tract and chest infections, causing persistent coughing and breathlessness. Sinusitis and nasal problems are also common... Later in life, people with cystic fibrosis are prone to bronchiectasis, bowel obstruction problems, failure to absorb food properly, infertility and cirrhosis (scarring) of the liver... The possible complications of the disease include: 'telescoping' (intussusception) of the bowel; secondary heart failure; pancreatitis; lung collapse; increased risk of developing diabetes; liver cirrhosis and its associated problems; obstruction within the biliary tract; most men with cystic fibrosis are infertile; women with cystic fibrosis have a slight risk of developing reduced fertility due to changes in the cervical mucus.

Despite the difficulties that will be experienced in lives with Down's syndrome or cystic fibrosis, on balance it may be fair to say that a person with one of these conditions will probably have a life she thinks is worth living, one that particularly *she* may also think is of reasonable quality. Indeed, there is evidence from positive psychological research on disability and disease that seems to suggest that in very many cases our subjective well-being is largely genetic, so that whether we have a condition of some kind matters a lot less than people may think.[68] So, although the severity of these conditions varies, even at their worst it seems that it would not have been against the interests of someone with one of them to have been born.[69] This means that prenatal screening and testing for such conditions would not be in their interests. Accordingly, we return to the broader picture of whose interests can be at stake in selection practices and begin to see the possible tension between the interests of prospective parents and their possible children. We now need to revisit the interests of those who are planning to have and raise a child.

### iii  Severity: whose interests?

The abortion of a fetus that would as a child develop Tay-Sachs is likely to be very emotionally painful for a couple. Despite this, the decision to end such a pregnancy may also be in their interests: it is unlikely that parents would think it in their interests to have a child whose life will be so short and apparently full of suffering.

---

[68] See A Fave and F Massimini 'The Relevance of Subjective Well-being to Social Policies: Optimal Experience and Tailored Intervention' in F Huppert, N Baylis and B Kaverne, *The Science of Well-being* (Oxford: OUP, 2005) 379.

[69] For interesting work on the views of people with conditions such as cystic fibrosis, Down's syndrome and spina bifida, both on their lives and on screening practices, see P Alderson 'Prenatal Counselling and Images of Disability' in D Dickenson (ed), *Ethical Issues in Maternal-Fetal Medicine* (Cambridge: Cambridge University Press, 2002) 195, discussed in S V. The HFEA/AGCT *Consultation Document*, above n 64, para 33, observes that 'many disorders vary in the severity with which they present. Cystic fibrosis can contribute to death within a few days of birth, but some individuals may survive into their thirties and beyond'.

However, we have also seen that there are cases of disease or disability in which a person would still think her life worth living and that here we cannot say that it is not in the interests of the possible person to be born. Despite this, a child's condition may still implicate his parents' interests in reproduction in serious ways: he might have significant mental impairment or serious health problems requiring repeated hospitalisation with an uncertain future. So, although people may reasonably disagree about this, and although the spectrum of severity of a given condition varies, it is arguable that some children born with a condition such as Down's syndrome or cystic fibrosis may fairly be judged to have a serious condition.[70]

At this stage, it is becoming apparent that screening, testing and selection decisions can in fact be made for either of two principal reasons: first, where the child's quality of life would be one of extremely low (sometimes called 'sub-zero') quality, as in the case of Tay-Sachs, primarily because of what that life would be like for the resulting child (here the parents' interests will also be implicated); second, where the child would in fact have a reasonable quality of life but its condition may nevertheless have the potential to impact adversely on its parents, because of their interests in the kind of child who will be born. (It should be noted here that other features in a child have the potential seriously to engage parental interests, so that impairment is not unique in this respect.[71]) Selection against Down's syndrome or cystic fibrosis (in some cases) may put special weight on the parents' interests rather than those of the child. Here we can also recall Shakespeare's analysis, in which he identified apparently both child-focused and parent-focused (or parent-accommodating) reasons for avoiding the birth of an impaired child.[72] Shakespeare also appears to support the distinction I endorse between, on the one hand, those rare cases in which birth might not be in the interests of the future child, given the severity of its impairment or condition and, on the other hand, cases in which selection is really, potentially, in the parents' interests or those of their wider family.[73]

In fact, unless parents have a well-informed picture of what life for someone with Down's syndrome may be like it is unlikely that they would see a decision to abort a fetus with Down's syndrome as really potentially concerning their own interests. To do so may be very painful and the idea that parents may want to avoid the birth of an impaired child for their own sake or that of their family is

---

[70] In *Rand v East Dorset Health Authority* [2000] 56 BMLR 39, discussed in Chapters 2 and 3, Newman J observed: '[t]here is an issue as to whether [the child in question] should be described as "seriously disabled"', noting that 'she is regarded as one of the most able and intelligent children among those who suffer from Down's Syndrome' (at 40). However, in due course he concluded that it was appropriate to describe her as 'seriously disabled' (at 45).
[71] I am grateful to Stephen Wilkinson here. Possible examples are an exceptionally gifted child, a black child in a racist society, or a female child in a sexist one.
[72] See text above at n 9.
[73] T Shakespeare, *Disability Rights and Wrongs* (London: Routledge, 2006) 97.

somewhat taboo.[74] Despite this, I have argued that prospective parents do have a legitimate moral interest in deciding whether to have a child with a serious condition of some kind and that this interest is one aspect of their broader interest in deciding whether to have *any* child. As we have also seen, in those rare cases where there is a serious risk that a subsequently born child would not have a life he thought worth living, abortion also may be justifiable in the interests of the fetus. Are parents morally required to avoid the birth of such a child?

## IV BIRTH AND HARM

### A  A Life that Someone May Think is Not Worth Living

We have seen that we can distinguish between cases where there is a high probability that a child would have a life of very low, or 'sub-zero', quality and ones where a condition or disease would nevertheless leave someone with a life worth living. Reflecting on the quality of the life that might be experienced encourages us to think not just about whether it is morally justifiable to avoid some lives at the prenatal stage (as we have done to some extent above and will do further below) but also about whether some lives *should* be avoided. We need to think about the relationship between existence and the experiences inherent in that existence and the possibility that a particular existence — a life — could or should have been avoided.

Any given embryo (past the possibility of twinning) or fetus can only later exist as one possible child. So the life of that child is the only life that embryo or fetus could come to have. If there is a serious risk that that child would have a life of very low quality, we need to ask whether birth is against its interests, even though this is the only life it could have. Clearly the child has interests once it is born (and from sentience onwards as a fetus), although prior to self-consciousness and the development of the capacity for autonomy it will not be able to take an interest in its welfare.[75] Do those interests include an interest in not being born under certain conditions?

Determining this might be thought to entail a comparison between existence and non-existence. We can understand that comparison in some cases. For instance, someone may be very ill and may contemplate refusing life-sustaining treatment because he thinks his life is no longer a benefit.[76] But we cannot

---

[74] In discussion, one anonymous obstetrician observed that she considers that clinicians tend always to cite and use the disability ground of the Abortion Act in relation to termination for fetal disability because this is easier for parents. I discuss this section in the next chapter.
[75] Steinbock, above n 35, 56.
[76] Buchanan *et al*, above n 7, 234.

meaningfully compare existence and non-existence at the start of life: non-existence is no state at all since there is no subject to experience it.[77] For some, this is a reason to reject the notion that a child could claim to have a 'wrongful life', one of such low quality that it would have been better not to be born. Rather than approach the issue by way of comparison, then, it may be more fruitful to focus instead on the experience of the person once born.

If pain and suffering are very severe — as seems highly likely in the case of Tay-Sachs — it might plausibly be claimed that it would have been better not to experience these conditions and so not to be born. This approach, advocated by Buchanan *et al*, concentrates on the burdens that come with or soon after birth and the lack of sufficiently compensating benefits or goods.[78] The thought is that the child's interests are so severely negatively affected that not to experience its life would have been preferable. This is an alternative way of understanding the notion of a 'wrongful life', one that does not entail notions of comparison.[79]

If such a person is born, has she been harmed? Traditionally understood, harm involves a comparison between one state and another in which one is made worse off. This brings us back to the difficulties of comparing non-existence and existence and tends again to lead to a rejection, morally or legally, of the idea of a wrongful life. However, on the above analysis, harm can also be understood as accruing at the point of existence, just as does the negative impact on the child's interests. This analysis can also be extended to include the notion of rights, which likewise accrue at the point of birth. As Buchanan *et al* have expressed this[80]:

> The right in question is the right of the child who does exist with a life not worth living not to have been brought into existence with such a life... The act of creating the person also creates the right that it violates — the person and his or her rights come into existence together.

Discussion of rights naturally invites discussion of duties. If prenatal testing reveals that a child would be born who would develop Tay-Sachs and if that child has a right not to be born, the implication would be that its parents are morally required to avoid its life by opting for a termination. If they decline to do so, it could be said that they are breaching a duty whose effects will be felt when the

---

[77] *Ibid* Heyd above n 11, 37, suggests that 'the comparison between life and nonexistence is blocked by two considerations: the valuelessness of nonexistence as such and the unattributability of its alleged value to individual subjects'.

[78] Buchanan *et al*, above n 7, 235.

[79] *Ibid*: 'The child in a wrongful life case has been given something — life — that because of its awful quality he or she should not have been given and has thereby been wronged'. As Buchanan *et al* note (at 236), a possible objection here is that before a child exists it can have no right and so that right cannot be respected by choosing not to allow the child to exist. The response is to observe that everyone has the right not to be born into a life not worth living, a right which is usually respected but not in the case of someone who has a 'wrongful life'.

[80] *Ibid* 236.

person is born with a life she does not think worth living.[81] (It should be noted here that sometimes a life of this kind of quality is described as a life 'worth not living'. The logical and practical difference here is that there may be nothing wrong with bringing into being someone whose life is merely not worth living, since it may not be not worth living. That is, it may just be neutral. For the sake of consistency with broader usage in the literature, however, I shall continue to use the phrase 'life not worth living'.[82])

At face value the idea that prospective parents might have such a duty seems quite onerous (at least psychologically, since such a moral duty could not be enforced). However, typically parents will not wish to continue with a pregnancy in which a fetus tests positive for a condition such as Tay-Sachs. Indeed, as noted earlier, usually their interest will be in avoiding the birth of such a child. In this way, the idea that they might have a duty to avoid its birth will not typically be a significant (psychological) constraint on their reproductive autonomy.[83] Rather, the avoidance of the birth might well be in line with their autonomous wishes and interests. But we can imagine cases where the idea of such a duty would be a significant constraint, for instance where parents have religious or other moral objections to the idea of termination, including in such circumstances.[84] Alternatively, to continue with an affected pregnancy may be a couple's last (or nearly last) chance of having a child.[85] Can it be said that even in these circumstances they have a duty not to permit the child to be born? Sadly, having a child who will develop the symptoms of Tay-Sachs and live at most four to five years may well be worse than having none at all, but people will have different views about this. In some cases prospective parents' moral beliefs may mean that they strongly disagree with the idea that they might have a moral duty not to allow the child's birth. In this light, it seems that we should only say, as Jonathan Glover has, that parents have a duty to avoid the birth of such a child 'where possible'.[86]

Indeed, another difficulty parents might encounter concerns the risks in any diagnostic testing at the prenatal stage, notably the risk of miscarriage following chorionic villus sampling or amniocentesis. The risk is typically described as being approximately one per cent.[87] For couples for whom conception was not easy, particularly where a woman is that much older, this risk may be of particular concern. (If a couple knows in advance of conception that there is a high risk of

---

[81] Ibid.
[82] I am grateful to Roger Crisp here.
[83] The typical lack of conflict between reproductive autonomy and the prevention of genetically transmitted 'harms' is also noted in *ibid* 255. As I have noted, this lack of conflict only applies in cases where a child would very probably have a life of very low quality.
[84] *Ibid* 237.
[85] A similar point is noted in *ibid* 241.
[86] Glover, above n 55, 60. Glover writes of a 'test' of 'urg[ing] avoidance where possible', noting that 'presumably [this is] in line with the thinking of most potential parents'.
[87] HGC, *Making Babies: Reproductive Decisions and Genetic Technologies* (2006), para 3.15.

transmission of a condition such as Tay-Sachs in their case, in fact they are likely to opt for IVF and PGD.) A different kind of difficulty may arise where access to testing and termination is restricted in some way.[88] For instance, parents may live in an area remote from the relevant prenatal services. This could make fulfilment of the duty difficult. In such a case, if the parents would wish to avoid having a child with a serious risk of a life of sub-zero quality but access to the means to identify and avoid this is hard, then in fact they are not readily able to exercise their reproductive autonomy.[89]

Overall, we might identify a spectrum of factors to consider in any appraisal of the potential wrongfulness of continuing with a pregnancy as a result of which someone could be born with a wrongful life, as Buchanan *et al* have done.[90] Such a spectrum needs to be sensitive to possible variations in circumstance, so that new factors might become relevant. In practice, this means that we should be receptive to parents' difficulties and concerns where we attempt to make a moral judgment in any given case.

## B  A Life that Someone Will Think is Worth Living

As we have seen, very few conditions are so severe that it can plausibly be said that it would be better not to have been born. Judgments as to the seriousness of less severe conditions are controversial, but there is a good chance that it is not against the interests of someone with Down's syndrome or cystic fibrosis to be born, despite the varying severity of those conditions. Indeed, people with these conditions have told us that they consider their lives worthwhile.[91] This does not mean that we must accept that such conditions are not disabling to some degree, including when a person is socially supported. Rather, it means that we should recognise that someone with a given condition thinks her life worth living. It also means that we cannot say that it would be better for the person not to have the given condition, if this would mean not being born. Here we return to the point that any given embryo (past twinning) or fetus can only become one possible child. To think of a given person without Down's syndrome and reflect on the

---

[88]  Buchanan *et al*, above n 7, 241.

[89]  See further Heyd, above n 11, 34: 'But how are we to decide whether parents eager to have children can be sued for conceiving a child with the knowledge that it has a 50 percent chance of suffering from a handicap?'

[90]  Buchanan *et al*, above n 7, 241: 'How bad is the child's life, and in particular how severe and unremitting is its suffering? How high is the probability of the child having a genetic disease incompatible with a worthwhile life? How weighty are its parents' interests in having the child? For example, is this likely its parents' only opportunity to become parents, or are they already parents seeking to have additional children? How significant is the possibility of the parents having an unaffected child if this pregnancy is terminated and another conception pursued? How willing and able are the parents to support and care for the child while it lives? These factors, and no doubt others unique to specific cases, will determine how strong the moral case is against individuals risking having a child who will not have a life worth living.'

[91]  See the work of Alderson, above n 69, discussed in S V.

ways in which this would have been to his advantage is in fact to think of a different person. Derek Parfit first explored this issue, dubbing it the 'non-identity' problem.[92]

So if a person is born with a condition that leaves her with a life worth living, there can be no question of a duty to prevent that life for *her* sake. On the contrary, at one level the issue is rather whether it is morally *permissible* to prevent that person being born. Another way of putting this, noted earlier, is to ask if it is morally justifiable to do so. It was suggested above that where prospective parents' interests in the kind of reproductive future they are able to undertake are seriously invoked — such as where a child may be significantly mentally impaired and/or at risk of serious and ongoing health problems — they may reasonably decide against the birth in question. Further, on a gradualist approach to the moral claims of the embryo or fetus, this decision will be morally acceptable, at least earlier rather than later. (I reserve discussion of late-term terminations to the next chapter.)

Importantly, there is another way of considering the moral issues at stake in avoiding possible lives, particularly those in which a child would have a life she thought worth living. This involves distinguishing between person- and non-person-affecting principles. At the outset, it should be noted that 'possible' has different meanings in the following discussion. It might mean 'not yet conceived'; it can also mean 'not yet born'. The moral implications in either case may be somewhat different.

## C  Person- and Non-person-affecting Principles

The discussion about possibly preventing lives affected by certain conditions has so far considered the interests of the person who would be born. Where there is a good chance that a person would have a life of reasonable quality, the discussion has also noted the potential interests of already-existing people — the parents. The wider family might be relevant here too. This kind of discussion is typically referred to as 'person-affecting' and on some moral views only person-affecting-principles are relevant to discussions about who should and who should not be born.[93] Since I have considered the interests of possible people as well as actual people, I am referring to person-affecting principles in their wider sense. An alternative way of reflecting on such discussions is to consider states of the world or states of affairs, a 'non-person-affecting' approach.

---

[92] D Parfit, *Reasons and Persons* (Oxford: OUP, 1984) Ch 16.

[93] eg, Heyd, above n 11, argues that only the interests of actual people (eg, parents, society) are relevant, not those of the possible child. He argues for a 'human-relative' conception of value and, on this basis, considers that the subjects of 'genesis problems' (those concerning the existence, number and identity of people) cannot themselves be the predicates of value. If the people whose existence is being debated do not have moral standing in either a person-affecting or a non-person-affecting theory, then all value must instead be located in the decision-making party, often the parents (14–15).

We can explore the relevance either of person-affecting or non-person affecting principles by comparing two ways of avoiding disability originating in the work of Derek Parfit and modified by Buchanan *et al*. In Parfit's work, the comparison is presented by means of two competing medical programmes. In Buchanan *et al's* work, the comparison is presented at the individual level of conception and pregnancy. I shall explore the comparison in the latter way. The means of avoiding disability are the same in either case.

In the first case, a couple is advised that they are at risk of having a disabled child (perhaps because of an infection in the pregnant woman) unless they delay attempting to conceive for two months. They do not do so and give birth to Child A, who is disabled. By waiting they could have conceived Child B (assuming their chance of conception two months later was equally good, an important caveat). In the second case, a pregnant woman does not take a pill needed by her fetus which is fully safe for her. The result is that Child C is born disabled. Child A and Child C are disabled to the same degree. Is the parents' or pregnant woman's conduct worse in either case?

In the first case, one question is whether Child A has been harmed. If not conceived with the disability, of course, the child would not have been conceived at all. Once again, this is the 'non-identity' problem. So, unless the child's existence is so awful that there are no compensating benefits in being alive (and it therefore has what might be termed a 'wrongful life') then on balance its existence is a good for it. In fact, however, both Child A and Child C have disabilities which leave them with lives they think worth living. This means, as Buchanan *et al* have noted, that the normal principles of beneficence and maleficence are not readily applicable to Child A, such that it is difficult to say that she has been harmed, is a victim or has had her rights violated.[94] Still, the couple could have waited and had a different child, B, without the disability. The result would be that someone would have been born with less (presumed) suffering and possibly greater opportunities and happiness. Would it have been better morally to wait and conceive Child B?

Arguably, given that Child A has a life she thinks worth having and living, this would only have been better if we were to adopt a non-person-affecting approach. On this basis it could be argued that, other things being equal (in particular that the same number of people exist), it is preferable if people are born who will not experience impairment or suffering and who will have greater rather than lesser opportunities (that is, by virtue of a congenital condition). The comparison here is between the lives of different possible people. This approach looks to the total degree of impairment, suffering or limited opportunity by comparing the world with Child A and the one with Child B. Of course, disability must be experienced by someone and for this reason the principle remains person-affecting, but what it does not require is that the same individual,

---

[94] Buchanan *et al*, above n 7, 247.

disabled and non-disabled, exists in either possible alternative.[95] The principle requires that we weigh not just less suffering but also more happiness or good; otherwise it could favour the birth of a person who would, overall, have a 'substantially worse life'.[96] On a non-person-affecting view, then, we could provisionally say that it would have been better if the couple had waited and conceived Child B and that they were wrong not to do so. I consider this further in due course.

Turning to the second case, a pregnant woman is advised that her fetus needs treatment by means of a pill which she needs to take and which is fully safe for her but, for no apparent reason, the woman declines to take the pill. Child C is subsequently born disabled. Given that this child could have been born without the disability, is this morally worse than the actions of the parents in the first case? Derek Parfit would argue that there is no difference since in both cases the same number of people are born with a disability. In the original example Parfit does admit that someone who was harmed *in utero* by a lack of treatment might well have a legitimate complaint, assuming he comes to know that his disability could have been avoided. But he 'controls' for this difference by stipulating that the person does not know about the avoidable nature of his disability.[97] However, as Jonathan Glover observes, even if he will not complain that his disability could have been avoided — because he does not know this to be the case — this does not mean that he should not have been treated *in utero* to avoid his disability: it is just that he did not know that we owed him this.[98] This thought appears consistent with the judgment that, other things being equal, harm to an actual person — by disabling him — is more morally serious than not preventing the birth of someone with an (unavoidably) disabled life that is worth living.[99] In this case, then, we might say that the woman has breached her moral duty to the child the fetus became, with the result that a person has been affected. It is also the case, and of less importance, that there is more disability in the world than if she had taken the therapeutic pill. (It is also true that there is more disability in the world if Child A is born.)

We can further bring out the moral force of harming an actual person by varying this scenario. Instead of the woman omitting to take the pill, we could create the (even more unlikely) example in which she deliberately intervenes in some way to harm the fetus *in utero*. For instance, Tony Hope has explored the idea of deliberately intervening, say, to deafen a child and concludes that this

---

[95] *Ibid* 249.
[96] *Ibid* 250.
[97] Parfit, above n 92, 367–9.
[98] Glover, above n 55, 49.
[99] Others agreeing with this view are Buchanan *et al*, above n 7, 254 and, by implication, Glover in *ibid*. This differs from Parfit, who holds that there is no moral difference between the various scenarios.

would be wrong.[100] Arguably, the only moral difference between failing to take the pill and deliberately intervening so that a child is later born with a disability may be that it is harder to judge the reasonableness of positive duties not to assist than negative ones not to harm.[101] That said, where a woman does not take a pill in pregnancy needed by the fetus which is safe for her and which she has no reason not to take, we can clearly judge this to be a breach of a positive duty to assist. In both cases, then, a person (the subsequently born child) has been wrongly harmed.

For a contrary view, however, consider an argument of John Robertson's that concerns a couple's desire for a deaf child.[102] When they learn that the woman is carrying a fetus who will be able to hear, they intervene during pregnancy to deafen it. On Robertson's view, the child has not been harmed because they would not otherwise choose to give birth to it: there is no 'alternative' way for the child to be born. Robertson's argument attempts to rely on the 'non-identity' problem, the point that the alternative is non-existence. His argument also relies on the idea that death will be worse for the child, from which it is spared by its parents' intervention to deafen it *in utero*. At one level, it is right that death would be worse, since being deaf is clearly compatible with having a life worth living. What his argument does not do, however, is to question whether the parents' intervention to deafen the fetus and thus the child who could otherwise be born with full hearing is itself morally acceptable.[103] In effect, where parents are only prepared to have a disabled child, his argument would legitimise the infliction of any harm on the fetus compatible with a life a person thought worth living. I consider the notion of parents wishing to have a disabled child in Chapter 6. For now, we might note that in Robertson's case it is not that the parents have 'selected for disability', as they might do by means of PGD, but rather that they have disabled a child who could otherwise, were it not for their desires, have been born able to hear. The question is not whether it is morally acceptable to want a deaf child, but whether the means to achieve such a child are. The problem here is that it is not true that there was not available to them the option of having the child and not deafening it.

The relationship between person-affecting and non-person-affecting principles in moral theory more generally is highly complex and unresolved.[104] Fortunately, I do not need to consider the issue more broadly here. I have used the two scenarios to illustrate the possible application of these principles. In the first pre-conception scenario the issue really concerned who should be born; in the

---

[100] T Hope and J McMillan 'Ethical Problems before Conception' (2003) 361 *Lancet* 2164, as discussed in Glover, above n 55, 50.
[101] For an argument on this point related to the maternal-fetal conflict see Scott, above n 31, Ch 2.
[102] Robertson, above n 2, 466.
[103] *Ibid*.
[104] As noted in, eg, Buchanan *et al*, above n 7, 250.

second it concerned the condition in which a given person is born. For now, it might be noted that both PND and PGD occur post-conception. The question that can lie behind them, however, is whether someone else could or should be born instead, either by means of termination followed by a subsequent pregnancy or by means of selecting one (or more) rather than other embryos. The moral implications in either case can be explored both by person- and non-person-affecting principles and we need to consider the application of these principles directly to PND, selective termination and PGD.

First, I would like to make an important preliminary point about the application of non-person-affecting principles. I have argued that one moral justification for termination where a child would have a life she thought worth living would be where its condition would nevertheless seriously affect its parents. This is a person-affecting consideration. I also suggested it was likely to be painful and difficult for prospective parents to acknowledge their potential interests in avoiding the birth of a child with a certain disability. In this light, one concern about the use of non-person-affecting principles may be that we could over-inflate the judgment of serious suffering, loss of opportunity or good that a condition may entail in order to be able to 'call in aid' non-person-affecting principles. We may have a tendency to do this rather than think honestly about how much as prospective parents we are in fact, and arguably sometimes legitimately, concerned about our own interests.

I now turn to consider the implications of non-person affecting principles for moral requirements and moral permissibility. Can such principles give rise to a duty to prevent a possible life where someone would have a life she thought worth living? And what is the relationship between these principles and the moral permissibility of preventing such a life? I turn first to the idea of duties, or moral requirements.

### i  Moral requirements

A non-person-affecting perspective could give rise to the following principle, proposed by Buchanan et al[105]:

> Individuals are morally required not to let any child or other dependent person for whose welfare they are responsible experience serious suffering or limited opportunity or serious loss of happiness or good, if they can act so that, without affecting the number of persons who will exist and without imposing substantial burdens or costs or loss of benefit on themselves or others, no child or other dependent person for whose welfare they are responsible will experience serious suffering or limited opportunity or serious loss of happiness or good.

On their analysis, it seems that on a non-person-affecting approach there may in fact be a duty to avoid the birth of a disabled person with a worthwhile life in favour of another non-disabled person. Indeed, since wrongful life cases are

[105] *Ibid* 249.

comfortably covered by person-affecting principles, in some ways what they call 'wrongful disability' cases are the main ones to which non-person-affecting principles might apply. (This does not mean the principles are not also applicable to wrongful life cases.) Somewhat puzzlingly, in discussing the potential wrongfulness of bringing a child into the world who would have a life she thinks worth living, Buchanan *et al* refer, at one end of the spectrum, to the notion of 'a condition that the child can reasonably be expected to live with', suggesting that in such a case the parents do not act wrongly.[106] It is not clear how this case is morally distinguishable from any other 'wrongful disability' case in which, by definition, a child has a life she thinks worth living, despite her disability.

On Buchanan *et al's* view, whether it is morally wrong to act so that a child is born who will experience serious impairment and loss of opportunity when another would not have done depends on how difficult it was to avoid this. There may be considerable costs or loss of benefits to parents at stake. In this respect, Buchanan *et al* again suggest a spectrum of factors that may be relevant, just as they did in relation to the potential difficulties facing parents at risk of having a child who would likely have a very low quality of life, a 'wrongful life'.[107] Once again, sensitivity is required in making judgments in this context.

In fact, a problem may occur if parents would not be able to 'replace' a disabled with a non-disabled child, perhaps because of fertility considerations. In such a case, Buchanan *et al* suggest that if they can only have a particular disabled child and that child will consider her life worth living, even on a non-person-affecting approach it is not wrong for them to have that child.[108] It is beyond my scope to engage in a discussion of the as-yet-unresolved complexities of so-called 'different number' cases.

Leaving these complexities aside, then, I want to discuss three important points about the idea of such a duty. The first concerns the stage at which non-person-affecting principles are applied: in particular, whether an embryo or fetus yet exists and, if so, how developed it is. The second concerns the difficult nature of the judgment, where a child would have a life she thinks worth living, that there is still 'serious suffering or limited opportunity or serious loss of happiness or

---

[106] *Ibid* 243.
[107] *Ibid*: 'Whether failure to prevent a disability is wrong in specific cases will typically depend on many features of that case. For example, what is the relative seriousness of the disability for the child's well-being and opportunities? What measures are available to the child's parents to prevent the condition — such as abortion, artificial insemination by donor, or oocyte donation — and how acceptable are these means to prospective parents? Is it possible, and if so how likely, that they can conceive another child without the disabling condition, or will any child they conceive have or be highly likely to have the condition? If the disability can only be prevented by not conceiving at all, do the couple have alternative means, such as adoption, of becoming parents? When the condition can be prevented or its adverse impact compensated for, what means are necessary to do so?'
[108] *Ibid* 255.

good'. The third concerns the costs or difficulties or loss of benefits for prospective parents in any given decision.

a   The stage of development of the fetus

Turning first to the fetus, there is an important feature which differentiates one of the scenarios in Parfit's work from the case of termination and even from PGD. Recall the couple who could avoid disability in a possible child by waiting to try to conceive. Since this is a choice made before conception, there need be no moral justification for it (assuming contraception, for instance, is not morally wrong). Indeed, the issue is not one of justification at all; rather, it is whether there is a duty to avoid the birth of a disabled child by failing to conceive it.

By contrast, most screening and diagnosis occurs at the prenatal stage when a woman is already pregnant. Prenatal screening, PND and selective abortion therefore entail choices regarding a being which, although not a person on many moral views, may have some moral claims, particularly later in pregnancy. However, when a non-person-affecting analysis is used in this context, the assumption is typically that the fetus has no moral status.[109] We can see, then, that the application of a non-person-affecting analysis dovetails well not only with the view that the fetus is not a person, but also with the view that personhood is central to any moral claims the fetus could have.[110] How satisfactory is this? Clearly, this depends on one's view of the moral status of the fetus.

Whilst on a gradualist approach the fetus is not at any stage a person, the fetus nevertheless has growing moral claims. The question that then arises is whether those moral claims can have any place in the application of a principle which assumes that claims short of personhood cannot count. The obvious answer is 'no'. But this answer is less than satisfactory where it is thought that the fetus has some moral claims, because it provides no way of taking account of those claims when we consider ending the life of the fetus in the interests of less disability and greater opportunities in other as yet non-existent people in the world. Recall in particular that the focus here is on a degree of disability which is fully compatible with a life worth living. In effect, if we ascribe some moral status to the fetus even though it is not a person (and some would reject this), it may make it difficult for there to be a duty which entails its destruction in these 'wrongful disability' cases. As the fetus develops, this difficulty increases. So, although we may not be as troubled about whether the moral claims of a four-week embryo could bar the determination of a duty to avoid its birth for the sake of less disability compatible with a worthwhile life in (another) future person, as the fetus develops we could

---

[109] For recognition of this point, see, eg, Sheldon and Wilkinson, above n 54, 95, who refer to the assumption that the fetus has 'very low' moral status.

[110] No doubt for this reason Buchanan *et al*, above n 7, consider that, at least for the first two trimesters, the fetus is not a person (at 240). Their argument does not appear to distinguish between pre-and post-conception scenarios and thus whether or not an embryo or fetus exists.

be increasingly concerned about this. By the time of a fetal anomaly scan at 20 weeks, we might really worry about whether there could be any duty to avoid the birth of the fetus for this reason. Rather, we may now be strongly concerned about the need morally to *justify* any termination. This contrasts sharply with the 'wrongful life' scenario, where a person would very likely not have a life she thought worth living, in which it is because we owe a duty to the child the fetus would become that termination may be morally required where possible.

Importantly, then, I am suggesting that with regard to decisions concerning a degree of disability or disease compatible with a life worth living, if we think the fetus has some growing moral claims (and many do not think this), non-person-affecting principles will have to compete with and give way to the fetus's growing moral status over the course of a pregnancy. Since the application of non-person-affecting principles in this context often assumes a very low or non-existent moral status for the fetus, such principles will be at their strongest applied pre-conception (as in one of Parfit's scenarios) or, to a lesser extent, at the stage of selection by PGD. However, whilst pre-conception it is possible to talk of moral requirements or duties, on a gradualist approach as a pregnancy begins and the fetus develops it may be that our focus should shift to the need for moral justification and so to the realm of moral permissibility. To further flesh this out we need to consider the second aspect of relevance to determinations of moral requirements (and to moral permissibility), notably the difficulty of judging that a disability is serious.

b    The difficulty of judging a disability to be serious

If on a gradualist approach the embryo has a lower moral status than the fetus, does this mean that parents are morally required to select against a child who would have a life she thought worth living when engaging in PGD or, if this were possible in their case, to take steps pre-conception to avoid a life of that quality (as in Parfit's example)? The moral status of the embryo (or fetus) is not the only relevant consideration here.

There is also the need to judge whether there will be in fact be 'serious suffering or limited opportunity or serious loss of happiness or good', to recall Buchanan *et al's* phrase. Arguably, the controversial and reasonably contested nature of judgments about the severity of a condition when a child would have a life she thought worth living will give the benefit of the doubt to parents here, potentially so as to deny the existence of a duty. Indeed, Buchanan *et al* themselves note the difficulty of judging the relevant 'seriousness'.[111] This means that, even pre-conception or at the stage of selection by PGD, if there is reasonable disagreement about the seriousness of a given condition it will be hard to say that parents are morally required to avoid the birth of a person with that condition.

---

[111]   *Ibid* 250.

c   Costs or difficulties or loss of benefits for parents

The costs or difficulties for parents will be a highly significant factor, as Buchanan *et al* acknowledge, and I would like to draw attention to some important issues in relation to this.

As noted, the embryo being tested in PGD may not have a very high moral status. This could be thought to clear the way for non-person-affecting duties in selection decisions. Yet the idea of a duty to avoid — by means of PGD — the birth of a child with a life worth living imposes the physical and emotional (and potentially financial) costs of PGD on prospective parents at what is likely to be an already very difficult time. Indeed, unless they have sought IVF and PGD because they are at high risk of having a child with a serious genetic condition of some kind (which could leave a child with or without a life she thought worth living) they are unlikely to use PGD. If using IVF because of fertility considerations, their concern will be to achieve a pregnancy and subsequent live birth. In this regard, they may be offered and accept the related technique of preimplantation genetic screening (PGS). The main (controversial) purpose of this technique is to improve IVF outcomes by detecting chromosomal abnormalities incompatible with life, although the technique also screens out embryos with a condition such as Down's syndrome.[112]

If couples do engage in PGD or PGS, they may be faced with some very difficult decisions or consequences. It may be that all their embryos prove to be ones that may be affected by a condition which nevertheless leaves a child with a life worth living. In this case, the Human Fertilisation and Embryology Authority (HFEA) licence conditions for clinics typically forbid the implantation of such embryos, even where a child would have a life she thinks worthwhile. In this way, the licence conditions do not discriminate between degrees of disability or disease (as I discuss further in the chapters on PGD). In such a case, a couple would then have no embryos to implant. Or it may be that those embryos that are not 'affected' do not appear to the IVF clinicians to be 'good' embryos for the purposes of achieving a pregnancy and/or do not survive to be implanted after PGD or PGS. Overall, prospective parents will always be constrained in their choice by the knowledge that the only way to attain more embryos is for the pregnant woman to undergo the first stages of another course of IVF, including stimulation by drugs and egg retrieval, often under general anaesthetic.

Importantly, when we combine these considerations with the difficulty of making the judgment about serious suffering and so forth, I suggest that we would conclude that there cannot be a duty either to undertake IVF and PGD or, if already undertaking IVF, to use PGD or, if already using PGD (or PGS) to avoid the life of a child whose life would *not* be worth living, then also to use the

---

[112]   Doubts about the use of PGS in relation to the improvement of IVF outcomes are expressed in, eg, D Hill 'Ten Years of Preimplantation Genetic Diagnosis-Aneuploidy Screening: Review of Multi-Center Report' (2004) 82/2 *Fertil & Steril* 300.

technique to avoid the birth of a child *with* a life worth living. So, for instance, if a couple were undergoing IVF and PGD for Tay-Sachs, they would not have a duty also to test their embryos for cystic fibrosis or Down's syndrome. Whether they would wish to do so is another matter.

When a pregnancy is established and we are considering PND, the twin issues of the moral claims of the fetus and the difficulty of judging seriousness will join the issue of the costs for parents. Once again, these costs may be very considerable. It is obvious that a couple is likely already to have formed an attachment to the fetus. They may also be concerned about whether they will be able to achieve another pregnancy if they terminate the current one. In this light, a termination may well be a distressing and demanding experience and will become increasingly so as a pregnancy progresses. For these kinds of reason, I think it would be very harsh to say that a couple has a duty, by means of a termination, to avoid the birth of a child who would have a life she thought worth living.

### ii  *Moral permissibility*

I have argued above that where we are considering the possible birth of someone with a life worth living, the strength of non-person-affecting principles will change over the course of a pregnancy in the light of the growing moral claims of the fetus. Arguably quite early on, the issue will shift from the notion of duties derived from non-person-affecting principles to the issue of the need for moral justification and so to the sphere of moral permissibility, rather than moral requirements. Indeed, even pre-conception or at the stage of selection by PGD, I highlighted the difficulty of judging seriousness and noted some possible costs or burdens for parents: both these factors may work to weaken the notion of a duty to avoid the birth of a child with a life worth living, even at these stages.

As a pregnancy progresses, then, the focus will shift from fairly weak notions of moral requirements to the question of what is morally permissible. In some ways we are also moving increasingly from non-person-affecting principles to person-affecting ones, even though the fetus may not at any stage be a person on the most stringent view of personhood.[113]

Importantly, the three factors discussed above will also be relevant to the issue of moral permissibility and so to the moral justification of the termination of the life of the fetus. First, the growing moral status of the fetus will mean that there is an increasing need morally to justify its termination. Second, as regards the difficulty of judging that a disability or disease compatible with a life worth living is serious, the contentious nature of these judgments could be thought either to be in the fetus's or its parents' favour. Here we can turn again to the gradualist approach to the fetus's moral status. The implication will be that the fetus will have a stronger moral claim the more advanced it is, which in turn will require

---

[113] Compare Buchanan *et al*, above n 7, 240, who leave the question open in the third trimester.

that the prospective parents' grounds for termination are that much more stringently justified. As regards the third factor — the costs or difficulties for parents — we should note that when we are discussing moral permissibility (rather than moral requirements), the costs or difficulties for parents are not those inherent in avoiding the current pregnancy. Rather, they concern those potentially inherent in *not* avoiding it, that is, in giving birth to a particular child. This also brings into view the parents' interests as a person-affecting consideration in its own right.

Overall, I have argued that both non-person-affecting principles and parents' interests (and so person-affecting principles) support the moral permissibility of avoiding the birth of a person who would have a life worth living, including at the fetal stage. However, the judgments as to the seriousness of a child's disability or disease and as to the costs or burdens for parents in having a given child must be that much more stringent as the fetus develops. It may be that after a certain stage termination is only morally justifiable if there is a serious risk that the child will have a life not worth living, so that termination can be said to be in the fetus's interests. I consider this further in Chapter 2 when I look at the issue of terminations after 24 weeks' gestation and the law.

## V THE INTERESTS OF PEOPLE WITH IMPAIRMENTS

I have already touched on the importance of sensitivity to the interests of people with impairments (or serious conditions of some kind) in debates about selection practices. In this section I try to identify the key issues relating to these interests that should be kept in mind throughout my discussion in this book. I say a bit more about models of disability, particularly in relation to the issue of discrimination. I also identify two particular concerns that people with impairments may have about prenatal, or preimplantation, selection practices. The first concern relates to the information that is provided to women or couples in the course of prenatal screening, PND or PGD; the second is that such practices, particularly through their increasingly routine nature,[114] express the view that people with impairments or disorders of some kind should not be (or have been) born. Overall, the issue of information provision emerges as a central one for policy-makers and health professionals.

### A  Models of Disability and Discrimination Issues

We saw earlier that some combination of the 'medical' and 'social' models is best placed to account for the significance of impairment or disability. I now want to address a concern about discrimination that relates to the two models.

---

[114] On the routinisation of prenatal screening, see in particular S Suter 'The Routinization of Prenatal Screening' (2002) 28 *Am JL & Med* 233, 268.

Where impairments can be alleviated with social support a question arises as to whether a decision selectively to terminate could be discriminatory. Sally Sheldon and Stephen Wilkinson have addressed this issue. Despite their criticisms of the social model for its failure to distinguish between disability and disadvantage, they suggest that there is one sense in which selective termination might be potentially discriminatory. As we shall see in the next chapter, these authors argue that, in the vast majority of cases in which being born is compatible with a good or reasonable quality of life, it is parental interests that to a large degree underlie the disability ground of the Abortion Act 1967 (as amended by the Human Fertilisation and Embryology Act 1990).[115] This is consistent with the arguments I have developed in this chapter and, accordingly, I agree with their view. One concern of Sheldon and Wilkinson is that where parental interests relate to the difficulties caused by any given impairment in itself, then selective termination is not discriminatory; by contrast, it might be otherwise where the underlying parental interests relate to the harms of social discrimination, notably where this results in 'lack of support services for the parents of disabled children or prejudice against those children'.[116] In a sense, the thought is that by screening and terminating for *disabilities* one may in fact be selecting against *impairments* that could be successfully alleviated with greater public support and that screening and termination therefore collude with discrimination against people with disabilities.

A question that then arises is how much we should do to address the latter harm. Social prejudice is always unacceptable. Is this always true of limitations in the degree of social support? Sheldon and Wilkinson note the necessity of resource allocation decisions.[117] This raises an interesting question about whether the connection between inadequate assistance and discrimination is a necessary one. Even if we could eradicate discrimination, in the sense of social prejudice, we may not have ideal levels of assistance for those with impairments and their parents. Buchanan *et al* have argued that, in the light of legitimate conflicting interests, society is not required to prioritise the interests of the disabled in reviewing social structures and arrangements.[118] They develop this point in relation to the requirements of the Americans with Disabilities Act, emphasising

---

[115] The relevant part of s 1(1) of the Abortion Act 1967 as amended by the Human Fertilisation and Embryology Act 1990 reads: 'Subject to the provisions of this section, a person shall not be guilty of an offence under the law relating to abortion when a pregnancy is terminated by a registered medical practitioner if two registered medical practitioners are of the opinion, formed in good faith... (d) that there is a substantial risk that if the child were born it would suffer from such physical or mental abnormalities as to be seriously handicapped'.
[116] Sheldon and Wilkinson, above n 54, 105.
[117] *Ibid* 108.
[118] Buchanan *et al*, above n 7, especially 291–3.

50   *Ethical Issues in Selection Practices*

that what the Act requires in the interests of equal opportunity is '"reasonable" accommodations' and that this implies that some weight should be given to the interests of others[119]:

> The addition of this qualifier signals a recognition that the interests of employers, of workers who do not have disabilities, and of consumers of the goods and services that public and private organizations produce are also legitimate and should be accorded some weight.

Acknowledging this point does not establish that more should not currently be done to support those with impairments and (where relevant) their carers. In this way, Shakespeare is right to emphasise the need 'for better provision of welfare services and financial benefits to parents of disabled children, in order to make it easier for parents to choose to… continue such a pregnancy'.[120] If justified, however, the recognition that, in the light of competing resources, society can at most provide reasonable support (however this is judged) would mean that eliminating discrimination does not *necessarily* entail the provision of optimal levels of assistance. And if this is so, then the decision to terminate a pregnancy that is in part based on concerns about the lack of support to an impaired child will not necessarily be discriminatory, in the United States, England or elsewhere.

However, parents might well be made more aware of the issue of discrimination and the role of social support in alleviating the effects of impairment as part of the officially non-directive counselling process that attends prenatal screening and testing practices. Indeed, to the extent that the decision to terminate or continue a pregnancy should be as informed as possible, such information could be seen as necessary. The resulting discussion would mean that the woman or couple would reflect on their reasons for seeking a termination in relation to issues of social support and discrimination. Yet, since the issue of discrimination is a moral one, to incorporate some information about or discussion of this issue into the ethos of non-directive counselling (discussed in Chapter 3) would entail careful thought about, and perhaps some re-evaluation of, that process.

## B   Information and Assumptions about Suffering or Difficulty

Assumptions about impairment can be helpfully challenged and informational issues explored through discussions with people with impairments. For instance, Priscilla Alderson undertook a series of interviews with adults who have one of a number of different conditions: cystic fibrosis, sickle cell anaemia, thalassaemia, Down's syndrome and spina bifida. She sought their views about their lives and about screening practices, setting out to 'challenge general assumptions, by showing how these interviewees did not fit the negative images propounded in the prenatal medical literature'.[121] To some degree, this observation relates to the

---

[119]   *Ibid* 292.
[120]   Shakespeare, above n 9, 672.
[121]   Alderson, above n 69, 203.

distinction between medical and social models of disability. Importantly, she found that those interviewed felt they suffered more from social stigma than from their actual physical conditions. A recurring theme was of 'adaptation, ingenuity and a resilience that grows through accepting and surmounting difficulties'.[122] (Alderson acknowledges that qualitative research of the kind undertaken here cannot claim necessarily to be representative.)

She compares this with the concern, which she thinks is inherent in prenatal screening practices, to avoid difficulties, noting that in any event these are an inherent aspect of human experience and suggesting that some degree of disability is inevitable at both ends of life. She is troubled by our '[f]earful avoidance of disability',[123] which she considers is 'liable to diminish people rather than freeing them into new achievement and confidence',[124] which she suggests would occur if we were instead to promote ways to support the lives of those with disabilities. She asks why there is not further discussion of the potential range of the severity of a condition, of the possibility of new treatments for some conditions and of the possibility that abortions may be preventing lives that are worth living. There may also be a 'mismatch' between the severity of a physical disability and the way a given life is enjoyed and valued. In this way, she challenges the assumption that it is 'kinder' to terminate because of the potential severity of the condition in any given case. (Of course, I noted above that indeed it would not be legitimate to argue that it is 'kinder' to terminate a fetus with, for instance, cystic fibrosis or Down's syndrome.) In effect, Alderson draws attention to the need for better information in the course of screening practices. What did her interviewees think about information provision in prenatal screening and PND and the practice of selective abortion more broadly?

Interestingly, those interviewed held a range of views. People with sickle cell anaemia, thalassaemia and cystic fibrosis tended to be in favour of PND, provided the information was accurate (currently unlikely, they thought). They also respected the parents' possible decision to terminate, whilst hoping that a given pregnancy would continue. (Indeed, it might be very difficult actively to support termination when this implies that one would not have been born.) By contrast, those with Down's syndrome and spina bifida, which are the subject of the most routine (therefore potentially the most unreflective, undebated) screening, were the least happy with the relevant practices.

These reactions confirm that a key moral issue in any consideration of the interests of people with impairments in selection practices concerns the nature of the information provided to women or couples in this process. Indeed, this point has been clearly made by Shakespeare. He discusses what he sees as the inadequacies of current counselling services and observes that '[d]ecisions about screening should be based on good information: rather than evaluating screening

---

[122] *Ibid* 208.
[123] *Ibid*.
[124] *Ibid*.

programmes in terms of those who undergo tests and terminations, programmes should be evaluated in terms of the proportion of people who were empowered to make an *informed choice*'.[125] The need for balanced information and, for example, the potentially unbalanced nature of information in relation to Down's syndrome has been more widely discussed in the literature.[126] Insight into the ways in which information-giving in this context should be developed has been offered by others well placed to do so.[127] Currently, there are few sources of information.[128]

The Nuffield Report also highlights the importance of the issue of information provision. Referring to the media coverage that used terms such as 'suffering' cited earlier, its report observes[129]:

> These examples show why it is important that accurate information is provided for pregnant women and for parents of newborn children about the nature and prognosis of the conditions of which their baby is at risk. There have been concerns about the adequacy of arrangements for informing parents about the disabilities that their baby is likely to develop, and his or her additional needs. In 2000, the Department of Health and Department for Education and Skills published joint guidance for parents and professionals (*Together from the Start*). This guidance identified several barriers to effective decision making at the time of early diagnosis. These include parents' perceptions of a lack of sensitivity, misunderstandings about the implications of a diagnosis, and the subsequent impact of a disability or health need on a child and his or her family. Some

---

[125] Shakespeare, above n 9, 685, my emphasis.

[126] See C Williams, P Alderson and B Farsides '"Drawing the Line" in Prenatal Screening and Testing: Health Practitioners' Discussions' (2002) 4(1) *Health, Risk and Society* 61, 73, for discussion of the value of this. For specific consideration of the information provided in relation to Down's syndrome, see C Williams, P Alderson and B Farsides 'What Constitutes Balanced Information in the Practitioners' Portrayals of Down's Syndrome?' (2002) 18 *Midwifery* 230.

[127] See, eg, B Bowles Biesecker and L Hamby 'What Difference the Disability Community Arguments Should Make for the Delivery of Prenatal Genetic Information' in Parens and Asch (eds), above n 7, 340.

[128] An exception is the ANSWER website developed by Tom Shakespeare and colleagues, the pilot version of which provides information about Down's syndrome, spina bifida, Turner's syndrome, Klinefelter's syndrome and cystic fibrosis, based on interviews and photographs of a range of people affected by each condition: <http://www.antenataltesting.info>, accessed 6 October 2007; T Shakespeare, above n 73, 100–101.

[129] Nuffield Council on Bioethics, above n 16, para 3.33, footnotes omitted. See also para 7.3, with reference to the future of a neonate who has experienced a period of critical care: 'In some cases, parents may be presented with overly negative images of the future lives of their children, which are not balanced by more positive information about the day-to-day lives of disabled people'. Footnote omitted (which cites: J Wyatt, *Matters of Life and Death: Today's Healthcare Dilemmas in the Light of Christian Faith* (Leicester: Inter-Varsity Press, 1998); J Campbell, (2005) former Chair of Social Care Institute for Excellence (SCIE) and a Disability Rights Commissioner, contributing to the Disability Rights Commission's Disability Debate; and C Eiser 'Children's Quality of Life Measures' (1997) 77 *Arch Dis Child* 350).

of the existing definitions of disability can be particularly insensitive, especially when it is not clear whether the child will develop disabilities or what the longer-term future might be. A template for good practice in discussing early identification, diagnosis and management of a disability or other special needs developed by the charity SCOPE in 2003 was rapidly adopted, disseminated and further developed in partnership with paediatric and other child health services and partners in health, education and the voluntary sector.

The Human Genetics Commission (HGC) likewise notes that[130]:

> [T]he information provided... is likely to focus on the medical difficulties that a child might have at present or in the future, and not on the potential that he or she might have for a rich and fulfilled life. It is especially important not to define any prospective children simply in terms of their potential impairments or diseases, but rather to acknowledge the wide range of factors that influence the length and quality of all our lives.

Although the medical model of disability has clearly been very influential in shaping the practice of prenatal screening and PND and the accompanying information processes, perhaps one difficulty with attempts to improve the quality of information — though arguably not a necessary one — stems from the ethos of non-directive counselling that accompanies PND, as hinted earlier. Although it is undesirable if a decision *not to terminate* an affected pregnancy is viewed negatively, the position in which parents come to fear that the decision *to terminate* will be viewed in this way likewise needs to be avoided. We should think clearly about what recognising the need for more 'balanced information' does and does not commit us to.

Arguably, calls for better-quality information about impairment, particularly the distinction between its intrinsic difficulties on the one hand compared with those that may be caused by discrimination or limitations in social support, do not in fact commit one to a view as to what is the better parental course of action in the face of a diagnosis of serious fetal anomaly. Rather, it commits one to giving the fetus's interests, and those of the child it would become, serious consideration. In practice, the result of better information about disability could be that in one case a woman (or couple) decides not to abort a given fetus. Assuming there has been sensitivity in the attendant discussions between the healthcare professionals and the pregnant woman, her existing legal options (to abort) would have remained intact. (These options are discussed in the next chapter.) The only change would be that, with better information about a possible child's impairment, the enhancement to her capacity to exercise her reproductive autonomy resulted in a decision not to abort. In another case, the same information and enhancement could well confirm a woman's (or couple's) pre-existing desire to abort. In yet a third case, it may be that a woman would not have aborted but, as a result of what is reasonably judged 'balanced information' instead decides to end

---

[130] HGC, above n 87, para 3.34.

her pregnancy. In all these cases, the interests of the fetuses, and the future children they would become, would be seriously considered and the women (or couples) would be making 'informed choices', to recall Shakespeare's phrase.

## C  The 'Expressivist Objection'

The 'expressivist objection' concerns the idea that prenatal and preimplantation selection practices send the message to people with impairments that they should not have been born and that their lives are in some sense worth less than other lives. As Shakespeare notes, the objection holds that PND expresses either negative or discriminatory views about people with disabilities.[131] Adrienne Asch has expressed the objection clearly, stating that 'prenatal diagnosis and selective abortion communicate that disability is so terrible it warrants not being alive'.[132] The view that PND expresses such opinions is strongly stated in the legal cases opposed to wrongful birth liability, discussed in Chapter 3. For instance, in the US case of *Dansby v Jefferson*, Wieand J noted that, in part, the wrongful birth statute banning the wrongful birth action 'reflect[s] the state's view that a handicapped person should not be deemed better off dead and of less value than a "normal child"'.[133]

It has been argued that, to be successful, the expressivist objection requires one of two positions: either that the fetus is a person or that 'it is motivationally impossible or irrational' both to seek to avoid disabilities because one devalues them and equally to value the disabled.[134]

### i  The fetus and personhood

Regarding the first of these points, it is often argued that if the fetus (or embryo) is *not* in fact a person, then no rights are violated when its life is terminated (or the embryo is placed *in utero*) and nothing is thereby said about the *rights* of born people, including those with disabilities.[135]

We know that — in the United States, England and more broadly in the Commonwealth — the fetus is not a legal person and arguably, as discussed earlier in this chapter, nor is it a moral one.[136] Nevertheless, although crucial in its ability

---

[131]  Shakespeare, above n 73, 89.
[132]  Asch, above n 65, 387.
[133]  *Dansby v Jefferson*, 623 A2d 816 (Pa Super 1993) 820. It could be argued that the state should pay the healthcare costs of impaired children if it wishes to promote their births, as of course it would in any event do in England. For the views of scholars opposed to wrongful birth actions see, eg, J Bopp, B Bostrom, D McKinney 'The "Rights" and "Wrongs" of Wrongful Birth and Wrongful Life: A Jurisprudential Analysis of Birth Related Torts' (Spring, 1989) *Duquesne Law Rev* 461.
[134]  Buchanan *et al*, above n 7, 280.
[135]  *Ibid* 297. See also L Gillam 'Prenatal Diagnosis and Discrimination against the Disabled' (1999) 24 *JME* 163, 169; E Jackson, *Regulating Reproduction* (Oxford: Hart Publishing, 2001) 98.
[136]  For discussion of the legal position, see Ch 2, S IV(B).

to protect the interests of a pregnant woman, the rule that the fetus is not a legal person (and the view that it is not one morally) can seem like a rather technical point that may not always be fully convincing when it comes to justifying fetal death. This is so even if the rule answers the charge of fetal rights violation. Indeed, this is why I suggested that to decide the question of the fetus's moral status by reference to whether or not it has the characteristics of personhood — and hence possesses rights — was unsatisfactory when I endorsed a gradualist approach to the moral status of the fetus earlier. So, to say that a pregnant woman has the right to refuse medical treatment because the fetus lacks legal status does not tell us anything about *why* she should have that right; it simply ensures that she has it.[137] A similar point could be made about the statement that abortion is legal because the fetus is not a legal person: an account of the justifiability of abortion that looks to the importance of a woman's interests in this context is much better placed to justify the abortion right, where it exists (for instance, in the United States).[138]

What are we to make, then, of the suggestion that because the fetus is not a person and abortion does not violate its rights, at most offence to people with disabilities can be caused when a fetus is selectively aborted? The accompanying thought, of course, is that offence cannot be the cause for the curtailment of freedoms in a liberal society. This may well be so, but offence can be a highly significant issue.[139] Further, and of greater concern, even if preimplantation and prenatal selection practices do not directly discriminate against people with disabilities (because neither the fetus nor the embryo is a person), nevertheless indirect discrimination may follow. This may occur where, as a result of partaking in such practices or simply due to awareness of the availability of these, people absorb or presume certain notions about the lives of people with disabilities. For this reason, people with disabilities may really be *harmed*, rather than simply offended, by the practices of prenatal screening, PND, selective abortion and PGD.[140]

For instance, one of the notions to which such practices apparently give rise is the idea that there is a connection between being responsible and avoiding the birth of a disabled child.[141] An unfortunate implication of this is that the

---

[137] The question of why she should have that right might be answered by reflecting on the significance of her moral and legal interests and rights in self-determination bodily integrity. See Scott, above n 31.
[138] For this kind of legal explanation, see, eg, *Planned Parenthood of Southeastern Pennsylvania v Casey* 120 LEd2d 674 (1992), discussed in Ch 3, S III.
[139] Buchanan *et al* acknowledge that offence can be taken, particularly given 'the shameful history of discrimination against and insensitivity toward persons with disabilities'. Buchanan *et al*, above n 7, 280–81.
[140] I am grateful to Jonathan Glover for emphasising this point in discussions.
[141] C Williams, P Alderson and B Farsides 'Too Many Choices? Hospital and Community Staff Reflect on the Future of Prenatal Screening' (2002) 55 *Social Science & Medicine*, 743, 751. See further M Saxton 'Why Members of the Disability Community

## 56  *Ethical Issues in Selection Practices*

widespread screening for Down's syndrome can mean that children born with this condition are regarded as 'mistakes'.[142] This kind of attitude is unlikely to enhance the opportunities that may be open to people with Down's syndrome. Rather, it is much more likely to be harmful to them. Having said this, it is very hard actually to appraise the extent of any harmful effects on people with disabilities. For instance, Shakespeare has observed that '[w]hile there is evidence that some disabled people *feel* offended and discriminated against by prenatal diagnosis, there is no strong empirical evidence that *material harms* to disabled people result from selective abortion'.[143]

Still, in the context of prenatal screening, PND, selective abortion and PGD, arguably we should think about how offence — and with it the potential for indirect discrimination and harm — can be minimised.[144] In essence, I think this returns us to the importance of striving to provide accurate and balanced information about life with a given disease or disability. James Nelson has questioned whether 'interfering' with reproductive autonomy is the right approach, or whether it would not be better to focus on educating people more widely about disability.[145] On this view, prenatal diagnosis is 'at worst the symptom, not the disease'. Although 'interference' with reproductive autonomy would be needed less if people were more informed about disability issues in the first place, the success of public education programmes will always be uncertain. This suggests that both approaches are required. Generally, more open debate about the moral issues in selection practices would enhance the development of better information and discussion. Indeed, health practitioners themselves may sometimes consider that they are working in a system that has not been the subject of overt critical reflection.[146]

---

Oppose Prenatal Diagnosis and Selective Abortion' in Parens and Asch (eds), above n 7, 147, 157 and N Press 'Assessing the Expressive Character of Prenatal Testing: The Choice Made or the Choices Made Available?' in Parens and Asch (eds), above n 7, 214, 219, on the potential for misunderstandings amongst pregnant women about the role and purpose of prenatal testing.

[142] R Hubbard observes: '[T]he child's disability is no longer an act of fate. [The woman] is now responsible, it has become her fault'. R Hubbard 'Eugenics: New Tools, Old Ideas' (1987) 13 *Women and Health* 225, 232.

[143] Shakespeare, above n 73, 96, my emphasis.

[144] A distinction should be drawn, perhaps, between the message received and the message sent. See Botkin, above n 7, 305. For thoughts on changing the way prenatal diagnosis is offered, see Asch, above n 14, 52.

[145] J Nelson 'The Meaning of the Act: Reflections on the Expressive Force of Reproductive Decision Making and Policies' in Parens and Asch (eds), above n 7, 196, 207.

[146] Williams *et al*, above n 141, 747–8, 749–50.

*ii Devaluing impairments but equally valuing those with impairments*

I now turn to the alternative idea on which it has been suggested that the 'expressivist objection' depends: that 'it is motivationally impossible or irrational' both to seek to avoid disabilities because one devalues them and equally to value the disabled.

I want first to return to non-person-affecting principles and to draw attention to a potentially unfortunate feature of discussions of these. To do so we need to compare the decision-making at stake in the scenarios discussed earlier, which originated in Parfit's notion of two competing medical programmes aimed at avoiding disability in future people, with decision-making outside the domain of reproductive ethics.

Turning to the latter, as Parfit has argued, choosing one economic or environmental policy rather than another could well result, over time, in different people being born.[147] If we choose a policy with worse environmental implications, however, and ultimately entirely different people are born, those people can have no complaint against us, since otherwise they would not have existed. This is the non-identity problem again.[148] Still, although we have chosen a policy in which different people will exist, who will nevertheless be happy to be alive, our policy has resulted in a world in which people have less well-being than another group of people might have had if we had chosen the other policy. The comparison is between the well-being of two different groups of people affected by different environmental or economic policies, as Jonathan Glover has noted.[149] Indeed, without a non-person-affecting approach we would have no way of caring, in the long term, about the consequences of choices we now make. To do so, although some reject this move,[150] we must resort to non-person-affecting principles.

In fact, there is a difference between the application of non-person-affecting principles in relation to the choice of an environmental or economic policy and such principles in relation to the direct choice of who should be born. This is so even though both are concerned with the overall degree of welfare of different people. In the first case, our critique of any given policy is based on the effect it will have on the environment and thereby *indirectly* on the well-being of actual, albeit different, people. In the second (whether we are thinking either at the level of policy or individually) the choices *directly* concern which people should be

---

[147] Parfit, above n 92, 377.

[148] In fact, it seems unlikely that any given environmental policy would completely change the identity of future people. That is, at least some of the same people may be born and in this sense our critique of the policy may also be constrained by what we might owe those people.

[149] Glover, above n 55, 46.

[150] eg, Heyd, above n 11, 14, because of his human-relative approach to value, in which value lies only in the decision-making party. His reasons concern the paradoxes of a non-person-affecting approach, which he explores in detail.

58  *Ethical Issues in Selection Practices*

born because we think that some people may have less well-being than others. On a non-person-affecting approach, the thought is that it is preferable if people without congenital disabilities and with greater opportunities and so forth are born. At one level, this seems right.

At the same time and at another level, *expressing the judgment* that the world is a worse place when disabled rather than non-disabled people are born could potentially be problematic for our relationship with people who have disabilities that leave them with lives they think worth living and also for their perception of themselves.[151] Of course, as applied to reproductive ethics, the non-person-affecting approach concerns who *should* be born, not who *was* born. However, since the relevant judgment hinges on a consideration of what the world would be like if some rather than others were born, it may sometimes seem hard fully to dissociate the perspective from a possible parallel judgment, looking around us, that it would *have been* better if certain disabled people had not been born and other non-disabled people — who may have had greater well-being — had been instead.

In response to this, Buchanan *et al* have suggested that there 'are many instances in which we devalue (and seek to avoid) certain characteristics that some individuals have without devaluing individuals who have them'.[152] They also observe that 'it is not the *people* with disabilities we devalue; it is the *disabilities*'.[153] In a similar vein, Walter Glannon has emphasised the distinction between physical conditions of the body and personhood.[154] Further, at the time a selection decision is made no person yet exists, a point to which I return below.[155] All of this is surely true.

At some level, however, it is preferable if it convinces the person with those characteristics. For this to occur effectively requires that that person can 'separate' themselves from their negative characteristic or impairment. This may be painful (though doable, since we can all imagine things that are impossible) because the avoidance of the impairment — through abortion (in the PND context) or embryo discard (in the context of PGD) — is equivalent to the avoidance of that particular person. A person with Down's syndrome, then, who might well have been aborted given the focus on this condition prenatally, may find it hard to accept both that Down's syndrome (particularly in its more severe manifestations) might be viewed negatively and yet that her life is said to be of equal value to that of her sibling without the condition. Although she might see this distinction, it would be understandable if she did not; indeed it may be particularly hard to

---

[151] It may be that RM Hare's idea of different levels of moral thinking could be useful here: RM Hare, *Moral Thinking: Its Level, Method and Point* (Oxford: OUP, 1981).
[152] Buchanan *et al*, above n 7, 280.
[153] *Ibid* 278, my emphasis.
[154] W Glannon, *Genes and Future People: Philosophical Issues in Human Genetics* (Oxford: Westview Press, 2001) 73.
[155] This is emphasised by Glannon in *ibid*, who cites Gillam, above n 135.

make the kind of separation that recognition of this distinction requires in the case of mental impairment (since this may more strongly affect perceptions of identity than some instances of physical impairment).[156] Further, Shakespeare has suggested that one of the strengths of the expressivist objection is that it 'captures the extent to which impairment is part of the identity of many disabled people, particularly those with congenital conditions: whereas non-disabled commentators see impairment as a separate aspect (like having influenza), disabled people argue that it is an important aspect of who they are'.[157] (In fact, this may be a case of two uses of 'identity', not two views of the same notion.) Indeed, as Jonathan Glover has observed and as noted earlier, this is why we need to be alert to 'possible biases' in accepting at face value the assessment an impaired person gives us of the impact the impairment has on his life.

The difficulty, in effect, is that while there is a highly valid conceptual distinction between the disvalue of the impairment on the one hand and the value of the life of someone with that impairment on the other, in the practice of PND and abortion (or PGD) the impairment and the actual life of the person in whom that impairment is situated are both avoided *one and the same*, so that that particular individual will never come to exist.[158] This requires some acknowledgement. With abortion in general, of course, it is also true that the person whom the fetus would have become is not and will never be known. The difference is that in this case there was never any concern about a feature of the *particular* fetus. Does it help to stress that selection practices aim at the *impairment*, such that one does not yet know — and will never know — the person whom the (discarded) embryo or (aborted) fetus would otherwise have come to be? This takes us into a discussion of what Adrienne Asch has called the 'any/particular' distinction.

### iii  The 'any/particular' distinction

The idea that PND and PGD aim at the impairment, not the future person, can itself be interpreted negatively: it is sometimes said that in such practices the

---

[156] As noted by L Carlson in 'Prenatal Testing and Selective Abortion' (2002) 75 *Phil and Med* 191, 207. Carlson discusses the work of disability theorists, such as S Edwards, who emphasise that 'disabilities are not detachable from selves' (at 206). It is not clear, however, how this reluctance or inability not to separate the two can be helpfully incorporated into the moral argument at this point other than to acknowledge, as I have done, that it may always be hard for those of us with impairments to make this conceptual separation, particularly where our impairments have a mental component.

[157] Shakespeare, above n 73, 89, citing, eg, S Edwards 'Disability, Identity and the "Expressivist Objection"' (2004) 30 *JME* 418.

[158] In this way, as Shakespeare acknowledges, attempts to prevent impairment through PND and selective abortion are different from attempts to prevent the same through, for instance, folic acid supplements. *Ibid* 91.

potential person has been *reduced* to his or her impairment.[159] In reality, of course, all that is known about the potential person at this time is that he or she will have an impairment. As Asch interprets this point, however, 'this one characteristic' is the basis for a decision to terminate (in the PND context).[160] Note that Asch's use of the word 'characteristic' obscures the point that, as she admits, 'the trait of disability may not be neutral'.[161] (On the other hand, she also criticises 'the majority' for 'see[ing] disability as a form of human difference that is worse than other types of difference'.[162])

Asch's point is part of her argument that while abortion in general may be defensible as being in a woman's interests, abortion of the disabled fetus in particular says something about the *fetus* rather than the interests of the pregnant woman, as is normally the case.[163] Her point is that in the case of an abortion that is not concerned with fetal anomaly a woman may have very strong reasons for wanting to avoid reproduction due, say, to her current life situation, but that in the case of an abortion of a fetus in whom a serious anomaly has been found, she wishes to have a child and her reasons for aborting simply relate to the *particular* fetus. The implication seems to be either that aborting the particular fetus does not have a strong relation to her reproductive autonomy interests, which Asch appears to want to limit to an interest in avoiding reproduction, or that to claim a connection between the reproductive interests of the parents and the characteristics of the fetus is problematic or offensive in some way.

With regard to the first point — that aborting the particular fetus does not have a strong relation to a woman's reproductive autonomy interests — the reproductive interests of the pregnant woman (and her partner) might not in fact be so easily separated from the characteristics of the particular fetus, as Asch would seem to require. I discussed this in earlier sections of this chapter. Recalling first the most straightforward of examples, the birth of a child with Tay-Sachs will impact hugely on parents, causing them great emotional distress as the child's condition deteriorates and he dies, having lived at most four to five years. Indeed, it might be said that by seeking to avoid the birth of such a child the parents are thereby expressing an aspect of their own interests in reproduction, which are thus more extensive than simply choosing whether or not to procreate.[164] In such a case, of course, parents can also be legitimately concerned to prevent a certain degree of suffering in the prospective child. The suffering has to be extreme, of course, for

---

[159] See, eg, B Jennings 'Technology and the Genetic Imaginary: Prenatal Testing and the Construction of Disability' in Parens and Asch (eds), above n 7, 138.
[160] Asch, above n 14, 236.
[161] *Ibid* 247.
[162] *Ibid* 252.
[163] *Ibid* 236–9.
[164] For critiques of the 'any/particular' distinction, see, eg, Jennings, above n 159, 200–205; Nelson, above n 145, 196.

it not to be in the fetus's interests (once it has these post-sentience), and those of the child it would become, to be born. This is the case of 'wrongful life'.

As discussed earlier, however, if being born in any given case is compatible with having a good or reasonable quality of life, then one cannot say that it is not in the fetus's interests to be born. This will be the case for a wide range of conditions for which we currently routinely screen. In such cases, if parents have an interest in being able to accept or avoid certain experiences that the birth of a given child might entail, parental and fetal interests may well come into conflict with one another. I have already suggested, in agreement with various others, that if one can decide whether to reproduce, some degree of control over roughly what that might involve is arguably entailed, both morally and legally.

Overall, the point I am making is that in either of the above cases the abortion of a particular fetus can and does have a strong and legitimate relation to a woman's (or couple's) reproductive autonomy interests, since these are not only invoked in the 'prior' decision, if you like, of whether to have a child.[165] As argued earlier in this chapter, this is because the large question of whether to have a child is not an entirely different question from that of whether to have a disabled child. In both cases, reflection on the issue entails consideration of the child's and the parents' life after the child's birth. In this regard, in both cases parents will come under extensive and ongoing positive moral (and legal) duties of care and some may reasonably feel that the degree of duty that may be entailed in the case of a severely disabled child is more than they can, or wish, to take on, particularly since such duties are likely to last that much longer if a child is unable ultimately to live and work independently (as may sometimes be the case).

Where does this leave us with regard to what might be a second interpretation of Asch's point — that to claim a connection between the reproductive interests of the parents and the characteristics of the fetus is in some way offensive? This second interpretation may be another way of expressing the view that one cannot both devalue an impairment and equally value the life of a person with that impairment.

If parents decide to abort a fetus affected by cystic fibrosis, does this say something about an already-born child with cystic fibrosis, the parents, or both? Cases have been made out for each of the first two possibilities. The likely complexities of meaning in this context have also been explored.[166] For instance, James Nelson argues that there may not be the direct relationship between meaning and intention that Buchanan *et al's* critique of the expressivist objection

---

[165] For apparent agreement, see also Shakespeare, above n 73, 93: 'It does not make sense to me that it is acceptable to have an abortion for social reasons — for example, the timing of the pregnancy is inconvenient, or the woman does not want a baby with this particular man, or the prospective parents do not want another addition to their family — but not for the morally significant reason that the foetus is affected by an impairment'.

[166] See, respectively, Nelson, above n 145, and Asch, above n 14. For a sophisticated discussion of the possible meanings, see Nelson, above n 145, especially 206–211.

may entail. Nelson's view 'is that even considered as a social practice, the meaning of testing and abortion remain both vague and ambiguous, and insofar as this practice does enfold objectionable meanings, the way to unseat them is not by restricting access to information and medical services'.[167] Overall, he observes that '[t]he meanings of decisions, practices and policies that involve screening and abortion cannot be determined outside the context of a broader set of decisions, practices, and policies as they affect people with disabilities, as well as women and family life more generally'.[168] To return to my question, on the one hand I think it is right that the action of aborting a child with cystic fibrosis is not *intended* to express anything about an already-born child with this condition. The action does mean, however, that the parents do not *themselves* want a child with cystic fibrosis.[169] On the other hand, then, that they prefer to abort such a child may in turn be offensive to children or adults with cystic fibrosis. Where do we go from here?

Arguably, consistent with the above thoughts, the case for justifying such offence can be made out in the case of serious impairments in a prospective child since these will significantly impact on its parents. In other words, in such cases the parents' reproductive interests will be seriously invoked. In this way, any offence to people with impairments caused by selecting against such impairments might be seen as unfortunate but justifiable. By contrast, since relatively trivial impairments or features do not begin seriously to implicate parental interests, it would be hard to argue that the expansion, say, of screening and abortion practices in relation to these could justify offence to those with impairments. In fact, such practices could be especially offensive to them, perhaps increasing the stigma felt by them.[170] Overall, once again it seems likely that ameliorating offence and the risk of indirect discrimination against people with impairments will best be achieved by the way in which screening and testing information is presented and discussed.

*iv   Interweaving parents' and children's interests*

Ultimately, in reflecting on the possible offence or indirect discrimination that prenatal screening, PND, selective abortion and PGD may cause to those of us with impairments or diseases, we are left to reflect on the significance of parental interests in this process and the legitimacy of parental reasons for wanting to avoid the birth of an impaired child. People (typically) choose to become parents and exist thanks to the various efforts of their parents. Whilst there are many senses in

---

[167]   *Ibid* 209.
[168]   *Ibid* 211.
[169]   Press, above n 141, 226–7, refers to surveys in which on the one hand people speak about equally valuing people with disabilities and on the other very strongly hope they will not have a child with disabilities.
[170]   Williams *et al*, above n 141, 748, note the comments of a psychologist to this effect, discussed further in Ch 5, S III(D)v.

which children are a gift, there is also a sense in which life itself is a gift to the child. (Since existence at the start of life is not a benefit, I refer to the idea of a gift here only in a metaphorical sense.) This is so even when, as is likely the case, reproduction is chosen as one way of enriching parental lives. Biologically, the giving of life happens through conception and gestation. In other senses, it happens through the way children are brought up and nurtured. If parents embark on this process at least partly to enrich their own lives, then at some level this enterprise will, understandably, be related to their conception of their lives. Again, metaphorically as it were, we might say that there has to be some 'give and take', some degree of compromise on both parts, although the embryo or fetus is not in a position to agree to this. Assuming the parents have been fully counselled about the medical and social aspects of the birth of a child with a certain condition (which, as we know, may not currently be the case) they may still decide that, with the necessarily limited knowledge they now have, they wish to avoid a certain kind of *potentially* more difficult or distressing reproductive experience. Alternatively, they may decide to proceed with an affected pregnancy, or not to seek PGD where they have a known risk.

It is helpful here to flesh out some of the sympathetic thoughts of those writing from a disability perspective. For instance Asch, writing about the work of the Hastings Center on PND, acknowledges[171]:

> Most project members believe that people with significant disabilities can have lives they experience as rewarding but worry that life with a disabled child would be more difficult than life with a child without disabilities. On this view, parents could or should not be expected to envision the family life that included a child with a disability as equivalent to family life where no children had disabilities.

In a similarly sympathetic vein, we saw earlier that Shakespeare apparently identifies what I called both 'child-focused and parent-focused (or parent-accommodating) reasons' for being able to make a decision about whether to accept or avoid the birth of an impaired child.[172] These observations point once again to parents' legitimate perception of their interests and limits. In a very sympathetic vein, Shakespeare concludes[173]:

---

[171] Asch, above n 14, 248.
[172] See text above at n 9.
[173] Shakespeare, above n 73, 102. And a little earlier he observes, at 99: 'All decisions about screening and termination are difficult, and can only be made by those people who have to live with the consequences — either the distress of abortion, or the potential stress of supporting a child, a disabled child, or an additional child. Society should support people to make good decisions, and support them with the consequences of their decisions. In particular, justice demands that the state should devote more resources to supporting families with disabled children, and to promoting the well-being of disabled adults, rather than acting as if prenatal diagnosis or other biomedical interventions will solve the problem of disability'.

> Testing should be limited to serious conditions which undermine quality of life for individuals and families... However, the privacy of those faced with these difficult decisions should be respected, and their autonomy supported. Everyone has an interest in helping prospective parents make better decisions, which they are less likely to regret at a future date. We should be on hand to offer counselling, good quality information and support, but we should not venture to dictate where the duties of prospective parents may lie.

Turning to other writers, David Heyd has subtly caught the interwoven welfare of parents and children: 'Not only is there a strong built-in impulse to have children, our own welfare is to a large extent dependent on theirs because each generation lives for quite a time with its dependants'; further, Thomas Murray has emphasised the interwoven nature of parents' and children's interests.[174]

### v  Opportunity — non-person-affecting principles again

Finally, a further strand of thought examining the legitimacy of parental reasons and the interests of people with impairments could focus on the degree of opportunity open to a child with cystic fibrosis, spina bifida or Down's syndrome, particularly since there is at least some agreement that a negative feature of impairment may be that it restricts opportunities, *despite* all social support.[175] Barring those cases where, for instance, deaf parents seek a deaf child (which I discuss in Chapter 6) it would, after all, be strange for a parent to *hope* for a child with health problems or limited opportunities,[176] however much the child may in fact successfully cope with these difficulties. Asch herself, in recognising that impairments are not neutral, suggests that '[w]e can agree that our disabilities impose limitations we might sometimes wish were not there'. She notes[177]:

> Fortunately, everyone in our project affirms that much of disability is socially constructed; what has remained a contentious and painful divide has concerned just how much is 'social', how much is irremediable, and how negative for child, family, or society those irremediable facets of disability turn out to be.

---

[174] Heyd, above n 11, 15, footnote omitted (cited again here). T Murray, *The Worth of a Child* (Berkeley: University of California Press, 1996) 138. For further thought on the expressivist objection and, in particular, prospective parents' evaluation of life with a disabled child compared with parents' retrospective evaluation of life with a disabled child, see J McMahan 'Preventing the Existence of People with Disabilities' in D Wasserman, J Bickenbach and R Wachbroit (eds), *Quality of Life and Human Difference: Genetic Testing, Health Care, and Disability* (New York: Cambridge University Press, 2005) 142.

[175] Parens and Asch, above n 26, 28.

[176] Asch, above n 14, agrees that it is appropriate for parents to 'have hopes and dreams for themselves, as well as for their children' (at 247–8). The difference, however, is likely to inhere in perceptions about whether a disability will mean that either a child or its parents will not have a rewarding life (at 248). Asch notes that she would not be a 'critic' if she thought that the child's or parents' hopes would be 'thwarted' by a child's disability. On the adjustment processes at stake in coming to terms with the prospective birth of an impaired child, see Bowles Biesecker and Hamby, above n 127, 345–6.

[177] Asch, above n 14, 247 and 243–4.

Further, the disvalue in constraint of opportunity was a point of extensive agreement amongst the Hastings Center working party that looked at these issues.[178] It is in this sense that the language of 'wrongful disability' with which mid-spectrum cases are often discussed — and which can be hard to reconcile with the views of disabled people themselves — may best be understood. In this light, one could argue that it is not undesirable if people with greater opportunities — including because of the inevitable and reasonable limits to social support where impairments exist — are born. This would be to incorporate a non-person-affecting perspective into this discussion. Recall, however, that I have argued that non-person-affecting principles have increasingly less weight as a pregnancy progresses.

The discussion of the interests of people with impairments has shown that the most important issue in relation to parents' interests in making reproductive decisions as well as to the interests of those with impairments concerns the enhancement of the information practices and deliberative processes attending these reproductive decisions, coupled with the education of the public more broadly about the impact (or lack thereof) of impairment in a person's life.

## VI EUGENICS

The concern is often expressed that selection by preimplantation and prenatal diagnosis is 'eugenic'.[179] Sometimes the concern may form part of the disability critique of selection practices, but it is also a free-standing issue in its own right. The topic of eugenics has been extensively discussed by others and my treatment of it will be brief.[180] My main purpose in raising it is to identify its possible relevance to current selection practices.

Historically, the notion of eugenics is associated most obviously with practices under the Nazi regime, but also in the United Kingdom, the United States and elsewhere in the earlier parts of the last century.[181] This kind of eugenics was typically driven by a mixture of nationalist and racist concerns[182] as well as fears of social degeneration. The eradication of social problems such as crime was thought to be linked to biology,[183] such that genetics affected morals and behaviour.[184] It was a government-led and coercive pursuit aimed at improving the population as

---

[178] Parens and Asch, above n 26, 28.
[179] See, eg, HGC, above n 64.
[180] See, eg, J Glover 'Eugenics: Some Lessons from the Nazi Experience' in J Harris and S Holm (eds), *The Future of Human Reproduction: Ethics, Choice and Regulation* (Oxford: OUP, 1998) 55.
[181] The example of sterilisation is discussed in D Kevles 'Eugenics and Human Rights' (1999) 319 *BMJ* 435, 436–7.
[182] See, eg, Glover, above n 180, 64, discussing the Nazis.
[183] Kevles, above n 181, 435.
[184] Ibid. J Gillott 'Screening for Disability: a Eugenic Pursuit?' (2001) 27 *JME* supp II, 21, 21.

a whole.[185] By contrast, whatever is practised today is *meant* to be a matter of individual choice in the course of reproduction and the facilitation of this. Whether this is in fact the case is an important question I consider further below and in Chapter 3, when I address the issue of consent to prenatal screening and PND.

Finding agreement on the meaning of such a broadly used term as 'eugenics' is not easy. Perhaps in recognition of this, John Gillot has suggested that a modern definition of eugenics might be 'any policy that alters the composition of the human gene pool'.[186] Stephen Wilkinson also notes the uncertain meaning of the term 'eugenics' and the way it is 'taken to be a negative moral term', though he suggests that perhaps there should be some intentional element in a so-called eugenic policy, thus potentially casting doubt on Kitcher's definition.[187] A detailed enquiry into the concept of eugenics is beyond my scope. More particularly, though, in the light of the disagreement that surrounds the word 'eugenic', its use tends not to be helpful, since it tends either to be wheeled out in a discussion-stopping way or simply to have this effect when it appears or is sensed on the horizon.[188]

What may be more helpful than labelling a selection decision 'eugenic' is to reflect on the reason or justification for it. Such a decision can be made (negatively) against a significant impairment, such as Tay-Sachs or Duchenne muscular dystrophy or perhaps Down's syndrome, or against a marginal feature, such as somewhat short stature. And hypothetically at least, notably in the PGD context, a selection decision can also be made (positively) for a marginal feature, such as height or eye colour, or for a feature which is considerably advantageous, such as intelligence, or for a disability. In practice, the techniques of PGD and PND currently enable selection against (or for) a number of serious impairments, but we may eventually come closer to being able to select, such as by PGD, for insignificant features, such as eye colour. Whether we could ever test for a

---

[185] For a thoughtful review of the alleged wrongs of eugenics, see D Wikler 'Can We Learn from Eugenics?' (1999) 25 *JME* 183. Wikler argues, in part, that a concern with the well-being of the group, rather than the individual, and with the costs to the group of the birth of any one individual was a fault of the early eugenics movements (eg, at 191, 192–3). Yet he also suggests (at 193): 'Done justly, the genetic well-being of the "group" is a proper object of concern. The question of moral importance is not whether this constitutes eugenics; it is whether it can be done fairly and justly. It wasn't, the last time it was tried'.

[186] Gillot, above n 184, 21, referring to part of the work of P Kitcher, *The Lives to Come: the Genetic Revolution and Human Possibilities* (London: Allen Lane, The Penguin Press, 1996).

[187] S Wilkinson 'Eugenics, Embryo Selection and the Equal Value Principle' (2006) 1 *Clinical Ethics* 46, 50; and S Wilkinson 'Eugenics and the Expressivist Argument' in his *Choosing Children: the Ethics of Selective Reproduction* (Oxford: OUP, forthcoming).

[188] This happened to some degree in the HFEA/AGCT, *Consultation Document* on PGD, above n 64, but especially the responses thereto. The responses are outlined and discussed in HFEA and HGC, *Outcome of the Public Consultation on Preimplantation Genetic Diagnosis*, 18 June 2001, discussed in Chs 4 and 5.

significant and complex trait such as intelligence is a matter of some doubt, but the hypothetical possibility can be noted.[189] In relation to all these, the helpful question is not which would be eugenic — since at one level they would all be — but how much we think it appropriate to make these different kinds of selection decision. The appropriateness of these decisions is the subject of discussion particularly in Chapter 5.

Since the *context* of decision-making is so important in the distinction between present and past selection practices, particularly individual rather than government decision-making, the way certain tests are offered and promoted is a highly important issue. For instance, in the United Kingdom, the recommendations of the National Institute of Clinical Excellence in relation to Down's syndrome screening may be relevant here and are discussed in connection with consent to prenatal screening and testing in Chapter 3. Generally, the way screening or testing is offered by service providers and the impact this has on prospective parents needs to be seriously considered. This is also an aspect to which Shakespeare has drawn attention. On the one hand Shakespeare is strongly critical of the use of the language of eugenics, especially 'Nazi eugenics' within the disability critique of prenatal screening, describing this as making for 'effective rhetoric but dubious argument'.[190] He emphasises the extent to which the developments in genetics are 'incremental, haphazard, contested and complex', clearly rejecting the notion of any 'government plan to eliminate disabled people'.[191] In this light, he notes that it is prospective parents, not doctors, who are responsible for the 'difficult decisions' made in pregnancy.[192] On the other hand, and importantly, Shakespeare has consistently emphasised what he calls the 'limitations on choice', noting the 'thousands of interactions, implicit expectations, subtle influences and restricted choices in which prospective parents find themselves'.[193] As he notes, this means that we cannot be complacent about the way in which current screening and testing practices are conducted.[194] Indeed, whilst he makes clear that he rejects certain arguments of the disability critique of screening practices, this does not mean he supports PND as it is currently practised.[195]

I return to this issue directly in Chapter 3. More generally, it is one that should be kept in mind throughout the discussion in this book.

---

[189] For optimism as to the possibilities of such breakthroughs, see W Henn 'Consumerism in Prenatal Diagnosis: a Challenge for Ethical Guidelines' (2000) 26 *JME* 444, 445; for pessimism, see E Kirk 'Embryo Selection for Complex Traits is Impracticable' (2003) 326 *BMJ* 53.
[190] Shakespeare, above n 73, 85.
[191] *Ibid* 87.
[192] *Ibid* 87–8.
[193] *Ibid* 88.
[194] *Ibid*.
[195] *Ibid* 85.

## VII  CONCLUSIONS

How our lives go — particularly how much we flourish — can be affected by whether we are impaired or have a disease of some kind. At the same time, it is obvious that many other factors will influence our lives, sometimes to a greater extent, including the attitudes of others throughout our lives and of our parents during our childhood. Hopefully — and also very probably — parents will love their child, so that we should not have to think of this as something parents 'owe' their children.[196] Where a child's condition is not of the extreme and rare kind that might give rise to a life he did not think worth living, parental love may be the factor that most contributes to his or her well-being or flourishing.

Reflecting on the degree of disability or disease in future people, I argued that prospective parents may have at least a *prima facie* duty to avoid a child's birth where there is a serious risk he would have a life not worth living, although we should always be sensitive to their interests and difficulties. However, the discussion has shown that it is rarely the case that a condition will be so severe that it would be against the interests of the future child to be born. In this light, I argued that we should recognise and reflect on the point that most prenatal and preimplantation selection practices are really, potentially, in the interests of prospective parents. I therefore began to consider the value and appropriate extent of reproductive autonomy in the context of selection practices, identifying this as the central focus of the book.

I argued that the reproductive autonomy that is at stake in having a say about the kind of child who will be born is not a completely different kind from that at stake in choosing whether to have any child. In both cases, taking on the duties of parenthood will involve assuming extensive positive moral (and legal) duties. Where prospective parents choose to avoid reproduction altogether before conception no justification of any kind is required for this exercise of their reproductive autonomy (barring the idea of a duty to maintain the human population and assuming that contraception is not morally wrong). By contrast, where a fetus is growing as part of an established pregnancy, or where embryos would have to be created for the purpose of testing them, unless one thinks that neither has any moral claims (and many people do think this), the exercise of reproductive autonomy will require some degree of moral justification.

On the gradualist approach to the embryo's and fetus's moral status that I have endorsed, stronger reasons must be offered morally to justify the fetus's demise as it develops. In the context of prenatal screening and PND, this means that the degree of impairment or disease the future child would have must be that much greater as a pregnancy develops if termination is to be morally justified. Overall, when a fetus already exists as part of an established pregnancy or embryos would need to be created so as to test them before transfer, the exercise of reproductive

---

[196] As noted by Glover, above n 55, 51.

## Conclusions 69

autonomy will be most justifiable (as regards the fetus or embryo), valuable (as regards the prospective parents' interests) and therefore worthy of protection when there are good or serious reasons for certain choices: these will imply that the moral interests derived from the value of reproductive autonomy are seriously invoked. This line of thought is fundamental to the analysis of a range of possible selection practices in this book. I develop the implications of a gradualist account for our treatment of the embryo particularly in Chapters 5 and 6.

Turning to non-person-affecting principles, I accepted that these can have some place in this context since, other things being equal, it seems right that we have reason to think it preferable that people at least begin life with potentially greater capacities for flourishing and well-being. Importantly, however, I resisted the idea that such principles give rise to a duty to avoid the birth of a child with a life she thinks worth living. This was on the basis of the possible moral claims of the fetus, particularly as a pregnancy progresses (so that the application of non-person-affecting principles would become somewhat disingenuous), the controversial nature of the judgment as to serious suffering and loss of opportunity in the life of a future child and the possible costs to parents at stake in such a duty. Such costs could be very considerable where termination is implicated, for instance because of the emotional burdens this may impose on parents, the physical ones that it would impose on a pregnant woman and the difficulties for a couple that may be involved in attempting to 'replace' one future child with another. Further, the emotional, physical and possible financial costs of undertaking IVF and PGD to avoid the birth of someone with a life worth living would also be very considerable, as I explore in further detail in Chapters 4 and 5 in particular.

The practices of prenatal screening, PND, selective abortion and PGD may also affect existing people with disabilities or disease. Discussion of this issue suggested that the best way to minimise that effect is to work on improving the information practices that accompany these forms of selection.

Lastly, I suggested that use of the term 'eugenic' tends to be question-begging, as others have recognised. We need instead to think about the justification for selection practices and also the extent to which women are in fact able to choose to accept or avoid the birth of a child with a disability or disease. I examine this issue particularly when I look at the question of consent to prenatal screening and PND early in Chapter 3.

In the next chapter, I turn to consider the operation and interpretation, morally and legally, of the law on selective abortion, building on the ethical groundwork established here.

# 2

# *Selective Abortion — The Interpretation and Operation of the Law*

## I INTRODUCTION

THIS CHAPTER EXPLORES the interpretation and operation of the law on selective abortion in England. Abortion is legal under section 1(1)(d) of the Abortion Act 1967 (as amended by the Human Fertilisation and Embryology Act 1990) if two doctors have formed an opinion in good faith that 'there is a substantial risk that if the child were born it would suffer from such physical or mental abnormalities as to be seriously handicapped'.[1] These terms leave considerable scope for interpretation, particularly about what is meant by 'seriously' and to date there has been no judicial interpretation of this section:

> [N]ot only would it be a bold and brave judge… who would seek to interfere with the discretion of doctors acting under the Abortion Act 1967, but I think he would really be a foolish judge who would try to do any such thing, unless, possibly, where there is clear bad faith and an obvious attempt to perpetrate a criminal offence.

So said Sir George Baker P in *Paton v BPAS*[2] and his view has been repeated at apposite judicial moments in subsequent cases.[3]

Relatively recently, however, a legal attempt was indeed made to question the discretion of doctors in *Jepson v The Chief Constable of West Mercia Police Constabulary*.[4] Reverend Joanna Jepson asked the West Mercia Police to investigate doctors who had authorised an abortion for bilateral cleft lip and palate at 28 weeks under the disability ground of the Act. When the police decided not to pursue a prosecution, the claimant succeeded in obtaining permission to proceed

---

[1] The relevant part of s 1(1) of the Abortion Act 1967 as amended by the HFE Act 1990 reads: 'Subject to the provisions of this section, a person shall not be guilty of an offence under the law relating to abortion when a pregnancy is terminated by a registered medical practitioner if two registered medical practitioners are of the opinion, formed in good faith… (d) that there is a substantial risk that if the child were born it would suffer from such physical or mental abnormalities as to be seriously handicapped'.
[2] [1979] QB 276, 282, in which a husband failed to obtain an injunction restraining his wife from having an abortion.
[3] eg, *C v S* [1988] QB 135, 153, in which a father, named as first plaintiff, failed to prevent his girlfriend from having an abortion of their unborn child, named as the second plaintiff.
[4] [2003] EWHC 3318.

with a claim for judicial review of that decision. However, the hearing was then suspended pending a renewed police investigation. In due course the Crown Prosecution Service (CPS) announced that, following an extensive review of evidence of various kinds, it would not prosecute the doctors in the case and, in turn, Reverend Jepson stated that she would seek legal advice as to whether to continue with her claim for judicial review.[5] Given the constraints of such an action, coupled with the CPS's view that the doctors formed a 'good faith' judgment about the abortion in question (which again underlines the words of Sir George Baker P in *Paton*), it seems unlikely that Reverend Jepson will be advised further to pursue her claim. Either way, we can consider the central questions the case raises. The obvious ones concern the terms of the disability ground of the Abortion Act, in particular the meanings of 'substantial risk' and 'serious handicap'. The underlying questions concern the balance between the moral and legal interests of the fetus and its mother (or parents).

Since Parliament entrusted the operation of the Abortion Act to doctors, a position which has been strongly criticised over the years,[6] apart from the now-halted *Jepson* case there has been only one legal case that considered the good faith of doctors in the operation of the Act.[7] Judicial deference to medical opinion is common in medical law. One problem with such deference in this

---

[5] For accounts of these developments, see, eg 'Cleft Lip Abortion to be Investigated' *The Guardian*, 17 April 2004; 'Curate Postpones Cleft Palate Late Abortion Action' *The Daily Telegraph*, 9 May 2004; and a CPS Press Release of 16 March 2005, entitled 'CPS Decides Not to Prosecute Doctors following Complaint by Rev Joanna Jepson' which reads, in part: 'The Chief Crown Prosecutor for West Mercia CPS, Jim England, said: "This complaint has been investigated most thoroughly by the police and the CPS has considered a great deal of evidence before reaching its decision… The issue is whether the two doctors who had authorised the termination were of the opinion, formed in good faith, that there was a substantial risk that if the child were born it would suffer from such physical and mental abnormalities as to be seriously handicapped. I consider that both doctors concluded that there was a substantial risk of abnormalities that would amount to the child being seriously handicapped. The evidence shows that these two doctors did form this opinion and formed it in good faith. In these circumstances I decided there was insufficient evidence for a realistic prospect of conviction and that there should be no charges against either of the doctors.' Mr England said the evidence considered by the CPS included medical records; guidance from the Royal College of Obstetricians and Gynaecologists; evidence from a number of professionals involved in the care, counselling and treatment in this case, and interviews of the two doctors. Opinions were also obtained from independent medical experts. 'We took all these matters into account when reaching our decision that there was no offence.' For Rev Jepson's reaction, see C Dyer 'Doctor who Performed Late Abortion Will Not be Prosecuted' (2005) 330 *BMJ* 668.

[6] See, eg, S Sheldon 'Who is the Mother to Make the Judgment?: The Construction of Woman in English Abortion Law' (1993) 1 *Fem Leg Stud* 3; S Sheldon 'The Law of Abortion and the Politics of Medicalisation' in J Bridgman and S Millns (eds), *Law and Body Politics: Regulating the Female Body* (Aldershot: Dartmouth, 1995) 105; E Jackson 'Abortion, Autonomy and Prenatal Diagnosis' (2000) 9(4) *Social and Legal Studies* 467.

[7] *R v Smith* (1974) 58 Cr App R 106, in which a doctor was convicted for lack of good faith in authorising an abortion under s 1(1)(a) of the Act.

context is that abortion is not only a medical matter in important respects (particularly since the legalisation of abortion has been highly important in preventing maternal mortality), but also a moral one, since it involves terminating the life of a being of controversial moral status and may involve, given the terms of the Act, a balancing of maternal and fetal claims. (Of course, preventing maternal mortality is itself a highly important moral issue.) This is so notwithstanding that, in the case of selective abortion, assessments as to the impairments that a born child would have require a certain but sometimes contested degree of medical input.[8]

Despite the dearth of directly relevant jurisprudence, there are in fact several sources that give indications as to how the disability ground of the Act might be interpreted, if it were to come under judicial scrutiny. I begin to explore these in Section II. The first, of somewhat limited assistance, is *Hansard*. The second is the Royal College of Obstetricians and Gynaecologists' (RCOG) guidelines on the interpretation of this section of the Act.[9] The third, perhaps surprisingly, is in fact in existing case law, notably the wrongful birth cases, which I introduce in Section III. These stem from the duty of care of health professionals to advise a woman or couple about the risk of disability in the child that would result from a woman's current pregnancy. The fourth source, more obviously, is in parts of the case law on abortion under the European Convention on Human Rights (ECHR), which I consider in Section IV. The Convention was directly incorporated into English law by means of the Human Rights Act 1998. Finally, in Section V, I consider the particularly acute question of the interpretation of the law with regard to termination after 24 weeks on the grounds of fetal anomaly. Some ethical argument is also required to link these pieces together.

## II EXPLORING THE TERMS OF THE DISABILITY GROUND OF THE ABORTION ACT

### A 'Substantial Risk'

#### i Hansard

The question of the degree of risk does not appear to have been of great concern in the Parliamentary debates surrounding the amendments to the Abortion Act.

#### ii RCOG guidelines

Turning immediately to the RCOG guidelines on abortion, these have no legal status. However, as with General Medical Council guidelines on issues such as

---

[8] On medical assessments of disability in this context, see, eg, T Shakespeare '"Losing the Plot?" Medical and Activist Discourses of Contemporary Genetics and Disability' (1999) 21/5 *Sociology of Health and Illness* 669, 678.

[9] Since May 2006 I have been a member of the RCOG Ethics Committee. Any views expressed here are mine and do not represent those of the committee.

confidentiality,[10] they would likely be treated with a good degree of judicial respect. To define 'substantial risk', the RCOG guidelines initially resort to dictionary definitions.[11] The guidelines then note the uncertain meaning of 'substantial': 'a risk may be substantial without satisfying the test of being more likely than not; equally the risk must be more than a mere possibility'.[12] The guidelines advise that obstetricians should 'err on the side of caution, bearing in mind that a decision to perform an abortion because there is a substantial risk rather than a certainty may result in the loss of a normal fetus'.[13] Although many anomalies can be diagnosed with 'near certainty', in other cases 'only a probability… can be provided'.[14] The guidelines advise that '[e]very effort should be made to obtain a positive antenatal diagnosis of fetal abnormality when this is practicable' and that '[t]he medical practitioners certifying that a risk is substantial should bear in mind that the risk should also be likely to be considered substantial by informed persons with no personal involvement in the pregnancy and its outcome'.[15] This suggests that the doctors who must make this assessment are not to be guided *only* by the woman's (or her partner's) perception of the risk. The guidelines identify relevant factors as the information diagnostic tests have revealed about the anomaly and the outcome for the fetus during pregnancy, when a child and when an adult, as gleaned from published studies.[16] So the guidelines implicitly refer to a woman's perception of risk in the negative sense by apparently ruling out a *solely* subjective risk assessment.

There is, however, an alternative section of the Abortion Act that may implicitly be used for selective abortion and, in effect, allows greater weight to be given to a woman's concerns. Section 1(1)(a) permits abortion where two doctors are of a good-faith opinion 'that the pregnancy has not exceeded twenty-four weeks and that the continuance of the pregnancy would involve risk, greater than if the pregnancy were terminated, of injury to the physical or mental health of the pregnant woman or any existing children of her family'. One set of RCOG guidelines implicitly notes the potential use of this ground for fetal anomaly in the following terms[17]:

> Women vary in their reaction to being told that their fetus is, or may be, abnormal. Occasionally a woman feels strongly that she is unable to accept a probability of risk or a degree of handicap that her medical practitioners consider less than substantial or

---

[10] GMC 'Confidentiality: Protecting and Providing Information' April 2004.
[11] RCOG, *Termination of Pregnancy for Fetal Abnormality in England, Wales and Scotland* (January, 1996) para 3.2.1.
[12] Ibid.
[13] Ibid.
[14] Ibid para 3.2.2.
[15] Ibid.
[16] Ibid.
[17] RCOG, above n 11, para 3.4.

serious. Under such circumstances, and only when the gestation is less than 24 weeks, the practitioners may decide that abortion has become necessary to protect her mental health.

The guidelines continue:

> After 24 weeks the grounds for abortion for mental health are more stringent; the continuation of the pregnancy must result in grave permanent damage to mental health. Such damage to mental health is unlikely to result from a woman's concern about a fetal abnormality that her doctors do not consider serious enough to satisfy the law. In effect this means that after 24 weeks the abortion decision must be based only on the anticipated risk that the child would be seriously handicapped.

So, where the pregnancy has not exceeded 24 weeks, section 1(1)(a) provides an alternative means of justifying abortion for impairment in the child that would be born, one that does not require that two practitioners consider the risk to be substantial or the condition serious.

Juxtaposed against the use of the disability ground itself, there is an element of a subjective assessment under the 'social ground' provided, of course, that two doctors judge there is a risk to the woman's mental or physical health (or any of her children) that is greater than if the pregnancy were terminated. On the question of health, the RCOG guidelines observe the World Health Organisation's definition of health as '... a state of physical, mental and social well-being and not merely an absence of disease or infirmity' and continue[18]:

> In determining whether there is a risk to mental health in a particular pregnancy the medical practitioners have to identify factors in the woman's life and personality that would threaten her mental health if the pregnancy were to continue: they do not have to certify that she has a mental illness.

Where section 1(1)(a) is used in relation to a fetal anomaly, in effect a woman's views about the degree of risk of a disability in the born child, or its seriousness, are being taken into account by use of a section of the Act that is not explicitly concerned with disability. To the extent either that a less serious condition or feature or that a low probability of a more serious one could create a risk to the woman's mental health, then an abortion could be in her interests according to the terms of this section. But the extent to which less serious features or relatively minor impairments could present this kind of risk to a woman will be limited. This section was not available for the abortion in *Jepson* because the pregnancy had gone beyond 24 weeks.

Strikingly, the allowance for some degree of attention, by use of section 1(1)(a), to a woman's reactions and feelings to the idea of a disability in the child to which she gives birth is in contrast to, if not an objective, then at least a more impersonal assessment of the degree of risk under the disability ground of the Act. However, although we have seen that the RCOG guidelines make clear that under the

---

[18] *Ibid.*

76  Selective Abortion — The Law

disability section of the Act certifying doctors should be aware that the degree of risk 'should also be likely to be considered substantial by informed persons with no personal involvement', it would be premature to conclude that some kind of impersonal or objective assessment is either required or, more particularly, truly possible regarding the criterion of seriousness.

**B  'Serious Handicap'**

*i  Hansard*

Parliament rejected the idea of a prescriptive list of serious conditions in relation to abortion for fetal anomaly on the basis that this would interfere with clinical discretion. This could be seen as wise in the face of variations in the severity of conditions.[19] Further, the Lane Committee's *Report on the Working of the Abortion Act 1967* decided that it would be inappropriate to define the statutory grounds more precisely.[20]

Not surprisingly, the Parliamentary debates on the amendments to the 1967 Act do not tell us what 'serious handicap' should mean. Indeed, the Lord Chancellor (as he then was) Lord MacKay of Clashfern observed: 'It is surely impossible to take an absolutely certain view of these cases. It is a matter of opinion, and the requirement is that the opinion should be formed in good faith'.[21] But the debates do give some indication as to what it was thought the term would *not* mean. In particular, there was a debate of sorts as to whether abortions might be performed for reasons of cleft lip. One speaker suggested that the idea that abortions could be conducted for such reasons was 'scaremongering'.[22] Regardless of whether or not this was so, the flavour of the debate suggests that such conditions would not have been viewed as serious in the requisite sense. By contrast, there is some indication that conditions such as spina bifida, hydrocephalus and cystic fibrosis would have been.[23] With reference to a proposed amendment that the type of disability should have to be recorded following a termination under this section of the Act, Kenneth Clarke said[24]:

> There is some point to the amendment. It would finally answer one way or the other the continual claim that abortion is carried out for a hare lip or other such condition. I share the doubts of those who say that that does not take place.

---

[19] On the approval of medical discretion generally in the application of the Act, see *Hansard*, 21 June 1990, vol 174, col 1156, per Mrs Maria Fyfe: 'If the law sets parameters that do not allow medical judgments to be freely exercised, it must be defective'.
[20] Lane Committee, *Report on the Working of the Abortion Act 1967* (1974) (Cm 5579) 211.
[21] HL Debs, vol 522, col 1098.
[22] Mr Frank Doran, *Hansard*, 21 June 1990, vol 174, col 1187.
[23] *Ibid* Miss Ann Widdecombe, col 1190.
[24] *Ibid* col 1201.

We know about the abortion in the *Jepson* case because the Department of Health gathers and records a great deal of statistical information about abortions carried out each year.[25] As regards the seriousness of the condition in that case we saw earlier that, in the light of a range of evidence, the CPS decided that the relevant doctors had formed a good-faith judgment on this issue. Without access to further information about this case, others cannot easily assess this judgment and, more particularly, it would be inappropriate to do so.[26] That said, it may be that in future doctors will be reluctant to put themselves at risk by performing an abortion for cleft lip/palate after 24 weeks, particularly since there was considerable discomfort amongst the fetal-medicine community about the *Jepson* case. In this sense, and importantly, although the doctors in *Jepson* have not been subject to legal sanction, practice may have changed.[27]

Despite the Parliamentary deference to 'good-faith' medical opinion, recently it has been suggested that '[s]ome degree of consistency amongst the medical profession is essential… and open debate about the terms may be the most effective way of achieving this'.[28] This may mean that we should at least try to identify which conditions can reasonably be judged as serious and thus may be the subject of reasonable disagreement. In the discussion that follows, I shall try to contribute to that debate.

### ii RCOG guidelines

Turning to the RCOG guidelines on 'serious handicap', if an 'abnormality' is untreatable and would lead to the death of the child once born, termination is always permissible. Aside from such cases a judgment has to be made as to 'whether the abnormality would be likely to result in "serious handicap"'.[29] The guidelines cite World Health Organisation definitions of disability, suggesting that '[a] person is only likely to be regarded as seriously handicapped if they need the support described in the WHO Points 3 and 4'. Point 3 says:

---

[25] Available at <http://www.publications.doh.gov.uk/public/sb0323.htm> accessed 8 October 2007.

[26] For interesting discussion of some of the issues that might arise in this context, see E Wicks, M Wyldes and M Kilby 'Late Termination of Pregnancy for Fetal Abnormality: Medical and Legal Perspectives' (2004) 12 *Med Law Rev* 285, 291: 'The more difficult question arises where an abnormality is seen which raises the possibility of handicap, but where the chances of the handicap being serious are uncertain, for example, with an apparently isolated cleft lip, or a minor abnormality of the hands or feet. The point here is that a full and frank discussion of any structural abnormality would leave open the possibility that the findings of the ultrasound scan could represent the first signs of a serious handicap which might not present itself until after birth.'

[27] Personal communication: Susan Bewley.

[28] *Ibid* 293.

[29] RCOG, above n 11, para 3.3.1

> Assisted performance. Includes the need for a helping hand (ie: the individual can perform the activity or sustain the behaviour, whether augmented by aids or not, only with some assistance from another person).

Point 4 states:

> Dependent performance. Includes complete dependence on the presence of another person (ie: the individual can perform the activity or sustain the behaviour, but only when someone is with him most of the time).

The RCOG guidelines also note, however, that a judgment that a child would be seriously disabled 'should be based on a careful consideration of the following factors, not all of which will be relevant in every case'[30]:

> The probability of effective treatment, either *in utero* or after birth; the probable degree of self-awareness and of ability to communicate with others; the suffering that would be experienced; the extent to which the actions essential for health that normal individuals perform unaided would have to be provided by others; the probability of being able to live alone and to be self supporting as an adult.

In all cases, the guidelines observe that judgments should be 'cautious', aware that there has been no judicial interpretation of 'seriously' disabled.[31]

I shall consider aspects of these RCOG factors in turn.

a   The probability of effective treatment *in utero* or after birth

As the RCOG makes clear, the probability of effective treatment is just one factor to be considered amongst possibly relevant others. However, the claimant in *Jepson* apparently wanted to make the legality of termination turn on just one criterion: she sought a declaration 'that "seriously handicapped" in section 1(1)(d) of the Abortion Act 1967 has to be understood by reference to the *remediability* of the condition'.[32] She or her counsel may well have read the RCOG guidelines on the point which cite the notion of 'treatment' but, since the case did not progress, we cannot know whether she saw 'treatment' and 'remediability' as the same. Perhaps one reason for the claimant's focus on the idea of remediability was that she herself was born with problems with her jaw, for which she had a number of successful corrective operations during childhood. The implication of a focus on the idea of remediability would be that where a condition can be remedied, there can be no justification for termination.

Although the idea of remediability may be thought to have a certain solidity to it, the meaning of the term in this context may not in fact be clear-cut. The term could refer to a medical cure or correction, as Reverend Jepson apparently obtained by means of her successful operations. Alternatively, it could imply

---

[30] *Ibid* para 3.3.3.
[31] *Ibid*.
[32] Above n 4, para 8 (my emphasis).

correction or alleviation to a significant degree by means of social support. This point relates to the distinction between medical and social concepts of disability noted in Chapter 1.

As outlined in the previous chapter, views of disability have been dominated by a medical conception of what it is to be disabled. We saw that John Harris is a proponent of this model, although he prefers to call this a 'harmed condition' model, and that he defines disability as a 'physical or mental condition which we have a strong [rational] preference not to be in'.[33] The alternative 'social model', as previously defended by Tom Shakespeare (amongst others) and now criticised by him to some degree, distinguishes between impairment as a medical condition of the body on the one hand and disability caused by social prejudice and discrimination on the other.[34] On this latter approach, whether an impairment leads to a disability will depend on the nature of the social environment the individual inhabits. With the medical model, then, disability is situated within the individual and with the social model, it is social in nature. The Nuffield Council on Bioethics' 2006 report *Critical Care Decisions in Fetal and Neonatal Medicine: Ethical Issues* (the 'Nuffield Report') discusses the two models, noting the contribution to understandings of disability made by the social model.[35] As noted in Chapter 1, Jonathan Glover has rightly observed that the debate as to which is the better model is now fruitless and that instead we should recognise the degree of truth in both. (For this reason I tend to use the terms 'disability' and 'impairment' interchangeably.)

There are two points to note about the relevance of these conceptions of disability here. First, in referring to 'treatment', the RCOG guidelines do not envisage the idea of a remedy through social support. For several reasons, this makes sense: first, it would be an unusual understanding of 'treatment' if it included social support; second, since the treatment might be *in utero*, social support could not be relevant at this stage; third, the notion of treatment is only one of several of the RCOG factors, some of the others of which appear — in effect — to refer to the notion of social support. Indeed, social support in the sense of aid from others is incorporated into the guidelines in the form of the last two factors cited above, namely 'the extent to which the actions essential for health that normal individuals perform unaided would have to be provided by others' and 'the probability of being able to live alone and to be self supporting as an adult'. The implication seems to be that the likelihood of a considerable degree

---

[33] J Harris 'Is There a Coherent Social Conception of Disability?' (2000) 26 *JME* 95, 97, citing Reindal's interpretation of Harris in S Reindal 'Disability, Gene Therapy and Eugenics — a Challenge to John Harris' (2000) 26 *JME* 89.

[34] T Shakespeare 'Choices and Rights: Eugenics, Genetics and Disability Equality' (1998) 13/5 *Disability and Society* 665, 665 (citing M Oliver, *The Politics of Disablement* (Basingstoke: Macmillan, 1990)). I refer to his more recent work later in this chapter.

[35] Nuffield Council on Bioethics, *Critical Care Decisions in Fetal and Neonatal Medicine: Ethical Issues* (2006), paras 35, 3.29–3.34 and 7.3.

of dependence may further support the idea of a termination. In this way, the idea of social support may be incorporated into the guidelines in a somewhat negative way and I return to this point below.

Second, the distinction between medical and social models of disability has implications for the *Jepson* claimant's assertion that 'serious' must be understood in terms of the remediability of the condition. If 'remediable' were only to refer to 'medical cure or correction', then 'serious' effectively has a very wide meaning, automatically incorporating a large number of conditions, such as Down's syndrome, which are not medically curable or correctable (although some of the health problems associated with Down's syndrome, such as heart conditions, may be). This may not be what Reverend Jepson intended, since her brother has Down's syndrome.[36] By contrast, if 'remediable' can include what we might call 'alleviation', then 'serious' becomes narrower in scope, since the health problems inherent in most instances of Down's syndrome can be alleviated to some degree. But there is an important and less obvious possible meaning of 'remediable', namely 'alleviation through social support'. If this is what is meant, the definition of 'serious' is considerably narrower in scope. This is because many conditions are alleviated by social support. It seems possible, then, that Reverend Jepson's choice of the term 'remediable' may have been intended to include both medical treatment and social support.

In fact, the RCOG guidelines have recently been criticised as relying on a 'potentially discriminatory' conception of disability. This was in the context of preimplantation genetic diagnosis (PGD) by the Human Fertilisation and Embryology Authority's (HFEA's) and Human Genetics Commission's (HGC's) 'Outcome Document' on the scope of PGD.[37] This concern about potential discrimination is not in fact analysed either in this document or (by means of record) in the minutes of background meetings prior to the publication of the document. But the report does recommend that the extent of social support available should be one of the relevant factors in decisions regarding PGD. Since it is also a factor in the RCOG guidelines, the implication would appear to be that in decisions about PGD the availability of social support might count, to some degree, as a reason *not* to offer PGD. That is, instead of the *need* for social support tending to support a negative view of disability, one that might count in favour of PGD, the *availability* of social support might instead count as a reason against it. (I explore the factors relevant to PGD in their own right in Chapter 4.) In this light, the idea of the need for and, particularly, the availability of assistance through social support could become, if not a *necessarily* positive, then at least a less negative factor in the assessment processes inherent in selective abortion. This may

---

[36] <http://www.telegraph.co.uk/opinion/main.jhtml?xml=/opinion/2005/03/20/do2001.xml&sSheet=/opinion/2005/03/20/ixop.html> accessed 8 October 2007.
[37] HFEA and HGC, *Outcome of the Public Consultation on Preimplantation Genetic Diagnosis*, 18 June 2001, Rec 15.

require a slight change of emphasis in the existing RCOG guidelines on the point. (I explore below the RCOG factors that are explicitly relevant to the idea of social support.)

Before turning to consider the next RCOG factor, we should consider the scope for treatment *in utero*. In fact, this is highly limited, as the Nuffield Report observes[38]:

> Advances in fetal diagnosis have not been matched by prospects for effective treatment with medicine or surgery. We are aware of the development of open fetal surgery as a possible means of correcting or lessening the impact of abnormalities in a limited number of conditions although we believe that the value of such procedures remains unclear at this time. Such procedures carry a high risk to the pregnant woman. *Our view is that in the UK, new procedures in fetal surgery should be offered only within a protocol approved by a research ethics committee.*

The report lists the small number of conditions for which 'effective fetal treatments are available'.[39]

b   The probable degree of self-awareness and of ability to communicate with others

The implication of this factor would appear to be that the less a born child would be self-aware and the less she could communicate with others, the more serious her disability is. Ultimately, the concept of self-awareness may be linked with the idea of suffering (another factor in its own right). For instance, a child may suffer less if she is less self-aware. Alternatively, a child may only be aware of pain and have no compensating pleasures, for instance through interaction with her parents.

A report by the RCOG Ethics Committee on the law and ethics of 'late termination' for fetal abnormality includes helpful discussion of a number of case studies.[40] Although these are intended to give guidance about termination after 24 weeks (third-trimester terminations), which I specifically discuss in the final section of the chapter, some factors from these studies help to illustrate the core RCOG factors on termination for disability in general. For instance, Case 1 includes some elements of relevance to self-awareness and the ability to communicate[41]:

> The fetus... developed severe microcephaly *in utero* and the neurological opinion was that the fetus had suffered cortical brain death. The prognosis was that the baby would

---

[38]   Nuffield Council, above n 35, para 17, referring also to paras 4.11 and 9.8. At para 9.8, the report also observes: 'There should also be careful scrutiny of the potential benefits and harms of new procedures'. Emphasis in original.

[39]   *Ibid* para 4.10.

[40]   RCOG Ethics Committee, *A Consideration of the Law and Ethics in Relation to Late Termination of Pregnancy for Fetal Abnormality* (RCOG Press, March 1998).

[41]   *Ibid* para 5.1.1 (my emphasis).

have severe spastic quadriplegia and possibly intractable fits, *be blind and deaf, with no sensation or human interaction except severe pain*. The life span could be as long as 20 years.

Clearly, this is a particularly extreme case and it is likely that where the factor of self-awareness and ability to communicate is particularly prominent in a decision, a child's condition could fairly be described as very severe.

c   The suffering that would be experienced

As explored in Chapter 1, in some mostly very rare conditions there is a serious risk of a very great degree of suffering, both physical and mental. In terms of genetic conditions, Tay-Sachs was the obvious example[42]:

> The classical form of Tay-Sachs disease (TSD) is a fatal genetic disorder in children that causes progressive destruction of the central nervous system… By about two years of age, most children experience recurrent seizures and diminishing mental function. The infant gradually regresses, losing skills one by one, and is eventually unable to crawl, turn over, sit, or reach out. Other symptoms include increasing loss of coordination, progressive inability to swallow and breathing difficulties. Eventually, the child becomes blind, mentally retarded, paralyzed, and non-responsive to his or her environment. To date, there is no cure or effective treatment for TSD.

As we saw before, in this extreme and rare case, arguably it is against the interests of a child who would have Tay-Sachs to be born.[43] The same might be said about the fetus in Case 1 above, whose condition in fact resulted not from a genetic cause but because the mother developed a severe reaction to a blood transfusion she had had at 25 weeks. In such cases, abortion can be said to be morally and legally legitimate on the basis of the suffering of the prospective child. In Chapter 1, ethically speaking this type of case was referred to as one of 'wrongful life', on the basis that in such cases there is a serious risk that the child will not think her life worth living, since the burdens of her existence will be insufficiently compensated for by benefits in it. Another example of a very serious genetic condition discussed in the previous chapter was Lesch-Nyhan syndrome. Broadly speaking, such conditions were contrasted with cases in which, although disabled, a person thinks her life worth living. These latter cases are more complex.

In fact, work with people who have this degree of disability shows that we should be careful not to make assumptions about a child's suffering and therefore that we should be cautious about the relevance of the language of suffering. For instance, in Chapter 1 I touched on Priscilla Alderson's interviews with adults who have one of a number of different conditions: cystic fibrosis, sickle cell

---

[42] National Tay-Sachs and Allied Diseases Association, Inc <http://www.ntsad.org> accessed 8 October 2007.

[43] Someone with strongly pro-life views would disagree.

anaemia, thalassaemia, Down's syndrome and spina bifida.[44] The severity of these conditions varies considerably and it seems likely that the interviews were with people who did not have the more severe versions of some of these conditions (such as spina bifida and cystic fibrosis).[45] As we saw previously, Alderson found that the interviewees felt they suffered more from social stigma than from their actual physical condition. (Sometimes the attitudes of the parents of a child with impairments may themselves affect the child's self-esteem, since some parents may adapt more easily or willingly than others to raising such a child.[46]) In part we might recall here the distinction between medical and social models of disability discussed earlier, although those models are about the causes of disability and only by implication, perhaps, the causes of suffering.

The lesson here, perhaps, is that we should not presume a connection between a given condition and suffering, at least of a mental kind.[47] This may tend to suggest that the factor of suffering in the RCOG guidelines is best understood as referring to physical suffering. Again, however, as those drafting the guidelines would have been aware, individual reactions to physical suffering vary a great deal and are influenced by mental attitudes and outlook. So, unless physical pain or discomfort is likely to be very severe, arguably particular caution should be exercised when reviewing suffering as a factor relevant to termination.

d   The extent to which the actions essential for health that normal individuals perform unaided would have to be provided by others

To some extent, I discussed this and the next factor when I considered the notion of 'remediability' suggested by Reverend Jepson as the only appropriate criterion for judging the legitimacy of termination for fetal anomaly. Earlier I suggested that there is perhaps scope for the need for the assistance of others to become a

---

[44] P Alderson 'Prenatal Counselling and Images of Disability' in D Dickenson (ed), *Ethical Issues in Maternal-Fetal Medicine* (Cambridge: Cambridge University Press, 2002) 195, 201.

[45] For one view of such conditions, see A Asch 'Can Aborting "Imperfect" Children be Immoral?' from A Asch 'Real Moral Dilemmas' *Christianity and Crisis* (1986) 46(10) 237. Reprinted in J Arras and B Steinbock, *Ethical Issues in Modern Medicine* 5th edn (Mountain View, Calif: Mayfield, 1999) 384, 386: 'Down's syndrome, spina bifida, cystic fibrosis, or muscular dystrophy cause degrees of impairment ranging from mild to severe, the degree indeterminable at the time of prenatal diagnosis. Most people with Down's syndrome are mildly or moderately retarded and thus have the potential to interact with friends and family, to learn many skills, and to live as adults in the community in supported living arrangements or on their own. Spina bifida can cause intellectual impairment but often does not, and adults with this disability today can be found as social workers, lawyers, and parents themselves. Cystic fibrosis and muscular dystrophy entail no intellectual impairment, and although they are degenerative conditions that often bring death in childhood or adolescence, many people with the latter disability and some with the former live into adulthood, are self-supporting, and are themselves parents.'

[46] I am grateful to Susan Bewley for drawing this point to my attention.

[47] The point has been well made by S Edwards, in 'Prevention of Disability on Grounds of Suffering' (2001) 27 *JME* 380.

84   *Selective Abortion — The Law*

less necessarily negative consideration in this context (though of course the RCOG's statement of this factor may not have been intended in this way) and I refer to that earlier discussion here. But I only suggested that there might be a change of emphasis in the way the idea of social support is viewed; I did not suggest that the need for social support should be irrelevant in this context.

Indeed, progress in the debate about models of disability has shown that the need for social support (whatever the degree of availability of this) should not necessarily be ruled out as a factor of some relevance in selective abortion. As noted in Chapter 1, for instance, John Harris has accepted that there may be 'social dimensions' to physical and mental conditions that disadvantage the individual[48] and, more particularly, Tom Shakespeare has acknowledged that some impairments can themselves lead to significant problems.[49] The implication is that some conditions will be disabling despite all possible support. The point is put well by Dorothy Wertz and John Fletcher[50]:

> Most physical and some mental disabilities can be overcome with social support and changes in the physical environment. Some mental and neurologic disabilities, however, require lifetime care and overwhelm parents' lives. Such disabilities may never be overcome even with massive economic and social support.

In this light, extensive dependence on others for crucial needs could legitimately continue to be a factor in selective abortion, though perhaps a less pronounced, or particularly reflective, one. We need to think more about the detail of this.

For instance, we can note the extent to which some people might need help in actions essential for health and, more particularly perhaps, the way in which this need might be associated with severe instances of other factors listed in the RCOG guidelines. Part of the point here is that in reflection on any given case there may be a delicate interplay of factors. Again, it is useful to refer to a case study from the RCOG Ethics Committee report on terminations after 24 weeks. Case 3 concerns a fetus with severe spina bifida with hydrocephalus[51]:

> A fetus was found at 34 weeks to have an open meningomyelocoele from T4 (mid-back down), kyphoscoliosis and severe hydrocephalus... It was thought that without surgery the baby was likely to die of overwhelming infection early in neonatal life. If the baby were operated upon and survived, repeated operations would be necessary and there would be a *high chance of mental retardation, wheelchair bound existence, urinary and faecal incontinence, and gross permanent multisystem disorders.*

---

[48] Harris, above n 33, 5, 95.
[49] Shakespeare, above n 34, 670.
[50] D Wertz and J Fletcher 'A Critique of Some Feminist Challenges to Prenatal Diagnosis' 175, as cited in B Steinbock 'Disability, Prenatal Testing and Selective Abortion' in E Parens and A Asch (eds), *Prenatal Testing and Disability Rights* (Washington, DC: Georgetown University Press, 2000) 108, 115.
[51] RCOG, above n 40, para 5.3 (my emphasis).

In such a case, I think it would be unhelpful to overemphasise the availability of help from others in relation to all of this child's needs and to downplay the need for such support. This is because such a child would be severely disabled, despite all the support he received.

e  The probability of being able to live alone and to be self-supporting as an adult

To some degree, I refer again to the earlier discussion about the concept of remediability and the way that the need for social support need not necessarily be viewed negatively. Compared with the previous factor, which may sometimes be of particular relevance when someone's condition is severe in a number of different ways (as in Case 3 above), the need for at least some degree of live-in help or support more generally as an adult does not appear a strong factor in favour of termination, at least by itself. Further and more generally, the RCOG might positively endorse the idea of social support, including in relation to conditions that are not diagnosable in pregnancy. The rate of termination for different fetal conditions varies considerably across Europe and it is likely that the availability of social support is influential here.[52]

It is helpful to note that the first three factors above only consider the interests of the person who would otherwise be born disabled (treatment, self-awareness and the ability to communicate and suffering). In one way this is also true of the latter two (actions associated with health needs performed by others and ability to live alone and without support). By implication, however, these latter factors also implicate third parties, perhaps particularly a child's parents. At this stage, we can recall part of a passage of Tom Shakespeare's that I quoted in the previous chapter[53]:

> [T]he decision to terminate pregnancy is not one that the majority of people take lightly. Moreover, there are reasons to want to prevent the birth of a child affected by impairment which do not reflect discrimination against disabled people: for example, the desire to avoid the early death or suffering of a loved child, or a feeling that a family will be unable to cope with the strain of looking after a very impaired member.

As I said previously, here Shakespeare has effectively alluded both to child-focused and parent-focused — or at least parent-accommodating — reasons for termination for reasons of disability.

When we review these factors, not all of which will be relevant in every case, it might also be noted that, morally speaking, a disability will need to be that

---

[52]  C Mansfield, S Hopfer, TM Marteau 'Termination Rates after Prenatal Diagnosis of Down's Syndrome, spina bifida, anencephaly, and Turner and Klinefelter syndromes: a Systematic Literature Review. European Concerted Action: DADA (Decision-making After the Diagnosis of a Fetal Abnormality' (1999) 19/9 *Prenat Diagn* 808; H Drake, M Reid, T Marteau 'Attitudes towards Termination for Fetal Abnormality: Comparisons in Three European Countries' (1996) 49/3 *Clin Genet* 134.

[53]  Shakespeare, above n 8, 681.

much more severe to justify termination as a pregnancy progresses. I discuss terminations after 24 weeks and the RCOG's endorsement of a gradualist approach to the fetus's moral status later in this chapter. Of course, English law also effectively endorses a gradualist approach to the issue of fetal legal protection, by requiring more stringent justifications for termination after 24 weeks, when section 1(1)(a) ceases to apply.[54] What this implies for our interpretation of the disability ground of the Act will be discussed specifically in the section on terminations after 24 weeks.

I now want briefly to recall some thoughts about prospective parents' moral interests in decisions relating to selective abortion. This is intended as a prelude to a consideration of whether the law on selective abortion does, can or should recognise that parents' interests may have a legitimate place in such decisions.

## III A WOMAN'S OR COUPLE'S MORAL AND LEGAL INTERESTS IN DECISIONS RELATING TO SELECTIVE ABORTION

### A Parents' Moral Interests in Being Able to Choose Whether to Have a Disabled Child

In Chapter 1, I began to consider the notion of reproductive autonomy and its place, value and extent in relation to disability in a future child. I argued that since people can decide whether to reproduce and since extensive positive duties are necessarily entailed in raising a child, arguably prospective parents should have some say about whether they give birth to any child, including a disabled one.[55] The wish to abort for reasons related to serious fetal anomaly may be justified because a significant degree of impairment in a future child may seriously invoke the parents' interests in reproductive autonomy and thereby determine whether or not they reproduce. We saw that there is considerable support for this position, including some from the perspective of disability interests, as noted at the end of the last section above.[56] To say that parents have an interest in being able to decide whether to give birth to a seriously disabled child is not to deny the positive aspects of raising a disabled or seriously ill child or to express a view as to the

---

[54] This is also noted by the Nuffield Council, above n 35, para 2.18.
[55] The classic statement of this view is found in J Robertson 'Genetic Selection of Offspring Characteristics' (1996) 76 *Boston U Law Rev* 421, 445.
[56] See, eg, A Buchanan, D Brock, N Daniels, D Wikler, *From Chance to Choice: Genetics and Justice* (Cambridge: Cambridge University Press, 2000); J Robertson, *Children of Choice: Freedom and the New Reproductive Technologies* (Princeton, NJ: Princeton University Press, 1994) and above n 55; Steinbock, above n 50, 108, 118, 119; J Botkin 'Line Drawing: Developing Professional Standards for Prenatal Diagnostic Services' in Parens and Asch (eds), above n 50, 288 and 'Fetal Privacy and Confidentiality' (1995) 25(5) *Hastings Center Report* 32. From a disability interests perspective, see, eg, Shakespeare, above n 34, 672.

balance of positive and negative experiences that might result.[57] It is simply to maintain that parents are entitled to form a view, which should be appropriately informed,[58] as to the broad kind of reproductive experience upon which they are able to embark.

As we have seen in Chapter 1, and in the discussion so far in this chapter, it is not straightforward to define the notion of 'serious disability', particularly in relation to less extreme conditions. This has been acknowledged in the literature, such as in an extensive study undertaken by the Hastings Center in the United States.[59] It has also been acknowledged in England by the HGC in relation to PGD[60]:

> It has proved impossible to define what 'serious' should mean in this context. We have listed some factors that should be taken into account when considering seriousness, but perhaps the most important is that this technique should not be used for the purposes of trait selection or in a manner which could give rise to eugenic outcomes.

The central difficulty with the definition of 'serious' is that clinicians, genetic counsellors, prospective parents and those with impairments (who may thereby have an insight into the interests of the child once born) may all have different views as to the meaning of seriousness. So would the child who would be born unless aborted. (I explore this with particular reference to the case of Duchenne Muscular Dystrophy, which is in fact typically thought of as a very serious condition, in Chapter 4.) In some ways, the question becomes 'serious for whom?'.[61]

As discussed in Chapter 1, if being born in any given case is compatible with having a good or reasonable quality of life, then we cannot say that it is not in the interests of a child who would have a condition compatible with such a life to be born. This will be the case for many conditions for which we currently routinely screen. In these cases, however, we have seen that parents may still have an interest in being able to choose to accept or avoid certain experiences that the birth of a given child might entail: there might be significant mental impairment or serious health problems requiring, for instance, repeated hospitalisation, perhaps with major operative procedures of uncertain success. In these cases the parents' interests and those of the future child are potentially in conflict, since it will not be against the latter's interests to be born. Turning to public perceptions of prenatal screening and PND, responses to the HGC's 2004 consultation entitled *Choosing the Future: Genetics and Reproductive Decision-Making* indicate that prenatal

---

[57] See Botkin, above n 56, 8, 300–301 for a discussion of the possible kinds of impact on parents.
[58] See the discussion in Ch 1, S V(B) and references therein.
[59] The essays resulting from this study are collected in Parens and Asch (eds), above n 50.
[60] HGC, *Response to the Human Fertilisation and Embryology Authority on the Consultation on Preimplantation Genetic Diagnosis*, para 6.
[61] Botkin, above n 56, 300, likewise notes this.

screening and PND are widely supported (though some clearly oppose these practices) and that there is a recognition both of a child's possible interests (in not being born when a condition is very severe) and generally those of its parents in this context.[62]

If parents do have a legitimate moral interest in choosing whether to continue or terminate a pregnancy where the fetus is at risk of being born seriously impaired, their views as to the seriousness of its impairment will have some moral weight, 'within reason'. The last point is an important caveat. This is because we do have a reasonably sure sense of the notion of seriousness at the extremes — for instance Tay-Sachs versus the webbing of two toes.[63] As suggested above, the problematic area is the large one of 'mid-spectrum' conditions in between.[64]

The important question to which I am now going to turn is whether parents' interests and views can be taken into account in the application of the disability ground of the Abortion Act. Of course, we have seen that in cases where doctors do not think there is a substantial risk or a serious disability, a woman's reactions to and views about the prospect of a disabled child can be taken into account by means of section 1(1)(a). But the key question is whether parents' views and interests can be taken into account by means of the disability ground itself. As we saw from earlier discussion about the meanings of 'substantial risk' and 'serious handicap', *prima facie* the answer to this is 'no'. After all, the section requires that

[62] HGC, *Making Babies: Reproductive Decisions and Genetic Technologies* (2006), para 3.7: 'The high uptake of prenatal screening gives some indication of the widespread public support for it, and for diagnosis. This was reflected by responses to our consultation. Many expressed support on the grounds of health benefits and reproductive choice. For those conditions for which treatment is not available, the health benefit was commonly seen in terms of relief from, or avoidance of, suffering through having the pregnancy terminated. Further, the potential emotional and physical suffering of the parents, because of the long-term care requirements, and the potential damage to siblings, because of the disproportionate needs of the new sibling, may also be reduced. Where parents decide to continue the pregnancy, early medical interventions may enable a safer pregnancy and delivery, and may facilitate earlier treatments to relieve some of the symptoms of the disease. In addition, early warning allows parents to prepare emotionally, physically and psychologically for their child as they learn about the implications of the disorder.'

[63] 'Webbing (syndactyly) refers to the union of two or more fingers or toes, which usually only involves a skin connection between the two, but may rarely also include fusion of bones in the affected digits. Webbing may extend partially up between the digits, frequently just to the first joint, or may extend the entire length of the digits Polysyndactyly describes both webbing and the presence of an extra number of fingers or toes.' MedLine Plus Health Information <http://www.nlm.nih.gov/medlineplus/ency/article/003289.htm#Alternative%20Names> accessed 8 October 2007. Note, however, that a minor anomaly may be an indication of a more serious anomaly as, for instance, Down's syndrome may be a relatively common cause. *Ibid*. A possible concern that 'that's not all that's wrong with [the] baby...' was noted by a midwife quoted in C Williams, P Alderson and B Farsides '"Drawing the Line" in Prenatal Screening and Testing: Health Practitioners' Discussions' (2002) 4(1) *Health, Risk and Society* 61, 68.

[64] D Wertz 'Drawing Lines: Notes for Policymakers' in Parens and Asch (eds), n 48, 261, 263 *ff* discusses the difference of views amongst practitioners as to what is serious.

two doctors judge these criteria to be fulfilled. In line with this, we saw that the RCOG guidelines describe 'substantial risk' in impersonal terms, and observe that the views of the certifying doctors should also be capable of validation by others with no personal involvement. As for 'serious handicap', although there is no reference to a personal or impersonal appraisal of 'serious handicap', in referring to the need that an individual may have for the assistance of third parties either in actions essential for health, or in aspects of the requirements of living alone or generally as an adult, the RCOG factors could perhaps be interpreted as subtly alluding to possible parental interests. Overall, given that bodies such as the HGC have suggested that it is impossible to define and agree upon seriousness, can doctors legally take account of the views of parents in certifying that a child would have a serious disability if born? The next section explores this hugely important, and currently unanswered, question.

## B Legal Interests

### i Parents' possible legal interests in the interpretation of the disability ground of the Abortion Act

The claimant in *Jepson* contended that a key error of law surrounding the abortion in that case was 'that the medical practitioners who signed the certificate... took into account the views of the parents involved' and 'that... in relation to the decision in question, the parents' views, as a matter of law, could have no weight'.[65] Certainly the Act states that two doctors must be 'of the opinion, formed in good faith' that the impairment is serious. Whether two doctors can decide in good faith that the condition is serious and mean (or also mean) in so doing, 'serious for this woman' (their patient for the purposes of a legal termination) is a crucial question. Doctors could decide that a woman's views as to seriousness are relevant to their opinion of whether the condition of seriousness is satisfied if they consider that the purpose of the disability section of the Act is to give women choice about the birth of a disabled child and recognise that, in making this choice, women (along with their husbands or partners, family and wider social network) will have views about the degree of impairment in a child they feel able to take on. Of course, sometimes women and their husbands or partners (where present) may disagree and in this case doctors will want to be clear as to the nature of the woman's feelings and wishes, which may sometimes be difficult to achieve.[66]

Some scholars have indeed suggested that where the fetus could have a reasonable quality of life as a born child, it is in fact the woman's or parents' interests that underlie this section of the Abortion Act. Glanville Williams laid the ground for this argument some time ago[67] and the basis of this section has been

---

[65] Above n 4, para 12.
[66] I am grateful to Susan Bewley here.
[67] G Williams, *Textbook of Criminal Law*, 1st edn (London: Stevens, 1978) 256.

reconsidered by Sally Sheldon and Stephen Wilkinson.[68] They argue that, because very few fetuses aborted under this ground would have lives of little or no quality if born, most abortions under this section cannot be seen as protecting the fetus from such a life. Rather, in most cases in which this section is invoked, the real concern is with the woman's or parents' interests. This is a moral argument as to the legal interpretation of this section of the Act and one with which I agree.

The legal objection to this argument, originally explored by Derek Morgan, is that a 'parental interests' interpretation of section 1(1)(d) of the Act would essentially repeat section 1(1)(a), making section 1(1)(d) redundant.[69] Sheldon and Wilkinson observe that, from an ethical viewpoint, it may simply be that there is more than one justification for section 1(1)(d) and, given the very different degrees of disability with which someone may be born, this must be right. From the viewpoint of statutory interpretation, however, they suggest that 'there are some grounds for questioning' whether Parliament can have intended that section 1(1)(d) should protect parents' interests.[70]

Of course, section 1(1)(d) can never be entirely redundant in that, unlike section 1(1)(a), it allows terminations up until birth. Apart from this point, and more fundamentally, it may be that as a society we have not necessarily been honest about whose interests the disability section of the Act is capable of protecting: it is to some degree taboo to say that parents have an interest in choosing to accept or avoid the birth of an impaired child and those debating the Act in Parliament may well have sensed this and therefore not stated it.

As indicated above, whether or not parents' interests could be relevant to the interpretation of the disability ground of the Act was set to be a key issue in the *Jepson* case. When the police investigated the matter, it contacted the RCOG. The original advice given to them by its Vice-President was (in part) as follows[71]:

> The termination was carried out under Ground E that 'there is a substantial risk that if the child were born it would suffer from such physical or mental abnormalities as to be seriously handicapped'. The abnormality is defined as bilateral cleft lip and palate and this had been diagnosed by ultrasound. There is no precise definition of 'serious handicap' and the decision is therefore one for the practitioner to make in consultation with the parents and other interested parties. In this case an expert in feto-maternal medicine as well as experts in the condition from the Birmingham Cleft Lip Team were involved. *The decision to abort under Clause E would always ultimately be with the mother having taken into consideration the perception of the parents to the serious nature of the handicap following counselling and information from experts with special knowledge of the condition.*

---

[68] S Sheldon and S Wilkinson 'Termination of Pregnancy for Reason of Foetal Disability: are there Grounds for a Special Exception in Law?' (2001) 9 *Med Law Rev* 85.
[69] D Morgan 'Abortion: the Unexamined Ground' [1990] *Crim LR* 687, 692.
[70] Sheldon and Wilkinson, above n 68, 100.
[71] Above n 4, para 6, per Miss Mellows (my emphasis).

*Selective Abortion — Parents' Moral and Legal Interests* 91

On behalf of the claimant, Reverend Jepson, it was argued that the Vice-President's statement was legally flawed. The arguments are recounted by Mr Justice Jackson[72]:

> The first error of law is that the medical practitioners who signed the certificate... took into account the views of the parents involved. Mr Gordon submits that in relation to the decision in question, the parents' views, as a matter of law, could have no weight. The second flaw which Mr Gordon contends exists is this: whether or not any reliance was placed on the parents' opinions, nevertheless the proposition that a cleft lip and palate could ever be a serious handicap within the meaning of section 1(1)(d) of the Abortion Act 1967 is wrong in law. The third error which Mr Gordon contends for is that the letter reaches conclusions about the nature of cleft lip and palate, which are inconsistent with the guidance published on other occasions by the Royal College of Obstetricians and Gynaecologists. As observed in argument, it seems to me that Mr Gordon's third point is, in truth, an aspect of, or a subsidiary part of, his second point.

Contrary to the claimant's position, are a woman's (or couple's) views relevant to the interpretation of the terms of section 1(1)(d) of the Abortion Act?

I first return to the letter to the police from the Vice-President of the RCOG. Regarding the place of a woman's (or couple's) views on the degree of risk or the seriousness of a disability, one sentence of her letter — which is of central importance to the interpretation of this section of the Act — is somewhat unclear. As emphasised above, she writes:

> The decision to abort under Clause E would always ultimately be with the mother having taken into consideration the perception of the parents to the serious nature of the handicap following counselling and information from experts with special knowledge of the condition.

On one reading, this means the woman is to take into account her own views, but this does not make sense and cannot be what is intended. Another reading, which makes more sense but is legally incorrect, is that legally the woman is required to take account of her partner's views. The question of what impact the relationship between a woman and her partner will have on her (or their) decision-making about selective abortion is an important one, but not one of central concern here. A further interpretation of this sentence is that although discussions about the seriousness of the impairment will take place between the woman (perhaps her partner), practitioners and relevant specialists, ultimately, *assuming* two doctors think that the legal criteria for an abortion are made out, it is the woman who decides whether to continue or to abort the pregnancy. This makes the most sense. By contrast, since the Act requires that two doctors consider the condition to be serious, the sentence cannot mean that *the woman decides whether the criterion of seriousness is satisfied*. Despite this, whether two doctors can certify in good faith that the condition is serious — and mean in so

---

[72] *Ibid* para 12. I cited part of this above.

doing (at least to some degree) *'serious for this woman or couple'* — is of course the crucial and currently unresolved question with which I am concerned. The claimant in *Jepson* was seeking to steer the law away from any such interpretation.

A further interpretation of this important sentence could be that it contained a 'typo' and that it should have read: 'The decision to abort under Clause E would always ultimately be with the *doctor* having taken into consideration the perception of the parents to the serious nature of the handicap following counselling and information from experts with special knowledge of the condition'.[73] (Alternatively, the 'typo' in fact entered the scene in the case report.) Indeed, this would be consistent with the earlier sentence in the Vice-President's letter which reads: 'There is no precise definition of "serious handicap" and the decision is therefore one for the practitioner to make in consultation with the parents and other interested parties.' On this point, one clinician comments that 'it would be normal good medical practice for a doctor to take account of parents' views'.[74] As I have indicated, whether this is consistent with the disability ground of the Abortion Act is the key question here. Reverend Jepson clearly thought it would not be. Given that the Vice-President alludes to discussions between a woman and her doctor, her statement may be describing the practice that typically occurs and has built up over the years. This practice may partly be a response to the discomfort some practitioners evidently feel at being the gatekeepers to abortion and the administrators of a system in which a pregnant woman's autonomy is deeply at stake but lacks legal protection in the form of a right to abort.[75] The question, however, is whether such a practice is lawful.

One way to think about this would be to try to reconcile use of section 1(1)(a) of the Act in relation to fetal anomaly with section 1(1)(d), the disability ground. What can we glean from the use of the former section for our interpretation of the latter?

As we have seen, the possible use of two different sections of the Abortion Act in relation to fetal impairment is not apparent from the terms of the Act itself. However, it seems right that section 1(1)(a) can be interpreted in this way given its concern with the mental (or physical) health of the woman. Where section 1(1)(a) is used in this fashion, in essence the thought is that although doctors do not think either that the risk is substantial or the condition serious, a woman may be seriously concerned about what she is able to take on, to the extent that there are risks to her physical or mental health greater than those inherent in

---

[73] Personal communication: Susan Bewley (my emphasis).
[74] *Ibid.*
[75] In discussions between health professionals, a philosopher and sociologists, one (unnamed) obstetrician said: 'I think things are probably made more difficult because most obstetricians and gynaecologists know that terminations for social reasons, or whatever, are done effectively on demand, and one of the main reasons for that is because of anxiety generated about the pregnancy continuing... our sort of baseline has shifted because of shifts in how the Abortion Act has been applied over the past 20 years or so'. Williams *et al*, above n 63, 66.

termination. Yet, since raising any child, but perhaps particularly a disabled one, has at least the potential to have considerable implications for the life of a woman (and her partner), any termination for serious fetal anomaly is likely seriously to implicate a woman's (and her partner's) interests, including where the termination is legally justified on the basis of section 1(1)(d).

On the one hand, then, section 1(1)(a) of the Act does not explicitly indicate that it might — in effect — be used in relation to fetal impairment, but arguably can be interpreted in this way to some degree, as evidenced in the RCOG guidelines[76]; on the other, the disability ground of the Act does not state that prospective parents' views about impairment can be a legitimate factor in the interpretation of this section but, on the argument presented here, arguably can be interpreted in this way. Notably, this may particularly be where a 'serious' condition may nevertheless result in a life that a child would think worth living, so that termination cannot be claimed, morally speaking, to be in the interests of the fetus or the child it would become. Indeed, assuming section 1(1)(a) can be used in relation to fetal impairment (which must be right), it would be hard to assert that prospective parents' views, particularly about the seriousness of an impairment, are legally irrelevant under section 1(1)(d), the disability ground, even though that section is not based on risks to the woman's mental or physical health. Rather, the use of section 1(1)(a) in relation to fetal anomaly confirms that the question of the degree of risk or, particularly, the seriousness of an impairment *cannot be a purely objective matter*. As we saw earlier, this has been acknowledged by the HGC. Significantly, we therefore have good reason to think that doctors can, to some extent at least, take the views and interests of a woman (and her partner) into account when deciding whether the criteria of the disability ground of the Act are satisfied. If this is so, then the practice to which the Vice-President alludes in her letter, which was also referred to by a clinician, is arguably defensible at law.

Although defensible, I have also suggested that there may be something of a taboo element to suggestions that parents have an interest in deciding whether or not to have a disabled child and so to contributing to discussions about the seriousness of a child's disability, or that doctors are entitled to take account of their views (particularly the woman's, a doctor's patient for the purposes of termination), especially about the impact of the birth of a disabled child on them (or her in particular). Further, perhaps especially where prospective parents are troubled about the morality of a possible abortion, sometimes it may be hard for them to express their views, even to sympathetic doctors. (Alternatively, the opportunity to discuss this may come as a huge relief.) Overall, the point is that the debate about selective abortion may be complicated by this element of taboo. However, when we move from the explicit context of abortion to that of related

---

[76] It is also arguable that the section could be used to support termination on the grounds of fetal sex if, for instance, a woman discovers that the fetus is female and advises doctors that her life will be made a misery by her husband or family if she has another girl.

case law, it seems that we have apparently found it somewhat easier,[77] implicitly at least, to accept the legitimacy of parental interests in and views about selective abortion. The cases on wrongful birth demonstrate this and are a further source as to the interpretation of the disability ground of the Abortion Act, including the relevance of parents' views and interests.

### ii   Implications of the wrongful birth cases

The idea of compensating parents for the lost opportunity to abort a fetus subsequently born as a child with a disability has been legally recognised for some time. The recognition of the wrongful birth claim progressed in response to scientific and legal developments in a way intended to enhance the deliberative quality of the abortion decision.[78] Such liability imposes on health professionals a duty to advise prospective parents about features or conditions in the fetus likely to result in a certain degree of disability or disease in the future child. Wrongful birth cases correspond (indirectly at least) to the terms of the Abortion Act, as discussed in more detail in the next chapter. In *Rance v Mid-Downs Health Authority*,[79] for example, one of the doctors was concerned that the couple might have had access to an abortion on the grounds of section 1(1)(d), it therefore being the relevant doctors' duty to inform them of information relating to a serious disability. Similarly, in *Rand v East Dorset Health Authority*, Newman J refers to the 'legal right accorded to parents by the 1967 Act as relevant to the ambit of the duty of care assumed by those having responsibility in connection with childbirth'.[80] Since there is in fact no such right, this statement makes more sense if we think of parents having an option, under certain circumstances, to terminate.

Importantly, at the outset it should be noted that the cases I am about to discuss largely post-date the new turn that the law took in the wrongful conception case

---

[77] By comparison, see in particular the US cases that reject the wrongful birth action, eg, *Schloss v Miriam Hosp*, No CA 98–2076, 1999 WL 41875, at 4 (RI Super Ct 11 January 1999): 'These cases are not about birth, or wrongfulness, or negligence, or common law. They are about abortion.' See also *Dansby v Thomas Jefferson University Hospital*, 623 A2d 816 (Pa Super 1993) 821, *per* Wieand J: 'The protection of fetal life has been recognized to be an important state interest. The legislature's expressed concern is to prevent lawsuits leading to eugenic abortions of deformed or unwanted children.' These cases are discussed in the next chapter.

[78] In the United States the catalyst for these cases was the leading abortion decision in *Roe v Wade* 35 LEd2d 147 (1973), discussed in the next chapter.

[79] [1991] 1 QB 587. The case concerned a failure to diagnose spina bifida and the legality of an abortion under the unamended Abortion Act 1967, in which the fetal disability ground of the Act was subject to time limits.

[80] [2000] 56 BMLR 39, 48 (my emphasis). This point is made in conjunction with a discussion of damages. Newman J also observes: 'The existence of the Act is sufficient to introduce into the relationship between the health authority responsible for a pregnancy and the parents, a duty to take reasonable steps to ensure the parents can exercise their choice under the Act'. *Ibid* 50.

of *McFarlane v Tayside Health Board*, which held that the birth of a healthy child following a negligent sterilisation constitutes pure economic loss that is outweighed by the 'blessing' inherent in the birth of the child.[81] It would be beyond my scope to consider the wrongful conception case law in itself, a topic of more central concern to others. However, I note with approval others' criticism of the way the jurisprudence in this area has developed following *McFarlane* so as to distinguish between the birth of a healthy child on the one hand and a disabled one on the other, thereby failing to attend appropriately to the autonomy interests at stake in being able to choose whether to have *any* child, whether 'healthy' or disabled.[82] (Indeed, this is consistent with my argument in Chapter 1 that the choice of whether or not to accept the birth of a disabled child is not a completely different kind of choice from that of whether to have any child. Rather, both choices are possible exercises of reproductive autonomy.) In general, the attention given to the notion of autonomy in the judgments of Lady Hale (as she now is) in several of the cases in this area is particularly worthy of attention.[83] For my purposes here, I note the way in which judges in the wrongful birth cases are necessarily operating against the background currently set by *McFarlane*.

Turning now to the wrongful birth action in itself, given that the scope of the action is effectively delineated by the terms of section 1(1)(d) of the Abortion Act, there has been no doubt that a wrongful birth action cannot succeed unless, amongst other factors, a woman was not informed of a substantial risk of a serious disability in the child that would be born. But there has sometimes been doubt as to whether the condition of seriousness of disability is itself fulfilled. This is illustrated by the case of *Rand*, which concerned the lost opportunity to choose whether to abort a fetus with Down's syndrome. Mr Justice Newman noted that '[t]here is an issue as to whether [the child in question] should be described as "seriously disabled"', observing that 'she is regarded as one of the most able and

---

[81] [2000] 2 AC 59.
[82] For further thought, see N Priaulx, *The Harm Paradox: Tort Law and the Unwanted Child in an Era of Choice* (London: UCL Press, 2007) especially Ch 3. I therefore agree with Priaulx's statement that '[s]ince caring for *any* child must be seen as bringing about a significant caring responsibility, if there is a difference in the burden and hardship that does result, this will be a matter of *extent*, not kind' (emphasis in original). See also JK Mason and GT Laurie, *Law and Medical Ethics*, 7th edn (Oxford: OUP, 2006) especially paras 6.20–6.30. 6.36–6.46.
[83] See in particular her judgment in *Parkinson v St James and Seacroft University Hospital NHS Trust* [2002] QB 266 in which she also devotes considerable attention to a woman's interest in bodily integrity and the way this is invoked by pregnancy and childbirth and its aftermath. See also the discussion of her judgments in Priaulx, above n 82 and Mason and Laurie, above n 82.

intelligent children among those who suffer from Down's syndrome'.[84] However, rightly or wrongly, in due course he concluded that it was appropriate to describe her as 'seriously disabled'.[85]

The issue of seriousness was also addressed in *Parkinson v St James and Seacroft University Hospital NHS Trust*, which concerned a negligent sterilisation and the subsequent birth of a child with 'severe learning difficulties', set against the backdrop of the decision in *McFarlane*. The Court of Appeal held that damages for the extra costs of raising a child with a disability were recoverable. On the question of the degree of disability, Brooke L.J. observed[86]:

> What constitutes a significant disability for this purpose will have to be decided by judges, if necessary, on a case by case basis. The expression would certainly stretch to

---

[84] Above n 80, 40.

[85] *Ibid* 45. He added, however, that 'the quality of her life, her ability, her personality and her potential have incalculable value'. Earlier he quotes Janet Carr, a clinical psychologist, who assessed K at the age of 4 years and 6 months: 'Where everyday life skills are concerned K is likely to be a very competent young woman with Down's syndrome, to be capable of living with some degree of independence, and even of being employed at a simple level and being paid a wage. She is however very unlikely ever to be able to live entirely independently; to marry, or to bring up children. She will need care and supervision for the rest of her life.' For more recent cases, see, eg, *Hardman v Amin* (2001) 59 BMLR 58, in which a GP had failed to diagnose that a pregnant woman was suffering from rubella and her child was subsequently born severely disabled. In this case Henriques J found that, amongst the damages to which she was entitled, the claimant should receive an award for her personal contribution to the child's care, which was to be calculated either by way of damages for loss of amenity or on a commercial basis with a discount of 25 per cent, following *Housecroft v Burnett* [1986] 1 All ER 332 and *Allen v Bloomsbury HA* [1993] 1 All ER 651. See also *Lee v Taunton and Somerset NHS Trust* [2001] 1 FLR 419. For further discussion, see Mason and Laurie, above n 82, paras 6.45–6.46, who observe that '[i]t can be said in general that the pattern developed in *Rand* has been widely accepted and, as a result, the underlying validity of the wrongful birth action bas been fully upheld. The extent of the available damages has, however, been modified in the light of *McFarlane* in that the costs of rearing a healthy child must, now, be deducted from the gross costs of caring for one who is disabled' (para 6.45, footnotes omitted).

[86] Above n 83, 283. The reference to 'severe learning difficulties' is at 271. Further, in answer to the question 'how disabled does the child have to be for the parents to be able to make a claim?' Hale LJ answers (at 293) 'that the law has for some time distinguished between the ordinary needs of ordinary children and the special needs of a disabled child'. She goes on to refer to statutory criteria. In supporting the award of damages for the extra costs of raising a child with a disability, she observed: 'A disabled child needs extra care and extra expenditure… The additional stresses and strains can have seriously adverse effects upon the whole family, and not infrequently lead, as here, to the break-up of the parents' relationship and detriment to the other children. But we all know of cases where the whole family has been enriched by the presence of a disabled member and would not have things any other way. This analysis treats a disabled child as having exactly the same worth as a non-disabled child. It affords him the same dignity and status. It simply acknowledges that he costs more'. The case was followed by *Groom v Selby* [2002] 64 BMLR 47, in which a doctor negligently failed to diagnose or test for pregnancy at a consultation with the claimant (so that she lost the chance to abort under s 1(1)(a) of the Abortion Act 1967) and

include disabilities of the mind (including severe behavioural disabilities) as well as physical disabilities. It would not include minor defects or inconveniences, such as are the lot of many children who do not suffer from significant disabilities.

Notably, in his allusion to a spectrum of seriousness, Brooke LJ's language shifts from 'disability' to 'defect or inconvenience'. While Brooke LJ's gloss on seriousness gives some sense of the meaning of 'serious' under the disability ground of the Act, he also makes plain that cases will have to be decided on a case-by-case basis. In cases of difficulty, then, judges in wrongful birth cases will have themselves to decide whether the criterion of seriousness is satisfied. In so doing, they may also have to address the question of whether, in answering this, it is legitimate to give weight to a woman's or couple's interests and views on this matter. It may be helpful at this juncture to reflect further on the purpose of the wrongful birth action and for what it supposedly compensates.

As noted earlier, the purpose of such actions is to protect prospective parents' interests in being able to choose whether or not to continue with a pregnancy in which the fetus will be born as a disabled child. These cases can result in awards of damages. If compensation were awarded solely for the extra costs of raising a disabled child — which have a very real monetary value — the cases would be unlikely to give any indication as to whether doctors (and later judges) can take a woman's (or couple's) views on seriousness into account in deciding that the grounds for section 1(1)(d) were made out. However, the courts have been prepared also to award damages for the impact on parents of raising a disabled child. In *Rand* (which, like *Parkinson*, post-dated *McFarlane*), Mr Justice Newman discusses such damages under the heading 'Damages for the additional mental, physical and emotional stress and wear and tear in bringing up a Down's syndrome child over and above that involved in bringing up a healthy child', and states[87]:

> It is obvious that the birth of a disabled child will dramatically affect the quality of life of both parents and it is to be inferred that a reason why they would have terminated the pregnancy was to avoid such a loss of amenity in their lives. As the law stands they cannot recover for any distress which causes no injury, but the loss of amenity caused by being required to expend time caring for a disabled child is a real and physical consequence. I have no doubt that it has sometimes led to exhaustion. In my judgment the law can recognise a claim for a continuing loss of amenity where a breach of duty has caused physical consequences giving rise to the loss of amenity.

It is unfortunate to describe the possible effects of the birth of a disabled child in such categorical terms. At the same time, as Newman J notes, given that the law

---

the subsequent child was in fact disabled. In this case, the child was born prematurely and about four weeks later developed salmonella meningitis complicated by bilateral front brain abscesses, which resulted in a severe level of disability.

[87] Above n 80, 57 (my emphasis). Of course, both parents will only be affected where both remain present.

currently limits the legitimate heads of damage (so that 'distress which causes no injury' cannot found a claim) he is in some ways obliged to overstate the point, emphasising the idea of 'exhaustion' and 'physical consequences giving rise to a loss of amenity'. Indeed, it would be preferable not to have to distinguish so completely between the impact of the birth of *any* child on the one hand and a *disabled* one on the other, but the decision in *McFarlane* precludes this. (This criticism is consistent with the point that, as I argued in Chapter 1, the birth of a disabled child may have a greater, rather than a completely different, kind of impact.) The general point about a possible impact on parents (here in fact in the light of the birth of a disabled child) is very important. In due course Newman J made an award of £30,000 to Mrs Rand and £5,000 to Mr Rand, thereby apparently distinguishing between the impact on each of the parents.

To support this head of damage, Newman J notes that the idea of damages for 'loss of amenity' in parents' lives was accepted by Brooke J in the earlier wrongful birth case of *Allen v Bloomsbury Health Authority*.[88] Additionally, he supports such damages with reference to the notion of a legally protected autonomy interest advocated by Lord Millett in the wrongful conception case of *McFarlane*.[89] Lord Millett observes of the parents in that case: 'They have suffered both injury and loss. They have lost the freedom to limit the size of their family. They have been denied an important aspect of their personal autonomy'. (It should be noted that the courts, appropriately, do not treat a woman's refusal to undergo an abortion as breaking the chain of causation in the tort of negligence.)

Although Lord Millet's point was not taken up by any of the other judges in *McFarlane* itself, his approach was approved by the majority of the House of Lords in *Rees v Darlington Memorial NHS Trust*.[90] This case concerned whether a disabled mother could recover damages (for the extra costs of child-raising associated with her own disability) for the birth of a healthy child following a negligently performed sterilisation. Although the majority in *Rees* decided that such recovery would be inconsistent with the principles of *McFarlane*, it approved the award of a 'conventional' sum in recognition of the 'legal wrong' done to her. Lord Bingham, whose wording was approved by Lord Millett in *Rees*, described the loss as follows: '[A] parent… has been denied… the opportunity to live her life in the way that she wished and planned'.[91] Arguably, in itself the creation of the award is one of the consequences of the difficulties created by the law in *McFarlane*.

[88] [1993] 1 All ER 651.
[89] Above n 81, 114.
[90] [2004] 1 AC 309. For criticisms of this case, see, eg, P Cane 'Another Failed Sterilisation' (2004) 120 *LQR* 189.
[91] *Ibid* 317. For criticisms of the conventional award in itself, and the attention it cannot pay to the individual effect on autonomy, see Priaulx, above n 82, 76 *ff*. Priaulx criticises *McFarlane* and *Rees* for the 'mere lip-service' the cases pay to autonomy and observes that '[w]hat is meant by autonomy in this context is a commitment to recognising the *diverse* situations of individuals, the varying degrees that individuals may be harmed through the negligent frustration of their reproductive choices' (emphasis in original). In fact, as noted

Returning to the wrongful birth case law itself, I am not suggesting that the cases currently overtly state that parents' views are relevant to the determination of the seriousness of a child's disability. However, we can see that damages are recognised for the possible impact on parents of raising a disabled child (beyond, that is, the financial costs of so doing) necessarily described, for the purposes of the law of negligence, as 'physical consequences giving rise to... loss of amenity' and further supported with reference to the protection due to autonomy interests (currently by means of a 'conventional award') in surrounding case law. In this way, I am simply suggesting that it is fair to say that there is at least a legal *opening* for the courts to state that parents' interests in making decisions about the birth of a disabled child — and so their views on seriousness — should carry some weight in the interpretation of the disability ground of the Act, at least in cases that are the subject of reasonable disagreement, and at least before 24 weeks. (I discuss termination after 24 weeks in the final section of this chapter.) These are the cases in the grey mid-spectrum area.

Potentially against the relevance of parental views, however, consider the following statement by Newman J in *Rand* itself[92]:

> I have concluded that there is a difference between the choice available to parents to limit their family on the grounds of size alone, and the choice available by virtue of the Abortion Act 1967 to terminate a pregnancy on *medical grounds*. The existence of the Act is sufficient to introduce into the relationship between the health authority responsible for a pregnancy and the parents, a duty to take reasonable steps to ensure the parents can exercise their choice under the Act. The lawful and proper operation of the Abortion Act anticipates and requires the opinions of medical experts to be available and *is firmly placed in the area of medical expertise*.

Of course, his reason for making the distinction between the choice not to have any child and the choice not to have a disabled one originates in the need to deal with and distinguish the decision in *McFarlane* to the effect that there is no liability for the birth of a healthy child following a failed sterilisation. Putting that to one side and turning now to his reflections on the operation of the disability ground of the Act, in strict legal terms Mr Justice Newman correctly emphasises that the operation of the Act is in the hands of doctors, in the sense that doctors must in good faith judge that the defence to what would otherwise be a crime is made out.[93] Yet, since he holds that the lawful operation of the Act 'is firmly placed in the area of medical expertise', at the same time he seems to be stating that the judgment that a decision selectively to terminate is justified must be a medical one. In the light of the work that has successfully been done on questioning, though not overturning, the medical model of disability, this is

---

above, in *Rand* Newman J does award more to Mrs Rand than Mr Rand. However, whilst this award is supported, in part, with reference to the award of 'conventional' damages in *McFarlane*, it is not an award of conventional damages *per se*.

[92] Above n 80, 48 (my emphasis).
[93] Offences Against the Person Act 1861, ss 58 and 59.

somewhat unfortunate, if unsurprising. Additionally, and more significantly, this kind of statement fails to capture the intrinsically moral nature of the decision to terminate any pregnancy, including one on the grounds of fetal anomaly. It is also potentially at odds with his own recognition, in the same case, of the possible impact that the birth of a disabled child may have on its parents, at least to the extent that that could give rise to a recognition of the relevance, within reason, of their views about seriousness.

Judges in future cases on wrongful birth could do well to take on board some of the criticisms of the exclusive role of doctors in evaluating disability.[94] These are criticisms implicitly recognised by bodies responsible for formulating legal guidelines in the parallel context of PGD, such as the HGC, whose views on the impossibility of defining seriousness I noted earlier. Judges could acknowledge these difficulties in their reflections on the meaning of 'serious handicap', including as they affect doctors themselves in their difficult task of operating legally under the Abortion Act. In so doing, given that the purpose of the wrongful birth action is to protect prospective parents' choice about whether to continue with a pregnancy in which the subsequently born child is at substantial risk of being seriously impaired, judges could decide that their views can legitimately be relevant, within reason, to the meaning of 'serious handicap' under the disability ground of the Act. Indeed, this would now be consistent with the recognition by the HFEA and HGC of the relevance of parents' views to testing and selection decisions in PGD (amongst other factors), as discussed in Chapter 4. (This is not to presume that the moral status of the embryo and fetus is necessarily the same.)

Strikingly, if parents' views about raising a disabled child and their thoughts about the seriousness of its disability were *irrelevant* to the legality of termination on the basis of the disability ground of the Act, then it is likely that the legality of many terminations that are currently performed should at least be questioned, as should the purpose of certain kinds of screening and testing. Indeed, this would probably be in line with Reverend Jepson's desires and beliefs in relation to selective abortion. For instance, given that it is most unlikely to be against the interests of someone with Down's syndrome to be born, screening, testing and termination for Down's syndrome could rarely, perhaps never, be said to be based on the seriousness of the condition from the child's point of view (although one in ten children do not survive the first year of life).[95]

Lastly on the wrongful birth cases, it should be noted that causation will limit the scope of a possible action from a woman's (or couple's) point of view. The test

---

[94] See, eg, Shakespeare, above n 34.
[95] Further, between screening and birth there is a high rate of stillbirth. C Julian-Reynier, Y Aurran, A Dumaret, A Maron, F Chabal, F Giraud 'Attitudes Towards Down's syndrome: Follow up of a Cohort of 280 cases' (1995) 32/8 *J Med Genet* 597; RH Won, RJ Currier, F Lorey, DR Towner 'The Timing of Demise in Fetuses with Trisomy 21 and Trisomy 18' (2005) 25/7 *Prenat Diagn* 608.

of causation will be whether the woman would have chosen to abort if she had been correctly advised of the fetus's health or condition. This is tested by a combination of subjective and objective factors.[96] In this sense, since the cases turn, in part at least, on what the woman (or couple) would have chosen to do when informed that the subsequently born child would be disabled, this is a further indication that parent's reproductive autonomy interests are recognised in the law, albeit to a limited degree.

Apart from reflecting on parents' possible interests in relation to degrees of disability that would nevertheless leave a child with a life he thought worth living, the only other way to view the question of seriousness, as discussed in Chapter 1, is in terms of non-person-affecting principles, although I am not suggesting that this could become part of legal reasoning. To recap, ethically speaking the idea is that, other things being equal, it is preferable if people at least start life without disabilities or disorders which may (though will not necessarily) impair their capacity for flourishing and well-being, including where these would be compatible with a life that a person would think worth living. Since not all people can start life this way, the implication is that it may be preferable if other, different, people do so in their stead.[97] However, in Chapter 1, I suggested that it was difficult to be swayed by non-person-affecting principles when a fetus (as the conceptus is called from eight weeks' gestation onwards) already exists and has increasing moral claims, even though the fetus is, arguably, not yet a person. By contrast, it may be that the potential interests of its parents, particularly its mother (a person-affecting consideration) can legitimately be weighed against the claims of the fetus, at least up to a certain point. Here I refer again to the gradualist account of fetal moral status that I endorsed in Chapter 1: where a subsequently born child would be seriously disabled but would nevertheless think her life worth living it may be morally justifiable to terminate the pregnancy because prospective parents may have a serious interest in avoiding her birth. (This would be an instance of a woman's (or a couple's) broader interest in reproductive autonomy in relation to the birth of any child.) However, morally to justify termination the condition must reasonably be judged that much more serious as the fetus develops. Whether a woman's or couple's interests in choosing whether to have a child with a disability or disease can justify termination after 24 weeks is a topic I consider specifically later in this chapter. Of course, where there is a

---

[96] *Smith v Barking, Havering and Brentwood HA* [1994] 5 Med LR 285. Fears of fraud are often expressed in conjunction with hostility to the wrongful birth action. See, eg, K Wilcoxon 'Statutory Remedies for Judicial Torts: The Need for Wrongful Birth Legislation' (Spring, 2001) *U of Cincinnati Law Rev* 1023, 1040. For a critique of the requirements of causation in the US context and suggestions for reform, see S Ryan 'Wrongful Birth: False Representations of Women's Reproductive Lives' (April, 1994) *Minnesota Law Rev* 857, 907. For further discussion of the wrongful birth cases, see Priaulx, above n 82.

[97] Ch 1, S IV(C).

serious risk that a subsequently born child would not think her life worth living, abortion may be justifiable in the interests of the fetus.

In the following chapter I explore in greater detail the legal duties accompanying screening and testing practices and their impact on decisions made about selective abortion. I now turn to consider the relevance of the European Convention on Human Rights to the law on selective abortion.

## IV CASES UNDER THE EUROPEAN CONVENTION ON HUMAN RIGHTS

The *Jepson* claimant sought declarations, amongst others, 'that the foetus at 24 weeks gestation and greater has a right to life pursuant to Article 2 of the European Convention on Human Rights, which is only subject to the competing Article 2 right of the mother' and 'that section 1(1)(d) of the Abortion Act is incompatible with Articles 2, 3, 8 and 14 of the European Convention on Human Rights'.[98] Since the case did not proceed, we do not know what arguments the claimant was planning to make, but aspects of ECHR case law can be discussed here. This is relevant to the issue ultimately underlying the meaning of the terms within the disability ground of the Abortion Act, namely the balance of legal interests between a pregnant woman and the fetus. The ECHR was of course directly incorporated into English law by means of the Human Rights Act 1998.

### A   Article 8

The first part of Article 8 of the Convention provides: 'Everyone has the right to respect for his private and family life, his home and his correspondence'. If an applicant can show an interference with this right, then it falls to the state in question to try to justify this under Article 8(2):

> There shall be no interference by a public authority with this right except such as is in accordance with the law and is necessary in a democratic society in the interests of national security, public safety or the economic well-being of the country, for the prevention of crime and disorder, for the protection of morals, or for the protection of the rights and freedoms of others.

In *Brüggemann and Scheuten v Germany*, the European Commission on Human Rights decided that although the decision to abort invokes a woman's private life, some regulation of pregnancy is consistent with respect for private life, since pregnancy 'cannot be said to pertain uniquely to the sphere of private life'.[99] Thus, abortion regulation does not need to be justified under Article 8(2). The reasoning of the dissenting Mr Fawcett is sometimes preferred because it places the onus of justification for regulation on the state; he held that '"private life"… must in my view cover pregnancy, its commencement and termination: indeed it would be

---

[98] Above n 4, para 8.
[99] (1981) 3 EHRR 244, para 59.

hard to envisage more essentially private elements'.[100] Despite this, he held a certain degree of regulation of abortion to be justified under Article 8(2). More recently, in *Tysiac v Poland* the European Court of Human Rights (ECtHR) has held that it is unnecessary to consider whether the Convention itself guarantees a right to abort and declined to consider this question, recalling in familiar terms that the way respect for private life is implemented in any given state will always require a fair balance to be found between the interests of the community and those of the individual.[101] The implication is that the lack of a right to abort in English law remains potentially compatible with Article 8.

The application of Article 8 focuses on the interests and rights of the pregnant woman, but does not tell us anything about the fetus. Is the fetus protected by Article 2, the right to life?

## B  Article 2

Article 2(1) states: 'Everyone's right to life shall be protected by law'. Is the fetus a legal person? English cases such as *C v S* and *Re F (in utero)* establish that it has no legal status.[102] Similarly, the Abortion Act itself implies that the fetus is not a legal person. Is this position compatible with Article 2?

The implications of a finding, sought by Reverend Jepson, that the fetus of 24 or more weeks has a right to life under Article 2 — which could only be overridden where 'the continuance of the pregnancy would involve risk to the life of the pregnant woman, greater than if the pregnancy were terminated' (under

---

[100] eg, by L Doswald-Beck 'The Meaning of the "Right to Respect for Private Life" under the European Convention on Human Rights' (1983) 4 *Human Rights Law Journal* 283, 291; D Feldman 'Privacy-related Rights and their Social Value' in P Birks (ed), *Privacy and Loyalty* (Oxford: OUP, 1997) 15; *Brüggemann*, above n 99, para 1.

[101] ECHR Appl No 5410/03 (2007). Here the Court in fact found a breach of Art 8 in relation to Polish law, on the basis of a lack of a clear procedure, in the face of disagreement, to review whether the criteria for a lawful abortion had been established. In this way, the case emphasised the need for a positive obligation to act. Note that where there is a positive obligation to act rather than merely a negative obligation to refrain from interference, the analysis under Art 8(1) and (2) is merged, as in *Rees v United Kingdom*, in which the Court observed: 'In determining whether or not a positive obligation exists, regard must be had to the fair balance that has to be struck between the general interest of the community and the interests of the individual, the search for which balance is inherent in the whole of the Convention. In striking this balance the aims mentioned in the second paragraph of Article 8 may be of a certain relevance, although this provision refers in terms only to "interferences" with the right protected by the first paragraph — in other words is concerned with the negative obligations flowing therefrom.' (1987) 9 EHRR 56, para 37.

[102] Respectively [1987] 1 All ER 1230, in which a man sought to prevent his girlfriend having an abortion; and [1988] 2 All ER 193, in which the Court of Appeal decided that it could not make the fetus a ward of court in response to a local authority's concerns about the lifestyle and mental condition of its mother.

section 1(1)(c) of the Act) — would be considerable.[103] In addition to creating the need for a declaration of incompatibility under the Human Rights Act as regards the disability ground of the Abortion Act (section 1(1)(d)), such a finding would also have implications for section 1(1)(b) of the Act, which permits abortion after 24 weeks where 'necessary to prevent grave permanent injury to the physical or mental health of the pregnant woman' (as well as for surrounding case law, notably that dealing with 'maternal-fetal conflict').[104] So, as regards the Abortion Act, her Article 2 argument would have had to have two prongs: not only would she have had to challenge the application of the disability ground after 24 weeks, she would also have had to challenge the application of section 1(1)(b). What does current case law tell us about the relevance of Article 2 to the fetus?

The case that considered the application of Article 2 to the fetus under English law was *Paton v UK*.[105] Since it concerned an abortion in the early stages of pregnancy performed in order to protect a woman's interests in physical and mental health, it left very open the extent to which Article 2 applies to the fetus. In fact, of the decision two leading commentators observe: 'It is difficult to conclude other than that the Commission was anxious to sidestep a controversial case'.[106] However, they also note the lack of consensus amongst Member States of the Council of Europe on the moral and legal issues surrounding abortion and thereby, in effect, what is called the 'margin of appreciation'. Following *Paton* it could only be said that, in the light of risks to the woman's physical or mental health, the early fetus has at best a limited right to life. In due course, *RH v Norway* extended *Paton* to abortions for social rather than health reasons.[107]

In 2004 the question of whether the fetus, including the third-trimester fetus, has a right to life under Article 2 was addressed by the ECtHR in *Vo v France*.[108] The case concerned a tragic mistake as to names in a French hospital that resulted in a doctor trying to remove an intra-uterine device from a woman who was in

---

[103] Section 1(1)(c) permits abortion where 'the continuance of the pregnancy would involve risk to the life of the pregnant woman, greater than if the pregnancy were terminated' but the framing of the declaration she sought suggests she was not seeking to challenge this ground.

[104] The cases in which a woman refuses a caesarean section are here in point. See, eg, *Re MB (Adult: Refusal of Medical Treatment)* (1997) 8 *Med LR* 217.

[105] (1981) 3 EHRR 408. See also *X v United Kingdom* (1980) 19 D & R 244.

[106] FG Jacobs and RCA White, *The European Convention on Human Rights*, 2nd edn (Oxford: Clarendon Press, 1996) 43.

[107] *RH v Norway*, Appl No 17004/90 (1992).

[108] Judgment of 8 July 2004, Appl No 53924/00. (In *Evans v United Kingdom*, Judgment of 10 April 2007, Appl No 6339/05, the ECtHR held also that an embryo does not have a right to life under Art 2, para 56. The case concerned a challenge to the consent provisions of the Human Fertilisation and Embryology Act 1990, specifically whether a man should be able to withdraw his consent to the continued storage of embryos created with his former partner when, as a result of treatment for cancer of her ovaries, she wished to use those embryos and had no other way of becoming a genetic mother. The ECtHR also found no violation of Articles 8 or 14.)

fact six months' pregnant. Several days later a scan showed that her pregnancy could not continue and an abortion was recommended. The applicant, Mrs Thi-Nho Vo, complained in relation to 'the authorities' refusal to classify the taking of her unborn child's life as unintentional homicide' and 'argued that the absence of criminal legislation to prevent and punish such an act breached Article 2'.[109] In the ECtHR it was argued on her behalf that her fetus had a right to life under Article 2.

At the outset the court identified the novel issue before it as 'whether, apart from cases where the mother has requested an abortion, harming a foetus should be treated as a criminal offence in the light of Article 2 of the Convention, with a view to protecting the foetus under that Article'.[110] It should immediately be noted that the facts of the case do not pit a woman's interests against those of her fetus. Rather, maternal and fetal interests are aligned. This is the hallmark of cases in which a third party harms the fetus (against the mother's will).

Following a review of prior case law, including *Paton*, the Court observed that[111]:

> [T]he unborn child is not regarded as a 'person' directly protected by Article 2 of the Convention and... if the unborn do have a 'right' to 'life', it is implicitly limited by the mother's rights and interests.

It noted, however, that 'the possibility that in certain circumstances *safeguards* may be extended to the unborn child' had not been dismissed.[112] At this point the majority appears to lay the ground for recognition of a distinction between granting rights to the fetus on the one hand and protecting its interests in a non-rights-based way on the other, to which I shall return.

Not surprisingly, the Court then called in aid the margin of appreciation. It said that, given that the interpretation of Article 2 in relation to the fetus had taken account of the difference of approach at the national level, the issue of the beginning of the right to life fell within the margin of appreciation. Here the Court noted both that the issue had not been decided in most of the contracting states (including in France, which was currently debating the issue in other contexts) and that 'there is no European consensus on the scientific and legal definition of the beginning of life'.[113] The only point of agreement is that the embryo or fetus is human. Despite this, the Court observed that since the fetus has the capacity to become a person and in some states is protected (for instance by means of inheritance laws), it requires 'protection in the name of human dignity, without making it a "person" with the "right to life" for the purposes of

---

[109] *Ibid* para 46.
[110] *Ibid* para 81.
[111] *Ibid* para 80.
[112] *Ibid* citing *Brüggemann and Scheuten v Germany*, above n 99, my emphasis.
[113] *Ibid* para 82.

Article 2'.[114] The Court might have noted here that the protection the fetus receives in contexts such as tort or inheritance is really protection of the born child, since the tort claim crystallises on the birth of the child and inheritance is only ultimately of concern if the child is born.[115] In this light, it is not clear that the idea of protection for the sake of human dignity is at all in issue in relation to either of these contexts. Still, there may be other contexts, notably abortion, in which the fetus's human dignity or, better perhaps, its human value, is in issue. This is explored below.

Reference to the margin of appreciation enabled the Court to avoid pronouncing on the application of Article 2 to the fetus. It considered that it was 'neither desirable, nor even possible' to decide the issue in abstract terms.[116] As for the particular circumstances of the case, it did not think it necessary to consider whether the ending of the fetus's life was within the scope of Article 2 because, even if Article 2 were applicable, France had not failed to comply with requirements concerning the protection of life in the sphere of public health.[117] In deciding this issue the Court considered whether France's legal protection of the fetus in this case complied with the procedural requirements inherent in Article 2.[118] Here it noted, in language reminiscent of that in *Paton*, that[119]:

> [T]he life of the foetus was intimately connected with that of the mother and could be protected *through her*, especially as there was no conflict between the rights of the mother and the father or of the unborn child and the parents, the loss of the foetus having been caused by the unintentional negligence of a third party.

For the avoidance of doubt the Court reiterated that '[t]he interests of the mother and the child clearly coincided', and that it therefore had to consider the effectiveness of the legal protection given to the mother in her claim that the doctor was liable for the loss of her fetus.[120] This is a very important observation. It emphasises that the negligent harm to the fetus in this case was also harm to the mother, who had wanted to continue with the pregnancy. This is not to say that the fetus is simply part of the mother. Rather, it is to underline the alignment of maternal and fetal interests on these facts. In such a case, the fetus can be protected through her. Accordingly, the Court rejected her argument that Article

---

[114] *Ibid* para 84.
[115] A Grubb 'Commentary: Killing the Unborn Child: Abortion and Homicide: *Attorney General's Reference (No 3 of 1994)*' 6 Med L Rev (1998) 256, 307. See also the discussion in J Seymour, *Childbirth and the Law* (Oxford: OUP, 2000) 199 *ff*.
[116] Above n 108, para 85.
[117] *Ibid*.
[118] *Ibid*.
[119] *Ibid* para 77 (my emphasis).
[120] *Ibid* para 87. This was criticised by Judge Ress (dissenting), who stated: 'As this case illustrates, the embryo and the mother, as two separate "human beings" need separate protection' (para 4). He gave no explanation of why this should be the case and I do not see how the facts support this.

2 required a criminal remedy, noting that 'if the infringement of the right to life or to physical integrity is not caused intentionally, the positive obligation imposed by Article 2 to set up an effective judicial system does not necessarily require the provision of a criminal-law remedy in every case'.[121] In this case, the applicant could have brought an action in negligence.[122] Therefore, even if Article 2 were applicable in this case (which, to recap, the Court decided was unnecessary to address either in abstract or particular terms) it had not been violated.[123]

In effect, in its approach to the application of Article 2 the Court adopts an approach similar to that of the Commission in *Paton* by holding, on the one hand, that a decision as to applicability was not required and, on the other, by giving an indication as to the legal position if Article 2 were held to apply.

The majority's judgment was criticised in various ways in the separate and dissenting judgments.[124] I shall briefly note one criticism and then turn to discuss a second.

One criticism was that, contrary to the majority's reasoning, prior Commission and Court case law had considered that Article 2 applied to the fetus, without deciding that it was thus a person, in the sense that the fetus deserved some protection which, however, must be balanced against the interests of the pregnant woman.[125] In fact, as noted above, we saw that in *Paton* the Commission had avoided deciding this issue whilst at the same time giving some indication as to how it would decide it. The criticism of the majority's judgment in *Vo* is therefore understandable, but not fully sustainable. A second, related, criticism and the one

---

[121] *Ibid* para 90. Note here that the English criminal case of *Attorney-General's Reference (No 3 of 1994)* [1997] 3 All ER 936, which concerned the criminal liability of a man who stabbed his pregnant girlfriend, of course concerned the *intentional* infliction of injury. In this case, Lord Mustill rejected 'the reasoning which assumes that since (in the eyes of English law) the foetus does not have the attributes which make it a "person" it must be an adjunct of the mother. Eschewing all religious and political debate I would say that the foetus is neither. It is a unique organism.' *Ibid* 943.

[122] *Ibid* para 91. Further, that an administrative law action was statute-barred was considered reasonable, since the right of access to courts is not absolute (*ibid* para 92). The applicant did not avail herself in time of this route, through which she could have established the doctor's negligence and claimed compensation (*ibid* para 94). This aspect was criticised by Judge Ress (dissenting), who notes that criminal law has an important deterrent role (*ibid* para 1). The same might be argued, however, of the law of tort.

[123] *Ibid* para 95

[124] *Ibid*. (a) Separate opinion of Mr Rozakis, joined by Mr Caflisch, Mr Fischbach, Mr Lorenzen and Mrs Thomassen; (b) separate opinion of Mr Costa, joined by Mr Traja; (c) dissenting opinion of Mr Ress; (d) dissenting opinion of Mrs Mularoni joined by Mrs Strážnická.

[125] *Ibid*. Separate opinion of Judge Costa, joined by Judge Traja, para 10. See also the dissenting opinion of Judge Ress, para 4.

I now want to discuss, is that the existence of national abortion laws shows that prenatal life is given some legal protection and that, accordingly, Article 2 should apply to the fetus.[126]

### C  Legal Protection: Fetal Rights or Fetal Value?

An important question raised particularly by this second criticism is whether giving some legal protection to the fetus has to imply the grant of a legal right, or a limited one. As we have seen, in England abortion is not legal for simply *any* reason; rather, abortion has to be justified according to one or more of the terms of the Abortion Act. This means that the fetus is legally protected to some degree. Could this also mean that the fetus has legal rights, or limited ones? Or could this instead mean, for instance, that Parliament has decided that the fetus has a value that should be recognised and protected?

The view that giving some legal protection to the fetus must imply giving it legal rights can be found in some of the separate and dissenting judgments in *Vo*. For example, in his separate opinion Judge Costa, joined by Judge Traja, states[127]:

> I see no good legal reason or decisive policy consideration for not applying Article 2 in the present case. On a general level, I believe (in company with many senior judicial bodies in Europe) that there is life before birth, within the meaning of Article 2, [and] that the law must therefore protect such life.

And in her dissenting opinion, Judge Mularoni, joined by Judge Strážnická, observes[128]:

> Although legal personality is only acquired at birth, this does not to my mind mean that there must be no recognition or protection of 'everyone's right to life' before birth. Indeed, this seems to me to be a principle that is shared by all the member States of the Council of Europe, as domestic legislation permitting the voluntary termination of pregnancy would not have been necessary if the foetus was not regarded as having a life that should be protected. Abortion therefore constitutes an exception to the rule that the right to life should be protected, even before birth.

I do not find this passage entirely clear. However, it is important to note that giving some protection to fetal life does not require that the fetus be given legal *rights*, particularly a right to life. There are other legal ways of protecting the fetus, albeit to a limited degree, that do not use the mechanism or language of rights.

To start, we might note that tort law protects the fetus from negligent injury by third parties (for instance, by means of the Congenital Disabilities (Civil Liability) Act 1976) though really it is the born child who is protected and ultimately has

---

[126] *Ibid*. See, eg, the dissenting opinion of Judge Ress, para 4. See also the dissenting opinion of Judge Mularoni, joined by Judge Strážnická.
[127] *Ibid* para 17.
[128] *Ibid*. No paragraph numbering is given in this judgment.

rights.[129] Protection of the fetus *itself* in English law is harder to detect, particularly since abortion is legal. But we have also seen that abortion is only legal if one or more of the grounds of the Abortion Act are satisfied, since otherwise it would be a crime according to sections 58 or 59 of the Offences Against the Person Act 1861; there is therefore is no legal right to abort on the woman's part.[130] Importantly, rather then being propelled towards the language of rights (which would have to be limited ones unless we were to disregard, say, the woman's interest in and right to life) we could instead see the conditions for legal abortion as ones that recognise that the fetus has moral and legal value, for this reason protecting it to a limited degree despite its lack of legal personhood. (To some extent, this is in line with Judge Mularoni's point, except that Judge Mularoni seems to imply at one point that therefore the fetus must have rights.) The significance of this move is that it avoids us stepping into the less subtle and more conflict-prone language of rights. Indeed, since no English woman currently has a legal right to abort, to start talking of fetal rights, even limited ones, seems uncalled for. There is in fact a certain subtlety to the English legal position, which involves a balancing of maternal and fetal interests and requires that the justification for abortion becomes that much more significant after 24 weeks (as discussed in the next section.)

---

[129] See my discussion of these issues in R Scott, *Rights, Duties and the Body: Law and Ethics of the Maternal-Fetal Conflict* (Oxford: Hart Publishing, 2002) Ch 6.

[130] To cite these grounds in full here, the relevant portion of s 1(1) of the Abortion Act 1967, as amended by the Human Fertilisation and Embryology Act 1990, reads: 'Subject to the provisions of this section, a person shall not be guilty of an offence under the law relating to abortion when a pregnancy is terminated by a registered medical practitioner if two registered medical practitioners are of the opinion, formed in good faith — (a) that the pregnancy has not exceeded twenty-four weeks and that the continuance of the pregnancy would involve risk, greater than if the pregnancy were terminated, of injury to the physical or mental health of the pregnant woman or any existing children of her family; or (b) that the termination is necessary to prevent grave permanent injury to the physical or mental health of the pregnant woman; or (c) that the continuance of the pregnancy would involve risk to the life of the pregnant woman, greater than if the pregnancy were terminated; or (d) that there is a substantial risk that if the child were born it would suffer from such physical or mental abnormalities as to be seriously handicapped'. Note also s 1(1) of the Infant Life (Preservation) Act 1929: 'Subject as hereinafter provided, any person who, with intent to destroy the life of a child *capable of being born alive*, by any wilful act causes a child to die before it has an existence independent of its mother, shall be guilty of felony, to wit, of child destruction, and shall be liable on conviction thereof on indictment to penal servitude for life. Provided that no person shall be found guilty of an offence under this section unless it is proved that the act which caused the death of the child was not done in good faith for the purposes only of preserving the life of the mother'. However, the 1929 Act is now irrelevant to the legality of abortion because of an amendment to the 1967 Act in the form of s 5(1): 'No offence under the Infant Life (Preservation) Act 1929 shall be committed by a registered medical practitioner who terminates a pregnancy in accordance with the provisions of this Act.'

In fact, even if a woman did have a right to abort under English law, this would not preclude the recognition that the fetus has value. This can be seen by looking comparatively at the construction of the relationship between the abortion right and the attendant state interests in the United States. For instance, although the jurisprudence of the US Supreme Court rejects the idea that the fetus is a legal person, it nevertheless asserts and continues to uphold the idea of a state interest in the potentiality of human life (as discussed further in the next chapter). *Planned Parenthood of Southeastern Pennsylvania v Casey* followed *Roe v Wade* in rejecting the idea of a fetal right to life, but gave increased attention to the State's interest in potential life originally asserted in *Roe*: it allowed states to take steps to try to ensure that a woman's decision to abort is thoughtful and informed as to the moral significance of the abortion decision.[131] (What this process can fairly entail is an important question in its own right, which I touch on in the next chapter.) The point here is that the idea of a woman's right to abort does not entail that the fetus has no value unless it is ascribed (limited) rights.

Overall, an important feature of the dissenting judgments in *Vo* is the revelation that protection of the fetus (and embryo) in the context of prenatal diagnosis, cloning and genetic engineering is clearly of current concern to members of the ECtHR.[132] In this light, the recognition and development of the idea that legal

---

[131] 120 LEd2d 674 (1992) and 35 LEd2d 147 (1973) respectively. For discussion see R Dworkin, *Life's Dominion: An Argument about Abortion and Euthanasia* (London: Harper Collins, 1993). Writing on abortion and the decision in *Casey*, Dworkin has distinguished between the state's 'derivative' interest in the fetus, which applies in the abortion context from viability onwards as the fetus acquires interests in its own right, and the state's 'detached' interest, developed in *Casey*, in encouraging responsible decisions which are duly respectful of the value of fetal life, eg, at 11, 24, 169–70.

[132] For instance, the dissenting Judge Ress observes: 'Even if it is assumed that the ordinary meaning of human life in Article 2 of the Convention is not entirely clear and can be interpreted in different ways, the obligation to protect human life requires more extensive protection, particularly in view of the techniques available for genetic manipulation and the unlimited production of embryos for various purposes. The manner in which Article 2 is interpreted must evolve in accordance with these developments and constraints and confront the real dangers now facing human life. Any restriction on such a dynamic interpretation must take into account the relationship between the life of a person who has been born and the unborn life, which means that protecting the foetus to the mother's detriment would be unacceptable' (above n 108, para 5). The dissenting opinion of Judge Mularoni, joined by Judge Strážnická, observes: 'since the 1950s, considerable advances have been made in science, biology and medicine, including at the prenatal stage. The political community is engaged at both national and international level in trying to identify the most suitable means of protecting, even prenatally, human rights and the dignity of the human being against certain biological and medical applications. I consider that it is not possible to ignore the major debate that has taken place within national parliaments in recent years on the subject of bioethics and the desirability of introducing or reforming legislation on medically assisted procreation and prenatal diagnosis, in order to reinforce guarantees, prohibit techniques such as the reproductive cloning of human beings and provide a strict framework for techniques with a proven medical interest.' And later the opinion continues: 'as with other Convention provisions, Article 2 must be interpreted in

protection of the fetus does not have to entail that the fetus has (limited) rights could be important. Indeed, the fetus can be legally protected to the same extent as if it had limited rights without resort to rights language. The idea that the fetus's human value can be protected to some degree by an expression of an interest in its life, formalised through national abortion laws, could be valuable within ECtHR case law on the fetus. In England, it is fair to say that we find this interest expressed in our abortion law. At the same time, a clearer distinction between the idea of a fetus as a rights-bearer on the one hand and a being of value on the other could also be helpful in English jurisprudence more generally.

Indeed, in some ways we do already find English judges attempting to express the idea that the fetus has value, despite its lack of legal status. This is not easy given the force of the language of rights, beside which other forms of moral and legal language sometimes appear insignificant. For instance, in *St George's Healthcare NHS Trust v S, R v Collins and others, ex parte S*, which concerned a pregnant woman's refusal of a caesarean section apparently needed by her fetus, Lord Justice Judge observes that '[w]hatever else it may be, a 36-week foetus is not nothing; if viable it is not lifeless and it is certainly human'.[133] He also states that 'the interests of the foetus cannot be disregarded on the basis that in refusing treatment which would benefit the foetus, a mother is simply refusing treatment for herself'. Judge LJ draws on the judgments in *Attorney-General's Reference (No 3) of 1994)*, notably Lord Mustill's statement that the fetus 'is a unique organism'.[134] Some have suggested that this kind of language is a prelude to granting the fetus rights.[135] But Lord Mustill observes of the fetus that '[t]o apply to such an organism the principles of a law evolved in relation to autonomous beings is bound to mislead'.[136] I take this to mean that he thinks that the application of rights-language to the implicitly non-autonomous fetus would be problematic. In this light, contrary to the fears that have reasonably been expressed about this aspect of his judgment,[137] here Lord Mustill might well be interpreted as showing some sensitivity as to the difficulties of granting the fetus legal rights. The central difficulty concerns the implications of this move for pregnant women. At the same time, he wishes to recognise the fetus's *sui generis* status. In my view, suppression of language which seeks to recognise the value of the fetus could ultimately be unhelpful to pregnant women, since the pressure to use rights

---

an evolutive manner so that the great dangers currently facing human life can be confronted. This is made necessary by the potential that exists for genetic manipulation and the risk that scientific results will be used for a purpose that undermines the dignity and identity of the human being.' No paragraph numbering is given in this judgment.

[133] [1998] 3 All ER 673, 687.
[134] [1997] 3 All ER 936, discussed in Grubb above, n 115.
[135] S Fovargue and J Miolá 'Policing Pregnancy: Implications of the *Attorney-General's Reference (No 3 of 1994)*' 6 Med L Rev (1998) 265, 288.
[136] Above n 121, 943.
[137] Fovargue and Miolá, above n 135.

112  *Selective Abortion — The Law*

language in relation to the fetus then increases. This tends to result in polarisation of what is typically called the 'maternal-fetal conflict'.[138]

If we do not grant (limited) rights to the fetus, however, its growing value must nevertheless be seriously considered. Returning to the abortion context, for instance, if the value of fetal life is to be recognised without the fetus having legal rights (or at best limited ones) then the provisions of the English Abortion Act must be taken seriously. The RCOG guidelines on termination in relation to fetal abnormality express this point well: 'The fetus is entitled to respect throughout pregnancy. Abortion is performed only after very careful consideration and only within the grounds permitted by the law'.[139] Fears that this is not always so in relation to section 1(1)(a) of the Act — the oft-called 'social ground' — are common and of course the *Jepson* case expresses this fear regarding the operation of the disability ground of the Act. The concern of some of the judges of the ECtHR about the legal situation of the fetus in the context of prenatal diagnosis[140] further reinforces the need for thought to be given to the appropriate protection of the fetus in existing practices of prenatal diagnosis and selective abortion. Clearly, it is important that this section of the Act protects the fetus where appropriate. But what might this mean or entail?

One way to emphasise the value of the fetus in whom a serious anomaly has been found, and the respect that it is due, would be to make a link between the issue of information about fetal anomaly in the course of prenatal screening, the fetus's interests (loosely understood prior to fetal sentience, as discussed in Chapter 1) and those of its parents in a way that recognises the need for a reasonable and fair balance between the possibly competing interests at stake. A key point here is that parents should as far as possible be accurately informed about a given impairment and what it may or may not entail. This is a loaded issue, since women and their partners should not be morally pressured either way. So perhaps the best way to express the point is that, if a woman (and her partner) are to make an informed, voluntary and therefore autonomous decision (assuming they have capacity), they will need to be given accurate information about a given disability in a possible child and to have time to reflect on this. If these conditions are fulfilled, then it might be said that due consideration is being given to the moral claims of the fetus to ongoing life. I discussed the issue of information provision in Chapter 1. I will revisit it, in relation to the idea of consent to screening and testing, and to the continuation or termination of a pregnancy, in the next chapter.

### D  Article 3

The remaining articles upon which Reverend Jepson would have sought declarations were Articles 3 and 14. A consideration of the fetus's claims in relation to

---

[138] For further discussion see Scott, above n 129.
[139] RCOG, above n 11, para 5.3.
[140] Above n 132 and text.

# Cases Under the European Convention on Human Rights 113

Article 3, which states that '[n]o one shall be subjected to torture or to inhuman or degrading treatment or punishment' would require careful reflection. We might see the issue under Article 3 as being whether abortion constitutes inhuman treatment, since this has been defined as treatment which causes intense physical and mental suffering.[141] The possibility that the fetus feels pain would be relevant here and is pertinent to a consideration of the balance of interests under the disability ground of the Abortion Act, since that section allows abortions up until birth.

The 1996 RCOG guidelines on abortion for fetal disability discuss the issue of fetal pain, citing the work of Maria Fitzgerald. She observes, in part[142]:

> The existing evidence shows that little sensory input reaches the developing cortex before 26 weeks and therefore... reactions to noxious stimuli cannot be interpreted as 'feeling' or perceiving pain... However, despite the lack of evidence for foetal pain, it cannot be denied that the foetal nervous system mounts clear protective responses to tissue injury and this cannot be ignored... The effects of trauma of any kind to the developing nervous system should be minimised as far as possible by whatever means are available to avoid changing the course of human development.

These latter observations may be particularly relevant where some form of treatment, such as fetal surgery, is in issue rather than abortion. With reference to Fitzgerald's review and abortion, the guidelines recommend[143]:

> This suggests strongly that the immaturity of the fetal central nervous system prevents conscious awareness of pain before 26 weeks gestation. It follows that up to this gestation the method of abortion should be selected to minimise the physical and emotional trauma to the woman. After 26 weeks it is not possible to know the extent to which the fetus is aware. So, in the later weeks of pregnancy, methods used during abortion to stop the fetal heart should be swift and should involve a minimum of injury to fetal tissue.

The RCOG Ethics Committee report on late terminations, two years later, likewise discusses the issue of fetal pain and refers to the report, the previous year, of an RCOG Working Party on Fetal Awareness.[144] The Ethics Committee notes the distinction between physical reactions to stimuli by the fetus and the cognitive awareness of pain and observes[145]:

> Sensory connections linking the skin and underlying organs through peripheral nerves to the spinal cord and brain stem, and from there to the thalamus and cerebral cortex, are necessary for the experience of pain.

---

[141] *Ireland v United Kingdom* (1978) 2 EHRR 25, para 167.
[142] RCOG, above n 11, para 9.2.
[143] *Ibid* para 5.3.
[144] *Report of the RCOG Working Party on Fetal Awareness* (London: RCOG, 1997).
[145] RCOG, above n 11, para 6.2.2.

The report then discusses the timing of neurological maturation in the thalamus at 25 weeks and in the cortex at 35 weeks and observes that the function of the thalamus, depending on feedback from the cortex, does not start before 22 weeks.[146] The report continues[147]: 'A functional cortex is essential for fetal awareness. Thalamocortical connections do not take place until 26–34 weeks' gestation. There is therefore no sensory input to the cortex before that time'. Having discussed the ability of drugs such as those used for anaesthesia to cross the placenta and build up slowly in the fetus, the report concludes[148]:

> For termination of pregnancy carried out at or after 24 weeks, it is therefore recommended that either feticide should be carried out using a technique, such as intra-cardiac injection of potassium chloride, that stops the heart rapidly, or premedication should be given to the mother, allowing time for it to build up in the fetus.

The suggestion of particular care from 24 weeks onwards appears to reflect a sensibly cautious approach to the research that indicates that the fetus can feel pain at 26 weeks at the earliest.

Not surprisingly, the research into fetal pain is ongoing. Vivette Glover and Nicholas Fisk (amongst others) have investigated this issue. They suggest that '[t]he fetus is currently treated as though it feels nothing, and is given no analgesia or anaesthesia for potentially painful interventions'.[149] Pain in the fetus cannot be measured directly but, on the basis of the available anatomical and physiological evidence, they consider it is 'likely' that the fetus can feel pain from 26 weeks (this accords with the RCOG review above), 'possible' that it can feel pain from 20 weeks and is caused distress by interventions from 15 or 16 weeks. Glover and Fisk suggest that analgesia for the fetus might be considered from this time, although the '[a]dministration of safe and effective analgesia to the fetus, without adverse effects in the mother, is a considerable challenge'.[150] They highlight the need for more research in this area.[151]

---

[146] *Ibid* para 6.2.3.
[147] *Ibid* para 6.2.4.
[148] *Ibid* para 6.2.7.
[149] V Glover and NM Fisk 'Fetal Pain: Implications for Research and Practice' (1999) 106 *British J of Obstet and Gyn* 881, 884.
[150] *Ibid* 885.
[151] *Ibid*. 'The physical system for nociception is present and functioning by 26 weeks and it seems likely that the fetus is capable of feeling pain from this stage. The first neurones to link the cortex with the rest of the brain are monoamine pathways, and reach the cortex from about 16 weeks gestation. Their activation could be associated with unpleasant conscious experience, even if not pain. Thalamic fibres first penetrate the subplate zone at about 17 weeks of gestation, and the cortex at 20 weeks. These anatomical and physiological considerations are important, not only because of immediate suffering, but also because of possible long term adverse effects of this early experience' (*ibid*). One of the questions the authors consider is the experience of the baby during birth, either by natural

The issue is also discussed at some length in the Nuffield Report, which draws on a range of work, including the most recent recommendations of the RCOG[152]:

> The question of whether a fetus can feel pain is almost impossible to answer. For adults, pain involves consciousness, thought, memory and fear. In the fetus, a grimace, physical withdrawal, movement or release of stress hormones into the blood stream does not necessarily mean that pain has been consciously perceived. Scientists disagree as to when the fetus has sufficient neurological development to perceive pain and whether there might be particular characteristics of the fetal environment that inhibit conscious perception of pain *in utero*. Even if the cerebral cortex (where pain and other sensations are perceived) is insufficiently developed before 26 weeks of pregnancy for the fetus to be conscious of pain, there may be negative consequences from distress associated with invasive procedures which affect subsequent development. In a report on fetal pain, the RCOG suggested that the potential for it should be considered in procedures involving fetuses from 24 weeks of gestation onwards (after which it is possible that the fetus may experience pain), while bearing in mind the potential harm that analgesic drugs may cause. The RCOG have recommended that fetal analgesia or sedation be considered for major intrauterine procedures, and... feticide or sedation be considered for late terminations of pregnancy.

The report also observes:[153]

> If fetuses can experience pain (itself a subject of some dispute...) it is reasonable to assume that a fetus has an interest in reducing the negative effects of pain and that interest gives us reason not to cause it.

Legally, if ever the application of Article 3 were to be considered in relation to the fetus, one objection may be that it cannot apply unless the fetus is considered a legal person and thus a rights-bearer, which could take us back to Article 2. Despite this, given that the majority in *Vo* emphasised the ways in which the fetus can and should be protected without granting it legal rights, a concern about fetal

---

or surgical means, noting the levels of various hormones present following either means of birth and speculating that in the future analgesia might be administered immediately before or after instrumental deliveries (*ibid* 884).

[152] Nuffield Council, above n 35, para 4.19, footnotes omitted (which variously cite KJ Anand, JV Aranda, CB Berde *et al* 'Summary Proceedings from the Neonatal Pain-control Group' (2006) 117 *Pediatrics* S9–S22; SWG Derbyshire 'Can Fetuses Feel Pain' (2006) 332 *BMJ* 909–12; DJ Mellor, TJ Diesch, AJ Gunn, L Bennet 'The Importance of "Awareness" for Understanding Fetal Pain' (2005) 49 *Brain Res Rev* 455–71; SJ Lee, HJP Ralston, EA Drey, JC Partridge, MA Rosen 'Fetal pain: A Systematic Multidisciplinary Review of the Evidence' (2005) 294 *J Am Med Assoc* 947–54; Glover and Fisk, above n 149; RCOG, above n 144; RCOG, *Further Issues Relating to Late Abortion, Fetal Viability and Registration of Births and Deaths* (2001) available at <http://www.rcog.org.uk/index.asp?PageID=549> accessed 8 October 2007.

[153] *Ibid* para 2.27, footnote omitted, which notes that '[a]llowing that a fetus has interests in this manner is compatible with holding a range of views regarding the moral status of a fetus as compared with a newborn baby' referring to paras 2.17–2.20.

pain could at least find legal expression, for instance through legal requirements that build on the recommendations of the RCOG. This could be particularly relevant to abortions over 24 weeks, including those under the disability ground of the Act.

### E  Article 14

Turning to the last article with regard to which Reverend Jepson was seeking a declaration, Article 14 states[154]:

> The enjoyment of the *rights and freedoms set forth in this Convention* shall be secured without discrimination on any ground such as sex, race, colour, language and religion, political or other opinion, national or social origin, association with a national minority, property, birth or other status.

As can be seen from the section of highlighted text, for Article 14 to apply requires that another Convention right can be invoked: it is not a free-standing guarantee against discrimination. However[155]:

> The application of Article 14 does not require a *breach* of another Article but merely that the facts of the case come within the ambit of another Article. Precisely what constitutes the 'ambit' of another Convention right is uncertain. In broad terms, Article 14 will come into play whenever the subject-matter of the disadvantage 'constitutes one of the modalities' of the exercise of a right guaranteed or whenever the measures complained of are 'linked' to the exercise of a right guaranteed.

It seems right, then, that the first question would remain whether, under judicial scrutiny, the fetus will be deemed to have another right, particularly a right to life. In the light of the recent ECtHR decision in *Vo v France*, this is unlikely. For the sake of argument, however, it is worth thinking a little more about what an Article 14 argument in this context would entail.

For a start, the fetus's right to life under Article 2 would have to be established. This could be limited just by the pregnant woman's right to life under section 1(1)(c) of the Act (Reverend Jepson's preference), or also by her interest in avoiding grave permanent injury to her physical and mental health under section 1(1)(b). This would establish that the fetus had invoked a right for the purposes of an Article 14 argument and would set the stage for the argument in favour of the declaration that the disability ground of the Act is incompatible with Article 14.

Turning to the Article 14 argument, the first hurdle would be to establish that the fact of disability was a 'status' within the terms of Article 14. The phrase 'other

---

[154] My emphasis.
[155] J Wadham, H Mountfield, A Edmundson, C Gallagher, *Blackstone's Guide to the Human Rights Act 1998*, 4th edn (London: Blackstone's, 2007) para 8.677, emphasis in original, footnotes omitted, which cite *Abdulaziz, Cabales and Balkandali v UK* (1985) 7 EHRR 471, *Botta v Italy* (1998) 26 EHRR 241, para 39 and *Peterovic v Austria* (2001) 33 EHRR 307, paras 22, 28.

status' has been interpreted broadly.[156] Further, in any event the prevention of discrimination on grounds of disability is considered so important that there is relevant legislation applying to disabled people.[157] So the fact of disability in the fetus would count as a relevant 'status'.

The next question would be whether there is in fact discrimination. This occurs when there is 'discriminatory treatment… in "relevantly similar" or analogous situations, and… no "objective or reasonable justification" for the distinction in treatment'.[158] In a domestic challenge in relation to the disability ground of the Abortion Act, this second question would entail asking whether there is 'enough of a relevant difference between X and Y to justify different treatment'.[159] In a challenge that went as far as the ECtHR, it would be for the state to justify different treatment. The ECtHR would consider whether there is a legitimate aim (none are specified in Article 14 itself), a reasonable relationship of proportionality between that aim and the means to achieve it and whether the margin of appreciation afforded to states further aids the case for the English state.[160] As noted earlier, the Strasbourg court allows a considerable margin in relation to moral matters such as abortion.

Turning now to the first question of whether there is different treatment of the fetus in whom an anomaly has been found compared with another fetus, if the fetus after 24 weeks could only be aborted to save a woman's life, then the permissibility of abortion after 24 weeks on the grounds of disability would be *prima facie* discriminatory. If it remained possible to terminate after 24 weeks also to protect a woman's very serious health interests under section 1(1)(b), again abortion on the grounds of disability would be *prima facie* discriminatory. This is because in both of the first cases, *any* fetus would be able to be aborted in order to protect the pregnant woman's life or serious health interests. However, after 24 weeks a fetus which is *not* at substantial risk of being born as a child with a serious handicap could not be aborted for any other reason than to protect the mother in these ways. By contrast, where a serious fetal anomaly has been found, such a fetus could be aborted up until birth. The *prima facie* case for discrimination is made out.

I turn now to the second question of whether that different treatment can be justified. This takes us to the heart of the matter. Tom Shakespeare suggests:[161]

---

[156] *Ibid* para 8.689.
[157] eg, Disability Discrimination Act 1995.
[158] Wadham *et al*, above n 155, para 8.692, footnotes omitted, which cite *National and Provincial Building Society v UK* (1997) 25 EHRR 127, para 88, *Lithgow v UK* (1986) 8 EHRR 329 and *Fredin v Sweden* (1991) 13 EHRR 784.
[159] *R (Carson) v Secretary of State for Work and Pensions* [2006] 1 AC 173, per Lord Nicholls (para 2) and Lord Hoffmann (para 31) as cited in Wadham *et al*, above n 155, para 8.742.
[160] See further the discussion in *ibid* paras 8.701–8.713.
[161] T Shakespeare, *Disability Rights and Wrongs* (London: Routledge, 2006) 95.

A simple charge of discrimination… fails, because here a distinction is being made on morally relevant grounds: a foetus with serious impairment is different from a healthy foetus, and to some this relevant difference is a sufficient reason for overturning usual protections.

Is he right?

Since the fetus (in whom no serious anomaly has been found) can currently be aborted after 24 weeks for reasons related to a woman's life and serious health interests, then one question could be whether there are any *sufficiently serious* maternal interests in abortion on the grounds of disability after 24 weeks. I explore this specifically in the next section. For now, if maternal interests could be seriously invoked in a way that is, in particular, judged commensurate with the way maternal interests may be invoked in sections 1(1)(b) and (c), then the case for discrimination would become harder to sustain. I presume this is what Shakespeare is, in effect, suggesting. (Conversely, if section 1(1)(b) had also been successfully challenged, the case would be easier, given the drastic nature of a risk to the woman's life.)

By contrast, if the case for maternal interests in terminating a disabled fetus after 24 weeks is *not* sufficiently strong, we would be left with the idea that the fetus might be terminated solely because of its disability. Where the fetus could as a child have a life it would think worth living, as is most often the case in relation to fetal anomaly, the justification for abortion looks thin in the absence of compelling maternal interests: why should such a fetus be aborted?

By comparison, could there be relevant and sufficient justification to terminate where a fetus would be born as a child at serious risk of having a life not worth living? In such a case, it would be hard to defend the argument that the fetus is *itself* the subject of discrimination. It is interesting to think through some of the legal ramifications of this scenario. Legally speaking, in English law a child does not have a claim for wrongful life, so that no-one could in fact argue that this kind of fetus has a legal right to be aborted.[162] At the same time, it may well not be in the interests of a child who would not think her life worth living to be born and therefore termination might, at least ethically speaking, be thought to be in the *interests* of the fetus, even if it did have a (limited) legal right to life after 24 weeks. At this juncture, since this discussion as to the possibility of the fetus acquiring an Article 2 right (in order to found an Article 14 claim) has been entirely speculative, I shall not further consider the legal reasoning that would be entailed. However, and more importantly given the current law, I do turn to give special consideration to the issue of terminations after 24 weeks in the next section.

Overall, we have seen that a review by English judges of the compatibility of the disability ground of the Abortion Act with the provisions of the ECHR would require judicial reflection on the balance of maternal and fetal interests in this

---

[162] *McKay v Essex AHA* [1982] 2 WLR 890.

context. Prior case law on cases of maternal-fetal conflict and abortion, including at the ECtHR level, coupled with the recent ECtHR decision in *Vo v France* all currently indicate that a finding would be made in favour of compatibility, such that the fetus of more than 24 weeks' gestation would not have a right to life either. Thus, existing ECtHR case law cannot be used to prompt a shift in the English legal balance of interests as between a pregnant woman and her impaired (or non-impaired) fetus.

## V ABORTION FOR FETAL ANOMALY AFTER 24 WEEKS

Finally, I turn to explore the application of the disability ground of the Abortion Act to terminations after 24 weeks in order to think about the extent to which such terminations can be justified. We should first note how extensive the practice of third-trimester abortions is. The Nuffield Report observes[163]:

> In England, Scotland and Wales the Abortion Act 1967 specifies that termination of pregnancy beyond 24 weeks of gestation is only legal if either a fetus is at substantial risk of serious handicap or there is a risk of grave permanent injury to the life, or the physical or mental health of the woman. In England and Wales in 2004, 124 terminations were carried out after 24 weeks of gestation, out of a total of 185,415 (less than 0.1%). Of these, 91 were for congenital malformations, 23 for chromosomal abnormalities and ten for other conditions, such as disorders related to gestation and growth.

By contrast, the number of terminations generally under the disability ground of the Abortion Act is estimated to be about 1,900 each year, approximately 1% of all abortions.[164] A further point to note from the outset concerns the significance of 24 weeks as a 'cut-off' point within the law. Sometimes it is suggested that 24 weeks represents the legal definition of viability. In fact, however, the relatively poor prospects for a fetus born at or near 24 weeks are noted by the Nuffield Report, which observes 'statistics indicate that most babies born below 25 weeks of gestation will die'[165] and that, 'at the time of writing, most babies born at 23 weeks die or survive with some level of predicted disability even if intensive care is given. Survival and discharge from intensive care for babies born between 22 and 23 weeks is rare'.[166] The Report also refers to media coverage of such

---

[163] Nuffield Council, above n 35, para 4.13, footnotes omitted.
[164] HGC, above n 62, para 3.6.
[165] *Ibid* para 23(b), emphasis in original.
[166] *Ibid* para 24. Note also that the way a pregnancy is calculated is crucial here: sometimes women who have had *in vitro* fertilisation (IVF) calculate their pregnancies from the date of embryo transfer, which is approximately two weeks later than the conventional dating method, since the latter 'counts' from the date of the last menstrual period. The result is that a birth might be described as being at 21 weeks plus 6 days, but would in fact be one at 23 weeks plus 6 days by conventional dating. Personal communication: Susan Bewley.

births[167]: 'This coverage tends to give a misleading impression that most babies born at the borderline of viability are healthy, whereas in reality, many do not survive and those who do often have disabling conditions ranging from mild to severe'.

As indicated in the previous section, one question about terminations after 24 weeks will be whether such terminations are ever justifiable on the basis of maternal interests. Another question will be whether these terminations can ever be defended on the basis of the fetus's interests. I shall consider these questions with reference to the RCOG Ethics Committee's report on third-trimester terminations for fetal abnormality.

A key ethical principle in the RCOG's report is stated as follows[168]:

> There is from the first a presumption in favour of life, not absolute but rebuttable for grave reason; and the rebuttal becomes harder to establish as gestation progresses. The ethics of termination in the late stages of pregnancy turns precisely on the gravity of the moral claim required to rebut this presumption in favour of life.

In essence, here the report states a gradualist approach to the moral status of the fetus, observing that the reason for termination must be ever stronger as pregnancy progresses. The report continues[169]:

> An alternative way of expressing this would be to speak of a presumptive duty to the fetus directed towards its good, from which the clinician could be released by an interposing duty. That duty might be to the mother as patient; or it might rest on the assumption that there are conditions with which it was for the fetus's own good not to be born. In either case, the duty to the fetus would persist in the obligation to protect it from distress as its life in the womb is terminated.

Here the report effectively identifies two potential reasons, or justifications, for terminations at all stages, one that concerns the pregnant woman and one the fetus. Ethically speaking, these are indeed the only possibilities (apart from the application of duties deriving from non-person affecting principles, which I have previously suggested are less than persuasive once a pregnancy is established). When we combine the statement of these possible reasons with the previous commitment to a gradualist view of the fetus's claims, the implication is that terminations after 24 weeks will require particularly strong instantiations of these reasons.

Another important question to consider at the start is why the issue of third-trimester termination ever arises. The RCOG report suggests three possible reasons: a pregnant woman books late for prenatal care; an abnormality is not found earlier; and an abnormality is found that can only be diagnosed late in pregnancy. Examples of the latter are 'achondroplasia, some genetic microcephaly,

---

[167] *Ibid* para 3.26.
[168] RCOG, above n 40, para 3.6.
[169] *Ibid* para 3.7.

severe growth retardation with organ failure, or intracranial haemorrhage, such as may occur with allo-immune thrombocytopenia or late viral infection with cytomegalovirus (CMV)'.[170] The increasing sophistication of ultra-sound technology, coupled with the use of invasive techniques, is partly behind detection later in pregnancy.[171] An important ethical point to note about anomalies that are only detectable or arise late is that there would not have been an opportunity to make a decision about them earlier. Another point to note about relatively late detection and the lack of a time-limit is captured well by the Nuffield Report[172]:

> Some specialists in fetal medicine have reported that the absence of an absolute cut-off in law at 24 weeks has relieved the pressure for hurried decision making in a small number of patients where further investigations, consultation and/or monitoring are necessary to help establish a prognosis, or where there are delays in access to screening.

On the one hand then, although the fetus's moral claims are constantly increasing, the lack of a time-limit means there is a better chance of making the most informed and well-judged decision in the circumstances. The overall advantages of the lack of a time limit are also endorsed by the HGC[173]:

> Changes to legislation that stop termination of pregnancy beyond the 24 week limit on the grounds of fetal abnormality could modify this picture in unpredictable ways. Changes in practice would be especially likely if this gestational age was close to that at which detailed fetal anomaly scans are commonly performed. While some late terminations would then not be performed, there is a possibility that other pregnancies might be terminated within the legal limit but before a full diagnostic process or consideration of implications had been completed. Decisions on whether or not to seek a termination would have to be made without full information.

I now turn to consider the two possible justifications of maternal or fetal interests for terminations after 24 weeks on the grounds of fetal disability.

---

[170] *Ibid* para 4.2.
[171] *Ibid* para 4.1. See also the example 'Case 2' discussed in Wicks *et al*, above n 26, 294, in which although a 20-week scan indicated that all was normal, a woman 'is admitted at 29 weeks with a small antepartum haemorrhage' and a 'scan performed shows placenta praevia (a low lying placenta) and severe hydrocephalus (excess fluid within the brain) with an adjacent porencepahlic cyst (cyst within the substance of the brain caused by loss of brain tissue)'. Upon investigation, the mother is found to have 'alloimmune thrombocytopenia (a low platelet count, implying the cause of the abnormal brain scan was probably bleeding)'. The woman 'wishes a termination of pregnancy, as the prognosis indicates that the risk of neurodevelopmental handicap is high'. As the authors note 'the case illustrates the potential for fetal abnormalities to present at any gestation'.
[172] Nuffield Council, above n 35, para 4.13, footnotes omitted.
[173] HGC, above n 62, para 3.11.

## A  The Pregnant Woman's Interests

The RCOG report observes, with reference to the possible late diagnoses above[174]:

> Such a diagnosis may lead to psychological harm or mental illness in the mother if she unwillingly continues the pregnancy with a baby that is diagnosed abnormal, delivers an unwanted child, and then has the difficulty of rearing, or sending for adoption, a baby who is handicapped.

As the report notes, the key question is whether 'these interests are grave enough to warrant late termination of pregnancy and whether unwillingness to rear a severely handicapped infant is a morally persuasive reason for termination'.[175] At this juncture, the report observes that since the *R v Bourne*[176] judgment of 1939, which allowed a woman's mental health to be of relevance to the legality of abortion:[177]

> [T]he well-being of the woman, as threatened by her attitude to the pregnancy, has been allowed increasing weight in rebuttal of the presumption in favour of life of the fetus and the public interest in maintaining that life. Her feelings would no longer be held to be irrelevant to the case.

The report then notes[178]:

> Many doctors today, therefore, would judge it to be both ethical and legal, in terms of the present law of abortion, to respect a settled maternal resentment at bringing to birth a gravely impaired fetus. They would so judge, partly out of concern for the feelings of the woman in her own person and partly out of anxiety lest an enforced upbringing of the child in an estranged, resentful relationship would result in a life so unhappy for the child as to threaten a disorder of personality. They would allow the considered judgment of the mother to be decisive.

There is much to discuss here. The Ethics Committee is right that, since the *Bourne* judgment, a concern with a woman's mental health has become part of English abortion law, although this is not to say that a doctor would now cite *Bourne* in defence, since the relevant defences to the crime of abortion are currently to be found in the Abortion Act. Upon which section of the Act would a doctor with the concerns detailed here seek to rely?

Arguably, a doctor could seek to rely on section 1(1)(b) which, to recall, permits abortion 'where necessary to prevent grave permanent injury to the physical or mental health of the pregnant woman'. Indeed, the reference to a 'settled maternal resentment' in the passage above may be intended to invoke the idea of 'grave permanent injury' to a woman's mental health. As for the concern

---

[174] *Ibid* para 4.3.
[175] *Ibid* para 4.4.
[176] *R v Bourne* (1938) 3 All ER 612.
[177] RCOG, above n 40, para 4.4.1.
[178] *Ibid* paras 4.4.1.

with the child that would be born and the risk of a 'disorder of personality', in some ways this requires that we think about whether this kind of disorder would give rise to a life not worth living. This seems unlikely. (The alternative is to apply the less-stringent non-person-affecting standard that allows us to think about the idea that it is preferable if people do not start their lives with certain difficulties compatible with a life worth living and that others start life in their stead but, as I have suggested at various stages, I think such principles cannot have real sway in the case of an established pregnancy, especially a relatively advanced one.) So, if it is indeed unlikely that any threatened disorder of personality could result in a life that was not worth living, then the only possible justification for termination will lie in the alleged necessity to protect a woman's mental health. People will disagree about whether this kind of resentment could morally and legally justify termination after 24 weeks, as the Ethics Committee itself notes[179]:

> The Ethics Committee, while some of its members might incline one way and some the other, can do no more than expose the tension between the moral claims and leave Fellows and Members of the College that liberty of conscientious decision which the law undoubtedly invests in them.

Clearly this question taxed the Committee, which can here be seen to emphasise the idea of individual conscience. It may be preferable if a woman were subsequently to give up a child for adoption, a possibility noted in the report and referred to as 'less drastic'.[180] However, as the report also notes, this requires that parents willing to adopt are found and that the woman is willing to give up her child.

Could a doctor concerned about a 'settled maternal resentment' rely on section 1(1)(d)? Previously I have argued that a woman's (and her partner's) views about the seriousness of a disability in a future child should be relevant to understandings of 'serious' in this section of the Act. This is on the basis that a woman (or couple) has an interest in deciding whether to have a seriously disabled child, joined with the fact that there cannot be a purely objective understanding of 'serious disability'. However, to say that a woman has an interest in making decisions of this kind and in having her views taken into account is not the same as saying that termination can be justified *in her interests up until birth*. This is in the light of the increasing moral claims of the fetus and the increased stringency in the grounds for legal abortion after 24 weeks. Weighing the fetus's claims after 24 weeks against her views on seriousness (effectively her *interests* where we are not directly considering fetal interests in not being born) is a very difficult moral and legal task and people will disagree about the answer here. Arguably, termination could still be in her interests where there is a serious threat to her mental or

---

[179] *Ibid* para 4.5.
[180] *Ibid* para 4.6.

124   *Selective Abortion — The Law*

physical health, but then legal justification would be sought under section 1(1)(b). As indicated above, whether this itself could be a legitimate use of section 1(1)(b) will also be a matter of disagreement.

I now turn to consider the idea of terminations after 24 weeks for serious fetal anomaly in the fetus's interests.

## B   The Fetus's Interests

In the discussion of Article 14 of the ECHR and section 1(1)(d) I raised the question of termination in the fetus's interests where there is a serious risk that a subsequently born child would not think his life worth living. Ethically speaking such a child could have a 'wrongful life', as first discussed in Chapter 1. By comparison, consistent with argument in this and other chapters, we could not say that termination could be in the fetus's interests where the subsequently born child would think his life worth living. Having recalled the standard that we are necessarily concerned with when we think about termination as potentially being in the fetus's interests, we can now think about termination on these grounds after 24 weeks. In this process I shall again refer to some of the case studies in the report of the RCOG Ethics Committee on late termination.

I referred to Case 1 earlier, since it had some some elements relevant to the general RCOG factors on termination for fetal anomaly, in particular those of self-awareness and the ability to communicate[181]:

> The fetus… developed severe microcephaly *in utero* and the neurological opinion was that the fetus had suffered cortical brain death. The prognosis was that the baby would have severe spastic quadriplegia and possibly intractable fits, *be blind and deaf, with no sensation or human interaction except severe pain*. The life span could be as long as 20 years.

In discussing this case, the RCOG Ethics Committee suggests that, although the condition was not lethal, the outlook for the child would mean that it would be lawful to withdraw treatment of him or her if born. Here the report refers to case law on withdrawal of treatment from neonates.[182]

Currently, the leading case is that of *Portsmouth Hospitals NHS Trust v Wyatt and another*.[183] The baby in this case was born prematurely at 26 weeks with respiratory problems. The question over a series of legal hearings was whether to ventilate her in the event that she succumbed to infection which led or might lead to a collapsed lung and which antibiotics would not cure. On the question of best interests, the Court of Appeal held that, in determining what was in a child's best interests, the welfare of the child was paramount and the court was obliged to consider that question from the assumed point of view of the patient. In terms highly familiar in medical law, it also held that there was a strong presumption in favour of a course of action that would prolong life, but that this could be

---

[181]  *Ibid* para 5.1.1 (my emphasis).
[182]  *Re J (a minor)* [1991] Fam 33; *Re C* [1990] Fam 26; *Re B* [1981] 1 WLR 1421.
[183]  (2005, CA) EWCA Civ 1181.

rebutted and that the term 'best interests' encompassed medical, emotional and all other welfare issues. It suggested that the court should undertake a 'balancing exercise', weighing up all the factors and perhaps draw up a 'balance sheet'.[184] Additionally, the court stated that suggestions by some judges in earlier cases that the concept of 'intolerability' was the key were incorrect, but that the concept could be a tool to help determine best interests.[185]

There are also important guidelines on the treatment of neonates from the Royal College of Paediatricians, entitled *Withholding or Withdrawing Life-sustaining Treatment for Children: A Framework for Practice*, reference to an earlier version of which is made in the RCOG report.[186] These guidelines list five situations in which it might be considered that treatment could be withdrawn or withheld. The first refers to a child who is brain-dead. The second discusses a child in a persistent vegetative state (PVS). The third, called a 'no chance' situation, refers to a child with such severe disease that life-sustaining treatment simply delays death without alleviation of suffering, in which case treatment to sustain life is deemed inappropriate. In the fourth 'no purpose' situation, although the child may be able to survive with treatment, its degree of physical or mental impairment will be so great that it is unreasonable to expect him to bear it. Finally, in the fifth so-called 'unbearable situation', a child and/or his or her family feel that, in the face of progressive and irreversible illness, further treatment is more than can be borne; here they wish to have a particular treatment withdrawn or to refuse further treatment regardless of medical opinion as to its potential benefit. It is interesting to note the reference, not just to a child's, but also to a family's feelings in this last scenario. But we should note that here the condition is progressive and irreversible. Overall, all the scenarios appear to contemplate a condition that is really very serious from the *child's point of view*: for instance, the first two concern brain death and PVS; in the third there is 'no chance'; in the fourth scenario the suffering is described as 'unbearable'; and in the fifth the illness is progressive and irreversible.

Further reflection on the treatment of neonates, and also on the moral and legal differences between the situation relating to neonates and fetuses, can be found in the Nuffield Report.[187] For my purposes, there are a number of important policy statements to note here. First, the Working Party considers 'the moment of birth, which is straightforward to identify, and usually represents a significant threshold in potential viability, as the significant point of transition not just for legal judgements about preserving life but also for moral ones'.[188] Second, the Working Party adopts the notion of 'intolerability', concluding that '[i]t would not be in a

---

[184] Ibid para 87.
[185] Ibid para 86.
[186] RCP, *Withholding or Withdrawing Life-sustaining Treatment for Children: A Framework for Practice* (2004, 2nd edn).
[187] Nuffield Council, above n 35.
[188] Ibid para 2.19.

126  *Selective Abortion — The Law*

baby's best interests to insist on the imposition or continuance of treatment to prolong the life of the baby when doing so imposes an intolerable burden upon him or her'.[189] The notion of 'intolerable':[190]

> ... embraces all three situations recognised by the RCPCH, as well as those that have features of more than one of these categories. We take 'intolerability' to encompass an extreme level of suffering or impairment which is either present in the baby or may develop in the future, and may be given more weight in the judgement of parents or doctors.

Third, the Working Party considers 'that the best interests of a baby must be a central consideration in determining whether and how to treat him or her', noting that this concept is enshrined in law but that the interpretation of the concept is 'far from straightforward'.[191] The Working Party discusses in some detail the 'weight of best interests, and interests of different parties'.[192] This discussion is of relevance also to a moral and legal consideration of the relationship between the interests of the fetus and those of its parents. The report notes that decisions about the care of neonates will impact on his or her parents and other family members, and that the Working Party 'does not consider that the baby's interests should invariably take precedence over the interests of these other parties', so that the interests 'of all those who may be affected' must be considered.[193]

In fleshing out the interests of parents and families, the report observes[194]:

> Consider for instance the interests of the parents of a baby who is born with a severe disability. There is no doubt that the interests of a baby are bound up with those of his or her parents, in that the degree of care that parents can devote to their child can make a very substantial difference to the quality of life that he or she can expect to enjoy. While often the adjustments that families have to make when a child has disabilities can readily be overcome, having a seriously disabled child can make a very substantial difference to the kind of life the parents can expect to enjoy... Caring for a seriously disabled child may significantly and deleteriously affect the lives of his or her parents: it can mean giving up employment, economic hardship, marital discord and divorce, great unhappiness, stress and ill health for which help from the state is limited... *The Working Party is clear that parents have interests and that it is reasonable for these interests to be given some weight in any relevant deliberations about critical care decisions for a child who is, or who will become, severely ill.*

The report then notes that 'equivalent interests of morally relevant parties of equal status have the same moral importance, and have equal weight'. However[195]:

---

[189] *Ibid* para 2.11.
[190] *Ibid* para 2.16.
[191] *Ibid* para 2.21.
[192] *Ibid* paras 2.28–2.32.
[193] *Ibid* para 2.29.
[194] *Ibid* para 2.29, emphasis in original.
[195] *Ibid* para 2.30, emphasis in original, footnote omitted.

*Abortion for Fetal Anomaly After 24 Weeks* 127

> In the circumstances concerning the decisions addressed by this Report, the interests of a baby which are at stake are often those of his or her very existence, whether he or she lives or dies, and of the quality of any life he or she might enjoy. These are usually a baby's very central or basic interests. *Thus, in according particular weight to the best interests of a baby, we are not viewing the baby as more important than other persons; rather we view his or her interests in living or dying, or in avoiding an 'intolerable' life… as more important than the interests that others may have in any significant decisions made about him or her.*

So, the consideration of strongest weight will always be the baby's interests in life, death or the avoidance of an intolerable life. Later the report proposes criteria for judging best interests in the case of a neonate.[196] The report considers that greater importance should be attached to parental views in the assessment of a chid's best interests, at least 'in cases when the outcome for their baby can reasonably be disputed', since this 'could potentially minimise disputes without prejudicing the welfare of the baby'.[197] I cannot further discuss the law and ethics relating to the treatment of neonates here, though I do note the much-debated case of *Re T (a minor) (wardship: medical treatment)*,[198] which gave some weight to the views of parents (who were health professionals) in deciding that it would be against the best interests of a child to receive a liver transplant.

We might note here that although the fetus likewise has interests in life or death or avoiding an intolerable life, given its lower moral and legal status the fetus's interests are arguably not of equal weight to those of its parents. Further, we have seen that the Nuffield Report endorses birth as a significant moment when a child has the same moral and legal status as those around it, thereby implying that before birth the fetus's interests would not be as strong as those of the neonate.

At this stage, I turn to consider the use that the RCOG report makes of the analogy between neonatal and obstetric practice.

The RCOG report notes that for the fetus 'there is no equivalent to withdrawal of treatment, unless induction of labour and detachment of the placenta can be equated with withdrawal of intensive life support'. The report continues with reference to Case 1[199]:

> If it would have been acceptable in this case to have withdrawn ventilation as a neonate, then logically it might be acceptable to deliver and detach the fetus from the life support

---

[196] *Ibid* paras 9.32–9.34.
[197] The report continues: 'A more transparent and structured set of criteria for judging best interests might also be useful. We propose such criteria in [a later chapter]. Such criteria would identify the questions that are relevant in making such decisions' (*ibid* para 8.54, emphasis in original). The report also observes: '*The current legal principles centred on seeking agreement between parents and professionals as to the best interests of the baby are, in principle, appropriate and sufficient*' (*ibid* para 38, emphasis in original, and referring to para 9.31).
[198] *Re T (a minor) (wardship: medical treatment)* [1997] 1 All ER 906.
[199] RCOG, above n 40, para 5.1.1, footnote referring to RCP guidelines omitted.

> provided by the uteroplacental environment. Since this case fulfils the criteria for non-treatment after birth, it would have been reasonable to have considered terminating the pregnancy.

The point here is clearly stated: the justification for termination in such a case stems from the justification for not treating the born child that this fetus would become who would, after all, have an even greater moral and legal status than the fetus. (Ethically speaking, such a child might have a 'wrongful life' though of course there is no legal claim for wrongful life in English law.) In due course the RCOG report suggests that the legality of terminations after 24 weeks on the grounds of fetal abnormality (a result of the 1990 reforms by the HFE Act) means that there is greater consistency between 'late obstetric practice and acceptable neonatal practice', observing that '[i]f it is held to be inappropriate to treat aggressively a newly born infant with the severest spina bifida, with a respiratory arrest or chest infection, it would be inconsistent to forbid termination of the life of the fetus, as severely damaged, before birth', but also cautioning that '[b]oth procedures require vigilant scrutiny lest, by over-familiarity, the moral claim of fetus and neonate alike be improperly diminished'.[200]

The idea of consistency between neonatal and obstetric practice is an important one and it must be right, as a matter of ethics and law, that if it is in the best interests of a neonate to withdraw treatment, it must also be justifiable to terminate the life of a fetus with a condition of the same degree of severity. The more difficult question arises when treatment would not be withdrawn from a neonate. In such a case there is no analogical guide which has the benefit of originating in reasoning concerning a being of greater moral and legal status and which can therefore comfortably 'cover' the situation of the fetus still *in utero*. The neonate is recognised as a moral and legal person when the fetus is not. However, this is not to say that moral or legal personhood settles issues of fetal treatment. This is because I have endorsed a gradualist account of fetal status that recognises the growing moral claims it has, claims that require ever-more serious reasons for harm to it. As we have seen, the RCOG also adopts a gradualist approach. In this light, we need to consider whether terminations after 24 weeks can be justified on the fetal disability ground of the Act when the fetus would otherwise become a child who would be treated.

It is useful at this point to compare further cases discussed in the RCOG report. Case 2 concerns Down's syndrome; Cases 3 and 4 reveal the spectrum of severity in relation to spina bifida; Case 5 is one of uncertain diagnosis; and Case 6 highlights the scope for different assessments of 'serious'.

Case 2 is described as follows[201]:

> A 27 year old married woman who had had a normal scan at 20 weeks was found to be 'small-for-dates' at 34. The fetus was noted to be below the third centile and to have a

---

[200] *Ibid* para 5.7.2(d).
[201] *Ibid* para 5.2.

complex cardiac abnormality, very abnormal limbs, hyper-extended head and peculiar movements *in utero*. A high likelihood of chromosomal abnormality was suspected and trisomy 21 was confirmed on fetal blood sampling. The mother was very keen to have a termination of pregnancy, even at this late stage, and this was performed by cardiac injection of potassium chloride followed by induction of labour. Post-mortem examination confirmed the findings.

The report then notes some key facts about Down's syndrome, describing it as 'a severely handicapping mental condition with an IQ usually varying between 50–80'.[202] The report also notes that the condition does not generally entail physical or mental suffering on the part of the person with the condition. The life expectancy is noted as 60-plus, though people who have Down's syndrome 'are seldom able to live unsupported'. The report observes that the condition is the commonest cause of mental disability and that screening and testing for the condition are available much earlier in pregnancy, as is termination. The report describes this 'largely as a second trimester issue'.

In fact, since the date of this report in 1998, first trimester screening for Down's syndrome has developed considerably with screening for nuchal translucency and other markers. However, in all cases when a pregnancy is screened in some way, this can only result in a risk assessment; and a certain diagnosis (in the face of a high risk assessment, say) can only occur following an invasive test such as chorionic villus sampling or amniocentesis. Both procedures carry an inherent risk of miscarriage, typically described as approximately one in 100.[203] So, while there are no risks to a pregnancy when a woman undergoes screening, there is a potentially very significant cost in obtaining an actual diagnosis.

The report discusses a number of reasons as to why Down's syndrome may become an issue later in the second trimester, or even in the third. One reason may be that the pregnant woman has declined screening earlier.[204] Assuming that she was properly informed about the purpose of such screening, it seems hard not to think that where a woman declines this relatively early in pregnancy, her possible wish to terminate in the face of a finding of Down's syndrome much later on may not be one that others feel should carry great weight. Other problems may arise of a more practical kind: 'results may have been lost or misfiled, there may have been inordinate delays in cell cultures or communication, or cultures may have failed to grow in the late second trimester'.[205] Then again, Down's syndrome may be diagnosed after 24 weeks because it is associated with physical anomalies, as in Case 2.

---

[202] *Ibid* para 5.2.1.
[203] HGC, above n 62, para 3.15. On the development of new tests that would avoid this risk, see J Buxton 'Non-invasive Pregnancy Test Shows Promise' 6 February 2007, 394 *Bionews* <http://www.bionews.org.uk/new.lasso?storyid=3340> accessed 8 October 2007.
[204] RCOG, above n 40, para 5.2.2.
[205] *Ibid*.

Strikingly, the report then observes[206]:

> Some specialists in fetal medicine are willing to offer late termination for 'Down's syndrome plus', for example, if there is an associated cardiac or gastrointestinal abnormality (although these may be correctable). Since a Down's syndrome child would usually be treated as any unaffected neonate and be given life-saving cardiac or gastrointestinal surgery, it is questionable, ethically and legally, whether it is acceptable to terminate for 'Down's syndrome plus'. The correctable abnormality appears to add only an opportunistic reason to terminate, unless it is acceptable to terminate in a case of Down's syndrome alone. This is in contrast to case 1, in which treatment of the neonate could reasonably have been withheld.

This is an insightful analysis of the possible reasons for deciding to terminate a third-trimester fetus found to have Down's syndrome. It emphasises that a child born with the condition will be treated in the same manner as any other, so that its medical and other needs will receive attention. In essence, morally and legally its best interests will require that it is treated. Indeed, as noted first in Chapter 1, a child with Down's syndrome will very likely think his life worth living.

Since the RCOG report has suggested that screening, testing and termination for the condition is justifiable earlier in pregnancy, what makes termination for Down's syndrome potentially unjustifiable later, particularly after 24 weeks, must be the growing moral claims of the fetus on the gradualist account of its moral status that the RCOG has endorsed. As I have indicated, I also share this view of the fetus's moral claims. The idea that termination for Down's syndrome after 24 weeks is morally questionable is also implied in an influential article in an obstetric journal.[207] However, although morally questionable, in my view we should be slow simply to declare such a practice immoral, since as third parties we are not involved in the consequences either way.

Where practical problems have arisen, such as that cell cultures have not grown and Down's syndrome is not detected until quite late, a woman who would have

---

[206] *Ibid* para 5.2.3.
[207] F Chervenak, L McCullough and S Campbell 'Third Trimester Abortion: Is Compassion Enough?' (1999) 106 *BJOG* 293. These authors conclude, at 295: 'It follows from the arguments we have presented here, based on virtues and ethical principles relevant to the concept of the fetus as a patient, that third trimester abortion should be restricted to pregnancies complicated by fetal anomalies in which either death or absence of cognitive developmental capacity is certain or near certain. Only in these cases should compassion for the pregnant woman be decisive. In all other cases, integrity requires that doctors refuse requests for third trimester abortion.' The influence of this article is discussed in C Williams 'Framing the Fetus in Medical Work: Rituals and Practices' (2005) 60 *Social Science & Medicine* 2085, who observes, at 2089: 'This was the article most frequently cited by practitioners as influencing their practice. One of the reasons it was so influential was that the article was "Editor's Choice" with the editor stating: "With the technology of the late twentieth century a fetus is considered to be viable at 24 weeks of gestation: after this point therefore the doctor has a duty of beneficence to the fetus, and should show it the intellectually disciplined compassion he affords to adults who are ill"' (Williams cites 'Editor's Choice' (1999) 106 *BJOG* vii).

preferred not to have a child with the condition may see herself as unlucky. Where results have been lost by others and not found till late in the day, late detection would essentially be the result of the negligence of health professionals. Should that negligence be permitted to prevent her having a termination? The problem here is that the fetus is also the innocent victim of that negligence and it is not clear that an ethical case could be made that justified a termination to 'make up for' the negligence of third parties. A woman may later be able to bring a wrongful birth action against the health professionals who negligently failed to inform her in a timely fashion (for instance, before 24 weeks) of the results of testing. In such a case, she would have to establish (on a balance of probabilities) that termination for Down's syndrome after 24 weeks is illegal under the Act. Since the Act trusts doctors to make 'good faith' judgments and since judges are, as noted earlier, reluctant to question that judgment, such a case could present the courts with a very real and difficult opportunity to evaluate the operation of the disability ground after 24 weeks. If such a woman could *not* in fact establish that a termination for Down's syndrome would have been illegal after 24 weeks, then the implication must be that while still pregnant she would have been legally entitled to find a fetal-medicine specialist who would conduct a termination after this time.[208] If such a case were ever to come to court, it may be that judges would cast some doubt on the morality of such a termination but ultimately be reluctant to condemn it legally. Alternatively, they may indeed take this step.

However, whilst it may be helpful for the law that an opportunity arises to clarify the legality of the operation of this section of the Act, particularly after 24 weeks, it is unlikely that it would generally be helpful for the courts to rule in and out certain conditions as being ones that would justify termination at any stage. This is because of the great variability in the prognosis in any given case, as the RCOG report also notes[209]:

> The factors of biological variability and medical uncertainty would make it inappropriate to draw up a list of conditions in order of severity that would enable practitioners to know which were seriously handicapping and thus legally or ethically acceptable, and which were not. This is also illustrated by the condition of spina bifida/hydrocephalus where the outcome is not completely predictable. There is a huge range between the following examples.

---

[208] On the practice of fetal-medicine specialists as an indication of the legality of late terminations, see Wicks *et al*, above n 26, 292: 'To proceed with a termination of pregnancy outside the normal boundaries of a doctor's medical practice would be grounds for exclusion from the register on a number of counts. It is our view, therefore, that the position taken by the fetal medicine team within each region of the UK is likely to represent the lengths to which a patient could go to secure a termination of pregnancy after 24 weeks gestation in the face of a "minor" congenital abnormality'.

[209] RCOG, above n 40, para 5.3.

## 132   Selective Abortion — The Law

Discussion of the next two cases illustrates this point. Case 3 is described as 'severe spina bifida with hydrocephalus'[210]:

> A fetus was found at 34 weeks to have an open meningomyelocoele from T4 (mid-back down), kyphoscoliosis and severe hydrocephalus. The mother had booked late because she was breastfeeding her one year old and had not realised that she was pregnant. The prognosis included a risk to mother of obstructed labour and the need for Caesarean section to deliver the baby. It was thought that without the surgery the baby was likely to die of overwhelming infection early in neonatal life. If the baby were operated on and survived, repeated operations would be necessary and there would be a high chance of mental retardation, wheelchair bound existence, urinary and faecal incontinence, and gross permanent multisystem disorders.

Case 4 is described as 'low spina bifida alone', as follows[211]:

> Another woman who booked late as she had only recently arrived in Britain was found to be carrying a fetus with a L3 lesion without obvious hydrocephalus. She was told there was a 90% chance of survival after operation and the baby would be likely to have normal intelligence but might require a wheelchair and might have incontinence. If walking were achieved it would be unlikely to be a normal gait. There was a small possibility of developing hydrocephalus later which might require shunting but would be unlikely to cause more than moderate developmental delay.

Of the two cases, the RCOG report observes that[212]:

> Although… both have neural tube defects there is clearly a very different outcome in terms of handicap. It is not possible to make rules regarding late termination by disease, as the prognosis can be very variable. Thus there is an ethical imperative to judge cases on their individual merits.

The implication would seem to be that although a termination may have been justifiable in the first case, it would not have been in the second. We do not know why the woman in the second case had not received relevant prenatal care prior to coming to Britain, though this could raise interesting issues of justice, for instance if she came from a country with inadequate prenatal care. Again, however, it would not be clear that this highly advanced fetus should 'pay' for that inadequacy.

The fifth case highlights the problem of uncertainty in some cases, so that a diagnosis cannot actually be made until after birth or a post-mortem. Case 5 is called 'uncertain diagnosis'[213]:

> Over a period of several weeks, increasing numbers of abnormalities were noted on the scans of a 17 year old in her first pregnancy. Initially only echogenic bowel was noted and the patient did not want further investigation. Then pericardial effusion and dilated

---

[210] *Ibid.*
[211] *Ibid.*
[212] *Ibid* para 5.3.1.
[213] *Ibid* para 5.4.

cerebral ventricles were noted and severe fetal anaemia was found at blood sampling for karyotyping. The fetus was then thought to have had a large unilateral intracerebral bleed, and a prognosis was given that the child was likely to live but be seriously handicapped. She was seen by 3 consultant fetal medicine specialists because there was some doubt about the underlying diagnosis. After extensive counselling, feticide was performed at 31 weeks and a post-mortem confirmed overwhelming virus infection with CMV, affecting many organs. One side of the brain was largely replaced with a clot and the other showed neuronal damage.

In a case of uncertainty, the RCOG report emphasises the need for 'further specialist opinion'.[214] It notes that '[u]ncertainty cannot be quantified, but is a matter of judgment, and in such circumstances the mother's opinion must carry some weight'.[215] Presumably, the thought here is that in the absence of a certain diagnosis, before any course of action is undertaken the mother's views as to whether she would want to continue the pregnancy should be given some weight. In the absence of definite knowledge as to the cause of the problems, and therefore the prognosis, this seems right.

The final case that I shall discuss, Case 6, is entitled 'subjective assessment of handicap'[216]:

A woman with achondroplasia (dwarfism) was found at 28 weeks to have a fetus with the same diagnosis which is not diagnosable earlier in pregnancy. The specialist explained that the condition was not considered to be seriously handicapping and would have refused termination in these circumstances. However the mother's compelling description of her own life and suffering and her genuine repeated request prompted a decision to perform feticide.

Commenting on the case, the Ethics Committee observes[217]:

This illustrates the difficulty in comparing objective judgment of function with the subjective suffering that might influence parental attitudes. There might be delight at having a child even though handicapped, or there might be despair at having a child with grave problems. Other people's attitudes have influence, and there is always the question whether facilities to help with rearing would be available and accessible.

This is a very interesting case. Clearly, the specialist was in no doubt that to have dwarfism does not mean that one is disabled. But here the pregnant woman, who herself has the condition, gives a 'compelling description of her own life and suffering'. It would be interesting to know more about what she said. Since the condition is not itself disabling or the cause of physical suffering, we might imagine here that her own difficulties and suffering were caused by aspects of the environment in which she lives. In effect, she may be alluding to social causes, in the way that the social model of disability emphasises. Indeed, in its comment on

---

[214] *Ibid* para 5.4.1.
[215] *Ibid*.
[216] *Ibid* para 5.5.
[217] *Ibid* para 5.5.1.

the case and reference to the influence of 'other people's attitudes' on the one hand and the 'question whether facilities to help with rearing would be available and accessible' on the other, the RCOG report effectively alludes to social conditions as causes of disability or difficulty. One interesting question that could arise here is whether, by agreeing to termination in the face of what are effectively social attitudes and inadequacies, one is colluding with those rather than challenging them, a point I discussed in Chapter 1. At the same time, there will be a reasonable limit to what society can offer in terms of support, given the constraints of resources. Given that the argument is often made that we should listen to and be more respectful of the views of those with a condition of some kind when we think about the ethics and legality of a particular termination, it seems hard in this case not to give some weight to this woman's views. At the same time, her fetus at 28 weeks was very advanced, and had very strong moral claims to life. Should its claims to life be overridden by her views about what its life would be like? It does appear as though this must have been the basis on which the clinician, who must have felt in a very difficult position, agreed to a termination.

## C  Factors Overall

I turn now to the RCOG's 'general commentary on the cases'.[218] At the outset this emphasises[219]:

> a vital need for medical accuracy, which requires both fetal medicine specialists and multidisciplinary input, as the prognosis will inevitably determine both the legality and ethical acceptability of any particular termination.

The RCOG suggests that the evidence should be discussed by doctors and parents together and that four factors might affect the 'ethical weighting which will be involved in their decision-making'[220]:

> a) The *suffering of the child*. This might involve pain and repeated operations, poor quality of life in severe cases, and awareness of difference and of discrimination if intelligence is normal. Yet life could be very fulfilling in milder cases.

> b) The *suffering of the mother*. Two types of suffering may be considered: on one's own behalf (disappointment, undue strain in caring with the risk of diminished care of siblings, demands of extra work, resentment of an unwanted child) and in empathy with the child (watching the cumulative operations and observing the struggles and developing self-awareness and apprehension). If abortion under a certain gestation is justified by risk to the mother's mental health, then logically it cannot be excluded late in pregnancy, unless the higher moral status of the more fully developed fetus makes the presumption in its favour the harder to rebut, a judgment which takes no necessary account of the normality or abnormality of the fetus.

---

[218] *Ibid* para 5.7.
[219] *Ibid*.
[220] *Ibid* (emphasis in original).

As regards the 'suffering of the child', as the report notes, conditions vary greatly in their severity. To refer to the key ethical distinction introduced in the last chapter: at one end there might be a real risk that a child would have a life she did not think worth living but once we move away from this extreme this will very likely not be the case. In such cases, it would be hard to say that termination could be justified in the fetus's interests. What about the 'suffering of the mother'?

As the report notes, the mother might suffer on her own behalf or on behalf of the child. The report's concern about observing a child's operations, struggles, increasing self-awareness and apprehension could perhaps be balanced beside a recognition that in some cases there may be the opportunity for strong rewards in watching a child face and overcome difficulties. The report implicitly alludes to the legality of abortion under 24 weeks where there is a risk to the mother's mental health under section 1(1)(a) and suggests that 'logically it cannot be excluded late in pregnancy, unless the higher moral status of the more fully developed fetus makes the presumption in its favour the harder to rebut'. It must be right that logically, as it were, a concern with a woman's mental health can always be present. What is in issue, as the report effectively notes, is what impact the increasing moral status of the fetus will have on that concern. In this regard, I am not clear what the report means to suggest. However, we should recall that before 24 weeks section 1(1)(a) only requires a risk to the woman's mental (or physical) health greater than if the pregnancy were terminated. After 24 weeks, the fetus's moral and legal claims are arguably greater and, as the RCOG report stated at the outset of its discussion, third-trimester terminations require more serious reasons. If this is so, it may be that a risk to the woman's mental health after 24 weeks could not be a sufficient legal justification for termination. Rather, section 1(1)(b) may be called into play, which is of course relevant where necessary to avoid grave permanent damage to her mental (or physical) health. It may be that the report is here alluding to the possible use of this section. As discussed in the section on maternal interests in termination after 24 weeks, it may sometimes be the case that termination on this basis could be justified, though it seems likely that this will be very rare and clearly people will strongly disagree about this.

I now turn to the last two factors[221]:

> c) The *burden on others*, in effect the wider family or the State, can be measured only in relation to the provision made by the community for the assistance of mothers bringing up children with special needs: provision of services or of social or financial support. In a wealthy country, State provision is determined by political will. It might be held that the principle of compassion, as well as the public interest in the preservation of life, should prompt such generosity as would remove the prospect of hardship from the number of adverse factors which lead to a request for termination. Voluntary or religious bodies often offer what the State does not.

---

[221] *Ibid.*

Here the report signifies the importance of social support in alleviating impairment. It might also refer explicitly to fathers, though clinicians may sometimes perceive that fathers may not in fact be supportive.[222] I cited part of the last factor in earlier discussion:

> d) *Severity of handicap*, as we have argued… above, does not diminish moral worth. It complicates the balance of moral claims by weighting the scale on one side against the other. The new legal liberty of late termination for grave fetal handicap brings more consistency between late obstetric practice and acceptable neonatal practice. If it is held to be inappropriate to treat aggressively a newly born infant with the severest spina bifida, with a respiratory arrest or chest infection, it would be inconsistent to forbid termination of the life of the fetus, as severely damaged, before birth. Both procedures require vigilant scrutiny lest, by over-familiarity, the moral claim of fetus and neonate alike be improperly diminished.

So, severity of disability adds a significant weight in favour of termination. This last factor confirms the thought that, both before and after 24 weeks, termination is justifiable in the fetus's interests if as a child it would be so impaired that it would not be in its best interests to continue to receive treatment. In such cases, we might say that there is a real risk that the subsequently born child would not think her life worth living.

Where this is not the case, however, the discussion overall has suggested that it cannot be said to be in the fetus's interests to have its life terminated, for instance in cases of Down's syndrome or milder cases of spina bifida. Where termination for Down's syndrome occurs relatively early in pregnancy when the fetus has a lower moral status, arguably this can be morally (and legally) defended on the basis of the parents' wish, if desired, to avoid the birth of a child with the condition, though many would disagree with this. Later in pregnancy, however, parents' interests and views cannot have the same moral weight given the increasing moral claims of the fetus. Of course, where a child would have a very severe condition their moral claims may have greater strength than in relation to a milder condition earlier in pregnancy, but in such a case termination is likely primarily to be in the fetus's interests, as noted above. By contrast, where a child would have a life worth living, then it may be that the only justification for third-trimester termination might be where this is judged necessary to avoid grave permanent damage to a woman's mental (or physical) health. It seems likely that this condition will rarely be fulfilled, particularly when we recognise that the woman would be entitled to ongoing social and emotional support and that we as a society would be morally obliged to provide this. However, I would not like categorically to rule out the possibility of a meritorious case. For instance, we may be able to imagine a case in

---

[222] 'Most of us in fetal medicine see many men being supportive but a minority of men a) pressurise women to abort otherwise wanted pregnancies (or else the relationship/support will end), or b) leave afterwards — leaving the woman literally "holding the baby".' Personal communication: Susan Bewley.

which a woman has mental health problems that could be exacerbated by the birth of a severely impaired child. Note that Shakespeare has suggested that after 24 weeks' gestation termination should only be permissible where a fetus would die *in utero* or as a neonate soon after birth or its mother's life would be in danger.[223]

## VI CONCLUSIONS

It seems unlikely that the *Jepson* case will be taken any further and hence that the disability ground of the Abortion Act will receive direct judicial consideration in the near future unless another case prompts a legal hearing. But we have a number of indications as to what its terms mean.

On the question of 'substantial risk', we saw that the RCOG guidelines suggest that the risk should *also* be seen as substantial by 'informed persons with no personal involvement in the pregnancy and its outcome'. This was in contrast to a direct focus on a woman's reactions to and feelings about the idea of a disability in the child to which she gives birth by use of section 1(1)(a) of the Abortion Act, which permits abortion where there is a risk to her physical or mental health greater than in termination.

Turning to the question of 'serious handicap', a brief study of *Hansard* revealed that there was concern at the time of the amendments to the Abortion Act that abortions on the ground of fetal impairment might be carried out for less than serious reasons. There was some indication that a cleft lip would not be considered serious but that conditions such as spina bifida, hydrocephalus and cystic fibrosis would be.

I discussed aspects of the RCOG guidelines on selective abortion generally. I considered the question of the probability of effective treatment *in utero* or after birth, one of several factors on the RCOG's list. I contrasted this with Reverend Jepson's claim that the criterion of whether a condition is remediable should determine the legality of termination under the disability ground of the Act. I explored different meanings of remediability, limited to a medical cure on the one hand and extended to alleviation, such as by means of social support, on the other. In the first case the meaning would automatically incorporate a wide range of conditions, including Down's syndrome, as ones justifying selective abortion (since at least the mental impairment is not treatable). By contrast, as Reverend Jepson probably intended, if 'remediability' includes alleviation by means of social support, then the scope for selective abortion solely on the basis of this criterion would necessarily be narrower.

I noted that the question of social support was in fact relevant to other factors within the RCOG guidelines, and that the need for social support should not necessarily be seen as a factor in favour of selective abortion. However, I also

---

[223] Shakespeare, above n 161, 95.

observed that where the need for social support was considerable in a child, particularly the extent to which the actions essential for health that normal individuals perform unaided would have to be provided by others (the first RCOG factor referring to the idea of social support), a child's condition could well be serious in ways implicating other factors. For instance, a child's degree of self-awareness and of ability to communicate with others might be seriously compromised and it may be that it would experience extensive suffering. In this way, although not all of the factors will necessarily be relevant to any one decision about termination, any decision is likely to involve a careful interplay and weighing of more than one factor. Turning to the second RCOG factor that implicates the idea of social support — the probability of being able to live alone and to be self-supporting as an adult — I suggested that on its own this does not appear to be a strong factor. I indicated that there might be a slight shift of emphasis in the way the reference, particularly to life as an adult, appears in the RCOG guidelines, in order to accommodate the contribution that the social model has made to our understandings of disability. However, I did not conclude that it would be inappropriate to exclude the need for social support as a factor potentially counting in favour of selective abortion. This is because some conditions, particularly 'mental and neurologic disabilities' as Wertz and Fletcher describe them, cannot be overcome, regardless of the degree of social support. Lastly, in relation to the relevance of the need for social support, I noted that where support is in issue, in terms of either of the 'social support' factors in the RCOG guidelines, the interests of third parties, notably the parents, are implicitly implicated.

One of the implications of the discussion of guidelines relating to the notion of seriousness is the recognition that it is not possible to agree upon and therefore to define 'serious disability', as the HGC has explicitly observed in relation to PGD. This point has also been observed in the literature more broadly.[224] In this light, a highly important question arises about the interpretation of the disability ground of the Act, namely whether a woman's or couple's views about the severity of a disability in a child they might have as a result of a current pregnancy can be taken into account when doctors decide that the criterion of seriousness is satisfied. In the previous chapter I argued that, since people can choose whether to have children and since raising a child entails extensive positive duties, prospective parents have a valid moral interest in having a say about whether to have any child, including a seriously disabled one. (Of course, this is not to deny that becoming a parent will inevitably involve taking risks, partly because not all fetal anomalies can be detected *in utero* and partly because a subsequently born child may well become ill or disabled after birth, a matter over which parents will have no control.) If we couple this with the difficulties of defining 'serious', the fair

---

[224] This is reflected in several of the essays resulting from the Hastings Center study, collected in Parens and Asch (eds), above n 50.

moral implication must be that they are entitled to have their views and interests taken into account in decisions about selective abortion, within reason. In turn, this should be recognised in the interpretation of 'serious' in the disability ground of the Act, at least before 24 weeks' gestation. Has the law done this or can it do so?

At this point, I turned to consider what the jurisprudence on wrongful birth might tell us. The wrongful birth cases were seen indirectly to correspond to the terms of the disability ground of the Act, since judges have been in no doubt that a wrongful birth action cannot succeed unless a child has a serious disability. In this regard, we saw that judges have been concerned to emphasise a distinction between 'significant disabilities' and 'minor defects or inconveniences'. There has yet to be clear judicial recognition of the moral (rather than medical) nature of the decision selectively to abort and hence of the limited weight that can be given to a purely medical account of disability and, in turn, to doctors' views in providing the justification, at least morally, for such a decision. Legally, however, judicial recognition of this point would be complicated by the legal role of doctors in securing a defence to the crime that abortion would otherwise be. Despite this, it was seen that there is at least an opening for judges to give some weight, in cases that are the subject of reasonable disagreement, to the views of a pregnant woman (and her partner) on the seriousness of an impairment in a prospective child. This lies in the fact that in wrongful birth cases damages are sometimes awarded for 'loss of amenity' to take account of the possible impact on parents of raising a disabled child. In *Rand* such damages were supported by reference to earlier wrongful birth case law and also by reference to the legitimacy of legally recognising and protecting parents' autonomy interests. This was advocated by Lord Millett in *McFarlane* and further developed and applied by the House of Lords in *Rees* in the form of an award of 'conventional' damages.

An exploration of ECHR jurisprudence suggested that the disability ground of the Act is compatible with Articles 2, 3, 8 and 14 of the ECHR. For this reason, ECHR case law cannot currently be used to question this section. Despite this, consideration of some of the separate and dissenting judgments in the ECtHR case of *Vo* highlighted a judicial concern with protection of the fetus. I suggested that this concern did not have to find expression in fetal rights, particularly since the application of the language of rights to a being inside another person is problematic. However, I noted that it is important that the increasing moral value of the fetus is respected and recognised within the law. English abortion law in fact achieves this by requiring reasons for abortion and by making the conditions for it more stringent after 24 weeks (overtly at least given that section 1(1)(a) no longer applies after this time). As regards the fetus at substantial risk of being a seriously disabled child and the need to value it, I suggested that we could link this with the need for fair and accurate information about disability in a child. The point here is that the fetus's claims to life will be given serious consideration if prospective parents are appropriately informed — and in turn reflect seriously — on what a child's life would probably be like. I discussed the issue of information further in Chapter 1.

Ultimately, it is the idea of potentially unjustified fetal death that is deeply at stake in the *Jepson* case. In *Jepson* this has two related aspects — a concern about the reasons, in particular, for terminating a third-trimester fetus and a concern that certain conditions in a future child are, more generally, inappropriately being viewed as serious.[225] (Of course, we have seen that the CPS, having reviewed a range of evidence, decided that a 'good faith' judgment was made as regards the seriousness of the condition in *Jepson* itself. Without access to further information about this case, it is not possible to assess this judgment. That said, as noted earlier, practice may have changed in that in future doctors may be reluctant to put themselves at risk by performing an abortion for cleft lip/palate after 24 weeks.)

As regards the third-trimester fetus, the pressure for abortions after 24 weeks to be for particularly serious reasons is rightly strong. We saw that the RCOG guidelines on abortion after this time assert that terminations must be for particularly serious reasons: 'As the protection due increases with embryonic development and fetal growth, reasons for termination, at no stage trivial, must be more pressing the longer pregnancy has progressed'.[226] The guidelines thus endorse a gradualist approach to fetal moral status, which holds that the longer a pregnancy has been allowed to develop, the greater must be the justification for in any way compromising it. As the RCOG Ethics Committee did in its report on late termination, I considered the idea of terminations after 24 weeks on the grounds of fetal anomaly, on the one hand in the interests of the pregnant woman and, on the other, in the interests of the fetus.

Can the disability ground of the Act be invoked on behalf of the pregnant woman (and her partner) after 24 weeks? Whilst I have argued that parental views about the seriousness of the disability that a child would have should be taken into account in the interpretation of the disability ground of the Act, at least where disabilities are the subject of reasonable disagreement, it does not follow that this means that their possible wish not to have a disabled child can carry weight up until birth. This is due to the increasing moral claims of the fetus. Since the law has to have a clear line, legally speaking the shift in the strength of those claims occurs at the 24th week, after which the reasons for abortion must be that much more stringent. Looking at the other grounds of the Act, we see this in the ongoing relevance only of the risk to a woman's life and the need to avoid grave permanent damage to her physical or mental health. It is therefore arguable that

---

[225] On the lack of a time-limit to s 1(1)(d) of the Act, see *Hansard*, 21 June 1990, vol 174, col 1198, eg, per Ms Richardson: 'Some handicaps are so severe that the foetus cannot survive. In a dramatic case, the brain or some other vital organ may be missing'. She also observes: 'There is no evidence that doctors have ever performed late abortions for trivial reasons'.

[226] RCOG, above n 40, para 7.4.

the disability ground of the Act should also be more stringently interpreted after this time. In this light, if termination on the grounds of fetal anomaly after 24 weeks is permissible in the interests of the pregnant woman, it may be that this can only be on the basis of section 1(1)(b). Although it seems unlikely that termination on the grounds of disability could be required, and therefore justified, to prevent grave permanent damage to her mental health under section 1(1)(b), a meritorious case cannot be categorically ruled out, particularly where there are other complicating factors.[227]

Turning to the fetus, I argued that at any stage of pregnancy a termination could only be said to be in its interests when there is a real risk that a subsequently born child would not think his life worth living. As the RCOG report on third-trimester terminations notes, termination in the fetus's interests will in effect be appropriate where as a neonate it would not be in its best interests to continue to receive life-sustaining medical treatment.

Overall, I have argued that there is a good moral case for doctors and judges to take parents' views on impairment into account, within reason. Although this aspect of the argument is a moral one as to the legitimate interpretation of the disability ground of the Abortion Act, the wrongful birth cases already provide a legal opening for the autonomy interests of prospective parents to receive greater protection. The irony is that many doctors probably already do recognise parents' interests in applying this section of the Act, as the Vice-President of the RCOG's letter to the police responding to Reverend Jepson's complaint effectively states. The law needs an opportunity to recognise that, within reason, this is correct.

In the next chapter, I turn to consider the way the law shapes the practice of prenatal screening and testing. In particular, I look at the way the law of wrongful birth influences the scope of healthcare professionals' positive duties to provide information about anomalies in the fetus. This is particularly important in the light of the fact that genetic knowledge and so the scope of genetic testing is constantly increasing.

---

[227] See, eg, the extreme hypothetical example 'Case 1' discussed in Wicks *et al*, above n 26, 292–4 in which, in addition to a limb reduction defect, the woman is a refugee who has been raped and tortured in her country of origin.

# 3

# *Informational Duties — the Impact on Prenatal Screening, Diagnosis and Selective Abortion*

## I INTRODUCTION

THIS CHAPTER CONSIDERS the extent of reproductive autonomy in relation to the question of impairment in a prospective child by focusing on health professionals' duties to inform a woman or couple about certain conditions or features of the fetus the woman is carrying. So, while the previous chapter considered how far reproductive autonomy extends mainly by exploring the law relating to selective abortion, this chapter particularly focuses on the wrongful birth cases that were briefly introduced in that chapter. Here I consider the standard of care to which health professionals' duties to inform are subject. This standard will determine the extent of information about the developing fetus that a woman is told. For this reason, the wrongful birth cases tell us for which kinds of reasons she will be able to terminate, if she chooses. In this way, the wrongful birth jurisprudence reveals more about the current legal scope of reproductive autonomy.

The cases are also an important indication about the future scope of this autonomy in two key ways. First, given the increasing extent of genetic knowledge, an analysis of the relevant case law helps us to explore whether parents will have a right to just *any* knowledge about the developing fetus, no matter how trivial. Second, and in the light of this increasing knowledge, if legislators were to consider creating a legal right to abort in England, including to selective abortion, one concern might be whether this could result in parents aborting fetuses because of really very minor concerns. With this in mind, a key question that this chapter asks is what difference, if any, it would make if a woman had a legal right to abort, at least up until a certain point in pregnancy. The best way to explore this question is by turning to a jurisdiction that does in fact have a rights-based abortion law, such as the United States. I do this in Section III. Strikingly, analysis of the relationship between the US law of abortion and that of wrongful birth tells us that a right to abort does not in fact entail a right to information about the fetus's condition. This has important implications for the reasons for which a woman will be able to exercise her abortion right.

In its analysis of the wrongful birth cases, the chapter considers the origins and basis of the liability established in such cases, both American and English, the question of the standard of care to which health professionals are subject, and the tensions between the interests of the medical profession on the one hand and a woman's or couple's interests in reproductive autonomy on the other. I address these issues in Section IV. Overall, but particularly in Section V, the chapter considers the ability of the law of tort now and in the future to affect what women or couples are told about their developing fetus and so which pregnancies may be maintained.

A second aspect of information provision is briefly discussed at the start of this chapter, in Section II: consent to screening and diagnosis. Without consent, screening or diagnosis that involve touching of a pregnant woman will constitute a battery.[1] At one level, the question of whether the requirements of a valid consent are satisfied in this context is easily answered. At another level, given the widespread and routine nature of these practices and the place, on occasion, of government policy, the question may be more complex. The place of counselling and its 'non-directive' nature is also briefly discussed here. At the outset, it is worth noting the distinction between screening and diagnosis. The Human Genetics Commission defines prenatal screening as 'a public health service that offers pregnant women a test to see if the baby is at an increased risk of having a particular disorder such as Down's syndrome'; and prenatal diagnosis as 'an individual procedure that aims to provide a diagnosis of a particular condition that the baby might have'.[2] The Nuffield Council on Bioethics' 2006 report, *Critical Care Decisions in Fetal and Neonatal Medicine: Ethical Issues* (the 'Nuffield Report') adopts the UK National Screening Committee's definition of prenatal screening as[3]:

> a public health service through which members of a defined population are offered a test. The purpose is to identify individuals who are more likely to be helped than harmed by further tests or treatment to reduce the risk of a disease or its complications.

## II CONSENT TO SCREENING AND DIAGNOSIS: INFORMATION AND COUNSELLING

In English (and United States) law a competent adult has the right to refuse treatment or tests, even where this will permanently damage health or lead to premature death. In *Re T* Lord Donaldson MR states[4]:

---

[1] *Chatterton v Gerson* [1981] 1 All ER 257.
[2] HGC, *Making Babies: Reproductive Decisions and Genetic Technologies* (2006), text box following para 3.3.
[3] Nuffield Council on Bioethics, *Critical Care Decisions in Fetal and Neonatal Medicine: Ethical Issues* (2006), para 3.7.
[4] [1992] 4 All ER 649, 653 (my emphasis).

The right of choice is not limited to decisions which others might regard as sensible. It exists notwithstanding that the reasons for making the choice are *rational, irrational, unknown or even non-existent.*

This was in line with the view of Lord Templeman in *Sidaway v Board of Governors of the Bethlem Royal Hospital*, that 'a patient is entitled to reject… [medical] advice for reasons which are rational, or irrational, or for no reason'.[5] The right has been approved in numerous subsequent cases.[6] If a woman is to give valid consent to, or to refuse, screening or testing in pregnancy, she must have capacity, act voluntarily and be informed as to the nature and purpose of the screening or testing, as I shall now explore.

## A  Capacity

English law presumes that adults have the requisite capacity. Traditionally the authority for this was in common law cases such as *Re MB*.[7] Since April 2007 this presumption has been present in statute in the form of section 1 of the Mental Capacity Act 2005.[8] This is a rebuttable presumption and the relevant test to rebut capacity focuses on a person's ability to understand and reason about the information presented to her.[9] Although it is possible that capacity could be in issue in this context, I shall not discuss it further here. I have discussed the issue of a woman's consent to, or refusal of, treatment apparently needed by her fetus elsewhere and this included a detailed consideration of cases in which capacity may be in issue.[10]

## B  Voluntariness: Offers of Screening and Testing

When a woman is given information about screening and testing in pregnancy, and is subsequently offered these services, ideally her autonomy is being facilitated in that she acquires information about options available to her in her pregnancy.

---

[5] [1985] 1 AC 871, 904. The case concerned a claim in negligence for non-disclosure of the risks of a surgical operation.

[6] eg, *Re C (Adult: Refusal of Medical Treatment)* [1994] 1 FLR 31; *Re MB* (1997) 8 Med LR 217; *Re JT (Adult: Refusal of Medical Treatment)* [1998] 1 FLR 48. Each of these cases concerned an adult's refusal of medical treatment.

[7] Above n 6.

[8] Section 1(2) of the MCA 2005 states: 'A person must be assumed to have capacity unless it is established that he lacks capacity'.

[9] Section 2(1) of the MCA 2005 states: 'For the purposes of this Act, a person lacks capacity in relation to a matter if at the material time he is unable to make a decision for himself in relation to the matter because of an impairment of, or a disturbance in the functioning of, the mind or brain'. Section 3(1) states: (1) For the purposes of section 2, a person is unable to make a decision for himself if he is unable — (a) to understand the information relevant to the decision (b) to retain that information (c) to use or weigh that information as part of the process of making the decision, or (d) to communicate his decision (whether by talking, using sign language or any other means)'.

[10] R Scott, *Rights, Duties and the Body: Law and Ethics of the Maternal-Fetal Conflict* (Oxford: Hart Publishing, 2002) especially Ch 3.

However, it is always possible that she will misunderstand the voluntary nature of this screening and testing, perhaps because in some way she receives the message that it is 'responsible' to accept these offers. The Human Genetics Commission has recognised this point, noting 'concerns that the existence of prenatal screening progammes puts pressure on individuals to take part because the very availability of the test may be taken to imply that it is a "good thing"'.[11] This kind of societal message might be surprisingly powerful and, at the same time, subtle. Certain forms of screening have become increasingly routine, such as that for Down's syndrome, and the routine nature of such screening has been specifically addressed in the literature.[12] In England in 2003 the National Institute for Health and Clinical Excellence (NICE) recommended that all pregnant women be offered screening for Down's syndrome.[13] Can the adoption of a national policy itself compromise voluntariness? The problem here is that the counter-factual scenario — of not offering such screening — also has the potential negatively to affect voluntariness. The ideal scenario is one in which women are provided with accurate information about Down's syndrome and clearly understand that they have the right either to refuse or to consent to such screening. Whether or not this has always been so, it is the scenario at which service providers should aim.[14] On this point, the HGC observes[15]:

> [S]creening must be presented and understood in such a way that to decline it is seen as a real option. It is equally important that those who choose to decline it are not viewed negatively by the medical profession or by society more widely. The UK [National Screening Committee] is currently looking at how consent for screening should be obtained.

The HGC also notes that the routine offer of screening may mean that it becomes the 'default option rather than the considered choice' and recommends[16]:

> In accordance with the NICE Guidelines, we consider that midwives and other professionals involved in prenatal screening should emphasise that participation is voluntary and that people are free to make their own decisions.

The law on the place of voluntariness in relation to the issue of consent is thinly drawn because there have been so few English cases on the issue, particularly in relation to consent (rather than refusal). The leading case of *Re T*, which

---

[11] HGC, above n 2, para 3.29. See also C Williams, P Alderson and B Farsides 'Too Many Choices? Hospital and Community Staff Reflect on the Future of Prenatal Screening' (2002) 55 *Social Science and Medicine* 743, 745, 750.
[12] eg, S Suter 'The Routinization of Prenatal Screening' (2002) 28 *Am J L and Med* 233.
[13] NICE 'Antenatal Care: Routine Care for the Healthy Pregnant Woman' Clinical Guideline, 6 October 2003, para 1.7.2.
[14] On the provision of information and Down's syndrome screening, see C Williams, P Alderson and B Farsides 'What Constitutes "Balanced Information" in the Practitioners' Portrayals of Down's Syndrome?' (2002) 18 *Midwifery* 230.
[15] HGC, above n 2, para 3.30.
[16] Ibid para 3.32.

concerned the validity of a woman's refusal of a blood-transfusion after a caesarean delivery, discussed the way in which 'undue influence' might invalidate consent and focused on the persuasive power of third parties and at what point this might result in undue influence. Lord Donaldson MR identified the strength of will of the patient, the relationship of the persuader to the patent and the types of arguments used as key factors in assessing undue influence, observing[17]:

> It matters not how strong the persuasion was, so long as it did not overbear the independence of the patient's decision. The real question in each case is: does the patient really mean what [she] says or is [she] merely saying it for a quiet life, to satisfy someone else or because the advice and persuasion to which [she] has been subjected is such that [she] can no longer think and decide for [herself]? In other words, is it a decision expressed in form only, not in reality?

In the context of prenatal screening and diagnosis, 'persuasion' should never be in issue when the offer of screening or testing is made. As indicated above, the question is the more subtle and complex one of whether the offer of such screening or testing and the culture of prenatal care in which a woman finds herself mean that she feels *pressured* to accept these. I cannot go into this issue further here, since it would require an extensive empirical investigation into the practice of screening and testing more suited to an overtly sociological, rather than legal and ethical, enquiry and the work of others in this regard should be noted.[18] However, throughout this chapter the ethical and legal importance of voluntariness to the validity of consent or refusal of testing should be borne in mind as an important background issue.

The other issue relevant to voluntariness that might be noted is the importance of non-directive counselling.[19] The culture of such counselling emerged in response to concerns about eugenic practices and is now very strong. In some ways, it is most relevant to the discussions that might ensue between a woman

---

[17] [1992] 4 All ER 649, 662. In this case a 34-week pregnant Jehovah's Witness who had been in a car accident contracted either pleurisy or pneumonia. In the first stages of labour, she refused a blood transfusion (as subsequent to the forthcoming caesarean-section) following discussions with her mother. Although she had been raised by her Jehovah's Witness mother, she was not herself of that faith. After she became unconscious her father and boyfriend applied to the court for assistance. The Court of Appeal held that doctors were justified in administering a transfusion on the basis of necessity because, at the time of the refusal and thereafter, she lacked the capacity to consent and had been subject to undue influence by her mother, which vitiated her refusal. See also *U v Centre for Reproductive Medicine* [2002] 1 FLR 927, in which a husband withdrew his consent to the posthumous use of his sperm following pressure from a nurse at an IVF clinic prior to treatment and it was later alleged that he had been subject to undue influence.

[18] See, eg, A Lippman 'Prenatal Genetic Testing and Screening: Constructing Needs and Reinforcing Inequities' (1991) 17 *Am J L and Med* 15. This article discusses the alleged 'geneticisation' of health problems and the alleged 'construction of a need' for PND which, it is claimed, is largely emerging out of the development of the technology itself.

[19] On this point see also R Green 'Parental Autonomy and the Obligation not to Harm One's Child Genetically' (1997) 25 *Journal of Law, Med and Ethics* 5, 5.

(and her partner) and a health professional *after* screening or testing. For instance, if a high-risk assessment results from screening for Down's syndrome, there may be discussions as to whether a woman wishes to undergo an invasive diagnostic test such as chorionic villus sampling or amniocentesis. Alternatively, there may be discussions after such diagnostic testing. At this latter stage, one question that may be in issue is whether a woman or couple wishes to continue with a pregnancy or to seek a termination. In this regard, the ethos of non-directive counselling, which is very strong, is predominantly about neutrality in relation to the issue of abortion. It is another question whether it is truly possible for health professionals to be non-directive, as has been discussed by others and noted by the HGC.[20] At the same time, the ethos of non-directive counselling should infuse initial discussions about the availability and purpose of screening and testing. In this way, this ethos is also relevant to questions about voluntariness when we review a woman's right to consent to, or refuse, screening or testing in pregnancy. At this point it might be noted that apparently a minority of professionals are in fact directive.[21] This is generally unfortunate, particularly where a child's impairment would be fully consistent with a life she would think worth living. Where this is so, there is the potential for the requirement for voluntariness in a woman's consent to screening, testing and — more seriously — also to termination to be compromised, and with it the legal validity of that consent.

A further highly important issue about voluntariness should be noted, namely the degree to which a woman or couple feels free either to continue or to

---

[20] For discussion of various aspects see, eg, Suter, above, n 12, 242–6, who notes the various ways in which genetic counsellors 'are far from neutral about many aspects of genetic counseling' (at 242), such as their commitment to the value of information itself. See also C Williams, P Alderson and B Farsides 'Is Nondirectiveness Possible within the Context of Antenatal Screening and Testing?' (2002) 54 *Social Science and Medicine* 339; and N Press 'Assessing the Expressive Character of Prenatal Testing: The Choice Made or the Choices Made Available?' in E Parens and A Asch (eds), *Prenatal Testing and Disability Rights* (Washington, DC: Georgetown University Press, 2000) 214, 230, who discusses possible interpretations of the place of such counselling within the practice of prenatal testing, either 'to counter any possibility of eugenic intent or explicit eugenic outcomes' or as 'a sort of bioethical window dressing that actually allows… a "backdoor" to eugenics'. See also HGC, above n 2, para 3.32.

[21] T Shakespeare, *Disability Rights and Wrongs* (London: Routledge, 2006) 101: 'If midwives, obstetricians and others working in maternity services imply that women have a duty to have tests or terminations, or if they are unsupportive to women who decline the screening offer, or if they are prejudiced about disability then, clearly, choice is undermined. There is evidence that professionals are frequently directive in this way, particularly from international surveys, but also sometimes in research in the UK. The majority of professionals may be non-directive and pro-choice, but individuals remain who make it clear to pregnant woman that they believe screening to be a great benefit which no sensible person could refuse.'

terminate an existing pregnancy after screening and diagnosis. The issue has been highlighted by the HGC. For instance, in relation to continuing an existing pregnancy, the HGC observes[22]:

> Unless prospective parents have a justified confidence in society's willingness to provide... resources and to offer a safe and nurturing environment for child and family, a positive screening result followed by a confirmatory diagnostic test may — by implying that abortion is the presumed choice — be seen as coercive.

And in relation to the decision to terminate[23]:

> Equally, they should have confidence that they would be treated with dignity and respect if they decide to seek to terminate the pregnancy and that support would be available afterwards to help them cope with the unhappiness and distress that can persist for months or years after a termination of pregnancy for fetal abnormality.

So, the element of voluntariness in decisions that a woman or couple make about continuing or ending a pregnancy also needs to be considered and protected.

## C  Information: Nature and Purpose, Not Results of Screening or Testing

To give valid consent, a woman must also be informed about the nature of any screening or testing. Arguably 'nature' includes purpose (rather than just the physical nature of a test, eg, the mechanisms of an ultrasound scan or the taking of blood) and in this context 'purpose' should include information about the condition that is the subject of screening.[24] If so, this means that a woman has a legal right to such information. As Tom Shakespeare has observed[25]:

> Work by the National Screening Committee is beginning to standardize the offer of screening across the country, so that all pregnant women are given access to good quality technology, regardless of postcode. Yet this work has not been matched by good quality information. In particular, screening information cannot simply be about the experience of having a test, the technical details of the test, and the reliability of the test. The most important question is what the test is for: in other words, information about conditions which the screening programme is intended to enable women to avoid, if they choose.

This is surely right and, as noted in the previous chapter, it is not clear that such information is always currently given, particularly in relation to the more routine screening such as that for Down's syndrome. As Shakespeare notes with regard to

---

[22] HGC, above n 2, para 3.21. See also para 3.31.
[23] *Ibid* para 3.31. See also para 3.34: 'Until there is proper support, there is no real choice'.
[24] In *Chatterton v Gerson*, above n 1, Bristow J refers to 'nature'. In *Re C*, above n 6, with reference to the legal requirement of capacity, Thorpe J refers to a patient understanding the 'nature, purpose and effects' of the proposed treatment. For relevant discussion see I Kennedy and A Grubb, *Medical Law: Text with Materials*, 3rd edn (London: Butterworths, 2000) 652.
[25] Shakespeare, above n 21, 100.

## 150  *Informational Duties – Impact on PND and Abortion*

Down's syndrome and other conditions detectable by means of an ultrasound scan, '[f]ailure to offer this information carries the implication that it is obvious that someone would want to avoid these conditions, the only question being whether the test is effective in providing the diagnosis'.[26] No doubt many of us have encountered women who have described their experiences of prenatal screening or have our own experiences in this context. I can recall a woman recounting that she opted for an amniocentesis test for Down's syndrome 'because those children have such terrible lives'. This may be a reminder that social attitudes to disability may affect the degree of choice prospective parents feel they have in PND. As Shakespeare observes:[27]

> for these reasons, achieving true choice in screening depends on a more extensive debate about the rights and potential of disabled people, and about the duty of society to accept and support those who need help and cannot achieve full independence.

Another woman I met did not realise that the major purpose of a 20-week ultrasound scan is to detect fetal anomaly and therefore that she could have been faced with difficult discussion and choices in the face of a positive finding.[28] The HGC also notes the lack of clear information that may surround screening practices, quoting a midwife who observes[29]:

> The tests are usually discussed at the booking (first) visit in the surgery or hospital antenatal clinic. There is so much other information to take in, that women feel overwhelmed. Couples have rarely thought through the full implications of the screening on offer — they assume 'it won't happen to me' — i.e. that 'something wrong' may be discovered.

The HGC also cites the observations of the Royal College of Nursing[30]:

> Some concern was expressed about the 'medical culture' which surrounds screening making it seem a 'routine' which some women may regard as reassuring without being sufficiently aware that it may lead to the diagnosis of a genetic condition.

The HGC therefore notes that it is:[31]

> essential that any individual undergoing screening procedures should understand that the test is intended to identify possible problems in the fetus and that, if an anomaly is discovered, difficult choices may have to be made, which may include a decision whether to continue or to terminate the pregnancy.

---

[26] *Ibid.*
[27] *Ibid* 101.
[28] Shakespeare also notes the possibility that some women or couples may not appreciate this purpose. *Ibid* 101.
[29] HGC, above n 2, para 3.29.
[30] *Ibid.*
[31] *Ibid* para 3.31.

Overall, in a recommendation that could be relevant both to the voluntary element of consent to testing and to the question of information provision, as well as to the voluntary nature of a decision to continue with or to terminate an existing pregnancy, the HGC recommends 'that a review of information, counselling and support services for those whose fetuses are diagnosed with a serious condition should be commissioned by the Department of Health'.[32]

I turn now from the question of the nature and purpose of screening or testing to the question of the information revealed in this process. Does a woman also have a right to just *any* information those scans or tests reveal and, if so, do health professionals have a duty to give her this? This is a central question in this chapter.

We know that English abortion law is not rights-based. However, there is evidence that some health professionals in this area, including doctors, are in fact concerned about whether they are sufficiently respecting a woman's autonomy and rights in the context of prenatal screening. One study, which addressed in part the difficulty of drawing lines in this context, found that one of the difficulties faced by practitioners was how to decide whether to provide information about fetal conditions or features that were not serious.[33] This concern may arise if information concerning relatively minor conditions happens to be found in the course of other screening or testing, which might well happen with the increasingly refined nature of screening and testing techniques. Although a minority of the participants in this study felt that they should try to draw some lines, the majority 'felt that individuals should have the right to make the choice'.[34] Just which choice they were concerned with here may not have been clear in these practitioners' minds. Overall, however, they were apparently troubled by the place of 'individual choice' in this context.[35] We should therefore clarify just what a woman can, theoretically at least (and thus leaving aside questions about social pressures to test that are relevant to the question of voluntariness), legally be autonomous about in this context.

As we have seen, a pregnant woman has the right to consent to, or refuse, prenatal screening or testing.[36] Following this, under English law, if the legal conditions are met, she has the option to abort. The answer to the legal question of what information the woman should receive about the fetus, however, cannot be predicated on her right to consent to or refuse the screening or testing. Rather, it must bear some relation to the terms of the Abortion Act. For instance, given

---

[32] *Ibid* para 3.35.
[33] C Williams, P Alderson and B Farsides '"Drawing the Line" in Prenatal Screening and Testing: Health Practitioners' Discussions' (2002) 4(1) *Health, Risk and Society* 61, 68.
[34] *Ibid*.
[35] 'Whilst there was little disagreement about screening for life-threatening conditions, many of the other categories provoked disagreement amongst practitioners, focusing mainly around whether or not individual choice should prevail'. *Ibid* 69.
[36] The general principles can be found in *Sidaway v Board of Governors of the Bethlem Royal Hospital*, above n 5 and *Re C*, above n 6. The principles as applied to a pregnant woman can be found in *Re MB*, above n 6.

the terms of section 1(1)(d), it would clearly be negligent not to advise a woman where her fetus was at 'substantial risk' of becoming a child with a 'serious handicap', whatever this means in practice.[37] In effect, a woman also has the legal right to this information. However, this is protected by the law of negligence, not the law of consent. That practitioners are apparently concerned that notions to do with a woman's autonomy should affect what information they convey to her in the course of screening or testing might be related to the ethos of non-directive counselling. In the light of the above points, however, it can be seen that that neutral ethos cannot *itself* guide or determine what information should be given. Rather, the neutral ethos can only give guidance as to how any given information regarding screening options and results should be presented and discussed.

In sum, while the law of consent protects a woman's right to consent to, or refuse, screening or testing, it is the law of negligence — in the form of the wrongful birth jurisprudence — that protects her right to a certain degree of information about the developing fetus. It is the latter that is the principal focus of this chapter.

The concern of health professionals as to whether they should advise of less serious or indeed relatively trivial features of the fetus's condition partly brings the interpretation of section 1(1)(a) of the Act into question. As we saw in the previous chapter, if a woman is concerned about a degree of risk or level of disability that her doctors do not think satisfy the criteria of section 1(1)(d), then they may decide that a termination under section 1(1)(a) is justified on the basis that going to term would create risks to her mental or physical health greater than if she were to terminate. Since outside the context of fetal anomaly this section may in general be interpreted in a relatively loose sense, it might seem unfair to allow one woman to abort on this ground (for 'social reasons') but deny another the chance to do so when she is concerned about a less than serious fetal impairment or a low risk of a more serious one. This is a problem inherent in a non-rights-based abortion law. The need to evaluate reasons and assign them to different boxes according to the terms of the Abortion Act may sometimes create a sense of unease for practitioners and a concern about whether women are being treated fairly in this process.[38] It is therefore not surprising that section 1(1)(a)

---

[37] The relevant part of s 1(1) of the Abortion Act 1967 as amended by the HFE Act 1990 reads: 'Subject to the provisions of this section, a person shall not be guilty of an offence under the law relating to abortion when a pregnancy is terminated by a registered medical practitioner if two registered medical practitioners are of the opinion, formed in good faith... (d) that there is a substantial risk that if the child were born it would suffer from such physical or mental abnormalities as to be seriously handicapped'.

[38] One (unnamed) obstetrician said: 'I think things are probably made more difficult because most obstetricians and gynaecologists know that terminations for social reasons, or whatever, are done effectively on demand, and one of the main reasons for that is because of anxiety generated about the pregnancy continuing... our sort of baseline has shifted because of shifts in how the Abortion Act has been applied over the past 20 years or so'. Williams *et al*, above n 33, 66.

might on occasion be used to support terminations for less serious fetal disabilities. There will be limits, however, to the extent to which less serious — especially relatively minor — disabilities could present this kind of risk to a woman.

One solution to concerns about fairness of treatment of women in the application of the Act would simply be to change the law so that women have the right to abort until a certain point in pregnancy. Then, concerns about the degrees of justification in practice as between the different grounds and whether the reasons presented on any occasion legally support abortion under a given ground would simply not arise. It is appropriate at this point to consider the alternative of a rights-based system as it has developed in the United States and so the place of a right to abort within the practice of prenatal screening. The question underlying this comparison is how possession of a right to abort affects the scope of reproductive autonomy in relation to fetal impairment. In this way, we can see what the implications of a rights-based approach to abortion would be in English law.

## III THE EFFECT OF A RIGHTS-BASED APPROACH TO ABORTION ON PRENATAL SCREENING AND TESTING

### A  The Right to Abort For Any Reason

As is well known, abortion law in the United States is rights-based. *Roe v Wade* [39] established a pregnant woman's right to abort her fetus for any reason until the end of the second trimester as an aspect of her right to privacy. In this process, the US Supreme Court also recognised two important state interests that are capable of limiting that right as pregnancy progresses: the state's interest in the health and life of the pregnant woman enables the state to regulate abortion from the end of the first trimester onwards; its interest in the potential life of the fetus becomes compelling after viability, such that abortion thereafter can be limited only to the need to protect the mother's life or health. Despite these state interests, since US abortion law is rights-based, a woman's ability to exercise her abortion right does not depend upon her underlying reasons. Further, since no distinction is made in the cases between a 'normal' as opposed to a disabled fetus, the abortion right is intended to apply to any abortion and thus any fetus (pre-viability). Indeed, none of the Supreme Court cases has been concerned in any way with whether the fetus was 'normal' or disabled. Rather, typically they have dealt with challenges to state regulations concerning 'informed consent' provisions (such as in *Akron v Akron Center for Reproductive Health* [40] or regulations concerning the standard of care in the abortion itself, such as in *Thornburgh v American College of Obstetricians*

---

[39] 35 L Ed 2d 147 (1973). Note that some state constitutions also protect the abortion right.
[40] 76 L Ed 2d 687 (1983).

154  *Informational Duties – Impact on PND and Abortion*

*and Gynecologists* [41]). In various ways, the issue in these cases was whether a woman's right to abort was the subject of illegitimate state interference.

This was also the issue in the important case of *Planned Parenthood of Southeastern Pennsylvania v Casey*.[42] In this case the Court reaffirmed *Roe's* core holdings, although it rejected the trimester framework established in *Roe* and revised the abortion right as a liberty interest derived from the due process clause of the Fourteenth Amendment. It also modified the standard under which the relation between the abortion right and state interests should be reviewed from that of 'strict scrutiny' in *Roe* [43] (which reflected a conception of the right as 'fundamental') to 'undue burden'. A state regulation imposes an 'undue burden' if it 'has the purpose or effect of placing a substantial obstacle in the path of a woman seeking abortion of a nonviable fetus'.[44] The case gave greater importance to the State's interest in the potential life of the fetus[45] and, in so doing, debated the merits of a number of provisions aimed at securing 'informed consent'. Some of these were intended to try to change a woman's mind and would thus burden her right to some degree (noted below). Since *Casey* gave more weight to the State's interest in potential life than *Roe*, it allowed states to create laws establishing a 'reasonable framework' to ensure that a woman's decision to abort is 'thoughtful and informed',[46] holding that 'what is at stake is the woman's right to make the ultimate decision, not a right to be insulated from all others in so doing'.[47] In *Casey* itself, for instance, the Court upheld the mandatory provision of literature on the risks of, and alternatives, to abortion, a 24-hour waiting period before an abortion, and limits on its availability to minors.[48] By contrast, it struck out an obligation that married women seek the formal consent of their husbands.[49] In fact, it is disputable whether the restrictions that the Court upheld do not in fact create an undue burden on a woman's abortion right. A number of states have

---

[41] 90 L Ed 2d 779 (1986).
[42] 120 L Ed 2d 674 (1992).
[43] This is the standard to which Justice Blackmun has repeatedly argued that restrictions on the right of privacy should be subject. By this standard a state must show that the restriction in question is 'both necessary and narrowly tailored to serve a compelling state interest'. *Griswold v Connecticut* 14 L Ed 2d 510 (1965), as cited by Blackmun J in *Casey* 120 L Ed at 749.
[44] Above n 42, 714, *per* the joint opinion.
[45] For a detailed discussion see Scott, above, n 10, Ch 4.
[46] Above n 42, 712 and 711 respectively. The joint opinion was supported in this respect by Justices Stevens (concurring in part and dissenting in part) and Blackmun (concurring in part, concurring in the judgment in part, and dissenting in part) (*ibid* 740 and 751 respectively). Thus, states could enact regulations informing women of the 'philosophic and social arguments of great weight that can be brought to bear in favor of continuing the pregnancy' (*ibid* 712). But note that Justice Stevens was concerned as to whether aspects of the regulations were in fact related to these arguments (*ibid* 744).
[47] *Ibid* 715.
[48] *Ibid* 885, 887 and 899 respectively.
[49] *Ibid* 895.

similar provisions and in such states it would seem considerably more difficult for women to exercise their abortion right.[50]

This broader aspect of the US context should be borne in mind in discussions of the federal position but cannot be further explored here. Likewise, it is beyond my scope to consider the US Supreme Court's most recent abortion decision of *Gonzales v Carhart* (2007), which concerned the question of abortion methods and in which the majority upheld Congress's Partial-Birth Abortion Ban Act 2003.[51] It should be noted, however, that although neither *Roe* nor *Casey* has been overruled, changes to the composition of the Supreme Court appear to be affecting the approach to abortion in the Supreme Court and the way that aspects of these earlier decisions, particularly the state's interest in potential life, are interpreted.

## B  The Role of the Medical Profession

Of course, a woman must consult a doctor in order to obtain an abortion and his or her role in this process should be considered, particularly in comparison with the English position. In *Roe*, Justice Blackmun held that, since the 'compelling' point of the state's interest in a woman's life and health is at the end of the first trimester (because until that point the risk of death through abortion may be less than through childbirth), up until this time a doctor 'in consultation with his patient, is free to determine, without regulation by the State, that, in his medical judgment, the patient's pregnancy should be terminated'.[52] This formulation

---

[50] For a record of those states that do have 24-hour waiting periods, such as Louisiana, see Center for Reproductive Rights <http://www.crlp.org/st_law_delay.html> accessed 9 October 2007. Note that prior to *Casey* Louisiana went so far as to enact a law allowing abortion only in cases of rape or incest or a threat to the woman's life (La Rev Stat Ann S 14.87 (1992). This was struck down as unconstitutional in *Sojourner T v Edwards* 974 F 2d 27 (5th Cir 1992) but it showed the willingness of states to test the waters in the light of US Supreme Court rulings, in this case *Webster v Reproductive Health Services* 106 L Ed 2d 410 (1989). In the latter case, Blackmun J (concurring in part and dissenting in part) observed that 'a plurality of this Court implicitly invites every state legislature to enact more and more restrictive abortion regulations in order to provoke more and more test cases, in the hope that sometime down the line the Court will return the law of procreative freedom to the severe limitations that generally prevailed in this country before January 22, 1973' (at 449).

[51] (2007) 127 SCt 1610. The Act states that theprocedure is never medically necessary. This was upheld by the Supreme Court,although previous decisions required an exception to protect a woman's health, not just her life, as in *Stenberg v Carhart* 530 US 914. Note the strong dissent in *Gonzales* by Ginsburg J, in which Stevens, Souter and Breyer JJ joined. In particular, Ginsburg J observes that '[t]oday's decision is alarming. It refuses to take *Casey*... seriously. It tolerates, indeed applauds, federal intervention to ban nationwide a procedure found necessary and proper in certain cases by the American College of Obstetricians and Gynecologists (ACOG). It blurs the line, firmly drawn in *Casey*, between previability and post-viability abortions. And, for the first time since *Roe*, the court blesses a prohibition with no exception safeguarding a woman's health.' (at 1641).

[52] Above n 39, 163.

appears to give some degree of decisional control to the doctor and the question then arises as to how this squares with *Roe's* pronouncement of a pregnant woman's *right* to abort.[53] Given that the context of concern at this point is the state's interest in the woman's life and health that becomes compelling in the second trimester, *Roe's* emphasis on the medical judgment of the doctor seems intended to grant doctors *medical* authority against the *state*, rather than *moral* or *legal* authority against the *pregnant woman*. (As we have seen in the last chapter, by contrast, to some degree the latter position represents English law.) This is reinforced by the statement that, until the end of the first trimester, 'the abortion decision in all its aspects is inherently, and primarily, a medical decision'.[54] If the concern here was with medical authority as to moral matters, there would be no reason to limit this exclusive authority to the end of the first trimester.[55] However, as regards a pregnant woman's right, although the decision in *Roe* does not appear to grant moral or legal authority to doctors, abortion is not available 'on demand'.[56] This is because medical judgment that an abortion is medically appropriate — or rather, perhaps, that it is not inappropriate — is still necessary.[57] Further, in the light of *Casey's* emphasis on the importance of the state's interest in potential life throughout pregnancy and its departure from the trimester framework, *Roe's* description of abortion in the first trimester as 'in all its aspects… inherently, and primarily, a medical decision', such that the state has no compelling interests during this period, might be read somewhat differently. Nevertheless, as regards a pregnant woman's right to abort, under neither *Roe* nor *Casey* do doctors appear to have moral or legal standing as a check on her *reasons*

---

[53] 'We, therefore, conclude that the right of personal privacy includes the abortion decision, but that this right is not unqualified and must be considered against important state interests in regulation' (*per* Blackmun J, *ibid* 154). 'That right necessarily includes the right of a woman to decide whether or not to terminate her pregnancy' (*per* Stewart J, concurring, *ibid* 170). The view, expressed by J Bopp, B Bostrom, D McKinney 'The "Rights" and "Wrongs" of Wrongful Birth and Wrongful Life: A Jurisprudential Analysis of Birth Related Torts' (Spring, 1989) *Duquesne Law Rev* 461, 497, that 'the Supreme Court's decision in *Roe* is grounded not upon the right of a woman to control her body, but on the right of the physician to administer medical treatment according to his professional judgment' (citing *Roe*, above n 39, 165) is thus misleading. This is not to deny the importance given to medical judgment in the abortion decisions.

[54] Above n 39, 166.

[55] In *Roe* itself, Blackmun J reviews medical attitudes to the regulation of abortion (*ibid* 141–6). He also reviews the history of abortion generally.

[56] 'Even the broadest reading of *Roe*, however, has not suggested that there is a constitutional right to abortion on demand. See, *eg, Doe v Bolton*… 35 L Ed 2d at 201… Rather, the right protected by *Roe* is a right to decide to terminate a pregnancy free of undue interference by the State.' (*Casey*, above n 42, 721, *per* the joint opinion).

[57] Note that in English law doctors cannot be required to treat a patient if to do so is against their clinical judgment. *Re J (a minor) (wardship: medical treatment)* (1990) 6 BMLR 25. I Kennedy has suggested that there must be limits to this principle: 'Commentary' (1993) 1 *Med Law Rev* 95.

for wishing to exercise her right.[58] It is true, however, that the doctor has a certain prominence in *Roe* that has been the subject of criticism over time.[59]

## C  Autonomy — Information That Aids, Not Burdens

The information process that is part of prenatal screening and diagnosis is intended to enhance and facilitate a woman's reproductive choices and, at the same time, not to burden them. (This is also true in England.) Could the state's interest in potential life from *Casey* be used at least to question a possible wish to abort for reasons relating to a relatively trivial disorder or condition, particularly as the fetus advances in development? Alternatively, would this be an undue burden on a woman's abortion right? (Of course, there is no federally protected *right* to abort after viability.)

The delivery of information in the context of prenatal screening and diagnosis is supposedly governed, as in England, by an ethos of non-directive counselling. It would therefore seem difficult for states to require that genetic counsellors incorporate the state's interest in potential life into their work, for instance by means of a framework designed to ensure the informed nature of a decision to abort an impaired fetus. Rather, this could be another form of information provision that could weigh against autonomy and 'unduly burden' it.

Let us think instead about aiding a woman's decision whether to continue or terminate a pregnancy by providing her with information as to the health or condition of the fetus. Since the Supreme Court's abortion decisions have typically been concerned with reviewing the potential of various information provisions to interfere with a woman's prior decision to abort, there is no abortion jurisprudence on the issue of *facilitating* her choice when the issue turns on the condition of her fetus.[60] It would be difficult to construe the state's interest

---

[58] That Blackmun J granted pregnant women the *right* to abort in *Roe*, despite the involvement of doctors in the process of obtaining an abortion, is a point repeatedly emphasised by him in later cases. For example, in *Casey* (concurring in the judgment in part and dissenting in part), he refers to a woman 'exercis[ing] her *fundamental right* with her responsible physician to terminate her pregnancy' (above n 42, 751, my emphasis). In *Webster v Reproductive Health Services* (concurring in part and dissenting in part) he holds that the majority's 'aggressive and shameful infringement on the *right* of women to obtain abortions in consultation with their chosen physicians, unsupported by any state interest, much less a compelling one, violates the command of *Roe*' (106 L Ed 2d 410 (1989), 450, my emphasis).

[59] See, eg, R Ginsburg 'Some Thoughts on Autonomy and Equality in relation to *Roe v Wade*' (January 1985) *N Carolina Law Rev* 375. 'Academic criticism of *Roe*, charging the Court with reading its own values into the due process clause, might have been less pointed had the Court placed the woman alone, rather than the woman tied to her physician, at the center of its attention' (at 382.) 'Overall, the Court's *Roe* position is weakened, I believe, by the opinion's concentration on a medically approved autonomy idea, to the exclusion of a constitutionally based sex-equality perspective' (at 386.)

[60] Compare S Gold 'An Equality Approach to Wrongful Birth Statutes' (1996) *Fordham Law Rev* 1005, 1036: 'Although *Casey* permits legislative curtailment of access to abortions,

in potential life (the fetus) as concerned with the *pregnant woman* and her possible wish to abort, thereby requiring that she be informed of the health or other condition of the fetus. Some thought might therefore be given to the possible relevance of the state's interest in a woman's health and life. The concept of health has been broadly interpreted to encompass both psychological and physical well-being (*United States v Vuitch*[61]) but never discussed — in the abortion cases at least — in terms of the avoidance of the birth of a seriously disabled child being potentially in the health interests of a pregnant woman. Nevertheless, this is an argument that might be made out in an appropriate case and that could in practice perhaps be the basis of a medically sanctioned abortion post-viability where states permit this. Apart from this line of thought, however, support for information provision about the specific fetus a woman is carrying is hard to establish on the basis of the abortion jurisprudence in itself.

Can support for the idea of facilitating autonomy in the decision whether to continue or end a given pregnancy be garnered more generally from the cases concerned with procreative liberty or autonomy, such as *Eisenstadt v Baird*? In that case, Justice Brennan observed[62]:

> If the right of privacy means anything, it is the right of the *individual*, married or single, to be free from governmental intrusion into matters so fundamentally affecting the person as the decision whether to bear or beget a child.

*Eisenstadt* indicates that this line of cases is essentially concerned with preventing interferences with a given right and hence with *negative* liberties,[63] as in the contraceptives case of *Griswold v Connecticut*.[64] Indeed, if the abortion right were construed as positive, then there may be abortion 'on demand', which the cases have denied.[65] Thus, to the extent that abortion requires positive medical assistance, there is no right to it, as the scope for medical discretion underlines.[66]

---

it is unlikely that the Court would support manipulation of health information as a method of limitation'. This may well be so, but it would entail judicial development of prior case law.

[61] 28 L Ed 2d 601 (1971).

[62] 405 US 438, 453 (1972), emphasis in original.

[63] Compare D Stoller 'Prenatal Genetic Screening: the Enigma of Selective Abortion' (1997/1998) 12 *J L and Health* 121, 139: 'This language shows that the Supreme Court recognized an individual's right to make decisions as to the terms under which he or she would procreate'. In essence, however, the effect of this recognition is limited.

[64] 14 L Ed 2d 510 (1965), in which the Court explicitly recognised a right to privacy for the first time and applied it to a married couple's right to use contraceptives.

[65] As noted above, n 56.

[66] This is consistent with the denial of a right to funding of abortions, eg, regarding *federal* funding, in *Harris v McRae* 65 L Ed 2d 784 (1986) the US Supreme Court held that the Hyde amendment, which forbids federal medical welfare funds from being used even for medically needed abortions, was constitutional. Regarding *state* funding, in *Maher v Roe* 53 L Ed 2d 484 (1977) the Court held that a state can deny financial assistance for non-therapeutic abortions, notwithstanding that it may help pay for childbirth.

Given that the choice to reproduce may be based on a certain conception, however approximate, of the kinds of experiences and burdens it will entail, one might well assert the importance of access to information that will affect that decision, as for instance John Robertson does.[67] However, the predominantly negative liberty inherent in the procreative liberty (including abortion) jurisprudence has important implications for the degree of information to which a woman or couple is entitled — at least on the basis of this area of law — regarding the characteristics or health of the developing fetus. Just as the legal right to abort including for reasons of fetal anomaly is negative in character, so is the right to information which it, at least, entails. Robertson acknowledges (in a footnote) that, the right being negative, it 'is a right against public or private interference, not a right to resources or to success in the efforts to select offspring traits'.[68] Somewhat confusingly, however, (in his text) he then states that 'denying a person information about the package of burdens, benefits, and rearing responsibilities that will ensue… would affect her decision whether to reproduce at all and would interfere with her procreative liberty'.[69] However, legally this would only be the case if procreative liberty entails a positive right to information. In Robertson's writing the issue is left uncertain, as is the boundary between what the procreative liberty jurisprudence actually supports and what it should support. But it seems clear that the ability of the established US abortion jurisprudence *in itself* to protect a woman's right to abort a fetus that would become an impaired child (by providing her with relevant information) is limited. Typically, this is due to its concern with a woman's pre-existing wish to terminate a pregnancy for whatever reason, rather than with fully enhancing her ability to decide to carry to term or to abort a particular fetus. Although this does not mean that US abortion law could not develop explicitly to acknowledge the importance of information about the health or other relevant state of the fetus, it has not yet done so. In essence then, and importantly, a legal right to abort does not necessarily entail a legal right to information about a specific fetus. Recognition of this has important implications for understanding the effects of a possibly rights-based approach to abortion in English law.

Still, the procreative liberty jurisprudence is not the only source of relevant law: the cases of wrongful birth are deeply concerned with providing information to enable choices associated with abortion. The rest of this chapter therefore turns to consider the law surrounding information disclosure as this has developed in the wrongful birth cases and associated case law. In what follows, I interleave discussion of US and English law. First I note the origin and broad scope of the duty as it developed in the wrongful birth cases.

---

[67] J Robertson 'Genetic Selection of Offspring Characteristics' (1996) 76 *Boston U Law Rev* 421, 427.
[68] *Ibid* 427, fn 27.
[69] *Ibid*.

## IV THE ROLE OF WRONGFUL BIRTH LIABILITY

### A  Tort's Concern to Protect Reproductive Autonomy, But Only So Far

The source of a positive duty to provide information about the developing fetus originates in the wrongful birth cases themselves, which were introduced in the previous chapter. Some of these interpreted *Roe* as the catalyst. In *Berman v Allan*, for instance, having acknowledged *Roe's* recognition of a woman's right to abort, Pashman J held that '[p]ublic policy now supports, rather than militates against, the proposition that she not be impermissibly denied a meaningful opportunity to make that decision'.[70] He further noted that '[a]ny other ruling would in effect immunize from liability those in the medical field providing inadequate guidance to persons who would choose to exercise their constitutional right to abort fetuses which, if born, would suffer from genetic defects'.[71] So the case does not say that *Roe itself* entails a positive right to information, but rather that public policy favours such a duty *so that* a woman can meaningfully exercise her established right to abort. Similarly, in *Smith v Cote*, having noted that the controversial issue of abortion had been settled by the Supreme Court, Batchelder J observed that the court's task was to 'decide only whether, given the existence of the right of choice recognized in *Roe,* our common law should *allow the development* of a duty to exercise care in providing information that bears on that choice'.[72] Later, he noted that in the light both of the technology of screening and of *Roe*[73]:

> Courts *accordingly* have recognized that physicians who perform testing and provide advice *relevant to* the constitutionally guaranteed procreative choice, or whose actions could reasonably be said to give rise to a duty to provide such testing or advice, have an obligation to adhere to reasonable standards of professional performance.

Wrongful birth cases in favour of liability consequently responded to scientific and legal developments in a manner intended to enhance the deliberative quality of the abortion decision.[74]

---

[70]  404 A 2d 8 (1979) 14. The case concerned a failure to advise a 38-year-old woman of the possibility of amniocentesis.
[71]  *Ibid*.
[72]  513 A 2d 341 (NH, 1986), 344, my emphasis. The case concerned a failure to detect rubella and to advise of its risks to the future child.
[73]  *Ibid* 346 (my emphasis).
[74]  Batchelder J also noted (*ibid* at 348): 'We must… do our best to effectuate the first principles of our law of negligence: to deter negligent conduct, and to compensate the victims of those who act unreasonably'. The existence of a web of federal and state regulation which either encourages or discourages access to genetic information should be noted but cannot be discussed here. See, eg, EW Clayton 'What the Law Says about Reproductive Genetic Testing and What it Doesn't' in KH Rothenberg and EJ Thomson (eds), *Women and Prenatal Testing: Facing the Challenges of Genetic Technology* (Columbus,

Importantly, while the impetus for wrongful birth liability in the United States came from the abortion right, the scope of the duty need not — and in fact does not — match that of the abortion right. For instance, in *Canesi v Wilson* Handler J held that although wrongful birth liability protects parental autonomy, the duty is 'premised' in tort and, most significantly, is therefore 'not coextensive with or measured by the woman's constitutional rights to decide the fate of her pregnancy'.[75] He observed, by contrast as it were, that *Roe* supports a woman's right to abort 'for any reason or no reason'.[76] Significantly then, in relation to prenatal screening and testing, there is an *asymmetry* between the US law of abortion and that of wrongful birth, explored further below.

By contrast, one of the most striking features of English wrongful birth law, touched on in the previous chapter, is the (indirect) correspondence or *symmetry* between it and the disability ground of the Abortion Act. Recall that in *Rance v Mid-Downs Health Authority*,[77] for example, one of the doctors was concerned that the couple might have had access to an abortion on the grounds of section 1(1)(d), it therefore being the relevant doctors' duty to inform them of information relating to a serious disability. Recall also that in *Rand v East Dorset Health Authority*, Newman J refers to the 'legal right accorded to parents by the 1967 Act as *relevant to the ambit of the duty of care* assumed by those having responsibility in connection with childbirth'.[78] In essence, English wrongful birth liability relatively straightforwardly responds to the limits placed on the legality of selective abortion.

So far we have seen that in both jurisdictions, despite the very different starting points in abortion law, the net position — by different means — is that decisional

---

Ohio: Ohio State University Press, 1994) 131. In California, doctors are required to inform women of the existence of alpha-fetalprotein screening: Cal Health and Safety Code, s 151 (West Supp 1990).

[75] 158 NJ 490 (1999) 510. In this complex case '[t]he parents' principal allegation was that the doctors were negligent in failing to warn them that a drug prescribed for the plaintiff mother posed the specific risk of fetal limb reduction and that the prescribed drug caused this defect. They also alleged other acts of negligence, including the failure to warn of general, unspecified fetal risks posed by the prescribed drug, and to take diagnostic measures during the mother's pregnancy that would have disclosed the presence of a fetal defect' (*per* Handler J at 498). The issue was 'whether it is necessary to establish medical causation in a wrongful birth action that involves the prescription of drugs without adequate warning of the fetal risks posed by those drugs' (*ibid* 499). This is not directly relevant to my discussion.

[76] *Ibid*.

[77] [1991] 1 QB 587. The case concerned a failure to diagnose spina bifida and the legality of an abortion under the unamended Abortion Act 1967, in which the fetal disability ground of the Act was subject to time limits.

[78] [2000] 56 BMLR 39, 48, my emphasis. This point is made in conjunction with a discussion of damages, which I have noted is beyond my current scope. Newman J also observes: 'The existence of the Act is sufficient to introduce into the relationship between the health authority responsible for a pregnancy and the parents, a duty to take reasonable steps to ensure the parents can exercise their choice under the Act' (*ibid* 50).

162   *Informational Duties – Impact on PND and Abortion*

control over the circumstances under which a fetus will be carried to term does not fully rest with the woman or couple. Although this is not surprising given the terms of English law, it reflects also the reality beneath the surface of US law. The rest of this chapter explores in more detail where decisional control actually lies in relation to prenatal screening, PND and abortion. It does this by exploring the impact that the law of negligence has on abortion options in both England and the United States. It also makes some brief suggestions as to where decisional control should lie and how extensive it should be. It does so by exploring the conscience issues for the medical profession, the basis of the wrongful birth action and the standard of care. Regarding the latter, I focus particularly on the potential tension between professional notions of practice on the one hand and reproductive autonomy on the other. Perhaps not surprisingly, some of these issues were significant in the judgments of those US cases that have rejected the wrongful birth action. These issues are also significant, however, in the cases in favour of wrongful birth liability themselves. Finally, I also consider the role that tort has to play — through wrongful birth liability — in shaping future screening practices.

## B   Issues of Conscience for the Medical Profession

Issues of conscience for the medical profession do not appear in English wrongful birth case law. This is likely to be because the terms of the Abortion Act set certain criteria for doctors, to which their legal informational duties, and those of other health professionals, broadly correspond. Having said this, I noted earlier that some health professionals in this context remain troubled by the issue of line-drawing. And in the next chapter I explore aspects of this in relation to the provision of preimplantation genetic diagnosis (PGD).

In the United States, conscience issues make a strong appearance in the handful of US cases that have rejected the wrongful birth action. Typically, such cases are also concerned at the very thought that the action hinges on the missed chance of an abortion. For instance, in *Schloss v Miriam Hosp*, a judge observes: 'These cases are not about birth, or wrongfulness, or negligence, or common law. They are about abortion'.[79] There is also a concern that there may be eugenic implications in the wrongful birth action. For instance, in *Dansby v Thomas Jefferson University Hospital*, Wieand J states: 'The protection of fetal life has been recognized to be an important state interest. The legislature's expressed concern is to prevent lawsuits leading to eugenic abortions of deformed or unwanted children'.[80] The rejection of wrongful birth liability, by legislative or judicial means, is seen in part as a way of giving doctors an escape route from being involved *in any way* with abortion, including simply by providing information which might lead to an abortion.[81]

---

[79] *Schloss v Miriam Hosp* No CA 98–2076, 1999 WL 41875, at 4 (RI Super Ct, 11 January 1999).
[80] *Dansby v Thomas Jefferson University Hospital* 623 A2d 816 (Pa Super 1993) 821.
[81] This emerges as a theme in the legislative history of Pennsylvania's wrongful birth and life statute, Title 42, section 8305 of the Pennsylvania Consolidated Statutes Annotated.

Scholars opposed to wrongful birth actions emphasise this issue, sometimes drawing attention to *Roe's* concern with protecting the interests of the medical profession (the point, in fact, which was discussed earlier).[82] These scholars have also interpreted information issues in cases subsequent to *Roe* as being concerned to protect the doctor from state interference just as much as the pregnant woman.[83] However, although the issue of state interference with medical practice is a recurring theme, it is far from clear that these cases were *equally* concerned to protect doctors. For instance, in *Akron v Akron Center for Reproductive Health*, Powell J held[84]:

> The Court also has recognized, because abortion is a medical procedure, that the *full vindication of the woman's fundamental right* necessarily requires that her physician be given 'the room he needs to make his best medical judgment.' *Doe v Bolton*... The physician's exercise of this medical judgment encompasses both assisting the woman in the decisionmaking process and implementing her decision *should she choose* abortion. See *Colautti v Franklin*.

Further, the suggestion by some scholars that the rejection of wrongful birth liability is necessary to protect the consciences of doctors is misleading in that there are alternative mechanisms in place in states that allow wrongful birth actions: doctors are never compelled to participate in abortions, although they are ethically obliged to refer patients seeking abortions.[85] (In England this obligation of referral may also be legal.[86])

---

See J Kowitz 'Not Your Garden Variety Tort Reform: Statutes Barring Claims for Wrongful Life and Wrongful Birth are Unconstitutional Under the Purpose Prong of *Planned Parenthood v Casey*' (Spring, 1995) *Brooklyn Law Rev* 235, 268 *ff*.

[82] See, eg, Bopp *et al*, above n 53, 497: 'the Supreme Court's decision in *Roe* is grounded not upon the right of a woman to control her body but on the right of the physician to administer medical treatment according to his professional judgment', citing *Roe*, 35 L Ed 2d at 165. This represents a selective focus on one aspect of the decision in *Roe*, discussed earlier.

[83] See eg, Bopp *et al* continue: 'Throughout the *Roe* progeny, the Court has continued to defer to the physician's privilege to exercise his professional judgment' (*ibid*). Again, this does not negate the importance of a woman's right. In essence, the authors manipulate questions about what information the courts have required or not required doctors to give pregnant women prior to an abortion (discussing cases such as *Colautti v Franklin* 58 L Ed 2d 596 (1979)) to assert that 'the imposition of wrongful birth liability upon physicians for failing to inform a prospective mother of complications that would result if she chose to give birth, or of available diagnostic procedures, creates an intrusion upon the professional judgment of medical personnel' (*ibid* 498).

[84] Above n 40, 697 (my emphases). *Doe v Bolton*, above n 56. *Colautti v Franklin*, above n 83.

In fact, the true effect if courts reject wrongful birth liability is to immunise from liability doctors who — either negligently or deliberately — fail to advise a woman of the possibility of screening or testing or of the results appropriate to her pregnancy. This is because the prospect of a wrongful birth action would require them to impart relevant information. An important question that then arises is whether the lack of a wrongful birth action in some states interferes with a woman's abortion right. This is a matter of some controversy amongst scholars.[87] Since, as we have seen, the abortion right is really negative in character — a freedom from interference — then, at least so far as the established abortion jurisprudence is concerned, it might be argued that the lack of a wrongful birth action does not interfere with the abortion right. As we saw, the concern with information issues in the leading abortion cases focused on not burdening, rather than assisting, the exercise of the right.

However, one question that arises under *Casey* is whether either legislative or judicial action banning wrongful birth actions could constitute state action imposing an undue burden on a woman's right to abort. We saw that *Casey* held

---

[85] *Hickman v Group Health* 396 NW 2d 10 (Minn 1986), *per* Simonett J, concurring specially, at 16: 'If a doctor, for reasons of personal ethics, does not wish to be involved in a patient's abortion decisionmaking, he is ethically bound to refer the patient elsewhere for the medical care the patient is entitled to receive'. The case concerned an alleged failure to advise a 34-year-old woman of the possibility of amniocentesis. See also D Wertz 'Drawing Lines: Notes for Policymakers' in Parens and Asch (eds), above n 20, 261, 269–70: 'Most professionals feel they have an obligation to offer referrals for services to which they are morally opposed' (she refers to survey evidence).

[86] I Kennedy and A Grubb, *Medical Law*, 3rd edn (London: Butterworths, 2000) 1446, interpreting the provisions of general practitioners' Terms of Service under the NHS (General Medical Services) Regulations 1992 (SI 1992, No 635, Sch2, para 12. Further, in *Barr v Matthews* (1999) 52 BMLR 217, Alliot J suggested that duty of referral may be legal as well as ethical, at 227: 'once a termination of pregnancy is recognised as an option, the doctor invoking the conscientious objection clause should refer the patient to a colleague at once'.

[87] For scholars arguing that it does, see, eg: A Stone 'Consti-tortion: Tort Law as an End-run around Abortion Rights after *Planned Parenthood v Casey*' (2000) *American University Journal of Gender, Social Policy and the Law* 471; A Silverman 'Constitutional Law — Pennsylvania's Wrongful Birth Statute's Impact On Abortion Rights: State Action And Undue Burden — *Edmonds v Western Pennsylvania*' (1993) *Temple Law Rev* 1087; J Gantz 'State Statutory Preclusion of Wrongful Birth Relief: a Troubling Re-Writing of A Woman's Right to Choose and the Doctor-Patient Relationship' (1997) *Virginia J of Social Policy and the Law* 795; Kowitz, above n 81, 89; Gold, above n 60. For scholars arguing that it does not, see Bopp *et al*, above n 53; M Pellegrino 'The Protection Of Prenatal Life: Tort Claims Of Wrongful Birth Or Wrongful Life And Equal Protection Under Pennsylvania's Constitution' (1999) *Temple Law Review* 715; K Wilcoxon 'Statutory Remedies For Judicial Torts: The Need for Wrongful Birth Legislation' (Spring 2001) *U of Cincinnati Law Rev* 1023.

that a state regulation is an undue burden on the abortion right if 'it has the purpose or effect of placing a substantial obstacle in the path of a woman seeking abortion of a nonviable fetus'. Indeed, where state courts have upheld anti-wrongful birth statutes, this has been on one or both of two grounds: that the ban on wrongful birth actions does not directly affect the right to abort and/or that the effect of the statute does not constitute state action.[88] Since it is difficult to show that banning wrongful birth (and life) actions has an 'effect' on abortion rights under *Casey*, however, it has been argued that use should be made of *Casey's* alternative 'purpose' analysis to show that such statutes are unconstitutional under the FourteenthAmendment. This was not a type of analysis conducted in *Casey* itself. In this way, the legislative history of such bans could be shown to have the *purpose* of substantially obstructing a woman's right to an abortion.[89]

The arguments either way are complex and cannot be explored here. What can be said, however, is that to the extent that the abortion decision is one of great import, the autonomy the right protects would be both enhanced and protected by providing a woman with information about the condition of the developing fetus. Sometimes this has not occurred, as in *Robak v US*, in which Swygert J observed[90]:

> In *Roe v Wade*, the Court held that it was the mother's constitutional right to decide during the first trimester of pregnancy whether to obtain an abortion. The staff at the OB-GYN clinic at Fort Rucker deprived Mrs. Robak of the opportunity to make an informed decision when they failed to tell her of her rubella and of the potential consequences on her fetus.

(Although this was indeed the net effect of their failure, as we have seen the positive duty to provide information relevant to the abortion decision is not in fact to be found within the established abortion jurisprudence.) In essence, giving the right to abort some positive protection in the form of the wrongful birth action enhances the capacity to exercise the abortion right autonomously, since health professionals are not then immunised from liability for failure to impart relevant information. In this light, the statement in one anti-wrongful birth case that, without wrongful birth liability, '[t]he two parties, doctor and patient, are still left free to make whatever decision they feel is appropriate'[91] may, unfortunately, be only partly true in some states. Indeed, to the extent that the lack of wrongful birth liability might well leave a woman uninformed (subject to her awareness of what questions to ask), she will not be truly free in exercising her decision not to abort. In support of the provision of such information and in

---

[88] Gantz, above n 87, 820.
[89] Kowitz, above n 81, adopts this approach.
[90] 658 F2d 471 (1981), 476.
[91] *Hickman v Group Health* 396 NW2d 10, *per* Yetka J, at 14.

opposition to Pennsylvania legislation banning the wrongful birth action, the then Governor Thornburgh (who was described as 'pro-life') observed[92]:

> [T]he Supreme Court… has clearly held that a woman has a constitutional right to an abortion… Under these circumstances, the intelligent exercise of that right should not be made to depend on the competence, diligence, integrity or philosophical views of a particular attending physician.

Whether wrongful birth action bans are constitutional remains unresolved at a higher level as the Supreme Court has so far declined to hear any relevant case.[93]

## C  The Basis of the Wrongful Birth Action

It is helpful now to understand what type of action may be at stake in a given wrongful birth action. There is no discussion in the English case law of the basis of the action, but this issue has been addressed in some of the US cases. Some put forward a standard of care analysis that suggests that the duty to inform is an aspect of a health professional's duty of prenatal care, for instance the US cases of *Reed v Campagnolo*[94] and *Smith v Cote*. Others, such as *Canesi v Wilson*, proceed on the basis of a negligent non-disclosure analysis. In the latter case, Handler J observed that '[t]he physician's duty to warn is thus limited by what risks a reasonably prudent patient in the plaintiff's position would consider material to her decision'.[95] A negligent non-disclosure analysis is traditionally concerned with risks inherent in *treatment* to which the complainant has consented.[96] In the United States this is an action for lack of informed consent, since the failure to inform of certain risks inherent in a given treatment may vitiate consent.[97] English law is different: as we saw earlier, in *Chatterton v Gerson* Bristow J held that to give valid consent the patient must only be broadly informed as to the nature of the treatment or procedure.[98]

The difficulty with applying a negligent non-disclosure analysis in this context has been observed in the cases. For instance, in *Reed v Campagnolo* Rodowsky J

---

[92] Pa Senate Leg J 2674 (17 September 1984) (veto message of Governor Richard Thornburgh dated 3 July 1984), as cited in Kowitz, above n 81, 269.

[93] See *Seipal v Corson* 637 A 2d 289 (Pa 1993), cert denied, 115 SCt 60 (1994); *Edmonds v W Pa Hosp Radiology Assoc* 621 A 2d 580 (Pa 1993), cert denied, 114 SCt 63 (1993); *Wilson v Kuenzi* 751 SW2d 741 (Mo 1988), cert denied, 488 US 893 (1988); *Azzolino v Dingfelder* 337 SE2d 528 (NC, 1985), cert denied, 479 US 835 (1986).

[94] 630 A 2d 1145 (Md, 1993). The case concerned a failure to advise of 'the existence or need for routine… AFP… testing' to detect severe conditions. The child suffered from multiple severe conditions.

[95] Above n 75, 511.

[96] For a discussion of the two possible approaches, see J Seymour, *Childbirth and the Law* (Oxford: OUP, 2000) 321. See also P Ossorio 'Prenatal Genetic Testing and the Courts' in Parens and Asch (eds), above n 20, 308.

[97] *Canterbury v Spence* 464 F2d 772 (DC, 1972).

[98] Above n 1.

observes: 'But one's informed consent must be to some treatment. Here, the defendants never proposed that the tests be done'.[99] And in *Karlsons v Guerinot* Moule J notes[100]:

> Here, the resultant harm did not arise out of any affirmative violation of the mother's physical integrity. Furthermore, the alleged undisclosed risks did not relate to any affirmative treatment but rather to the condition of pregnancy itself. Allegations such as these have traditionally formed the basis of actions in medical malpractice.

(Whether this is always so will vary between jurisdictions.[101])

Indeed, a wrongful birth action in the context of prenatal screening and testing will be concerned with either one or more of the following: whether appropriate screening or testing (or both) was offered[102]; whether the results of these were accurately interpreted[103]; and whether the results were effectively communicated to the woman or couple. If appropriate screening or testing are *not* offered, a woman's consent will not be in issue. If appropriate screening or testing *are* offered, although she must consent for these not to constitute a battery (assuming touching is involved), the woman herself is not being treated. Further, the risks of which she may negligently not be advised are risks pertaining to the *fetus* discovered as a *result* of the testing; they are not risks inherent in the testing.[104] For the purposes of a wrongful birth action, there are therefore some difficulties in

---

[99] Above n 94, 1152. The Reeds alleged that they were not informed of the possibility of amniocentesis and alpha-fetoprotein (AFP) testing.

[100] 394 NYS2d 933 (1977) 939. In this case 'although defendants were informed of her medical history, including the fact that she was 37 years old, had a thyroid condition and had previously given birth to a deformed child, they failed to inform and advise her and her husband of the risks involved in the pregnancy, particularly with regard to the likelihood of giving birth to another deformed child. Defendants also failed to inform her of the existence of an amniocentesis test which, when administered, could detect whether the fetus was in fact deformed' (at 934).

[101] Ossorio, above n 96, 325.

[102] For an English case in which it was found that a 37-year-old woman had not received counselling in relation to the offer of screening for Down's syndrome, see *Enright v Kwun* [2003] EWHC 1000.

[103] For a case concerned with the standard of care in sonography, in this case of the fetus's brain, see *Lillywhite v University College London Hospitals NHS Trust* [2005] EWCA Civ 1466. See also *P v Leeds Teaching Hospitals NHS Trust* [2004] EWHC 1392, which concerned alleged negligence relating to checks on the fetus's bladder.

[104] But note that where the risk of miscarriage inherent in amniocentesis or chorionic villus sampling was not disclosed and a miscarriage ensued, this would give rise to an action in wrongful death, at least in the United States. *Verkennes v Corniea* 38 NW2d 838 (1949) was the first case to permit recovery for the death of the fetus *in utero* under a wrongful death statute. In England, wrongful death actions are not recognised as regards the fetus, although damages have been awarded to a mother for a stillbirth which resulted from negligent treatment: *Bagley v North Herts Health Authority* [1986] NLJ Rep 1014. Damages under the Fatal Accidents Act 1976 were not permitted on the basis that the child had died *in utero* as a result of the negligence.

applying a negligent non-disclosure analysis in this context. Perhaps not surprisingly, then, the English cases appear implicitly to be analysed as regular breaches of the standard of care.

Nevertheless, given that the prenatal screening and testing project is concerned with whether certain screening or testing should be offered and the accurate interpretation and communication of the results of these, *information* — rather than treatment — is the central issue. This is despite the possibility, on rare occasions, of some treatment for the fetus *in utero*. This gives to the prenatal screening and testing context something of a *hybrid* quality, with elements both of information disclosure and regular standard of care. The law of information disclosure, despite its customary concern with risks inherent in treatment, thus comes naturally to mind. A feature of this area of the law is its concern, at least in the United States, Canada and Australia, with patient autonomy.[105] Somewhat infamously, England took a doctor-oriented approach to this issue in the leading case of *Sidaway v Board of Governors of the Bethlem Royal Hospital*,[106] although there may now be signs of a shift towards a more patient-oriented approach.[107] In this light, and importantly, we will see that the question of the appropriate standard of care must ultimately be related to the importance of reproductive autonomy.

Whether a standard of care or a negligent non-disclosure (that is, in the United States, an 'informed consent') analysis is used, either has controlling devices. In

---

[105] In the United States, *Canterbury v Spence*, above n 97; in Canada, *Reibl v Hughes* (1980) 114 DLR (3d) 1; in Australia, *Rogers v Whittaker* (1992) 67 ALJR 47.

[106] Above n 5.

[107] *Pearce v United Bristol Healthcare NHS Trust* [1999] PIQR 53. In this case a woman gave birth to a stillborn baby. Her doctor had advised no induction or caesarean section when her baby was late. Induction carried a risk to the fetus but a caesarean only carried a risk to the mother, who said she would have run that risk had she been properly advised or had a second opinion that there was a risk of stillbirth if she waited. Lord Woolf MR held, at 59: 'if there is a significant risk which would affect the judgment of a reasonable patient, then in the normal course it is the responsibility of a doctor to inform the patient of that significant risk, if the information is needed so that the patient can determine for him or herself as to what course he or she should adopt'. On the one hand Lord Woolf's statement may seem to be moving towards the more patient-centred approaches of the United States, Canada and Australia; on the other, it is not clear that it really goes any further than Lord Bridge's position in *Sidaway*, to which Lord Woolf MR immediately refers after this passage: 'In the *Sidaway* case Lord Bridge recognises that position. He refers to a "significant risk" as being a risk of something in the region of 10 per cent'. In fact, the woman in *Pearce* lost the case. See also *Chester v Afshar* [2004] 4 All ER 587. In this case a neurosurgeon advised the complainant to undergo an elective surgical procedure on her spine; she reluctantly agreed and the procedure was carried out three days later; she subsequently developed *cauda equina* syndrome which was a known small risk of the procedure. The judgment in favour of the complainant involved a modification of the traditional approach to causation. Overall, the value of autonomy is a strong theme in the majority judgments in *Chester*, but *Sidaway* still seems to be the governing authority, albeit with a new emphasis on the more pro-autonomy sections of the judgments in *Sidaway*, for instance in that of Lord Hope.

both jurisdictions a standard of prenatal care analysis will require medical evidence as to the relevant standard, as noted by the court in *Reed v Campagnolo*.[108] In the United States, the standard in a negligent non-disclosure analysis will be determined by the idea of what is material to a reasonable patient.[109] In this context it would mean that a health professional must advise of tests or disclose observations or results of which a reasonably prudent woman in the woman's position would want to be informed.[110]

Further, issues in causation will also limit the scope of a possible action from a woman's or couple's point of view. In the wrongful birth context both a standard of care and a negligent non-disclosure analysis employ the test of causation from the negligent non-disclosure cases — thus, whether she/they would have aborted if she/they had been correctly advised of the fetus's health or condition or the risks in relation to this. In the United States this may be tested by purely objective factors[111] and in England by a combination of subjective and objective ones.[112] In this sense, since the cases turn, in part at least, on what the woman (or couple) would have chosen to do when informed that the fetus would certainly or very likely become a disabled child, autonomy interests are recognised — to some degree at least — in either type of action.[113] As regards US law, this fits with the development of the wrongful birth action in response, partly, to *Roe*. In England, it fits with the option to abort that the Abortion Act grants a woman in the case of a fetus that will certainly or very likely become a seriously disabled child.

## D  The Standard of Care: Traditional Negligence or Negligent Non-disclosure

We now need to consider directly the question of the standard of care in these cases. In fact, it is not only conscience issues that are related to the interests of the

---

[108] Above n 94, 1154.
[109] 'A risk is… material when a person, in what the physician knows or should know to be the patient's position, would be likely to attach significance to the risk or cluster of risks in deciding whether or not to forego the proposed therapy' (*Canterbury v Spence*, above n 97, 787, *per* Robinson J). *Canesi v Wilson*, above n 77, 510, *per* Handler J, emphasis in original: 'The physician's obligation, therefore, does not "compel disclosure of *every* risk… to any [pregnant] patient" but rather only "*material* risks to a *reasonable* patient"' (citing *Largey v Rothman* 110 NJ 204, 213).
[110] See, eg, *Canesi v Wilson*, above n 75.
[111] *Canterbury v Spence*, above n 97.
[112] *Smith v Barking, Havering and Brentwood HA* [1994] 5 Med LR 285. Fears of fraud are often expressed in conjunction with hostility to the wrongful birth action. See, eg, Wilcoxon, above n 87, 1040. For a critique of the requirements of causation in this context and suggestions for reform, see S Ryan 'Wrongful Birth: False Representations of Women's Reproductive Lives' (April 1994) *Minnesota Law Rev* 857, 907.
[113] For an English case ultimately turning on the issue of causation, see *Deriche v Ealing Hospital NHS Trust* [2003] EWHC 3104, in which a woman had contracted chicken pox during pregnancy and there was conflicting evidence about the warnings she had been given about the possible consequences for the fetus.

medical profession. The question of the standard of care also relates partly to these interests.[114] Indeed, we will see that some of the cases reveal a concern with the degree of burden that information practices put upon the profession and with the degree of control it has over these.[115]

For instance, in settling on the reasonably prudent patient standard (hence a negligent non-disclosure analysis), it was noted in the pro-wrongful birth case of *Canesi v Wilson* that[116]:

> These constraints serve to place reasonable bounds on the extent of disclosure required by doctors and, so bounded, the standard comports with basic considerations of fairness and public policy that are relevant in determining the scope of a duty of care and the extent of liability that may be placed on the medical profession.

*Reed v Campagnolo* exhibits similar concerns but with a difference of emphasis. Rejecting the complainant's proposal that the standard should be governed by what a reasonable person in the complainant's position would want to know (and thus rejecting a negligent non-disclosure analysis), the court emphasised that[117]:

> [T]he rule cannot focus exclusively on the plaintiff. A fair rule would have to look at all of the possible tests that might be given and evaluate the reasons for excluding some and perhaps recommending one or more others. That approach requires expert testimony.

Here the concern seems not only, or so much, with burdensomeness for the medical profession, but rather with the idea that the complainants in these cases should not be able to *drive the action*.[118] Concern to protect the doctor becomes a concern with the complainants not being permitted to shape or direct medical practice in this area. The *Reed* court thus directly raises the issue of control over the information that is the focus of prenatal screening and testing.

At this point, we should ask to what extent the standard of medical practice is, or more particularly should be, a *medical* issue. This is an old question in medical law that needs to be considered here in relation to prenatal screening and

---

[114] Although it would also be possible to analyse the cases in terms of the *scope of the duty*, the cases themselves hinge upon a standard of care analysis.

[115] See, eg, *Dansby v Jefferson* 623 A 2d at 820, *per* Wieand J, observing that the statute banning wrongful birth 'reflects a refusal to dictate to the medical profession how to practice in the field of obstetrics'. Attention should be paid to the use of language in this context, which may be offensive to people with disabilities. Adrienne Asch has suggested that we should review the use of the word 'risk', as opposed to 'possibility' or 'likelihood', in relation to the birth of a disabled child. A Asch 'Why I Haven't Changed My Mind about Prenatal Diagnosis: Reflections and Refinements' in Parens and Asch (eds), above n 20, 234, 252. In the discussion of negligence issues which follows I try to avoid the use of the word 'risk' where possible. Sometimes, however, in making use of negligence cases from other areas, this would be artificial and unnecessary.

[116] Above n 75, 511, *per* Handler J.

[117] Above n 94, 1154, *per* Rodowsky J. But note that there is a lack of medical consensus on the issue of which tests should be offered (Seymour, above, n 96, 317).

[118] This is also noted by Seymour, *ibid* 268.

diagnosis. The *Reed* court suggests that medical evidence is relevant to this issue. Similarly, in *Smith v Cote* the court observes that the standard of care will be determined by the 'standards and recommended practices and procedures of the medical profession, the training, experience and professed degree of skill of the average medical practitioner, and all other relevant circumstances'.[119] The latter are not elaborated upon. It is interesting to recall here, given their emphasis upon medical evidence in defining the standard of care, that *Reed* and *Smith* were important cases in developing the wrongful birth action in response to *Roe*. The real question, however, is whether medical evidence should be not just relevant but *determinative*. This depends on the importance we attach to a woman's (or couple's) autonomy in this context. As screening becomes more sophisticated and at the same time perhaps cheaper (for instance by means of DNA chip technology)[120] and as at least some portions of the community become more aware of the possibilities,[121] so this issue will become more pressing.

To begin to address this issue, the current method of determining the standard of care in medical practice should be noted. In the United States the standard is essentially determined by medical practice.[122] In England the doctor-oriented standard enshrined in *Bolam v Fiern Hospital Management Committee*[123] lost some ground in *Bolitho v City of Hackney HA*.[124] This meant that medical decisions must not only be responsible according to a body of medical opinion,[125] but must also be mindful of comparative risks and benefits and have some 'logical basis'. This, a distinctly narrow criterion, is not a very promising tool to review practices in the highly value-laden and moral area of prenatal screening and testing. Given the impact that the Abortion Act will have on the shape of medical practice in this area it would clearly be 'illogical', say, for a health professional not to advise a woman of test results indicating that the fetus has a serious disability (and surely, in any event, also irresponsible according to *Bolam*) but this leaves a great deal of uncertainty. Which screening or testing should be offered? And to whom should these offers be made?

---

[119] Above n 72, 346, *per* Batchelder J.
[120] See, eg, J Botkin 'Line Drawing: Developing Professional Standards for Prenatal Diagnostic Services' in Parens and Asch (eds), above n 20, 288, 295, for a description of this technology.
[121] Seymour, above n 96, 106, 324, notes the possibility of potential liability becoming a product of what is technologically possible. On the question of consumer pressures, see also Williams *et al*, above n 11, 748.
[122] See, eg, *Bardessono v Michels* 3 Cal 3d 780 (1970).
[123] [1957] 2 All ER 118.
[124] [1997] 4 All ER 771.
[125] Above n 123, 587, *per* McNair J in *Bolam*: a doctor 'is not guilty of negligence if he has acted in accordance with a practice accepted as proper by a responsible body of medical men skilled in that particular art'.

### i  The risk of a given fetal condition

Turning first to the question of to whom screening and/or testing should be offered, an assessment of the risk of a given condition is likely to be relevant to this issue. For instance, since more than 90 per cent of neural tube defects develop in pregnancies where there is no known risk, population-based screening has been adopted for some time.[126] For other conditions such as those caused by chromosomal abnormalities, a woman's age is the most significant risk factor. For this reason, traditionally a woman in her early twenties would not be routinely offered an amniocentesis actually to diagnose the presence or absence of a condition such as Down's syndrome, since medical practice in the United States was to offer such invasive testing routinely only to women over 35.[127] The rationale for this partly related to an increase in the likelihood of bearing such a child at this age and partly to the fact that the risk of miscarriage inherent in amniocentesis would then be less than a woman's age-related risk of the fetus having a chromosomal abnormality. Describing this policy, for instance, Jeffrey Botkin notes[128]:

> Before age thirty-five, the risk of bearing a child with a chromosome abnormality is 3.6 per 1,000 (1 in 278 births). At age thirty-five, the incidence increases to 4.9 per 1,000 (1 in 204 births). Part of the justification for this particular cut-off was the perception that the risk of bearing a child with a chromosome abnormality at age thirty-five exceeds the risk of losing the pregnancy through complications of the procedure (approximately 1 in 200). Of note, this policy was not based on any empirical data that couples considered the risk at thirty-five to be sufficiently greater to justify screening.

(I discuss more recent developments and policy initiatives in relation to detection of chromosomal abnormalities below.) Statistical evidence thus supported the standard of care, so that the practice was that a woman in her early twenties, say, would not be routinely offered diagnostic testing. Regarding much less common conditions, it has always been the case that in the absence of a family history of a condition there will be no indication to screen or test for it.[129] On a standard of care approach to these cases tort seems to focus on the defendant — the relevant health professional — and considers what risks he/she should reasonably be concerned to warn about (by offering screening or testing). In making this assessment health professionals would be influenced partly by the risk of a given

---

[126] Press, above n 20, 218. Sometimes there is the possibility of some treatment shortly after birth, the need for which can be indicated by screening.

[127] Botkin, above n 120, 296.

[128] *Ibid* (footnote omitted).

[129] *Ibid* 294. The duty to look into family history will, however, be limited. Thus, a wrongful birth action failed regarding the birth of a child with Tay-Sachs in *Munro v Regents of University of California* 263 Cal Rptr 878 (Cal App 2 Dist 1989). There, the doctor's practice was to advise testing only if one of the parents was of known Ashkenazic origin. In fact the great-grandparents had been part of a community which had a slightly increased prevalence of the disease.

condition and partly by how significant they consider it to be.[130] The alternative is for tort also to focus, at least in part, on the autonomy interests of prospective parents that are at stake (akin to, if not in exactly the same way as, the law relating to negligent non-disclosure).

One way this could occur — in either jurisdiction — would be to think about paying less attention to the risk of certain conditions and to offer at least certain sorts of screening or testing to *all* women. Indeed, as noted earlier in the chapter, NICE recommended that this should be so in England, at least in relation to serum screening for Down's syndrome (discussed further below, along with more recent US developments).[131] However, unless such a decision has been made for policy reasons of some kind, to decide that Down's syndrome (or other) screening and testing should be offered more widely probably requires some assessment as to the possible uptake. From the law of negligent non-disclosure that keeps insisting on a front-row seat in this context, the criterion of materiality would seem to be a useful tool. *Canterbury v Spence* held that[132]:

> A risk is... material when a person, in what the physician knows or should know to be the patient's position, would be likely to attach significance to the risk or cluster of risks in deciding whether or not to forego the proposed therapy... The factors contributing significance to the dangerousness of a medical technique are, of course, the *incidence of injury* and the *degree of the harm* threatened.

So, when we turn to think about a more reproductive autonomy-focused approach, we again find the twin factors of the degree of risk on the one hand and of harm on the other. In other words, these are key factors not just in a regular standard of care but also on a negligent non-disclosure analysis. This can be brought out by reflecting more closely on the example of screening for Down's syndrome.

Thinking about the 'degree of harm', what would the 'reasonable' pregnant woman in her early twenties, say, think was significant in the sense of serious or meaningful? This is an issue addressed principally in the next section. For now, she may or may not be concerned about the possibility of a child with Down's syndrome. This will depend on how she perceives the birth of such a child, a perception that may be either more or less informed. Arguably, Down's syndrome can sometimes be a significant impairment and is at least a condition the potential implications of which parents may wish to reflect on.[133] Indeed, what many of the

---

[130] 'Nevertheless, current professional standards have established a risk of approximately 1 in 200 for chromosome abnormalities as sufficiently high to justify routinely offering a relatively expensive and invasive diagnostic procedure' (*ibid*). On risk in general as a factor within the standard of care, see, eg, *Bolton v Stone* [1951] AC 850.
[131] NICE, above n 13.
[132] Above n 97, 787–8, *per* Robinson J (my emphasis).
[133] The Down's Syndrome Association, in 'Your Baby has Down's Syndrome: a Guide for Parents', provides a mixture of information, some of the flavour of which is given by the following: 'Children with Down's syndrome can and do grow up to live long and

wrongful birth cases show is that couples typically do want a choice about whether to have a child with Down's syndrome (though this may have been affected by the information provided as to what raising such a child may entail, an issue I touched on in Chapter 1).

Whatever she thinks of the seriousness of Down's syndrome, what will probably be relevant to whether the 'reasonable' woman in her early twenties takes up an offer, say, of preliminary screening is how great she thinks her risk of having a child with Down's syndrome is. If she is informed that, at the age of 21, this is approximately 1 in 1500,[134] she may decline to have a preliminary blood test or nuchal translucency scan. Alternatively, she may accept the offer of initial screening but stop there in the absence of a risk result that could prompt her towards invasive diagnostic testing.

This seems to show that the *risk* of a condition on the one hand and its *significance* on the other are unlikely to be fully disconnected in the mind of the 'reasonable' parent. In effect, in our concern to concentrate more on the autonomy of the 'reasonable' parent, we find that the question of the significance that may attach to the fetal condition cannot do all the work: the question of the chance of it occurring may also play a role.[135] In turn, this supports *Canterbury's* formulation of materiality for the 'reasonable patient' as hinging on the twin factors of the risk and significance of the harm. Strikingly, we might also note that it supports the Abortion Act's criteria of 'substantial risk' of 'serious handicap', though of course the key question in relation to the Act, explored in the previous chapter, is whether doctors can legally take parents' interests and views into account in deciding that these criteria, particularly the latter, have been fulfilled.

As I have noted, then, at least in the United States, these two elements of the degree of risk and of harm are central both to a negligent non-disclosure and to a

---

fulfilled lives. Provided they are allowed the opportunities they need to develop self-help skills and independence, people with Down's syndrome can thrive well into their fifties and beyond, facing many of the challenges we all encounter: school, further education, work and a home of one's own. Many children with Down's syndrome are now being integrated successfully into mainstream schools' (at 11). 'People with Down's syndrome all have a certain degree of learning disability (mental handicap). The degree of disability varies from person to person and it is impossible to tell at birth what that degree will be' (at 4). 'About one in three children born with Down's syndrome has a heart defect. Some heart defects are quite minor, such as murmurs; some defects are severe, requiring medication and/or surgery' (at 8). One of various possible heart conditions is an atrioventricular (septal) defect which 'can be corrected by major heart surgery in infancy, but for a few babies the operation is not medically advisable' (at 18).

[134] NHS, 'Looking for Down's Syndrome and Spina Bifida in Pregnancy' <http://www.midirs.org/nelh/nelh.nsf/TOPICVIEW?OpenForm&id=0CF97F7937C651B980256B9100504576>. This document also observes: 'Nearly every pregnant woman is offered screening tests for Down's syndrome… as part of her antenatal care'.

[135] Of course, the risk of miscarriage in diagnostic tests is also at stake here, particularly when the chances of a given fetal condition are low.

regular standard of care analysis. However, there is an important difference between them, concerning who is at the centre of the assessment in either case. If a regular standard of care approach is used to determine the extent of the duty in the prenatal screening and testing context, the health professional decides whether to offer screening or testing based on the profession's assessment of the degree of risk and the significance of the disability or disorder that a child would have, although a sense of possible parental concerns will probably inform, particularly, the latter assessment. By contrast, if a negligent non-disclosure analysis is used, the health professional decides whether to offer screening or testing based explicitly on his/her perception of what would be material to a 'reasonable' parent. In practice, this may or may not lead to significant differences, particularly since many health professionals (perhaps most) will also be parents. But the difference is still worth noting.

Generally, the above analysis suggests that when the risk of a given fetal condition is very low, it is hard to see why screening or testing should be routinely offered in the absence of a particular policy initiative. Further, this appears the case either in terms of a regular standard of care or a negligent non-disclosure analysis that hinges on the concerns of the 'reasonable parent'. In both cases the degree of risk and the seriousness of the condition will be relevant. At stake in this analysis may also be the idea that the costs of offering such tests can legitimately be taken into account on either approach.[136] Thus, in England, the fact that prenatal screening and testing predominantly occurs within a publicly funded and highly pressured healthcare system will be an important factor, except where the government has decided to adopt a specific policy, as it has in relation to Down's syndrome screening. In the United States, access to tests may depend on health insurance, the terms of which may themselves be mindful of risk assessments, effectively giving coverage for diagnostic testing to the over-35-year-old, but not to the 21-year-old.[137] In this case the capacity to protect reproductive choice, at least as regards certain kinds of serious fetal disability, will turn on a woman's ability to pay for such tests and thereafter, potentially, for an abortion.

When testing becomes both more accurate and safer, however, this issue will need further reflection. The question of how extensively screening and/or testing should be offered when the chances of a given fetal condition are low may well take on a new complexion when developments in prenatal testing (such as DNA

---

[136] The standard of care in negligence may, of course, typically take the cost of prevention into account: *Latimer v AEC* [1953] AC 643. Likewise, a negligent non-disclosure analysis hinges on the idea that not all information can be offered.

[137] M Malinowski 'Coming into Being: Law, Ethics and the Practice of Prenatal Genetic Screening' (1994) 45 *Hastings L J* 1435, fn 220; C Powell 'The Current State of Prenatal Genetic Testing in the United States' in Parens and Asch (eds), above n 20, 44, 49. For a discussion of the criteria on the basis of which US health medical organisations might offer currently available and future tests, see Wertz, above n 85, 272–8. Wertz does not include the criterion of seriousness, which she suggests that only parents can judge (*ibid* 275).

chip technology) mean that testing, all at once, for a huge range of sometimes rare conditions is inexpensive and safe. (But note that the predictive value of such tests is likely to vary.[138]) Although the importance of the risk of a certain condition may be marginalised with such developments, it seems likely that the question of its *seriousness* will continue to have some impact, since the question of the 'degree of harm' is significant either in a negligent non-disclosure or a standard of care analysis. For instance, in deciding what information to disclose to prospective parents as the result of a range of tests, in England health professionals will inevitably be mindful of the scope of the Abortion Act and its requirement of a 'serious handicap'. Recall also the power of the causation requirements to limit the success of any wrongful birth actions for trivial or minor features. The implication of this latter point would be that, if information about relatively trivial concerns was not passed onto parents, they would not be able to say they were deprived of the opportunity to abort and so could not found a wrongful birth claim. I discuss this further in the next section.

Before I turn to focus on the significance or seriousness of any given condition in a child, it should be noted that, over time, invasive diagnostic testing for chromosomal abnormalities has become less dependent on age as a risk factor. This is because there have been significant improvements in screening: these modify a woman's *age*-related risk and instead determine her *actual* risk. Screening therefore results in a more accurate assessment of the probability of chromosomal abnormalities in any given pregnancy. Such screening occurs either by means of increasingly accurate blood tests, or through the refinement of ultrasound techniques (such as scans to assess nuchal translucency and other markers) or both.[139] To some extent these developments respond to the idea that the possibility of a child with a chromosomal abnormality such as Down's syndrome may be one that a woman or couple would want to reflect on during pregnancy and so give importance to the possible significance that a woman or couple may attach to the condition.

The result is that reproductive autonomy now receives greater protection: on the one hand younger women, who may not previously have been offered screening and may have been very surprised by the birth of a child with a chromosomal abnormality, will also be offered screening that assesses their actual, rather than low age-related, risk; on the other, older women who may nevertheless attach significance to a chromosomal abnormality can more easily decide *not* to risk an invasive test where their high age-related risk has subsequently been reduced by screening. This is highly beneficial not only for pregnant women but also for the fetuses they are carrying, approximately one in 100 of which would otherwise miscarry due to amniocentesis. The risk with

---

[138] Botkin, above n 120, 295, 297.
[139] See NICE, above n 13, for a review of the options.

chorionic villus sampling (CVS), which has the advantage of being able to be performed earlier in pregnancy, is approximately the same.[140]

These developments have been instantiated in specific policy changes or recommendations in both England and the United States. In England, for instance (as noted early on in this chapter), current UK guidelines, issued by NICE in 2003, recommend that all pregnant women should be offered either nuchal translucency screening or serum screening for Down's syndrome (or some combination thereof).[141] If a woman is found to be at high risk of carrying a fetus with Down's syndrome, she is then offered either amniocentesis or CVS, depending on the stage of her pregnancy. This kind of policy has only just been recommended in the United States. In January 2007 the American College of Obstetricians and Gynecologists (ACOG) issued a Practice Bulletin developed jointly by the ACOG and the Society for Maternal-Fetal Medicine.[142] Until now, as discussed above, a maternal age of 35 has been used to determine who should routinely be offered screening as opposed to who should be offered invasive diagnostic testing, so that invasive tests such as amniocentesis or CVS were only routinely offered to women older than 35. The new guidelines recommend that all pregnant women should be offered screening for Down's syndrome (by a combination of nuchal translucency scanning and blood testing) during the first trimester, regardless of their age. If a woman is found to be at high risk for Down's syndrome she should then be offered either CVS or amniocentesis. So, the same policy is now in place in both jurisdictions.

Is such a policy eugenic? I raised this question at the end of Chapter 1. There I suggested that prenatal screening and testing today are meant, at least, to be a matter of facilitating individual choice. To the extent that policy recommendations by bodies such as NICE or professional bodies such as the ACOG serve the purpose of facilitating individual choice, such policies do not have the negative connotations of state-led eugenic programmes of the last century. What is crucial, however, is that women are well informed about a condition that is the subject of screening and testing, such as Down's syndrome, and do not feel pressured to accept screening in the first instance. This goes back to the issue of voluntariness and its relationship to the validity of consent raised at the start of this chapter. A further point to note in connection with facilitating autonomy concerns the reason why such policies have been adopted. Apart from the desire to protect

---

[140] HGC, above n 2, para 3.15. On the development of new tests that would avoid this risk, see J Buxton 'Non-invasive Pregnancy Test Shows Promise' 6 February 2007, 394 *Bionews* <http://www.bionews.org.uk/new.lasso?storyid=3340> accessed 10 October 2007.
[141] NICE, above n 13.
[142] ACOG, Press Release 2 January 2007 'New Recommendations for Down's Syndrome Call for Screening of All Pregnant Women' <http://www.acog.org/from_home/publications/press_releases/nr01-02-07-1.cfm> accessed 10 October 2007. Practice Bulletin No 77 'Screening for Fetal Chromosomal Abnormalities' is published in the January 2007 issue of *Obstetrics and Gynecology*.

women and fetuses from the risks of invasive testing, as indicated above the drive to improve such screening practices by more accurately determining the risk of a woman bearing a child with a chromosomal abnormality must also have been related to the thought that chromosomal abnormalities could well be thought 'significant' by a woman or couple.

At this stage, we need to shift attention to this issue of significance. Indeed, since the latter part of this discussion has tended to concentrate on the *risk* of a condition in order to explore the place and role of medical opinion and its relationship to reproductive autonomy interests in shaping the standard of care, it has only partially addressed the significance of a given condition to a woman or couple. A discussion of the parents' perception of the *seriousness* of the actual condition that the child might have is now required. The following discussion explores this with reference to the value of reproductive autonomy.

## V THE RELATIONSHIP BETWEEN THE SERIOUSNESS OF A FETAL CONDITION AND THE REASONS FOR EXERCISING REPRODUCTIVE AUTONOMY

### A   Reasons: A Moral Framework

The significance of reproductive autonomy in this context and the place and weight of parental views were first discussed in Chapter 1. Broadly speaking, I accepted the value of reproductive autonomy. In any event, we saw that the difficult questions always concern its limits. In this context what is really at stake is how extensive we think autonomy should be and in what ways, if any, it might be both protected and limited. Morally speaking, given that parents can choose whether to reproduce, arguably they should also be able to choose to avoid reproduction under certain conditions, because of what caring for a severely disabled child may entail. It is important, however, that in making any choice they are appropriately informed.

As we first saw in Chapter 1, screening, testing and abortion can, in effect, be undertaken for either of two principal reasons. First, where a child's quality of life could be one of extremely low (or 'sub-zero') quality, as appears likely in the case of the progression of a condition such as Tay-Sachs, selection can fairly be said to be undertaken because of what that life would be like for the resulting child (though here the parents' interests will also be implicated). Second, where a child would actually have a reasonable quality of life but its condition may still have the ability negatively to impact on its parents, selection will really be undertaken because of their interests in being able to make some choices about the kind of child who will be born. Screening for Down's syndrome and cystic fibrosis (in some cases) may put particular weight on the parents' interests rather than those of the child. Even if it would have not have been against the child's interests to be born (that is, it would *not* have had a 'wrongful life'), to terminate a pregnancy affected by either condition may be justifiable — particularly that much earlier in pregnancy — because parental interests will likely be seriously invoked. This will be the case for a large range of conditions for which we currently routinely screen but regarding which it would be disingenuous to say that there is a risk that the child would have a life she did not think worth living. In such cases, if parents have an interest in choosing whether to accept or avoid certain experiences that the birth of a given child might entail, parental and fetal interests become opposed to one another since, on the gradualist approach to the fetus's moral status that I endorsed in Chapter 1, the fetus will have a growing moral claim to life.

As argued in Chapter 1, in this event, even if the fetus is arguably not a moral person, unless we hold that it has no moral value there should be some moral justification for aborting it. This means that reasons should be offered to justify fetal demise. This can only plausibly occur when the reasons are of a good, that is, serious, nature. Arguably, the question of the moral justification for aborting in such cases should be related to the seriousness of the condition that the future child might have. (The very difficult issue of determining the seriousness of a child's condition in any given case is revisited below.) This is because serious conditions have the potential significantly to affect parents' lives and hence seriously invoke their reproductive interests. In this way, our perception of the appropriate extent of reproductive autonomy in this context might be related to the severity of the child's condition and the impact of that condition on the parents. Thus, a concern about a relatively trivial feature of the fetus's condition may be hard to construe as seriously implicating the parents' interests in reproduction. On a gradualist view of the fetus's moral status, which is committed to according some moral value to the fetus despite its lack of moral personhood and rights (and can acknowledge the significance of the development of fetal interests), the pressure for reasons for termination to be serious will grow with the fetus. I explored the legal implications of this particularly in Chapter 2.

This line of argument, originally developed in earlier work of mine, has been criticised by Nicolette Priaulx, who implies that the idea that serious disabilities in a child may seriously affect parents is circular.[143] The point is misplaced, because it is in fact a matter of correlation, as others have implicitly noted.[144] Further, nothing in this line of argument or in my earlier expression of it suggests that the choice to avoid a particular disabled child is a choice of a completely

---

[143] N Priaulx, *The Harm Paradox: Tort Law and the Unwanted Child in an Era of Choice* (London: UCL Press, 2007) 67. (Priaulx refers to my 'Prenatal Screening, Autonomy and Reasons: the Relationship between the Law of Abortion and Wrongful Birth' (2003) 11 *Medical Law Review* 265.)

[144] As J Botkin observes, in 'Fetal Privacy and Confidentiality' (1995) 25(5) *Hastings Center Report*, 32, 37: 'the more severe the condition is for the child, generally the greater the harm will be to the parents'. Botkin suggests that the impact of certain conditions on family life can be described in terms of four characteristics: 'First, there is the likely severity of the condition with respect to health. Second is the age of onset of the condition, and third is the probability that the child's genotype will manifest as a significant clinical disease. Fourth is the probability that the condition will occur in those without specific risk factors'.

different kind from the choice to avoid the birth of any child, as discussed in Chapter 1 and contrary to a puzzling assumption by Priaulx.[145] Priaulx is also critical of the suggestion that the exercise of reproductive autonomy in relation to a fetus might best be justified with reference to the reasons for its exercise. It is legitimate to criticise the reference to reasons provided that one fully acknowledges the implications of this, which must be that the fetus has no moral claims of any kind. In relation to a gradualist account and reasons, Priaulx asks[146]:

> [M]ight not the exercise of reproductive autonomy itself, by a woman already invested with full moral personhood and legal rights, constitute a 'serious reason' for trumping the claim of a foetus who is, 'arguably not a [full] moral person'. Why then, morally speaking, should we be concerned about the presence of a serious fetal condition?

This is an interesting point, because it highlights that a woman is a moral and legal person but a fetus is not. Indeed, in Chapter 1, I suggested that it was problematic to ascribe rights to the fetus, because of the difficulties that may be created by the presence of an additional right-holder within the woman's body. However, Priaulx's criticism misunderstands the gradualist approach to the moral status of the fetus, as developed by scholars such as Joel Feinberg, because she does not appear to appreciate, at least in what is expressed here, that the approach focuses on the reasons for treating the fetus in a detrimental way and whether these are commensurate with the fetus's growing moral claims. The gradualist approach is not concerned with whether the fetus is a person, or whether the woman is one, and in this way helpfully sidesteps the ultimately question-begging nature of the rights-based arguments that accompany discussions of personhood and often dominate debate about the maternal-fetal relationship. Indeed, a gradualist approach effectively focuses on imperfect moral obligations, those that are not correlated with rights. At the same time, as explored in Chapter 1, a gradualist approach is compatible with aspects of other approaches to the maternal-fetal relationship. In particular, we can still acknowledge, as I have above, the difficulties that would be created if the fetus, which resides in the woman's body, also has rights. Finally, in relation to Priaulx's criticisms, and foreshadowing an important part of the discussion to follow, although a gradualist approach to fetal moral status implies that the more advanced the fetus is the greater should be the justification for terminating its life, I do not suggest that we can (or should attempt) *in practice* to judge seriousness, particularly in relation to the mid-spectrum disability whose seriousness will inevitably be the subject of reasonable

---

[145] Priaulx, above n 143, 66. On the choice to avoid the birth of a disabled child as one instance of the choice to avoid reproduction, see my discussion in Ch 1, S II and further argument in S V(C)iii of that chapter.

[146] Priaulx, above n 143, 66–7.

disagreement.[147] In such cases, as I discuss below, arguably we should defer to prospective parents' interests and views. Priaulx has missed this highly important point.

## B Reasons: The Law

Against this reminder of one view of the moral balance of the parental and fetal interests at stake, I turn to explore the link between reproductive autonomy, reasons and their weight within the law. In the discussion that follows, exploring the issue of the seriousness of a given fetal impairment helps explain the extent to which reproductive autonomy is valuable and hence worthy of protection in this context.

### i  Reasons in abortion law

Regarding abortion law in general, we have seen that English law opted for a medically operated system of justificatory grounds (reasons) on the basis of which abortion is legal. By contrast, US abortion law decided that autonomy prevails, but that it is the ultimate right, not the process of decision-making, that it is most important to protect. This is evidenced by the increased attention the state now permits the potential life of the fetus to be given following *Casey*, such that states can take steps to ensure that a woman's decision to abort is thoughtful and informed as to its moral significance. The negative liberty inherent in the abortion right is severely limited, however, when the state's interest in the fetus becomes compelling following viability, potentially much more so than in England. Those states that allow terminations after this time on the basis of fetal disability face definitional issues, akin to those at stake in the interpretation of the English Abortion Act, about seriousness.[148] In England, then, reasons for abortion matter *restrictively* throughout pregnancy and in the United States after viability. Put another way, theoretically at least (however liberally aspects of English law are in fact interpreted), in England fetal interests might be said to be *asserted against* a woman's interests in a potentially restrictive sense throughout pregnancy and simply *acknowledged* in US law until viability, following which they are asserted in a restrictive way.

Moving now to abortion in the context of prenatal screening and diagnosis (PND) the question is whether and, if so, how the importance of reasons is accounted for in either jurisdiction. We have seen that the terms of the English Abortion Act will affect the standard of care as regards the offer of screening and testing and that, as regards disability in the possible child, a serious one is required. In this sense, English abortion law might itself be said to entail, in some way, the

---

[147]  I first highlighted the difficulty with the practical application of a gradualist account in Scott, above n 10: see the last section of Ch 1 and discussion in Ch 2 in that work. However, this difficulty does not mean that the account is of no value, as discussed further there.
[148]  For discussion of this issue, see Stoller, above n 63, 136–7.

provision of information to the effect that the fetus is at substantial risk of becoming a child with a serious disability. Otherwise a woman will not be able to choose whether or not to continue with such a pregnancy and so to avail herself of the degree of reproductive autonomy (the option to abort if certain conditions are fulfilled) that English abortion law allows. Further, the corresponding wrongful birth duty is unlikely to support the lost opportunity to abort for reasons relating to a condition that doctors do not think serious, unless section 1(1)(a) could have been invoked on the woman's behalf. To succeed, however, a wrongful birth action would have to establish that, in relation to a condition that the doctors did not think satisfied the criteria of section 1(1)(d), a woman who had been very distressed by the prospect of the birth of a given child was negligently not informed of the possibility that doctors might legally grant an abortion on the basis of section 1(1)(a) (on the basis that the risks to her mental or physical health of going to term were greater than in termination). Further, the action would have to show that a risk to her health had indeed materialised. Moreover, if her mental health were at stake, she would have to show that she had thereby suffered a clinically recognised condition, as required by the law on psychiatric injury.[149] That is, either in relation to mental or physical health, she would have to show legally recognised 'damage' for the purposes of the law of negligence.

The fact that the Abortion Act requires a serious disability within the terms of section 1(1)(d) perhaps explains why the English wrongful birth cases have not been troubled by questions about seriousness versus triviality in relation to degrees of fetal anomaly for which a woman might have aborted. As noted in the previous chapter, although there has sometimes been doubt as to whether the condition of seriousness of disability is itself fulfilled, there has been no doubt that this is what is required. This is not true of the US cases, as we shall now see. Indeed, given the necessarily open nature of the *right* to abort recognised in *Roe*, the question of the possible *reasons* for an abortion — and so the seriousness of impairment in a future child — have been very important to judges in deciding wrongful birth cases.

*ii Reasons in wrongful birth case law*

When we turn again to the United States, perhaps somewhat surprisingly given the rights-based nature of abortion, we find that the US law of wrongful birth might well also require serious reasons if the lost chance to abort is to be actionable. Indeed, as part of the concern with determining the reasonableness of the potentially negligent health professional's conduct, there is also a concern with the *seriousness* of the disability in issue. Strikingly, in *Smith v Cote* the court observes that the relevant 'standard does not require a physician to identify and disclose every chance, no matter how remote, of the occurrence of *every possible*

---

[149] See, eg, *Alcock v Chief Constable of South Yorkshire Police* [1991] 2 All ER 907.

birth "defect", no matter how insignificant'.[150] In other words, both the degree of risk and the seriousness of the condition are critical in establishing the standard of care. We also find a concern with this issue in the anti-wrongful birth case of *Azzolino v Dingfelder*, in which the court looked askance towards those jurisdictions which did recognise the action, asking[151]:

> When will parents in those jurisdictions be allowed to decide that their child is so 'defective' that given a chance they would have aborted it while still a fetus and, as a result, then be allowed to hold their physician civilly liable? When a fetus is only the carrier of a deleterious [sic] gene and not itself impaired? When the fetus is of one sex rather than the other? Should such issues be left exclusively to the parents with doctors being found liable for breaching their duty to inform parents of any fetal conditions to which they know or should know the parents may object? When considering such questions it must constantly be borne in mind that pregnant women have been recognized as having an absolute constitutional right, at least until a certain point in their pregnancy, to have an abortion performed for any reason at all or for no reason... *Roe v Wade*...

The fear that parents might force the disclosure of information of doubtful significance, on the basis of which they might then abort, drives this court to reject outright the wrongful birth action. But the court assumes, wrongly as we have seen, that the parameters of abortion law will govern what parents are told in this context if a wrongful birth action is permitted. Indeed, earlier we saw that *Canesi* explicitly notes that the two areas of law are not coextensive. In essence, the extracts from *Azzolino* demonstrate a concern with the seriousness of the reasons on the basis of which an abortion might have been sought.[152] In a parallel fashion, in *Arche v US Department of Army* the court makes clear that in recognising a cause of action for wrongful birth 'we assume that the child is

---

[150] Above n 72, 347, my emphasis.
[151] 337 SE 2d 528 (NC, 1985) 535, *per* Mitchell J. The case concerned a failure to advise of the possibility of amniocentesis. For rejection of the wrongful birth claim, see also *Atlanta Obstetrics and Gynecology Group v Abelson* 398 SE 2d 557 (Ga, 1990) and *Grubbs v Barbourville Family Health Center* 120 SW 3d 682 (Ky, 2003). See also D Heyd, *Genethics: Moral Issues in the Creation of People* (Berkeley: University of California Press, 1992) 34, for relevant discussion of wrongful life suits.
[152] See also Bopp *et al*, above n 53, 505: 'Recognition of wrongful birth is a "slippery slope" which will... encourage and increasingly lead to abortion for lesser reasons...'. These scholars also suggest that to avoid liability doctors will recommend abortions and that this interferes with a pregnant woman's choice (*ibid* 483). To conform to the standard of care, however, only requires that the parents be informed to the degree that the standard supports. The decision is then the parents'. The idea that wrongful birth liability itself skews parental choice (*ibid* 486–7) is thus far-fetched. It was noted earlier, however, that the very existence of screening technologies will likely affect choices during pregnancy.

severely and permanently handicapped'.[153] Further, *Smith v Cote* defines a wrongful birth action as 'a claim brought by the parents of a child born with *severe* defects'.[154]

Despite taking different legal paths — either for or against liability — these cases demonstrate a concern at the prospect of the wrongful birth action being used for the lost opportunity to abort for insignificant or trivial concerns. The implication is that the public policy that supported the development of the wrongful birth action in cases such as *Berman v Allan* — partly in response to *Roe* — cannot go as far as to allow legal actions concerned with less serious or trivial features. Indeed, we saw that *Berman* itself speaks of giving a woman the opportunity 'meaningfully' to exercise the abortion right.

In the United States, then, whilst a woman has the *right* to abort for a trivial fetal anomaly, there is a question as to whether she will learn about it. The means by which the standard of care in negligence traditionally has regard not only to the probability of the harm (as discussed earlier in relation to the incidence of a given condition) but also to its seriousness[155] would suggest that the standard will not require 'warnings' of such conditions or characteristics. Indeed, even on the strongest autonomy-oriented approach of the negligent non-disclosure cases, health professionals would have in mind the *reasonably prudent* parent, who is defined as being partly influenced by the 'degree of the harm' (as well as by the degree of risk).[156]

Additionally, since a wrongful birth action — however it is constructed — will always turn, ultimately, on whether the complainant would in fact have aborted and (as noted earlier) causation in the United States is typically tested by objective factors, this will tend to rule out actions regarding trivial fetal impairments. The *Canesi* court is thus right to hold that whilst protective of autonomy, the wrongful birth duty is premised in tort. This, coupled with the underlying policy rationale of the pro-wrongful birth cases — to facilitate *meaningful* exercises of the autonomy recognised in *Roe* and *Casey* — suggests that there would not be a duty to look for or advise of trivial features of the fetus's condition.[157] This is not to say

---

[153] 798 P2d 477 (Kansas, 1990) 480, *per* Miller CJ: 'By handicapped, we mean, in this context, that the child has such gross deformities, not medically correctable, that the child will never be able to function as a normal human being'.

[154] Above n 72, 344, *per* Batchelder J (my emphasis).

[155] *Paris v Stepney Borough Council* [1951] AC 367.

[156] Interestingly, Botkin, above n 120, 303, suggests that there is no reason why autonomy rights in the reproductive context should be stronger than in the medical context generally. He also observes: 'do professional standards follow popular attitudes or are popular attitudes shaped by professional standards? The answer is probably both' (*ibid* 292).

[157] Wertz, above n 85, 278, discussing the criteria for offering multiplex testing by means of DNA chip technology, poses the following hypothetical example: 'Will a test for webbed toes be on the multiplex offered to women of advanced maternal age? No. Knowing that a fetus has webbed toes makes no difference in terms of prenatal treatment

that in practice relatively trivial features might not happen to be noted and communicated to the parents, for instance in the course of a routine scan for more serious anomalies. It means, however, that the standard of care would not require this.[158]

There are very important implications for any changes to English abortion law here: if the law were ever to become rights-based to some degree, health professionals would not automatically have a duty to advise prospective parents of relatively insignificant features of a fetus's condition (even though causation in tort is tested in England by a combination of objective and subjective factors). For this reason, fetuses would not in practice be aborted for reasons relating to relatively trivial features. In any event I think this kind of concern, though common, is highly speculative and one that takes a somewhat cynical view of prospective parents. In reality, particularly in a chosen pregnancy, parents become very attached to their developing fetus.

So, for health professionals to decide to screen or test for and advise of any given condition or characteristic would require, in the first place, that it be thought serious or meaningful. This brings us to the question of how 'serious' or 'meaningful' will be defined in tort.

### iii  Defining seriousness in wrongful birth case law

Although there is a divergence of views as to whether it is appropriate to try to draw lines in this area and hence to determine degrees of seriousness,[159] the above

---

or birth management. It *makes no difference to most people's reproductive plans*. Therefore, there is no reason to offer it or even to tell women about its existence, unless there is a family history... We need a balance between personal autonomy and the requirements of a health care system that cannot offer everything to everyone' (my emphasis). The implication is that such information would not be material or meaningful. Wertz suggests it would be different if the woman has a family history of webbed toes, adding '[i]t is for her to decide just how great a "disaster" having webbed toes may be for the child'. Wertz suggests she might also obtain such a test if she is able to persuade a mental health professional of serious psychiatric reasons for having it. She suggests, in effect, that the woman should have the right to make the 'wrong' decision. As I have made clear, she has this legal right by means of *Roe v Wade*. The question under discussion here concerns the extent of the duty to advise her of such conditions. A medical definition of webbing is noted in Ch 2, n 63.

[158] Botkin, above n 120, 301, observes: 'a few parents might claim severe impact of the birth of an infant with color blindness or of the "wrong" gender. While a plausible case might be made in individual circumstances based on idiosyncratic values, such exceptions need not form the basis of professional standards'. Note that in England, if a woman were to *ask* about trivial aspects of the fetus's condition, arguably there would be a duty to answer honestly, if the information were known as the result of an already-performed test. But of course this does not mean that she could necessarily abort thereafter. On the duty to answer questions, see *Pearce v United Bristol Healthcare NHS Trust*, above n 107, 54.

[159] For arguments *against*, see Wertz, above n 85, 274, 275, who considers that only parents should have the right to draw lines. For arguments in *favour*, see Botkin, above n 120, 288, who argues that practitioners can draw lines as part of establishing a standard of care. T Shakespeare '"Losing the Plot?" Medical and Activist Discourses of Contemporary

discussion has shown that the law of tort will need to do so for the purposes of the wrongful birth action. How? As noted above, operation of the causation and reasonably prudent patient tests in certain jurisdictions (as in *Canesi*) would come into play here, thereby forestalling the possible concern that courts cannot distinguish between the severity of disabilities because the injury — the denial of choice — is the same. But these tests require some normative input. What do 'meaningful' and 'serious' mean? This issue was discussed in previous chapters.

As noted before, the degree of disagreement about what counts as 'serious' is one of the most difficult issues in this context.[160] In the English context, we saw in Chapter 2 that there are Royal College of Obstetrician and Gynaecologists (RCOG) guidelines concerning the meanings of the terms in the disability ground of the Abortion Act. But we also noted that judgments as to seriousness become increasingly difficult as we move away from examples of disabilities that can be seen as very severe, such as Lesch-Nyhan syndrome and Tay-Sachs (conditions that might give rise, philosophically speaking, to a 'wrongful life'). Although it is likely that we have some hold on these issues at the extremes — for instance Tay-Sachs versus the webbing of two toes[161] — difficulties attach to the large range of 'mid-spectrum' conditions in between.[162] Further down the scale[163] in this 'grey' area might be cystic fibrosis, spina bifida and Down's syndrome, the seriousness of which (depending on the prognosis, especially in the first two cases) are very much a matter of debate.[164] Moving still further down the scale might be missing hands, feet or digits, and susceptibility to diseases, perhaps especially

---

Genetics and Disability' (1999) 21:5 *Sociology of Health and Illness* 669, 685, notes (in relation to preimplantation genetic diagnosis) that 'disabled people may welcome a list of conditions for which screening is prohibited'.

[160] E Parens and A Asch 'The Disability Rights Critique of Prenatal Genetic Testing: Reflections and Recommendations' in Parens and Asch (eds), above n 20, 3, 33: 'our project group could not reach a consensus about drawing lines between reasonable and unreasonable tests'.

[161] A medical definition of webbing is noted in Ch 2, n 63. Note, however, that a minor anomaly may be an indication of a more serious anomaly as, for instance, Down's syndrome may be a relatively common cause. *Ibid*. A possible concern that 'that's not all that's wrong with [the] baby…' was noted by a midwife quoted in Williams *et al*, above n 33, 68.

[162] Wertz, above n 85, 263 *ff* discusses the difference of views amongst practitioners as to what is serious.

[163] Botkin, above n 120, 304, notes the relative nature of severity, so that conditions need to be compared with other conditions.

[164] For one view of such conditions, see A Asch 'Can Aborting "Imperfect" Children be Immoral?', from A Asch 'Real Moral Dilemmas' *Christianity and Crisis* (1986) 46(10) 237, reprinted in J Arras and B Steinbock, *Ethical Issues in Modern Medicine* 5th edn (Mountain View, Calif: Mayfield, 1999) 384, 386: 'Down's syndrome, spina bifida, cystic fibrosis, or muscular dystrophy cause degrees of impairment ranging from mild to severe, the degree indeterminable at the time of prenatal diagnosis'.

late-onset ones, such as Huntington's.[165] In some cases there will also be medical uncertainty about how severe a given condition might be in the born child[166]; in others there will be uncertainty in the screening process about whether a given condition will ever manifest itself. Then there is the question of 'serious for whom': the parents or the child. 'Serious' for the child the fetus will become may have its own set of meanings and uncertainties, which may hinge in part upon its own mental attitude, the reactions of others and the social conditions it encounters. The perspective of people with disabilities may also be helpful to parents in their perceptions of what may lie ahead if they continue with the pregnancy of an 'affected' fetus.

Overall, where birth is compatible with a good or reasonable quality of life for the child but the parents wish to avoid a potentially more difficult or distressing rearing experience, we return to the potential conflict of interests between the fetus and its parents. In such a case, it is the parents' interests that may be particularly at stake when we reflect on the question of seriousness. I therefore argued in Chapter 2 that doctors would be right to take account of parents' interests and views, within reason, in the interpretation of the criteria in the disability ground of the Act, particularly before 24 weeks. What are the implications of this for the future scope of health professionals' duties in prenatal screening and PND?

*iv Implications for the current and future scope of the wrongful birth action*

Turning again to the law and the scope of the wrongful birth action in particular, if selective abortion in many cases protects parental interests and if the wrongful birth action developed as a further means of protecting these, one implication is that parents will, on balance, be the most important (if not the sole) judges of the seriousness of a prospective child's condition. As indicated briefly in the previous chapter, this could be explicitly recognised in the wrongful birth action itself. Importantly, recalling the concerns of some of the US wrongful birth cases, this does not mean that parents will thus be in control of informational issues. Earlier

---

[165] Robertson, above n 67, 445, suggests that a woman should be able to abort for a late-onset condition in the fetus. Legally, of course, she can do so in the United States. Regarding the English context, Kennedy and Grubb, above n 24, 1428, observe: 'although it is more difficult to interpret [the disability ground] as covering [late-onset conditions], once it is accepted that the handicap need not manifest itself at birth, it would seem to undermine the purpose of the provision narrowly to restrict it to childhood'. If parental interests are understood as underlying the disability ground to a large degree, one question here might be how much weight parental interests should be given across the life-span of offspring: see further discussion in Ch 4, S IV(B)vii. Wertz, above n 85, 267, notes that professional societies are opposed to testing children for late-onset conditions, unless this will be of some benefit to the child, for instance by prevention.

[166] Williams *et al*, above n 33, 72; M Saxton 'Why Members of the Disability Community Oppose Prenatal Diagnosis and Selective Abortion' in Parens and Asch (eds), above n 20, 147, 155, 149, observes that 'the medical system tends to underestimate the functional abilities and overestimate the "burden" of these disabled citizens'.

188  *Informational Duties – Impact on PND and Abortion*

I suggested that whether parental reasons for wanting to end a pregnancy are serious (and hence justified given the growing moral claims of the fetus) will be related to the severity of the prospective child's condition.[167] This is because parents will inevitably reflect on the possible impact on them of that condition. There will thus be some kind of 'reality check' on parents' perceptions. In this way, just as it would be hard for a parent to present a truly trivial impairment or feature in a child in such a way as to have a serious impact on them, so it would be hard to deny the legitimacy of a parent's concerns about a child with Tay-Sachs.

It is the mid-spectrum disability, however, that creates difficulties and is effectively the subject of discussion here. The question is whether such a disability is *sufficiently serious* for the parents' interests in being able to choose to merit legal protection. In such cases, although a child may well have a good or reasonable quality of life his condition may still significantly affect his parents, perhaps because he has learning difficulties or often requires hospital treatment. Arguably, parents do have an interest in choosing whether to continue a pregnancy with these kinds of implication (in addition to an interest in being well-informed about them).[168] In these kinds of case, then, the point of recognising that parents will be the most important judges of the impact on them of a child's condition is to suggest that, given that there is room for doubt about seriousness in the mid-spectrum area, parents' perceptions may legitimately tip the balance. In effect, this means that parents have an interest in being informed about conditions in the mid-spectrum area. (That they also have an interest in being informed about extreme conditions such as Tay-Sachs is very clear.) As for what is 'mid-spectrum', we might say that these are the conditions which are the subject of reasonable disagreement.

For parents' interests in being informed about such conditions to receive legal protection, a duty to screen, potentially test for and advise of information in relation to relevant fetal conditions would have to be recognised in tort. Sometimes, a fear of wrongful birth liability may mean that certain screens and tests in any event become part of the standard of care. Apart from such cases, tort will muddle its way through this process as and when the need arises. In so doing, courts' perceptions of the reasonable parent will be crucial.[169]

---

[167] Above, in S V(A).
[168] Interestingly, Botkin, above n 144, suggests that, as a determinant of when prenatal testing is *not* required as part of the standard of care '[a]t least five classes of conditions can be distinguished on the basis of likely availability and effectiveness of therapy, age of onset, and likelihood of manifestation of the disease' (at 38).
[169] Research by Press shows that some conclusions can be drawn about what parents consider 'serious': N Press *et al* 'Provisional Normalcy and "Perfect Babies": Pregnant Women's Attitudes toward Disability in the Context of Prenatal Testing' in S Franklin and H Ragone, *Reproducing Reproduction: Kinship, Power and Technological Innovation* (Philadelphia: University of Philadelphia Press, 1998) 46.

In fleshing these perceptions out, courts might partly reflect on the reasons for which wrongful birth actions have been brought to date. For instance, English case law already supports an action in wrongful birth in relation to Down's syndrome and spina bifida.[170] Public policy — which, in the absence of public debate, will lag somewhat behind the reality of current screening and testing — will also play a role. In this regard, courts could resort in part to certain reports to ascertain views as to how far the wrongful birth action should go in compensating for a failure to provide information relating to the fetus's condition. Examples might be the Human Fertilisation and Embryology Authority's (HFEA's) and HGC's report following the consultation exercise on the related issue of preimplantation genetic diagnosis, discussed in Chapters 4 and 5.[171] Although the issues of prenatal and preimplantation genetic diagnosis raise many similar issues about the scope and legitimacy of parental control in the reproductive process, however, they are far from equivalent. Of particular relevance would be the HGC's 2006 report, *Making Babies: Reproductive Decisions and Genetic Technologies*, in which the HGC notes the difficulties of defining seriousness in this context.[172] The HGC observes[173]:

> One way of doing this would be to draw up a list of conditions that are considered to lead to a very poor quality of life, and to restrict consideration to these conditions. However, this approach fails to recognise that quality of life judgments are subjective, and that genetic disorders are variable in terms of severity and health outcomes.

The HGC endorses the UK National Screening Committee's role 'in ensuring that possible new screening tests are properly evaluated against clear criteria'.[174] As for other possible sources of assistance in judging the reasonable scope of screening and testing, in one of the English wrongful birth cases — *Parkinson v St James and Seacroft University Hospital NHS Trust* — Hale LJ notes the possibility of referring to related statutory areas in order to help define seriousness, citing section 17(2) of the Children Act 1989[175]:

---

[170] On spina bifida, see *Rance v Mid-Downs Health Authority* [1991] 1 QB 587. The case concerned a failure to diagnose spina bifida and the legality of an abortion under the unamended Abortion Act 1967, in which the fetal disability ground of the Act was subject to time limits. On Down's syndrome, see, eg, *Rand v East Dorset Health Authority*, above n 78, discussed in Ch 2, S III(B)ii.

[171] HFEA and HGC, *Outcome of the Public Consultation on Preimplantation Genetic Diagnosis*, 18 June 2001. Or, in the United States, the work of the Hastings Center on prenatal testing: see Parens and Asch, above n 20.

[172] Above n 2, para 3.27.

[173] *Ibid*.

[174] *Ibid* para 3.26.

[175] [2002] QB 266, 293. Regarding the US context, the Americans with Disabilities Act is sometimes thought to be helpful to discussions in this context. See, eg, Parens and Asch, above n 160, 31.

190  *Informational Duties – Impact on PND and Abortion*

> A child is disabled if he is blind, deaf or dumb or suffers from mental disorder of any kind or is substantially and permanently handicapped by illness, injury or congenital deformity or such other disability as may be prescribed.

Such definitions would have some value but it would also have to be borne in mind that they were formed in a different legal context and for different legal purposes. Overall, if parental interests are recognised as being arguably the most significant before birth, especially earlier in pregnancy and before the shift in the stringency of the grounds for abortion generally at 24 weeks, this should lend weight to deciding this issue, when in doubt, in favour of the parents.[176] There will be limits, however, regarding the extent to which these issues reach the courts. Given this, and failing public debate resulting in some form of overt regulation in this area, health professionals will be left, perhaps unwillingly, to decide these issues. Some approximate notion of the 'reasonable parent' may likewise be relevant to their deliberations. I return to their role in my conclusions.

Concluding this part of the discussion, although a wrongful birth action based on trivial reasons is inherently unlikely,[177] the fear of such reasons is both strong and persistent. Reflection on the seriousness of reasons tests what we think in different cases, thereby helping us to explore when autonomy is (and is not) important in the context of PND and selective abortion and hence when it should be legally protected in the face of the growing moral claims of the fetus. Arguably public policy would *not* support an action in wrongful birth concerning trivial features of the fetus's condition because of some sense that it would be inappropriate or unnecessary to sue for the lost opportunity to abort for such reasons, despite the fetus's lack of legal personality, although this is an issue in need of open debate. Underlying this is probably some sense that parental

---

[176] Note that Williams *et al*, above n 33, 72, observe that if lines cannot be drawn, choice becomes the 'default' option (citing A Kerr, S Cunningham-Burley and A Amos 'Drawing the Line: an Analysis of Lay People's Discussions about the New Genetics' (1998) 7 *Public Understanding of Science* 113. Wertz, above n 85, 268: 'Drawing lines within this broad category, which includes most prenatal tests, is not only practically difficult but also offensive, both to individuals' autonomy and to some people with disabilities, who might consider their conditions labeled inappropriately. It therefore seems most appropriate to let the people who will raise the child — the parents — make the decisions within this broad category'.

[177] See Wertz, above n 85, 275 (citing survey evidence in support): '"frivolous" choices and… abuses… may be few… It appears that the American public is not eager to abort for most fetal conditions'.

autonomy interests are unlikely seriously to be invoked in such a case.[178] In any event, in such a case the damages would surely be nominal.[179]

In some ways, then, reasons matter. This is not only about the fairness or otherwise of the burden on health professionals of a very extensive duty to advise of information gleaned or potentially to be gleaned about the fetus, perhaps in the course of an ultrasound scan. It also concerns the point or value of the wrongful birth action in itself. In effect, then, the positive liberty that is at stake in, but not protected by, US abortion law is only partially protected by tort (where a wrongful birth action exists). Importantly, this does not mean that there is any justification for interfering with the US abortion right *per se*. It simply means that a woman is not assisted to abort for reasons of trivial fetal anomaly by the legal requirement that such information be provided her. In this sense, to the extent that the scope of the wrongful birth action may affect what she is told about her fetus, then in practice the scope of the reasons for which she can abort will to some degree be limited. This is not to deny that people with the financial resources and requisite assertiveness will be able to obtain a great deal of information.[180] As we have seen, in English law, by contrast, there is more of a correspondence between wrongful birth liability and abortion law.

Given that the fetus is not a legal person, these limits to wrongful birth liability might be thought of as in some way 'symbolic'. John Robertson has made a similar point in relation to abortion.[181] That the fetus is not a legal person, however, is only partly determinative of its value within the law. The main function of the rule is to prioritise the pregnant woman's interests over those of the fetus. Arguably, this is a highly important move both in terms of principle and policy but it does not mean that the fetus is 'nothing' in the eyes of the law, either in England or the United States. In the United States, the fact that the fetus has a value, despite lacking legal personhood, is inherent in the state's interest in potential life. Although English law has no formal language to express a concern

---

[178] This would be consistent with an account of rights that gives at least some weight to the notion of interests: see Ch 1, S II(E). Bopp *et al*, above n 53, refer to the idea of a parent's 'subjective emotional state' (at 513) and the 'subjective value' a parent chooses to assign to a child's life in a discussion of fears of fraudulent claims. Thus, they ignore the possibility of underlying moral interests being seriously invoked. Given the existence of these interests, it is unlikely to matter if the parents are not advised of trivial aspects of the fetus's condition.

[179] The issue of damages in a wrongful birth case is highly complex and, as noted earlier, cannot be explored here.

[180] Wertz, above n 85, 270: 'People with the money will find a way to get most of the services [which might not otherwise be on offer]'.

[181] Robertson, above, n 67, 445: 'True, abortion may not violate anyone's rights, but it does involve the destruction of a potential human life, and thus signifies the reduced importance of that life, and by extension, other human life'.

for the fetus's value, I noted in the previous chapter the attempt by some English judges to express this, thereby perhaps recognising the moral claims of the developing fetus.[182]

In fact John Robertson himself, generally renowned for a strongly pro-reproductive autonomy approach, distinguishes between concerns that will be 'central' or 'material' to reproductive autonomy and will thus determine whether reproduction occurs on the one hand and mere 'preferences' on the other.[183] On the question of how 'centrality' or 'materiality' should be measured, he suggests that some combination of subjective and objective factors is likely to resolve this issue and thus decide which features of reproductive autonomy receive protection.[184] Although at one point Robertson suggests that certain choices might be protected simply because someone would base her reproductive decision on it,[185] he also acknowledges that, at 'the outer limits, questions of the materiality of prebirth selection practices to reproductive decisions will ultimately require judgments that are constitutive of why reproductive freedom receives heightened protection'.[186] Such judgments will ultimately depend on the strength of the reproductive interests invoked and in the realm of the trivial reason those interests will be very weak or, we might say, trivially invoked. The implication would be that line-drawing at this end of the spectrum is not that difficult.

## VI CONCLUSIONS

There is clearly a delicate balance of interests at stake in this context, particularly between a fetus and its prospective parents. Over the course of the first three chapters, I have argued that parents have a legitimate moral and legal interest in

---

[182] As Judge LJ noted in *St George's Healthcare NHS Trust v S, R v Collins and others, ex parte S* [1998] 3 All ER 673, 687: 'Whatever else it may be, a 36-week foetus is not nothing; if viable it is not lifeless and it is certainly human'. He was discussing the House of Lords' decision in *Attorney-General's Reference (No 3)* [1997] 3 All ER 936 (which concerned the criminal liability of a man who stabbed his pregnant girlfriend). In that case, the House of Lords had criticised the Court of Appeal's conclusion that the fetus should be regarded as an integral part of its mother in the same way as if it were part of her body. Judge LJ cited Lord Mustill's rejection of 'the reasoning which assumes that since (in the eyes of English law) the foetus does not have the attributes which make it a "person" it must be an adjunct of the mother. Eschewing all religious and political debate I would say that the foetus is neither. It is a unique organism. To apply to such an organism the principles of a law evolved in relation to autonomous beings is bound to mislead' (*ibid*, citing *Attorney-General's Reference (No3)* [1997] 3 All ER 936 at 943).
[183] Robertson, above n 67, 429.
[184] Note that his concern at this juncture is with procreative liberty generally.
[185] Robertson, above n 67, 430.
[186] *Ibid* 430–31. See also J Robertson, *Children of Choice: Freedom and the New Reproductive Technologies* (Princeton, NJ: Princeton University Press, 1994) 160 (footnote omitted): 'The scope of legal remedies for wrongful birth will affect physicians' behavior [regarding trivial reasons] and women's access to prenatal screening for controversial indications'.

being able to decide whether to give birth to a child who can reasonably be seen as seriously disabled, at least in the first six months of pregnancy. The issue of late terminations was discussed particularly in Chapter 2.

In English law parental interests are protected principally by means of the fourth ground of the Abortion Act, with corresponding wrongful birth liability. In this way this ground is in itself, in effect, a control mechanism as regards the duty in tort. In the United States, reproductive autonomy is recognised at the federal level in the sense that a woman is free to abort for any reason before viability. As far as a potentially disabled fetus is concerned, however, wrongful birth duties will be limited to duties to advise of serious disabilities (and however these are judged, they will not include the very trivial). So reproductive autonomy will only be protected by means of the wrongful birth action in situations in which it might be seriously invoked. (In some states, of course, there is no wrongful birth action.) By contrast, in neither jurisdiction is a desire to abort the fetus for a trivial anomaly or negatively viewed feature legally protected by wrongful birth law in the prenatal screening and PND context. The difference is that, in the United States, *if* a woman had such information about the fetus, she would have the legal right to abort for that reason pre-viability. (The same would be true in England if abortion law became rights-based.) A woman does not, however, have a positive right to information about trivial features or conditions, a position arguably supportable in public policy terms. Here the distinction between negative and positive aspects of the US abortion right comes to the fore. In effect, although she would have the right to abort for a trivial fetal anomaly before viability in the United States, the potential exercise of the right in this way is, in a sense, the subject of moral condemnation by means of limits expressed in the wrongful birth action, since only serious conditions or mid-spectrum conditions judged sufficiently serious will be the subject of health professionals' duties. Given that a woman may thus not receive information about trivial features of the fetus's condition, in effect (as regards fetal anomaly) there is really only a fully protected right (whatever the practice may be) to abort for serious anomalies or conditions deemed sufficiently serious to be part of healthcare professionals' informational duties. By very different means, the position is effectively the same in English law.

We know that there are fears about the increasing number of genetic tests and the extent to which some of these might concern conditions whose seriousness is a matter of doubt. But we have seen in this chapter that mechanisms are already in place within the existing law to control, particularly, whether one could sue for the lost opportunity to abort on the basis of a relatively insignificant condition, but also — perhaps more strikingly, given the rights-based nature of abortion law in the United States — whether one would have been able to abort on this basis in the first place. The indirect nature of this sort of control is particularly marked in the United States, since the wrongful birth action is distinctly out of alignment with the scope of the abortion right. For any new screening or testing to become part of the standard of care in England, this must ultimately have some connection with the terms of the disability ground of the Abortion Act. At the same time, the terms of this section are in line with the twin concepts of the degree of risk and harm central to the standard of care in negligence. In the United States, the latter considerations are the key. Although a woman's (or couple's) autonomy interests might increasingly come to bear on the formulation of the standard of care, in any event even a negligent non-disclosure analysis will always limit the extent of the recognition and protection that these will receive, essentially by constructing a picture of the reasonable parent. This will occur by means of the tests of materiality and/or causation (depending on the jurisdiction). Thus, can we really envisage a successful action for the lost opportunity to abort a fetus in whom the skin of the fourth and fifth toes was fused? Such an action is also extremely unlikely. For these reasons, and importantly, if English abortion law were to become rights-based to some degree, we should not be unduly concerned that fetuses would be aborted for reasons related to relatively trivial features.

Since there will be limits as to how much the courts become involved in these processes, health professionals will play an important role in the formation of policy and the shape of practice.[187] It has been argued that public policy would support limits to reproductive autonomy in this context, at least in terms of the legal requirements for information-giving rather than by limiting access to abortion itself (where freely available). But of course this does not necessarily entail that health professionals should be the only people involved in setting those limits, even if some medical involvement is appropriate. In England we have had a public consultation exercise on preimplantation genetic diagnosis. More recently, the HGC consulted, in part, about prenatal screening and testing in general and several of its recommendations were discussed in the early stages of this chapter.[188]

Where societal agreement is limited, however, or public regulation is simply not forthcoming, medicine and the law will be left to (and will have to) work this out. Given the widely recognised highly moral nature of the practices at stake, this is unfortunate. No doubt it is also burdensome to health professionals. In England, such an outcome may be softened by the recognition that our (statute-based) law on abortion specifically addresses, in part, the issue of disability in a subsequently born child (although this still leaves questions about the meaning of 'seriousness') and that the law of wrongful birth effectively corresponds to this. In the United States, by contrast, the rights-based nature of abortion opens a vista on a vast spectrum of suits relating to fetal anomaly that only doctors and, on occasion, the

---

[187] This will be so regardless of whether they feel in control of this process, which it appears they do not: Williams *et al*, above n 11, 747–8.

[188] HGC, above n 2. The lack of regulation in the area of assisted reproduction and genetic testing has recently been lamented in the United States, with a call for 'public participation in the development of public policy on genetic testing' (Dr Hudson, Director, Genetics and Public Policy Centre, Johns Hopkins University). Dr Hudson noted that consideration was being given to establishing a body similar to the HFEA in Canada: C Marwick 'Monitoring of Assisted Reproduction Techniques is Inadequate, US Experts Say' (2003) 326 *BMJ* 1352.

courts are left to address by determining the standard of care and through it the extent of the wrongful birth action. In this process, judges or health professionals could proceed on the basis that prospective parents' interests are the strongest, especially pre-fetal sentience.

Overall, as regards the relationship between autonomy, abortion and wrongful birth in the context of prenatal screening and diagnosis, the law in effect does — and arguably should — require serious reasons as the basis for a legal action hinging on the lost opportunity to abort for reasons of fetal anomaly in both jurisdictions. This means that the risk must be substantial and the disability in the future child serious, including from the parents' reasonable point of view. Importantly, this is not meant to suggest that an autonomy-based approach to abortion is not a good thing (and that it would not be preferable for English law to be autonomy-based, at least to some degree) or that where the abortion right exists, the state has any legal grounds to interfere with a proposed abortion for reasons relating to trivial fetal anomaly. So, autonomy or liberty in this negative sense should remain intact. The reason for this lies in highly important concerns about not coercing pregnant women. Of course, it might be argued that a woman *is* coerced if not informed of trivial features of the fetus's condition that would in fact have caused her to abort. If so, it can only be said that the coercion would be insignificant.

Overall, the discussion has revealed some curious features about the relationship between autonomy and reasons in this context. Somewhat surprisingly, US abortion law has been seen to be less autonomy-focused than it might at first have seemed, since it is not overtly concerned with facilitating autonomy by providing information about the health or other status of a developing fetus. Rather, the law of wrongful birth does this, but in a limited way. Attention has thus been drawn to the distinction between negative and positive aspects of reproductive liberty. By contrast, to the extent that section 1(1)(d) of the English Abortion Act can be used to protect parental interests and recognise that in relation to serious disabilities parents may well elect to terminate a pregnancy, English abortion law (somewhat paradoxically given that it is not autonomy-based) might well be seen as at least partly concerned with reproductive autonomy. This is backed up by corresponding wrongful birth liability. Importantly, the discussion has not doubted that reproductive autonomy matters but it has suggested that, when the growing moral claims of a fetus are at stake, reasons do as well, thereby implying that reproductive autonomy matters most when seriously invoked. This is consistent with my argument in Chapters 1 and 2.

In the next three chapters I move from prenatal screening and diagnosis to PGD. In the next chapter I explore the interpretation and operation of the law on PGD in England, with particular reference to the interplay between the views of health professionals and those of prospective parents. A key question concerns the extent to which prospective parents' views and interests are and can be taken into account and so the current scope of reproductive autonomy in PGD.

# 4

# *Preimplantation Genetic Diagnosis — The Interpretation and Operation of the Law*

## I INTRODUCTION

IF A COUPLE knows or is concerned that they are at risk of having a child with a genetic condition or disease they may seek *in vitro* fertilisation (IVF) and preimplantation genetic diagnosis (PGD). Although success cannot be guaranteed, the purpose of PGD is to enable parents to have a child without a genetic impairment and, in so doing, to avoid moral or other difficulties in the termination of an already-begun pregnancy. PGD can currently be performed where there is a 'significant risk of a serious genetic condition being present in the embryo', the criteria established by the Human Fertilisation and Embryology Authority (HFEA) and the Human Genetics Commission (HGC).[1] (If the wording in the Human Tissue and Embryos (Draft) Bill, published as this book goes to press, were to become law, under the corresponding relevant criteria the technique would be available where there is a 'significant risk that a person with the abnormality will have or develop a serious physical or mental disability, a serious illness or any other serious medical condition'.[2]) PGD involves genetic

---

[1] HFEA and HGC, *Outcome of the Public Consultation on Preimplantation Genetic Diagnosis*, 18 June 2001, rec 11.

[2] Given the timing of the publication of the Draft Bill, I am unable to give it detailed consideration. However, I note the key relevant provisions in this and subsequent chapters. Human Tissue and Embryos (Draft) Bill, May 2007 (amending Sch 2 of the HFE Act 1990): 'After paragraph 1 insert 1ZA… (1) A licence under paragraph 1 cannot authorise the testing of an embryo, except for one or more of the following purposes — (a) establishing whether the embryo has a gene, chromosome or mitochondrion abnormality that may affect its capacity to result in a live birth, (b) in a case where there is a particular risk that the embryo may have any gene, chromosome or mitochondrion abnormality, establishing whether it has that abnormality or any other gene, chromosome or mitochondrion abnormality, (c) in a case where there is a particular risk that the embryo may have an abnormality affecting the X or Y chromosomes, establishing the sex of the embryo, (d) in a case where a person ("the sibling") who is the child of the persons whose gametes are used to bring about the creation of the embryo (or of either of those persons) suffers from a life-threatening medical condition which could be treated by umbilical cord blood stem cells, establishing whether the tissue of any resulting child would be compatible with that of the sibling, and (e) in a case where uncertainty has arisen as to whether the embryo is one of those whose creation was brought about by using the gametes of particular persons,

testing of a cell extracted from a six-to-ten-cell (day three) embryo fertilised and grown *in vitro*. This chapter focuses on the interpretation and operation of the law on PGD. The key question on which it focuses is what weight, if any, is and should be given to a pregnant woman's (or the couple's) views on the issues of the degree of risk and the seriousness of a disability in a future child. The chapter explores this issue particularly by considering the views and experience of some health professionals who provide PGD.

When a couple approaches a PGD clinic, they may find that the condition of concern to them is one for which the HFEA has already granted a licence (through a licence committee). Or it may be that, as a result of discussions with a couple, the clinic applies for a licence on their behalf in relation to a given condition for the first time. Either way, prospective parents will discuss with clinicians and other professionals who provide PGD their concerns and reasons for seeking treatment. Moreover, these health professionals and scientists will have views about the criteria indicating a 'significant risk of a serious genetic condition' and the operation of these in practice, particularly the extent to which a given condition can be regarded as 'serious'. Here I explore these views by considering, in Section IV, the experience and thoughts of health professionals and scientists working at one English site which provides PGD. (There is, of course, no claim that this sample is representative of those working in the area more generally.) I consider these views with reference to the factors that the HFEA and HGC recommend that clinics should consider in deciding whether to offer PGD for a given condition, such as 'the view of those seeking treatment of the condition' and 'the likely degree of suffering associated with the condition'. The views of these health professionals and scientists are drawn from transcripts both of interviews with individual staff members and of ethics discussion groups. These groups consisted of four to six members of staff and were facilitated by a philosopher. I also relate staff's views and experiences to some key arguments about the appropriate scope of PGD (and prenatal diagnosis (PND)). In particular, I consider the question of whether, and if so how, prospective parents' interests and views should be taken into account in decision-making.[3]

---

establishing whether it is. (2) A licence under paragraph 1 cannot authorise the testing of embryos for the purpose mentioned in sub-paragraph 1(b) or (c) unless the Authority is satisfied — (a) in relation to the abnormality of which there is a particular risk, and (b) in relation to any other abnormality for which testing is to be authorised under sub-paragraph 1(b) that there is a significant risk that the person with the abnormality will have or develop a serious physical or mental disability, a serious illness or any other serious medical condition.' See further below n 53 for criteria relevant to sub-paras 1(b) and (c); and see further below n 18 for criteria relevant to sub-para 1(d).

[3] I would like to thank all those who participated in this research and also the Wellcome Trust Biomedical Ethics Programme for its grant (Grant no: 074935). The project was entitled 'Facilitating Choice, Framing Choice: the Experience of Staff Working in PGD', January 2005–June 2007 and was conducted with Clare Williams (principal researcher),

Before I begin the substantive work of this chapter, in Section II I give some background about PGD and its legal context; and in Section III I discuss the principal recommendations of the HFEA and HGC in relation to PGD, focusing on the terms 'significant risk' and 'serious genetic condition' and outlining the PGD guidance that is discussed in detail in Section IV.

## II BACKGROUND AND LEGAL CONTEXT

The technique of PGD 'typically involve[s] several stages: the creation of an embryo *in vitro*, the removal of one or more blastomeres, the genetic testing of those blastomeres for certain conditions and the transfer of suitable embryos to a woman'.[4] The blastomere(s) (cells) are removed when the embryo consists of six to ten cells. PGD is helpful for three main categories of disease[5]: sex-linked disorders such as Duchennemuscular dystrophy[6]; single gene defects, for instance, cystic fibrosis; and chromosomal disorders such as translocations, inversions, and chromosomedeletions. A related technique is preimplantation genetic screening (PGS). This focuses on aneuploid embryos, which may be inherently non-viable (so that they either fail to implant or miscarry) and is therefore particularly associated with attempts 'to improve the success of IVF treatments', although this is a matter of some controversy.[7] Aneuploid embryos may also become fetuses with a condition such as Down's syndrome. PGS was approved some time after the Outcome Document.[8] 'It is expected that... [it]... will only... be used' in relation to[9]:

> (i) Women over 35 years of age (ii) Women with a history of recurrent miscarriage not caused by translocations or other chromosomal rearrangements (iii) Women with several

---

Kathryn Ehrich, Bobbie Farsides, Clare Sandall and Peter Braude. I would also like to thank these colleagues for their very helpful comments on an earlier draft of this chapter.

[4] HFEA, *Code of Practice*, Sixth Edition (2003) para 14.1.

[5] F Flinter 'Preimplantation Genetic Diagnosis Needs to be Tightly Regulated' (2001) 322 *BMJ* 1008, 1008–9.

[6] For information, see, eg, The Muscular Dystrophy Campaign <http://www.muscular-dystrophy.org/information_resources/factsheets/medical_conditions_factsheets/duchenne.html> accessed 11 October 2007.

[7] The quotation is from HFEA/HGC, *Minutes of Joint Working Party on Preimplantation Genetic Diagnosis*, 20 December 2000, para 4. Doubts about the use of PGS in relation to the improvement of IVF outcomes are expressed in, eg, D Hill 'Ten Years of Preimplantation Genetic Diagnosis-Aneuploidy Screening: Review of Multi-Center Report' (2004) 82/2 *Fertil & Steril* 300.

[8] A Ferriman 'UK Approves Preimplantation Genetic Screening Technique' (2001) 323 *BMJ* 125. The HFEA and HGC were clearly worried about the human rights implications of the fact that the technique was already available elsewhere in Europe. HFEA/HGC, above n 7, para 8.

[9] HFEA, above n 4, para 14.27. '"Expected to" or "expected that"... indicates what is to be regarded as the proper conduct of licensable activities or as suitable practice within licensed centres' (*ibid* 123).

previous failed IVF attempts where embryos have been transferred or (iv) Women with a family history of aneuploidy not caused by translocations or other chromosomal rearrangements.

PGD is regulated by means of the Human Fertilisation and Embryology Act 1990 (the HFE Act) as this governs the provision of IVF, the HFEA's licensing function and guidance in the HFEA's sixth Code of Practice. The criterion of 'a significant risk of a serious genetic condition... in the embryo', evolved as a result of a Consultation Document[10] produced by the HFEA and the Advisory Committee on Genetic Testing (AGCT) and a final report by the HFEA and HGC, the 'Outcome Document'.[11] The report contains a number of further recommendations about the provision of PGD, and these have been incorporated into the Code of Practice. There has also been judicial consideration of the legal scope of PGD in relation to the very particular issue of 'saviour siblings' in *The Queen on the Application of Quintavalle v Human Fertilisation and Embryology Authority* (discussed below), as well as further HFEA pronouncements.

A brief consideration of the *Quintavalle* case demonstrates the current relationship between key sections of the HFE Act and the practice of PGD. The issue in this case was whether the HFEA could license HLA-typing by PGD to enable a child to be born who would be a tissue match for a sibling with beta thalassaemia major. In the Court of Appeal,[12] Phillips, Schiemann and Mance LJJ all held that PGD for the purpose, not simply of ensuring that a woman was able to bring a pregnancy to term (as Maurice Kay J had held below), but also to ensure that a child would be free from genetic abnormalities, is lawful under the HFE Act 1990. The key statutory provisions requiring interpretation are section 2(1) and Schedule 2, paragraph 1(1)(d). Section 2(1) states:

> (1) In this Act... "treatment services" means medical, surgical or obstetric services provided to the public or a section of the public for the purpose of assisting women to carry children.

Schedule 2, paragraph 1(1)(d) provides:

> (1) A licence under this paragraph may authorise any of the following in the course of providing treatment services — ... (d) practices designed to secure that embryos are in a suitable condition to be placed in a woman or to determine whether embryos are suitable for that purpose...

Paragraph 1(1)(3) might also be noted:

> A licence under this paragraph cannot authorise any activity unless it appears to the authority to be necessary or desirable for the purpose of providing treatment services.

---

[10] HFEA and AGCT, *Consultation Document on Preimplantation Genetic Diagnosis*, November 1999.
[11] Above n 1.
[12] [2003] EWCA Civ 667.

In July 2004 the HFEA announced that selection of an embryo that would have the same tissue type as an existing ill sibling would be legal even where the embryo itself was not at risk of a serious genetic condition. Permission must still be sought from the HFEA in each case and the procedure should be a 'last resort'.[13] The earlier decision on the case of the Whittaker family was contrary to this position. In April 2005 the House of Lords unanimously dismissed the appeal against the Court of Appeal judgment, which also questioned the HFEA's revised policy.[14] Lord Brown defined the issue raised by the case as 'whether the [HFEA]... is empowered by the 1990 Act to license tissue typing...'.[15] He went on to state that[16]:

> The critical question... is whether tissue testing is a practice designed to determine whether an embryo is suitable for placing in a woman (paragraph 1(1)(d)) and necessary or desirable for the purpose of providing a medical service which itself is to assist a woman to carry the child (section 2(1)).

The House held, per Lord Hoffman, 'that both PGD and HLA typing could lawfully be authorised by the authority as activities to determine the suitability of the embryo for implantation within the meaning of paragraph 1(1)(d)'.[17] Although I make further reference to the *Quintavalle* case, this chapter concentrates on PGD in the general (ie, non-HLA typing) case. As can be seen from the above, each time the HFEA grants a licence for PGD, it must decide whether it is 'necessary or desirable for the purpose of providing treatment services', according to Schedule 2, paragraph 1(1)(3) of the Act. (Note here also the proposed amendments to the Act by virtue of the Human Tissue and Embryos (Draft) Bill.[18])

It is also important to consider the possible relevance of section 13(5) of the HFE Act. This requires that, in considering whether to treat the woman or

---

[13] HFEA Press Release 'HFEA Agrees to Extend Policy on Tissue Typing' 21 July 2004.
[14] [2005] 2 All ER 555.
[15] *Ibid* para 42.
[16] *Ibid* para 49.
[17] *Ibid* para 35. For discussion of the issue of HLA-typing in this context see S Sheldon and S Wilkinson '*Hashmi and Whittaker:* An Unjustifiable and Misguided Distinction?' (2004) 12 *Med Law Rev* 137; G de Wert 'Preimplantation Genetic Diagnosis: the Ethics of Intermediate Cases' (2005) 20/12 *Human Reproduction* 3261.
[18] Above n 2 (amending Sch 2, HFE Act 1990): 'After paragraph 1 insert 1ZA... (4) In considering under paragraph 1(3) whether the testing of embryos for the purpose mentioned in subsection (1)(d) is necessary or desirable for the purpose of providing treatment services, the Authority must have regard to — (a) any alternative sources of tissue which are or may become available for treating the sibling, and (b) the likely long-term effect of awareness of the testing on any child who results from an embryo that was subject to testing'. (For subsection (1)(d) see above n 2.) The proposed new Regulatory Authority for Tissue and Embryos (RATE) will have to consider whether tissue-typing is necessary or desirable on a case-by-case basis. By contrast, licences for testing under paras 1ZA(a), (b) or (c) can be considered on a general basis.

couple, the clinicians and other professionals consider the welfare of the future child.[19] It is uncertain whether this controversial provision[20] also has relevance in deciding which tests to perform and which embryos to select, rather than the preliminary question of whether to grant access to IVF.[21] Indeed, if we apply the requirement in the case of decisions about testing embryos and think, particularly, about the child that will result from the selection of any given embryo, we run into the conceptual difficulties surrounding the 'non-identity problem', first discussed in Chapter 1.[22] Any given embryo can only exist as one possible child (or twins) and it might be argued that it is only if this child would be at risk of having a life she did not think worth living (in philosophical terms, a 'wrongful life') that a welfare-of-the-child judgment could be made against selecting the relevant embryo.[23] The point here is that, as long as the subsequently born child will think her life worth living, it will not be against her interests to be born or, put another way, incompatible with her welfare. (In fact, a similar point can be made about the application of the 'welfare principle' in IVF more generally.)

The alternative way of considering the interests of future people is, of course, to adopt a non-person-affecting perspective, as discussed in the latter half of Chapter 1. On this approach, since the balance of burden and benefit in any *one* person's life is not at stake, it is possible to depart from the 'wrongful life standard' as the one that determines when it may be wrongful to select for possible implantation a given embryo. This is because we would instead be thinking of the lives of different possible people and recognising that, other things being equal, it may be preferable if people are born who at least start life without impairments or disorders that may impede their capacity for flourishing and welfare. However, not surprisingly perhaps, no distinction is made between a person- and a non-person-affecting approach in the HFE Act, nor in the HFEA's sixth Code of Practice, nor in the *Quintavalle* case. In Chapter 1 I suggested that, ethically

---

[19] The HFE Act, s 13(5) states: 'A woman shall not be provided with treatment services unless account has been taken of the welfare of any child who may be born as a result of the treatment (including the need of that child for a father), and of any other child who may be affected by the birth'.

[20] For thoughtful criticism, see especially E Jackson 'Conception and the Irrelevance of the Welfare Principle' (2002) 65(2) *MLR* 176. In January 2005 the HFEA launched a consultation document on this issue, entitled 'Welfare of the Child — Tomorrow's Children'. It then issued new guidance, which replaces Part 3 of its Code of Practice, above n 4.

[21] E Jackson notes the possibility that the section is relevant in *Regulating Reproduction* (Oxford: Hart Publishing, 2001) 245. In the Court of Appeal decision in the *Quintavalle* case, above n 12, Mance LJ held (at para 122) that the 'requirement… must not only apply before, but continue throughout the administration of treatment services'. This consideration formed part of the argument towards allowing tissue typing, since s 13(5) allows account to be taken of 'any other child who may be affected by the birth'. This aspect was not addressed in the House of Lords' decision.

[22] D Parfit, *Reasons and Persons* (Oxford: OUP, 1984) Ch 16.

[23] That is to say, in line with Parfit's arguments in *ibid*.

speaking, non-person-affecting principles might have some weight in decisions about embryos, although not as much as they might have if we could make decisions before two gametes fuse. This suggestion does not imply that the embryo is a person, but it does recognise that the embryo has the huge potential to be one. (As regards the fetus in an established pregnancy, I suggested that it was hard for non-person-affecting principles to have ongoing force.)

As a general rule, I shall not further discuss non-person-affecting principles in this chapter, essentially because these were not identified as relevant by the professionals whose views and experience I am going to discuss (with one possible exception). This does not mean, however, that non-person-affecting principles are irrelevant to testing and selection decisions in PGD and here I refer back to the discussion in Chapter 1, as well as forward to the discussion in Chapters 5 and 6. However, I do refer to such principles briefly later in this chapter when I touch on PGD for lower-penetrance, late-onset conditions.

Turning to the relevant parts of the discussion of the welfare of the child in the HFEA's Code of Practice, the HFEA observes that the assessment 'is expected to take into account the following factors relating to patients:... (v) The risk of harm to children including: (a) inherited disorders or transmissible disease...'.[24] As can be seen from this statement, the HFEA does not make any comment about the severity of a given condition or whose interests might be implicated by any given condition: there is no statement about the way in which the severity of a given condition might or might not leave a child with a life she thinks worth living or the ways in which parents' interests — rather than those of any particular child — might really be implicated by a given condition. In some ways this may be understandable in the sense that to make such a statement would require the HFEA to commit to a particular ethical analysis. In any event, presumably the HFEA is leaving consideration of these issues to clinics, though in fact it seems unlikely that clinics themselves will overtly make these distinctions, perhaps because of the somewhat taboo nature of recognising any possible conflict between a future child's interests and those of its parents.

Compatible with argument in earlier chapters, the point I wish to make here is that even if a possible child from a given set of embryos would have a reasonable quality of life — hence a decision to choose it would be compatible with a welfare assessment of its interests — parents may have an interest in choosing whether to avoid the birth over and above this possible child's interests. The parents' interests may therefore remain a valid consideration regardless of any particular judgment (however this is made) about the welfare of a possible child under the HFE Act. In fact, some of the guidance that I shall explore in this chapter specifically lists 'the view of those seeking treatment of the condition' as a

---

[24] HFEA, above n 4, para 3.12.

factor to be considered in the decision to offer PGD. Other factors of possible relevance here are 'the family circumstances of those seeking treatment' and 'their previous reproductive experience'.

Turning now to the question of which tests can be performed on the embryo, the HFEA's and HGC's Outcome Document makes clear that this is not necessarily in the hands of the woman (and her partner), nor those of the clinicians and other professionals at the treatment centre. To perform a particular new test, the centre must seek a licence from the HFEA. In so doing, it must provide 'evidence about the safety and efficacy of the tests and the centre's competence in the techniques used, as well as notification of the information given to patients and the means by which the decision to use PGD has been reached'.[25] (The HFEA has now simplified the provision of PGD by deciding that once a clinic has been licensed to offer a certain form of testing, others licensed to perform PGD can do so without having to obtain fresh licences themselves, provided that they use the same techniques.[26]) Where decisions are 'ethically difficult', centres may seek the guidance of a treatment ethics committee, whose views may in turn be taken into consideration by HFEA licence committees. A minimum of two peer reviewers considers each application on the basis of 'the scientific and clinical information currently available, and in the light of prevailing moral attitudes towards the proposed treatment'.[27] The Outcome Document recommends that the list of peer reviewers involved in the interim licensing system 'should be expanded to include clinical geneticists, molecular geneticists, cytogeneticists, and genetic counsellors'.[28] The two accompanying recommendations are that '[p]eer reviewers should also be asked to comment on the seriousness of the disorder for which the centre is applying to use PGD in the light of the guidance given in the Notes for Centres' and that '[c]entres should include in their application a paragraph describing in lay terms the condition for which they are applying to use PGD, incorporating descriptions of the full range of the experiences of affected individuals and their families where appropriate'.[29]

The nature of the professionals at treatment centres should also be noted. Recommendation 5 of the Outcome Document states that the team should

---

[25] Above n 1, para 4.

[26] HFEA Press Release 'HFEA Announce New Process to Speed up Applications for Embryo Screening' 19 January 2005: 'Under the new guidelines, if a clinic, with proven expertise in performing embryo biopsies, applies for a licence to carry out screening for a particular condition, which is already being carried out successfully in another clinic — such as screening for sickle cell anaemia, cystic fibrosis and Duchenne's muscular dystrophy — the HFEA will approve the application without having to go through the full HFEA licence committee process, providing the same technique and methods are used'.

[27] Above n 1, para 4. The meaning of 'prevailing moral attitudes' is uncertain. One interpretation, suggested by a referee for the article on which this chapter is in part based, could be 'what the public will tolerate'.

[28] *Ibid* rec 1.

[29] *Ibid* recs 3 and 4 respectively.

include 'reproductive specialists, embryologists, clinical geneticists, genetic counsellors, cytogeneticists and molecular biologists'. Following their referral to a centre these are the people with whom those seeking treatment may interact. At a treatment centre for PGD, then, a couple may discuss very personal issues with a number of different specialists. Further, the HFEA licence committees are distanced from the couple and their discussions with the staff of treatment centres. This means that a couple's reasons for wishing to have a new test will be conveyed via the treatment centre itself.

Overall, it is clear that PGD entails a considerable degree of positive assistance from others (as do screening and termination for fetal disability). This was emphasised in one of the HGC's meetings prior to the finalisation of the Outcome Document. One clinician commented on the highly technically demanding nature of these techniques and their requirement of a 'commitment of time and effort from a large team', concluding that 'the team should be able to influence what tests were carried out and what embryos were implanted'.[30] (Within the NHS, the cost of PGD probably has some relevance here.) This emphasises the extent to which the entire process of creating a child through IVF with PGD hinges on the involvement of third parties. As for the extent of the practice, although it was initially licensed at only a handful of centres, following the Outcome Document any centre with the technical ability and expertise can apply to the HFEA to be licensed to offer this technique. More generally, and looking to the future, the potential scope of PGD will broaden with increasing genetic knowledge.

## III THE RECOMMENDATIONS ON RISK AND SERIOUSNESS

The criteria for PGD, and the views of those who sit on the HFEA's licence committees and of health professionals and scientists who provide PGD will each have a bearing on the extent to which a couple can choose to try to avoid the birth of a child with a certain condition and so upon the extent of their reproductive autonomy. The appropriate scope of such autonomy is controversial, particularly in this context when I am considering to what extent a couple should be able to try to avoid the birth of a particular child, for instance because of a certain genetic condition, in favour of another child without that condition.

Before I turn to explore the way health professionals and scientists perceive and experience the criteria governing PGD and the factors to take into account in deciding whether to offer any given test, it is worth considering how the HFEA and HGC decided on these criteria and how they envisaged they would operate, especially the way in which access to treatment would be discussed and

---

[30] HGC, *Minutes of Plenary Meeting*, 2 March 2001, para 4.5, *per* Professor Burn, as paraphrased in the minutes.

negotiated. For instance, how did the HFEA and HGC foresee the relationship between health professionals and prospective parents?

Prior to the consultation exercise, PGD had been licensed in line with the criteria of the disability ground of the Abortion Act 1967 (as amended by the Human Fertilisation and Embryology Act 1990). As discussed in earlier chapters, that ground requires that two doctors consider that there is a 'substantial risk' of a child being born 'seriously handicapped'.[31] Following the consultation, the HFEA and HGC decided to continue the 'precautionary principle' of broadly aligning the criteria for PGD with those for selective abortion.[32] Recommendation 11 contains the chosen criteria for PGD: 'The guidance should indicate that PGD should only be available where there is a significant risk of a serious genetic condition being present in the embryo'.

We can immediately see that there are differences between the wording in the disability ground of the Abortion Act and that in Recommendation 11. Most obviously, perhaps, the level of risk is not the same. For selective abortion this must be 'substantial'; for PGD it must be 'significant'. The first term implies a certain quantitative level of risk; it is not clear what the second implies. It could refer to a quantitative element, including a degree of risk that is less than substantial but still of some weight. In this sense, the concern would be with the statistical risk of the condition (depending on whether it is dominant, recessive, random but high, or sporadic but low). Or the term 'significant risk' could imply a degree of risk with a certain meaning to the couple seeking treatment: that is, the perception, or experience, of the couple of the impact of the disorder. Then again, the term could be intended to mean both of these. Indeed, if we explore more deeply the recommendations governing PGD, we see that whilst the HFEA and HGC profess broadly to align the criteria for PGD with those for selective abortion, the discussion and recommendations within the Outcome Document explicitly mention and give weight to the views of prospective parents on the two criteria. This is in contrast to the disability ground of the Abortion Act. As we first saw in Chapter 2, this makes no mention of the views of prospective parents and explicitly requires that two doctors are of the view, formed in good faith, that the criteria of 'substantial risk' and 'serious handicap' are satisfied.

For instance, one section of the Outcome Document on PGD notes that the Joint Working Party (JWP) of the HFEA and HGC agreed that 'the nature of the decision to pursue treatment involving PGD... meant that a central role in the judgement about the significance of the risk and the seriousness of the condition

---

[31] The relevant part of s 1(1)(1) of the Act reads: 'Subject to the provisions of this section, a person shall not be guilty of an offence under the law relating to abortion when a pregnancy is terminated by a registered medical practitioner if two registered medical practitioners are of the opinion, formed in good faith... (d) that there is a substantial risk that if the child were born it would suffer from such physical or mental abnormalities as to be seriously handicapped'.

[32] Above n 1. The reference to the 'precautionary principle' is in para 25.

should be given to the people seeking treatment'.[33] Another stresses the 'crucial importance of the views and experiences of those seeking treatment in decision-making'.[34] Here the personal nature of the issues in question is apparently being emphasised. This may begin to explain the difference in the nature of the risk specified in the Abortion Act on the one hand and the criteria for PGD on the other. While there may be a personal element to the question of the degree of risk and the seriousness of a condition in the context of selective abortion, arguably the growing moral and legal status of the fetus also temper the degree to which personal considerations can be valid, as discussed in Chapters 1 and 2. By contrast, on the gradualist approach to the moral status of the embryo and fetus that I have endorsed, the embryo's moral claims will carry some, but less, weight. The appropriate degree of risk in PGD compared with prenatal screening and PND was discussed by the JWP[35]:

> Some members pointed out that the risk should be substantial, and that people seeking treatment should not be allowed to pursue treatment where there was only a minimal risk (as they would not in PND), although it was acknowledged that this could potentially invite a conflict between people seeking treatment involving a particular test and clinicians who do not consider that the risk warrants it.

The passage seems to show two concerns: first, that parents might want to test too freely; second, that to require a substantial degree of risk could be problematic in relations between those seeking treatment and clinicians. So what is a 'significant' risk?

## A  'Significant Risk'

The JWP recommended that 'the significance of the risk to people seeking treatment, not the level of risk itself, should be judged by agreement between the people seeking treatment and the clinical team'.[36] This passage seems to acknowledge that the way a couple perceives a risk is not governed solely by how great that risk is in percentage terms. The passage also suggests that the couple and the clinical team should discuss and agree upon the significance of the risk. There is a further recommendation of relevance here, as Recommendation 13 states: 'The guidance should indicate that the perception of the level of risk by the people seeking treatment is an important factor in the decision-making process'. If we look at minutes of a JWP meeting on this point, we find 'that what [is] intended [is] the *subjective evaluation* of the level of risk in the minds of the people seeking

---

[33] Above n 1, para 32 and rec 13. Para 34 addresses the issue of information provision, especially the need for balanced information which includes 'that provided by disabled people and their families', an issue to which we return later.

[34] *Ibid* para 21. This paragraph is concerned with the relevance of RGOG guidance on termination of pregnancy, to which I return in due course.

[35] HFEA/HGC, *Minutes of Joint Working Party on Preimplantation Genetic Diagnosis*, 30 March 2001, para 5.4.

[36] *Ibid* para 5.11.

treatment'.[37] Ultimately, then, prospective parents' perception of the risk is described as '*an* important factor'; at the same time, 'agreement' is required as to the significance of the risk. In this way, the term 'significant risk' in Recommendation 11 should perhaps be understood as one that acknowledges the weight of prospective parents' views but also requires that they discuss their views with clinicians, who may or may not agree that a risk is indeed 'significant'. The implication is that if they do not, the criteria for PGD are not satisfied. In fact, it is highly unlikely that any of the health professionals or scientists at a clinic will be or have been in the same position as those seeking PGD. This may or may not create difficulties for agreeing upon the significance of the risk.

## B 'Serious Genetic Condition'

When the HFEA and HGC turned to consider the criterion of seriousness, there was a concern, which seems to reflect that in relation to the degree of risk, 'that the decision should not be made solely by the parents as some had very wide definitions of what counts as serious, which many others would not agree with'.[38] The final recommendation implicitly recognises that prospective parents will have views on this matter, but also requires that those views are discussed with clinicians: Recommendation 14 states 'that the seriousness of a condition should be a matter for discussion between the people seeking treatment and the clinical team'.[39] We do not find quite the same attention here (as we did in relation to the degree of risk) to the views of parents and there is no overt suggestion that seriousness is a subjective matter. Yet since the recommendation explicitly requires that seriousness should be a matter of discussion, there appears to be a realisation that there may be a range of views on the matter. Again, this is in contrast to the disability ground of the Abortion Act, which we saw makes no reference to the views of prospective parents or to discussions between them and health professionals. (It should be remembered here that abortion itself is a crime, to which the opinion of two doctors that one of the grounds for abortion is made out provides a defence.[40]) It may well be that increasing awareness of the difficulty of defining

---

[37] HFEA/HGC, *Minutes of Joint Working Party on Preimplantation Genetic Diagnosis*, 11 May 2001, para 5.15 (my emphasis).
[38] HGC, *Minutes of Genetic Testing Sub-group*, 12 January 2001, para 5.4, *per* Dr Flinter.
[39] Above n 1. The recommendation goes on to state that 'information provided to those seeking treatment... should include genetic and clinical information about the specific condition; its likely impact on those affected and their families; information about treatment and social support available; and the testimony of families and individuals about the full range of experiences of living with the condition'. Curiously, a somewhat puzzling variation of the point in Rec 14 can be found in the Summary of the responses to the Consultation Document which at one point observes that '80% *agreed* that the seriousness of a genetic condition should be a matter of *clinical judgment* based on general guidance' (HFEA/HGC, *Analysis of the Responses to the Joint HFEA/AGCT Consultation on PGD*, para 56(iv) (my emphases)).
[40] Offences against the Person Act, 1861, ss 58, 59.

'serious' underlies this recommendation. As noted in earlier chapters, the HGC has itself observed: 'It has proved impossible to define what "serious" should mean in this context'.[41]

On the whole, the HFEA and HGC seem to have tried both to recognise, to some extent at least, the personal nature of the issues at stake in PGD but also to observe limits to the acceptability of the views of prospective parents and so, ultimately, to reproductive autonomy. This is clearly expressed in the statement that[42]:

> The JWP agreed the importance of placing greater emphasis on the role of those seeking treatment in reaching the decision about when treatment was appropriate, whilst at the same time maintaining that this should not imply that this treatment should be available on demand.

The idea, it seems, is that this delicate balance will be achieved by means of the stated criteria ('significant risk of a serious genetic condition') as discussed, interpreted and agreed between prospective parents and health professionals and scientists on the one hand and clinics and licence committees on the other.

What is it like for PGD health professionals and scientists to operate under these criteria? How do they feel about trying to achieve the balance between respect for personal views on the one hand and the acceptable limits to reproductive autonomy on the other that seems to be sought by the HFEA and HGC? How do health professionals and scientists perceive the risks and the seriousness of the genetic conditions in question? What do they think about prospective parents' views about these matters? Do they see themselves as being some kind of a 'check' on the potentially excessively wide views of prospective parents? Before I turn to consider this issue, I need to outline the specific PGD guidance.

## C  The PGD Guidance

The HFEA and HGC rejected the idea of a 'prescriptive list of "serious conditions" for which the technique was thought to be appropriate'.[43] (As noted in Chapter 2, Parliament made a similar rejection in relation to abortion for fetal anomaly on the basis that this would interfere with clinical discretion. This is particularly important in the face of variations in the severity of conditions.[44]) Whilst the interim guidance had made use of the RCOG document *Termination*

---

[41] HGC, *Response to the Human Fertilisation and Embryology Authority on the Consultation on Preimplantation Genetic Diagnosis*, para 6.
[42] Above n 1, para 23.
[43] Ibid.
[44] On the approval of medical discretion generally in the application of the Act, see *Hansard*, 21 June 1990, vol 174, col 1156, *per* Mrs Maria Fyfe: 'If the law sets parameters that do not allow medical judgments to be freely exercised, it must be defective'.

of *Pregnancy for Fetal Abnormality in England and Wales*,[45] both the responses to the consultation and the JWP had concerns about this. These took two forms: first, the 'crucial importance of the views and experiences of those seeking treatment in decision-making'; second, 'the dependency of the RCOG guidance on the World Health Organization (WHO) definition of "serious disability" which was felt to be based on a view that emphasised a discriminatory conception of disability'.[46] Whether these are linked issues is not immediately clear. In the succeeding paragraph they appear to be linked. Here it is noted that the WHO standard of judging serious disability was not felt to be 'appropriate to the very personal decision to seek PGD treatment'.[47] The Outcome Document then recommends the use of 'dedicated PGD guidance', suggesting that '[t]his reflected the view that PGD guidance should support difficult parental choices rather than appearing to discriminate against individuals with certain conditions'. What is being stated here is not immediately apparent. On the one hand, reproductive autonomy is certainly being given considerable weight. On the other, this occurs in conjunction with a rejection of guidance that seems to be perceived as discriminatory in relation to disability. This suggests that some wider point may be being made, perhaps that PGD decisions are at some level about giving weight to reproductive autonomy rather than discriminating against people with disabilities (although the Outcome Document's fears about, rather than explicit analysis of, discrimination through PGD were noted above).[48] A similar point might be made about selective abortion. Arguably, both PGD and selective abortion are really about supporting reproductive autonomy (albeit to a limited degree) and cannot fairly be said to discriminate against people with disabilities, particularly where serious parental concerns are in issue.[49]

The Outcome Document states that '[i]n line with responses to the consultation... the JWP considered that it would be appropriate to specify factors that should be taken into account in reaching a decision to provide PGD treatment'.[50] This list is contained in Recommendation 15[51]:

> The guidance should indicate that in any particular situation the following factors should be considered when deciding *the appropriateness of PGD*: the view of those seeking treatment of the condition; their previous reproductive experience; the likely

---

[45] RCOG, *Termination of Pregnancy for Fetal Abnormality in England, Wales and Scotland* (January, 1996).
[46] Above n 1, para 21.
[47] *Ibid*, para 22: 'It was noted that the WHO's revised classification, ICIDH-2—International Classification of Functioning, Disability and Health (WHO, 2000), was currently in prefinal draft'.
[48] See also HGC, above n 41, para 5, which refers to 'concerns that PGD should not be used to... further disadvantage disabled people now and in the future'. The concern requires further analysis.
[49] I discussed this particularly in Ch 1, S V.
[50] Above n 1, para 37.
[51] *Ibid* (my emphasis). See also HFEA, above n 4, para 14.23.

degree of suffering associated with the condition; the availability of effective therapy or management now and in the future; the speed of degeneration in progressive disorders; the extent of any intellectual impairment; the extent of social support available; and the family circumstances of the people seeking treatment.

By itself it is unclear whether 'the appropriateness of PGD' means the decision to offer PGD and with it the choice of which conditions to test for, or also the question of the selection of embryos thereafter. This is clarified by a later paragraph, which states[52]:

> Embarking on preimplantation testing presents patients and clinicians with a *further set of choices* to be made after the outcome of the test is known. Difficult choices might arise if the test is inconclusive, if only affected embryos are available for transfer, or if collateral information about the genetic status of other family members was discovered.

So it seems that the list of factors applies to the decision to *offer* PGD and to the question of what PGD itself will entail, notably which conditions should be the subject of testing. (Note also here the proposed amendments to the HFE Act by virtue of the Human Tissues and Embryos (Draft) Bill.[53])

I now turn to consider the views of the professionals working in one clinic that offers PGD.

## IV HEALTH PROFESSIONALS' AND SCIENTISTS' VIEWS AND EXPERIENCE

This central section of the chapter considers health professionals' and scientists' experience and views of the twin criteria of 'significant risk' and 'serious genetic condition'. In due course the discussion is developed with explicit reference to the factors that the HFEA and HGC recommended should be considered in the decision to offer PGD and listed above, such as 'the view of those seeking treatment of the condition' and 'the likely degree of suffering associated with the condition'. In effect, these factors help elucidate the meaning of the criteria for PGD.

---

[52] *Ibid*, para 8 (my emphasis).
[53] Above n 2, amending Sch 2, HFE Act 1990: 'After paragraph 1 insert 1ZA... (3) In considering under paragraph 1(3) whether the testing of embryos for the purpose mentioned in sub-paragraph (1)(b) or (c) is necessary or desirable for the purpose of providing treatment services, the Authority must have regard to — (a) the extent to which the disability, illness or other medical condition involves intellectual, physical, emotional or psychological impairment, having regard to the treatment available, (b) where relevant, the likely age of onset of the disability, illness or other medical condition in question, (c) where any illness or other medical condition is a progressive disorder, the likely rate of degeneration, (d) the proportion of those having the abnormality in question who are likely to be affected, and (e) the reliability of the test to be applied'. (For sub-para (1)(b) and (c) see above n 2.)

## A 'Significant Risk'

The question of the degree of risk facing a couple was touched on in several of the ethics discussion groups (EDGs). Some members of staff appear to see the issue of risk in quantitative terms. For instance, Scientist 19 refers to the idea of a 'significantly increased risk above population risk'.[54] This same scientist also states that there is no need for additional tests that will compromise accuracy, when people are not 'at risk'.[55] Another member of staff (Nurse 13) comments that if the risk is greater, this helps '[you to] feel easier maybe about what you're doing'.[56] The relationship between the criteria is also touched on in discussions. For instance, Scientist 2 comments that although there may only be a risk rather than a certainty of a condition occurring in a child, the risk could relate to a very serious condition.[57]

Some of the health professionals and scientists also work in the area of prenatal screening, PND and termination and the recognition that risk may have a subjective component is clearly revealed in the account of a woman who was already pregnant and undergoing prenatal screening. The account is given by Counsellor 28.[58] The woman in question had previously given birth to a child with a 'very nasty disease' who 'died very horribly'. She now had a new partner, so that her risk of having another affected child was 'really very small'. 'But… she was at the stage of her life that she was so anxious about what might happen and the pregnancy brought back all the kinds of memories and feelings that losing her baby obviously reminded her of'. A test for the condition that affected her child was negative but a scan revealed a relatively mild and unconnected physical malformation that could be corrected once the child had been born.

> And that was the only abnormality with this baby, but the girl became so convinced that this was like a sign, a premonition, you know, a sort of marker, that this was all going to go wrong again. And as a result of that, she became… very mentally unstable. And I really felt that if she had been forced to continue with that pregnancy, she may have ended her life.

This case highlights the potentially subjective nature of risk. Clearly, it also raises questions about seriousness. Indeed, Counsellor 28 notes that the relatively trivial malformation would not have satisfied the requirement of seriousness under the disability ground of the Abortion Act. However, in the light of the woman's fears about something else being wrong with the fetus, the health professionals were in

---

[54] Ethics Discussion Group (EDG) 1, Scientist 19, 6.
[55] EDG 1, Scientist 19, 11.
[56] EDG 3, Nurse 13, 8. For a detailed discussion of the staff's attitudes to embryos, see also K Ehrich, C Williams, B Farsides, J Sandall and R Scott 'Choosing Embryos: Ethical Complexity in Staff accounts of Preimimplantation Genetic Diagnosis' (2007) 29/7 *Sociology of Health & Illness* 1.
[57] EDG 5, Scientist 2, 19.
[58] EDG 2, Counsellor 28, 13–14.

fact concerned about a risk to her mental health. Although the account does not record on what grounds an abortion was sanctioned, it is likely that this would have been under section 1(1)(a). As discussed in Chapter 2, this permits abortion where 'the pregnancy has not exceeded twenty-four weeks and... the continuance of the pregnancy would involve risk, greater than if the pregnancy were terminated, of injury to the physical or mental health of the pregnant woman or any existing children of her family'. In such circumstances, in effect, a woman's views about the degree of risk or the seriousness of the disability are being taken into account by use of another ground of the Abortion Act. As noted previously, the actual disability ground of the Act makes no mention of a woman's (or her partner's) views about disability. Curiously perhaps, the Outcome Document on PGD makes no reference to the use of section 1(1)(a) of the Abortion Act in the context of disability.

It is interesting to speculate what would have happened if, instead of becoming pregnant with her new partner, the woman had instead sought PGD, for instance for the condition which had affected her first child. As noted above, her risk (with her new partner) of having another child with the same condition was now 'very small'. Understandably, however, she was very fearful of something going wrong with a subsequent pregnancy. To what extent could these fears have been relevant to a decision to provide PGD of some kind? Two of the factors that the HFEA and HGC recommend should be considered when deciding the appropriateness of PGD (discussed further below) could have been particularly relevant: the view of those seeking treatment of the condition and their previous reproductive experience. However, although the woman may have been very fearful, where the risk is in fact 'very small' it is not clear that her subjective experience can gain her access to PGD. Indeed, as we saw above, whilst the HFEA and HGC intended the term 'significant risk' to mean 'the subjective evaluation of the level of risk in the minds of the people seeking treatment' and this is 'an important factor', agreement is still required as to the significance of the risk. It seems unlikely that health professionals and scientists would have agreed that the risk was 'significant'. No doubt resource considerations will also be relevant here in the NHS context. Further, since the woman in this revised scenario is not already pregnant there would not be the immediate concern with her mental health — and the need, in some sense, to 'rescue' her — that there was in the original case.

## B 'Serious Genetic Condition'

I have touched on a case from the context of prenatal screening and selective abortion that highlighted the potentially subjective nature of risk and speculated on the degree to which this can be relevant in the context of PGD. The case also raised issues about seriousness, a question about which health professionals and scientists had a great deal to say in the interviews and discussion groups. By way of introduction to this issue, it may be useful to note that recollection of the case above led Counsellor 28 to observe[59]:

> I've always thought, perhaps it's one of the reasons it hasn't been done in law, is that you can't kind of... write a list of things or conditions that you consider serious... And I think one of the reasons it's not been done in law is that it — the perception and the reality of seriousness isn't just about the condition itself.

Strikingly, this observation supports the HFEA's and HGC's rejection of a prescriptive list in favour of the development of the PGD guidance. Having recounted the above case, Counsellor 28 continued: '[I]f you did have a list, I think you would be less of a clinician, because the notion of clinical judgement and care of your patient or family would have to go out the window'.[60] The suggestion here seems to be that the perceptions of the prospective parents and the situation of the wider family may be relevant to an assessment of seriousness. As we shall see, this suggestion is given further weight by the views of other staff.

I now turn to explore their views with specific reference to the PGD guidance. Although each of these factors could be helpful in my exploration of health professionals' and scientists' views on seriousness, some particularly so, I do not have the scope to give them equal weight here. Further, I do not necessarily look at them in the order listed above.

At the outset, it is worth noting how decisions about seriousness are made in this clinic. Given that different professionals will hold a range of views about the seriousness of conditions and the appropriateness of testing for them, the clinic discusses decisions on a case-by-case basis. Where it wishes to start testing for a new condition, the clinic holds multidisciplinary meetings approximately every six weeks prior to applying for a licence from the HFEA. Present at these meetings are reproductive clinicians, geneticists, molecular biologists, counsellors, clinical geneticists, embryologists, cytogeneticists, specialist clinicians in haematology and dermatology, and administrators involved in planning cases.

### i  The view of those seeking treatment of the condition

This factor explicitly refers to the need to take into account prospective parents' views. As we have seen, the HGC has stated that it is 'impossible' to define seriousness. What we might call the 'subjectivity' of seriousness was a much-discussed issue in the groups. For instance, Doctor 24 says '[w]hat I feel is serious, minor, is a very subjective issue especially to parents'.[61] He/she expands[62]:

> Maybe for a parent having a child with six fingers, is minor. That's the only thing I can think of myself. Anything beyond that, any handicap in a child, I would not consider *not*

---

[59] EDG 2, Counsellor 28, 13.
[60] *Ibid* 14.
[61] EDG 1, Doctor 24, 7.
[62] My emphasis.

serious. So, I have to — it's a very personal opinion as to — I mean I can't off hand think of any condition which should not be tested because it's not serious.

Similarly, Counsellor 18 says of the notion of seriousness that '[w]e all have a different idea of what it is'.[63] In the light of the developments in PGD technology ('it's just going to develop and progress over the centuries') Counsellor 18 continues[64]:

> [T]here will always be people pushing the boundaries, and it's a serious condition this week, but like we've said, nobody can really define seriousness… and what is serious for you won't be for me. And I think it's this, and you think it's that. And in ten years' time, they'll think…

Differences of view about seriousness are also noted by Embryologist 33[65]:

> I think how one person copes with it and how another person copes with 'serious' is going to be different as well… What one person thinks is a serious condition, the next person might not.

Importantly, however, within the groups there was also a sense that although there is a subjective element to seriousness, at the same time there must be a limit to what could in any sense be regarded as a 'serious genetic condition': it cannot be that 'anything goes'. For instance, in response to the last comment above, Scientist 2 observes[66]: 'No, but, when it's serious, their life is completely debilitated by it… it's medically serious'. Later, he/she adds: 'If we said the possibility is it's going to be mild, we wouldn't do PGD for it. But if the possibility is there that it's going to be fairly serious, that's why it's done'. Further, as we saw above, Doctor 24 suggested that having an extra finger could not in any sense be 'serious', thus seeming to place extra digits at the non-serious end of the spectrum of 'abnormality'. As for other conditions that may not be serious, Nurse 13 suggests that a condition such as cleft palate is not serious, although 'people are clamouring for' the relevant testing.[67] Not surprisingly, these observations show that health professionals and scientists have views — though not necessarily homogeneous ones — about which conditions will satisfy the criterion of 'serious genetic condition'. In any event, as we know, the HFEA and HGC require (in Recommendation 14) 'that the seriousness of a condition should be a matter for discussion between the people seeking treatment and the clinical team'.

So far, we have seen that although these health professionals and scientists consider that 'serious' has a subjective component, at the same time several members of staff think it is not a 'free-for-all'. It may now be helpful to think more closely about the possible meanings of 'serious' by considering whose

---

[63] EDG 3, Counsellor 18, 15.
[64] EDG 3, Counsellor 18, 23.
[65] EDG 5, Embryologist 33, 19.
[66] EDG 5, Scientist 2, 19.
[67] EDG 3, Nurse 13, 24.

interests may be at stake in PGD. In this regard, a very important question was posed by Doctor 11: 'Is seriousness... [about] the person that's going to be affected by that condition? Is it serious at their level, not so much our level?'[68]

As seen in earlier chapters, this question has been considered in the related context of PND and selective abortion. For instance, Sally Sheldon and Stephen Wilkinson have helpfully clarified this issue in relation to the interpretation of the disability ground of the Abortion Act. Sheldon and Wilkinson argue that when the fetus would be born as a child with what many would regard as an extremely serious condition (perhaps Tay-Sachs),[69] termination may well be in the fetus's interests, a position in accordance with other philosophical analyses.[70] Since it *may* be that if born such a child would say her life was not worth living (see further below) it may also be that, if not terminated *in utero*, the subsequently-born child could claim, ethically speaking, to have a wrongful life.[71] Yet there are remarkably few conditions that might be potentially serious in this way. Recognition of this requires that we recall the other possible justifications for PND and termination and indeed for PGD.

Where a child would be born with a condition that would mean she still thought she had a life worth living, a more satisfactory rationale for use of the disability ground of the Abortion Act might be found in the notion of 'parental interests', as Sheldon and Wilkinson have argued and as I discussed at length in Chapter 2.[72] This type of argument could also be applied in the context of PGD,

---

[68] EDG 4, Doctor 11, 27.

[69] 'The classical form of Tay-Sachs disease (TSD) is a fatal genetic disorder in children that causes progressive destruction of the central nervous system... By about two years of age, most children experience recurrent seizures and diminishing mental function. The infant gradually regresses, losing skills one by one, and is eventually unable to crawl, turn over, sit, or reach out. Other symptoms include increasing loss of coordination, progressive inability to swallow and breathing difficulties. Eventually, the child becomes blind, mentally retarded, paralyzed, and non-responsive to his or her environment. To date, there is no cure or effective treatment for TSD.' National Tay-Sachs and Allied Diseases Association, Inc <http://www.ntsad.org> accessed 8 October 2007.

[70] S Sheldon and S Wilkinson 'Termination of Pregnancy for Reason of Foetal Disability: are there Grounds for a Special Exception in Law?' (2001) 9 *Med Law Rev* 85, 88 *ff*. A second rationale for the disability ground of the Abortion Act discussed and ultimately rejected by Sheldon and Wilkinson is the so-called 'replacement argument', which relies on non-person-affecting principles (*ibid* 93 *ff*). As discussed in Ch 1, the distinction between cases in which a child might have a wrongful life and ones in which this would not be the case is endorsed by others, such as A Buchanan, D Brock, N Daniels, D Wikler, *From Chance to Choice: Genetics and Justice* (Cambridge: Cambridge University Press, 2000) 235.

[71] See, eg, Buchanan *et al*, above n 70, *ibid*. As Sheldon and Wilkinson note, however, such a claim has not been recognised in English law. Sheldon and Wilkinson, above n 70, 89, and referring to *McKay v Essex AHA* [1982] 2 WLR 890.

[72] Sheldon and Wilkinson, above n 70, 99 *ff*. The legal objection to this argument, originally explored by Derek Morgan (D Morgan 'Abortion: the Unexamined Ground' [1990] *Crim LR* 687, 692) is that a 'parental interests' interpretation of s 1(1)(d) of the Act

the rationale for which is of course the main consideration here. The thought is that PND or PGD for conditions that are not as serious as (for instance) Tay-Sachs, coupled with the option of termination or embryo discard, may potentially respond to parents' concerns and interests.

Of course, before leaving the PND context, we should recall that if parents are to have the legal option of termination in any given case, two clinicians must judge in good faith that the condition is 'serious', as explored in detail in Chapter 2. Indeed, as discussed in Chapter 3, it is likely that parents would only have been offered screening or testing aimed at 'serious' conditions of some kind, although a less serious feature might happen to be found on an ultrasound scan. In effect, then, where a fetus would be born as a child with a life she thought worth living but clinicians still judge a given condition to amount to a 'serious handicap' for the purposes of the disability section of the Abortion Act, they are effectively determining that although the condition would leave a child with a life worth living, it has an element of seriousness that implicates its parents' interests in child-raising and, moreover, to an extent that justifies termination. Since there is a dearth of case law on the Abortion Act, there is as yet no overt recognition of this point, although we saw in Chapters 2 and 3 that the law has recognised that parents can sue for the lost opportunity to abort a disabled child and that to some extent this is because of their interests in child-raising.[73]

With this recollection of parental interests, it should immediately be noted that, although this chapter discusses staff's views about parents' concerns and relates these to ethical arguments about whether it can be appropriate to take account of parents' interests in the evaluation of 'seriousness', as noted in earlier chapters, nothing of what follows should be taken as implying that raising a child with a disability is necessarily more demanding than raising a non-disabled child. Further, I make no judgment as to the balance of rewards and demands in raising a disabled, as compared with a non-disabled, child. Clearly, this is a judgment for parents to make. Experiences will vary widely and some or many people may say that raising a disabled child is particularly rewarding.

---

would essentially repeat s 1(1)(a) of the Act, making s 1(1)(d) redundant. Sheldon and Wilkinson observe that, from an ethical viewpoint, it may simply be that there is more than one justification for this section. From the viewpoint of statutory interpretation, however, they suggest that 'there are some grounds for questioning' whether Parliament can have intended that s 1(1)(d) should protect parents' interests. Of course, s 1(1)(d) can never be entirely redundant in that, unlike s 1(1)(a), it allows terminations up until birth. Apart from this point and more fundamentally, it may be that as a society we have not necessarily been honest about whose interests the disability section of the Act is capable of protecting: it is to some degree taboo to say that parents have an interest in choosing to accept or avoid the birth of an impaired child and those debating the Act in Parliament may well have sensed this.

[73] For discussion of relevant wrongful birth case law (and interpretation of the disability ground of the Abortion Act generally), see Chs 2 and 3 above.

Returning directly to PGD, here too we face the point that very few genetic conditions might be so serious as to give rise to a life that a child thought was not worth living. (I consider health professionals' and scientists' thoughts about some specific contenders for the description 'very serious' below.) This means it may be appropriate to recognise that at least some forms of PGD are conducted for the prospective parents. Scientist 21 makes this point very clearly[74]:

> I was at a conference… Parent Project UK, which is a charity which is aimed at… therapy for Duchenne muscular dystrophy people, and they were all parents. So one presented a talk actually which I found very interesting, and they looked at the quality of life for families with boys with Duchenne muscular dystrophy, which is a severe disease. The average lifespan now is about 19. And the quality of life of — the perception of the quality of life of the affected boy was rated differently by parents, by the clinicians looking after them and by the boys themselves. And the boys themselves… gave their rating of quality of life the same as any healthy controlled sample. And the parents gave them the lowest quality and the clinicians gave them somewhere in between the two, which was interesting, I thought… *So that implies we're doing this for the parents and not for the child in some respects.*

Earlier, Scientist 21 observed[75]: 'Obviously people want to have children and when they have children with disability or handicap, to some extent that makes their life a bit more miserable compared to what they're hoping for'. The potential impact of a child's disability on parents was observed by a number of participants. Scientist 8 refers to the 'huge burden' that parents may experience.[76] He/she also alludes to the idea of undoubtedly serious conditions on the one hand and conditions about which parents may disagree on the other[77]:

> I mean I think there are conditions which are under all circumstances, horrendous. And can be put very firmly on that list. But I completely agree with [the participant], I mean I think there are lots of conditions which aren't clear-cut and which for some families might be considered serious and others not.

Further, Administrator 31 observes: 'I think you need to look at people's — you know seriousness, to a certain extent, has to be based on people's perception of their ability to cope'. Ethically speaking, we could relate the idea of the 'ability to cope' to the question of the extensive positive moral duties that parents must undertake in child-raising and to the idea that people might reasonably disagree about how much is reasonable to have to 'take on' (assuming there is a choice at the stage of selection by PGD or PND), as discussed in Chapter 1. So, each of these members of staff seems to recognise and accept that parents' interests are significantly implicated in the possible wish to avoid a child with a serious genetic condition.

---

[74] EDG 2, Scientist 21, 3–4 (my emphasis).
[75] EDG 2, Scientist 21, 2.
[76] EDG 2, Scientist 8, 5.
[77] *Ibid* 14.

Turning now to the interaction between health professionals and prospective parents, in which they may (explicitly or otherwise) discuss the notion of seriousness, it appears that meeting the couple and learning something about their experience can considerably affect the views of staff. For instance, Doctor 11 observes[78]: 'knowing the couple can have an amazing effect on how you feel about them'. And Counsellor 17 adds[79]:

> I guess if you do get the opportunity to see, hear a little bit more about the whole story behind... the couple, you've got more of an idea of the issues then, for them too. So I think... even if you are discussing cases that you've not been actually involved in, I guess having seen some of these then it perhaps puts you in a better position in thinking, 'Oh yes, I know what you're trying to get at, I understand where you're coming from, but I actually think that's wrong'. Or, 'Yes, I agree with that'. You know.

The philosopher facilitating the discussion suggested to one of the groups[80]:

> BF: So you think if someone has personally experienced something, they're in a position to tell you, in a real sense, how serious it is to them, in a way that might not seem obvious from the outside?
>
> Doctor 11: That's where it sits with me, is that if they feel that it's serious enough, that if they found that their child was affected by it, and tested prenatally, they would consider terminating the pregnancy, because they would not want their child to go through this, mum's gone through all this, sister's gone through this, even though, as a penetrance issue, if they feel strongly enough that they would go to those lengths, then I wouldn't... have difficulty offering them PGD.

('Penetrance' refers to the degree of risk.) This perspective is echoed by Embryologist 15[81]:

> I find it very difficult to draw the line between what is natural — I don't know — it was very easy first of all because it was very defined for diseases where the children would be, would die, basically. Or have a very reduced life. There are... some cases where the children would have problems, maybe developmentally or physical problems. But that can perhaps be overcome with surgery or — so that's a bit more of a sort of a grey area. But, in general, if I was pushed about it, I would probably still lean towards the side of the parents for opting to go through it because they obviously have either seen their child go through that or someone in their family. And if they're willing to go through the treatment, then I would probably be leaning towards that as well.

In general, there did not seem to be any strong disagreement with the idea, expressed by Scientist 2, that 'you have to be able to see patients' perspectives'.[82] Referring to the way the clinic works as a team, he/she continues 'and then [you]

---

[78] EDG 4, Doctor 11, 24.
[79] EDG 4, Counsellor 17, 24.
[80] Bobbie Farsides, EDG 4, 28.
[81] Interview, Embryologist 15, 2.
[82] EDG 5, Scientist 2, 27.

open it to everyone who works in the unit, and then their perspectives as well'. On the one hand, then, there are discussions between people seeking treatment and one or more members of staff; on the other, the staff will then discuss a given request for PGD amongst themselves (as noted earlier). Since the staff are actively involved in all the processes in PGD, they need to feel as comfortable as they can with the acceptability of PGD for a given condition. The ethical dimensions of staff involvement in PGD was a much-discussed issue in the groups, but not one on which I can focus here.[83]

In this section I have reviewed these health professionals' and scientists' thoughts about the 'subjective' notion of seriousness, but at the same time noted that they do not necessarily think that *any* condition can reasonably be seen as serious. I have also noted, in response to Doctor 11's question ('Is it serious at their level, not so much our level?'), that in reflecting on seriousness it is important to think about 'serious for whom?'. As explored in earlier chapters, there is a distinction between conditions that are so serious that it may, conceivably, not be in the embryo's or fetus's interests to be born on the one hand, and conditions that are less serious on the other.[84] In the latter case, it will not be against the interests of someone with a given condition to be born; at the same time, however, parents may have an interest in deciding whether to give birth to such a child. I then considered the recognition, by staff, of the importance of the views of prospective parents about the seriousness of a condition.

We now need to look at something of the spectrum of possible conditions in order further to disentangle the embryo's interests from those of its parents or the wider family, where these may diverge. I do this with reference to another factor that the HFEA and HGC recommended should be considered in relation to the decision to offer PGD, namely 'the likely degree of suffering associated with the condition'.

### ii   The likely degree of suffering associated with the condition

a   Very serious conditions

Clearly, suffering could be of a mental or physical form. Either way, it may affect someone's quality of life. As we saw in Chapter 2 with reference to the Royal College of Obstetricians' and Gynaecologists' (RCOG) guidelines on selective abortion, the difficulty with this important factor is that we have to estimate the degree of suffering in conditions we have not experienced. Arguably, anyone with

---

[83] eg, in EDG 1, 2 and 5. The issue was also referred to by various members of staff in interview, eg, Scientist 2, Doctor 6 and Embryologist 15.

[84] The reference to interests is used loosely, since it may be argued that the embryo has none until it acquires them at sentience. On the link between interests and sentience, see B Steinbock, *Life Before Birth* (New York: OUP, 1992) 24, fn 24. On the notion of interests, see J Feinberg, *Harm to Others* (New York: OUP, 1984) 34: 'In general, a person has a stake in X… when he stands to gain or lose depending on the nature or condition of X'.

a given condition will be the best informed about it and, in the PGD context, sometimes prospective parents will themselves be in a position to offer insights. I start with some of the conditions staff mentioned that are often regarded as undoubtedly serious. Recall, for instance, Scientist 2's reference to a life being 'completely debilitated' by a 'medically serious condition'.

'I think I would consider a serious condition, for instance, a genetic condition called Tay-Sachs disease, where the children die in childhood... I would consider that a serious condition because a child being so sick in early life, and going through all the things...', observes Doctor 32.[85] Tay-Sachs is often cited as a classic case of a very serious condition (and I have relied on it as a clear instance of a very serious case since Chapter 1). Since a child with Tay-Sachs lives such a short time, and in a state of rapid and marked physical and mental deterioration, it may not be feasible to obtain the views of such a child on his or her suffering. Looking from the outside, however, it may be plausible to say that the suffering would be very great.

Another condition that is often regarded as very serious, and that was discussed in one of the groups, is Duchenne muscular dystrophy.[86] Recall that Scientist 21 (above) referred to this as a 'severe disease' and said (in part):

> The average lifespan now is about 19.... [T]he boys themselves... gave their rating of quality of life the same as any healthy controlled sample. And the parents gave them the lowest quality and the clinicians gave them somewhere in between the two...

On this basis, it may be that if we asked these boys whether Duchenne muscular dystrophy entails significant suffering, they would say 'no'. In fact, the boys' response is not surprising and is in line with other research in which people with a given illness or condition report greater quality of life compared to that

---

[85] EDG 3, Doctor 32, 18.

[86] 'The muscular dystrophies are a group of over 20 hereditary muscle disorders in which slow, progressive muscle wasting occurs, leading to increasing weakness and disability... Duchenne's muscular dystrophy is the most common and most severe type... The first signs of the Duchenne type of dystrophy usually appear before the age of three. In most cases the muscles appear bulkier than normal. Even so, there is progressive weakening. This initially affects the muscles of the buttocks and legs, and causes a characteristic waddle when walking. The child may therefore be slow to walk and have slower development. Children overcome the effects of the weakness by doing things differently, such as getting up by "hand-walking" up their legs. By about 8 to 11 years boys become unable to walk and by their late teens or twenties the condition is usually severe enough to shorten life expectancy... There is no treatment that will cure the muscular dystrophies. Physiotherapy can help to prevent deformity and rigid joints in the later stages... Possible complications are: curvature of the spine, breathing difficulties, weak heart muscle, severe chest infections.' NHS Direct Health Encylopaedia 'Muscular Dystrophy' <http://www.nhsdirect.nhs.uk/articles/article.aspx?articleId=257> accessed 13 October 2007.

attributed to them by others.[87] Despite this, it is clear that their parents thought that their quality of life was severely affected and the clinicians likewise, though to a lesser extent. Why might this be so?

Presumably, there may be several elements that will affect parents' views. They may agonise for the experience of their children, for the things they cannot do, and for their relatively short life-span. In this process, the predominant consideration will very likely be for the children. But it seems inevitable that part of the parents' assessment about the quality of life of their boy(s) will stem from their own experience of parenting him (or them). Further, they may have increased physical demands in parenting, commensurate with the increasing disability of the child and its need, for instance, for wheelchairs, lifting devices and so forth. Moreover, the death of children, in this case just on the cusp of adulthood, clearly affects parents and was a factor noted generally in one of the discussion groups. For instance, Doctor 32 observed: 'For the parents, the death of a child is very serious'.[88] In many ways, then, it does not seem surprising that parents should rate the quality of life of their children with Duchenne muscular dystrophy the lowest.

Clinicians' views, we may recall, were recorded as being in between those of the boys and their parents. It may not be surprising that clinicians would think a condition less serious than the boys' parents: however caring they are, they will be much less emotionally and physically involved. As for clinicians thinking that Duchenne muscular dystrophy results in a lower quality of life, compared with what the boys thought, clinicians are likely to have very much in mind the clinical features of the condition and will be trying to ameliorate its symptoms. For this reason, the clinical features may be more prominent in their minds than in those of the boys. Further, since they are not experiencing the condition themselves, they will not have the same sense (as the boys) of the impact (or lack thereof) of the condition on life overall. Clinicians' possible tendencies to think of disability in medical terms (as first noted in Chapter 1 and as discussed below) may also be relevant here.

---

[87] See, eg, the work of P Alderson 'Prenatal Counselling and Images of Disability' in D Dickenson (ed), *Ethical Issues in Maternal-Fetal Medicine* (Cambridge: Cambridge University Press, 2002) 195, first discussed in Ch 1. Alderson interviewed adults who have one of a number of different conditions: cystic fibrosis, sickle cell anaemia, thalassaemia, Down's syndrome and spina bifida. She sought their views about their lives and about screening practices. See also the Nuffield Council on Bioethics, *Critical Care Decisions in Fetal and Neonatal Medicine: Ethical Issues* (2006) para 3.19: 'As they grow up, children who develop disabilities report a more positive outlook than their carers… It is therefore particularly important that stereotypes or prejudices against states of disability are not fostered during the decision-making process'. The report also observes: 'Research has shown that families are generally more positive about a baby's health problems than the neonatal doctors and nurses who provide his or her care'. This last statement presents a different picture from the account given here of Duchenne muscular dystrophy.

[88] EDG 3, Doctor 32, 20.

Both parents and clinicians may compare the boy's experiences with their own experience of life and its possibilities and reflect particularly, in so doing, on the things the boys cannot do. It may be useful at this point to think about the significance of the potential losses — of experiences, activities or opportunities — involved in disease or disability. In this respect a key idea explored in Chapter 1 was that of flourishing. Jonathan Glover writes about disability in this way. We saw previously that he suggests that disability is a 'functional limitation, which (either on its own or — more usually — in combination with social disadvantage) impairs the capacity for human flourishing'.[89] When we have not experienced a given condition, he asks whether and if so how we can make the judgment that it amounts to a disability. Glover suggests that strong weight should be given to the accounts and views of those with disabilities. This implies that we should take the views of the boys with Duchenne muscular dystrophy very seriously. However, because people's identities are to some degree inherent in their disabilities, we saw before that Glover suggests that these views 'need to be interpreted with alertness to possible biases'.[90] As we saw, he also notes that, in reflecting on whether a condition amounts to a disability, we have other sources upon which we can draw: on the one hand, ideas about the components of human flourishing; on the other, the knowledge that people who can see and hear, for instance, can give about these senses and their experience of them.[91]

In this light, and returning to the example of Duchenne muscular dystrophy, although these boys rated their quality of life as high as that of healthy boys, it could be argued that the condition brings with it the possibility of suffering and loss of the opportunity to flourish. In this way, Duchenne muscular dystrophy may reasonably be viewed, as Scientist 21 suggests, as a 'severe' disease and perhaps a 'very severe' one. However, since judgments by third parties about the quality of life of possible others are obviously difficult and sensitive, as noted in Chapter 1, we saw that Jonathan Glover has suggested that, rather than attempting to make clear-cut judgments about conditions that we have not experienced, it may be better to restrict ourselves to the question of whether there is a *serious risk* that a child would have a life that was not worth living.[92] Glover thinks this might be true of a condition such as Lesch-Nyhan disease.[93] It also seems likely that we can

---

[89] J Glover, *Choosing Children: Genes, Disability and Design* (Oxford: Clarendon Press, 2006) 9.
[90] *Ibid* 22.
[91] *Ibid* 22–3.
[92] *Ibid* 60.
[93] 'Lesch-Nyhan syndrome (LNS) is a rare, inherited disorder caused by a deficiency of the enzyme hypoxanthine-guanine phosphoribosyltransferase (HPRT). LNS is an X-linked recessive disease — the gene is carried by the mother and passed on to her son. LNS is present at birth in baby boys. The lack of HPRT causes a build-up of uric acid in all body fluids, and leads to symptoms such as severe gout, poor muscle control, and moderate retardation, which appear in the first year of life. A striking feature of LNS is self-mutilating behaviors — characterized by lip and finger biting — that begin in the second year of life.

say there is such a risk in the case of Tay-Sachs. At the same time, it is *not* clear that we can say this in relation to Duchenne muscular dystrophy. With regard to the boys who have Duchenne muscular dystrophy, Scientist 8 observed[94]:

> I think what's not predictable is that they would not see themselves as having any different quality of life than normal boys. I think it's quite predictable that they would say that they're glad they're alive.

However, in all these cases the impact on parents could be considerable. On this point, Doctor 32 added in relation to Tay-Sachs that the condition would be serious 'for the child, for the parents, just as bad. So that I would consider serious on those two accounts'.[95]

Glover's warning about making judgments that there is a risk that someone will have a very low quality of life is salutary. In one of the discussion groups, Scientist 8 observed that one clinician had given a talk in which he/she had said that the only condition in relation to which he/she could ever recall that people said they would prefer not to be born was epidermolysis bullosa (EB).[96] Indeed, the Nuffield Council report *Critical Care Decisions in Fetal and Neonatal Medicine: Ethical Issues* (the 'Nuffield Report') observes of the 'extreme form of the condition' that '[t]he intractable pain and consquent disablity imposed on a child... could be said to make continuing life "intolerable"'.[97] This suggests that EB would be a strong contender for being at the top of the list of very serious conditions, although we have noted that it may be very hard to obtain the views of a child with Tay-Sachs, who will be subject to rapid physical and mental deterioration and will die very young.

---

Abnormally high uric acid levels can cause sodium urate crystals to form in the joints, kidneys, central nervous system, and other tissues of the body, leading to gout-like swelling in the joints and severe kidney problems. Neurological symptoms include facial grimacing, involuntary writhing, and repetitive movements of the arms and legs similar to those seen in Huntington's disease. Because a lack of HPRT causes the body to poorly utilize vitamin B12, some boys may develop a rare disorder called megaloblastic anemia... The prognosis for individuals with LNS is poor. Death is usually due to renal failure in the first or second decade of life.' National Institute of Neurological Disorders and Stroke <http://www.ninds.nih.gov/disorders/lesch_nyhan/lesch_nyhan.htm> accessed 13 October 2007.

[94] EDG 2, Scientist 8, 48.
[95] EDG 3, Doctor 32, 19.
[96] EDG 2, Scientist 8, 4. 'Epidermolysis bullosa (EB) is the name given to a group of genetic disorders that lead to fragile skin. This fragility leads to blistering and shearing of the skin as a response to friction and everyday knocks and bumps... There are three major types of EB, but the general symptoms in all forms of EB are skin fragility and blistering. In some types the internal linings of the body can be affected, as well as the cornea of the eye. Healing with scarring seen in some forms of EB can also lead to worsening disability. Within each type there are sub-groups with a huge variety of symptoms and prognosis.' NHS Direct Health Encylopaedia 'Epidermolysis bullosa' <http://www.nhsdirect.nhs.uk/articles/article.aspx?articleId=560&PrintPage=1> accessed 13 October 2007.
[97] Nuffield Council on Bioethics, above n 87, para 2.14.

### b   Less serious conditions

I now move away from conditions that some people might reasonably regard as very serious (even though a person with a given very serious condition may not say that his or her life is not worth living). As first noted in Chapter 1, conditions that might be seen as less serious include cystic fibrosis and Down's syndrome, amongst others. What do PGD health professionals and scientists think about testing for these conditions? I turn first to cystic fibrosis.

### 1   Cystic fibrosis

A number of members of staff discussed cystic fibrosis. Since someone with this (or any genetic) condition could only ever exist with cystic fibrosis, we need to think about how severe the condition is and whether it should be avoided for the 'person's sake', as it were. What did members of staff think about the condition? Scientist 21 observes:[98]

> I would say our role was to enable somebody to have a healthy baby when, in the first instance they've got a fairly substantial risk of having an unhealthy baby. And so I guess... the dividing line then is, what you classify as healthy and unhealthy and how severe.

He/she later refers to cystic fibrosis as 'major'. Scientist 19 describes the condition as 'quite serious'.[99] Doctor 24 thinks it is 'fairly serious'.[100] 'Major', 'quite serious' and 'fairly serious' all seem to indicate a degree of uncertainty about the severity of cystic fibrosis. The issue was touched on in one of the discussion groups. The philosopher made the following point[101]:

> BF: There's also the lesson to be learnt from the disability literature more generally, about society's attitudes towards disability. I mean it's not something we've touched upon in our discussion. But, for example, one of the groups that might... have serious questions to ask of the work you do, are people who are born with and living with disability, because what they might say is, 'Actually I live perfectly good lives, I enjoy a good quality of life. Yet if you match up the lives we're living against the lives you're selecting out, they don't look much different.'

In response, Doctor 11 observed: 'You could use that argument quite easily for cystic fibrosis, couldn't you?' This suggests we need to reflect again on whose interests are being protected, or most protected, in PGD, this time in relation to cystic fibrosis testing.

In this regard, Doctor 20 recalls an interesting couple[102]:

---

[98]   Interview, Scientist 21, 13.
[99]   Interview, Scientist 19, 4.
[100]  Interview, Doctor 24, 5.
[101]  Bobbie Farsides, EDG 4, 32.
[102]  Interview, Doctor 20, 20.

> We saw a couple last week who came for cystic fibrosis, a fertile, intelligent couple, who have a cystic fibrosis child. And I said, 'What are you doing this for? Why don't you just have another pregnancy?' And they couldn't consider terminating a Cystic child because, firstly they said, 'we do not want to have another child that I have to watch die or be very ill. But on the other hand, if we kind of [terminate the] pregnancy it's like terminating [our existing child]… And we feel we can't do that. And we want some other way of approaching this.'

In this case, the testing seems very much in the interests of the parents: although PGD is not 100 per cent accurate, these parents clearly saw the possibility of a pregnancy achieved through PGD as a way of avoiding the potentially very painful issues they might face if a fetus tested positive for cystic fibrosis. The question of trying to avoid the dilemmas around termination is extremely important in PGD and is often referred to by members of staff, both in interviews and in the discussion groups.[103] The issue may be particularly acute because, as with the parents in Doctor 20's example, the parents have already had another child with the relevant condition; or they may have terminated one or more pregnancies; or they may have miscarried earlier pregnancies and want to avoid the risk of miscarriage inherent in diagnostic testing in pregnancy.

On the question of the seriousness of cystic fibrosis, it is also interesting to delve more deeply into Doctor 24's views who, recall, describes the condition as 'fairly serious'[104]:

> I always, I don't think of myself as an embryo. I think of myself as the parent. What if I had this problem? Would it be acceptable to me or would it not be acceptable? So I don't think there's any parent in the world, or there may be, who knowingly would want an affected child. So anything to do, anything science can offer to help in that aim, is fine.

Doctor 24 suggests here that it is the parents who would not want a child with cystic fibrosis. The interviewer continues:

> KE: Right, okay. Again, I'm playing Devil's Advocate a bit here, but some people would say that if you eliminate all people who have anything wrong with them, these diseases or these conditions, then you're — how does that then impact on the bigger society if I make it so that there are fewer and fewer people who are born with anything wrong with them? First of all, what does that say to the people who do have those conditions?
>
> Doctor 24: You see, I mean, you have to ask those people themselves, say cystic fibrosis, would they want a child with cystic fibrosis? Would they want — I don't think they would.

Here Doctor 24 seems further to be suggesting that people who actually have cystic fibrosis may not themselves want to have a child with the condition. This

---

[103] eg, EDG 5, Scientist 2; and in interview Scientist 8, 5, 17.
[104] Interview, Doctor 24, 13–14. The interviewer to whom I refer shortly is Kathryn Ehrich.

does not mean it is not worth living with cystic fibrosis; rather, it means that also people with the condition may sometimes think it is better to avoid having it if possible (and so to avoid some lives rather than others).

Overall, then, it may be defensible to describe cystic fibrosis (which can of course vary in its severity) as 'serious' provided that we recognise that it does not seem to be so serious as to give rise to a risk of a life of very low quality, one that may not be worth living. Further, since someone with cystic fibrosis could only ever exist as that person, the seriousness of the condition may really relate more to their parents' interests. (Remember that, for now, I am leaving to one side a non-person-affecting analysis, on which we could compare the lives of different possible people with lives each thought worth living, because such principles do not appear to have been discussed by the staff on whose views I am focusing, with one possible exception.) Recall again Scientist 21's comment (in relation to another condition): 'So that implies we're doing this for the parents and not for the child in some respects'. What we have seen so far is that although this could be true in relation to what might be seen as very serious conditions (such as Tay-Sachs), it is particularly the case in relation to less serious ones. I discuss the moral acceptability of PGD that may ultimately predominantly be in the parents' interests below when I turn to consider Down's syndrome.

Of course, when prospective parents discuss the seriousness of a given condition with members of staff they need to know what that condition involves. The question of information provision is in fact part of Recommendation 14 in the Outcome Document, the recommendation (to recap) that states 'that the seriousness of a condition should be a matter for discussion between the people seeking treatment and the clinical team'. The recommendation in fact goes on to state[105]:

> [I]nformation provided to those seeking treatment... should include genetic and clinical information about the specific condition; its likely impact on those affected and their families; information about treatment and social support available; and the testimony of families and individuals about the full range of experiences of living with the condition.

In turn, this is embodied in the HFEA's Code of Practice.[106]

Now, an important aspect of PGD for a condition such as cystic fibrosis is that the people who seek PGD for this condition will have reason to think they are at risk. This may be because they have had a child with cystic fibrosis; or someone in their wider family may have the condition; or one of the couple has the condition. (By contrast, in dominant conditions — such as Huntington's Chorea, achondroplasia and myotonic dystrophy — one of the parents is *always* affected, or will be in due course if it is late-onset, and will therefore have a particularly

---

[105] Above n 1, para 32 and Rec 13. Para 34 addresses the issue of information provision, especially the need for balanced information which includes 'that provided by disabled people and their families', an issue to which we return later.
[106] Above n 4.

personal view of the situation.) Indeed, it will probably be for one of these reasons that they come to the clinic seeking PGD. The couple will therefore have some knowledge of what living with cystic fibrosis is like. This in turn would mean (for instance, if PGD for cystic fibrosis had not yet been licensed and a decision therefore had to be made about whether to offer such testing) that their views as to its seriousness would carry considerable weight. Generally, it may mean that these couples are likely to have less need for information about the condition than other people may have. By contrast, if a couple presented for consultation having had a child who was very mildly affected by cystic fibrosis, they may well need to know more about the condition. The general point here is that people seeking PGD for cystic fibrosis will typically have a good idea of what it involves, even if they may benefit from further information about (say) the spectrum of severity. Such information may help them gauge the severity of what they have 'experienced' so far.

An additional point to note here is that when people approach a clinic about the possibility of PGD for something they have experienced in some way, they must think that it is important enough to try to 'do something about it'. As one member of staff put this, 'of course it must be serious for them to come here'.[107] This does not tell us 'for whom' the condition is serious, but it does tell us that people have experienced something as a problem and have decided to go out of their way to try to avoid it. In relation to experience of a condition and subsequent knowledge of it, the situation may be very different in relation to the second condition I now discuss, Down's syndrome.

2   Down's syndrome

At the time of the interviews and discussion groups, one of the issues the clinic was considering was whether to offer PGD for Down's syndrome to prospective parents coming through for PGD for other conditions. New developments in PGD technology are behind this move, which would mean that identification for trisomy 21 could be 'added in' to other PGD testing. I now explore some of the issues at stake in this idea, as revealed through the interviews and discussion groups.

To offer women testing for Down's syndrome under these circumstances would be to offer them testing for a condition which was the not the primary focus of their PGD attempt. It would typically mean that staff took the initiative of offering this test in the course of discussions with a couple. Of course, for older women the issue of Down's syndrome may well be in their minds before any overt offer of a test. Indeed, Scientist 2 observes[108]:

---

[107] Interview, Doctor 6, 13.
[108] EDG 5, Scientist 2, 33–4. The Down's Syndrome Association, in 'Your Baby has Down's Syndrome: a Guide for Parents', provides a mixture of information on the condition, some of the flavour of which is given by the following: 'Children with Down's syndrome can and do grow up to live long and fulfilled lives. Provided they are allowed the

[A] lot of our PGD patients are in the older bracket... The patients are asking about screening the embryo for Down's as well, because one day we are going to put something back that's normal for the disease they have, and it's going to come out Down's, and they're going to have to terminate then or not terminate because a lot of them don't have amnios anyway because... What do we do?

For many younger women, the issue of Down's syndrome may not be so prominent although it is likely that, if they were to become pregnant, they would face the issue later given the current national screening programme for Down's syndrome, discussed in Chapter 3. At the PGD stage, however, since the offer of testing for Down's syndrome would be in addition to testing for another condition, and since the primary focus of couples in coming to the clinic would have been on that other condition, testing for Down's syndrome would be different in various ways from testing for conditions such as Duchenne muscular dystrophy or cystic fibrosis. I would like to explore some of these differences with reference to staff's views about Down's syndrome and PGD for this condition.

A preliminary point to make is that the accuracy of testing for Down's syndrome is an important issue. This is noted by Scientist 21, who seemed to be in favour of PGD for Down's syndrome, subject to concerns about accuracy in the test itself and the possibility of then having to exclude what were in fact normal embryos.[109] I cannot discuss the scientific aspects here. My discussion can only proceed on the basis that testing for Down's syndrome is or could become sufficiently accurate to justify its inclusion at the PGD stage. To some degree this is a matter of judgment which needs to be related to the significance of the risk and the perceived seriousness of the condition. As we have seen, these are not purely objective matters.

What are some of the attitudes of staff to Down's syndrome? In one of the discussion groups, Embryologist 33 says that 'people [with Down's syndrome] can still have fully functional lives'.[110] Scientist 2 later observes: 'and they feel they have a fulfilling life, and that's what counts, how they feel. If they feel it's fulfilling, it doesn't matter what anyone else says, if they feel they have had a worthwhile life and what they've achieved...'.[111] In another discussion group, Scientist 8 observes[112]: 'You mentioned earlier about Down's, which used to be the end of the world, and now it's a much more accepted condition. And as time moves on

opportunities they need to develop self-help skills and independence, people with Down's syndrome can thrive well into their fifties and beyond, facing many of the challenges we all encounter: school, further education, work and a home of one's own. Many children with Down's syndrome are now being integrated successfully into mainstream schools' (at 11). 'People with Down's syndrome all have a certain degree of learning disability (mental handicap). The degree of disability varies from person to person and it is impossible to tell at birth what that degree will be' (at 4).

[109] Interview, Scientist 21, 23–4.
[110] EDG 5, Embryologist 33, 33–4.
[111] *Ibid* Scientist 2.
[112] EDG 2, Scientist 8, 14–15.

and people's ideas change, you can't have hard and fast rules'. None of these comments suggests that these members of staff thought that Down's syndrome should be avoided for the sake of the person with the condition. Those groups that did touch upon the issue of Down's syndrome then had to face the question of why there might be screening for this condition.

To begin, there was some discussion of screening for Down's syndrome in the PND context. For instance, in response to Scientist 8's comment above about ideas changing, Counsellor 28 observes[113]: 'Right, but it's still the most common condition for which we've screened'. In another group, Doctor 24 observes: 'there's such a lot going on about Down's syndrome. There's so much work going on, there's so much apprehension going on'.[114] Who is this work for? Although the severity of Down's syndrome varies considerably, the idea that it is better not to be born than to have Down's syndrome is highly implausible. We must face the recognition then (and leaving aside a non-person-affecting analysis) that Down's syndrome screening is really aimed at prospective parents. Is this morally acceptable? To offer any thoughts on this we need to think both about prospective parents and about the embryo or fetus.

Turning to the parents, I have argued in earlier chapters that they should have some choice in reproduction about whether to have a child with a disability, including one that is not so serious as to lead to an extremely low quality of life for a child, such as cystic fibrosis or Down's syndrome. As we have seen, the idea that reproductive autonomy should include, to some extent, the ability to avoid congenital disability in future children is supported by a number of different writers, some from a broadly liberal perspective.[115] Further, perhaps most strikingly, there is some support for this idea from the disability critique of prenatal screening and selective abortion.[116] For instance, Tom Shakespeare observes generally[117]:

> The role of prospective parents has largely been ignored by disabled radicals. Because these are predominantly non-disabled people, it is likely that they will hold some of the prejudicial attitudes to disability which are common in society. Yet the decision to terminate pregnancy is not one that the majority of people take lightly. Moreover, there

---

[113] EDG 2, Counsellor 28, 14–15, part cited above.

[114] EDG 1, Doctor 24, 13.

[115] eg, Buchanan *et al*, above n 70; J Robertson 'Genetic Selection of Offspring Characteristics' (1996) 76 *Boston U Law Rev* 421; B Steinbock 'Disability, Prenatal Testing and Selective Abortion' in E Parens and A Asch (eds), *Prenatal Testing and Disability Rights* (Washington, DC: Georgetown University Press, 2000) 108; J Botkin 'Line Drawing: Developing Professional Standards for Prenatal Diagnostic Services' in E Parens and A Asch, *ibid* 288.

[116] See, eg, T Shakespeare 'Choices and Rights: Eugenics, Genetics and Disability Equality' (1998) 13/5 *Disability and Society* 665, 672.

[117] *Ibid* 681. He also emphasises the need 'for better provision of welfare services and financial benefits to parents of disabled children, in order to make it easier for parents to choose to… continue such a pregnancy' (*ibid* 672).

are reasons to want to prevent the birth of a child affected by impairment which do not reflect discrimination against disabled people: for example, the desire to avoid the early death or suffering of a loved child, or a feeling that a family will be unable to cope with the strain of looking after a very impaired member.

Turning now to the embryo or fetus, the acceptability of selection will depend, in part, on the question of the moral status of each. The argument that parents are entitled to have some choice about whether to have a child with a disability entails the view that the moral status of the embryo (at the time of PGD) or the fetus (for instance at the time of a nuchal translucency scan for Down's syndrome and chorionic villus sampling) is not so great as to outweigh the prospective parents' reproductive autonomy interest in avoiding disability in a future child. By contrast, if we were to give greater moral importance to the embryo or fetus, or both, we might say that it is only morally acceptable to test (with possible discard or termination) where there is a serious risk that a child would have a life she would not think worth living. (For some, of course, even this would not be acceptable.) As we have seen, however, several members of staff at this PGD clinic seem to think that it is appropriate to take account of parental interests in PGD and were prepared to say so quite explicitly in relation to very serious conditions as well as in relation to cystic fibrosis. This suggests that they consider that in such cases the parental interests outweigh the moral claims of the embryo.

More specifically, why might parents be interested in the option of avoiding the birth of a child with Down's syndrome and how might this compare with their interests in relation to cystic fibrosis? In the latter case, it may be that prospective parents are likely to think primarily about the avoidance of suffering. Arguably, they can think of cystic fibrosis testing as 'testing which avoids suffering'. This is so even though to be born with this condition often appears compatible with a reasonable quality of life and a life worth living. In the case of Down's syndrome, there may be physical suffering in severe cases and prospective parents may worry, in particular, about the risk of cardiac defects, particularly inoperable ones. But it may be that prospective parents are more likely to think about the question of mental impairment and to worry about how severe this may be. Although mental impairment may give rise to a loss of opportunity in the life of someone with Down's syndrome, it will not necessarily mean that that person is unhappy or feels unfulfilled themselves, although they may suffer from social stigma. Despite this, in the light of the potential health problems and a degree of mental impairment, it seems unlikely that prospective parents would *hope* for a child with Down's syndrome. At the same time, it may be hard for prospective parents to face — let alone admit to — the possibility that Down's syndrome testing may really be about their own potential interests and concerns.

Interestingly, this difficulty appears to be echoed amongst the staff at the clinic (many of whom are likely to be parents) in their discussions of Down's syndrome, since it seemed hard for anyone explicitly to state that testing for Down's syndrome might really concern parental interests, although Scientist 8 (below) touches on this. Further, out of the 26 interviews conducted at this site, only four interviewees themselves brought up the example of Down's syndrome in their one-to-one interviews, although the interviewer occasionally raised it.[118] (Of course, in part this is not surprising in that PGD for Down's syndrome had only just become part of the agenda for discussion at the clinic.) Rather, typically the issue was brought up by the philosopher in the discussion groups.

Indeed, the important point about whose interests may be at stake (and why) in testing for Down's syndrome was put to one of the groups by the philosopher[119]:

> [I]n the past people were very ready to make quite sort of broad sweeping statements about the quality of life of somebody with Down's syndrome. But people now no longer feel happy making [those statements]. The shift of emphasis is on, 'Well what does it mean to the family to have a child that will remain dependent for much longer in their life, that might have… health problems etc? What does it mean to the other siblings?' And some people are less comfortable with that sort of more global calculation than they would be with the calculation in the case where you actually look at the condition and…

Here she suggests some plausible reasons as to why parents may be concerned to be able to choose whether or not to have a child with Down's syndrome and, at the same time, acknowledges that recognition of these reasons may be uncomfortable or unacceptable for some. Of course, if we do accept that parents are entitled to avoid the birth of children even where they would have conditions, such as cystic fibrosis, that might well enable them to have a reasonable quality of life, then we have no reason to say that it is not acceptable for parents to be concerned with the similarly less serious (though of course very different) condition of Down's syndrome. However, it could be argued that it may be harder openly to acknowledge this in the case of Down's syndrome because of the element of mental impairment: in particular, it may be easier for parents to say they want to avoid suffering (for instance as in cystic fibrosis) than to say that they want to avoid mental impairment in their child (in the case of Down's syndrome). What did staff think about the philosopher's suggestion about what may be the real purpose of Down's syndrome testing?

---

[118] Scientist 9 raises the issue of PGD for Down's syndrome in addition to testing for other conditions. Scientist 3 mentions Down's syndrome, but this is simply in connection with analysing amniocentesis results. Administrator 12 comments on whether people necessarily abort a fetus with Down's syndrome. Counsellor 17 raises the issue of adding in PGD for Down's syndrome in relation to concerns about decreasing the accuracy of test results. Scientist 21 discusses Down's syndrome and PGD for Down's syndrome, although the interviewer was the first to mention the issue. Doctor 6 responded to a question about Down's syndrome by the interviewer; Doctor 24 responded to two such questions; Nurse 25 responds to a question about Down's syndrome in connection with PGD.

[119] Bobbie Farsides, EDG 2, 5.

At this point Doctor 22 commented that 'those children are very happy children often aren't they?'. Scientist 8 responded[120]:

> But that's exactly the point. In that situation we're talking about existing individuals and their quality of life. When we're looking at a PGD family, we're not saying, we're not making any judgement about an existing individual by saying that on average these people do not have the opportunities and quality of life that normal people have, the parents have a huge burden. So we're not, there's no living person that we're saying we're going to take away their life, this is not about that. We're not going to deprive some individual, of life, by doing the test. I mean it is different — a non-existing person does not have the same weight in the balance as the existing person. Isn't that right?

Scientist 8 seems to envisage here the idea of PGD for Down's syndrome, although he/she may also be alluding to PGD more generally. There are a number of important ideas embedded in what he/she says and it is worth trying to spell these out: first, that when people reflect that children with Down's syndrome often seem 'very happy', they are thinking of people who actually exist and their quality of life; and therefore, second, deliberations in PGD do not entail judgments about the quality of lives of existing people; rather, third, they entail general reflection on the opportunities and quality of life 'on average' (this may be reminiscent of a non-person-affecting perspective); fourth, there is the suggestion (which may or may not include Down's syndrome) that parents 'have a huge burden'; and fifth, the point is made that no-one's life is being taken away by doing 'the test', coupled with the thought that 'non-existing' people have less weight in any moral equation than existing ones. Arguably, if we were to take the gradualist view that the fetus has greater moral status than the embryo (and various members of staff seemed to think this was the case, while others did not)[121] this last statement would apply more strongly in the PGD than the PND context. However, since on many moral views also the 12-week fetus is not a person,[122] the statement may also apply in the context of PND. Each of these statements seems concerned to justify the idea of PGD, including PGD for Down's syndrome, and amongst them we find the notion of a 'burden' for parents. Interestingly, we find the statement about parents' interests mixed in with a number of important statements about the justifiability of testing. This may again highlight the difficulty people may seem to feel about pointing too overtly to parents' potential interests in relation to Down's syndrome testing.

---

[120] EDG 2, Scientist 8, 5.

[121] Examples of staff in favour of a gradualist approach to the embryo's and fetus's moral status were Scientist 8, 4, and Embryologist 15, 16; an example of a member of staff who attributed a high moral status to the embryo was Scientist 2, 15–16. We do not attempt here to represent the proportion of staff with given views.

[122] By contrast, even the embryo has the moral status of a born child on a potentiality account. For an adherent, see J Finnis 'The Rights and Wrongs of Abortion: A Reply to Judith Thomson' (1973) 2 *Phil & Pub Aff* 117.

Since Down's syndrome is a condition about which people may be fearful, they may also be misinformed. In particular, people may overestimate the impact on them of the birth of a child with Down's syndrome. Being well or fully informed about the life of someone with Down's syndrome will most probably not be true of the majority of the couples coming through for PGD for another condition. One reason for this is that the syndrome arises from a chromosomal trisomy and is generally not inherited. Even if a couple has met or known a child or an adult with Down's syndrome, they will not necessarily know about the range of severity of effects, both physical and mental. Information provision in relation to a condition such as Down's syndrome would therefore be very important if PGD for Down's syndrome were offered at the clinic. Indeed, as noted in Chapter 1, Tom Shakespeare has suggested that[123]:

> Decisions about screening should be based on good information: rather than evaluating screening programmes in terms of those who undergo tests and terminations, programmes should be evaluated in terms of the proportion of people who were empowered to make an informed choice.

As also noted in Chapter 1, the possibly unbalanced nature of information about Down's syndrome has been explored in the context of PND.[124] It would therefore be crucial that this issue is adequately addressed in the context of PGD.

In one of the groups staff showed an awareness of the importance of information provision. With reference to Down's syndrome being the most common condition for which there is prenatal screening, Scientist 8 observed[125]: 'But that's presumably because the women who accept the screening and prenatal testing, are ones who know about the condition enough to know that they will not necessarily want to have a Down's baby'. However, Counsellor 28 responded: 'Except I think they don't…'. The concern that people may take up the offer of Down's syndrome testing without adequate reflection (either in the PND or PGD context) is well caught by Counsellor 10[126]:

> I think it is, society evolves and obviously it will influence personal decisions. And, but regardless of that, there are so many people who are so individual that they just won't go with whatever everybody is saying. *As long as the medical profession is vigilant in providing unbiased, accurate information, and not just putting these couples or women on a conveyor belt, you know, like what sort of has happened with the Down's syndrome screening, then I think you're empowering people to make an individual choice.* And almost stopping them in their, yes we'll have it — 'hang on a second, why do you really want to have it?'

---

[123] T Shakespeare '"Losing the Plot?" Medical and Activist Discourses of Contemporary Genetics and Disability' (1999) 21:5 *Sociology of Health and Illness* 669, 685.
[124] See C Williams, P Alderson and B Farsides 'What Constitutes 'Balanced Information in the Practitioners' Portrayals of Down's Syndrome?' (2002) 18 *Midwifery* 230.
[125] EDG 2, Scientist 8, 14–15.
[126] EDG 1, Counsellor 10, 29 (my emphasis).

The reference to a 'conveyor belt' in relation to Down's syndrome screening generally is worrying and would raise concerns about the voluntariness, and so validity, of consent to testing, first discussed early in Chapter 3.

So far, I have suggested why parents may want to be informed about Down's syndrome and why they may or may not want to accept the offer of testing for it. I have also suggested that there are arguments as to why testing for Down's syndrome may legitimately be seen as part of reproductive autonomy, just as testing for other conditions that leave someone with a life they think worth living, such as cystic fibrosis, may be. These arguments apply to selection by PGD and earlier rather than later in an established pregnancy, and therefore arguably not after 24 weeks, as discussed in Chapter 2.

My final thoughts about Down's syndrome testing concern the specific reasons for offering it as an *addition* at the PGD stage. On this point, Counsellor 28 observes: '[B]ut I think if we have it on the screening test, then it is by definition, thought to be medically sensitive to have it, because otherwise why would we be offering this test?'. It would be interesting to know what he/she means by 'medically sensitive'. The term may refer to the possibility of being responsive to the concerns of people seeking PGD. It is not difficult to imagine these concerns and they are very clearly spelt out by Nurse 4[127]:

> [With] nuchal screening [women are given]... a risk factor, it's about 80%+ accurate, but it doesn't give you a definitive diagnosis for — and, you know, the main focus is for Down's... [F]or the Down's thing, I can imagine there would be a great temptation for it to be either done at the PGD stage, because you only get — you're not getting a definitive answer at the nuchal test, and if someone — a lot of anxiety is raised, even if someone doesn't go into a high risk group, if you change their risk to make it worse from their background age risk, you're introducing a lot of anxiety into that pregnancy. And if they fall into a high risk group, that they've got a 1 in 250 chance of having a Down's child, they're sent for an amniocentesis which carries a risk of miscarriage. So I can imagine, in the future, that there will be a big temptation to be adding it in at that stage just to pre-empt that sort of... I'm not saying that's a good thing.
>
> BF: No, but you would see it as — ?
>
> Nurse 4: When there is a choice to do something like improve... screening, I think it becomes probably tempting, and will that be a start of the thing to...

Nurse 4 seems to want to see this development as an 'improvement' in screening practices, but without expressing a view overall as to whether this is a 'good thing'. Once again, this may reflect the reluctance people have, including staff at the clinic, to express a view about Down's syndrome testing. Would the offer of Down's syndrome testing as an addition to other PGD testing be valuable for women and their partners?

---

[127] EDG 1, Nurse 4, 9–10.

Women who are undergoing IVF and PGD for another condition that they and the clinical staff have agreed is sufficiently serious may previously have had a child with the condition that is now the subject of PGD; or they may have had one or more terminations in relation to that condition; or they may have had one or more miscarriages due to the condition or another cause. As Nurse 4's account demonstrates, women may also worry about the risk of Down's syndrome and what a nuchal translucency scan may reveal and whether they will then feel the need to opt for a diagnostic test with its risk of miscarriage.[128] Additionally, one could speculate that after all the help the IVF/PGD clinic has given them, some women may also feel concerned about 'letting the clinic down' if they were to miscarry as a result of a diagnostic test or decide they want to end a pregnancy if that test shows the fetus has Down's syndrome. These are potentially heavy burdens for women and their partners to carry.

In this light it could be argued that, provided these women are informed to an appropriate extent about Down's syndrome, it could reasonably seem to staff to be morally appropriate to offer these women PGD for Down's syndrome in addition to their other testing. Indeed, for anyone who holds a gradualist approach to the moral status of the embryo or fetus, as I do (and, as noted before, some staff at this clinic do and some do not), it is morally preferable to test for Down's syndrome at the PGD stage and then possibly to discard an embryo than to test at the 12-week or more point in the PND context and then terminate an established pregnancy. (This is not to say that the latter is unjustifiable.) Further, the possibility of avoiding a more morally problematic outcome is likely to be an issue for many parents, particularly since they may be seeking PGD in the first place to avoid PND and termination.[129] In this light, since staff frequently observed how important it is for them to feel comfortable about the procedures with which they are involved, they could also feel that by 'adding on' testing for Down's syndrome by PGD, they may be helping women avoid a morally more problematic outcome at a later stage. They will certainly be helping them to reduce their risk of Down's syndrome and therefore also their possible stresses in a subsequent pregnancy.

It may also be that it is easier for women and their partners to reflect on the information they receive about Down's syndrome in advance of an existing pregnancy, rather than in the midst of one, and thus to make a more informed decision at the IVF stage. Having said this, since there may be fewer 'costs' to a couple (for instance, they would not be putting an established pregnancy at risk by invasive testing) they may be inclined to test more readily for Down's syndrome at the PGD than the PND stage (assuming the addition of a test for Down's syndrome does not compromise the accuracy of their other testing or leave them with little or no choice of embryos). Once again, however, arguably this would be morally acceptable provided they have been fully informed and

---

[128] The risk is typically cited as about 1%. HGC, *Making Babies: Reproductive Decisions and Genetic Technologies* (2006), para 3.15.

[129] eg, this is referred to in EDG 1 by Scientist 2, 21.

have carefully reflected on the possibilities of raising a child with Down's syndrome. What many may perceive as the lower moral status of the embryo, compared with the fetus, will also strengthen the argument for selection at the PGD stage.

I now turn very briefly to note the remaining factors that the HFEA recommends should be considered in relation to the decision to undertake particular PGD tests and to draw out some relevant comments of the clinic's staff. There is only scope to give a flavour of the views of health professionals and scientists in relation to these factors.

### iii  The extent of any intellectual impairment

The possible distinction between a child's and its parents' interests can also be noted in relation to 'the extent of any intellectual impairment'. A child with moderate intellectual impairment may well make considerable educational progress and subsequently lead a life of some independence.[130] This may be the case with more mild expressions of Down's syndrome. Yet if the people seeking treatment have some interest in which children are born, then their views and interests will have some weight. Apparently in support of this, Administrator 12 observed[131]:

> I don't say that a child with learning difficulties or anything like that isn't going to be able to live a good life, good quality of life. But I think the couples should be able to make that decision themselves.

Presumably the reference to 'that decision' is to whether or not to give birth to such a child.

### iv  The extent of social support available

Clearly, good social support will be in the interests both of a child and of its parents. The issue was touched on in one of the discussion groups, as Doctor 32 observed: 'But if you talk about it basically, you know, why can't a child with a disability, with Down's syndrome or something else, not be perfectly okay if it's adequately supported?'[132] We can relate this observation to the distinction between 'medical' and 'social' models of disability discussed first in Chapter 1. The medical model has tended to dominate understandings of what it is to be disabled.[133] We may have seen an example of this above when Scientist 2 observed: 'No, but, when it's serious, their life is completely debilitated by it... it's *medically* serious'.[134] The medical model has been subject to a critique in the form

---

[130] On Down's syndrome, see above n 108.
[131] Interview, Administrator 12, 12.
[132] EDG 3, Doctor 32, 26.
[133] See, eg, J Harris 'Is There a Coherent Social Conception of Disability?' (2000) 26 *JME* 95.
[134] My emphasis.

of the 'social' model.[135] The former locates disability within the individual, the latter in the social environment the individual inhabits, so that the individual is 'impaired', not 'disabled'. Over time, some proponents of either model have accepted to some degree the limitations of their respective approaches.[136] As noted in Chapter 1, it is now clear that some combination of the models is best placed to account for the significance of impairment.[137] In turn, it can reasonably be acknowledged, as Tom Shakespeare has, that despite good social support there may still be considerable difficulties in raising an 'affected' child.[138] Therefore, if prospective parents' interests are relevant to selection decisions, there may still be reason to test for a given condition, even when good social support would be available (which it will not always be).

### v  The family circumstances of the people seeking treatment

There are various elements of possible relevance here. Prospective parents may already have other affected children. Or this factor might allow for concern as to the possible effects, one way or another, of the birth of a seriously impaired child in a family generally. The welfare-of the-child requirement of the Human Fertilisation and Embryology Act allows for the interests of other children to be considered.[139] Whether 'family circumstances' is confined to the nuclear family or whether a couple must already have children in order for this factor to be relevant is unclear. Arguably, some flexibility here is desirable given the variation in families' experiences. The relevance of family circumstances to all the conditions discussed here was noted implicitly or explicitly in earlier discussion, for instance in relation to Duchenne muscular dystrophy, cystic fibrosis and Down's syndrome. Further, there were numerous observations in the discussion groups and interviews that revealed great empathy with couples in the light of their family experience to date. For instance, in relation to cancer in the family, Nurse 4 observes[140]:

> So if someone felt so passionate about it, I don't feel that I can judge or say what they — because I don't know, unless you're in someone else's shoes, I don't feel that I can make such a judgment really. So if someone has got a family history, a very strong family history of cancer, then… who am I to say?

---

[135] See, eg, Shakespeare, n 113
[136] eg, Harris and Shakespeare, above nn 133 and 135.
[137] Glover, above n 89, 7–8.
[138] See, eg, Shakespeare, above n 116.
[139] The HFE Act, s 13(5) states: 'A woman shall not be provided with treatment services unless account has been taken of the welfare of any child who may be born as a result of the treatment (including the need of that child for a father), and of any other child who may be affected by the birth'.
[140] Interview, Nurse 4, 8.

Doctor 6 also alludes generally to the experience with which a couple presents at the clinic[141]:

> There are very few grey areas that I find in my mind. I think that anybody... that comes here seeking PGD has been on such a roller coaster ride and been through so much, that one has to appreciate just the sheer emotional turmoil they've been through.

Doctor 6 also notes the difficulty of making judgments about seriousness unless one has experience of a condition:

> I think you can only make decisions on such subjects if you have experience in that. I don't. I couldn't tell you whether... was serious enough, but I bet if I had a roomful of parents and families with children affected with it, I'm sure they would voice their opinion — in their situation it is a hugely important, devastating thing.

Further, Counsellor 17 observes that 'at the end of the day, it should be — we should be led by what parents want to do, they're in the best position to know what's right for them and their family'.[142]

### vi  The availability of effective therapy or management now and in the future

The current availability of therapy or management now is potentially relevant to many conditions. The possibility of future treatment is of particular significance in relation to testing for late-onset disorders. In some cases, the 'effectiveness' of therapy will be a matter of discussion and, perhaps, disagreement. For instance, in one of the discussion groups Scientist 34 observed[143]: 'with breast cancer you can have all this, you know, preventative treatment and treatment is a lot better'. Later the discussion proceeded as follows:

> Scientist 2: But it's treatable to the point where you will have a normal lifespan...
>
> Embryologist 33: Not in everybody.
>
> Scientist 2: No, but it can be now because you can have a mastectomy and that's it, you're cured for life.

There is not scope here to discuss other aspects of treatment by mastectomy and the suitability of PGD for breast cancer. It would be interesting to know whether there would ever be a situation in which the clinical staff thought that the relevant treatment was sufficient but prospective parents did not. Given the empathy with a couple's family experience that we saw in relation to the previous factor, it is possible that most members of staff would defer to patients on the question of the acceptability of a given treatment. Inevitably, however, there remains the issue of uncertainty as to future treatments.

---

[141] Interview, Doctor 6, 4.
[142] Interview, Counsellor 17, 18–19.
[143] EDG 5, Scientist 34, 25.

### vii  The speed of degeneration in progressive disorders

Once again, both the child's and the prospective parents' interests could be relevant. In the extreme case of Tay-Sachs, where a child will live at most four to five years and will suffer greatly during this time, birth is unlikely to be either in its or its parents' interests and so PGD for Tay-Sachs is arguably strongly supportable. The clinic's staff was highly sensitive to the impact of a child's death on its parents. For instance, from one of the discussion groups[144]:

> Doctor 32: For the parents, the death of a child is very serious... I can only, of course, judge from the outside experience, you know, because I've been an oncologist for a long time. And I've seen children die and what that did to the parents throughout the illness and the death and everything. So that's where I'm coming from...

I touched on the question of the quality of life of someone who dies in their late teens in the discussion of Duchenne muscular dystrophy, when I noted the divergence in views between clinicians, parents and the boys themselves.

This is an appropriate point at which to discuss PGD for late-onset conditions. Testing for Huntington's Chorea, a fully-penetrant condition, has taken place for some time. Generally, the staff were very open to the views of people who had experience, in one way or another, of Huntington's Chorea. For instance, in interview Nurse 4 observed: 'when you've got something like Huntington's... I mean the parents are so aware of how devastating it is'.[145]

Relatively recently, the HFEA issued a public consultation document on the use of PGD for lower-penetrance conditions, later-onset conditions such as inherited breast, bowel and ovarian cancer.[146] As advised in this document, the HFEA thought it appropriate to consult on this issue because of perceived differences between such conditions and others for which PGD had to date been licensed. The HFEA emphasises[147]:

> [T]hey are *lower-penetrance* (i.e. not everyone with the faulty gene will develop the cancer); the occurrence of cancers have a *later age of onset* — in adult life in many cases; there is a possibility for preventative surgery, early detection and effective *treatment* for these cancers in susceptible individuals. The HFEA has licensed PGD for conditions that may have one or two of the features listed above... like Huntington's. However, lower penetrance conditions have all three features and it is the combination of these features that makes these conditions different...

Fleshing out these issues, the HFEA notes that the penetrance of the cancers in question ranges from 30% to 80%; that a person is unlikely to be affected until their 'late thirties, forties or fifties'; that '[m]any people are successfully treated and this number is increasing as better treatments are developed' and that '[i]t is also

---

[144] EDG 3, Doctor 32, 19, partly noted earlier.
[145] Interview, Nurse 4, 7–8.
[146] HFEA, *Choices and Boundaries* (November 2005).
[147] *Ibid* para 1.3, emphasis in original.

possible for people who know they are at risk to have regular checks and/or preventative — prophylactic — surgery to remove tissue that is likely to be affected... such as the breasts... or bowel'.[148] The consultation document observes the importance of '[t]he perception of the condition by those seeking treatment' as 'an important factor' and here notes that people's views may be affected by 'their attitude towards their own risk or that of their partner and how optimistic they are about treatment options in the future', the likelihood that those seeking PGD 'will have first-hand experience of the impact this has on the affected person and the rest of the family' and that at least one member of a given couple will themselves 'have experience of how being at risk of the condition affects a person'.[149] In this light, the document observes that 'people seeking treatment are in many ways best placed to judge the seriousness of the condition'.[150]

Following the consultation process and discussion, the HFEA indeed decided to licence PGD for these conditions, stating[151]:

> Taking into account the range of views expressed in the public discussion and the recommendations of the Ethics and Law Committee, the Human Fertilisation and Embryology Authority believes that, in principle, it is appropriate that PGD be available for serious, lower penetrance, later-onset genetic conditions such as inherited breast, bowel and ovarian cancer. This decision does not fetter the discretion of a Licence Committee which will consider the individual merits of each application.

The HFEA's reasoning is apparently contained in the preceding paragraph, which states[152]:

> Carrying the faulty gene can cause significant anxiety which is not lessened by the fact that the condition is not fully penetrant. The Authority considers conditions of this type to be serious genetic conditions. It also recognises that the impact of carrying a gene that increases risk of developing a given condition differs between individuals. The impact can differ both in terms of how an individual might perceive the risk as well as,

---

[148] Ibid.
[149] Ibid para 4.4.
[150] Ibid.
[151] HFEA Press Release 'Authority Decision on the Use of PGD for Lower Penetrance, Later Onset Inherited Conditions' (10 May 2006). The HFEA also states: 'The Authority decided that applications for lower penetrance conditions should initially be considered on a case-by-case basis because of the difference in the way that families are affected by these conditions and also because this is a new class of PGD conditions. This will be reviewed in two years when the Authority has more knowledge and experience of dealing with such applications.' The first licence in relation to breast cancer has now been sought: see J Buxton 'UK Couples Request Breast Cancer Embryo Test' 30 April 2007, 405 *Bionews* <http://www.bionews.org.uk/new.lasso?storyid=3423> accessed 13 October 2007. For current developments in relation to early-onset Alzheimer's Disease, see A Thornhill, G Grudzinskas and A Handyside 'PGD for Early Onset Alzheimer's Disease: Preventing Disease... Not the Cure' Week 10–16 April, 403 *Bionews* <http://www.ivf.net/ivf/index.php?page=out&id=2647> accessed 18 October 2007.
[152] HFEA, above n 151.

more practically, the way that the condition will manifest in any particular family. Therefore the Authority considers it essential that the views of the individuals seeking treatment be taken into account in the decision making process.

Strikingly, the HFEA here emphasises the importance of attending to the views of those seeking treatment. This is of course one of the key factors amongst the HFEA's and HGC's list of factors to be considered in relation to the decision to offer PGD generally. As we have seen in this chapter and in relation to PGD for Huntington's Chorea (above), health professionals and scientists appear to approve of, and give weight to, this factor in their work.

Ethically speaking, arguably it is appropriate both to view the kinds of lower-penetrance, later-onset conditions discussed by the HFEA as ones satisfying the criteria of a 'significant risk of a serious condition' provided, of course, that we recognise that having one of these conditions is most unlikely to make someone think that their life is not worth living (and there is no indication that the HFEA does think this). Since this is not the case, we are necessarily thinking about conditions compatible with a life worth living. Consistent with previous analysis, since any given person born at risk of one of these cancers is unlikely to regret being born, we need to clarify the ethical justification for such testing. Where someone is unlikely to contract cancer until their late thirties, forties or fifties, it may be that prospective parents' interests, at least as *parents*, may have less weight than where a child would have a serious genetic condition. However, parents are also more broadly part of the family of any adult child and, since we are discussing inherited conditions, certain families will bear the impact of cancer very strongly. These are all person-affecting considerations. More generally, the thought that it may be appropriate to test for these lower-penetrance, later-onset conditions is perhaps best justified on the non-person-affecting principle that, other things being equal, we have reason to select people with greater potential for flourishing and welfare. Importantly, this is not to presume that being at risk of having or developing one of these conditions will *necessarily* affect welfare; rather, recalling my discussion of Jonathan Glover's work in Chapter 1, it is to emphasise the way illness and disability *may* negatively affect people's lives.[153]

### viii   Their previous reproductive experience

Lastly, great sensitivity to a couple's reproductive past was shown in very many of the interviews and discussion groups. There was discussion of the experience of couples with another affected child (or children), of couples who had frequently miscarried and of couples who had felt the need to terminate previous pregnancies.

---

[153] See Ch 1, S III(B). For further discussion that touches on selection in relation to late-onset conditions, see W Glannon, *Genes and Future People: Philosophical Issues in Human Genetics* (Oxford: Westview Press, 2001) Ch 2.

In relation to the advantages of PGD over PND, Scientist 8 observes: 'I would look at it very much from the woman's point of view, that it's rescuing women from having to make those appalling decisions'.[154] Similarly, Embryologist 15 observes[155]:

> I think I've got a leaning towards PGD more from a patient-orientated view, inasmuch as what the patients have actually been through to actually be at that stage, and offering a treatment that doesn't involve termination of a fetus when it's actually growing inside them, I think it's a really viable way of bypassing a lot of problems with terminations of pregnancy for what are often the most atrocious diseases, you know, really they've been through a lot of trauma by the time they actually come to see us.

The avoidance of further difficulties or suffering was also relevant in relation to patients who had experienced miscarriages due to chromosomal translocations. Doctor 14 observes[156]:

> And, to me, it is legitimate to avoid them going through this heartbreaking experience and the anticipation and the torture of not knowing a) that it will happen, b) that if it happens and they became pregnant and that pregnancy would be doomed to another miscarriage — so, in my mind, that is a sensible indication to give them the benefit of treatment and the technique that will increase the probability of them having a continuous pregnancy as opposed to going through that experience again.

Here there is the highly compassionate suggestion that a couple should not be expected to suffer just because the risk of miscarriage in relation to a given translocation is not certain.

## V CONCLUSIONS

At the start of this chapter I reviewed the HFEA and HGC recommendations and discussions relating to the PGD criteria of 'a significant risk of a serious genetic condition'. We saw that the recommendations sought to recognise, at least to some extent, the personal nature of the issues at stake in PGD but also to observe limits to the legitimacy of prospective parents' views. In essence, this was to be achieved by requiring discussion between prospective parents and health professionals and scientists about the degree of risk and the seriousness of any given condition. I suggested that the HFEA and HGC had, in effect, put these professionals in the position of being something of a 'check' on what these bodies

---

[154] Interview, Scientist 8, 2.
[155] Interview, Embryologist 15, 2.
[156] Interview, Doctor 14, 8. For ethnographic work on PGD that particularly considers the concerns of prospective parents, see S Franklin and C Roberts, *Born and Made: An Ethnography of Preimplantation Genetic Diagnosis* (Princeton: Princeton University Press, 2006).

saw as the potentially excessively wide views of those seeking treatment.[157] Have the views of staff that I have explored here indeed shown these health professionals to be in this 'gatekeeper' role?

In relation to the degree of risk, we saw that health professionals and scientists tended to view risk in quantitative terms. (Of course, the Abortion Act relies on a quantitative notion of 'substantial risk'.) This was interesting given that a possibly more subjective notion of risk was intended by the JWP.[158] One exception to this is Scientist 21, who commented on how his/her own experience of pregnancy changed his/her perception of risk[159]:

> So, what I'm saying, actually putting myself in that position of the patient, it completely changed my perspective... subsequently, when I've been giving risk figures out to people, because I can imagine what it's like getting that figure, that result myself now.

Of course, as we have seen, the HFEA and HGC also envisaged that the degree of risk should be a matter for discussion and agreement.

Most of my discussion concentrated on the thorny issue of seriousness. We saw that health professionals and scientists saw some conditions as being very definitely serious, such as Tay-Sachs, but that many saw less serious conditions, such as cystic fibrosis (and potentially Down's syndrome) as sufficiently serious to meet the criteria for PGD.[160] Given that these conditions were less serious, however, the question then arose 'serious for whom?'. Here we saw the view, at least on the part of some staff, that sometimes seriousness concerns possible parental interests. In relation to Down's syndrome this tended to be implied rather than stated. In line with the recognition generally of the legitimacy of parental interests, great weight was given by staff to the views of prospective parents. They were mindful of couples' previous reproductive experience — particularly the traumas of abortion and miscarriage — and also of the experience that those seeking treatment might have of a given condition, for instance through the previous birth of an affected child. In this process staff were, in effect, attending to many of the factors that the HFEA and HGC recommended should be considered in the decision to offer PGD.

However, although staff were sensitive to prospective parents' views and experiences, this did not mean that they necessarily thought that 'anything goes'. While they were often prepared to defer to prospective patients in relation to 'grey areas', this was largely because they thought it would be inappropriate to judge the seriousness of a condition of which they had no experience. Further, by definition of course, a 'grey area' is not one that concerns trivial features or

---

[157] HFEA licence committees are of course a further possible check. But it is likely that if a clinic supports an application for PGD, the licence committee will usually agree.
[158] Above text before and n 36.
[159] Interview, Scientist 21, 27.
[160] The possibility of testing for Down's syndrome, as an addition, was of course the subject of discussion at the clinic.

conditions. Indeed, there was a recognition that people would only be motivated to seek PGD and, in particular, go through with the attendant IVF, where they truly experienced something as a problem — as 'serious'. In these cases, it is likely (though not certain) that staff (and perhaps HFEA licence committees when the case is made out by staff) will agree that a condition is sufficiently serious to justify PGD. This is not to deny that there may always be conditions that provoke debate and disagreement, perhaps between staff and perhaps also, though not necessarily, between staff and prospective parents. The clinic's regular case-by-case and multi-disciplinary meetings (to discuss new conditions) were noted above.

In essence, then, it appears that if these health professionals and scientists were truly to doubt the seriousness of a given condition for which a couple were seeking PGD, they would indeed act as a check on their views, and would be likely to deny the provision of PGD. In any event, in response to the idea that relatively mild conditions might be the subject of testing, Scientist 8 reminds us of the 'limitations of PGD in terms of the number of embryos you have available'.[161] The implication of this limitation is that at some point a couple's desire to have a child could come into conflict with their desire to have a child without a very much less serious condition. In other words, they would have to reflect carefully on their true goal.

Overall, these health professionals and scientists showed great empathy with the experiences of prospective parents and were likely to defer to their views. However, in response to the interviewer's question, 'Should we always give patients what they want?', Doctor 14 replies: 'No, no. It's not in absolute terms. They want it for a legitimate reason.'[162] Of another staff member, the interviewer asks: 'If they wanted to do something, anything, would it be acceptable because it is what they wish?'. Scientist 9 responds: 'I think it depends on, it's within reason, isn't it?'[163] This notion of reason is crucial. The scientist continues: 'But what is reason, whose reason, whose reason is it?' More generally, this is of course a central question in any analysis of the scope of reproductive autonomy. The best answer that I can give in this context is that as long as a condition lies in that 'grey area', its seriousness can be a matter of reasonable disagreement. For this reason, it could be appropriate to offer PGD.

As we saw in Chapters 2 and 3, PND and selective abortion may be appropriate in the same way, though late abortions raise particular issues. One of the points demonstrated in this chapter is that, by contrast with the context of PND, there is an overt, if limited, recognition of the interests of prospective parents in the legal criteria governing the provision of PGD. I argued in Chapter 2 that it would be appropriate for the law to recognise the interests of prospective parents in PND and selective abortion and that the wrongful birth cases provide

---

[161] EDG 2, Scientist 8, 19.
[162] Interview, Doctor 14, 2. The interviewer was Kathryn Ehrich.
[163] Interview, Scientist 9, 7. The interviewer was Kathryn Ehrich.

an opening for this. Prospective parents' interests could also receive more overt recognition in the professional guidelines surrounding selective abortion, such as in those of the RCOG.

In the next two chapters I turn to consider whether there is a moral and legal case for broadening the criteria for PGD, a question that arises in the face of the constant increase in developments in genetic knowledge and testing. In Chapter 5, I start by asking whether in English law PGD should continue only to be available on the basis of criteria broadly consistent with those of the disability ground of the Abortion Act.

# 5

# *The Future Scope of Preimplantation Genetic Diagnosis*

## I INTRODUCTION

IN THIS CHAPTER I turn to consider some moral arguments for and against expanding the scope of what we currently allow in preimplantation genetic diagnosis (PGD). The unfortunate phrase 'designer baby' is now familiar in debates surrounding assisted reproduction. As a reference to current possibilities the term is misleading, but the phrase indicates a societal concern of some kind about control and choice in the course of reproduction. People can choose whether to have a child. As first discussed in Chapter 1, they also have a moral interest in choosing, to some degree, the conditions under which they do so, such as whether this will entail caring for a severely disabled child, though some would dispute this. In general, people disagree about the appropriate limits of reproductive autonomy, by which I mean the degree to which people should be free to make certain choices or take certain actions in the reproductive context. (In this way, the term 'procreative liberty' could also be used.) In the context of PGD there is concern about the degree to which we should permit 'negative' testing and selection, that is, selection against impairments at the embryonic stage. As we saw in Chapter 4, the current UK legal position on PGD adopts the 'precautionary principle'[1] of broadly aligning the criteria for PGD with those of section 1(1)(d) of the Abortion Act 1967 (as amended by the Human Fertilisation and Embryology (HFE) Act 1990). Further, as we saw in Chapter 2, that section requires that, in authorising an abortion, two doctors judge there to be a 'substantial risk' of a 'serious handicap' in the child that would be born.[2] In this way, just as serious reasons are legally required for selective abortion, so are they required for PGD. For this reason, negative selection against marginal or trivial features (if technically possible) would not currently be permitted. In this context

---

[1] HFEA and HGC, *Outcome of the Public Consultation on Preimplantation Genetic Diagnosis*, 18 June 2001, para 25.

[2] The relevant part of s 1(1) of the Abortion Act 1967 as amended by the HFE Act 1990 reads: 'Subject to the provisions of this section, a person shall not be guilty of an offence under the law relating to abortion when a pregnancy is terminated by a registered medical practitioner if two registered medical practitioners are of the opinion, formed in good faith… (d) that there is a substantial risk that if the child were born it would suffer from such physical or mental abnormalities as to be seriously handicapped.'

there is also concern about the possibility of 'positive' selection, that is, selection in favour of features, be they marginal or significant. Overall, this chapter asks whether there are reasons why people should only be able to select against serious impairments and why they should not be able to select 'positively' in favour of certain features, be they marginal or significant.

The distinction between 'negative' and 'positive' selection is by no means clear-cut. In fact, in either case one is implicitly selecting both for and against a given aspect at the same time. With this important caveat in mind, it may be that the terms represent, to some extent, a useful shorthand way of describing any given kind of selection. Indeed, as Jonathan Glover has noted, although the distinction 'is sometimes a blurred one… often we can at least roughly see where it should be drawn'.[3]

On an introductory theoretical note, recall that I have adopted an approach in which it is particularly those interests associated with autonomy that may be sufficiently important to ground the ascription of rights.[4] On this approach, autonomy is not itself rights-based. Rather, as Joseph Raz argues, it is a value to which we can relate certain interests, and which may in turn found certain rights.[5] Making a related point, Buchanan *et al* are of the view that rights arguments need support, which can be found by showing how rights protect important underlying interests and choices; on self-determination (which is taken also to include decisions as a parent or a prospective parent) they observe that '[o]ther things being equal, the more central and far-reaching the impact of a particular decision on an individual's life, the more substantial a person's self-determination interest in making it'.[6]

With regard to PGD, the key value is reproductive autonomy: it spawns a moral interest in being able to determine the kind of child who may be born. However, this interest is controversial in scope because of the disagreement that surrounds the moral status of the embryo. Accordingly, the question here is how great that interest is and whether it is sufficiently important to ground a moral, and ultimately a legal, right to PGD. Combining this approach to the link between autonomy, interests and rights with a gradualist approach to the embryo's (and

---

[3] J Glover, *What Sort of People Should There Be?* (Harmondsworth: Penguin, 1984) 31–2.
[4] See Ch 1, S II(E).
[5] See Ch 1, S II(E). Generally see also A Buchanan, D Brock, N Daniels and D Wikler, *From Chance to Choice: Genetics and Justice* (Cambridge: Cambridge University Press, 2000) 207 for the view that rights arguments need support, which can be found by showing how rights protect important underlying interests and choices.
[6] Buchanan *et al*, above n 5, 207 and 216. The text preceding this quotation states: 'A… point about the value of self-determination is that its exercise can be more or less important or valuable on different occasions and in different decisions. One of the most important determinants of this differential importance or value is the nature of the decision and subsequent action in question. *Deciding what to have for breakfast tomorrow is vastly less significant than deciding* what career to pursue, whom to marry, or *whether and under what conditions to have children.*' My emphasis.

fetus's) moral status first discussed in Chapter 1, the exercise of reproductive autonomy will be most justifiable (as regards the creation, testing and possible discard of the embryo) and valuable (as regards prospective parents' interests) when there are good or serious reasons for certain choices: these will mean that the moral interests derived from it are seriously implicated. In this way, the exercise of reproductive autonomy will be most worthy of protection where, for instance, the purpose is to select against a serious genetic condition (either in the interests of the future child or its parents or both, as first explored in Chapter 1).

However, given that the embryo's moral status is arguably lower than that of the fetus, we need to consider whether less serious reasons for testing and selection could suffice. Indeed, it may be that choices for 'lesser' reasons will not necessarily be morally impermissible. For instance, we might instead say that there is a much weaker interest in making such choices, so that that there is less reason to admit a moral right in such cases and, in turn, that such choices may be less worthy of third-party assistance. In turn, one of the questions to consider will be whether 'lesser' choices are justifiably legally prohibited.

In what follows, I begin in Section II by identifying various fears about the use of PGD. In Section III, the central section of this chapter, I turn to consider the interests at stake in this context. I revisit the question of the moral and legal status of the fetus and embryo, particularly the latter, and also ask who is the subject of moral concern in this context — the embryo or the future child or both? I then consider why PGD for serious genetic conditions is defensible; this echoes discussion in earlier chapters but with particular reference to PGD. Following that, I consider the idea of selection against or for marginal or minor features, such as aesthetic ones. With reference to such selection I ask a number of questions. First, might such choices be important to parents? Second, what harm, if any, could result for the future child? Third, is it acceptable to create and destroy embryos for the purposes of such testing? Fourth, since the assistance of various medical and scientific parties will be required in this process, are the interests or concerns of these third parties relevant? Fifth, recalling the discussion in Chapter 1, what might people who have disabilities think about this kind of selection and are their views relevant? Sixth, whatever people might think about the moral permissibility of such practices, does society have the right to forbid them or should they instead be legalised? I then turn to discuss selection in favour of serious features, such as (if this were possible) intelligence.

## II FEARS OF TRIVIAL OR EUGENIC USE OF EMBRYOS

As discussed in Chapter 4, the Human Fertilisation and Embryology Authority (HFEA) and the Advisory Committee on Genetic Testing (AGCT) issued a

Consultation Document on PGD in 1999.[7] The 'Outcome Document' of 2001 contains the HFEA's and Human Genetics Commission's (HGC's) recommendations in the light of this consultation.[8] Those of particular relevance to my concerns were explored in detail in the previous chapter.

One theme that apparently characterised the responses to the consultation is expressed clearly in the following quotation from the Outcome Document: 'Respondents to the consultation… indicated strongly that restrictions should be placed on the use of PGD to prevent it being used for frivolous or "social" reasons, or for eugenic purposes.'[9] In fact, the Outcome Document here affirms a fear[10] originally identified and put to the public in the Consultation Document.[11] This may raise some questions about the phrasing of consultation documents. Noting the current limitations on the number of tests that can be performed, the HGC observes that this 'itself seems to be the best protection against its misuse' but that, should the number of possible simultaneous tests increase, 'these guidelines will have to be revisited as a matter of urgency'.[12]

These fears are also expressed in *The Queen on the Application of Quintavalle v Human Fertilisation and Embryology Authority*, the 'saviour sibling' case.[13] The background to this case, which also served to explain the relationship of PGD to the Human Fertilisation and Embryology (HFE) Act, was outlined in the previous chapter.[14] Turning directly here to the fears of trivial or eugenic use revealed in the case, in the Court of Appeal Mance LJ observed that '[t]he crucial distinction has been put as being between "screening out abnormalities" and "screening in preferences". That distinction raises a spectre of eugenics and "designer babies"'. He continued as regards the facts in the case: 'But it is a crude over-simplification to view this case as being about "preferences". The word suggests personal indulgence or predilection and the luxury of a real choice.'[15] He appears, in effect, to be pointing to the moral seriousness of the reason for testing in the *Quintavalle* case, namely to provide a life-saving cure for the affected sibling.

---

[7] HFEA and AGCT, *Consultation Document on Preimplantation Genetic Diagnosis*, November 1999.
[8] HFEA and HGC, above n 1.
[9] *Ibid* para 25.
[10] For discussion of this fear, see HGC, *Minutes of Plenary Meeting*, 2 March 2001. Para 4.7 refers to 'concerns about "designer babies"'. The theme of 'trivial use' in the responses is noted in HGC, *Minutes of Genetic Testing Sub-group*, 16 February 2001, para 8.5. The idea of 'designer babies' and 'social uses' is also noted in HGC, *Minutes of Plenary Meeting*, 2 March 2001, paras 4.6 and 4.7.
[11] HFEA and AGCT, above n 7, para 26.
[12] HGC, *Response to the Human Fertilisation and Embryology Authority on the Consultation on Preimplantation Genetic Diagnosis*, para 7.
[13] [2003] EWCA Civ 667 (CA); [2005] 2 All ER 555 (HL).
[14] Ch 4, S II.
[15] Above n 13, para 134.

## Fears of Trivial or Eugenic Use of Embryos   251

More generally, as noted in Chapter 4, the potential latitude of the meaning of 'suitable' for the purposes of Schedule 2, paragraph 1 of the HFE Act 1990 was an issue of concern in this case. To recall, this paragraph provides:

> A licence under this paragraph may authorise any of the following in the course of providing treatment services — ... (d) practices designed to secure that embryos are in a suitable condition to be placed in a woman or to determine whether embryos are suitable for that purpose...

Addressing this point in the House of Lords, Lord Brown observed[16]:

> The fact is that once the concession is made (as necessarily it has to be) that PGD itself is licensable to produce not just a viable foetus but a genetically healthy child, there can be no logical basis for construing the authority's power to end at that point. PGD with a view to producing a healthy child assists a woman to carry a child only in the sense that it helps her decide whether the embryo is 'suitable' and whether she will bear the child. *Whereas, however, suitability is for the woman, the limits of permissible embryo selection are for the authority*. In the unlikely event that the authority were to propose licensing genetic selection for *purely social reasons, Parliament would surely act at once to remove that possibility*, doubtless using for the purpose the regulation making power under section 3(3)(c). Failing that, in an extreme case the court's supervisory jurisdiction could be invoked.

As we know, by means of its Consultation and Outcome Documents, the HFEA (with the AGCT and then HGC) has indeed determined 'the limits of permissible embryo selection' in the general (ie, non-HLA, human leukocyte antigen, typing) case, such that a 'significant risk of a serious genetic condition' is required. Testing and selection is only permissible under these terms.[17] Given that Schedule 2, paragraph 1(3) provides that '[a] licence under this paragraph cannot authorise any activity unless it appears to the authority to be necessary or desirable for the purpose of providing treatment services', then in a sense the question in this chapter is whether the HFEA could or should consider it either 'necessary' or 'desirable' to extend the scope of PGD and license other forms of testing. Alternatively, could the government have considered it appropriate to extend the scope of PGD in its review of the HFE Act and subsequent (draft) Human Tissue and Embryos Bill?[18] (Although I make further reference to the *Quintavalle* case, this chapter concentrates on PGD in the general — that is, non-HLA typing — case.)

---

[16] Above n 13, para 62 ( my emphasis).
[17] Further, the key recommendations from the Outcome Document are repeated in the HFEA's *Code of Practice — Sixth Edition* (2003) (and also in the HFEA's document *Guidance on Preimplantation Testing*, sent to clinics on 15 May 2003).
[18] Department of Health, *Review of the Human Fertilisation and Embryology Act: Proposals for Revised Legislation (including Establishment of the Regulatory Authority for Tissue and Embryos)*, December 2006, para 2.43, discussed in my conclusions; Human Tissue and Embryos (Draft) Bill, May 2007. The draft bill was published just as this book was going to press and therefore I have not been able to give it detailed attention. The proposed criteria

Overall, the responses to the Consultation Document and aspects of the judgments in the *Quintavalle* case appear to show two main and possibly related fears at stake in this area: one concerns the 'slippery slope' towards 'trivial' or 'social' use; the other concerns the idea of eugenics.

Turning first to the issue of eugenics, I noted in Chapter 1 that there is no agreement about the term 'eugenics' and the way, as Stephen Wilkinson observes, it may be 'taken to be a negative moral term'.[19] In itself the word 'eugenic' may not be helpful, since it tends to inhibit discussion, as happened to some degree in the Consultation Document but especially the responses thereto. As observed in Chapter 1, rather than calling a selection decision 'eugenic', it may be more useful to reflect on the reason or justification for it. We can do this in relation to negative testing against conditions such as Tay-Sachs, Duchenne muscular dystrophy, or Down's syndrome; in relation to the currently hypothetical notions of testing for features such as height, hair or eye colour; and in relation to the similarly hypothetical idea of testing for a polygenic feature that is considerably advantageous, such as intelligence.[20]

## III THE INTERESTS AT STAKE: THE REASONS FOR CHOOSING BETWEEN POSSIBLE LIVES

Would it be morally acceptable to extend the scope of PGD? Subject to scientific possibility, should we think about broadening the range of conditions or features for which we allow testing? In effect, as noted in the Introduction, this is to ask whether the criteria for PGD should continue to be aligned with those for selective abortion. The HFEA and AGCT Consultation Document states that both 'raise the same general issues in relation to the seriousness of inherited conditions'.[21] The Outcome Document observes that although the Joint Working Party (JWP) of the HFEA and HGC 'appreciated that significant differences existed between the techniques of PGD and post-implantation prenatal diagnosis (PND) it agreed as a precautionary principle that the use of PGD should be

---

of particular relevance were noted in detail in Ch 4, n 2. Amending Sch 2, HFE Act 1990: 'After paragraph 1 insert 1ZA... (2) A licence under paragraph 1 cannot authorise the testing of embryos for the purpose mentioned in sub-paragraph 1(b) or (c) unless the Authority is satisfied — (a) in relation to the abnormality of which there is a particular risk, and (b) in relation to any other abnormality for which testing is to be authorised under sub-paragraph 1(b) that there is a significant risk that the person with the abnormality will have or develop a serious physical or mental disability, a serious illness or any other serious medical condition.'

[19] S Wilkinson 'Eugenics, Embryo Selection and the Equal Value Principle' (2006) 1 *Clinical Ethics* 46, 50.

[20] The polygenic nature of such traits is noted in HGC, *Making Babies: Reproductive Decisions and Genetic Technologies* (2006) para 7.42.

[21] HFEA and AGCT, above n 7, para 27.

consistent with the use of PND'.[22] Of course, the Outcome Document is in part a response to the views expressed through the consultation exercise. The framing of the questions in that process was in turn influenced by the fact that PGD had been licensed on a preliminary basis in terms of a 'substantial' risk of a 'serious' condition, that is, on the basis of the criteria for selective abortion.

The view that the criteria for PGD should not be the same as those for PND has been expressed by John Harris[23]:

> [T]his comparison is seriously misleading if not fallacious. The fallacy is that a decision to abort must... be endorsed by two medical practitioners and comply with the requirements of various Acts of Parliament... On the other hand, a decision not to implant embryos requires no legal justification whatsoever. The decision not to implant embryos *in vitro* is within the unfettered discretion of any woman.

In effect, Harris is pointing out that the death of embryos in the case of IVF with PGD requires no legal justification. This is correct. Despite this, there can be no quarrel that the current criteria governing testing and selection processes in PGD are broadly in line with those of the disability ground of the Abortion Act. The question is whether this should be so, particularly when there is no legal obligation to save any of the embryos. The answer will partly turn on the underlying moral issues. Harris observes that 'the decision to select between embryos is constrained by morality' such that, for instance, we 'should not choose between them in ways which might constitute unfair discrimination',[24] but does not elaborate here. However, he considers it most likely that the decision to implant in any given case could be shown to be 'rationally, ethically defensible', such that others may be hard-pressed to challenge it.[25]

To appraise the broad alignment of the PGD criteria with those for selective abortion, and so whether it is appropriate that only serious genetic conditions should be the focus of testing in PGD requires, first, some consideration of the moral and legal status of the embryo and fetus.

## A  The Moral and Legal Status of the Embryo and Fetus

There are various approaches to the issue of moral status, which I have outlined in Chapter 1 and explored in more detail elsewhere.[26] For instance, the embryo has

---

[22] HFEA and HGC, above n 1, para 25.
[23] J Harris 'Rights and Reproductive Choice' in J Harris and S Holm (eds), *The Future of Human Reproduction: Ethics, Choice and Regulation* (Oxford: OUP, 1998) 5, 32–3.
[24] Ibid 33.
[25] Ibid.
[26] See R Scott, *Rights, Duties and the Body: Law and Ethics of the Maternal-Fetal Conflict* (Oxford: Hart Publishing, 2002) Ch 1. For an elegant discussion of the possible views, see, eg, J Feinberg 'Abortion' (1979) in his *Freedom and Fulfillment* (Princeton: Princeton University Press, 1992) 37.

the moral status of a born child on a potentiality account.[27] On many other views, its moral status is non-existent or very low when compared with that of a three- or six-month-old fetus, such that it lacks moral rights. On most moral views also the fetus lacks these.[28] As discussed in Chapter 1, in common with various others, my view is that the status of the embryo and then the fetus increases gradually throughout pregnancy. In my view at least, this does not imply that the embryo has no moral value. The approach is compatible with the view that there is an increase in the strength of the fetus's moral claims with the acquisition of interests at sentience,[29] but that it never acquires rights. The development of sentience approximately coincides with the point of viability. On the significance of viability, however, I noted in Chapter 2 the relatively poor prospects for a fetus born at or near 24 weeks. On this gradualist approach, the longer a pregnancy has been allowed to develop, the greater must be the justification for terminating it. Attractively, the approach allows for an interplay of maternal and fetal (and in this context, paternal) interests.

To some degree this approach is reflected in the law relating to the fetus. Although no legal rights are granted to the fetus through the Abortion Act and relevant case law states that the fetus lacks legal personality and therefore rights,[30] the availability of legal abortion depends on one of the grounds of the Abortion Act being satisfied. In fact, another way of thinking about the protection granted to the fetus by means of the Abortion Act would be to say that it has some kind of limited right, such as the right that its life not be terminated without some moral and legal justification. Overtly, however, the law has shied away from any reference to fetal legal rights and clearly the fetus lacks a legal right to life, as explored in Chapter 2. After 24 weeks' gestation, the less stringent ground of the Abortion Act no longer applies.[31] Notwithstanding this, of course, the fetus in

---

[27] For an adherent, see J Finnis 'The Rights and Wrongs of Abortion: A Reply to Judith Thomson' (1973) 2 *Phil & Pub Aff* 117.

[28] Since even the late-gestation fetus lacks the characteristics underpinning the criteria for moral personhood. On fetuses, moral personhood and rights, see MA Warren 'On the Moral and Legal Status of Abortion' (1973) 57(1) *The Monist* 43.

[29] For a philosopher supporting the link between interests and sentience, see B Steinbock, *Life Before Birth* (New York: OUP, 1992) 24, n 24. On the notion of interests, see J Feinberg, *Harm to Others* (New York: OUP, 1984) 34: 'In general, a person has a stake in X... when he stands to gain or lose depending on the nature or condition of X'.

[30] See *Re MB (Cesarean Section)* [1997] 8 Med LR 217 amongst other cases.

[31] Section 1(1)(a) is time-limited to terminations before 24 weeks. The relevant portion of s1(1) of the Abortion Act 1967, as amended by the Human Fertilisation and Embryology Act 1990, reads: 'Subject to the provisions of this section, a person shall not be guilty of an offence under the law relating to abortion when a pregnancy is terminated by a registered medical practitioner if two registered medical practitioners are of the opinion, formed in good faith — (a) that the pregnancy has not exceeded twenty-four weeks and that the continuance of the pregnancy would involve risk, greater than if the pregnancy were terminated, of injury to the physical or mental health of the pregnant woman or any existing children of her family'. See Ch 2 for further discussion.

which a serious anomaly has been found can be aborted up until birth if the conditions of section 1(1)(d) of the Act are met.[32] This was discussed particularly in Chapter 2. Importantly, that the law can protect the fetus to some degree even though it might be thought to lack moral rights and does lack legal ones reminds us that rights are not the only mechanism compatible with a degree of legal protection.

Turning now to the embryo, how much protection should it receive and, in particular for current purposes, should it only be legal to test embryos — and therefore also possibly discard them — on the basis of criteria that are broadly the same as those for the selective abortion of the fetus?

The embryo is usually three days' old when tested in PGD and consists of six to ten cells.[33] No-one has let it live very long, although several people have actively engaged in the process of creating it. Should the embryo be treated in a manner broadly consistent with the impaired fetus, that is, with reference to the requirements of 'a significant risk of a serious genetic condition'?

Prior to the formulation of the recommendations in the Outcome Document, discussions within the HGC itself revealed a concern that 'there was a real risk in the future that, with PGD becoming available for more people… it could be used for *selecting* babies'.[34] At one level, this fear may arise precisely because on many (though not all) views the embryo has a relatively low moral status. At another level, this is ironic since what some might judge to be the relatively low moral status of the embryo could imply that such use is unproblematic.[35] However, although relevant, the moral status of the embryo is not necessarily fully determinative in this context. The Warnock Report (which preceded the HFE Act 1990) held that, although of low moral status, embryos are entitled to 'respect'.[36] The notion of respect is somewhat vague and all too easy to criticise. At the same time, it is hard to come up with a better term when what we may be

---

[32] Or possibly those of s 1(1)(b), as discussed in Ch 2, S V(A).

[33] F Flinter 'Preimplantation Genetic Diagnosis Needs to be Tightly Regulated' (2001) 322 *BMJ* 1008, 1008.

[34] HGC, *Minutes of Genetic Testing Sub-group*, 12 January 2001, per Dr Albert, para 5.4 (my emphasis). See also HGC, *Minutes of Genetic Testing Sub-group*, 16 February 2001, para 8.2: 'Dr Albert… felt that there was a eugenic danger to this procedure with future technological developments such as gene chips, and it was important to state clearly that PGD should be used for specific testing and not screening. Dr Draper felt that what the Sub-group was trying to do was to pick a line between allowing PGD for anything people requested and not allowing it at all, and which would reflect concerns raised in many of the consultation responses.'

[35] J Robertson, *Children of Choice: Freedom and the New Reproductive Technologies* (Princeton, NJ: Princeton University Press, 1994) 156: 'because the embryo is so rudimentary in development, selection for less serious reasons should be less objectionable than screening of fetuses for those same reasons'. See also his 'Genetic Selection of Offspring Characteristics' (1996) 76 *Boston U Law Rev* 421, 450.

[36] Warnock Report (Cmnd 9314), *Report of the Committee of Inquiry into Fertilisation and Embryology*, republished as *A Question of Life* (Oxford: Blackwell, 1985).

trying to do, perhaps, is simply to say that the embryo may have some moral value. I shall therefore use the term 'respect' in relation to the embryo to convey this thought. As for the Warnock Committee's emphasis on respect for the embryo, as a matter of public policy it could be argued that it is important to give the embryo some legal protection so as to accommodate to some degree different moral perspectives on it. In fact, in its very liberal and controversial report, *Human Reproductive Technologies and the Law* (2005), the House of Commons Science and Technology Committee observed[37]:

> We accept that in a society that is both multi-faith and largely secular, there is never going to be consensus on the level of protection accorded to the embryo or the role of the state in reproductive decision-making… We believe, however, that to be effective this Committee's conclusions should seek consensus, as far as it is possible to achieve. Given the rate of scientific change and the ethical dilemmas involved, we conclude, therefore, that we should adopt an approach consistent with the gradualist approach, of which the Warnock Committee is one important example.

Further, in its report *Making Babies: Reproductive Decisions and Genetic Technologies* (2006), the HGC noted[38]:

> To date, society as a whole has been unable to reach a consensus about how the status of the embryo relates to the moral principle that requires us to protect human life. As a result there is no social consensus about the extent to which the embryo is to be protected, and about when and why and at what stages of embryonic development protections are required.

In thinking now about whether it should only be permissible to test the embryo on the basis of criteria compatible with those of the Abortion Act, it would be helpful to consider the degree to which our concern in selection practices is indeed with the embryo or fetus.

### B  The Subject of Moral Concern

Decisions about reproduction entail the creation (or avoidance) of new people and accompanying relationships. Ideally, such decisions will entail moral reflection, for instance about the ability of the woman or couple to care for a child. Notice that here the interests at stake are not those of the embryo (or fetus) but those of the future child that the embryo (or fetus) will become. However, at the stage of selection by PGD, the subject of testing is an embryo. Further, on many moral views the embryo's moral status is lower than that of the fetus and much lower than that of the future child it has the potential to become. Where an embryo or fetus exists, decisions about reproduction therefore have a curious binary nature: on the one hand they concern the existence or otherwise of a future child and the conditions under which that child will be born; on the other,

---

[37] House of Commons Science and Technology Committee's report *Human Reproductive Technologies and the Law* (2005), observation in rec 2 (in part), para 46.
[38] HGC, above n 20, para 1.17.

at the time of the selection decision, they concern a subject in embryonic or fetal form, whose respective moral statuses are arguably, to different degrees, considerably lower than that of any future child.

This binary feature of these decisions means that when we think about the moral appropriateness of selection decisions, we need to attend both to the welfare of the future child and to the moral claims of the embryo or fetus. On the one hand, then, when we think about the future child, we need to think about the extent to which certain choices could harm it, if at all, remembering here that if an embryo is not selected it will not in fact come to be a child. On the other, when we think about the embryo or fetus, we need to think about the extent to which a given test and subsequent choice, which could well entail its destruction, is morally (and ultimately legally) justifiable. In relation to embryos and PGD, we also need to observe that a desire to test embryos may also involve their creation. In the discussion that follows, I shall try to attend to concerns about both the embryo and the future child to see what light they may shed on the moral permissibility of different kinds of selection decision.

## C  Selecting Against 'Serious' Genetic Anomalies

I argued in Chapter 1 that, in the light of the positive moral duties that raising a child will entail, people should be able to choose whether to reproduce and also, to some extent, the conditions under which they do so. For instance, they should be able to avoid the birth of a seriously impaired child, including by selective abortion. As we saw in Chapter 2, it could be argued that after sentience and viability (not in fact a clear-cut concept, given the high risks of severe disability in children born around the time of viability) abortion is only clearly morally defensible if there is a risk that a child would have a life she did not think worth living, although there may be exceptions here.

A central difficulty in discussions about 'seriousness' is that it is probably impossible for people to agree on the meaning of this term, as noted in earlier chapters. Previously, I identified two applications of 'serious' in the literature. As we first saw in Chapter 1, in some cases a future child may be so severely impaired that it might be against its interests to be born: Tay-Sachs may be one example. In such a case, there is no real conflict between the future child's interests and those of its parents, who are unlikely to want to proceed with an affected pregnancy. But as we diverge from the extreme and unusual case, judging seriousness is much more difficult. It is made more complex by the potentially competing perspectives — parental, medical and those of the impaired — on this issue. In recognition of this, the HGC has observed[39]:

> It has proved impossible to define what 'serious' should mean in this context. We have listed some factors that should be taken into account when considering seriousness, but

---

[39] HGC, above n 12, para 6, and as also noted in earlier chapters.

perhaps the most important is that this technique should not be used for the purposes of trait selection or in a manner which could give rise to eugenic outcomes.

Further, the HFEA's and AGCT's Consultation Document observes: 'individual judgments on seriousness will vary depending on personal and family circumstances and on the nature and severity of the condition and the likelihood of transmission'.[40] In some cases, although a possible child may have the prospect of a reasonable quality of life, his impairments may still implicate his parents' interests in reproduction in serious ways. Thomas Murray has similarly identified these kinds of parental interests.[41]

In line with these two applications of 'serious', testing and selection decisions in PGD could be made for either of two principal reasons, as discussed first in Chapter 1. First, it may be that there is a serious risk that a subsequently born child would not think his life worth living because the burdens of his existence are not sufficiently outweighed by any compensating benefits; here, in effect, philosophically speaking he would have a 'wrongful life'. In this case, it can fairly be said that PGD is conducted to avoid breaching a moral duty to that child that would otherwise crystallise on its birth. Of course, the parents' interests will also be implicated. Further, from a non-person-affecting view we could also say that it is preferable that such a child is not born. Second, there is the case in which a child would have a reasonable quality of life and think his life worth living but his condition may have the potential negatively to impact on his parents. Here PGD is effectively conducted because of *their* possible interests in the kind of child to which they give birth, rather than his. Testing for Down's syndrome or cystic fibrosis (in some cases) may attend particularly to the parents' interests rather than those of the child, although each condition varies considerably in severity, as discussed in Chapter 2.[42] For instance, the HFEA's and AGCT's Consultation Document observes that 'many disorders vary in the severity with which they present. Cystic fibrosis can contribute to death within a few days of birth, but some individuals may survive into their thirties and beyond'.[43] Arguably, selection against either condition through PGD may be justifiable because parental interests could be seriously invoked, even if it would not have been against the child's

---

[40] HGC and AGCT, above n 7, para 31.

[41] T Murray, *The Worth of a Child* (Berkeley: University of California Press, 1996) 138. As we saw in Ch 2, Sally Sheldon and Stephen Wilkinson have argued that, other than in extremely severe cases, parental interests represent the most plausible justification for the disability ground of the Abortion Act. S Sheldon and S Wilkinson 'Termination of Pregnancy for Reason of Foetal Disability: are There Grounds for a Special Exception in Law?' 9 *Med Law Rev* (2001) 85.

[42] For interesting work on the views of people with conditions such as cystic fibrosis, Down's syndrome and spina bifida, both on their lives and on screening practices, see P Alderson 'Prenatal Counselling and Images of Disability' in D Dickenson (ed), *Ethical Issues in Maternal-Fetal Medicine* (Cambridge: Cambridge University Press, 2002) 195, discussed in Ch 1, S V(B).

[43] Above n 7, para 33.

interests to be born. Once again, non-person-affecting principles could also be used to support this second kind of selection. As argued in Chapter 1, such principles would be strongest before the creation of any given embryo, although they may have some weight against the embryo, but arguably have increasingly less weight against the growing moral claims of the fetus, even if the fetus is not a person.

At this stage we should recall a conceptual point relating to the application of the welfare-of-the-child requirement in section 13(5) of the HFE Act to the PGD context. In the traditional sense, the welfare requirement is a concern attaching to *any* child a couple might have through IVF. An attempt to apply the requirement in the case of the child who will result from the selection of a particular embryo runs into the conceptual difficulties surrounding what Derek Parfit has called the 'non-identity problem', first explored in Chapter 1 and identified again with reference to PGD in Chapter 4.[44] As we saw in that chapter, in offering guidance on the interpretation of section 13(5), the HFEA (in its Sixth Code of Practice) observes that the assessment in relation to the welfare of the child 'is expected to take into account the following factors relating to patients:... (v) The risk of harm to children including: (a) inherited disorders or transmissible disease...'.[45] In this way, the HFEA does not make any comment about the severity of a given condition or whose interests might be implicated by any given condition. As the previous chapter has tried to show through ethical argument and consideration of the factors relevant to the PGD guidance (such as 'the view of those seeking treatment of the condition') prospective parents' interests may be a valid consideration in testing and selection decisions, regardless of any particular judgment about the welfare of a possible child under the HFE Act. However, it seems unlikely that the possible distinction between prospective parents' and children's interests is openly acknowledged in discussions between prospective parents and a clinic's staff. Similarly, and perhaps unsurprisingly, non-person-affecting principles are not identified by the HFEA and, as we saw in the previous chapter, appear rarely, if at all, to be present in the minds of a clinic's staff.

So far, I have suggested that the creation, testing and selection of embryos for the serious reasons discussed above is highly justifiable. Discussion in the previous chapter also pointed towards this conclusion. Does this mean that PGD tests and choices that do not in some sense concern a serious genetic condition are morally impermissible? For instance, what about selection for hair, eye colour or height, which are aesthetic features? What does the binary nature of these decisions tell us about the permissibility of these kinds of selection? Although such choices are entirely hypothetical, reflection on them helps us work out what we think about different kinds of selection practices.

---

[44] D Parfit, *Reasons and Persons* (Oxford: OUP, 1984) Ch 16.
[45] HFEA, *Code of Practice — Sixth Edition* (2003) para 3.12.

## D  Selecting Against Or For Purely Aesthetic or Generally Trivial Features

At the outset, I should say something about the 'serious/trivial' distinction around which I am structuring this discussion, because there are of course important judgments at play in my use of this distinction. Since my primary concern is always with the appropriate scope of reproductive autonomy (or liberty) of prospective parents, I am particularly interested in the question of which features in a child, such as serious disability, have the potential significantly to impact on parents' lives and thereby seriously invoke their interest in reproductive autonomy. My thoughts here are consistent with those of Buchanan *et al*, cited earlier, that '[o]ther things being equal, the more central and far-reaching the impact of a particular decision on an individual's life, the more substantial a person's self-determination interest in making it'. As I shall argue below, although some parents might wish to select a future child on the basis of its hair or eye colour, such features will not in fact have a serious impact on parents' lives. (I do not suggest that this settles the issue of moral permissibility.) So, this is one way in which I have constructed the 'serious/trivial' distinction. At the same time, I do not presume the distinction is clear-cut, as I discuss below.

A second way of viewing the 'serious/trivial' distinction is to relate it to the non-person-affecting perspective (first discussed in Chapter 1) that encourages us to think about bringing people into the world with greater potential for flourishing and welfare. As observed in Chapter 1, although there is no necessary connection between severe disabilities and diminished flourishing and welfare, severe disabilities could seriously disrupt our potential for flourishing. By contrast, although features such as the colour of our eyes or hair may well affect how we feel about ourselves and may affect how others react to us, it is not clear that, other things being equal, these features have very great ability to determine the extent to which we flourish. Rather, it seems more likely that, whilst such features may have some impact, this will be relatively trivial compared with the impact of other features, such as our health and physical functioning. From a non-person-affecting perspective then, there would not be a strong reason to select on this basis. This gives further weight to a broad distinction between the 'serious' and the 'trivial'.

The 'serious/trivial' distinction can also be related to the so-called 'treatment/enhancement' distinction. The latter is related to the idea of selection against serious impairments on the one hand and in favour of 'better than normal' features on the other. On a non-person-affecting approach the reason to make any given choice between different possible people (at the embryonic stage) would always be to increase the potential for flourishing and welfare in future people. For this reason, rather than being understood as a clear-cut distinction, the 'treatment/enhancement' distinction is probably best understood as applying to a spectrum of selection choices, with choices against impairments and disorders at one end and choices in favour of certain features, be this better health or greater intelligence or positively viewed aesthetic features at the other. (I return to this point and to others' discussion of it later in the chapter.) The connection I now want to make between what might therefore be better termed the 'treatment/enhancement' *continuum* and the 'serious/trivial' distinction (perhaps this too is a continuum) entails observing that in relation either to selection against relatively trivial negative features or in favour of relatively trivial positive ones, the 'treatment' or 'enhancement' effect (on flourishing and welfare) will be relatively small, compared with selection against a serious genetic disorder or selection in favour of a feature such as significantly enhanced health. Again, this reinforces my use of a broad distinction between the 'serious' and the 'trivial'. As noted above, however, I acknowledge that there will be disagreement about what counts as one or the other.

In due course I shall relate the above observations to the question of the moral status of the embryo (and fetus) amongst other issues: when we think about the extent to which, other things being equal, a given feature would affect the life of a future person, this may have some implications for the moral acceptability of any given choice from the point of view, as it were, of the 'cost' to those embryos that are created for the purposes of testing but which are not selected. Having flagged some connections with the ideas I am going to develop in this chapter, I turn now directly to consider whether selection for relatively trivial features is morally problematic.

I can think of six main questions that we could ask about the idea of such practices. First, could such choices be important to parents and does the answer to this matter? Second, what harm, if any, could come to the resulting child? Third, is it acceptable to create and destroy embryos in order to carry out such testing? Fourth, given that the assistance of various medical and scientific parties will be required in this process, are the interests or concerns of these third parties relevant? Fifth, what might people who have impairments think about this kind of selection and are their views relevant? Sixth, whatever we might think about the moral permissibility of such practices, does society have the right to proscribe such practices or should they instead be legalised?

### i  Parents' interests and attitudes: central versus marginal features

We could first ask what features in a child are directly related to the goals and experiences prospective parents might seek in parenthood. Some features will be central and others marginal, although there will inevitably be disagreement about where to draw the line.[46] A central feature could be that the child will have the

---

[46] The distinction between central and peripheral features has also been observed in relation to reproductive autonomy by John Robertson: 'The objective materiality of some traits to reproductive decisions will attenuate as we move from genes for severe genetic disease to susceptibility genes to genes for hair and eye colour, and from negative to positive methods of selection... at some point the divergence from what most people view as central to reproductive meaning will diminish the perceived importance of the

prospect of a reasonably long and healthy life (thus, not Tay-Sachs) or that it will be free from significant mental impairment or health problems (thus, not at least some cases of Down's syndrome). The process of parenting, in which parents seek to encourage a child in the pursuit of valuable activities, to facilitate the child's education and to instill certain moral values — all ideally aimed at the flourishing of the child — may (other things being equal) be somewhat harder if a child is mentally impaired or suffers from debilitating health problems, especially ones that will shorten its life. In these ways, features in a possible child that would affect to some extent whether or with what degree of difficulty a parent can fulfil these parental aims could be seen as central ones. Of course, finding that one's child is significantly impaired, either mentally or physically, may itself affect one's perception of the goals and experiences of parenting.[47] Moreover, it is likely that additional demands will be accompanied by additional rewards. Despite this, before any given child is born, I argued in Chapter 1 that prospective parents may reasonably have some sense, however imperfect and potentially subject to change, of what they wish or feel able to embark on. In this process, they may reflect on which features seem in some way central and these might include such things as health and lack of mental or physical impairment.

By contrast, a marginal feature would be whether a child will be short or tall, or whether he or she will have brown or green eyes. Some prospective parents might argue that the 'colouring' of their future child is important to them. Once they have given birth to a child, however, and experienced something of child-raising, it seems implausible that they would continue to regard this aspect as important — relative, that is, to other more central features in their child. In this light, it seems safe to say that the goals and experiences of parenthood would not be seriously affected by the hair or eye colour of a child. This means that parents do not have a serious interest in being able to test and select one way or the other. In turn, this may imply that there are no strong grounds to admit a moral and legal right to such choices, particularly since these would entail the assistance of third parties. But it is too early either to conclude this or to decide whether, legally speaking, such choices should not be permitted.

---

reproductive interest at stake, and indicate that selection on that basis should not be part of procreative liberty... Drawing the line between protected and unprotected traits and methods is likely to be difficult.' Note that his concern at this juncture is with procreative liberty generally. J Robertson 'Genetic Selection of Offspring Characteristics' (1996) 76 *Boston U Law Rev* 421, 431. He suggests, somewhat speculatively, that US courts might seek to protect less material interests on the basis of another right, such as the right to 'family autonomy in raising offspring' (*ibid* n 12), citing *Wisconsin v Yoder*, 406 US 205 (1972) (in which Amish parents were permitted to control the 'religious future' and education of their children). He goes on to discuss the idea of a subjective preference which may be too far removed from reproductive meaning.

[47] I am grateful to Bobbie Farsides here.

Now, it might be noted here that autonomy consists in being able to make serious *and* trivial choices.[48] It is valuable to be able to make such choices and the ability to do so highlights the value of autonomy generally in our lives. However, as noted in Chapter 1, our autonomy is most valuable to us when it concerns decisions relating to important questions in our lives, ones that will have a significant impact — such as whether to have a child, or whether to have one with a serious impairment. In case of doubt, consider having a choice between being able to test for a serious genetic condition in a future child on the one hand and eye colour on the other. In fact (assuming the existence of a test for eye colour) this could be a very real choice, in the sense that testing for eye colour could compromise the accuracy of testing for the serious genetic condition.[49] If this were the choice facing you, which would you choose (if either)?

This point having been addressed, morally speaking does it matter — in our appraisal of the legitimate scope of testing and selection in PGD — that whether a child has green or brown eyes will really be of marginal or even no importance to a prospective parent either at the time of selection or, alternatively, once a child is in fact born and developing? In other words, does it matter that this will not be a choice of great import or value? There are other possible objections, beside the lack of any real importance to such choices, that people might make.

For instance, Allen Buchanan *et al* observe: 'the greater the harm would be to another as a result of respecting a particular reproductive choice, the weaker is the overall moral case provided by self-determination for respecting that choice'.[50] This must be right. But we should recall here that, so far as current techniques are concerned, the 'determination' that may occur in the context of genetic selection is not so much the determination of what another will be like — in the sense of shaping a *given* person — but rather the determination of who will exist. To what extent is this about self-determination from the point of view of prospective parents? If they choose to select a child without a serious genetic condition rather than one with that condition, they are in one sense determining an important aspect of the shape of their *own* future lives, that is, whether they become the parents of a child with a serious impairment. At this stage, however, they are not determining the shape of their *child's* future life. Rather, they are determining who will exist. Alternatively, if they choose to select a child with green rather than brown eyes, given the lack of real importance to them of this choice, they are not in fact determining an important aspect of the shape of their lives. Rather,

---

[48] I am grateful to Roger Crisp here.
[49] On the question of a decrease in accuracy with additional tests, note the comments of one of the members of staff at the clinic that provides PGD, the work of which was discussed in Ch 4. Counsellor 17 observes: 'Well, so far, the evidence doesn't really stack up... and my greatest worry is, you know, that you start adding in all these sorts of tests, and compromise the test results that you initially set up PGD for... I think that will always be a problem.' Interview, Counsellor 17, at 20.
[50] *Ibid* 218.

they are selecting between children — and so determining who will exist — on the basis of a purely aesthetic feature. Overall, the point is that the technique of genetic selection under discussion here (PGD) does not entail the determining, or shaping, of an actual other.

At this stage we might explore another concept that has featured in relevant critiques — that of 'self-expression'. Onora O'Neill, writing about autonomy and reproduction, observes that abortion concerns the avoidance of the birth of another; by contrast, in reproduction the creation of another is at stake. For this reason it would not be appropriate to construe the autonomy at stake in the latter context 'primarily' as a form of 'self-expression'.[51] In fact, it does not appear that writers such as Ronald Dworkin, John Robertson and John Harris, whose work on 'reproductive autonomy' or 'procreative liberty' she critiques here, consider that these concepts are concerned with self-expression. Rather, the focus in their work would appear to be on aspects of self-determination.[52] O'Neill's repeated use of the term 'self-expression' is therefore somewhat puzzling. At face value, however, when applied to the wish to select on the basis of purely aesthetic features, O'Neill's term 'self-expression' may capture something of what some people may find troubling about this desire, as if parents were putting together elements that aesthetically pleased them or accorded with some ideal notion of a child's appearance in their minds. Having said this, once again we should recall that current methods of genetic selection really concern *who* will exist, not the features of any one possible person. It is just that who exists will depend on the reason for the choice between embryos. (It would be different if the traits of embryos were actually manipulated.)

Still, to give further consideration to concerns about excessive determination of others, or self-expression, we need now to think about the interests of the future child.

### ii  *The child's interests: autonomy and flourishing*

There are several ways to reflect on the interests of the future child. We could think about its welfare, either physically or emotionally. In this process, we are likely to think about the degree to which it is loved, nurtured, taught, accepted and so forth. We could then think about the extent to which these things are promoting its autonomy. In thinking about a child's autonomy, we can distinguish between the promotion of a child's capacity for autonomy on the one hand, which might include such things as the ability to reason and carefully to reflect on emotional responses, and a child's actual or apparently autonomous choices on the other. (The extent to which the latter should be promoted and respected by parents is a huge question in its own right, not of concern here.) And in turn, to

---

[51] O O'Neill, *Autonomy and Trust in Bioethics* (Cambridge: Cambridge University Press, 2002) 61. See generally her Ch 3.

[52] See, eg: Robertson, above n 35; Harris, above n 23; R Dworkin, *Life's Dominion: An Argument about Abortion and Euthanasia* (London: Harper Collins, 1993).

some extent we could link ideas about the child's autonomy with thoughts about its capacity to flourish and its actual experience of flourishing.

Concerns related to the notion of a child's autonomy have been present in the literature for some time. For instance, one worry that has been expressed about testing (of all kinds) relates to the idea, originally developed by Joel Feinberg, of a 'child's right to an open future'.[53] Whether there is such a right is a matter of considerable debate. Some writers clearly have sympathy with the idea. For instance, fleshing out the idea of such a right in terms of the 'kind of neutrality' that parents should practice, Buchanan et al state[54]:

> The idea is that parents have a responsibility to help their children during their growth to adulthood to develop capacities for practical judgment and autonomous choice, and to develop as well at least a reasonable range of the skills and capacities necessary to provide them the choice of a reasonable array of different life plans available to members of their society.

(In fact, we should note that these thoughts address the way a child is actually brought up.) There are two ideas at stake here: one concerns the idea of promoting autonomous capacities; the other concerns the development of a range of options from which the subject can choose. The latter is really also about facilitating autonomy, since without education (for instance) a child's choices, and so her autonomy, will be limited.[55] In this light it seems, as Stephen Wilkinson argues, that what really underlies the idea of a right to an open future is a more straightforward and comprehensible concern with a child's autonomy.[56] Perhaps the notion of an 'open future' is best understood as a catching metaphor.

We can now relate some of the ideas sketched above in relation to a child's welfare to the 'trivial' choice concerning a marginal feature. We can think first about the child's autonomy. If chosen for his green eyes and red hair, has his autonomy been interfered with? As we know, he can only exist as that child and so, if chosen for those features, there can be no sense in which the genetic choice *per se* has interfered with his autonomy. Further, the genetic choice can be

---

[53] J Feinberg 'The Child's Right to an Open Future' in W Aiken and H LaFollette (eds), *Whose Child? Children's Rights, Parental Authority and State Power* (Totowa, NJ: Rowman and Littlefield, 1980). See also D Davis 'Genetic Dilemmas and the Child's Right to an Open Future' (1997) 27(2) *Hastings CR* 7, 12: 'Good parenting requires a balance between having a child for our own sakes and being open to the moral reality that the child will exist for her own sake'; E Schmidt 'The Parental Obligation to Expand a Child's Range of Open Futures when Making Genetic Trait Selections for their Child' (2007) 21/4 *Bioethics* 191.

[54] Buchanan *et al*, above n 5, 170.

[55] As N Levy interestingly observes: 'We have no way of marking a precise boundary, within which… choices are the necessary preconditions of the child's own decisions, and beyond which too many options are foreclosed. All we can do is try to make some sort of judgment.' N Levy 'Deafness, Culture, and Choice' (2002) 28 *J Med Ethics* 284, 284.

[56] S Wilkinson 'Parental Duties and Virtues' in his *Choosing Children: the Ethics of Selective Reproduction* (Oxford: OUP, forthcoming).

cosmetically modified: if he wishes, he could become free of these features to some extent with the use of coloured contact lenses and hair dye. Will he have an interest in doing so? This is unlikely unless his parents chose him with these features because they — a failed model and actress — dreamt that he would grow up to be successful where they were not and, consequent on their PGD choices, raise him very much with these expectations in mind. This could be frustrating for him: for instance, he may feel that his own desires and interests are not encouraged. Or he may feel insufficiently loved and accepted for himself. Clearly, however, this is a highly implausible scenario. And in any event, it is worth thinking about how much influence, at least over his autonomy, these parents can really have. Legally, they are obliged to send him to school so that, whilst they may not actively encourage his educational opportunities, they cannot actually curtail them.

Importantly, what this fanciful example shows is that if there are problems when parents attach great importance to a child's purely aesthetic features, these do not lie in the genetic selection *per se*, but rather in the parental expectations attendant or consequent on such choices, as in this necessarily forced example. In essence, these would be 'environmental' harms. We might be inclined to think of these parents as shallow. However, we should notice that this will characterise them and their approach to child-raising regardless of whether they have access to genetic selection for aesthetic features. So, while the shallow focus of these parents may have led them to seek certain testing (if it were available), those attitudes are essentially independent of that testing. In such a scenario, since the child's autonomy is likely to be marginally affected at best and possibly not at all, the potential for harm may rather lie in the parents' own inadequacies in relation to the nurturing and acceptance of their child.

This notion of acceptance to which I am drawing attention stems particularly from recent work by Stephen Wilkinson who argues, rightly I think, that the parental virtue that may be required once a child is born as a result of a process of genetic selection is that of acceptance. Having examined several arguments in the literature, including those relating to the parental virtue of acceptance and those relating to the idea of unconditional parental love, Wilkinson distinguishes between '(a) a prenatal commitment to accepting and loving your child, *once it arrives*, whatever characteristics it has and (b) refraining from selective reproduction', observing that '(a) does not logically require (b); or at least we are still waiting for an *argument* that links (a) and (b)'. (As Wilkinson notes, whether selective reproduction might be followed by a lack of acceptance *empirically* speaking can only be a matter of speculation.) Further, with reference to the idea of unconditional love, Wilkinson suggests that what is really required is that *'parental love ought not to be withheld or withdrawn on trivial or morally irrelevant grounds'*.[57]

This line of thought also appears relevant to objections to selective reproduction based on the notion of 'commodification' of children, which have been noted by the HGC.[58] If a child's autonomy is unlikely seriously to be affected by selection practices, it might be that what people really worry about is the notion of children being 'commodified' if parents wish to select a child with a particular eye or hair colour. It is not clear to what extent this kind of concern stems from notions of appropriate parental values or from fear of harm to future children. It probably relates to a very understandable concern with the quality of the parent-child relationship and worries about the impact of selection practices on that relationship, such as that parental love is 'withheld' unless a child has certain features or characteristics. However, once again we can note that any harm to a resulting child or children will come from the parents' attitude to child-raising itself, rather than from the genetic selection *per se*. Arguably, then, this concern might be addressed by again emphasising the importance of the virtue of parental acceptance following any form of genetic selection. In general, whatever the focus of genetic selection (the avoidance of a serious genetic condition or of a relatively minor feature), it is of course to be hoped that parents will greatly love whatever child is born so that, as Jonathan Glover has observed (as noted in Chapter 1), we do not have to think of this as something that is 'owed' to children. Whether children are loved and accepted could well be the factor that most influences their flourishing and well-being.

On the question of possible harms to future children, however, there are two very important points to note here. One is that there is still some uncertainty about the long-term effects on a child of the removal of either one or two cells at the preimplantation stage.[59] The former Chair of the HFEA observed that this is a

---

[57] *Ibid*, emphasis in original. Wilkinson discusses the work of several scholars, including R McDougall 'Acting Parentally: An Argument against Sex Selection' (2005) 31 *JME* 601. See further R McDougall 'Parental Virtue: A New Way of Thinking about the Morality of Reproductive Actions' (2007) 21/4 *Bioethics* 181.

[58] HGC, above n 20, para 4.5. Further, G McGee 'Parenting in an Era of Genetics' (1997) 27(2) *Hastings CR* 16, 18, writes about the idea of 'systematic choices' and parental expectations.

[59] G White and M McClure 'Introducing Innovation into Practice: Technical and Ethical Analyses of PGD and ICSI Technologies' (1998) 26 *JL Med and Ethics* 5, 5: 'Scientific concerns about PGD center on possible harm to the early embryo resulting from the extraction of a single cell...'. According to Stuart Lavery, Sub-specialist in Reproductive Medicine, the Hammersmith Hospital, London, the initial data on safety are 'reassuring', although continuing surveillance is needed ('PGD and the "Welfare of the Child"' talk at 'Moral Dilemmas in Reproductive Medicine', British Fertility Society VIIth Ethics Study Day, RCOG, 27 February 2004). The latest study indicates that there is no increase in anomalies at birth: J Buxton 'Embryo Tests Carry No Extra Health Risk' 24 June 2007 412 *Bionews* <http://www.ivf.net/ivf/index.php?page=out&id=2780> accessed

reason to limit testing to serious conditions.[60] If we continue to take a cautious approach because of this, it will take some time to rule out these concerns, since PGD was first conducted in 1990, so that the oldest resulting child is now about 17. This is a point of potential relevance to any kind of testing and selection in PGD.

A second extremely important point about the practice of PGD, in any form, lies in its association with IVF and the higher risk of multiple births that currently attends IVF pregnancies. The HFEA recently published a report, written by the Expert Group on Multiple Births after IVF, entitled *One Child at a Time: Reducing Multiple Births After IVF*, which highlights the risks to the mother, fetus and future child from multiple (including twin) pregnancies. My focus in this section is on harm to the future child. In this regard, the report makes it very clear that it is in the best interests of every child to have developed in a singleton pregnancy. In its Executive Summary, the report states[61]:

> The biggest risk factor for twins is prematurity and low birth weight, which often necessitates hospitalisation at the beginning of life, and is linked to a significant risk of neonatal death of one or both twins, beside longer term health and cognitive effects. For example twins are at least six times more likely than singletons to suffer from cerebral palsy... A multiple pregnancy should not be regarded as the ideal outcome of IVF treatment. The problem is not that two healthy babies might be born, but that too often adverse outcomes occur for the mother and one or both of the babies. IVF clinicians, embryologists, nurses and counsellors, the professional bodies, patient organisations and IVF patients themselves need to acknowledge that IVF children (like all other children) are entitled to the best possible start in life: their chances of being born as full term singletons with a normal birth weight need to be maximised... The only way to reduce the multiple birth rate after IVF is to transfer only one embryo to those women at most risk of having twins. Overall, eSET [elective Single Embryo Transfer] needs to be made the norm in IVF treatment.

---

14 October 2007, noting findings reported at a meeting of the European Society of Human Genetics which studied babies at birth and two years thereafter.

[60] Suzi Leather, debate 'Saviour Siblings', Progress Education Trust, 16 October 2003. This consideration was previously at stake in the issue of tissue typing. In the Court of Appeal decision in the *Quintavalle* case, above n 13, para 132, Mance LJ observed that 'the HFEA, exercising its judgment, considered that the invasive procedure of a biopsy should only be undertaken on an embryo if it was necessary in the first instance from the point of view of the embryo, in other words to confirm the embryo's genetic normality. If a biopsy was necessary in any event on that ground, then there was no objection to allowing it for the further purpose of tissue testing'. The HFEA's current position on this matter was discussed in Ch 4, S II.

[61] HFEA Expert Group on Multiple Births after IVF, *One Child at a Time: Reducing Multiple Births After IVF* (October 2006) 8–9.

The HFEA has now issued a consultation document seeking advice on how UK practice can be modified to avoid the problems that may be associated with multiple births.[62]

Morally speaking, it would be somewhat paradoxical to use IVF and PGD to avoid disease or impairment in a future child, particularly of a degree compatible with a life the child would think worth living, with the result that twins are born with, say, cerebral palsy. As both the report and the consultation document make clear, careful thought needs to be given to which women are more likely to have a multiple pregnancy and this needs to be balanced against the aim of achieving a live birth. As for the other possible purposes of PGD under discussion here, namely the use of IVF and PGD to select for purely aesthetic or other relatively trivial features, arguably the risks to the future child associated with multiple births would always be a very strong reason against allowing transfer of more than one embryo. In theory, this could become a relevant ethical guideline in this context. That said, however, where a couple already needed IVF to have a child and was 'adding in' selection of some kind, there would need to be a more complex appraisal of their wish to achieve a live birth on the one hand and the desirability of avoiding a twin pregnancy on the other. Since it could be difficult effectively to monitor who 'needed' IVF (to achieve a live birth) and who did not, this could become highly complex. I do not further address this issue here, other than to emphasise that the severity of possible harms to a child when part of a multiple pregnancy is a moral issue of potentially very great significance in this context.

So, should we legally permit testing for marginal or aesthetic features? In one way, to allow such testing could be seen as encouraging some kinds of prospective parents to focus on unimportant features of a possible child. This is in the sense that, once a practice is legalised, it has apparently received a 'stamp of approval'. *Prima facie* this does not appear to be a hugely attractive policy move. This is particularly so if concerns beyond harm to the interests of a future child were allowed to come into play. For instance, we could explore whether there are some broadly (though not necessarily fully) shared societal notions or values about what is important in reproduction and child-raising. People will obviously disagree about this, but I am simply thinking here of nurturing, teaching, loving, accepting and so forth. The kinds of aesthetic features of a child that might be able to be selected, such as colouring, bear no relation to these activities, feelings, aims and virtues. Whether this line of thought would give us a reason to proscribe aesthetic selection, however, is unclear. This is because the standard for restraining freedom in a liberal democracy is typically that of harm, particularly of a serious kind, to others. Having said this, it should be noted that the restrictions on the right to respect for private life embodied in Article 8 of the European Convention on

---

[62] HFEA, *The Best Possible Start to Life: A Consultation Document on Multiple Births after IVF* (April 2007).

Human Rights (ECHR), which was incorporated into English law by means of the Human Rights Act 1998, include 'morals'.[63] I return to this point later.

Before concluding whether selection for aesthetic or other trivial features should be legalised, we still need to consider a number of other issues, the first of which was whether the moral claims of the embryo can tell us anything about the permissibility of this kind of selection.

### iii   The claims of the embryo and the processes in PGD

PGD must accompany a cycle of IVF. Doctors will prescribe hormonal drugs, including injections, to a woman. She will most likely administer these herself. Her ovaries will be monitored by ultrasound scan for the production of eggs. In due course, these will be retrieved by a doctor, sometimes under general anaesthetic. The woman's partner's sperm will be mixed with the eggs and those that have fertilised and developed to an appropriate size (six to ten cells) on the third day (typically) after the egg collection can then be tested by the appropriately trained specialist in PGD. There are a number of things to notice about this process.

First, while normally one of a woman's ovaries would release one egg a month, the injections will stimulate her ovaries to produce as many eggs as possible. Women's responses to these drugs vary considerably; a cycle could yield about eight to ten eggs.[64] If all fertilise, eight to ten embryos will then exist. If the purpose of using IVF is purely to use PGD for aesthetic features, these embryos will have been created simply for the purposes of testing and selecting them for these features. So, we are not just talking of testing and discarding some embryos, but rather also of creating them for the purposes of this testing and selection in the first place. Is this morally problematic?

While some people clearly hold that the embryo has the same moral status as a born child, others do not think this. Although the gradualist approach that I endorse recognises that the embryo and fetus at each stage has potential and is developing (all going well), the status of the three-day embryo is not very great. This is not to say that the embryo has no moral status because the embryo's possibly huge potential is an important (though not morally decisive) consideration. I say 'possibly huge potential', however, because not all embryos have the same potential for life, such as those that carry a chromosomal abnormality

---

[63] Art 8(1) reads: 'Everyone has the right to respect for his private and family life, his home and his correspondence'. If an applicant can show an interference with this right, then it falls to the state in question to try to justify this under Art 8(2): 'There shall be no interference by a public authority with this right except such as is in accordance with the law and is necessary in a democratic society in the interests of national security, public safety or the economic well-being of the country, for the prevention of crime and disorder, for the *protection of morals*, or for the protection of the rights and freedoms of others' (my emphasis).

[64] An example with 12 eggs is given by the HGC, above n 20, text box following para 4.5.

incompatible with life. Whilst others may have a normal complement of chromosomes, they may still fail to implant in a woman's uterus if given the chance. Sometimes these differences in the potential of embryos will be apparent to the relevant IVF or PGD professionals, either because there are certain observational criteria on which they can judge the potential of embryos (such as how well the cells in the embryo are multiplying) or because certain tests have revealed fatal chromosomal anomalies or genetic conditions of some kind. In other cases, only time will tell, so that the potential of any one embryo can only be proved by what happens to it on transfer to a woman's uterus (at which point, other factors may also come into play). On the basis of a gradualist approach and also in the light of these facts about the varying potential of embryos, should we allow testing for aesthetic features (assuming this became possible)?

Moving to some degree from ethics to public policy, would aesthetic selection be compatible with the Warnock Report's recommendation, and the House of Commons Science and Technology Committee's apparent recent endorsement, of 'respect' for the embryo? An important question here is what this 'respect' should entail. People will think differently about this. A starting point could be that it entails not treating or taking the embryo 'lightly', but what would this mean? It is possible to imagine things that some people would think were disrespectful: some years ago, for instance, there was a case about the freeze-drying of fetuses for use as earrings, but we can also imagine this scenario in relation to embryos.[65] Personally I think this kind of use would be, for want of a better word, disrespectful of the embryo. This may seem surprising since I think the embryo has a lower moral status than the developing fetus. However, because of the enormous potential of the embryo, particularly one with good live-birth potential, it seems right that some purposes that may entail its destruction are more morally acceptable than others. Where embryos are created through IVF and PGD is conducted to avoid the birth of a child with a serious genetic condition, I have suggested that there are legitimate moral purposes at stake (be they person- or non-person-affecting or both). In the United Kingdom, we also license the use of discarded IVF embryos for purposes connected with the treatment of infertility and related issues and also for the treatment of disease.[66] For my part, I would agree with such use. Returning to the hypothetical case of the use of freeze-dried embryos as earrings, of course the embryos would most likely already have perished and so it is doubtful that this use would have entailed their destruction. But we can imagine a scenario in which this would have been the case. Either way, though particularly in the latter scenario, personally I think it would be disrespectful to create jewellery out of a pair of embryos.

[65] *R v Gibson and Sylveire* [1991] 1 All ER 439 concerned earrings made from freeze-dried fetuses. Both the artist and the owner of the gallery in which the earrings were displayed were convicted of outraging public decency.

[66] HFE Act 1990, Sch 2, para 3; Human Fertilisation and Embryology (Research Purposes) Regulations 2001 (SI 2001 No 188).

It also seems likely that at least some people would think that genetic testing for aesthetic features does not 'respect' the embryo. I think that, to the extent that excess embryos have to be created for the purpose of this selection, there is some force in this. Moreover, I think that the notion of 'respect' can be understood, not just as a notion of public policy, but also as capturing or alluding to an important part of what those who do not attribute full moral status to the embryo may nevertheless feel and think about it. In what follows, I shall try to imagine some possible scenarios in which aesthetic selection may take place.

Before this, I note that the HGC helpfully describes a possible PGD cycle (where the purpose is to avoid a serious genetic condition) and it is worth working through this in order to appreciate the very real constraints in any attempt to secure a live birth following IVF and PGD. In the example they give, ovarian stimulation results in twelve eggs, which produce ten embryos following IVF, of which eight prove suitable for biopsy.[67] Of these, seven are successfully diagnosed, of which two are normal (in relation to the condition that is the subject of testing). Of these two, one is rated as 'good' and suitable for implantation, the other 'poor'. Accordingly one embryo is transferred and the pregnancy rate per cycle is fifteen to twenty per cent (and the risk of a misdiagnosis is less than one per cent). We can extrapolate from this example to that of attempts to select for aesthetic features.

Consider first the 'pure' case of PGD solely for aesthetic reasons. On the one hand, it could be that, once tested, no embryos have the desired feature or features, and so it could be — if selection of a particular aesthetic feature (or features) were so apparently important — that none were selected for transfer. On the other hand, this is highly implausible: a couple who had gone through the demands and risks (such as of ovarian hyper-stimulation syndrome)[68] of IVF, which of course physically mainly implicates the woman, would be very unlikely to feel emotionally or morally comfortable about discarding these embryos, that is, about not giving them the chance of continued life. Rather, at this point it is more likely that one or more would be selected for possible implantation. This underlies the point that, most likely, anyone who had committed to the demands of IVF would ultimately strongly want a child, and not just one with, say, green eyes. Given the choice between no chance of a child (or a further and unpredictable cycle of IVF) and a child without the chosen aesthetic features, it is very likely that these prospective parents would choose to have the more certain

[67] HGC, above n 20, text box following para 4.5.
[68] For an account of these risks see, eg, HFEA, *Guide to Infertility* (2006/7) (available at <http://www.hfea.gov.uk/en/1131.html> accessed 14 October 2007) 24, in which the condition is described as '[a] potentially dangerous over-reaction to fertility drugs used to stimulate egg production. Cysts develop on your ovaries and fluid collects in your stomach. In severe cases (about 1–2 per cent) your ovaries become vary swollen and fluid may fill the stomach and chest cavities. A fall in the concentration of red blood cells can lead to blood clots and blood flow to the kidneys may also be reduced'.

chance now (that is, because embryos had been successfully created in the current cycle) of a child. Here we see again the way in which some autonomous wishes are more meaningful and so stronger than others, as others have similarly recognised.[69] So in this scenario, if the parents were to choose to transfer one or more embryos anyway, embryos created for the purpose of testing for purely aesthetic features would in fact have been given the chance of life as a person. (I do not mean to imply here that existence itself can be understood as a benefit, as first discussed in Chapter 1; I note merely that not all the embryos would be wasted.) By contrast, if all the embryos were indeed discarded, which I have suggested is highly implausible, then it is hard not to think that this would in some sense be 'disrespectful' of them. Further, it should be noted that PGD makes it very unlikely that embryos will successfully freeze: this means that, if the couple were unsuccessful in their first attempt at a live-born child, or wanted in due course to have another child from the same group of original embryos, most likely this would not be possible because all the embryos that were not transferred would have perished.

An alternative and arguably more likely scenario would be one in which a couple already needed IVF to achieve the birth of a child. *Prima facie* this appears less problematic in the sense that embryos, particularly excess ones, are already being created for what most people would probably regard as a highly legitimate purpose (the relief of fertility problems). That said, only some embryos (or perhaps none, as above) will test positively for the desired aesthetic features. Indeed, the embryo's aesthetic features will always be related to the genetic make-up of its parents. There may be a strong chance of the desired features or a weaker one; if the former, there would be less reason to test for them in the first place. Now, if testing does take place and if some embryos test positively, the question will also always arise as to whether these are the embryos with the best chance of implantation and live birth, as judged by the various criteria available to the embryologists.

Given the choice between a better chance of the live birth of a child *without* the desired features and a smaller chance of a live birth *with* them, any couple who actually really wanted a child would abandon the quest for particular insignificant aesthetic features in a child. This does not indicate whether such testing should be permissible; it merely reinforces the strength of certain reasons and choices over others. *Prima facie*, then, there does not appear to be a reason not to allow such testing, on behalf of the embryos' sake at least, given that these already have to be created for the normal purposes of IVF and assuming (which is fair) that some will in any event be transferred, regardless of their aesthetic features. The only caveat here would be the point about the likely inability of embryos that have been the subject of PGD to freeze: this distinguishes the case from another cycle

---

[69] See Buchanan *et al*, above n 5, 216.

of IVF in which no PGD takes place. That said, the chances of success with frozen embryos are somewhat lower than with fresh embryos.[70]

Another scenario could be one in which a couple already feel they need PGD for a serious genetic condition of some kind, and 'add on' testing for aesthetic features. However, here it may be that the 'add-on' testing compromises the accuracy of the testing for the serious genetic condition, since in general the more conditions that are the subject of testing, the less accurate is the testing. Even if or when this is overcome, the chance of finding good embryos (ones with promising 'live-birth' potential) that are *also* free from the serious genetic condition in question and that *also* possess the chosen aesthetic feature(s), is really very small. Recall that an average IVF cycle will yield approximately eight to ten eggs. Once again, then, a couple would be forced to think about what is most important for them and, if they have gone through the hurdles of IVF and PGD, it is very unlikely that they would contemplate discarding normal embryos with good potential for implantation but without the chosen aesthetic features. Of course, once more this has not told us that testing for aesthetic features should be impermissible; it has simply highlighted the realities of attempting to engage in such choices.

Overall, perhaps the claims of the embryo to 'respect' are most threatened where embryos are created, tested and discarded for lack of the chosen features, purely for aesthetic reasons. However, given that PGD embryos are very unlikely to freeze, there may also be thought to be an element of 'disrespect' where a couple who needs IVF adds in testing for purely aesthetic features: where they are unsuccessful in their first attempt or wanted to come back for another child they would have to start from scratch and create another set of embryos, since most likely none from the original set would have frozen.

### iv   The professionals involved in IVF and PGD

At this point, we need to bring into view the role of the many third parties involved in IVF and PGD. These include doctors, nurses, embryologists, cytogeneticists and scientists. I noted at one point in the last chapter, when I referred to (qualitative) research at one UK clinic that conducts PGD, that some staff have strong concerns about the extent to which they feel comfortable engaging in certain practices.[71] For instance, we saw that the seriousness of certain genetic conditions is a matter of regular discussion, and sometimes disagreement, at this clinic. There was also an indication, in many of the interviews and ethics discussion groups, that many members of staff would have problems moving away from the criterion of a 'serious genetic condition' because, in various ways, they felt that the purpose of their work was to enable parents to have healthy

---

[70] HFEA 'Understanding Clinic Success Rates' <http://www.hfea.gov.uk/en/820.html> accessed 14 October 2007.
[71] Ch 4, S IV (B) i.

children.[72] They do not see their role as one of providing other kinds of selection methods to parents. Sometimes this seemed to flow from their own sense of what was morally appropriate in work with embryos; at other times they were also concerned about media perceptions and portrayals of their work. Overall, however, it seemed as though many members of staff themselves have a sense of a limit to the appropriate extent of embryo testing and selection.

None of these processes is possible without the involvement of these medical and scientific staff. If they, or some of them, would not feel comfortable about creating and testing embryos for purely aesthetic features (in any of the ways discussed above), even after the arguable lack of any possible harm to future children has been discussed, they cannot be compelled to engage in these practices unless the law has permitted these and not allowed staff conscientiously to object. Is there a good case for such legalisation, with or without a conscientious objection mechanism? I shall return to this after I have touched on the interests of those with impairments in such practices.

### v  The interests of those with impairments

One concern about PGD is what, if anything, it says about people with disabilities.[73] I discussed aspects of this issue in Chapter 1. I refer again to that discussion, and here add only some comments about the possible implications for people with impairments of purely 'trivial' kinds of selection.[74]

The Outcome Document expresses a concern about the practice of PGD devaluing or discriminating against the interests of people with impairments,[75] although it does not in itself explain how PGD might in fact be discriminatory. Although support for PGD had been expressed through the consultation exercise, there were 'concerns about 'designer babies' and about the technology not being

---

[72]  eg, Scientist 21 observes: 'I would say our role was to enable somebody to have a healthy baby when, in the first instance they've got a fairly substantial risk of having an unhealthy baby. And so I guess… the dividing line then is, what you classify as healthy and unhealthy and how severe…'. Interview, Scientist 21, at 13.

[73]  On the fears that prenatal screening (and by implication PGD) might constitute discrimination against people with disabilities, see, eg, M Saxton 'Why Members of the Disability Community Oppose Prenatal Diagnosis and Selective Abortion' in E Parens and A Asch (eds), *Prenatal Testing and Disability Rights* (Washington, DC: Georgetown University Press, 2000) 147, 151, who suggests that discrimination issues affecting people with 'chronic diseases or disability' are overlooked in discussions about medical decision making (at 154). She also suggests that it is hard 'to assess the true impact of disability on the individual's life experience' due to the impact of 'oppressive social conditions' on the public's perceptions, which people with disabilities may have 'internalize[d]' (at 150).

[74]  See Ch 1, S V.

[75]  HFEA and HGC, above n 1, para 22: 'PGD guidance should support difficult parental choices rather than appearing to discriminate against individuals with certain conditions'.

used to discriminate further against disabled people now or in the future'.[76] Minutes of discussions preceding the document also note, but do not record, an analysis of this concern.[77]

We have already seen that people with disabilities may consider that testing and selection for serious genetic conditions in some way devalues or discriminates against them. I suggested in Chapter 1 that the best way to address this concern was to focus on improving the information practices in PND and PGD. Turning now to selection for relatively trivial features, might people with impairments feel offended, disrespected or harmed by PGD for trivial reasons? As we know, there is no clear moral purpose (be it person- or non-person-affecting or both) for testing and selection in such cases, either because such aspects of a possible child do not begin seriously to implicate parental interests or (from a non-person-affecting perspective) because purely aesthetic features are unlikely significantly to affect a child's welfare. Given their possible association with a quest for 'perfection' such practices may be worrying to someone with impairments, perhaps increasing the stigma felt or, more seriously, actually experienced by them. For instance, a psychologist interviewed in qualitative research on PND (not PGD) observed[78]:

> If there is a society in which one can make an individual informed choice that you don't want to have a baby with a minor abnormality, then over a period of years we will see less and less babies with abnormalities born on the whole… then the social pressure on those who are disabled will rise and rise, and the stigma that will be attached to them will be even greater.

The authors who conducted this research later observed[79]: 'Serious concerns were expressed during the groups about what the eventual impact of individual consumer choice might be for wider society, including increased stigma for the disabled…'. If such stigma resulted in actual harm, the issue would be more serious than that of unjustified offence.

Overall, in any policy move to extend the scope of PGD (or other testing), it would be important to establish what people with disabilities might think about such practices. How much weight should be given to any one set of views is another question. But the views of those who already have to deal with disadvantage and difficulties arising from impairment — who may object on the

---

[76] HGC, *Minutes of Plenary Meeting*, 2 March 2001, para 4.7.
[77] HGC, *Minutes of Genetic Testing Sub-group*, 12 January 2001, para 5.7: 'Dr Draper felt that to reflect the views expressed in the consultation responses any guidance should make clear that PGD should not be used in a way that leads to systematic discrimination'. See also HGC, *Minutes of Plenary Meeting*, 2 March 2001, para 4.7.
[78] Quoted in C Williams, P Alderson and B Farsides 'Too Many Choices? Hospital and Community Staff Reflect on the Future of Prenatal Screening' (2002) 55 *Social Science & Medicine* 743, 748.
[79] *Ibid* 750.

grounds of possible further stigmatisation — may plausibly have greater weight than where the case for a certain kind of testing is in fact strongly made out, as it is in relation to serious conditions.

### vi  The issue of legalisation

So far, the preliminary indications are that parents do not have a strong interest in testing and selecting for purely aesthetic reasons: the above discussion of the possible results of testing and the actual choices with which prospective parents may be faced has underlined the relative lack of importance of aesthetic choices compared with the goals at stake in IVF by itself, or IVF with PGD for serious genetic conditions. This lack of importance means that the prospective parents' interest in the kind of child they will have is not strongly invoked by aesthetic choices, a point made earlier in the discussion of 'central' versus 'marginal' features. One implication of this could be that there are no strong grounds to say that these parents have a moral right to such testing. If we couple this with the possible concerns of health professionals and those of people with impairments about selection for aesthetic features, again the case for granting a right, allowing such testing and thereby (at least in the absence of a conscientious objection mechanism for the relevant health professionals and scientists) compelling assistance in this matter, is not very strong. By implication, the case for legalising such testing, coupled with a conscientious objection mechanism, is somewhat stronger. However, to what extent does a case have to be made in *favour*, rather than *against*, legalisation?

Indeed, at this point it might be noted that an important value in a liberal society is the protection of freedoms to which some or many do not themselves give importance. One way of looking at the issue would be to consider whether reproductive autonomy is so important in itself, regardless of the reason for which it is exercised on any given occasion, that we should allow such testing in a liberal society or, put another way, do not have the right to ban it. Some people will think that reproductive autonomy *per se* is so important that there should not be a restriction of this kind (at least as regards PGD rather than selective abortion, given the arguably higher moral status of the fetus.) For the reasons stated at various points in the book, I do not think reproductive autonomy is always important in itself regardless of the reason, that is, for which it is exercised. Rather, it matters to people and is therefore *most* deserving of protection, when their interests in the kind of child they will have are meaningfully invoked. But this does not necessarily mean that the exercise of reproductive autonomy without good reason, if you like, is not deserving of *any* protection. John Harris has discussed the importance of protecting even unimportant freedoms[80]:

> As I argued... even idle preferences command respect and their denial requires justification. But serious moral claims require the greatest respect and the weightiest

---

[80] J Harris 'No Sex Selection Please, We're British' (2005) 31 *JME* 286, 287.

reasons must justify their denial, even where those claims are just that, 'claims' and not established moral rights. It is not the particular liberty that has to be so important, what is important is that the burden of proof is on those who would curtail liberty... I... maintain... that reproduction clearly is an important liberty by any standards and while maybe not itself... constitutive of liberal democracy it is by any reckoning of an importance which requires serious engagement if it is to be set aside.

As Harris reminds us, the onus of justification for prohibition is typically on the prohibitor. Further, the more serious the moral claim, the greater the need to justify the prohibition.[81]

Indeed, when we turn from the context of philosophical ethics to that of political philosophy and law, we see that this is indeed the case, as both Mill's famous dictum[82] and the structure of Article 8 of the ECHR show. Article 8(1) reads: 'Everyone has the right to respect for his private and family life, his home and his correspondence'. If an applicant can show an interference with this right, then it falls to the state in question to try to justify this under Article 8(2):

> There shall be no interference by a public authority with this right except such as is in accordance with the law and is necessary in a democratic society in the interests of national security, public safety or the economic well-being of the country, for the prevention of crime and disorder, for the protection of morals, or for the protection of the rights and freedoms of others.

However, and this is sometimes the catch, what comes within 'private and family life' has to be decided afresh in relation to any given issue. The closest legal decision we have concerning Article 8 relates to abortion. In Chapter 2 I noted that in *Brüggemann and Scheuten v Germany* the European Commission on Human Rights held that although the decision to abort invokes a woman's private life, some regulation of pregnancy is consistent with respect for private life, because pregnancy 'cannot be said to pertain uniquely to the sphere of private life'.[83] This meant that the regulation of abortion did not have to be justified under Article 8(2). The alternative approach was represented in the dissent of Mr Fawcett, who held that '"private life"... must in my view cover pregnancy, its commencement

---

[81] For a contrasting view, see, eg, J Botkin 'Ethical Issues and Practical Problems in Preimplantation Genetic Diagnosis' (1998) 26 *JL Med and Ethics* 17, 24, who suggests that despite the speculative nature of concerns over the parent-child relationship arising from choices made in PGD 'the fundamental importance of the parent-child relationship suggests that a burden of justification must rest with parents or professionals who would use PGD for the selection of offspring for characteristics other than significant health conditions. Parental desires to use technology in the fine-grained selection of children must be justified through claims of legitimate interest'.

[82] '[T]he sole end for which mankind are warranted, individually or collectively, in interfering with the liberty of action of any of their number, is self-protection... the only purpose for which power can be rightfully exercised over any member of a civilized community, against his will, is to prevent harm to others.' *On Liberty* (1859) in Mill, *Utilitarianism*, M Warnock (ed) (Fontana: London, 1962) 135.

[83] (1981) 3 EHRR 244, para 59.

and termination: indeed it would be hard to envisage more essentially private elements'.[84] Notwithstanding this, he held a certain degree of abortion regulation to be justified under Article 8(2). So there could be two possible approaches to the regulation of PGD with respect to Article 8: either PGD does not come within private and family life, so that the state does not have to justify limits on the practice; or PGD does fall within private and family life, so that the onus is on the state to justify any restrictions on it. The result could be the same on either reasoning, but in one case the state would have to justify any limits. What are the possible grounds for justification?

One difference between Mill's dictum and Article 8 is, as noted earlier, that 'harm' is not the only criterion for the limitation of freedom in Article 8, which also allows scope for consideration of 'morals'. The problem, of course, is 'whose morals?' Should the views of the (apparent) majority dictate what is permissible? As I shall explore in the next chapter, this at least strongly influenced the HFEA in deciding, a few years ago, that sex selection for non-medical reasons should not be legalised. (More recently, this also influenced the government in deciding not to legalise sex selection in its review of the HFE Act.) In this regard, the views of the (apparent) majority contained a mixture of concerns about what we may label as 'values' of various kinds and about harms, though of course the latter were necessarily speculative. I will explore in more detail the question of possible legalisation in the next chapter, when I focus more explicitly on Article 8 reasoning in the context of my discussion of sex selection.

For now, we might note that if genetic testing and selection for aesthetic or other relatively trivial reasons were to be allowed, we do not always have to correlate moral and legal interests and rights. For instance, although we would then legally permit such choices — for example because we do not think the case to ban them is sufficiently made out, particularly in terms of possible harms — we might also say that in such cases parents' interests in genetic selection are not really seriously morally implicated. In turn, parents would not really have a moral right — or at least a strong one — to such testing. Put another way, we could say that they do not have a strong moral justification for exercising the legal right they would have been given. However, for reasons of political philosophy and law, we would have decided to give them this legal right. I shall return to the issue of legalisation in my conclusions as well as, in a more legally oriented discussion, in the next chapter.

## E  Selecting in Favour of 'Serious' Features

The discussion so far has concentrated on negative selection against serious impairments and both negative and positive (hypothetical) selection in relation to trivial features, such as aesthetic ones. This section discusses the idea of positively selecting for what we might call 'meaningful' features.

---

[84] *Ibid* para 1.

### i  Selecting for intelligence

An example, if it were possible, would be selecting the embryo with the potential to be the most intelligent child of a given set of embryos. At the outset, the polygenic nature of traits such as intelligence should be noted. This means, as noted by the HGC, that the possibility of such kinds of selection is actually very unlikely.[85] However, as with aesthetic choices, it is useful to discuss the entirely hypothetical prospect of such tests because it helps us tease out our thoughts about different kinds of selection decision.

Consider first the prospective parents. For a start, all prospective parents will be limited in their choices of genetically related children by the strength or weakness of their own genetic material. If there will in fact be limited variation between embryos in this respect, it is unlikely to be worth parents' while to undertake IVF and PGD for this kind of selection. Still, we need briefly to consider some of the arguments for and against such a practice.

Selecting for higher intelligence may appear desirable to some or even many parents. However, it is in fact debatable whether selecting for heightened intelligence, rather than against significant intellectual impairment, seriously invokes parents' interests in reproduction: it is unlikely that their goals and desires as parents will be thwarted by the birth of a somewhat less intelligent child. If so, there is no strong case in favour of such a practice for their sakes. However, as we have already seen, since it may be important to grant freedoms that are not in fact very significant, the less than serious impact on parents' experience of child-raising is not in itself decisive.[86]

Consider now the interests of the future child. If it had not been selected it would never have existed, so in this way (assuming that we cannot meaningfully compare existence and non-existence at the start of life) there is no sense of a conferral of benefit on it by being selected for its higher intelligence. What about harm? Of course we can think of highly speculative examples in which hyper-ambitious parents attempt to select for intelligence and then raise a child with huge expectations of her. However, as noted in the discussion of selection for aesthetic features, not only is the idea that a child might be harmed by this kind of selection entirely speculative; in any event, any harm can in fact only come from her environment — here the way her parents subsequently raise her.

---

[85] HGC, above n 20, para 7.42. For further discussion of this kind of selection, see K Birch 'Beneficence, Determinism and Justice: an Engagement with the Argument for the Genetic Selection of Intelligence' (2005) 19/1 *Bioethics* 12.

[86] If competitive advantage is actually sought (vicariously through and for the child, whose own interests are considered below) because heightened intelligence is really a positional good, widespread selection of this kind may be self-defeating. For discussion of the self-defeating aspects of these choices, see Buchanan *et al*, above n 5, 186. However, it is not clear that heightened intelligence is merely a positional good, just as height may not be: I am grateful to Roger Crisp here.

As for the embryo, if it were possible, selecting for intelligence would mean that one or more embryos are selected over others. If we again take the view that the acquisition of interests hinges on sentience, such that the embryo does not have interests until as a fetus it acquires sentience, it does not matter to the embryo whether or not it is selected. However, as explored earlier, excess embryos that are very unlikely to freeze will typically be created and will therefore perish. If we are thinking about the embryo's potential and the idea of 'respect' for the embryo, as before this may be problematic to some degree either where IVF is undertaken just to attempt to select a feature such as intelligence or, though to a lesser extent, where IVF is needed but PGD is not. That said, reflecting on embryo discard, people might think it more 'worthwhile' to select for intelligence than for green or blue eyes. Put another way, we might say there is a somewhat stronger moral case to do so, at least from a non-person-affecting perspective and assuming (a large assumption that would require investigation) that heightened intelligence has the potential to increase welfare and flourishing.

Once again, people working in IVF and PGD will clearly have views about this kind of selection. Further, selecting for intelligence might be offensive to some people with impairments and, if such practices were to risk harm to them, this could be a reason in favour of prohibition. In both cases I refer again to earlier discussion.

What about society's interests in this kind of selection? Might it be a benefit or a good in general that a child of higher intelligence exists? This would be to consider the issue from a non-person-affecting perspective. If more intelligent (different) children were chosen, there would be a class of brighter children.[87] In other words, since it does not matter strongly (or strongly enough) to the parents, or at all to the children, could it be argued that the only real benefit may be to society — in a manner akin to society's interest in well-educated citizens?[88] In this light, the question would be whether as a society and for society's benefit we think it appropriate to allow selection for heightened intelligence, rather than for the avoidance of mental impairment.

It is doubtful that society would really have an interest in facilitating this although, for reasons related to liberal democratic values, it may not have a sufficient interest in disallowing it.

---

[87] I first discussed non-person-affecting principles in Ch 1, S IV(C). For the contrasting view that only person-affecting principles count, see D Heyd, *Genethics: Moral Issues in the Creation of People* (Berkeley: University of California Press, 1992) 170–77.

[88] I do not see how else the idea of having a duty beneficently to select for such a feature might be understood. For discussion of a duty to select the embryo with the most advantageous features and characteristics, see J Savulescu 'Procreative Beneficence: Why We Should Select the Best Children' (2001) 15(5/6) *Bioethics* 413, 418. Savulescu employs a non-person-affecting analysis.

Focusing on the issue of facilitation, IVF and PGD are expensive and widespread demand for such selection would be an unnecessary drain on public healthcare resources.[89]

Turning to private use, this could raise the issue of fairness, an issue that might also be thought to be raised by some forms of aesthetic selection (even though here we are not talking about advantages to a given child but rather to different possible children).[90] Wealthy parents can already advantage their children in various ways, for instance through private education[91]; in this sense inequity is already present in the environmental factors shaping a child's future. However, with the regulation of PGD in the United Kingdom we have the opportunity, if we wish, to make a public statement about fairness that is not available in many other contexts.[92] We would have to weigh such notions about fairness with notions about the value of permitting the exercise of both important and unimportant freedoms. In this process, we might note that, since for genetic reasons intelligent parents may tend to have children with at least the potential for intelligence (though environmental factors will probably play a large role in determining the ultimate intelligence of the child), it is not clear that any

---

[89] On the idea that the implications for resources may give some right to society, see D Heyd 'Prenatal Diagnosis: Whose Right?' (1995) 21 *JME* 292, 295. Heyd adopts a person-affecting approach and argues that 'we should... negotiate carefully between the rights of the parents and those of society'. For thoughts on funding, PGD and the NHS, see Department of Health 'Preimplantation Genetic Diagnosis (PGD) — Guiding Principles for Commissioners of NHS Services' (September 2002) at <http://www.dh.gov.uk/assetRoot/04/11/89/35/04118935.pdf> accessed 14 October 2007.

[90] As noted by, eg, L Silver 'How Reprogenetics will Transform the American Family' (1999) 27 *Hofstra L Rev* 649, 657.

[91] Silver, writing about the US context, believes with some apprehension that power in relation to these issues lies in the 'marketplace' (*ibid* at 658).

[92] Buchanan *et al*, above n 5, 202, suggest that there is 'no reason to object in general to using genetic influences any more than environmental ones in the pursuit of... advantages' but that 'some efforts to pursue advantage (whether genetic or environmentally influenced) may reasonably be restricted' either because they 'are self-defeating and pose threats to public goods' or because they raise 'objections of fairness' (or in cases of genetic manipulation, which is not under consideration here, because of inherent risks). On the question of expanding the scope of genetic testing, see also J Glover, *Choosing Children: Genes, Disability and Design* (Oxford: OUP, 2006) 103: 'perhaps the medical boundary is not the right one to defend. But, if we do cross it, we may want to set limits to the free market. Here, this means limits to the programme of liberal eugenics. These limits may be to prevent social inequalities becoming even more deeply rooted genetic inequalities, and to escape falling into the competitive trap set by the pursuit of genetic positional goods. They may sometimes be based on protecting the right of our children to an open future. And, perhaps most fundamentally of all, the limits may be needed to protect parts of human nature needed for the containment of our dark side or else in a more positive way for the good life, parts of our nature that it would be tragic to lose... But we should also be aware that the boundaries we lay down and the values behind them are unlikely to be permanent.'

'advantage' would really be bestowed by genetic selection for heightened intelligence. For this reason, fairness may not in fact be seriously in issue.

### ii  Selecting for better health

In the absence of a specific genetic indication to test for a given condition (including lower-penetrance or late-onset conditions, such as those discussed in the previous chapter), given the genetic and environmental complexity of health it seems unlikely that PGD will generally become a powerful selection tool for 'enhanced' health. The HGC observes[93]:

> It is... clinically undesirable to do more [tests] as most markers for a predisposition to certain illnesses are insufficiently predictive to be of any practical use and could, potentially, produce anxiety where none is warranted.

Nonetheless, we can again think about some of the moral issues in relation to such testing.

For instance, we could work through the prospective parents' interests (not very strong, at least compared with the avoidance of a child with actual health problems or impairments), the child's interests (not particularly strong, though we could look at the matter differently by thinking about the well-being of different possible children from a non-person-affecting perspective), the 'claims to respect of the embryo' (arguably not necessarily threatened given the value of health, including enhanced health), the views of those who work in this area (some third parties may be more favourable towards selection for 'enhanced' health) and of people with impairments (perhaps potentially threatened, but not in any necessary, that is, conceptual way). Provisionally, there may well be a stronger *prima facie* moral case for this kind of selection. The case is supported by John Harris[94]:

> Suppose some embryos had a genetic condition which conferred complete immunity to many major diseases — HIV/AIDS, cancer and heart disease for example, coupled with increased longevity. We would, it seems to me, have moral reasons to prefer to implant such embryos, given the opportunity of choice.

I think Harris is right that, from what must be a non-person-affecting perspective, we would have reason to choose to implant the embryos that would as people (so far as we can tell at the point of genetic selection) have enhanced health, 'given the opportunity of choice'. However, as I imagine Harris would recognise, reflecting on this 'opportunity' requires that we think about public resources and so about society's moral priorities. In this regard, Buchanan *et al* suggest, rightly I

---

[93] HGC, above n 20, para 4.30.
[94] J Harris 'Is There a Coherent Social Conception of Disability?' (2000) 26 *JME* 95, 100. See also L Bortolotti and J Harris 'Disability, Enhancement and the Harm-Benefit Continuum', in JR Spencer and A du Bois-Pedain (eds), *Freedom and Responsibility in Reproductive Choice* (Oxford: Hart Publishing, 2006) 31.

think, that although the so-called 'treatment/enhancement' distinction does not map onto a distinction between what is morally required and what is morally permissible, 'the boundary between treatment and enhancement offers a plausible, publicly usable boundary for saying what society's primary obligations are in the delivery of health care'.[95] (I say a bit more about this distinction below.) The HGC has also emphasised the question of funding priorities.[96]

As for private use, we could revisit the concern about fairness. This concern may be more real, compared with the genetic selection for intelligence by intelligent parents, but then here perhaps concerns about fairness could be outweighed, not only by the importance of liberal freedoms, but also by the thought that, from a non-person-affecting perspective, it is good if people who are less likely to succumb to certain diseases will be born. As Harris notes, this thought 'would not imply that normal embryos had lives that were not worth living or were of poor or problematic quality'.[97] Nor, of course, would it imply this of people with impairments or other diseases or disorders.

A further point to note here concerns the implications of the above discussion for the so-called 'treatment/enhancement' distinction. As I noted earlier in this chapter, rather than being a clear-cut distinction, the terms are best understood as forming part of a continuum. As before, one way to bring out this point is to observe that it is the same non-person-affecting perspective that gives us reason to choose a world inhabited by people with better health prospects that also gives us reason to avoid disability in future people. Stephen Wilkinson has noted (in connection with a discussion of Parfit's work) that, *at least on its own,* a non-person-affecting perspective cannot distinguish between not selecting for

---

[95] Buchanan *et al*, above n 5, 202. For further discussion of Buchanan *et al's* work relating to this distinction, see P Wenz 'Engineering Genetic Injustice' (2005) 19/1 *Bioethics* 1.

[96] HGC, above n 20, para 4.8: 'On average, a PGD cycle in the UK currently costs between £4,500 and £6,000 and whether NHS patients have access to this treatment depends on funding decisions by their primary care organisations. About half obtain NHS funding; the rest must pay for their own treatment. In contrast, NHS funding for more conventional prenatal diagnosis and termination of pregnancy is generally available. PGD was considered in some detail by the Public Health Genetics Unit in their response to our consultation. They concluded that as PGD is a complex and expensive procedure with a limited success rate that will only benefit a small number of people, it is not appropriate at this time to devote limited health care resources to making it more widely available and that regulated use with close monitoring should continue.'

[97] Harris, above n 94, 100.

'better than normal' features on the one hand and selecting for disability on the other.[98] The HGC has made a related point, observing[99]:

> [I]t may be difficult to determine where the line between preventing harm, and enhancement, is to be drawn. Indeed, it could be argued that there is no line, and that the two are one and the same thing, with the common objective of ensuring that a child is born with as few disadvantages as possible.

However, what we can do in order to make some important distinctions is to show the moral relevance of other factors. For instance, in various ways in different chapters I have identified the moral status of the embryo or fetus as a factor of particular relevance to discussions about the moral permissibility of certain testing and selection decisions. Further, with reference to the possible suggestion that non-person-affecting principles imply that prospective parents might be morally required to maximise welfare in selection choices, I have also noted the multiple costs to prospective parents of engaging in IVF and PGD (say, to select an embryo with enhanced features), or the various costs of terminating an established pregnancy (say, where the future child, despite having an impairment, would have a life worth living).[100]

### iii  Selecting for specific aptitudes or abilities

A further type of selection could be for specific aptitudes or abilities, such as in music, though again this is purely hypothetical. John Robertson has discussed this kind of choice, comparing it with the case of aesthetic selection. Although generally renowned for a strongly libertarian approach, in fact he observes that creating embryos so that the hair or eye colour of a possible child can be chosen may not be supportable 'by a reasonable explanation of the need'.[101] Here he is

---

[98] S Wilkinson 'Selecting for Disability and the Welfare of the Child', in above n 56. Wilkinson discusses non-person-affecting principles in the context of Derek Parfit's 'Same Number Quality Claim': 'the Same Number Quality Claim cannot on its own justify banning selecting for disability, because this would entail (absurdly, or at least unpalatably) an "in principle" commitment to forcing parents to have the "best possible" child in all cases'. For the purposes of my discussion, I ignore the further and as yet unresolved implications of the Same Number Quality Claim, which are pointed out by Wilkinson: 'This in turn seems to rely on the Impersonal Total Principle which… entails the Repugnant Conclusion'. Parfit expresses this conclusion as follows: 'For any possible population of at least ten billion people, all with a very high quality of life, there must be some much larger imaginable population whose existence, if other things are equal, would be better even though its members have lives that are barely worth living'. Parfit, above n 44, 388. Generally, philosophical debate has not yet found a way to avoid this conclusion.

[99] HGC, above n 20, para 1.25. This is in fact in the context of a discussion about manipulating the genetic make-up of a given embryo, but the point would seem to apply also in the non-person-affecting sense.

[100] I discuss and reject the idea of a duty to maximise in R Scott 'Why Parents Have No Duty to Select "the Best" Children' (*Clinical Ethics*, forthcoming 2007).

[101] J Robertson 'Extending Preimplantation Genetic Diagnosis: Medical and Non-medical Uses' (2003) 29 *JME* 213, 215. It is not clear how this view rests with his

weighing parental interests against the claims of the embryo. The implication may be that an individual's view of the importance of doing so should not be decisive. He compares such a scenario with one in which parents have a 'strong enough preference to seek PGD for [a given] purpose… and that preference rationally relates to understandable reproductive goals',[102] in which case they have shown its importance. Robertson's example in the latter case is of highly musical parents for whom, unlike most of us perhaps, perfect pitch is very important. This could be seen as different from the aesthetics of colouring in that it relates, on the one hand, to the parents' conception of valuable activities in life and, on the other, to the cultivation of worthwhile abilities in a child. We could see the example, at least potentially, as combining in a serious way parental and offspring interests. For these parents, it could at least be argued that the child's musical ability may, reasonably, be seen as a central feature, one that could potentially be deserving of greater protection than the desire to select hair or eye colour.

To choose the embryo for its perfect musical pitch (if ever possible) would itself be to choose the potentially musically-gifted child. If not chosen for this reason, that child would not exist. So it would be hard for the child to claim that, if selected for this reason, its interests in autonomy and flourishing had been harmed. This is the 'non-identity' problem again. As before however, in the context of PGD we could instead focus on a child's interest in not being harmed by her parents' expectations consequent on their PGD decisions. In essence, the 'musically-selected' child needs to be able to reject music if she wishes. This is consistent with a concern for the child's autonomy and flourishing. That said, once again it is entirely speculative to imagine that such expectations could be so harmful as to have made the original selection decision by PGD impermissible. After all, the choice here is between existence or non-existence for this child: if she had not had great musical potential, she would not have been chosen and so would not have existed.

At the same time, since earlier I noted that to allow aesthetic choices could, at least in some cases, be seen as encouraging shallow parents to focus on trivial concerns, we could also think that allowing parents to select for features of specific importance and interest to them could be seen as actually promoting particular kinds of parental expectations, to the possible (though not necessarily very great) detriment of a child. That said, the possession of musical ability is clearly a tremendous gift and so, generally speaking, the development and flourishing of that ability could be a significant good in a child's life. Here then, it is more likely to be the case that allowing such choices could be seen as encouraging something of potentially great value and satisfaction in a future person's life. Ultimately, of course, the real test for these parents will be to accept their child's rejection of music, if that is what the child decides.

statement, a little earlier in the passage, that '[u]ltimately, the judgment of triviality or importance of the choice within a broad spectrum rests with the couple'.
[102] *Ibid.*

As for the other issues that we might consider, first, reflecting on the claims of the embryo to 'respect', embryo creation and discard for musical ability is arguably more justifiable than for aesthetic features, though not strongly justifiable where otherwise neither IVF nor PGD would be undertaken. As before, people working in IVF and PGD will clearly have views about this kind of selection. It is not obvious what people with impairments or diseases would think about this kind of selection; once again, their views would be relevant. Overall, it may be hard to make the case for prohibition although, when we think about the creation of excess embryos, IVF and PGD solely for this purpose could be thought somewhat problematic. In this way, we might say that the *prima facie* case for selection for specific aptitudes or abilities is less strong than for health, and so perhaps more easily overridden, for instance, by the claims to respect of the embryo.

Finally, the hypothetical nature of all the possible choices discussed apart from selection against serious genetic conditions cannot be stressed enough. There are two reasons why such choices are likely to remain in the domain of fiction. First, as the HGC has recently stressed[103]:

> The kind of physical and behavioural characteristic that some people might want to select — such as beauty, intelligence or personality — will involve a large number of genes with complex and unpredictable interactions with each other and with the environment.

The HGC also observes that[104]:

> For practical reasons, the number of conditions for which PGD can be offered is limited, and few tests can be done on the DNA extracted from a single cell taken from an embryo. Only one test, or occasionally two, is normally performed.

Second, recall the limitations on the number of embryos and their varying potential for implantation and live-birth. I discussed this earlier in the chapter when I highlighted the very real pressures and actual choices facing a couple trying to engage in any kind of embryo selection where they actually very much wanted a child. As the HGC addresses this aspect[105]:

---

[103] HGC, above n 20, para 7.42.
[104] *Ibid* para 4.30. Note also the development of preimplantation genetic haplotyping (PGH), discussed in P Renwick 'Proof of Principle and First Cases using Preimplantation Genetic Haplotyping — a Paradigm Shift for Embryo Diagnosis' (2006) 13/1 *Reproductive Biomedicine Online* 758, 748: 'PGH represents a paradigm shift in embryo diagnosis, as one panel of markers can be used for all carriers of the same monogenic disease, bypassing the need for development of mutation-specific tests, and widening the scope and availability of preimplantation genetic testing'. However, limits in the number of available embryos will always mean that not many tests can be performed at the same time; otherwise there may be no embryos suitable for transfer.
[105] HGC, above n 20, para 7.42.

Even if we were able to understand and predict these complex relationships, the limited number of embryos available in PGD would make selection for one with a specific combination of gene variants virtually impossible. The hope of making a designer baby is fanciful.

## IV CONCLUSIONS

Serious reasons for testing and selecting embryos are currently required in the United Kingdom. The current criteria are that there must be a 'significant risk of a serious genetic condition in the embryo'. Reflecting on the conditions for which testing presently occurs, it appears that these criteria will be satisfied either where there is a significant risk that a possible child would be destined by its impairments to have no prospect of a reasonable quality of life or where this is not so, but there is a significant risk that parental interests in reproduction could be seriously implicated, for instance in the possible wish to avoid the birth of a less, but nevertheless seriously, impaired child. As technology improves (and there will always be limits here) we could consider moving away from the 'precautionary principle' and licensing more forms of testing. Whether the current criteria should be modified will depend on the degree to which other reasons for selection between embryos are thought problematic. Early on in this chapter I noted that Schedule 2, paragraph 1(3) of the HFE Act provides that '[a] licence under this paragraph cannot authorise any activity unless it appears to the authority to be necessary or desirable for the purpose of providing treatment services'. This means that the question we have been considering in this chapter is whether the HFEA could or should consider it either 'necessary' or 'desirable' to extend the scope of PGD and license other forms of testing. It seems unlikely that it could be 'necessary' to do so, and so the question is rather whether it would be 'desirable'. Alternatively, although this looks improbable given the terms of the Human Tissue and Embryos (Draft) Bill, the government could decide explicitly to make other forms of selection legal by means of revisions to the HFE Act itself.[106]

Turning first to selection for relatively trivial, such as aesthetic, features, we have seen that it is implausible that selection against or for relatively insignificant features could seriously implicate parental interests in reproduction or count as serious reasons for exercising reproductive autonomy. Put another way, clearly parents do not *need* testing for such features in the way that we may reasonably understand at least some prospective parents to need the option of testing for serious impairments in a possible child. For this reason, there would be no question of devoting NHS resources to testing for such features. However, this does not mean that such choices are therefore morally impermissible and should never be legalised.

---

[106] See the proposed criteria of particular relevance, above n 18 and as stated in detail in Ch 4, n 2.

With regard to possible concerns for the embryo, some may not think such choices problematic or not sufficiently so,[107] whilst others may be strongly troubled. My view is that the trivial choice, though unnecessary, would not in itself be problematic where PGD is already being conducted for serious concerns. In this case, a couple is seeking to have a child without a serious genetic impairment and needs IVF with PGD to do so. This means that excess embryos will already be created (assuming a reasonable number of eggs and that these or many of these are all fertilised); further, the couple will also choose to transfer one or more embryos (assuming the existence of one or more that are not affected by the serious genetic condition). Alternatively, where a couple needs IVF for fertility reasons and PGD is conducted solely for trivial selection, although the couple is likely to choose one or more embryos for transfer (whatever their apparent features), since PGD will compromise the ability of any spare embryos to freeze, the scenario has the potential to be morally problematic from the point of view of the embryo if, for instance, a couple is not successful in their first attempt at a live-born child or if they wish to have a second child and therefore need to create a fresh collection of embryos when otherwise they could have transferred previously frozen ones. The other scenario I discussed above was one in which a couple would wish to engage in IVF and PGD *solely* for the purposes of aesthetic selection. In this case, excess embryos will be created for no other reason than selection for aesthetic features. Accordingly, personally, I would be the least comfortable with this scenario. This is because, although I think the embryo has a lower moral status than the fetus, generally speaking (and putting to one side the differences between embryos) the embryo's huge potential is morally relevant (though not morally decisive, as it would be for someone who thinks we should ascribe full moral status to the embryo on the basis of this potential). The situation is mitigated or 'rescued' somewhat by the fact that, as I have discussed, a couple would be most likely to choose to transfer one or more embryos, despite the absence of the desired aesthetic or other trivial feature. But of course we are assuming here that they did not need IVF to give birth to a child and so excess embryos did not have to be created. In this scenario, we might then question whether, either in an ethical or a public policy sense, the embryo is 'respected'.

Turning from the embryo to the future child, what could be problematic in at least some cases is simply the approach to child-raising of parents who wish to make such choices — such as a shallow conception of parenting or overbearing parental expectations — rather than any genetic selection *per se*. That is, it is implausible that genetic selection for aesthetic features in itself could lead to real harm to a child. In the absence of serious harm (or a risk of such harm) to a child, which is highly unlikely in this kind of case, a concern for the future child cannot be decisive against such selection.

---

[107] See, eg, Robertson, above n 35 (1996) 451–2.

Turning to the other issues, I suggested that if at least some health professionals and scientists would not be prepared to engage in such choices and, if such choices were to be legally permitted, there would be a good case for allowing conscientious objection to them. The trivial choice may also be problematic if people with impairments are strongly and not unreasonably offended by it and policy-makers should take account of this.

As a society, some might wonder if we would wish to be seen to be encouraging relatively trivial choices by allowing PGD in the private sector for them. Since concerns about harm seem far-fetched we may in fact have to focus all the more carefully on the justification for prohibition, although this would depend on whether the right to private and family life under Article 8 of the ECHR is interpreted to include choices in PGD. I examine the operation of Article 8 in more detail in the next chapter. For present purposes, and assuming for the moment that choices in PGD were found to be protected by the first part of Article 8 (perhaps unlikely), I think the strongest reason not to allow such selection may inhere in the legitimacy of an ethical and public policy concern with the embryo, given the reasonable disagreement that surrounds the question of the value of the embryo. This is clearly a matter for debate. I suggested above that where a couple engaged in IVF and PGD solely for aesthetic selection, we might well question whether the embryo is valued and, albeit to a lesser degree, also where such testing was added in with IVF for fertility reasons. At the same time, although the latter scenario may be less problematic, 'policing' when a couple needs IVF in the first place (so that excess embryos would already have to be created) would be likely to be difficult. Generally, if concern for the embryo is sufficiently strong, this may be a reason to prohibit aesthetic or other trivial selection including, for simplicity perhaps, where PGD is already taking place for serious genetic conditions. What would be unusual about this is that it would not be a traditional concern with harm (since arguably embryos do not have interests until they acquire them as fetuses with sentience). However, as noted earlier, the justifications for proscribing the Article 8 right to respect for private and family life include a concern with what are rather aridly described as 'morals'. In this regard, a legitimate moral concern for the importance of 'respecting' the embryo could perhaps justify any prohibition of aesthetic or other relatively trivial selection. Conceivably, another ethical concern would be to emphasise the more important aspects of reproduction and child-rearing — loving, caring, teaching and so forth — but this rapidly becomes quite amorphous and potentially that much more contentious.

If I were pressed as to whether I think we should legalise selection for relatively trivial reasons, I would be torn between the arguably attractive ethical and public policy move of making a statement about not overtly disregarding the point that the embryo has some moral value, coupled with emphasising those aspects that seem more important in reproduction and child-rearing on the one hand, and the importance of not forbidding practices that are not clearly harmful and that some people might wish to engage in on the other. Ultimately, I may consider that we would have good reason not to legalise the trivial choice, in the light of the reasonable disagreement about the value of the embryo on the one hand and the relative unimportance of selection for trivial features on the other, but I would be open to argument on the point.

With regard to the people who might wish to select in these ways, earlier in the chapter I tried to draw attention to the realities of engaging in IVF and PGD and the choices (and particularly lack thereof) with which women and couples are very likely to be faced. In this process, we saw that ultimately they would almost always have to focus on their real goal — achieving the live birth of a child. And it is fair to assume that this is indeed their real goal, given the physical and emotional demands and physical risks of IVF itself. All of this means, I think, that if we were to decline to legalise such choices (if ever they became technically possible) on the grounds, say, of concern for the embryo, we would not in fact be denying something that some people really found important but others did not. Rather, it seems fair to say that the people who had wished to have these choices would not ultimately see aesthetic features as important, given the other issues at stake — such as avoiding a seriously impaired child, or simply achieving the live birth of a child, or the way some may feel about preventing the possible birth of a live child by failing to select *any* of the deliberately created embryos. (This is not to suggest that no justification is required to proscribe relatively unimportant freedoms.)

Further, given the realities of IVF and PGD, it is also likely that, despite good counselling, if we were to permit aesthetic selection we would be raising false expectations about what is entailed with possibly difficult, particularly emotional, consequences. Already in relation to PGD for serious genetic conditions there is a large drop-out rate from the point of initial referral — and this is in relation to serious conditions.[108] The emotional consequences of IVF and PGD are especially unpredictable. For instance, a couple who had, understandably perhaps, thought relatively 'lightly' of embryos might nevertheless find themselves being powerfully affected by the existence of their own. When we combine these considerations with the other reasons that tended to count against a strong case for permitting aesthetic choices, I think it might be thought reasonable not to permit them, though perhaps somewhat paternalistic. As I have indicated, however, the dilemma appears quite finely balanced and, in particular, there are no convincing arguments of harm to children from such practices in themselves. By contrast, I have indicated that if harm to people with impairments were a serious concern, this could be a good reason counting against the legalisation of such choices.

As for the purely hypothetical notion of positive selection for serious features, such as intelligence or 'enhanced' health, we saw earlier that there is no strong case for such selection from the parents' or the child's point of view (in the sense that the child is not benefited by being selected for these features) and that the

---

[108] This emerged from discussions with staff at the clinic discussed in Ch 4.

only possible benefit could be to society as a whole, in the sense that it would consist of different, more intelligent and/or healthier people. But I also doubted that this was a very serious societal interest, at least in the sense that there would be no reason to support public provision for such selection. Selection in the private sector may raise issues of fairness, although there was also reason to doubt this: here I suggested that we would have to weigh up such concerns, where they exist, against the importance of permitting certain choices. If this proves finely balanced, once again it may be appropriate to consider the worries about creating false expectations in prospective parents, and also about the possible emotional strains and consequences of IVF and PGD: while it may not be too difficult to imagine the physical experience and burdens of IVF, it may sometimes be harder for women or couples to predict their emotional reactions. We could also think about the claims of the embryo to respect (though these do not appear threatened by selection for serious positive features), the views of relevant professionals, and of people with impairments. Ultimately, however, I stressed the likely continuing hypothetical nature of such choices due to the complexity of the genetic components of an attribute such as intelligence and the limits in the number of available embryos, particularly ones with good potential for implantation and live birth.

As noted in earlier discussion, an important point that could plausibly affect *any* policy decision on the future of PGD is that there is some uncertainty about the long-term effects on a child of the removal of a cell at the preimplantation stage. Importantly, if really serious problems were found with born children who had undergone PGD, in fact we would have to reassess whether it was justifiable to test for serious conditions: where a condition such as Tay-Sachs is at stake, the answer is likely to be affirmative; by contrast, since it is generally not against the interests of a child with Down's syndrome to be born, we would have to weigh up the harm to the future child from such testing against the parents' possible wish to be able to choose whether to have such a child. If no long-term negative effects are found, this concern will fall away. For now, if PGD for a serious condition is already taking place, then any additional testing of that already-removed cell cannot add to the possible harm to the future child.[109] recent US study concluded that there is currently no evidence, at least at birth, of harm to the child who will be born; however, the study only considered a small number of such births.[110] Long-term follow-up studies are required. Whether we should continue to be cautious in the light of fairly remote risks is another issue that could be considered.

---

[109] Of course, this was central to the HFEA's prior policy of allowing HLA tissue-typing only if the embryo is itself at risk of a serious genetic disorder, as in the *Quintavalle* case, above n 13.

[110] Y Verlinsky, J Cohen, S Munne, L Gianaroli, JL Simpson, AP Ferraretti and A Kuliev 'Over a Decade of Experience with Preimplantation Genetic Diagnosis: A Multicenter Report' (2004) 82/2 *Fertility and Sterility* 292.

Although I have offered some arguments either way and indicated my views about these, the most recent indications are that, even if technically possible, it will not become legal to test for aesthetic features or features such as intelligence, as discussion in the Department of Health's White Paper on the future shape of the HFE Act demonstrates[111]:

> The Government will propose that the law is changed to include explicit criteria for the testing of embryos. In broad terms, legitimate purposes will be: to allow screening-out of genetic or chromosomal abnormalities which may lead to serious medical conditions or disabilities, or miscarriage; to enable the identification of a tissue match for a sibling suffering from a life-threatening illness, where umbilical cord blood is to be used in treatment of the sibling. Deliberately screening-in a disease or disorder will be prohibited.

I discuss this last type of selection in the next chapter. The government envisages that the HFEA will continue to license PGD, in accordance with the relevant criteria.[112]

Finally, I want now to leave aside notions of extending the current criteria to selection for less than serious features or conditions or in favour of positively viewed serious features, and to focus on the current broad alignment of the criteria for PGD and selective abortion.

Arguably, if PGD is safe for the future child, it should be sufficient moral justification that the object of testing is a serious impairment. Morally speaking, it is unnecessary also to require a 'significant risk', at least to the extent that this includes a quantitative component. In the case of abortion, the requirement of a 'substantial risk' forms part of the moral justification for aborting the fetus, which might well be considerably advanced in development. Since it is widely accepted that the fetus has greater moral status, this requirement has a legitimate purpose. In PGD, since the embryo is thought by many (though not all) to have a considerably lower moral status, and since the regulatory scheme of the HFE Act reflects this in public policy, the death of any embryos created, tested but not transferred is less important than the death of the fetus in the case of selective (or any) abortion. So, in the case of PGD, the desire to test for a serious condition where the risk is nevertheless viewed as less than significant (in a quantitative sense) could be morally sufficient. As matters stand, then, and to the extent that some importance may be given to a quantitative notion of risk in the term 'significant', the embryo appears overvalued by the current arrangements. In a somewhat similar vein, the House of Commons Science and Technology Committee observes: 'our gradualist approach to the status of the embryo leads us

---

[111] Department of Health, above n 18, para 2.43.

[112] *Ibid* para 2.44: 'The Government sees an ongoing role for the regulator in ensuring consistency in practice, and the licensing of screening in accordance with criteria relating to the seriousness of the disorder in question. Further, the Government proposes that licensing of screening to identify a tissue match for a sibling with a life-threatening disease will, as now, be undertaken on a case by case basis.'

to conclude that there is a mismatch between the protection afforded an embryo created in vitro before it is implanted and one at a later stage of development in the woman's uterus'.[113] This statement occurs in the context of a discussion of sex selection, a topic I address in the next chapter.

Of course, it should not be forgotten here that 'significant risk' has another meaning beyond the quantitative: in its alternative form the term captures the 'significance' of the risk to a given woman or couple. This is an important aspect if we are to say, as I have, that parents' views and potential interests should carry some weight in this context. Further, as we saw in the last chapter, the current recommendations on PGD require 'agreement' as to this significance between health professionals and prospective parents and it is of course possible that some health professionals will give less importance to quantitative meanings of risk in agreeing to provide PGD. Still, at least where public health resources are implicated, it seems likely that a quantitative component will have some relevance to this 'agreement'. Where this is the case, the current requirement of a 'significant risk' in the case of PGD may indeed have a legitimate moral role in the allocation and distribution of public funds within the NHS.[114]

In terms of the general alignment of the criteria for PND and PGD, although the HGC (with the HFEA) originally endorsed the 'precautionary principle' of aligning these, in fact more recently it has questioned this position[115]:

> Having reconsidered the matter, we accept the argument that a distinction may be drawn between the moral status of an unimplanted embryo and a fetus in an established pregnancy, and that this distinction may be used to justify the use of PGD for certain conditions where PND cannot be regarded as appropriate or acceptable and for which termination of pregnancy is seldom sought. For some conditions where PND is considered to be inappropriate, PGD might be permissible.

The HGC then turns to late-onset and lower-penetrance conditions (which I discussed in Chapter 4 since there is currently some licensing in relation to these), observing[116]:

> We support a cautious approach to the extension of the use of PGD to further conditions. We expect that some serious late onset conditions, and also other conditions of lower penetrance, may be considered appropriate for PGD should parents wish to use

---

[113] House of Commons Science and Technology Committee, above n 37, rec 26 (in part), para 119.

[114] For relevant thoughts, see HGC, *Choosing the Future: Genetics and Reproductive Decision-Making — Analysis of Responses to the Consultation*, para 4.5, entitled 'The Economic Cost of PGD': 'There seems to be some consensus that, at this stage of development in the technology, NHS-funded testing should be limited by a set of strict criteria; these may include the severity of the disorder, the risk of an affected pregnancy (for example, whether the patient has a family history of a genetic disorder) and the efficacy of the test'. See also HGC, above n 20, para 4.8, cited at above n 96.

[115] HGC, above n 20, para 4.17.

[116] *Ibid* para 4.18.

the technique to avoid the birth of an affected child. But... this should be in the context of systematic paediatric follow up of the children.

The HGC also discusses 'saviour siblings' here, which I likewise touched on in Chapter 4.

Looking to the future of PGD, there may be a tendency to assume that there are lower costs in choosing between embryos (at least once several embryos exist) than in terminating an existing pregnancy. Theoretically at least, there is greater scope to focus on less serious considerations, including ones that would be unlikely to influence prospective parents in deciding to abort.[117] However, we have seen that the greater the number of conditions or features that are the subject of testing, the less may be the accuracy of that testing and the fewer embryos there may be to transfer: indeed, there may be none. We have also seen that not all embryos will be judged to have good live-birth potential. Overall, the physical and emotional burdens of undergoing IVF will always be considerable. In this light, the concerns of people engaging in PGD are likely to be very serious indeed, given their past reproductive experience and possible reproductive future. They will have in mind both the interests of their possible child and, particularly when a child's impaired existence is nevertheless compatible with a reasonable quality of life but they remain concerned about the possible impact of such a birth on them, their own interests in reproduction. As with selective abortion, then, where a given child would have a reasonable quality of life, parental interests may be the ones that are most often potentially invoked by PGD. We should recognise and accept this more clearly by legal and other means.

In the next chapter I turn to consider two special cases of PGD: selecting for disability and sex selection. These are distinguishable from the issues in this chapter in two main ways: first, there is evidence that some people really want either to select for disability or to select the sex of their child and second, these choices are currently possible through PGD.

---

[117] As noted earlier, this concern is recorded in HGC, *Minutes of Genetic Testing Sub-group*, 12 January 2001, para 5.4: 'Dr Albert felt that there was a real risk in the future that, with PGD becoming available for more people... it could be used for selecting babies'. The concern here is presumably with selection on the basis of insignificant features. In outlining the respective scope of selective abortion and PGD, the Consultation Document notes that 'some may fear it will be too easy to test and discard [embryos] where no serious disorder exists'. However, the Document also notes that since PGD necessitates IVF it is by no means an 'easy option' and therefore will not be 'undertaken lightly or offer any guarantee of success'. HFEA and AGCT, above n 7, para 26.

# 6

# *Uses of Preimplantation Genetic Diagnosis — Two Particular Cases*

## I INTRODUCTION

MOST OF THE discussion in this book has concerned the moral and legal permissibility of selection, either by prenatal screening and diagnosis (PND) or preimplantation genetic diagnosis (PGD) against genetic impairments, disorders or diseases in future children. Though controversial in the various ways discussed here, PND has developed over time and become commonplace and PGD will become increasingly so, though not nearly as widespread. Relatively recently, debates about selection practices have been infused by references to a kind of selection that seems to turn traditional concerns about avoiding disability on its head: the case of prospective parents who seek a child with an impairment such as deafness. This is the first topic of this chapter, addressed in Section II.

The chapter also explores the very real wish that quite a number of prospective parents apparently have to choose the sex of their child. This desire apparently surprises people less but troubles many. In turning to consider sex selection for non-medical reasons in Section III, I pay particular attention to the policy analyses and conclusions of the Human Fertilisation and Embryology Authority (HFEA) in its most recent report upholding a ban on sex selection and of the government in its review of the HFE Act. I relate these to an analysis of the possible application of the right to respect for private and family life under Article 8 of the European Convention on Human Rights (ECHR), incorporated into English law by means of the Human Rights Act 1998, considered more briefly at points in earlier chapters. In this way, I focus on the important question of to what extent society has the right to proscribe certain practices. This is a fitting final topic for the book as a whole.

## II SELECTING FOR DISABILITY

I start by recalling some background thoughts about person-affecting and non-person-affecting principles and the idea of harm, first discussed in Chapter 1. I then look at the views of two scholars, John Harris and Ronald Green. After that I consider parents' possible interests in selecting for disability and the implications for third-party assistance. I then reflect on selection for deafness and the idea of opportunity. In the final sections I look briefly at selection for achondroplasia (or dwarfism) and the idea of selection for Down's syndrome or cystic fibrosis. At the outset, it should be noted that the idea of selecting for disability, although a very specific possible use of PGD, is another instance of a type of selection in which people might consider that particular attention needs to be given to the welfare of the future child.[1]

## A  Person-Affecting and Non-Person-Affecting Principles and Harm Revisited

From earlier discussion, particularly in Chapter 1, it can be said that being born with a disability would not harm a child unless that disability entails a condition that is so severe that there is a serious risk that the child will not think her life worth living. If she did not think her life worth living, we might say that she has a 'wrongful life'. On the understanding advocated by Allen Buchanan *et al* that I endorsed, someone has a wrongful life when the burdens that come with or soon after birth are insufficiently compensated by benefits or goods.[2] In such a case, a person's interests are so severely negatively affected that not to experience her life would have been preferable. So, those who deliberately selected her existence would have breached a moral duty, the effects of which crystallised at the point of her birth. By contrast, the reason why a child cannot be said to be harmed (in the comparative sense at least) where, despite having some impairment such as the inability to hear, she would nevertheless think her life worth living, is that she can only exist as that child and so with that impairment. This is the 'non-identity' problem that we have encountered at various stages.[3] Accordingly, as long as she considers her life to be worth living she cannot be said to have been harmed, comparatively speaking. However, not all would agree, as I discuss below.

If a child is not harmed by being selected for an impairment, the only sense in which it could be wrong deliberately to select an embryo that would come to be a child who could not hear or see, or would have any other impairment compatible with a life she would very likely think worth living, would be in a non-person-affecting sense. This is the sense in which it could be wrong to select for people with impairments and possibly fewer opportunities when other, *different*, people could have existed without these things. The application of non-person-affecting principles in this context dovetails well with the thought that it is preferable that people start life without avoidable impairments or diseases. This is not to make any judgment about the quality of life of people who do not start life in this way. It is simply to observe that it is preferable for any one of us to

---

[1] As noted by S Wilkinson 'Selecting for Disability and the Welfare of the Child', in *Choosing Children: the Ethics of Selective Reproduction* (Oxford: OUP, forthcoming 2007). As Wilkinson notes '[q]uality of life arguments are not confined to disability'.
[2] A Buchanan, D Brock, N Daniels, D Wikler, *From Chance to Choice: Genetics and Justice* (Cambridge: Cambridge University Press, 2000) 235.
[3] D Parfit, *Reasons and Persons* (Oxford: OUP, 1984) Ch 16.

begin life with full capacities for functioning and so full potential for flourishing. This recalls my discussion of Jonathan Glover's analysis of disability in Chapter 1.[4] As Stephen Wilkinson notes with reference to Glover's work, the idea is not that there will necessarily be a connection between disability and lack of welfare or flourishing, but that people born with impairments may have a reduced capacity to flourish.[5] So, since not all people will be able to start life with full capacities, non-person-affecting-affecting principles here suggest that it would be preferable if other people start life in their place, so to speak. At one level, this sounds harsh and judgmental. At another level, of course, since existence in itself (rather than continued existence, say, assuming someone thinks his life is worth living) is not a benefit, it does not really matter *who* comes to exist and therefore non-person-affecting principles can have considerable sway.

If it is preferable that people at least begin life with greater capacities and opportunities and so forth, then we might say that there is at least a *prima facie* duty not to select for disability. Since this is a *prima facie* duty, we should also consider what those prospective parents who wanted to select for disability could tell us about their reasons for doing so. In effect, we would have to evaluate their reproductive autonomy interests in making such a choice against the strength of non-person-affecting principles at the stage of embryonic selection. I consider this in due course.

In addition, an important caveat in relation to the idea of any *prima facie* duty will concern whether we are discussing selection between embryos or the termination of a pregnancy with the idea that another pregnancy will be begun in due course. I made some points about this question in Chapter 1. There I explored the relevance of non-person-affecting principles, not in relation to *selecting* for disability, but *avoiding* it. This was particularly in the context of prenatal screening, diagnosis (PND) and selective abortion. I suggested that, because of the possible moral claims of the fetus (at the time when prenatal screening and PND begins at 11–12 weeks and onwards), the controversial nature of judgments about the severity of disabilities that leave people with lives worth living and the possible costs to parents of terminating an established pregnancy, non-person-affecting principles might best be understood as one of the reasons grounding the *moral permissibility* of avoiding impairment, rather than as giving rise to *requirements* to do so. If this were not so, parents would be morally required to terminate a pregnancy in which a fetus had a condition compatible with a life worth living and, for the reasons just cited, I do not think this is an acceptable conclusion. As indicated in Chapter 1, the point about the fetus here is not that it is a person, even perhaps in the third trimester of pregnancy. Rather, I think it becomes harder to be swayed by non-person-affecting principles given the increasing development of the fetus and the fact that, if applied in the context of

---

[4] Ch 1, S III(B).
[5] Above n 1.

an established pregnancy, the principles could give rise to a duty to abort a fetus. In essence, I think these principles are strained by such application. By contrast, given that arguably the embryo has fewer moral claims than the fetus of 11–12 weeks and more, there is greater scope for non-person-affecting principles to carry weight in the context of PGD. That said, arguably such principles would be at their strongest before the fusion of gametes.

What these thoughts again show is that, whilst non-person-affecting principles on their own cannot distinguish between the idea of obligations not to select for disability, obligations to avoid it and obligations to select embryos or fetuses with in some way 'better' features or characteristics (such as enhanced health),[6] we can draw on other moral ideas from the very real contexts about which we are thinking to make important distinctions and draw crucial lines.

At this stage, I shall consider the views of two writers, in order to deepen our understanding of what selection for disability does or does not actually entail.

## B  Choosing a Deaf Embryo Versus Failing to Cure a Deaf Child

John Harris writes: 'I do not believe there is a difference between *choosing* a preimplantation deaf embryo and refusing a cure to a newborn. Nor do I see an important difference between refusing a cure and deliberately deafening a child.'[7] I touched on Harris's notion of harm in Chapter 1 and I would now like to consider this in more detail by considering these two claims in turn. At the outset it is worth drawing on Harris's own clarification about what he thinks about selection for disability[8]:

> I argued… in some detail about cases like this, suggesting that whereas the parents would be harming their children, in that they brought children into the world in a harmed condition when they had the alternative of bringing healthy children into the world, they did not wrong those children because the children would clearly have a life worth living. In a case like this the parents have wronged no one, but have harmed some children unnecessarily, but those who were harmed had no complaint because for them the alternative was non-existence.

On this view, when a child has been selected for disability, it has been harmed. This is because Harris considers 'that disabilities are… physical or mental conditions that constitute a *harm* to the individual, which a rational person would wish to be without'.[9] Further, in the passage quoted above, he refers to the parents as having 'harmed' the children. On its face, this sounds as if it must be a comparative use of harm but in fact it cannot be that the person selected for disability has been harmed in this sense, provided she thinks her life worth living,

---

[6] See discussion in Ch 5.
[7] J Harris 'Is There a Coherent Social Conception of Disability?' (2000) 26 *JME* 95, 97, emphasis in original.
[8] *Ibid* 97.
[9] *Ibid* 98 (my emphasis).

because the alternative for the child was not to exist. What one could perhaps say is that an individual is harmed, or is worse off, compared to another possible individual: this would be a non-person-affecting understanding and comparison. Harris also describes a disabling condition as 'harmful to the person in that condition', which perhaps avoids the risk that people might think he is using 'harm' comparatively.[10] Focusing now on the individual who has been selected for disability, since the alternative for her was non-existence and since she thinks her life is worth living, on Harris's view the child can have no complaint against its parents. This is surely right. Harris also tells us that a child has not been wronged where it has a condition, such as deafness, that is compatible with a life worth living. This must be right too. The implication is that only those people with a condition so severe that they do not think their lives worth living have been wronged: the case of 'wrongful life'. Overall, he thinks it is 'wrong to bring avoidable suffering into the world'.[11] As suggested above, the application of non-person-affecting principles tells us that it is at least preferable not to select for people who will start life with fewer capacities. So in principle I would agree with Harris's last statement, though I am reluctant to use the terminology of suffering, since there will not necessarily be any, particularly of a psychological kind.

Let us now examine Harris's claims in more detail:

> I do not believe there is a difference between *choosing* a preimplantation deaf embryo and refusing a cure to a newborn. Nor do I see an important difference between refusing a cure and deliberately deafening a child.

Harris is right that there is no difference between selecting Embryo A, who will become the deaf Child A, and not curing the newborn Child B, in the sense that in both cases (assuming selecting Embryo A results in the live birth of a child) the *result* will be that a child will exist who cannot hear. To be more explicit, on the one hand, selection of Embryo A has resulted in the birth of the deaf Child A; on the other, the refusal to cure the deaf Child B has resulted in the continuing existence of a deaf child. Alternatively, to turn the facts around, on the one hand, if deaf Embryo A had *not* been selected, another different child (Child C) with the ability to hear might have existed instead; on the other, if the young deaf Child B were indeed offered (via its parents, say) a cochlear implant, instead it would have been able to hear (assuming the success of the cure). In both cases, either there is a deaf child or there is not. The lack of difference here relies on a non-person-affecting understanding of the selection of Child A rather than, say, Child C such that it is preferable not to seek to bring people into the world with impairments when other people without these could have existed instead. But, as Harris will recognise, non-person-affecting principles are not the only ones of relevance.

---

[10] *Ibid* 97.
[11] *Ibid* 96.

I shall now develop the cases a little further. Embryo A could only be born as the deaf Child A and, since we understand that deafness is compatible with a life worth living, it cannot really be said that it is against Child A's interests (when it possesses these, once born, that is) to have been selected for its deafness. However, if she has some residual capacity for hearing, it may come to be *against* her interests not to be offered, at the appropriate time after birth, a cochlear implant: indeed Jonathan Glover has suggested, as discussed below, that arguably her parents will owe this to her. Child B has not been selected for deafness but happens to be deaf. Once more — if she too has some residual capacity for hearing — it will be against her interests not to be offered the same assistance in hearing at the appropriate time. So again, in one way there is no difference between the cases in the sense that, once the two children are at the appropriate stage to try a cochlear implant, they should both be offered this. Further, we could even say that, assuming the availability of the relevant medical resources, the medical appropriateness of the cure and the lack of any harm through the cure itself (important caveats), failing to do so would be as morally culpable as deliberately deafening yet another child, say Child D. In this sense, I am inclined to agree with Harris's second sentence above: 'Nor do I see an important difference between refusing a cure and deliberately deafening a child'. Importantly, in developing the two cases in a parallel way and thinking about the duties that will be owed to either child to offer them assistance in hearing, we are entirely within the realm of person-affecting duties: we are thinking about the duties that each of these existing children may be owed. And the same person-affecting duties will be owed to both as *children*.

We should now revisit Harris's first sentence to remind ourselves of its claim: 'I do not believe there is a difference between *choosing* a preimplantation deaf embryo and refusing a cure to a newborn'. In the preceding paragraph, I explored the implications of either course of action in terms of the moral duties that will be owed to both Child A and Child B. However, it should not be forgotten that Harris's real comparison is between the actual selection for deafness in the first place and the failure to cure in the second: between these he sees no difference, presumably in terms of result. And indeed, as indicated at the start of the discussion, there is indeed no difference between the two in the non-person-affecting sense that in either case the result will be that a child will not be able to hear. Further, as just explored, as *children*, each will be owed various person-affecting duties, including the offer of assistance in hearing.

However, to say that the actual decision to select Embryo A, who will not as Child A be able to hear (rather than Embryo C, who could have done so) and who otherwise would not be born, is no different from the failure to offer a cochlear implant to the already-existing Child B is to ignore the point that, at the moment of selection, no duty is owed to Embryo A and the Child A it will become *not* to select it, since deafness is compatible with a life worth living. Indeed, on Harris's own analysis this would be to say that Child A is not wronged. By contrast, a very real duty is currently owed to the already-existing Child B who is deaf and who may well benefit from being offered a cochlear implant: in this case, a person already exists to whom duties are owed and the failure to offer the cochlear implant may adversely affect, indeed harm and also wrong, a person. But the selection of Embryo A does not adversely affect or harm (at least in a comparative sense) or wrong a person, since the Child A who will (all going well) emerge from the selection of Embryo A could *only* have existed without the ability to hear *and* this inability is compatible with a life worth living.[12] Indeed this is why, as Harris states, this child can have no complaint against its parents for having been selected.

Still, on Harris's analysis, Child A has been harmed. As we saw above, in his view one can be 'harmed', and be in a 'harmful condition', despite the absence of any comparative state, that is, despite the fact that the only alternative is non-existence. This is a legitimate view, provided one understands that 'harm' is not being used here in its comparative sense, at least not as it affects *people* (rather than in non-person-affecting comparisons between the lives of different possible people). Importantly, given this — and other things being equal — I suggest that any harm (in Harris's sense) to Child A must be less significant than the harm to Child B when we do not cure him. This is compatible with the thought that — again (and critically) other things being equal — person-affecting principles and duties may have greater moral significance than non-person-affecting ones. Since both Child A and Child B are deaf (unless cured), the sense of significance here must lie in our moral accountability in relation to and responsibility for the respective states of affairs, rather than in these states themselves. In essence, I think this may be where the difference between the cases lies. (Of course, after birth, as I have explored, it will be morally appropriate to offer Child A, just as Child B, assistance in hearing.)

In sum, Harris is right that, in the non-person-affecting sense, there is no difference between selecting a deaf embryo (who comes to be a child) and failing to cure, or indeed deafening, an already-existing child: in both cases the result is a deaf child. He would also be right to point out that after the birth of Child A, both children will be owed (person-affecting) duties, including the same offer of a cure. But there are differences between the two scenarios when we compare the failure to cure with the act of selection, since at this point we see that the already-existing Child B is clearly owed (person-affecting) moral duties whilst, at the point of selection, Embryo A/the future Child A is not. Although when Child A is born she too will be owed duties, and we might say she is in a 'harmful condition', those duties do not include a duty (which could have crystallised at the point of her birth) to have prevented her birth. This is because she is very likely to think her life worth living. Lastly and importantly, as suggested above and

---

[12] This point is made in a similar way by M Häyry in 'There is a Difference between Selecting a Deaf Embryo and Deafening a Hearing Child' (2004) 30 *JME* 510, 510. As Häyry notes in relation to legal analysis, for instance, in England s 1 of the Children Act 1989 sets out the principle of best interests in relation to the welfare of the child.

other things being equal, any harm (in Harris's sense) to Child A must I think be less significant than the harm to Child B when we do not cure him. Since both Child A and Child B are deaf (unless cured), I am referring here to the degree of our moral responsibility for their deafness. Of course, Harris may not think this is a significant difference or may disagree with this.

Finally, in relation to Harris, it is worth noting what he says immediately after the two claims I have been discussing: 'But even those who differ from me on these points will, I think, have some anxiety about these cases. Whether or not they are exactly the same, they are sufficiently morally similar to raise doubts in our minds.' Ultimately, I do not think the cases in his first claim are exactly the same, essentially due to what may be the lesser significance of our responsibility for the harm (in Harris's sense) to Child A. But, as indicated at the start of this section, for non-person-affecting reasons I do indeed have some anxiety about selecting for disability at the embryonic stage, which I shall explore further below; and likewise I do think the cases are sufficiently similar as to raise doubts and therefore also to require further analysis. An important issue that I have not yet considered is the strength of parents' possible reasons for selecting for disability; I shall do this shortly.

In order further to deepen our analysis of selection for disability, I shall now consider the views of Ronald Green.

## C  'Sarah Can Hear, But I Can't'

Ronald Green has criticised the reliance, in the logical sense, that has to be placed on non-existence in analyses of selection practices. He proposes[13]:

> Parents have a *prima facie* obligation not to bring a child into being deliberately or negligently with a health status likely to result in significantly greater disability or suffering, or significantly reduced life options *relative to the other children with whom he/she will grow up.*

Green stresses that[14]:

> It is this reasonably expected health condition and the level of life prospects of others in the child's birth cohort, not the state of non-existence, that is the appropriate benchmark for assessing harm in reproductive decision-making.

In a sense, this is an application of non-person-affecting principles. Of course, Green recognises the logical force in the non-existence point, such that in one very significant way a child has not in fact been harmed (comparatively speaking), since otherwise he/she would not have existed (and assuming he thinks his life is worth living). Nevertheless, moving somewhat between the language of harming and of wronging, he suggests that a child is morally wronged when his parents

---

[13] R Green 'Parental Autonomy and the Obligation not to Harm One's Child Genetically' (1997) 25 *Journal of Law, Med and Ethics* 5, 10, my emphasis.
[14] Ibid.

*Selecting for Disability* 305

breach the stated *prima facie* obligation without 'adequate justifying reasons' and writes here about the idea of 'significant' harm.[15] Given that he has stated a *prima facie* obligation of parents, he thinks that parents' interests must be weighed in the balance, as I do. Green also thinks that the 'willingness and ability' of parents to make up for 'less than desirable'[16] features of the child's congenital condition should be taken into account. This seems right.

Despite the power of the non-identity problem as a possible response to a child who thinks he has been harmed by being selected for deafness, Green may be right to encourage us at least to think about the way a child might look around him and in some way consider that he is unfairly disadvantaged compared with his friends and classmates. The question, I think, is how far this can take us. Green suggests that we can evaluate whether we have 'significantly' harmed someone by asking that person not whether he would prefer not to have been born, but rather whether he would have preferred to live without the specific condition that he has, such as deafness.

In fact, it is very unpredictable to what extent people would answer in the affirmative in relation to this second question. Here we might recall what we learnt about the boys with Duchenne muscular dystrophy and their views about their quality of life in Chapter 4, particularly the somewhat surprising point that they did not rate their own quality of life any lower than that of other children around them.[17] Further, we should recall that a central problem in establishing what people think about their life with their condition may be that their identities may be very much bound up with their disorders or impairments, as first explored in Chapter 1. This may be so the stronger the disorder or impairment. As noted there, Jonathan Glover observes that it is because of this that we need to be alert to 'possible biases' in people's accounts of the quality of their lives.

Still, if children might tend to look around them and wish they did not have a given condition, then perhaps it is not entirely satisfactory in defence simply to rely on the point that otherwise they would not have existed. Generally speaking, it may indeed be preferable not (deliberately) to select people who might have these feelings. If so, this would be another reason to support at least a *prima facie* obligation not to select for disability. The difference this time is that Green's analysis focuses more on person-affecting considerations, even though it involves people looking around them and thinking about the lives of other people and, in a psychological rather than logical sense, whether they could have lived those lives. However, since the primary focus is on person-affecting notions, we need to think further about Green's idea and, in particular, standard of harm.

First, Green's notion of '"significantly greater" suffering or disability'[18] sets a lower threshold than the wrongful life standard I have endorsed as the measure of

---

[15] *Ibid* 9.
[16] *Ibid*.
[17] Ch 4, S IV(B)ii.
[18] R Green, above n 13.

when we would wrong someone in allowing him to be born (assuming this could reasonably have been avoided). Green suggests that it is preferable to be cautious and avoid even 'moderate degrees of harm for those we bring into being'.[19] I am wary of moving away from the wrongful life standard. On the one hand I would be concerned that we may start to make quite presumptuous judgments about what can and cannot give rise to a good or reasonable quality of life. Indeed, as matters stand, we already have to be careful to avoid this in relation to the notion of 'wrongful life'. On the other, moving away from the wrongful life standard may allow greater scope for an unnecessary degree of criticism of, or lack of sympathy for, parents' interests and concerns to be brought into this kind of analysis (not in fact by Green, since in due course his analysis gives careful consideration to this point).[20]

Yet, despite the relatively clear-cut nature of the wrongful life standard, I think Green's worry about the possibility, at least, of children looking around them and wishing that they too could hear, or run, or see cannot be fully dismissed by reference to the non-identity problem. In essence, then, I think that Green's concerns give us another reason (of uncertain weight) to think that selection for impairment at the embryonic stage is not morally preferable, subject to analysis (below) of the strength of parents' possible interests in this kind of selection. However, given the 'safety net' of the wrongful life standard, I think it would be going too far to say that a child is harmed or wronged, in a serious sense, if selected for an impairment compatible with a life worth living. For similar reasons, I think Bonnie Steinbock and Ron McClamrock set the threshold too low, when they suggest a principle of 'parental responsibility' under which it is not morally acceptable to have a child unless it can be given 'a decent chance of a happy life',[21] since 'bringing children into existence under very adverse conditions is unfair to the children themselves'.[22]

Second, I am concerned about the scope of Green's argument. We saw that he argues that:

> Parents have a *prima facie* obligation not to bring a child into being deliberately or negligently with a health status likely to result in significantly greater disability or suffering, or significantly reduced life options *relative to the other children with whom he/she will grow up*.

For reasons cited earlier, I do not think that parents have an obligation to terminate a pregnancy, particularly when a fetus would become a child with a life

---

[19] Ibid 9.
[20] For instance, Green observes: 'In the special case of parents who carry a genetic disease and who are at risk of passing the condition on to their offspring, we must also be especially careful not to burden their lives further by ill-considered moralistic judgments and intrusions' (*ibid* 6).
[21] B Steinbock and R McClamrock 'When is Birth Unfair to the Child?' (1994) 24 *Hastings C Rep* 15, 17–18.
[22] Green, above n 13, 19.

she thought worth living. To recap, the reasons here concern the relative weakness (and, if you like, the somewhat disingenuous nature) of non-person-affecting principles when applied in relation to the developing fetus (even though it is arguably not yet a person), the possible costs to parents of termination and the highly debatable severity of impairments compatible with a life worth living. Nor do parents have an obligation, when using IVF for reasons relating to fertility, to test embryos in order to avoid the birth of a child with a life worth living. For reasons discussed in the previous chapter, particularly concerning the limits on the number of embryos and the pressures they will face to select those with the best live-birth potential, this could well make their main aim of achieving the birth of a child that much harder. In addition, to require parents to use IVF (so as to employ PGD) where otherwise they would not do so, would be excessively burdensome. Moreover, unless the parents are aware of the genetic possibility of giving birth to a child who might have a wrongful life, they will not have a reason to seek the relevant testing. By contrast, if they were aware of such risks, they may instead be seeking IVF simply so as to avail themselves of PGD.

Overall, then, I think that Green's argument has some, but necessarily limited, force. At most, I think it is a point of view that we might consider when we reflect on the idea of parents using PGD deliberately to try to select a child with an impairment. But even here, where a child has a life she thinks worth living I do not think it can be said that she has been harmed or wronged.

## D  Parents' Possible Interests in Selecting for Disability and Implications for Third-Party Assistance

I now turn to consider prospective parents' interests in selecting for an impairment such as deafness. I shall also bring a further and by now familiar ethical aspect into view — the involvement of third parties in selection practices. To some degree I discuss these in tandem.

Where parents wish to use IVF and PGD to choose a child with an impairment such as the inability to hear, as with any couple engaging in these processes to *avoid* disability in a possible child and, in a different way, any woman or couple engaging in PND and selective abortion, they need the help of others to do so. This could bring the ethical concerns of scientific and medical third parties into view. I discuss this aspect below. It might also bring into question the appropriate use of public resources, for instance where prospective parents would wish to use the National Health Service (NHS), to select for disability. (The implications for the NHS or other kinds of public resources *after* a child is born are arguably more controversial and highly sensitive.[23])

---

[23] This point is also made in Häyry, above n 12, 511, footnote omitted: 'The real clash occurs between the family's interest to have the kind of child they prefer, and society's claim that production of yet another individual with special needs will place a burden on scarce resources. The real policy choice must be made between reproductive autonomy and socio-economic considerations.'

Let us imagine a deaf couple who seek a deaf child through the NHS or another publicly funded health system. The couple may increase their chances of achieving this with IVF and PGD. However, particularly if public resources are at stake, we may be entitled to appraise the strength of these parents' interest in having a disabled child. After all, when we reflect on *avoiding* disability, although the severity of disability is contentious, currently screening and diagnostic practices are offered in relation to disabilities that can reasonably be judged to be serious: the purpose of screening is not to search for trivial features (although of course these might happen to be found on an ultrasound scan); nor, thinking about the law, would the disability ground of the Abortion Act support a termination in relation to them. I discussed this in detail in Chapter 3. In other words, by the same token in the PND context we appraise the strength of parents' interests in choosing whether or not to have a *non-disabled* child and do not currently assist them simply to avoid a purely aesthetic or other trivial feature that may concern them. So, reflection on the strength of the parents' interests in selecting *against* disability must entail, in part, reflection on the disability in question in any given case. In the context of PND, arguably the moral claims of the growing fetus are particularly relevant and stronger than those of the embryo, and previously I have suggested that, on a gradualist approach, it would not be permissible to abort a fetus on the basis of an aesthetic or other trivial feature.

When we return to reflect on prospective parents' interests in selecting *in favour* of disability, it also seems right that we should think, in part, about the severity of the disability in question. We need to consider whether their interest is strong enough to outweigh the idea of a *prima facie* duty, originating in non-person-affecting principles, not to engage in PGD so as to select a child with an impairment. Unlike the context in which parents are seeking to avoid disability in their future child, where we can fairly say that the more severe the disability the stronger may be the parents' interest in making a decision in relation to it (such as to avoid it), here it could be that the more severe the disability, the weaker the parents' interests in making a choice in relation to it (here to select for it), as I shall explore.

Let us think further about the deaf couple who very seriously want a deaf child and the strengths of their interests in achieving this. Perhaps these parents will try to convince us that without IVF and PGD they could not contemplate having a child because the feature of deafness is so central to their undertaking: they want a deaf child because of the overlap this will bring between its experiences and their own, perhaps as part of Deaf Culture, in a predominantly hearing world. They argue that this feature is so important that to deny them the deaf child will be to deny them any child. Whilst such claims have been described as selfish,[24] in

---

[24] 'To intentionally give a child a disability, in addition to all the disadvantages that come as a result of being raised in a homosexual household, is incredibly selfish.' Ken Connor, president of the (Australian) Family Research Council, cited in M Spriggs 'Lesbian Couple Create a Child Who is Deaf Like Them' (2002) 28 *JME* 283, 283. The

some ways they are very understandable and could seriously weaken our concern with the non-person-affecting principles that have some strength at the point of embryonic selection.[25] At this stage, we need to try to think more about being deaf and the extent to which this is disabling, that is, about the severity of deafness.

## E  Deafness and Opportunity

In support of the idea of greater opportunities for non-deaf people, Nancy Rarus (of the Australian National Association of the Deaf) observes that people who are deaf 'don't have as many choices'.[26] The strength of this point about greater opportunities for hearing people needs to be assessed with reference to the question of whether the disadvantages that may flow from being deaf are entirely a result of inadequate social support and/or discrimination. For reasons first discussed in Chapter 1, I agree with those who think it implausible to maintain that the potentially negative impact of being deaf is entirely due to social causes. Neil Levy addresses this point well[27]:

> Though much has been done... [to eliminate disadvantage] and a great deal more could be achieved, we can expect the deaf always to be at some disadvantage. We are, in many ways, a logocentric culture — one which is centred around the voice. The deaf will always be cut off from the buzz of conversation, always restricted to a narrower range of jobs, always slightly alienated from the mainstream of political, social and cultural life. Deaf culture may have its compensations, but they cannot entirely make up for this arrangement. Choosing deafness is, therefore, choosing a real (though not necessarily an especially severe) limitation. To that extent, deaf children have their future narrowed. Moreover, there is a sense in which this future is uncompensated. For the children of the deaf, access to deaf culture is not the compensation they receive for their disability, it is their birthright.

This last point is a particularly salient way of viewing what is usually seen as a real compensation. Levy's reference to deaf children having 'their future narrowed' implies a comparison with other, hearing, children and echoes Green's point that

---

reference to homosexuality is to the lesbian couple in the US, discussed below. The notion of 'giving' a child a disability if of course conceptually flawed. But this is how many people appear to understand the notion of selecting for disability.

[25] Similarly, N Levy 'Deafness, Culture, and Choice' (2002) 28 *JME* 284 (whose work is discussed further below) observes that 'we ought to react to... [such parents] with compassion and understanding, not condemnation' (at 285).

[26] Cited in Spriggs, above n 24, 283.

[27] Levy, above n 25, 284. Levy continues: 'Culture, like language, is normally passed on without effort. Any baby, hearing or deaf, will pick up sign language and speak it as a first language, so long as it is exposed to it regularly... The hearing child of deaf parents might be said to have a maximally open future, since she participates, as a full member and not merely an onlooker, in two cultures... deaf parents do not need to choose to exclude their children from the hearing world in order to include them in theirs; both are open to them' (at 284–5).

the appropriate comparison is not with non-existence, but with other, hearing, children. Strikingly, in one sense Levy's point about conversation is also made by one of the women who selected a child for deafness in the United States (as noted in more detail below). At high school she had an interpreter and, looking back, she observes that '[n]o teenage conversation can survive the intrusion of third-party interpretation'.[28] Of course, in her mind in some way this is a point in favour of selection for deafness, where deafness is promoted and supported in its own right as it were, since by contrast in growing up she herself 'felt flawed'.[29] Her feelings require that we think further about the social dimensions of disability.

On this issue John Harris has suggested: 'The crucial question is whether, if all the social dimensions of disability could be resolved, there would be any other dimensions left and if so how important they would be?'[30] We have already seen Levy's answer (in effect) to Harris's question in the above quotation: there would be a significant residue. Harris's answer is[31]:

> The harm of deafness is not exhausted by the possible social exclusion. Its harm is the deprivation of worthwhile experience… Social factors may exacerbate the problem of having such disabilities but they are disabilities because there are important options and experiences that are foreclosed by lameness, blindness and deafness. There are things to be seen, heard and done, which cannot be seen, or heard, or done by the blind, the deaf and the lame *whatever the social conditions*. Some of these things are very worthwhile. That is not to say that people who are blind, or deaf or lame cannot find other and different worthwhile things to do and to experience. It is just that there are pleasures, sources of satisfaction, options and experiences that are closed to them. In this lies their disability. Their social exclusion, of course, given that it is added to these disabilities is simply gratuitous, in a way that the disabilities may not be, and it may indeed be worse than the disabilities.

Since I agreed in Chapter 1 that disability cannot be entirely social by cause, and in the light of Levy's and Harris's comments here with particular reference to deafness, I think it is fair to say that it is preferable to be able to hear. But I have also said that we need to weigh up the parents' possible interests in selecting for deafness and put these beside the non-person-affecting principles that guide us against this kind of selection. How is this now to be resolved?

Here I think we must come back to the point that, as Jonathan Glover has suggested, selection for deafness could simply be self-defeating: if it turns out that their child when born has some residual capacity for hearing, and particularly as cochlear implant technology improves, the parents will probably owe it to him to

---

[28] As cited in Spriggs, above n 24, 283.
[29] *Ibid.*
[30] Harris, above n 7, 95.
[31] *Ibid* 98 (emphasis in original).

make this available by seeking the requisite medical help and advice.[32] As I understand it, it will not be predictable which child, if born, might have some residual capacity for hearing. Since this will always be a possible outcome, then parents may always become obliged in due course to offer their child assistance in hearing. To this extent, the strength of parents' reasons for wanting to select for a deaf child appears to diminish considerably, since public resources in such selection could well be wasted.[33] In turn, this leaves us with the relatively strong non-person-affecting principle that, at the point of embryonic selection, it is preferable not to select for people who will start life without a capacity such as hearing, and even though such a person would have a life she thought worth living.

As indicated above, selection for deafness has in fact occurred by use of a deaf sperm donor to a lesbian couple in the United States (in fact without IVF and PGD). In this case, although the couple specifically sought a deaf child, in due course it did transpire that the child had some potential for hearing and it was suggested that he should start to use a hearing aid when he is young.[34] For the reasons just discussed, these parents will indeed owe it to their child to allow it take advantage of such an aid at an early age. In this case, the parents have apparently said that he can choose to use the aid later if he wishes. Since early use is recommended to help facilitate language skills,[35] it is not clear whether they are currently doing what is best for this child.

If public resources were not implicated, to some degree the issue might be thought simply to concern the idea of not interfering (that is, negatively) with reproductive freedom. But of course even in the case of private clinics the positive assistance of third parties would still be required. What might staff at such clinics think of this kind of selection?

Morally speaking (that is, leaving to one side any questions about the relevant law), it would be a matter for the relevant clinical team to decide whether to assist the deaf couple who wanted a deaf child. Here, for instance, if it identified non-person-affecting principles as being relevant the team could weigh up the relative strength of these at the embryonic stage on the one hand (so that arguably it is preferable not to select for disability at this point) and the strength of the parents' interests in doing so on the other. On the above analysis, however, which noted the potentially self-defeating nature of selection for deafness in any given case, non-person-affecting principles may tend to hold out against parental reasons, though perhaps with less strength where there could be no concern with potentially wasting public resources. In fact, and as discussed particularly in

---

[32] J Glover, *Choosing Children: Genes, Disability and Design* (Oxford: OUP, 2006) 26. The potentially self-defeating nature of such a choice is also noted by Wilkinson, above n 1.
[33] The possibility of resources being wasted is also noted by Wilkinson, above n 1.
[34] Spriggs, above n 24, 283.
[35] *Ibid.*

## 312  *Uses of Preimplantation Genetic Diagnosis*

Chapter 4, the health professionals and scientists who work at a given clinic are very likely to have their own moral views and, potentially, concerns about helping to create a child with a disability, including one that is compatible with a life worth living, particularly since they may well see their professional role as one of helping parents to have 'healthy' children. For instance, Scientist 21 observed:[36]

> I would say our role was to enable somebody to have a healthy baby when, in the first instance they've got a fairly substantial risk of having an unhealthy baby. And so I guess… the dividing line then is, what you classify as healthy and unhealthy and how severe…

Further, turning now to the law, clinicians and scientists may well perceive a clash between selection of this kind and their obligation, under section 13(5) of the Human Fertilisation and Embryology (HFE) Act, to consider the welfare of any future child. Although they might be persuaded that this kind of selection is not a wrong to the child in the way that selecting a child with what would amount to a 'wrongful life' would be, they may still feel considerable discomfort about the idea. If so, any legalisation of such choices should arguably be accompanied by a conscientious objection mechanism.[37]

Overall, the above analysis has suggested that, at least in the case of selection for deafness, there are unlikely to be sufficiently compelling reasons to assist, given that deafness is an impairment, coupled with the potentially self-defeating nature of the choice. Further, in reality clinics are unlikely to have any choice in this matter. Current HFEA licences for PGD typically forbid the implantation of 'abnormal' embryos. Further, the Department of Health White Paper on the reform of the HFE Act states that '[d]eliberately screening-in a disease or disorder will be prohibited' (and this is further reflected in the Human Tissue and Embryos (Draft) Bill).[38]

Ultimately, the above analysis has partly hinged on the judgment that deafness is in fact an impairment. Notice that, if it did not, we could not justify granting public resources to selection *against* deafness, or an impairment of similar severity.

---

[36] Interview, Scientist 21, 13.

[37] It appears that Green, above n 13, would implicitly agree with this analysis: 'The fact that these technologies require the cooperation and assistance of medical personnel takes them beyond the private sphere of parental decision making' (at 7). 'On balance, I believe the issues here are not compelling enough to lead us to say that we *must* establish legal or professional norms impeding such a choice on the parents' part. However, neither is it clear that the parents' rights are strong enough to lead us to conclude that genetics professionals *must*, as a matter of professional responsibility, bow to the parents' wishes regardless of counselors' personal views. When no pressing moral reasons counsel otherwise, medical professionals have a right to decide to whom they will offer their services and for what reasons' (at 11–12, emphasis in original).

[38] Department of Health, *Review of the Human Fertilisation and Embryology Act: Proposals for Revised Legislation (including Establishment of the Regulatory Authority for Tissue and Embryos)*, December 2006, para 2.43; see Human Tissue and Embryos (Draft) Bill, May 2007 (amending Sch 3 of the HFE Act 1990), Cl 20(4).

Indeed, in this light it seems likely that we would give serious consideration to the claims to publicly funded IVF and PGD of a deaf couple who were concerned *not* to have a deaf child and otherwise had a high chance of doing so. Since deafness is compatible with a life worth living, in this last case the parents' interests might be thought to be particularly at stake, though in a non-person-affecting sense the life of one child rather than another would be too.

At the same time, if instead we were using public resources to help a deaf couple with fertility problems simply to have a child by IVF, there would be no strong moral reason also to employ PGD to select a *non-deaf* child, unless the couple themselves wanted this. This might seem curious given the non-person-affecting principle that it is preferable that people are born with greater opportunities and so forth. However, I have also noted the inability of non-person-affecting principles themselves to distinguish in important ways between different contexts and choices. As noted first in the previous chapter, the processes of PGD may themselves compromise parents' ability to have a child through IVF. There could be several reasons for this: an embryo is damaged by the removal of the cell for testing[39]; testing reveals that no embryos will become children who can hear; or the embryo or embryos that test normal are of poor quality with low prospects for live birth. Further, PGD compromises the ability of embryos to freeze, so that if the chosen (fresh) embryo or embryos fail to implant or miscarry, a couple must start another IVF cycle from scratch (since they are unlikely to have any frozen embryos on which they could draw). Another reason in support of the idea that deaf parents would not have an obligation to employ PGD to avoid deafness is simply that being deaf is clearly fully compatible with a life that a child would think worth living. Indeed, throughout my analysis this has further supported the idea that parents are not morally obliged to (go out of their way to) avoid giving birth to children with lives of this kind of quality.

However, moving from the ethics to the law, it is not clear that an IVF clinic's interpretation of the welfare-of-the child principle in section 13(5) of the HFE Act, coupled with the guidance in the HFEA's Sixth Code of Practice (first discussed in Chapter 4),[40] would mean that clinical staff would be content *not* to test the embryos of a deaf couple for deafness, so as to avoid the birth of a deaf child. In particular, clinics may be concerned about the statement in the Code that clinics 'are expected to take into account... the risk of harm to children including... inherited disorders or transmissible disease'.[41] As I discussed in the previous chapter, the HFEA does not differentiate between the severity of conditions and so whether they are likely to be compatible with a life that someone would think worth living.

Finally, it is worth thinking briefly about different kinds of selection for disability, even though none is likely to be legal in the United Kingdom.

---

[39] The incidence of this appears to be typically quoted as about 1%.
[40] See Ch 4, S II.
[41] HFEA, *Code of Practice — Sixth Edition* (2003) para 3.12.

## F  Selecting for Achondroplasia

In some cases, selection for a given condition will not be self-defeating because a condition is not medically correctable. This is true of achondroplasia, or dwarfism. In fact, having achondroplasia need not mean that one is disabled,[42] though it may complicate the process of doing certain things. However, as Jonathan Glover has noted, in these cases the adjustments appear relatively easily achieved, such as 'needing a stool to boost height when speaking in public'; in this light, dwarfism need not be seen as a disability.[43] Although relatively few of us have experienced this condition, it seems unlikely that one could really say that it was very bad to be born with it.[44] This means that there could be no strong grounds for criticising the desire of parents who have the condition to select such a child. Instead, are there grounds to help them achieve this?

In one sense, there may be a certain neutrality to the choice, such that to have achondroplasia is simply to be different in one aspect, albeit a pronounced and very visible one. If so, it might be thought that parents are unlikely to have a serious interest in having a child with this condition and thus to have a very strong reason to select such a child.[45] By the same token, there would be no strong reason for us to help them achieve the birth of such a child, just as there is no strong reason for us to help parents achieve a child with or without certain aesthetic features, as I explored in the previous chapter. To grant these parents public resources to select a child with achondroplasia would be to ensure that more instances of a given type of difference existed, but we have no obligation to replicate difference (though we may sometimes be obliged to protect or promote it where it exists). If this selection choice does indeed have a certain neutrality to it, it would also be likely to mean that, if this were legal, parents could use a private clinic, whose clinicians may (or may not) feel they would have no strong reason to question their choice. (As noted above, however, even though achondroplasia is not a disability, selection for it would probably currently be seen as illegal and will remain so.)

In another sense, however, we can imagine some reasons for parents who have dwarfism to want to select a child with the condition. For instance, their accommodation may be highly adapted to living with the condition. Further, Ronald Green notes that he has been told by some people with achondroplasia that they are worried about disciplining a child *without* the condition and the ultimate effect on the child's well-being if they are not successful in this.[46]

---

[42] For instance Harris, above n 7, 98, suggests that to have this condition is not to be in a harmed condition.
[43] Glover, above n 32, 10.
[44] However, see discussion in Ch 2, S V(B) of the woman with this condition who very much wanted a termination of a fetus found late in pregnancy to have this condition.
[45] Ronald Green has likewise observed that there may be 'possibly fewer pressing parental reasons' in this case. Green, above n 13, 12.
[46] *Ibid.*

Another reason could be an important medical one: there may be increased dangers for a pregnant woman with achondroplasia in giving birth to a child without this condition.[47] Arguably, this last could be a very strong reason to help a couple have a child with this condition, one that could perhaps ground a challenge to the illegality of this kind of selection, although women with dwarfism typically deliver by caesarean-section.[48] Overall, as others have noted, in some ways selection for achondroplasia is a harder case than that of selection for deafness.[49] On balance, however, the case for selection for the condition, at least using public resources, does not appear strong.

A final point to note about achondroplasia is that a couple with the condition has a one-in-four chance of having a child who will be homozygous for the gene. In this case, the born person will die as a child following a rapid and steep decline.[50] We might note in passing that selection for a homozygous child, though highly implausible as a choice, would arguably breach a duty to the future child to avoid it having a wrongful life.

Deafness and achondroplasia are the conditions that have dominated the debate about selection for disability. In the case of deafness there is a strong and independent culture of people who are deaf — Deaf Culture. Further, the discussion in the literature is always of prospective parents who have a given condition and who want to have a child with that same condition. In this light, it would seem right to question from the outset the desire, say, of hearing parents to have a deaf child (though such a desire is likely to be hypothetical for obvious genetic reasons). In essence, I cannot see that there would be any moral reason to accede to the parents' desire in this case. What about selection for other conditions typically thought compatible with a life worth living, such as cystic fibrosis or Down's syndrome?

## G  Selecting for Down's Syndrome or Cystic Fibrosis

Let us think first about the case in which either one or both of the prospective parents has Down's syndrome. (In fact, fertility is typically impaired in the case of Down's syndrome, but I shall leave this to one side.[51]) In theory, such selection could be achieved by selecting an embryo with three copies of chromosome 21. A couple with Down's syndrome might well want to have a child with the condition and, given the mental characteristics of the condition, this could be very understandable. The situation could then be analysed as above: we could weigh the relative strength of non-person-affecting principles at the point of embryonic

---

[47] Personal communication: Peter Braude.
[48] Green, above n 13, 12 (citing TE Kelly, *Clinical Genetics and Genetic Counseling* (Chicago: Book Medical Publishers, 2nd edn, 1986) 292–3).
[49] Ibid.
[50] Ibid 6.
[51] Down's Syndrome Association <http://www.downs-syndrome.org.uk/DSA_FAQs.aspx#faq31> accessed 15 October 2007.

selection against the strength of the parents' interests and reasons. These latter may well be that much stronger where a condition is not medically correctable (in terms of the mental element, that is) and so where the choice is not self-defeating and therefore potentially wasteful of public resources. However, what about the health problems inherent in Down's syndrome? In at least one sense of health, these immediately distinguish the case from that of selection for deafness. Still, although the health problems inherent in Down's syndrome may weaken the parents' case, it is implausible to say that someone with Down's syndrome will not think his life worth living, despite his health problems. At the same time, turning to a non-person-affecting sense, we might be somewhat troubled by the idea of the selection for the health problems that would also be entailed. These vary unpredictably in severity but it could, for instance, be of particular concern that one in ten children with Down's syndrome die in their first year of life.[52] (In such a case, which could perhaps raise concerns about a possibly wrongful life, person-affecting principles would also be implicated.) Overall, as before, a typically non-person-affecting concern with the health problems must be weighed against the very personal interests of the parents with Down's syndrome who may very much want a child with the condition. To help resolve this issue, some might point to the possible need for assistance in child-raising from third parties in this kind of case, but I am not sure if it would be fair to raise this given the disadvantages that people with Down's syndrome clearly experience in our society.

I turn now to selection for cystic fibrosis. If one or more parents themselves had the condition, given the health problems in which the condition consists and the lack of any particular mental characteristics, it would seem much less understandable to want to select for the condition. Such a desire also seems inherently unlikely. Indeed, there is strong evidence that parents with some experience of cystic fibrosis (and therefore awareness of their reproductive risk in this regard) try to avoid having children with it. I deduce this from the fact that cystic fibrosis is a relatively common condition for which testing occurs in PGD, for instance at the clinic studied and discussed particularly in Chapter 4.

Turning to parents *without* either Down's syndrome or cystic fibrosis, it seems very unlikely that they would want actually to select for either of these conditions. This will probably be because the conditions both involve health problems to some degree (or a high chance of them in the case of Down's syndrome) and that in the case of Down's syndrome there is also a varying degree of mental impairment. For these reasons, it seems unlikely that such parents would want actively to seek children with these conditions. Importantly, to say

---

[52] Further, between screening and birth there is a high rate of stillbirth. C Julian-Reynier, Y Aurran, A Dumaret, A Maron, F Chabal, F Giraud 'Attitudes Towards Down's syndrome: Follow up of a Cohort of 280 cases' (1995) 32/8 *J Med Genet* 597; RH Won, RJ Currier, F Lorey, DR Towner 'The Timing of Demise in Fetuses with Trisomy 21 and Trisomy 18' (2005) 25/7 *Prenat Diagn* 608.

this is not to say that parents will not greatly want and love the children they have who happen to be born with one of these conditions. In addition, unlike the case of deafness, there is not a culture around either of these conditions, although there are usually associations of parents who have children with these conditions and in this way a sense of community around these children and their families.[53] The lack of such a culture (to which, of course, the parents here would *not* already belong) further reduces the likelihood of a desire to select for these conditions.

For all these reasons, it seems unlikely that parents without Down's syndrome and parents with or without cystic fibrosis would have an interest, let alone a strong one, in going out of their way to select a child with one of these conditions. As we have often seen, it is the strength of their interest, coupled with a reflection on the nature of the disability in question and the moral status of the embryo (or fetus), that is at stake, amongst other issues, in all selection cases. In this light, there is nothing to suggest that such choices would be morally permissible. (The factors just recalled were also at stake in the spectrum identified by Buchanan *et al* in relation to 'wrongful life' and 'wrongful disability cases' where the *avoidance* of disability is at stake, discussed in Chapter 1.) Ultimately, we should always be attentive to prospective parents' concerns and reasons.[54] At the same time, I think we would be right to pause and question the motivations of parents who wanted help in selecting a child who could reasonably be seen as being seriously disabled where this involves health problems, except perhaps where one or both of the parents have Down's syndrome. This is not because conditions such as Down's syndrome or cystic fibrosis are not compatible with a life worth living. Rather, it is because we can fairly say that it would be unusual for parents without these conditions (or with them in the case of cystic fibrosis) to want actively to make such a choice; we can also say that they would have no strong interest in doing so. For these reasons, the strength of non-person-affecting principles in such cases (as applied at the embryonic stage) — which point towards the view that it is preferable that people do not start life with impaired capacities for flourishing — would be considerable. We might also note that, where a child has health problems, public health resources (where available, as in the United Kingdom), will be implicated, though I noted earlier that this is highly sensitive. As observed at several points above, in any event this kind of selection looks set to remain illegal.

Most importantly, this last reference to public health resources does *not* imply that parents who do *not* want to terminate a pregnancy where a fetus has one of these conditions should be criticised for implicating public resources in the future. Such parents are likely not to want to terminate because of emotional, religious or other moral difficulties about doing so. They may also rightly think that if the

---

[53] For example, the Down's Syndrome Association in the UK.
[54] As Green, above n 13, is also keen to emphasise, 12. Further, the views of staff working at a PGD clinic reveal strong concerns of this kind, though not necessarily ones that would support selection for disability: see generally Ch 4.

woman gives birth to a child with one of these conditions, that child will think its life worth living. This is not so much a case in which we are evaluating parents' *interest in having a disabled child*. Rather, we are concerned with the *costs to them of avoiding this* when a woman is already pregnant. The increased moral status of the fetus, compared with the embryo, will particularly be an issue here. It would be unthinkable that, because of the future implications for public resources, where a child would have a life she thinks worth living, we would try to persuade, let alone coerce, a couple into termination. By contrast, there may be at least a *prima facie* case for diverting from a policy of non-directive counselling in wrongful life cases, but this would depend very much on the details of the case. Further, the reasons here would concern the interests of the child, not the public purse.

## H   Implications Overall

For non-person-affecting reasons that may have some strength at the point of embryonic selection (albeit less strength than the moment before any gametes fuse to create an embryo), I have argued that it is *prima facie* morally preferable not to select a child who will start life with reduced capacities for flourishing, even though these may well leave her with a life worth living and even though, of course, she may well in fact flourish in other ways. However, I said that this is only a *prima facie* position, one that must be weighed against the strength of parents' possible reasons for wanting to select a child with an impairment. That said, at least in the cases that I have been able to discuss here, we do not seem to have found an instance in which parents in fact have a sufficiently strong case to outweigh these non-person-affecting principles, particularly where public resources in IVF and PGD would be implicated. The possible exception here was selection for Down's syndrome where one or more parents has this condition, because of the mental characteristics of the condition. Even here, however, it was hard not to be concerned — in a non-person-affecting sense — about the condition's inherent health problems. All of this tends to suggest that it is very unlikely that public resources should be devoted to selection for disability or that private clinics should ever be compelled to assist: that is, staff should always have the option of conscientious objection.[55] I have also noted that these kinds of selection are currently illegal (by means of HFEA licence conditions) and are

---

[55] Consider also Ronald Green's conclusion, which gives strong weight to parents' views but concludes that *sometimes* selection for disability may be not just morally not preferable, but also morally impermissible, compatible with his rejection of the wrongful life standard as a measure of harm overall: 'in most cases, we will defer to parents' thinking about these matters and recognize that *their* global judgment about the prospects facing their children is normally to be respected. *This is perhaps especially true where parents with a disability are concerned*, because they can be expected to approach these decisions with utmost seriousness about the stakes for their child. Only when clear evidence indicates that the parents are unconcerned about their child's wellbeing or that their judgment about their child's prospects is clearly wrong can we conclude that they may be acting in a morally irresponsible way.' Green, above n 13, 11, first emphasis in original; second added.

likely to remain so by means of a revised HFE Act. On balance, given that for non-person-affecting reasons it is arguably morally preferable not to select an embryo for disability and that we have found it hard to find sufficiently strong countervailing parental reasons for this kind of selection, this may well be acceptable. But an alternative would be to allow a case-by-case assessment of such requests by means of specific HFEA licenses. Even though we might find it hard to imagine one, this would at least allow for the possibility of a sufficiently compelling case. However, it seems that the government has set its face against this option, by recommending that such selection explicitly be made illegal in the new Act itself.

At the same time, in the course of this discussion I have suggested that parents are not morally required to terminate a pregnancy in which the fetus would come to be an impaired child who thought her life worth living. Nor are parents required to undertake IVF or, if already doing so, to add in PGD to select against a child who would have such a life. In each case, this would be an excessively burdensome demand; further, in the case of IVF and PGD, a moral requirement to add in such testing could compromise the important aim of having a live-born child.

### III SEX SELECTION

Sex selection for non-medical reasons raises many of the issues that have been discussed in the previous chapter and for this reason my treatment of it will be relatively brief.[56] Yet the topic perhaps deserves attention in its own right because determining the sex of an embryo is currently possible, because this may well be a kind of selection in which a number of prospective parents would wish to engage, and because the issue has twice received direct attention from the HFEA, by means of two public consultation exercises and subsequent reports.[57] Although a major focus of the latest HFEA consultation was to consider whether sperm sorting should in future be regulated, as well as sex selection by PGD, since my focus in this book is on PND and PGD I shall restrict my discussion to sex selection by PGD.

---

[56] There is an enormous literature on this topic. For arguments in favour, see, eg, R Rhodes 'Ethical Issues in Selecting Embryos'(2001) 943 *Ann NY Acad Sci* 360 and S Savulescu 'Sex Selection: The Case For' (1999) 171(7) *Med J Aust* 37; for arguments against see, eg, R McDougall 'Acting Parentally: An Argument against Sex Selection' (2005) 31 *JME* 601 and JM Berkowitz and JW Snyder 'Racism and Sexism in Medically Assisted Reproduction' (1998) 12 (1) *Bioethics* 25. For a review of some of the relevant literature, see C Waldby, *Literature Review and Annotated Bibliography: Social and Ethical Aspects of Sex Selection*. This forms Appendix D of the HFEA's report, *Sex Selection — Options for Regulation: A Report on the HFEA's 2002–3 Review of Sex Selection including a Discussion of Legislative and Regulatory and Options* (2003).
[57] HFEA, above n 56. HFEA, *Sex Selection* (1993).

I first consider the idea of sex selection with reference to the main issues I identified in the previous chapter: parents' possible interests, the future child's interests, the claims of the embryo and the processes in PGD, the people working in IVF and PGD and the interests of those with impairments. I shall also consider the idea of any broader social impact. I then turn to consider aspects of the HFEA's most recent conclusions on the subject, criticism of these and the government's recommendations in connection with the review of the HFE Act. As noted at the start of this chapter, the reason for discussing the HFEA's latest report on this issue is to take the opportunity to reflect on a policy analysis and to do this in conjunction with a more detailed look at Article 8 of the ECHR, considered briefly in earlier chapters. In this way, I focus on the important question of to what degree society has the right to forbid certain practices. This is a suitable topic with which to conclude the book as a whole.

At the outset it should be noted that in the United Kingdom recent studies show 'no significant overall preference for one sex over the other'.[58] Assuming for present purposes that people answer honestly when asked if they have any preference, in this light two otherwise potentially legitimate concerns about the practice of sex selection might be thought to fall away: that sex selection would create an imbalance in numbers between the sexes[59]; and that sex selection would be an instance of discrimination against women. Accordingly, I shall not discuss these here. By contrast, both of these are known to be highly pertinent concerns in countries such as India and China.

However, the objection to sex selection on the grounds of discrimination is not necessarily overcome at this point. This is because although, taken as a group, prospective parents in the United Kingdom apparently have no overall preference for one sex rather than another, individuals clearly do. Some people might find this objectionable. Here it may be helpful to think of an analogy with a society with no racism on the one hand, and one in which 50% of the population is against black people and 50% against white people on the other.[60] Arguably, the former society would be a better one in which to live. Is a parental preference for one sex rather than another an instance of discrimination in the same way? I consider this below.

Note that the ensuing discussion concerns legalisation and availability of the practice within the private sector, since I cannot think that there would be a good enough case for the use of public resources, given the competition for these. To

---

[58] HFEA, above n 56, para 26. However 'a disproportionately high percentage of those actively seeking sex selection were from ethnic populations originating outside Europe'. Although there was a preference for male children amongst couples who already had more than one female child and had little reproductive time left, the HFEA concludes that '[t]hese findings did not demonstrate that permitting controlled sex selection for non-medical reasons would lead to a skewing of the sex ratio in the UK'.
[59] As the HFEA itself concludes, *ibid* para 138.
[60] I am grateful to Roger Crisp here.

begin, I interleave discussion of the interests that parents might have in sex selection with the interests of their future children.

## A  Parents' and Children's Interests

For some people, the sex of their future child will be of no importance; for others, this will not be so. A typical example of the latter may be a family with two boys in which the parents would also like to have the experience of raising a girl. This may give rise to the desire for sex selection for what is often termed, rather oddly perhaps, 'family balancing'. This is sometimes seen as the form of sex selection that would be most justifiable: for instance, the House of Commons Science and Technology Committee recently suggested that there was insufficient evidence to ban the practice of sex selection for family balancing.[61] But of course many people are opposed to sex selection of all kinds, as is clearly demonstrated in the HFEA's latest report. Where sex selection is not for the purpose of having the additional experience of raising a child of the opposite sex, the desire is simply to select a child of one sex rather than another. This seems to create particular problems in people's minds. In part, this may be because to want to select a child of one sex rather than another means that one has a strong preference for a child of one sex, so that one implicitly wants to *avoid* the other sex. We may therefore wonder why this is the case.

It is possible to think of reasons for this desire. Some people may think that raising either a boy or a girl will entail experiences they might prefer. However, here perhaps one worry would be whether they are presuming certain facts about girls or boys, such as (to use the stereotypical examples) that girls will enjoy shopping and boys football, or that girls are quieter than boys. Alternatively, is it indeed possible to point to certain facts about the differences, if any, between the sexes? This depends on whether we think and agree that girls inherently have stronger instantiations of certain features, such as empathy. Clearly, this is highly controversial and raises the familiar and probably irresolvable nature/nurture debate. So we are unlikely to agree on facts about the nature of boys or girls. In this light, we are left with the idea of parents wanting to select the sex of their child on the basis of what we can at best agree are ideas that give rise to preferences. Is this morally problematic? In particular, is it discriminatory?

Arguably, discrimination involves acting in ways that result from unjustified beliefs about certain kinds of people. If this is so, then we would have to think about whether the beliefs that prospective parents have that incline them to choose one sex over another are justified. The problem we return to here is that we are unlikely to agree on this point. So, leaving this to one side for now and moving on, if we were in some way able to decide that there is in fact

---

[61] House of Commons Science and Technology Committee's report *Human Reproductive Technologies and the Law* (2005), rec 30, para 142.

discrimination, where does its wrong or harm lie? Is it in the act of discrimination, its effect, or both? People will think differently about this. Thinking along the lines of harm, in the context of successful sex selection, the girl who has been selected for her sex is not the subject of discrimination. Rather, the non-existent boy is. Such a boy cannot be harmed. So perhaps instead we should be concerned about the risk of harm to other boys whom, for instance, these prospective parents will meet through social activities with their now-born girl. It seems unrealistic to think that these boys will be harmed, particularly in a serious way, by the attitudes of these parents. Still, maybe it is the act of discrimination that is troubling. This may be so. However, we will always return to the point that it is going to be very hard to establish whether the actual choice of one sex over another is based on unjustified beliefs. According, I shall leave the idea of discrimination at the individual level to one side.

If instead we think simply about the interests of the future children who might be selected on the grounds of their sex, if parents do have particular ideas about girls or boys, then when they have either a boy or a girl *without* sex selection, they are very likely in any event to raise a child according to these ideas, at least to some extent. If the child they happen to have is not seriously harmed by these presumptions — and it seems inherently unlikely that it would be harmed — then we can also say that sex selection itself would not risk serious harm to another child selected according to its sex.

A very different kind of reason for sex selection from that of 'family balancing' may be where, say, a prospective father had a troubled relationship with his own father and worries about patterns repeating themselves if he has a son. In his mind this could be a very serious reason to want to select a girl, though here it might be said that the solution lies in counselling for this man. This example is rather different in that here the welfare of any future child may be thought potentially to be an issue if sex selection is *not* permitted. But unless a prospective father was abused by his own father and fears doing the same in relation to his own son, then the welfare of any future son is unlikely seriously to be in issue in a sense that points strongly in favour of sex selection. At the same time, here perhaps the father's interests in a potentially less-troubled parent-child relationship could in some ways be seen as those that could justify or at least explain the desire for sex selection.

Clearly, we can think of other examples of possible parental reasons. In general, however, some people will always dispute that parents could have a strong reason to choose the sex of their child, including where they want to add either a boy or a girl to a family in which there is only a child (or children) of the opposite sex. Others will think there may well be quite strong reasons in at least some cases. Whatever the reason for the selection, it seems implausible that the practice (particularly in itself, rather than the expectations consequent on it) would result in harm, especially of a serious kind, to children. Of course, since sex selection is not currently legal, some may not be convinced by this statement because we have not had the opportunity to test it.

Indeed, turning to some of the objections to sex selection raised by respondents to the HFEA consultation on the question of harm, the now-familiar concern about effects on the parent-child relationship and the idea that one should not be able to determine too much about one's future child was a major concern in the responses. For instance, one concern that was expressed was about one's relationship to the 'outcome' if one actually chose the sex of one's child, since 'hopes' would be replaced by 'expectations'[62]:

> In particular, where the outcome that is wished for is the creation of another human being, respect for the future child's value as an individual precludes the exercise of control by parents over the kind of child it is to be, including over its sex.

In some ways this worry relates to concerns I identified in the previous chapter in the discussion of purely aesthetic or other relatively trivial choices. For instance, I referred to Onora O'Neill's concerns about the appropriate extent of reproductive autonomy, though I questioned whether her term 'self-expression' was really what was entailed in making choices between embryos. Rather, I suggested that varying degrees of (parental) self-determination were at stake, depending on the significance of the feature that is the subject of testing and selection (for example, serious impairment versus eye colour). In relation to the idea of self-determination, although I noted Buchanan *et al's* suggestion that the appropriate moral scope to 'determine' others is much less than the scope to 'determine' ourselves, in the context of genetic selection, we are (currently) determining *who* will exist — here, boy or girl — rather than *what they will be like*. Determining the latter in fact happens after birth and, ironically, gives people much less cause for concern. In the previous chapter I also touched on the worry about 'commodification' that often arises in this context. It is not clear to what extent this latter is a concern with values rather than with harm, but the discussion earlier suggested that ultimately worries about harm to future children from genetic selection (itself at least) are really very speculative.

So far, then, there appear to be no strong reasons to say that sex selection should not be permissible, at least if an important criterion is the welfare of the future child. (However, in due course I again refer to the important question of the possible harms to future children associated with multiple births as a result of IVF.) I have also suggested that there may sometimes be legitimate parental reasons for the choice. Let us think now about the claims of the embryo (or fetus).

## B  The Claims of the Embryo and the Processes in IVF and PGD

I have suggested that sometimes parents may have a strong reason for wishing to select the sex of their child. In earlier chapters I have also suggested that, on a

---

[62] HFEA, above n 56, para 95. 'In particular, where the outcome that is wished for is the creation of another human being, respect for the future child's value as an individual precludes the exercise of control by parents over the kind of child it is to be, including over its sex.'

gradualist approach to the moral status of the fetus, legitimately strong parental reasons can justify fetal demise. Despite this, personally I would not feel comfortable with termination on the grounds of fetal sex, including relatively early on. This is because I tend to doubt that a parental desire for a child of one sex rather than another could be a sufficiently serious reason to terminate an already-established pregnancy (notwithstanding that in all pregnancies there is approximately a one-in-five chance of miscarriage). However, there could be legitimate cases. For instance, there may be women from certain ethnic minorities who are pregnant with a female fetus and who are subject to such family and cultural pressure that their mental or physical health is at risk. In such a case, section 1(1)(a) of the Abortion Act 1967 (as amended by the HFE Act 1990) may be called into play.[63] Generally, apart from the case in which a woman from an ethnic minority is under extreme pressure, morally speaking we may want to reflect not just on prospective parents' reasons for not wanting a child of a given sex, but also on the degree of their responsibility for the relevant pregnancy. What about the not-yet-implanted embryo, whose moral status is somewhat lower, though not non-existent?

As in the previous chapter, we can think about three different scenarios: IVF for the purposes of using PGD solely to select the sex of a child; IVF where needed for reasons of fertility, with sex selection by PGD added on; and IVF and PGD for a serious genetic condition (not sex-linked, since here sex selection is already entailed), with sex selection for 'social' reasons added on. Given the public policy position in the United Kingdom that the embryo should be respected, would selection in these cases be 'respectful' of it? Alternatively, simply ethically speaking, would this be the case? Recall here that I suggested in Chapter 5 that where people do not grant full moral status to the embryo and where they may also think that it has a lower moral status than the fetus, they may nevertheless want to attribute some value to it that may be captured by use of the term 'respect', in recognition of its huge potential. For instance, on the gradualist approach of which I am in favour, I feel this way. Let us look briefly at these three scenarios.

The first scenario entails IVF and PGD solely for sex selection. Since approximately fifty per cent of embryos are likely to be of a particular sex then, assuming there are a reasonable number of embryos from an IVF cycle, there will be a roughly even chance that a couple will be able to choose one or more embryos of the 'right' sex with good live-birth potential. So the choices facing them may well be less limited and therefore less pressured than those facing parents who want to select for a particular genetic trait, as discussed in Chapter 5. Overall they may well have a good chance (subject to the variables necessarily inhering in any given couple's IVF attempt) of the live birth of a child of the 'right' sex. This means that, of the embryos tested for sex, one or more may end

---

[63] See discussion of this section in Ch 2.

up as a child, so that not all the embryos will be wasted. That said, it is always possible that the best-quality embryos will not be of the desired sex and at this point the prospective parents may well feel very pressured indeed, given the choice between discard of all their embryos or selection for transfer of one or more of the 'undesired' sex. If they choose an embryo of the 'right' sex but of lesser quality in the hopes that it will implant, it will be hard for them not to be conscious of the fact that they are, in effect, discarding those with greater potential for life. This realisation will be reinforced if the chosen embryo (or embryos) does not in fact implant or miscarries. On the question of the creation of excess embryos, we might also recall that, after PGD, any not selected will be unlikely to freeze and therefore have a future chance at transfer (if the couple is unsuccessful in their first attempt or if another child were desired).

Whether one thinks that the claims of the embryo make IVF and PGD solely for sex selection impermissible may depend on how concerned one is about embryo discard. Clearly, this was an issue of concern to some respondents to the HFEA's consultation.[64] As with all aspects of selective reproduction, including that against disability, I think it makes sense to weigh the claims, particularly of the discarded embryos, against the strength of possible parental reasons for selection. This allows scope for the potential legitimacy of these reasons. In saying this, I recognise that some will think that no parental reasons for sex selection will ever be strong enough. On a gradualist approach, however, particularly when we are concerned with an embryo that only has a potential (of a varying degree) to implant, then on occasion parental reasons may appear sufficiently strong.

What about the scenario when IVF is already needed? Here excess embryos already have to be created. Further, given their fertility problems, prospective parents may feel that much more pressured to select the best-quality embryos. If these happen to be of the right sex, things will be easier for them; if not, then given that their primary aim will be to have a child, they are very likely just to select the embryo(s) with the best live-birth potential. Indeed, most probably they would be considering the idea of sex selection as an addition 'if possible'. Overall, the point in this case is that they already need IVF and so there is a good chance that they will be creating excess embryos. In this case, if we think that IVF is justifiable (as I do) then so, at least from the point of view of our moral concerns about embryos, will be sex selection. There is a caveat here, however, which relates to the point that any embryos tested will be unlikely to freeze and so have a chance at transfer in the future (again, if the couple is unsuccessful in their first attempt or if they desire another child). That said, as noted before, the implantation-potential of frozen embryos is lower than that of 'fresh' ones.

Lastly, if a couple were using IVF and PGD for a serious genetic condition, their choices would be likely to be strongly governed by the desire to avoid

---

[64] HFEA, above n 56, para 74. As the report notes, for some this makes PGD for any reason unacceptable. See also paras 92, 93.

embryos with the relevant condition. If this leaves them with one or more embryo of their chosen sex, they will be particularly fortunate. If it does not, it is highly unlikely that they would choose not to implant any embryos, given their primary concern to have a child without a serious genetic condition. Once again, excess embryos will be created but this will be for the primary purpose, which I have suggested is highly defensible, of avoiding a serious genetic condition in the future child. Although the embryos tested will be unlikely to freeze if not chosen, they already have to be biopsied for the purposes of the original PGD. Further, there are also not likely to be many embryos that are both free from the genetic condition and of good quality (in terms of live-birth potential). In any given cycle at most two could be implanted according to current HFEA policy (if the woman is under 40).[65] (But note that this policy may be revised in the light of concerns about further reducing the incidence of multiple births, as first discussed in Chapter 5.) In the unlikely event that there is a choice of more than two that are free of the genetic condition (for instance, where two are male and two are female) then, from the point of view of the embryos, it does not matter which comes to exist (assuming that the interests of the embryo, metaphorically understood since it lacks sentience, are not very strong at this point). Here, then, the outcome for the embryos is really no different than if sex selection were not conducted.

As in the previous chapter, then, when I discussed selection for purely aesthetic features, at least from the point of view of concern for the embryo, the first scenario has the potential to be morally problematic, the second quite a bit less so, whilst the third is not morally problematic. In the first two cases, however, arguably the moral balance will turn on the parents' possible reasons for sex selection (given that harm to the future child from the genetic selection seems too speculative to be of serious concern) and here, compared with selection for purely aesthetic features, it may be that parents sometimes have quite strong reasons.

### C  The Views of Clinicians, Scientists and Those With Impairments

As before, the clinicians and other staff involved in PGD are likely to have moral views about the legitimacy of sex selection. Some may think this a justifiable wish of parents; one clinic that responded to the HFEA's consultation indeed indicated this, at least for reasons of 'family balancing'.[66] Other staff may disagree with the idea of this practice. Overall, this may be a case where, if the practice were legalised, conscientious objection should be allowed.

---

[65] HFEA Press Release 'HFEA Reduces Maximum Number of Embryos Transferred in Single IVF treatment from Three to Two' 8 August 2001 <http://www.hfea.gov.uk/en/959.html> accessed 15 October 2007. The HFEA's commitment to reducing the number of multiple births has been strengthened in its *Code of Practice — Sixth Edition*, which states (in para 8.20) that 'centres are expected to ensure that' only two embryos are implanted in women under 40 and three in women over 40.

[66] HFEA, above n 56, para 82.

In Chapters 1 and 5 I also touched on the interests of people with impairments in genetic selection practices. Apart from referring to those discussions here, I note that one response to the HFEA consultation suggested that allowing people to engage in sex selection would encourage them to think lightly of selection against disability; if valid, this point is likely to apply to any selection that is not against disability.[67] This is a striking concern, though given what is entailed in sex selection by PGD it also seems unlikely that anyone would really embark on this process who did not have very strong desires and reasons for wanting to do so.

Generally, what we have seen is that where a couple would have strong reasons for wanting to select the sex of their child, the case may be morally justifiable; where they do not, this is less likely to be so although, as just noted, it is very unlikely that they would engage in IVF and PGD in the absence of such reasons. So, should sex selection be legalised?

## D  The Views of the HFEA and Government: Is Legal Prohibition Justified?

I now turn to consider the views of the HFEA and, more briefly, those of the government in its review of the HFE Act 1990. As noted earlier, this is an opportunity to reflect on a given policy analysis and its compatibility, in particular, with Article 8 of the ECHR. At the same time, it is an occasion further to consider the question of society's right to proscribe certain selection practices, a suitable final topic for this book.

One solution to the question of whether to legalise sex selection would be to allow the practice in cases where prospective parents have strong reasons. However, judging people's reasons is in reality very difficult. So, although the absence of strong reasons is likely to make the case less morally justifiable, most likely the question would be whether or not to legalise it in *all* cases. Indeed, the HFEA itself suggests that in its view sometimes sex selection will be for good reason but that distinguishing between cases on the basis of parental motives is 'not possible or desirable'.[68] This brings us back to the issues of liberty, harm and democracy first discussed in the previous chapter. In what follows, I focus on the HFEA's conclusions and those parts of its report related to these.

Towards the end of its report, which surveys the various types of evidence emerging from the consultation process, the HFEA observes[69]:

> The main argument against prohibiting sex selection for non-medical reasons is that it concerns that most intimate aspect of family life, the decision to have children. This is an

---

[67] *Ibid* para 77.
[68] *Ibid* para 137. Some respondents also thought it would be hard to 'police' sex selection for family balancing, particularly where step-children or adopted children are present in a family: para 94.
[69] *Ibid* para 132. The evidence included a 'Scientific and Technical Literature Review', a 'Social and Ethical Literature Review', 'Qualitative Research Findings' and 'Quantitative Research Findings', all of which can be found in the appendices to the report.

area of private life in which people are generally best left to make their own choices and in which the state should intervene only to prevent the occurrence of serious harms, and only where this intervention is non-intrusive and likely to be effective.

John Harris calls this the 'democratic presumption'.[70] In effect, here the HFEA is in fact recognising (though not necessarily agreeing with) the argument that sex selection falls within the arena of private and family life, so that interference with the practice would have to be justified. We have not had any legal cases establishing this. However, if sex selection were indeed held to fall within the parameters of the right to respect for private and family life protected by Article 8 of the ECHR, the question would then be whether the state could justify interfering with the right.[71] As we saw in Chapter 5, the relevant restrictions on this right include those that are 'necessary in a democratic society… for the protection of morals, or for the protection of the rights and freedoms of others'. Alternatively, a court could decide that sex selection does *not* in the first instance fall within the scope of Article 8, so that it did not have to justify interference or restrictions of any kind.

In its conclusion, the HFEA states[72]:

> In reaching a decision we have been particularly influenced by the considerations set out above relating to the possible effects of sex selection for non-medical reasons on the welfare of children born as a result, and by the quantitative strength of views from the representative sample polled by MORI and the force of opinions expressed by respondents to our consultation. These show that there is very wide-spread hostility to the use of sex selection for non-medical reasons. By itself this finding is not decisive; the fact that a proposed policy is widely held to be unacceptable does not show that it is wrong. But there would need to be substantial demonstrable benefits of such a policy if the state were to challenge the public consensus on this issue.

Here the HFEA suggests that a concern with harm to future children, coupled with the strength of opinion against the practice, has led it to decide in favour of a continued ban. Whilst the HFEA suggests that public opinion cannot demonstrate that a policy would be wrong, it suggests that there must be 'substantial demonstrable benefits' for the state to reject the public's opinion. Harris argues that this conclusion has 'emptied' his earlier so-called democratic presumption 'of

---

[70] J Harris 'No Sex Selection Please, We're British' (2005) 31 *JME* 286, 287.

[71] Article 8(1) reads: 'Everyone has the right to respect for his private and family life, his home and his correspondence'. If an applicant can show an interference with this right, then it falls to the state in question to try to justify this under Art 8(2): 'There shall be no interference by a public authority with this right except such as is in accordance with the law and is necessary in a democratic society in the interests of national security, public safety or the economic well-being of the country, for the prevention of crime and disorder, for the protection of morals, or for the protection of the rights and freedoms of others.'

[72] HFEA, above n 56, para 147.

content'.[73] I am not clear what Harris means by the 'democratic presumption', since in general this term appears to be used in a number of different ways.

I shall therefore look at the HFEA's two statements in more detail. As noted above, in the first passage quoted the HFEA has merely acknowledged the argument that sex selection might be deemed to fall within the realm of the right to private and family life, so that intervention with the practice would have to be justified. That is, it has not said that sex selection *does* in fact fall within the scope of this right. In this way, arguably this is one statement about the delineation and operation of freedoms in a democracy, but so too is its second set of statements from its conclusions. Turning to the latter, clearly it is correct that the majority of those who were asked or who responded to the consultation do not think that sex selection for non-medical reasons should be legalised. Here the HFEA effectively suggests that its decisions on policy should be in tune with the democratic will, unless strong benefits can be shown to justify rejection of that will. I do not have the scope here to engage in a detailed discussion of the formation of policy in a democracy. However, arguably it is *prima facie* correct that the state should take decisions on policy that reflect the views of the majority. (It is not immediately clear where the segment about 'demonstrable benefits' originates, and this clearly bothers Harris. Later, however, I suggest a legitimate interpretation of this point in conjunction with a discussion of the justification for interference with the Article 8 right.)

In sum, across the two passages the HFEA is referring to different mechanisms that determine the scope of freedoms in a democracy. Ultimately, since these are potentially conflicting mechanisms, the question will be how to reconcile these. In particular, is the democratic will compatible with the rights of the individual?

Turning to the HFEA and the way it makes decisions, the HFEA is of course a statutory body established under the HFE Act 1990, part of whose remit is to regulate, by means of policy formation, the area of assisted reproduction. This requires it to consult the public, interested professionals and other parties. Only a small percentage of those consulted will ever respond to a public consultation exercise. Likewise, the election of English governments does not reflect the view of all enfranchised adults, since a number do not bother to vote. So the problem that the respondents to the HFEA consultation processes do not constitute all or even a majority of the UK population is not unique. Typically only those with a particular interest or with strong views on the topic are likely to take the trouble to respond. But it is not clear that this problem could ever be overcome. All of this suggests that, if it is bound to make certain decisions in accordance with the public view on a matter, where it pays attention to that view the HFEA cannot really be criticised.

However, the HFEA would be deemed to be a public authority which means that, by virtue of section 6(1) of the Human Rights Act, it has a duty to act in

---

[73] Harris, above n 70, 287.

330  *Uses of Preimplantation Genetic Diagnosis*

ways compatible with Convention rights.[74] It would therefore be open to an interested party to challenge its policy on sex selection, mounting an argument (the one that the HFEA recognised above) that sex selection falls within the right to respect for private and family life. Is this argument plausible?

### i  Analysis under Article 8(1) of the ECHR

It has been suggested that Article 8 covers self-determination in a general way.[75] However, autonomy and privacy are not necessarily the same and the relationship between them has been the subject of considerable debate.[76] On one view, for instance, although not a proxy for autonomy, privacy might be a subset of it.[77] On another view, however, a major flaw in work on privacy has been the notion that privacy and autonomy are synonymous concepts; rather, privacy should not be confused with, and indeed is unrelated to, autonomy.[78] The diversity of interpretations has been noted by David Feldman, who concludes that the debate centres around the question of whether control over information on the one hand or notions of personal autonomy, dignity or moral integrity central to liberalism on the other lie at its heart.[79] In connection with the ECHR in particular, Feldman has observed[80]:

> [T]he idea of private life must not stretch to the point at which it subsumes other autonomy-related rights and loses its rationale. The interest in private life… is *related to*, but is not the *same as*, autonomy, moral integrity, dignity, or intimacy…

In *Pretty v United Kingdom* (which concerned whether the illegality of assisted suicide in the United Kingdom was compatible with the ECHR) the European Court of Human Rights (ECtHR) observed[81]:

> Though no previous case has established any right to self-determination as being contained in Article 8 of the Convention, the Court considers that the notion of personal autonomy is an important principle underlying the interpretation of its guarantees.

---

[74]  Section 6(3) says that '"public authority" includes… (b) any person certain of whose functions are functions of a public nature'.

[75]  H Nys 'Physician Involvement in a Patient's Death' (1999) 7 *Med L Rev* 209, 214.

[76]  I discuss this in more detail in R Scott, *Rights, Duties and the Body: Law and Ethics of the Maternal-Fetal Conflict* (Oxford: Hart Publishing, 2002) Ch 4.

[77]  T Halper 'Privacy and Autonomy: from Warren and Brandeis to *Roe* and *Cruzan*' (1996) 21 *J of Med and Phil* 124, 133.

[78]  WA Parent 'Recent Work on the Concept of Privacy' (1983) 20 *Am Phil Q* 341, 345.

[79]  D Feldman 'The Developing Scope of Article 8 of the European Convention on Human Rights' [1997] 3 *EHRLR* 265, 265–6. See also Parent, above n 78, who identifies no fewer than five interpretations of privacy, each with a band of supporters slightly varying the themes within these interpretations.

[80]  Feldman, above n 79, 273 (my emphasis).

[81]  (1998) 26 EHRR 241, para 32.

In this way, the Court appears to recognise that although self-determination is not the same as privacy, nevertheless the idea of self-determination or personal autonomy may be important to the interpretation of Convention rights, including that in Article 8.

Turning now to some of the ECtHR's interpretations of the right to respect for private and family life, the Court has generally avoided the need to define a core meaning of 'private life'. Instead, it has interpreted this in various ways,[82] for instance: as including the right to 'establish and develop relationships with other human beings especially in the emotional field, for the development and fulfilment of one's own personality'[83]; as including sexual orientation and activity, which concern 'an intimate aspect of private life'[84]; and as protecting a person's 'physical and moral integrity'.[85] Overall, it has been held that the essential purpose of the article is to protect the individual from arbitrary action by public

---

[82] D Feldman 'Privacy-related Rights and their Social Value' in P Birks (ed), *Privacy and Loyalty* (Oxford: OUP, 1997) 15–50, 41. In turn this is consistent with the notion that the Convention is a 'living instrument' the interpretation of which requires that the notion of 'private life' will create new rights as social conditions require it: *Tyrer v United Kingdom* (1978) 2 EHRR 1, para 31. Indeed, the process of trying to produce an 'exhaustive list' does not, as E Barendt observes, look 'very sensible': E Barendt 'Privacy as a Constitutional Right and Value' in Birks, *ibid* 1–14, 13.

[83] Appl No 6825/74, 5 DR 86. The applicant wished to keep a dog, which certain regulations prohibited. See also *Niemietz v Germany* (1992) 16 EHRR 97, para 29, regarding the first part of this definition. The applicant's law offices were searched by German police looking for information about a third party who was the subject of a criminal investigation. The Court held it 'would be too restrictive to limit the notion to "an inner circle" in which the individual may live his own personal life as he chooses and to exclude therefrom entirely the outside world' (at para 29). For a defence of Art 8 based on the notion of personality, see LG Loucaides 'Personality and Privacy under the European Convention on Human Rights' (1990) 61 *BYBIL* 175, who argues that freedom can only be effective if the individual can be self-defining and self-determining, hence that the relationship between the individual and the state or society must not be conceived in abstract terms but in a way which takes account of the personal qualities of the individual. This conception, it is argued, has been influential in the interpretation of the Convention (at 177).

[84] *Laskey, Jaggard and Brown v United Kingdom* (1997) 24 EHRR 39, para 36. The applicants appealed against their conviction in the UK for various offences including assault and wounding relating to sado-masochistic activities over a ten-year period, which were filmed on video-tape, on the basis that this was a violation of Art 8. The Court found the convictions did not unjustifiably interfere with their private life.

[85] *Costello-Roberts v United Kingdom* (1995) 19 EHRR 112 (which concerned an unsuccessful application in respect of corporal punishment at a private school) para 35, citing *X and Y v Netherlands* (1986) 8 EHRR 235 (which concerned an application on behalf of a mentally handicapped young woman of 16 who had been raped at a special-needs home and the fact that the Netherlands' criminal law only recognised a complaint if made by the victim herself, of which she was incapable).

authorities.[86] Most recently, in *Evans v United Kingdom*, the ECtHR held that 'the right to respect for the decision to become a parent in the genetic sense, also falls within the scope of Article 8'.[87]

Of the ECtHR's interpretations above, a case might at least be made that, if the right to respect for private life has been interpreted as including a right to 'establish and develop relationships with other human beings especially in the emotional field, for the development and fulfilment of one's own personality', and also to include 'the right to respect for the decision to become a parent in the genetic sense', then sex selection falls within private life. For instance, it could be argued that prospective parents have the right to try to select either a girl or a boy and thus to establish a relationship with one or the other. There is also the possibility that sex selection might be held to fall within the right to respect for family life. The ECtHR has found that 'the mutual enjoyment by parent and child of each other's company constitutes a fundamental element of family life'.[88] Perhaps an argument in favour of sex selection could be mounted that builds on this.

For present purposes, let us assume that the *prima facie* case is made out that sex selection falls within the right to respect for private and family life under Article 8(1). The issue would then turn on whether the HFEA (within the domestic context) or the government (should a case proceed to Strasbourg) had justifiably interfered with the right and so, in effect, with whether a ban on the practice is 'in accordance with the law' and is 'necessary… for the protection of morals, or for the protection of the rights and freedoms of others', according to Article 8(2).

### ii   Analysis under Article 8(2) of the ECHR

I shall first outline the way the justifiability of an interference with the right to respect for private and family life would be assessed. I shall then look at the HFEA's and government's reasons for proscribing sex selection, in order to try to evaluate whether the ban would survive a legal challenge. I will concentrate on the idea of a case reaching the Strasbourg court.

#### a   In accordance with law

To be in accordance with law, an interference with the right must occur by means of legal regulation.[89] It seems likely, given the licensing function granted to the

---

[86]  *Kroon v Netherlands* (1994) 19 EHRR 263.

[87]  *Evans v United Kingdom*, judgment of 10 April 2007, Appl No 6339/05, para 72. The case concerned a challenge to the consent provisions of the HFE Act 1990, specifically whether a man should be able to withdraw his consent to the continued storage of embryos created with his former partner when, as a result of treatment for cancer of her ovaries, she wished to use those embryos and had no other way of becoming a genetic mother. The ECtHR found no violation of Art 8 (or Arts 2 or 14).

[88]  *Ahmut v Netherlands* (1996) 24 EHRR 62.

[89]  *Halford v United Kingdom* (1997) 24 EHRR 423, which concerned office phone-tapping.

HFEA by the HFE Act, that its policy decision on sex selection by PGD would qualify as a form of legal regulation. The policy can also be accessed by the public and is certain.[90] (Clearly, if the government indeed amends the HFE Act to make the legal criteria for PGD explicit within the Act, and thereby puts the prohibition of sex selection on a statutory footing, this would also be in accordance with law.) Since it appears that this first criterion would currently be satisfied by the HFEA policy, I shall not further consider it.[91]

b   Legitimate aim

As noted earlier, the legitimate aims within Article 8(2) that are relevant to the prohibition of sex selection are 'the protection of morals, or… the protection of the rights and freedoms of others'. If challenged in the Strasbourg court, the United Kingdom would have to establish that a ban on sex selection was truly directed at promoting one or more of these aims. It appears that whether there is a 'legitimate aim' cannot be interpreted independently of the question of whether the means to achieve it are proportionate.[92] Further, the aims in Article 8(2) should be interpreted with reference to Article 18, which states: 'The restrictions permitted under this Convention to the said rights and freedoms shall not be applied for any purpose other than those for which they have been prescribed'. It should also be noted that the 'rights and freedoms of others' does not necessarily refer to the Convention rights held by others. Commenting on the wide range of acceptable reasons for restricting rights, John Wadham *et al* observe that '[i]t is not difficult for a country facing an allegation of a breach of human rights to find a reason relevant to any case'.[93]

c   Necessary in a democratic society

Lastly, the United Kingdom would have to establish that the interference was 'necessary in a democratic society', a test that hinges on the idea of proportionality. This term received considerable attention in *Handyside v United Kingdom*.[94]

---

[90]   Indeed, the rules of a professional body may also suffice if valid and publicly available: *Barthold v Germany* (1985) 7 EHRR 383.
[91]   Note, however, the discussion of the development of the concept of legality within domestic jurisprudence, and the potential differences between this and Strasbourg jurisprudence, discussed in J Wadham, H Mountfield, A Edmundson and C Gallagher, *Blackstone's Guide to the Human Rights Act 1998* 4th edn (London: Blackstone's, 2007) paras 2.77–2.88.
[92]   *A v Secretary for State for the Home Department* [2004] UKHL 56.
[93]   Wadham *et al*, above n 91, para 2.96.
[94]   (1976) 1 EHRR 737. This case concerned the English publication, for children, of the *Little Red School Book*, which contained a part on sex. The police seized the book and obtained a forfeiture order on the basis that the book was contrary to the Obscene Publications Act 1950. The applicant pleaded a violation of Art 10 (freedom of expression) whilst the government argued that the restriction was necessary for the 'protection of morals'. Accepting that the limitation was 'prescribed by law' the court had to consider whether it was proportionate and 'necessary in a democratic society'. In answer, with

334  *Uses of Preimplantation Genetic Diagnosis*

In this case the ECtHR observed that whilst 'necessary' is not the same as 'indispensable', nor is it as flexible as words such as 'ordinary', 'useful', 'reasonable' or 'desirable'.[95] Rather, 'necessity' must imply a 'pressing social need'. Here the court referred to the doctrine of the 'margin of appreciation', by which it allows states some leeway in the protection of Convention rights having regard to national traditions and conditions.[96] (As an international doctrine this does not have any place under the Human Rights Act, that is, within the domestic context.[97]) The court in *Handyside* reflected on the principles characterising a democratic society, identifying these as 'pluralism, tolerance and broadmindedness'.[98] This meant, for instance, that 'every 'formality', 'condition', 'restriction' or 'penalty' imposed in this sphere must be proportionate to the legitimate aim pursued'.[99] Further, in *Sunday Times v United Kingdom*, the court held that when the necessity doctrine is applied, exceptions to the right 'must be narrowly interpreted'.[100] The *Sunday Times* case in fact established a commonly used

reference to the doctrine of the margin of appreciation, the court noted that 'the domestic margin of appreciation... goes hand in hand with a European supervision' (at para 49). See also *Dudgeon v United Kingdom* (1981) 4 EHRR 149, in which the applicant alleged that Northern Ireland's criminalisation of all homosexual behaviour was a breach of Art 8. The Court agreed on the basis that the legislation 'by reason of its breadth and absolute character, is, quite apart from the severity of the possible penalties provided for, disproportionate to the [government's] aims' (at para 61). At para 53 the court said that 'a restriction on a Convention right cannot be regarded as "necessary in a democratic society" (two hallmarks of which are tolerance and broadmindedness) unless, amongst other things, it is proportionate to the legitimate aim pursued' (footnote omitted).

[95] Above n 94, para 48.

[96] In practice, this doctrine means that the court (or the Commission, when it existed) allows governments 'the benefit of the doubt'. L Doswald-Beck 'The Meaning of the "Right to Respect for Private Life" under the European Convention on Human Rights' (1983) 4 *HRLJ* 283, 307.

[97] Wadham *et al*, above n 91, para 2.165: 'The margin of appreciation is an international doctrine, based on the limitations of the international court. It has no place in domestic arrangements for protecting human rights and should not be used when the Convention is applied by the national courts.' This means that at the stage of a domestic challenge to the prohibition on sex selection, the English courts would find themselves looking more closely at issues that the Strasbourg court can in effect avoid by reference to local conditions. In so doing, they have to balance the interests of the individual with those of the community at large, consistent with the ECtHR's approach to these issues in earlier cases, eg, *Keegan v Ireland* (1994) 18 EHRR 342 and *Stjerna v Finland* (1994) 24 EHRR 194, as noted in Feldman, above n 82, 41.

[98] Above n 94, para 49. For application of these principles, see *Dudgeon*, the case concerned with the illegality of homosexuality in Northern Ireland, in which we have seen that the court noted that two 'hallmarks' of a democratic society are tolerance and broadmindedness (para 53). The issue of homosexuality obviously raises questions about majority and minority public opinion and central to democracy is the notion of protecting minorities against oppression by the majority, as noted by F G Jacobs and R CA White, *The European Convention on Human Rights* 2nd edn (Oxford: Clarendon, 1996) 33.

[99] Above n 94, para 49.

[100] (1979) 2 EHRR 245, para 59.

three-fold test, which asks first whether the interference corresponds to a 'pressing social need', whether it is 'proportionate to the legitimate aim pursued' and whether the reasons offered to justify the interference are 'relevant and sufficient'.

1   Pressing social need

The requirement for a pressing social need is a stringent one, entailing that a right can only be restricted proportionately, that the pressing social need must fit with the requirements of a democratic society identified in *Handyside* — 'pluralism, tolerance and broadmindedness' — and that the actual restriction rightly aims at the end in question and does not surpass what is 'strictly necessary' to achieve it.[101] The assessment of the pressing social need will attend closely to the importance of the right so that, for instance, interference with an intimate aspect of the right to private life will require very strong justification.[102]

2   Proportionate to the legitimate aim pursued

This is the most important part of the necessity test.[103] In *Soering v United Kingdom*, the ECtHR observed[104]: 'Inherent in the whole of the Convention is a search for the fair balance between the demands of the general interest of the community and the requirements of the protection of the individual's human rights'. As Wadham *et al* note, in this light '[t]he principle of proportionality is concerned with defining that "fair balance". It requires a reasonable relationship between the goal pursued and the means the state has chosen to achieve that goal'.[105] Factors of possible relevance to the question of proportionality include[106]: 'the extent to which the interference impairs the "very essence" of a right' (so that, for instance an interference with an intimate aspect of Article 8 requires particularly strong justification, whilst the ECtHR gives greater freedom to a state in assessing whether it has complied with its positive obligations under Article 8); 'whether a less restrictive alternative, yet equally effective, measure is available to the state to achieve the legitimate aim pursued' (which could, for instance, be relevant to the question of a policy operating in a blanket way); and 'whether there are any effective safeguards or legal controls over the measures in question' (including the sufficiency of compensation or legal remedies for those affected). Further, 'whilst Article 8 contains no explicit procedural requirements, the decision-making process leading to measures of interference must be fair and such as to afford due respect to the interests safeguarded by Article 8'.[107]

As can be seen, there is some conceptual overlap between the requirements inherent in a 'pressing social need' on the one hand and the idea of 'proportionate

---

[101]   Wadham *et al*, above n 91, paras 2.106–2.107.
[102]   *Ibid* para 2.108.
[103]   *Ibid* para 2.109.
[104]   (1989) 11 EHRR 439, para 89.
[105]   Wadham *et al*, above n 91, para 2.110.
[106]   *Ibid* para 2.113.
[107]   *McMichael v United Kingdom* (1995) 20 EHRR 205.

to the legitimate aim pursued' on the other. This is not surprising given that the idea of proportionality is relevant to the whole Convention. (I do not have the scope specifically to consider the idea of proportionality within the domestic context.)

### 3  Relevant and sufficient reasons

Finally, the ECtHR would have to determine whether the United Kingdom's reasons for interfering with the right to respect for private and family life are 'relevant and sufficient'.[108] This is an objective test that assesses the adequacy of the reasons, so that the Court would have regard to the evidence or the facts on the basis of which it was thought that sex selection threatened either the rights or freedoms of others or morals, so that there was a pressing social need to protect these.[109] Since the right to respect for private and family life is a particularly important right, the assessment would be strict.

### 4  Implications: justifiable interference?

So, if sex selection *were* held to fall within the right to respect for private and family life, restricting or proscribing it would have to be in accordance with law, have a legitimate aim and be necessary in a democratic society. We have seen that the latter requires a 'pressing social need', that the restriction is 'proportionate to the legitimate aim pursued' and that there are 'relevant and sufficient reasons'. Does the HFEA's reasoning supporting a continued ban suggest that these conditions would be fulfilled? I now turn to consider the points to which the HFEA apparently gave particular attention in forming its conclusions and whether these would survive legal challenge in the event that the ECtHR did decide that sex selection by PGD falls within the first part of Article 8. As will be seen in due course, it appears that the government leaned on the HFEA's reasoning in its review of the HFE Act; this suggests that the HFEA's policy analysis would become relevant to a review by the Strasbourg court.

In the first paragraph subsequent to its recognition of the possibility that sex selection might fall within the right to respect for private and family life, the HFEA refers to 'risk to health'.[110] It is not clear what the HFEA has in mind here, but it may be implicitly referring to the fact that it is not yet known whether there are any long-term risks to the child from PGD. If it is thought that we should adopt a precautionary approach to the issue of such risks, since this attends to the rights and freedoms of others this could be a contender for a legitimate aim in the interference with the right to respect for private and family life. The HFEA discusses this question briefly in earlier parts of its report.[111] I first identified this issue in the discussion of purely aesthetic or other relatively trivial choices in the

---

[108] *Jersild v Denmark* (1995) 19 EHRR 1.
[109] As implied in Wadham *et al*, above n 91, para 2.116.
[110] HFEA, above n 56, para 133.
[111] *Ibid* para 133, discussed also at paras 100, 102 and 121.

previous chapter. The report also refers at this point to 'other social and moral considerations' and observes that '[m]any of these were set out at length in the consultation document', though some were also put forward by respondents.[112] Here another legitimate aim is potentially at stake, though not fleshed out, namely the protection of morals and I return to this below. The reference to 'other social... considerations' is somewhat vague and it is not clear whether the 'rights and freedoms of others' could be implicated here. Two paragraphs later the report refers to the suggestion that selection for sex alone could be discriminatory or that selection against serious genetic conditions could be 'eugenic'.[113] Discrimination could bring the 'rights and freedoms of others' into play, whilst a reliance on the notion of 'eugenics' would be question-begging and would require further analysis. In fact, the HFEA dismisses the idea of eugenics (in relation to selection against disability), but states that 'objections to sex selection on the grounds of discrimination raise serious issues'.[114] This seems wise given the unhelpful nature (as discussed in Chapter 1) of arguments based on the notion of eugenics. However, the HFEA does not develop the discrimination point. Instead, the report moves on to observe (as noted earlier) that sometimes parents may have good reason for sex selection but that judging reasons in practice would be problematic.[115] This may be intended as a rebuttal to the concern about discrimination. The report then observes a concern about the development of a sex imbalance, but notes that although it found 'little relevant evidence about the effect of sex selection in countries like the UK... what evidence there is does not suggest that such an imbalance would result'.[116] However, it suggests that this concern would give good reason to monitor sex selection if it were legalised, so that the practice could be prohibited or limited if an imbalance resulted.[117] This is in fact consistent with a suggestion by John Harris.[118] Arguably, the prevention of a sex imbalance could be a further legitimate aim. However, given the current indications that a sex imbalance would *not* in fact result and in the absence of a trial period indicating the contrary the question, perhaps, is whether there is now a pressing social need to prevent a sex imbalance, one that is proportionate to the legitimate aim to ban the practice.

The HFEA then highlights the arguments it has found 'most persuasive': in addition to the 'health risks', it cites concerns about the 'welfare of families and children' and refers here to respondents' 'alarm' about psychological damage to children selected for their 'sex alone'.[119] This is strongly criticised by John Harris

---

[112] *Ibid* para 133.
[113] *Ibid* para 135.
[114] *Ibid* para 136.
[115] *Ibid* para 137.
[116] *Ibid* para 138.
[117] *Ibid*.
[118] Harris, above n 70, 288.
[119] HFEA, above n 56, para 139, for all points within my paragraph.

who points out, rightly, that one cannot really be selected for one's sex alone.[120] The HFEA also refers to suggestions that children selected for sex might be treated prejudicially or 'moulded' to fit parents' expectations. As noted in my earlier discussion, whether or not selected (in part) for their sex, children may be subject to parents' expectations, including about their sex, so it is doubtful that this is a valid concern. The HFEA then records the apprehension that children *not* selected for sex might be 'neglected' compared with other children. I think this takes a strikingly pessimistic view of human nature. The final concern observed at this point relates to the risk of misdiagnosis with sperm sorting. Although discussion of this technique is beyond my scope, it is perhaps worth noting that here the worry focuses on the potential suffering of a child as the result of 'parents' frustrated expectations'.[121] Perhaps counselling could address this concern where necessary. It is also worth recalling Stephen Wilkinson's point (noted in Chapter 5) that arguably the parental virtue that is required following any kind of selection is that of acceptance; Wilkinson also notes that it is possible for parents not unconditionally to love and accept their child whether or not they are using techniques of sex (or other) selection.[122] In general, although the concerns noted in this paragraph would be purporting to attend to the rights and freedoms of others, it seems doubtful that they are really legitimate aims, given their highly speculative basis.

At this point, the HFEA report turns to observe the 'positive benefit' that could result from allowing sex selection, such as reducing the number of '"unwanted" children or aborted fetuses, the effects of parental disappointment or the threat to the welfare of children in large families where the parents keep trying to conceive a child of a particular sex naturally'.[123] (In this way, in fact, the HFEA seems implicitly to acknowledge Wilkinson's point that parents may or may not accept their children regardless of whether they have undertaken any kind of selective reproduction.) These are all significant benefits that would appear to weigh strongly against the very speculative harms and risks to which the report has just given attention. More particularly, such benefits could be thought to undermine the idea that there is a pressing social need to ban sex selection that is

---

[120] Harris 'Sex Selection and Regulated Hatred' (2005) 31 *JME* 291, 293. 'This is the point which derives from Kantian ethics, that individuals must be treated as ends in themselves and not as *mere* means. However, it is very difficult to find evidence or even persuasive anecdotes that if people are treated as means they are treated as *mere* means or even *exclusively* as means. It is very unlikely that children selected for their sex would be selected *solely* for their sex. Indeed it is difficult to understand what that might mean.' Emphases in original.

[121] HFEA, above n 56, para 139.

[122] Wilkinson 'Parental Duties and Virtues' in above n 1. With regard to the idea of unconditional love, Wilkinson accepts a limited version of this principle, such that '*parental love ought not to be withheld or withdrawn on trivial or morally irrelevant grounds*' (*ibid,* emphasis in original).

[123] HFEA, above n 56, para 140.

proportionate to the legitimate aim, namely the aim of guarding against highly speculative infringements of the rights and freedoms of others. The report then acknowledges that many of the concerns cannot be answered unless sex selection is tried (which, in itself, tends to undermine the case for a pressing social need) and states: 'Whilst it is not clear that the practice of sex selection would always be incompatible with the welfare of the child born as a result there is *clearly ample reason* to be cautious'.[124] On what we have seen so far, given the speculative nature of the harms on the one hand and the rather less speculative nature of the possible benefits on the other, I think it is fair to say that the latter part of this statement cannot be justified. One might wonder, at this point, if the reasons for a ban are relevant, but more particularly sufficient.

It is worth thinking a bit further here about the HFEA's reference to possible benefits and the question of whether there is a pressing social need to ban sex selection. As noted above, the HFEA has in fact identified a number of possible benefits flowing from sex selection, such as reduced numbers of abortions. (This is an interesting benefit to have observed when, in fact, abortion on the grounds of fetal sex is not, by itself, legal. The thought here must be that section 1(1)(a) of the Abortion Act is sometimes being used for this purpose, on the basis that there is a risk to the pregnant woman's physical or mental health that is greater than if the pregnancy were terminated.) In the light of these positive benefits, it would be important to think very carefully about whether there is a pressing social need to proscribe sex selection by PGD. Here, ideally, it may be relevant to consider the extent of abortions that are really for sex selection on the one hand as opposed to the extent to which the opportunity for sex selection by PGD may be taken up by couples. However, it is not clear how either of these, particularly the former, could be determined.

The next five paragraphs of the report address the risks in sperm-sorting, and here the HFEA notes that the issue may be revisited if one of the methods proves safe,[125] but there is no further mention of PGD. The HFEA then arrives at its conclusion, cited in full above.[126] As a reminder, here the HFEA observes that it has been particularly influenced by the 'considerations... relating to the possible effects of sex selection for non-medical reasons on the welfare of children born as a result, and by the quantitative strength of views from the representative sample... and the force of opinions expressed by respondents' which show 'very wide-spread hostility' to the practice. It is at this juncture that the HFEA states that although these factors cannot be decisive, there are insufficient 'demonstrable benefits' for the 'state... to challenge the public consensus'. As we have seen so far, overall it is not clear that, on this reasoning, the HFEA would be able to establish that interfering with a *prima facie* right to sex selection under Article 8 would be necessary in a democratic society, in the sense that it is not clear that it has

---

[124] *Ibid* para 141 (my emphasis).
[125] *Ibid* para 143.
[126] *Ibid* para 147.

established a legitimate aim, at least in its attention to the rights and freedom of others, and that the interference is necessary (entailing a pressing social need, that the restriction is proportionate to the legitimate aim pursued and that there are relevant and sufficient reasons).

In general, it is hard to determine whether the risk of psychological or physical harm (to the future child from sperm-sorting or PGD) or whether the various moral objections put forward by respondents are more prominent in these conclusions and the paragraphs leading to them. I have suggested that the concerns about psychological harms seem particularly speculative. If there is a real worry about physical harm to the future child from PGD then, and importantly, in fact this should make us think about the extent to which PGD for any reason, medical or non-medical, is justifiable. I discussed this in Chapter 5. Of course, since the risk is unknown, so is the degree of harm. But if the harm were considerable, we would have to think about the extent to which PGD to avoid the birth of someone with a life worth living, which is typically really in *parents'* possible interests (except on a non-person-affecting approach) is justifiable. Indeed, if the harm were relatively severe, it might be that PGD could only be justified to avoid the birth of someone who would be likely to have a wrongful life, one he did not think worth living. At this stage, since the oldest PGD child is now about 17[127] and no harm has been detected, it seems unlikely that the risk of physical harm should be a major concern. If this is the case, the only harms in the context of sex selection would remain these highly speculative ones of a psychological nature. In any event, on the HFEA's reasoning at least, these should be weighed against the benefits that might result (such as a reduced number of abortions). Further, I have suggested that this question is itself relevant to the assessment of whether there is a pressing social need proportionate to the legitimate aim.

Arguably, these speculative harms should also be weighed against the strength of parents' possible reasons for wanting to select the sex of their child. Indeed, this would be to give closer attention to the question, in particular, of whether the prohibition of sex selection is proportionate to the legitimate aim pursued. In fact, the HFEA seems to have underplayed parents' interests in its review. In a sense, this might be thought to be compatible with the way the HFEA has acknowledged the possible *prima facie* position that sex selection is part of the right to private and family life, but concentrated on alleged harms to others and other moral objections. In other words, it has focused on the issue of interference with the right to private and family life and, in particular, the possible grounds for such interference, rather than also on the prior question of whether the Article 8 right might indeed include the practice of sex selection by PGD. However, in doing so

---

[127] PGD was first conducted in about 1990 in the US. See Y Verlinsky, J Cohen, S Munne, L Gianaroli, JL Simpson, AP Ferraretti and A Kuliev 'Over a Decade of Experience with Preimplantation Genetic Diagnosis: A Multicenter Report' (2004) 82/2 *Fertility and Sterility* 292.

arguably it has failed sufficiently to consider whether, or at least to explain why, the interference (with a supposed *prima facie* right) is in fact *justifiable*. This is unfortunate because, given the importance of the Article 8 right, the proportionality of the interference would be stringently assessed.

As the HFEA itself acknowledges, we cannot know what the result will be unless we legalise the practice of sex selection, at which point we can also monitor it.[128] As noted before, this might be thought to undermine the case for a pressing social need. Instead of a 'trial run', however, the HFEA has opted for the precautionary principle of a continued ban. The HFEA could instead have adopted the same approach that it has taken in relation to 'saviour siblings'. (This does not imply that the moral case for selecting for sex is as strong as selecting for a saviour sibling.) As we know from the *Quintavalle* case discussed in Chapters 4 and 5, it is now legal to select an embryo that would be a tissue match for an affected sibling and not only where the embryo is itself at risk of becoming an affected child.[129] In the context of saviour siblings the HFEA has suggested that the ongoing welfare of children selected in this way be monitored. This also accords with the HGC's recommendations on the point.[130] This policy shows that the HFEA is currently prepared to expose saviour siblings to the risk of harm from PGD where there can be no possible benefit to them from the use of that technique (since existence is not a benefit in itself at the start of life). The only difference I can see here is that, as noted above, the moral case for sex selection could presumably never be as great as that for selection for a child whose cord blood could provide a life-saving cure to an affected brother or sister, which could indeed be relevant to an assessment under Article 8(2).

A very significant possible harm to the future child that could result from sex selection by PGD and IVF, to which the HFEA does not in fact refer in its report, relates to the rate of multiple births associated with IVF. I drew attention to the importance and potential relevance of this issue to discussions of selection by PGD in the previous chapter. There I suggested that there would be a particularly strong case for single embryo transfer where the reason for selection was *not* to avoid a serious genetic condition and where a couple did not already 'need' IVF to have a child and was 'adding in' selection on the basis of relatively trivial features. However, I also acknowledged that 'policing' when a couple did and did not need IVF would be difficult, a point we have already encountered in this chapter. For present purposes I would emphasise again that the severity of the possible harms to a child when part of a multiple pregnancy is an issue of potentially very great significance in this context that could count in favour of a continued ban on sex selection by PGD.

As we know, Article 8 allows scope for interference with the right to respect for private and family life, not just on the grounds of harm to others, but also on the

---

[128] HFEA, above n 56, para 138.
[129] [2003] EWCA Civ 667 (CA); [2005] 2 All ER 555 (HL).
[130] HGC, *Making Babies: Reproductive Decisions and Genetic Technologies* (2006) para 4.22.

grounds of morals (in addition to other irrelevant grounds). I would now like to give some attention to the idea of morals as a possible legitimate aim. If a case were to proceed to the ECtHR, we might recall the case of *Vo v France*, discussed in Chapter 2.[131] We saw that a significant feature of the dissenting judgments in *Vo* is the revelation that protection of the fetus (and embryo) in the context of prenatal diagnosis, cloning and genetic engineering is of current concern to members of the ECtHR. Given the potential for embryo discard inherent in the practice of sex selection by PGD, this could suggest that a UK ban would not be seen as inconsistent with Article 8, though whether this would constitute a majority view of the Court is another question. In determining whether the ban fulfils a pressing social need, in relation to an acutely moral issue such as embryo discard the Court would be likely to invoke the margin of appreciation, giving leeway to the United Kingdom in its policy and legal approach to the protection of the embryo. Indeed, in *Evans v United Kingdom*, the Court recently observed[132]:

> [S]ince the use of IVF treatment gives rise to sensitive moral and ethical issues against a background of fast-moving medical and scientific developments, and since the questions raised by the case touch on areas where there is no clear common ground amongst the Member States, the Court considers that the margin of appreciation to be afforded to the respondent State must be a wide one... The Grand Chamber, like the Chamber, considers that the above margin must in principle extend both to the State's decision whether or not to enact legislation governing the use of IVF treatment and, once having intervened, to the detailed rules it lays down in order to achieve a balance between the competing public and private interests.

In fact, it is worth noting here that the United Kingdom has one of the most liberal approaches in all of Europe to the availability of PGD and the protection of the embryo.[133] This could be thought to reinforce the application of the margin of appreciation. The doctrine of the margin of appreciation may be a particularly useful tool when the protection of morals is invoked as a legitimate aim because otherwise it is not clear how one would assess whether such an aim attends to a pressing social need and is proportionate to the legitimate aim pursued.

---

[131] Judgment of 8 July 2004, Appl No 53924/00.
[132] Above n 87, paras 81 and 82, with regard to an analysis of the application of Art 8.
[133] This point emerged particularly strongly in a paper by Judge Christian Byk, Court of Appeal, Paris and Secretary General, International Association of Law, Ethics and Science, entitled 'Preimplantation Genetic Diagnosis: an Ambiguous Legal Status for an Ambiguous Medical and Social Practice' presented at a symposium entitled *Comparative European Approaches to Preimplantation Genetic Diagnosis*, organised by the Centre for Bioethics and Policy, London, 1 May 2007. Judge Byk appeared to characterise Germany, Austria and Italy as adopting a 'prohibitive' approach; Sweden, Iceland, Norway, Denmark, Spain, Portugal, Greece, Belgium, France and Switzerland as adopting a 'restrictive regulatory' approach; and the Netherlands and the UK as adopting a 'moderate liberal' approach.

We can reflect further at this point on the concerns within the United Kingdom that might be thought to attend embryo discard, ones that might be protected with reference to the margin of appreciation. Since, with the HFEA, I have suggested that it would be hard to 'police' the use of PGD for sex selection, so that only those with supposedly 'good reasons' or only those with fertility problems (therefore already undertaking IVF and potentially discarding embryos) availed themselves of the practice, then there may be a real concern about widespread use of the practice and, with it, embryo discard. (In turn, this difficulty could support a blanket ban and thus support the proportionality of the interference.) Indeed, earlier I suggested that unless a couple already needed IVF, the embryo discard that would attend sex selection by PGD could reasonably be seen as a legitimate moral concern. That said, we should remember the discouragingly high costs to a couple, of a physical (for the woman), emotional and financial nature of IVF in general. These costs might suggest that any given couple who did in fact engage in sex selection by PGD would have good reason to do so, therefore helping (to some extent at least) to justify embryo discard. However, as noted earlier, some people will be of the view that prospective parents could never have a good reason to try to choose the sex of their child, a reason that could justify embryo discard.

At this stage, is there any prospect of sex selection being legalised? Not surprisingly, in the light of the HFEA report, the answer seems to be negative. In its review of the HFE Act, which followed a public consultation by the Department of Health, the government has ruled out any such development. In considering the responses to the consultation the White Paper notes that 'it was clear that responses generally favoured measures such as a ban on sex selection of offspring for non-medical reasons' (and this is further reflected in the Human Tissue and Embryos (Draft) Bill).[134] In its next reference to sex selection, the paper observes that the HFEA has not licensed sex selection for non-medical reasons.[135] In due course the White Paper notes the 'strong opposition' to the practice found in the HFEA's consultation.[136] As noted earlier, in this way the paper appears to give some considerable weight to the HFEA's consultation and report. Shortly thereafter the paper observes that the government has considered a range of views and evidence on this matter, including the view of the House of Commons Science and Technology Committee that there 'was insufficient

---

[134] Department of Health, above n 38, para 1.11; Human Tissue and Embryos (Draft) Bill, above n 38 (amending Sch 2 of the HFE Act 1990): 'After para 1 insert 1ZB... (1) A licence under paragraph 1 cannot authorise any practice designed to secure that any resulting child will be of one sex rather than the other'. Further amendments make clear that sex selection associated with medical reasons will still be permitted.
[135] *Ibid* para 2.41.
[136] *Ibid* para 2.45.

## 344  Uses of Preimplantation Genetic Diagnosis

evidence to justify a ban on "family balancing"' where a family already has several children of the same sex.[137] However, the White Paper concludes[138]:

> [T]he Government is persuaded that sex selection for nonmedical reasons within treatment services should be prohibited, including for 'family balancing'. This reflects, in part, the strength of public opinion on this matter that this should not be a matter of choice open to potential parents. It also takes account of the possible effects — including internationally — on cultures where there is a clear preference for male children. The ban will apply both to embryos and to gametes...

On the one hand, then, the government has been persuaded by what it takes to be the majority of public opinion; on the other hand, it is concerned about the effects, both nationally and internationally, on cultures that prefer male children. Leaving aside the issue of public opinion (which we have seen from the HFEA report to be based, typically, on highly speculative concerns about harm, though also on arguably legitimate concerns with morals, such as the question of embryo discard), it is not clear that a concern about international effects can be sufficiently strong to justify prohibition of the practice in the United Kingdom. By contrast, to the extent that the government is genuinely concerned about effects on communities within the United Kingdom, this concern requires further analysis. I cannot go deeply into this issue here but one question may be whether the potential harm of allowing sex selection by PGD is really greater than not allowing it. For instance, where women of certain ethnic minorities may be pressured to keep trying to have a son they may undergo repeated abortions, if not in the United Kingdom then in another country. In this light, we may be faced with a question of which is the 'worse of two evils', as those working in the IVF clinic whose work was discussed particularly in Chapter 4 observed in relation to cases of certain ethnic women they had encountered. In effect, staff who also worked in the area of PND were sometimes wary of divulging the sex of a fetus in the course of an ultrasound scan, but at the same time worried that, if they did not do so, a woman may return to another country and be exposed, necessarily later in her pregnancy, to possibly unsafe abortion practices.[139] In

---

[137] *Ibid* para 2.47.
[138] *Ibid* (emphasis in original).
[139] Ethics Discussion Group (EDG) 5. In the course of the relevant discussion, Scientist 34 observes: 'One woman, we had a DMD [Duchenne muscular dystrophy] lady, she was a carrier, she couldn't tell her husband — because of religious — she thought that he would beat her up, whatever. And she kept getting pregnant and having a DMD test, "Oh it's a girl," and she would disappear to India and come back a few months later saying she wasn't pregnant any more. I think this happened about eight times. And I think by this point, all of us in the lab seemed a bit uneasy about that. So I don't know. So we've stopped actually telling her now, I think, or not treating her, I'm not sure what decision was made, but, I mean is it easier in a way to give her the option straightaway of having her choice so that she doesn't have to go through so many abortions, and doesn't have the family pressures? I think she was very, very scared. She didn't particularly enjoy it. Or is it, I don't know, I don't particularly think it's right, but she's obviously had a bit of a hard time.'

Conclusions    345

essence, if concern for the effect on certain cultures within the United Kingdom is a reason to ban sex selection, it is one requiring much greater analysis if a pressing social need that is proportionate to the legitimate aim is to be established on the basis of relevant and sufficient reasons. (That said, of course, no case has yet established that the practice of sex selection falls within the right to respect for private and family life, so that there is currently no legal requirement to justify interference with the right. Rather, my discussion has proceeded on the basis of a *prima facie* right, in order to explore the case for the justification of a ban.)

Indeed, if a considerable number of fetuses are being aborted, including relatively late, and women from ethnic minorities are being exposed either to repeated abortions here or to less-safe and necessarily later abortions abroad, any claim that a continued ban on sex selection by PGD responds to a pressing social need would require further justification. To assess this, ideally we would need evidence about the number of abortions for reasons of fetal sex (either here or by UK women abroad) and to review this in the light of concerns about the potentially high uptake of the practice of sex selection by PGD and therefore about the extent of possible embryo discard. Two other points might be noted here. First, women have a much higher moral (and legal) status than embryos. This means that we should be more concerned to protect them (for example, from possibly unsafe abortions abroad) than to protect embryos. Second, however, women who may currently abort a fetus on the grounds of its sex may not or may not be able to afford sex selection by PGD. This means that legalising the practice will not necessarily significantly reduce the number of abortions and therefore may have no protective effect on significant numbers of women (or fetuses). In turn, it might be argued that this counts against the suggestion that a ban does *not* fulfil a pressing social need, since we could be left with a concern about a significant degree of embryo discard due to the uptake of the practice generally within the population. As suggested above, however, a lot more evidence about the practice of abortion on the grounds of sex would be required, including the extent to which such abortions are undertaken by women from ethnic minorities. Whether this evidence could be obtained is uncertain. Further, since women have a much higher moral and legal status than the embryo, we should also think about whether preventing harm to a few women could in fact justify larger numbers of embryo discard.

## IV CONCLUSIONS

I return first to selection for disability. In line with my overall analysis, which draws on the distinction between cases where there is a serious risk that a life would not be worth living and those where a person could in fact have a reasonable quality of life, but also emphasises the relative strength of non-person-affecting principles at the point of embryonic selection (at least compared with the situation of an already-established pregnancy), it is *prima facie* morally preferable not to select for disability, even where a child would think her life worth living. However, against this we must weigh parents' interests in this kind of selection. When we do this, however, at least with regard to the cases examined in this chapter, it seems hard to find a case in which parental reasons could really be sufficiently compelling, particularly so as to justify the use of public resources. As we have seen, it is likely that the government will explicitly outlaw such choices (which are currently illegal by means of HFEA licence conditions) in the new HFE Act. It is always possible that this will proscribe some legitimate cases, though at the same time it is hard to envisage these in the abstract.

Turning to sex selection for non-medical reasons, here I suggested — as the HFEA has itself acknowledged — that sometimes parents may in fact have sufficiently serious reasons for wanting to engage in this practice, at least in relation to embryonic (rather than fetal) sex selection, though people will reasonably disagree about this. (In some cases, women from certain ethnic minorities may indeed have very strong reasons for termination if their lives are made very difficult by family members in the event that they give birth to a girl.) Focusing on the claims of the embryo, although sex selection where IVF is *not* already needed (so that excess embryos are not already being created) is the most troubling case morally, I suggested that here the thought that the embryo has some moral value could be weighed against the strength of possible parental reasons for selection. As for the future child, I emphasised the highly speculative nature of concerns about psychological and physical harm to children. In turn, I discussed the extent to which such concerns (particularly about the former type of harm) had been put forward by respondents to the HFEA's consultation and in turn influenced the HFEA in its report. Here I suggested that the HFEA had missed an opportunity properly to weigh these speculative harms against the benefits that it suggested might flow from sex selection in certain cases and that a harm/benefit ratio could in fact be thought relevant to the question of whether there is a pressing social need to proscribe sex selection, one that is proportionate to the legitimate aim. Lastly, on the question of harm, I suggested that the HFEA has inconsistently overplayed the risk, particularly, of physical harm to children from PGD, since it has let this concern drop away in the case of selection for saviour siblings (albeit a much more pressing moral case).

Focusing now on the issue of morals, as we have seen, a concern with morals can be a legitimate aim for the purposes of Article 8(2). If an English court, and ultimately the ECtHR, were to agree that there were sufficient moral concerns about sex selection, then the case for interference could be made out, particularly if reinforced by (albeit speculative) concerns about physical or psychological harm to future children (another form of moral argument, in fact). However, this would depend on establishing that a ban fulfils a pressing social need, that it is proportionate to the legitimate aim pursued and that there are relevant and sufficient reasons for it. Thinking about how a concern with morals could be fleshed out, I drew attention to the arguably legitimate nature of concerns about embryo discard and the fact that the ECtHR would be likely to invoke the margin of appreciation in relation to the moral question of the protection of the embryo. Within the United Kingdom itself, it appears that there is reasonable disagreement about the need to protect the embryo. Such disagreement will be reinforced by the fact that people will also reasonably disagree about whether parental reasons for sex selection could ever be sufficiently strong to justify embryo discard.

By focusing on possible harms and benefits, as well as the issue of morals, the HFEA has underplayed the importance of attending to parental interests in themselves. This may have been because its discussion and argument appeared to be set against the hypothetical (and therefore not seriously considered) backdrop in which sex selection was deemed to fall within the right to respect for private and family life. At the same time, however, its lack of attention to this issue means that it insufficiently attended to the need to consider whether interference could really be justified, rather than what the possible grounds of interference are. (This does not mean that the case for a ban cannot in fact be justified but it does suggest that, on its own terms, the HFEA's report does not really do this. The House of Commons Science and Technology Committee was also of the view that the analysis in the HFEA report is inadequate.[140])

The same might be said of the government in its review of the HFE Act, though of course the government was not reasoning under the hypothetical assumption, which seemed to infuse the HFEA's report, that sex selection could *prima facie* be protected by the right to respect for private and family life. Thus, leaving to one side any need to justify interference with this right, to the extent that the government's review hinges on public opinion it could, of course, be said that it is acting democratically in proposing to continue the ban on sex selection. That said, if it could be demonstrated, say, that many people were basing their disapproval of the practice on ill-conceived concerns, then the democratic argument would be weakened, but it is not clear how this could be demonstrated other than by legalising and carefully monitoring the practice. Such a move could attend to and might even allay concerns about harms, but for some people residual concerns about moral issues independent of harm might remain, such as a concern with the embryo (which lacks interests prior to fetal sentience).

Overall, if the ECtHR *were* to find that sex selection falls within the right to respect for private and family life, a concern with moral objections might be thought sufficient to justify a continued ban, with particular reference to the margin of appreciation. It should be remembered, however, that there have been no legal cases on the question of whether sex selection by PGD is part of the right to respect for private and family life in Article 8 of the ECHR, nor even on PGD itself within the Strasbourg court. Therefore, and most importantly, there is no

---

[140] House of Commons Science and Technology Committee, above n 61, para 142.

current legal requirement under ECHR jurisprudence overtly to justify prohibition of the practice. Nor, indeed, has any Strasbourg decision yet established that the practice of abortion falls within Article 8 and, of course, English law itself grants no actual legal right to abort.

With reference to embryo discard and also to different approaches within Europe, the relationship between the legal approaches to the embryo and fetus needs always to be well considered. In this regard, we might note the previous legal position in Italy, in which PGD was banned in 2004, a position only recently reversed.[141] In my view, with regard to the embryo and fetus, the irony of the prior legal position was that couples could still terminate a fetus, arguably a being of greater moral status, on the grounds of a genetic or other anomaly. (This is not to suggest that such terminations should be illegal.) In effect, then, there was a piecemeal approach to preimplantation and prenatal selection in Italy. An additional feature of the law there is still that all embryos must be implanted at the same time (from the limit of three eggs that can be legally fertilised). The risks to future children from multiple births, arguably beings of very much greater moral status than the embryo, are considerable, as noted particularly in Chapter 5. In my view, this is the kind of irony and, more particularly, potential harm that may result from what we might think of as an 'absolutist' approach to these moral issues, under which the embryo is protected, so to speak, 'at all costs'.

Finally, it is worth noting the potential relevance of the above relatively detailed analysis of Article 8 and its possible application to PGD for sex selection to the various largely hypothetical uses of PGD discussed in the previous chapter.[142] It seems likely that reasonable disagreement about the moral question of embryo creation and discard, coupled with the thought that prospective parents cannot have strong reasons to select for relatively trivial features, would continue to be central points in any analysis. Where selection is for serious 'positive' features such as enhanced health, as suggested in the previous chapter, the moral balance would become more complex. However, reasonable disagreement is particularly likely to attend discussions about the embryo whenever we move away from consideration of selection against serious genetic conditions. Of course, this would also be the case as regards the fetus in relation to prenatal screening, PND and selective abortion. In any discussion of selection practices, at least where there is no risk of a wrongful life from the point of view of the future child, a central issue will

---

[141] Judge Byk, above n 133. For further discussion and an account of the subsequent referendum on the issue see F Turone 'Italy to Pass New Law on Assisted Reproduction' (2004) 328 *BMJ* 9. See also F Turone 'Italians Fail to Overturn Restrictive Reproduction Law' (2005) 330 *BMJ* 1405 for an account of further developments, including the Vatican's attempt successfully to discourage people from voting in an attempt to keep the turnout below quorum. For the most recent developments, see F Turone 'Italian Court Upholds Couple's Demand for Preimplantation Genetic Diagnosis' (2007) 335 *BMJ* 687.

[142] The potential relevance of an Art 8 analysis was of course noted in Ch 5, but I reserved a fuller discussion of the possible application of Art 8 to PGD until this chapter.

always be how to balance the claims of the embryo or fetus on the one hand and the reason for selection and the question of whose interests or what purpose that selection serves on the other.

# Bibliography of Works Cited

ALDERSON, P 'Prenatal Counselling and Images of Disability' in D Dickenson (ed), *Ethical Issues in Maternal-Fetal Medicine* (Cambridge: Cambridge University Press, 2002) 195
ANSWER, <http://www.antenataltesting.info>
ASCH, A 'Real Moral Dilemmas' (1986) 46/10 *Christianity and Crisis* 237
—— 'Reproductive Technology and Disability' in S Cohen and N Taub (eds), *Reproductive Laws for the 1990s* (Clifton, NJ: Humana Press, 1989)
—— 'Why I Haven't Changed My Mind about Prenatal Diagnosis: Reflections and Refinements' in E Parens and A Asch (eds), *Prenatal Testing and Disability Rights* (Washington, DC: Georgetown University Press, 2000) 234
BAILY, M 'Why I Had Amniocentesis' in E Parens and A Asch (eds), *Prenatal Testing and Disability Rights* (Washington, DC: Georgetown University Press, 2000) 64
BARENDT E 'Privacy as a Constitutional Right and Value' in P Birks (ed), *Privacy and Loyalty* (Oxford: OUP, 1997) 1
BERKOWITZ, JM and SNYDER, JW 'Racism and Sexism in Medically Assisted Reproduction' (1998) 12 (1) *Bioethics* 2
BIRCH, K 'Beneficence, Determinism and Justice: an Engagement with the Argument for the Genetic Selection of Intelligence' (2005) 19/1 *Bioethics* 12
BOPP, J, Bostrom, B, and McKinney, D 'The "Rights" and "Wrongs" of Wrongful Birth and Wrongful Life: A Jurisprudential Analysis of Birth Related Torts' (Spring, 1989) *Duquesne Law Rev* 461
BOTKIN, J 'Fetal Privacy and Confidentiality' (1995) 25(5) *Hastings CR* 32
—— 'Ethical Issues and Practical Problems in Preimplantation Genetic Diagnosis' (1998) 26 *JL Med and Ethics* 17
—— 'Line Drawing: Developing Professional Standards for Prenatal Diagnostic Services' in E Parens and A Asch (eds), *Prenatal Testing and Disability Rights* (Washington, DC: Georgetown University Press, 2000) 288
BOWLES BIESECKER, B and HAMBY, L 'What Difference the Disability Community Arguments Should Make for the Delivery of Prenatal Genetic Information' in E Parens and A Asch (eds), *Prenatal Testing and Disability Rights* (Washington, DC: Georgetown University Press, 2000) 340
BUCHANAN, A, Brock, D, Daniels, N and Wikler, D, *From Chance to Choice: Genetics and Justice* (Cambridge: Cambridge University Press, 2000)
BUXTON, J 'Non-invasive Pregnancy Test Shows Promise' 6 February 2007, 394 *Bionews*, <http://bionews.org.uk/new.lasso?storyid=3340>
CANE, P 'Another Failed Sterilisation' (2004) 120 *LQR* 189
CARLSON, L 'Prenatal Testing and Selective Abortion' (2002) 75 *Phil and Med* 191
CHERVENAK, F, McCullough, L and Campbell, S 'Third Trimester Abortion: Is Compassion Enough?' (1999) 106 *BJOG* 293
CLAYTON, EW 'What the Law Says about Reproductive Genetic Testing and What it Doesn't' in KH Rothenberg and EJ Thomson (eds), *Women and Prenatal Testing: Facing the Challenges of Genetic Technology* (Columbus, Ohio: Ohio State University Press, 1994) 131

DAVIS, D 'Genetic Dilemmas and the Child's Right to an Open Future' (1997) 27(2) *Hastings CR* 7

DEPARTMENT OF HEALTH 'Preimplantation Genetic Diagnosis (PGD) — Guiding Principles for Commissioners of NHS Services' (Sep 2002)

——, *Review of the Human Fertilisation and Embryology Act: Proposals for Revised Legislation (including Establishment of the Regulatory Authority for Tissue and Embryos)* (December 2006)

DOSWALD-BECK, L 'The Meaning of the "Right to Respect for Private Life" under the European Convention on Human Rights' (1983) 4 *Human Rights Law Journal* 283

DOWN'S SYNDROME ASSOCIATION 'Your Baby has Down's Syndrome: a Guide for Parents' <http://www.downs-syndrome.org.uk/pdfs/new_parents.pdf>

DRAKE, H, Reid, M, and Marteau, T 'Attitudes towards Termination for Fetal Abnormality: Comparisons in Three European Countries' (1996) 49/3 *Clin Genet* 134

DWORKIN R (ed), *The Philosophy of Law* (Oxford: OUP, 1977)

——, *Life's Dominion: An Argument about Abortion and Euthanasia* (London: Harper Collins, 1993)

DYER, C 'Doctor who Performed Late Abortion Will Not be Prosecuted' (2005) 330 *BMJ* 668

EHRICH, K, Williams, C, Farsides, B, Sandall, J, and Scott, R 'Choosing Embryos: Ethical Complexity in Staff accounts of Preimplantation Genetic Diagnosis' (forthcoming 2007) *Sociology of Health & Illness*

EDWARDS, S 'Prevention of Disability on Grounds of Suffering' (2001) 27 *JME* 380

—— 'Disability, Identity and the "Expressivist Objection"' (2004) 30 *JME* 418

FAVE, A and MASSIMINI, F 'The Relevance of Subjective Well-being to Social Policies: Optimal Experience and Tailored Intervention' in F Huppert, N Baylis and B Kaverne, *The Science of Wellbeing* (Oxford: OUP, 2005) 379

FEINBERG, J 'The Child's Right to an Open Future' in W Aiken and H LaFollette (eds), *Whose Child? Children's Rights, Parental Authority and State Power* (Totowa, NJ: Rowman and Littlefield, 1980)

——, *Harm to Others* (New York: OUP, 1984)

—— 'Abortion' (1979) in his *Freedom and Fulfillment* (Princeton: Princeton University Press, 1992) 37

FELDMAN, D 'Privacy-related Rights and their Social Value' in P Birks (ed), *Privacy and Loyalty* (Oxford: OUP, 1997) 15

—— 'The Developing Scope of Article 8 of the European Convention on Human Rights' [1997] 3 *EHRLR* 265

FERGUSON, P, Gartner, A and Lipsky, D 'The Experience of Disability in Families: A Synthesis of Research and Parent Narratives' E Parens and A Asch (eds), *Prenatal Testing and Disability Rights* (Washington, DC: Georgetown University Press, 2000) 72

FINNIS, J 'The Rights and Wrongs of Abortion: A Reply to Judith Thomson' (1973) 2 *Phil & Pub Aff* 117

FLINTER, F 'Preimplantation Genetic Diagnosis Needs to be Tightly Regulated' (2001) 322 *BMJ* 1008

FOVARGUE, S and MIOLÁ, J 'Policing Pregnancy: Implications of the *Attorney-General's Reference (No 3 of 1994)*' 6 *Med L Rev* (1998) 265

FRANKLIN, S and ROBERTS, C, *Born and Made: An Ethnography of Preimplantation Genetic Diagnosis* (Oxford: Princeton University Press, 2006)

GANTZ, J 'State Statutory Preclusion of Wrongful Birth Relief: a Troubling Re-Writing of A Woman's Right to Choose and the Doctor-Patient Relationship' (1997) *Virginia J of Social Policy and the Law* 795
GILLAM, L 'Prenatal Diagnosis and Discrimination against the Disabled' (1999) 24 *JME* 163
GILLOTT, J 'Screening for Disability: a Eugenic Pursuit?' (2001) 27 *JME* supp II, 21
GLANNON, W, *Genes and Future People: Philosophical Issues in Human Genetics* (Oxford: Westview Press, 2001)
GOLD, S 'An Equality Approach to Wrongful Birth Statutes' (1996) *Fordham Law Rev* 1005
GLOVER, J, *What Sort of People Should There Be?* (Harmondsworth: Penguin, 1984)
—— 'Eugenics: Some Lessons from the Nazi Experience' in J Harris and S Holm (eds), *The Future of Human Reproduction: Ethics, Choice and Regulation* (Oxford: OUP, 1998) 55
——, *Choosing Children: Genes, Disability and Design* (Oxford: OUP, 2006)
GLOVER, V and FISK, NM 'Fetal Pain: Implications for Research and Practice' (1999) 106 *British J of Obstet and Gyn* 881
GMC 'Confidentiality: Protecting and Providing Information' April 2004
GREEN, R 'Parental Autonomy and the Obligation not to Harm One's Child Genetically' (1997) 25 *JL Med and Ethics* 5
GRUBB, A 'Commentary: Killing the Unborn Child: Abortion and Homicide: *Attorney General's Reference (No 3 of 1994)*' 6 *Med L Rev* (1998) 256
HARE, RM, *Moral Thinking: Its Level, Method and Point* (Oxford: OUP, 1981)
HARRIS, J 'Rights and Reproductive Choice' in J Harris and S Holm (eds), *The Future of Human Reproduction: Ethics, Choice and Regulation* (Oxford: OUP, 1998) 5
—— 'Is There a Coherent Social Conception of Disability?' (2000) 26 *JME* 95
—— 'No Sex Selection Please, We're British' (2005) 31 *JME* 286
—— 'Sex Selection and Regulated Hatred' (2005) 31 *JME* 291
HÄYRY, M 'There is a Difference between Selecting a Deaf Embryo and Deafening a Hearing Child' (2004) 30 *JME* 510
HENN, W 'Consumerism in Prenatal Diagnosis: a Challenge for Ethical Guidelines' (2000) 26 *JME* 444
HEYD, D, *Genethics: Moral Issues in the Creation of People* (Berkeley: University of California Press, 1992)
—— 'Prenatal Diagnosis: Whose Right?' (1995) 21 *JME* 292
HFEA, *Sex Selection* (1993)
——, PRESS RELEASE 'HFEA Reduces Maximum Number of Embryos Transferred in Single IVF treatment from Three to Two' (8 August 2001)
——, *Code of Practice — Sixth Edition* (2003)
——, *Sex Selection — Options for Regulation: A Report on the HFEA's 2002–3 Review of Sex Selection including a Discussion of Legislative and Regulatory and Options* (2003)
——, PRESS RELEASE 'HFEA Agrees to Extend Policy on Tissue Typing' (21 July 2004)
——, PRESS RELEASE 'HFEA Announce New Process to Speed up Applications for Embryo Screening' (19 January 2005)
——, *Choices and Boundaries* (November 2005)
—— 'Welfare of the Child — Tomorrow's Children' (2005)
——, PRESS RELEASE 'Authority Decision on the Use of PGD for Lower Penetrance, Later Onset Inherited Conditions' (10 May 2006)
——, EXPERT GROUP ON MULTIPLE BIRTHS AFTER IVF, *One Child at a Time: Reducing Multiple Births After IVF* (October 2006)

——, *The Best Possible Start to Life: A Consultation Document on Multiple Births after IVF* (April, 2007)
HFEA and AGCT, *Consultation Document on Preimplantation Genetic Diagnosis* (November, 1999)
——, *Minutes of Joint Working Party on Preimplantation Genetic Diagnosis* (20 December 2000)
——, *Minutes of Joint Working Party on Preimplantation Genetic Diagnosis* (30 March 2001)
——, *Minutes of Joint Working Party on Preimplantation Genetic Diagnosis* (11 May 2001)
——, *Outcome of the Public Consultation on Preimplantation Genetic Diagnosis* (18 June 2001)
HGC, *Minutes of Genetic Testing Sub-group* (12 January 2001)
——, *Minutes of Genetic Testing Sub-group* (16 February 2001)
——, *Minutes of Plenary Meeting* (2 March 2001)
——, *Making Babies: Reproductive Decisions and Genetic Technologies* (2006)
HALPER, T 'Privacy and Autonomy: from Warren and Brandeis to *Roe* and *Cruzan*' (1996) 21 *J of Med and Phil* 124
HILL, D 'Ten Years of Preimplantation Genetic Diagnosis-Aneuploidy Screening: Review of Multi-Center Report' (2004) 82/2 *Fertil & Steril* 300
HOPE, T and MCMILLAN, J 'Ethical Problems before Conception' (2003) 361 *Lancet* 2164
HOUSE OF COMMONS SCIENCE and TECHNOLOGY COMMITTEE, *Human Reproductive Technologies and the Law* (2005)
HUBBARD, R 'Eugenics: New Tools, Old Ideas' (1987) 13 *Women and Health* 225
JACOBS FG and WHITE, RCA, *The European Convention on Human Rights*, 2nd edn (Oxford: Clarendon Press, 1996)
JACKSON, E 'Abortion, Autonomy and Prenatal Diagnosis' (2000) 9(4) *Social and Legal Studies* 467
——, *Regulating Reproduction* (Oxford: Hart Publishing, 2001)
—— 'Conception and the Irrelevance of the Welfare Principle' (2002) 65(2) *MLR* 176
JENNINGS, B 'Technology and the Genetic Imaginary: Prenatal Testing and the Construction of Disability' in E Parens and A Asch (eds), *Prenatal Testing and Disability Rights* (Washington, DC: Georgetown University Press, 2000) 138
JULIAN-REYNIER, C, Aurran, Y, Dumaret, A, Maron, A, Chabal, F and Giraud, F 'Attitudes Towards Down's Syndrome: Follow up of a Cohort of 280 cases' (1995) 32/8 *J Med Genet* 597
KENNEDY, I 'A Woman and her Unborn Child' in his *Treat Me Right* (Oxford: OUP, 1992) 364
—— and GRUBB, A, *Medical Law: Text with Materials*, 3rd edn (London: Butterworths, 2000)
KEVLES, D 'Eugenics and Human Rights' (1999) 319 *BMJ* 435
KIRK, E 'Embryo Selection for Complex Traits is Impracticable' (2003) 326 *BMJ* 53
KITCHER, P, *The Lives to Come: the Genetic Revolution and Human Possibilities* (London: Allen Lane, The Penguin Press, 1996)
KOWITZ, J 'Not Your Garden Variety Tort Reform: Statutes Barring Claims for Wrongful Life and Wrongful Birth are Unconstitutional Under the Purpose Prong of *Planned Parenthood v Casey*' (Spring, 1995) *Brooklyn Law Rev* 235
LANE COMMITTEE, *Report on the Working of the Abortion Act 1967* (1974) (Cm 5579)
LEVY, N 'Deafness, Culture, and Choice' (2002) 28 *JME* 284
LIPPMAN, A 'Prenatal Genetic Testing and Screening: Constructing Needs and Reinforcing Inequities' (1991) 17 *Am J L and Med* 15

LOUCAIDES, LG 'Personality and Privacy under the European Convention on Human Rights' (1990) 61 *BYBIL* 175

MALINOWKSI, M 'Coming into Being: Law, Ethics and the Practice of Prenatal Genetic Screening' (1994) 45 *Hastings LJ* 1435

MANSFIELD, C, Hopfer, S and Marteau, TM 'Termination Rates after Prenatal Diagnosis of Down syndrome, spina bifida, anencephaly, and Turner and Klinefelter syndromes: a Systematic Literature Review European Concerted Action: DADA (Decision-making After the Diagnosis of a Fetal Abnormality' (1999) 19/9 *Prenat Diagn* 808

MARWICK, C 'Monitoring of Assisted Reproduction Techniques is Inadequate, US Experts Say' (2003) 326 *BMJ* 1352

MASON, JK and LAURIE, GT, *Law and Medical Ethics*, 7th edn (Oxford: OUP, 2006)

MCDOUGALL, R 'Acting Parentally: An Argument against Sex Selection' (2005) 31 *JME* 601

—— 'Parental Virtue: A New Way of Thinking about the Morality of Reproductive Actions' (2007) 21/4 *Bioethics* 181

MCGEE, G 'Parenting in an Era of Genetics' (1997) 27(2) *Hastings CR* 16

MCMAHAN, J 'Preventing the Existence of People with Disabilities' in D Wasserman, J Bickenbach and R Wachbroit (eds), *Quality of Life and Human Difference: Genetic Testing, Health Care, and Disability* (New York: Cambridge University Press, 2005) 142

MORGAN, D 'Abortion: the Unexamined Ground' [1990] *Crim LR* 687

MURRAY, T, *The Worth of a Child* (Berkeley: University of California Press, 1996)

NATIONAL INSTITUTE OF NEUROLOGICAL DISORDERS and STROKE <http://www.ninds.nih.gov/disorders/lesch_nyhan/lesch_nyhan.htm>

NATIONAL TAY-SACHS and ALLIED DISEASES ASSOCIATION, INC <http://www.ntsad.org>

NELSON, J 'The Meaning of the Act: Reflections on the Expressive Force of Reproductive Decision Making and Policies' in E Parens and A Asch (eds), *Prenatal Testing and Disability Rights* (Washington, DC: Georgetown University Press, 2000) 196

NICE 'Antenatal Care: Routine Care for the Healthy Pregnant Woman' Clinical Guideline 6 (October 2003)

NUFFIELD COUNCIL ON BIOETHICS, *Critical Care Decisions in Fetal and Neonatal Medicine: Ethical Issues* (2006)

NYS, H 'Physician Involvement in a Patient's Death' (1999) 7 *Med L Rev* 209

O'NEILL, O, *Autonomy and Trust in Bioethics* (Cambridge: Cambridge University Press, 2002)

OSSORIO, P 'Prenatal Genetic Testing and the Courts' in E Parens and A Asch (eds), *Prenatal Testing and Disability Rights* (Washington, DC: Georgetown University Press, 2000) 308

PARENS, E and ASCH, A 'The Disability Rights Critique of Prenatal Genetic Testing: Reflections and Recommendations' in E Parens and A Asch (eds), *Prenatal Testing and Disability Rights* (Washington, DC: Georgetown University Press, 2000) 3

PARENT, WA 'Recent Work on the Concept of Privacy' (1983) 20 *Am Phil Q* 341

PARFIT, D, *Reasons and Persons* (Oxford: OUP, 1984)

PELLEGRINO, M 'The Protection of Prenatal Life: Tort Claims of Wrongful Birth or Wrongful Life and Equal Protection Under Pennsylvania's Constitution' (1999) *Temple Law Review* 715

PRESS, N 'Assessing the Expressive Character of Prenatal Testing: The Choice Made or the Choices Made Available?' in E Parens and A Asch (eds), *Prenatal Testing and Disability Rights* (Washington, DC: Georgetown University Press, 2000) 214

PRIAULX, N, *The Harm Paradox: Tort Law and the Unwanted Child in an Era of Choice* (London: UCL Press, 2007)

RAZ, J 'Right-based Moralities' in J Waldron (ed), *Theories of Rights* (Oxford: OUP, 1984)

——, *The Morality of Freedom* (Oxford: Clarendon Press, 1986)

REINDAL, S 'Disability, Gene Therapy and Eugenics — a Challenge to John Harris' (2000) 26 *JME* 89

RENWICK, P 'Proof of Principle and First Cases using Preimplantion Genetic Haplotyping — a Paradigm Shift for Embryo Diagnosis' (2006) 13/1 *Reproductive Biomedicine Online* 758

RCOG, *Termination of Pregnancy for Fetal Abnormality in England, Wales and Scotland* (January 1996)

——, *Report of the RCOG Working Party on Fetal Awareness* (London: RCOG, 1997)

RCOG ETHICS COMMITTEE, *A Consideration of the Law and Ethics in Relation to Late Termination of Pregnancy for Fetal Abnormality* (RCOG Press, March 1998)

RCP, *Withholding or Withdrawing Life-sustaining Treatment for Children: A Framework for Practice* (2004, 2nd edn)

RHODEN, N 'Trimesters and Technology: Revamping *Roe v Wade*' 95 *Yale LJ* (1986) 639

RHODES, R 'Ethical Issues in Selecting Embryos'(2001) 943 *Ann NY Acad Sci* 360

ROBERTSON, J, *Children of Choice: Freedom and the New Reproductive Technologies* (Princeton, NJ: Princeton University Press, 1994)

—— 'Genetic Selection of Offspring Characteristics' (1996) 76 *Boston U Law Rev* 421

—— 'Extending Preimplantation Genetic Diagnosis: Medical and Non-medical Uses' (2003) 29 *JME* 213

RYAN, S 'Wrongful Birth: False Representations of Women's Reproductive Lives' (April, 1994) *Minnesota Law Rev* 857

SAVULESCU, S 'Sex Selection: The Case For' (1999) 171(7) *Med J Aust* 37

—— 'Procreative Beneficence: Why We Should Select the Best Children' (2001) 15(5/6) *Bioethics* 413

SAXTON, M 'Why Members of the Disability Community Oppose Prenatal Diagnosis and Selective Abortion' in E Parens and A Asch (eds), *Prenatal Testing and Disability Rights* (Washington, DC: Georgetown University Press, 2000) 147

SCHMIDT, E 'The Parental Obligation to Expand a Child's Range of Open Futures when Making Genetic Trait Selections for their Child' (2007) 21/4 *Bioethics* 191

SCOTT, R, *Rights, Duties and the Body: Law and Ethics of the Maternal-Fetal Conflict* (Oxford: Hart Publishing, 2002)

—— 'Why Parents Have No Duty to Select "the Best" Children' (2007) *Clinical Ethics* 3/3 149

SEYMOUR, J, *Childbirth and the Law* (Oxford: OUP, 2000)

SHAKESPEARE, T 'Choices and Rights: Eugenics, Genetics and Disability Equality' (1998) 13/5 *Disability and Society* 665

—— '"Losing the Plot?" Medical and Activist Discourses of Contemporary Genetics and Disability' (1999) 21/5 *Sociology of Health and Illness* 669

——, *Disability Rights and Wrongs* (London: Routledge, 2006)

SHELDON, S 'Who is the Mother to Make the Judgment?: The Construction of Woman in English Abortion Law' (1993) 1 *Fem Leg Stud* 3

—— 'The Law of Abortion and the Politics of Medicalisation' in J Bridgman and S Millns (eds), *Law and Body Politics: Regulating the Female Body* (Aldershot: Dartmouth, 1995) 105

—— and WILKINSON, S 'Termination of Pregnancy for Reason of Foetal Disability: Are there Grounds for a Special Exception in Law?' (2001) 9 *Med Law Rev* 85

—— 'Hashmi and Whittaker: An Unjustifiable and Misguided Distinction?' (2004) 12 *Med Law Rev* 137

SILVER, L 'How Reprogenetics will Transform the American Family' (1999) 27 *Hofstra L Rev* 649

SILVERMAN, A 'Constitutional Law-Pennsylvania's Wrongful Birth Statute's Impact On Abortion Rights: State Action And Undue Burden-*Edmonds* v *Western Pennsylvania*' (1993) *Temple Law Rev* 1087

SPRIGGS, M 'Lesbian Couple Create a Child Who is Deaf Like Them' (2002) 28 *JME* 283

STEINBOCK, B, *Life Before Birth* (New York: Oxford University Press, 1992)

—— 'Disability, Prenatal Testing and Selective Abortion' in E Parens and A Asch (eds), *Prenatal Testing and Disability Rights* (Washington, DC: Georgetown University Press, 2000) 108

—— and MCCLAMROCK, R 'When is Birth Unfair to the Child?' (1994) 24 *Hastings CR* 15

STOLLER, D 'Prenatal Genetic Screening: the Enigma of Selective Abortion' (1997/1998) 12 *JL & Health* 121

STONE, A 'Consti-tortion: Tort Law as an End-run around Abortion Rights after *Planned Parenthood v Casey*' (2000) *American University Journal of Gender, Social Policy and the Law* 471

STRONG, C 'Overview: a Framework for Reproductive Ethics' in D Dickenson (ed), *Ethical Issues in Maternal-Fetal Medicine* (Cambridge: Cambridge University Press, 2002) 17

SUTER, S 'The Routinization of Prenatal Screening' (2002) 28 *Am JL & Med* 233

THOMSON, JJ 'A Defence of Abortion' (1971) 1 *Phil & Pub Aff* 47

THORNHILL, A, Grudzinskas, G and Handyside, A 'PGD for Early Onset Alzheimer's Disease: Preventing Disease... Not the Cure' 17 April 2007, 403 *Bionews*, <http://bionews.org.uk/commentary.lasso?storyid=3411>

TURONE, F 'Italy to Pass New Law on Assisted Reproduction' (2004) 328 *BMJ* 9

—— 'Italians Fail to Overturn Restrictive Reproduction Law' (2005) 330 *BMJ* 1405

VERLINSKY, Y, Cohen, J, Munne, S, Gianaroli, L, Simpson, JL, Ferraretti, AP and Kuliev, A 'Over a Decade of Experience with Preimplantation Genetic Diagnosis: A Multi-center Report' (2004) 82/2 *Fertility and Sterility* 292

WADHAM, J, Mountfield, H, Edmundson, A and Gallagher, C, *Blackstone's Guide to the Human Rights Act 1998*, 4th edn (London: Blackstone's, 2007)

WARNOCK REPORT (Cmnd 9314), *Report of the Committee of Inquiry into Fertilisation and Embryology*, republished as *A Question of Life* (Oxford: Blackwell, 1985)

WARREN, MA 'On the Moral and Legal Status of Abortion' (1973) 57(1) *The Monist* 43

WENZ, P 'Engineering Genetic Injustice' (2005) 19/1 *Bioethics* 1

DE WERT, G 'Preimplantation Genetic Diagnosis: the Ethics of Intermediate Cases' (2005) 20/12 *Human Reproduction* 3261

WERTZ, D 'Drawing Lines: Notes for Policymakers' in E Parens and A Asch (eds), *Prenatal Testing and Disability Rights* (Washington, DC: Georgetown University Press, 2000) 261

WHITE, G and MCCLURE, M 'Introducing Innovation into Practice: Technical and Ethical Analyses of PGD and ICSI Technologies' (1998) 26 *JL Med and Ethics* 5

WICKS, E, Wyldes, M and Kilby, M 'Late Termination of Pregnancy for Fetal Abnormality: Medical and Legal Perspectives' (2004) 12 *Med Law Rev* 285

WILLIAMS, C 'Framing the Fetus in Medical Work: Rituals and Practice' (2005) 60 *Social Science and Medicine* 2085

——, ALDERSON, P and FARSIDES, B '"Drawing the Line" in Prenatal Screening and Testing: Health Practitioners' Discussions' (2002) 4(1) *Health, Risk and Society* 61

—— 'What Constitutes "Balanced Information in the Practitioners" Portrayals of Down's Syndrome?' (2002) 18 *Midwifery* 230

—— 'Is Nondirectiveness Possible within the Context of Antenatal Screening and Testing?' (2002) 54 *Social Science & Medicine* 339

—— 'Too Many Choices? Hospital and Community Staff Reflect on the Future of Prenatal Screening' (2002) 55 *Social Science & Medicine* 743

WILLIAMS, G, *Textbook of Criminal Law*, 1st edn (London: Stevens, 1978)

WILKINSON, S 'Eugenics, Embryo Selection and the Equal Value Principle' (2006) 1 *Clinical Ethics* 46

——, *Choosing Children: the Ethics of Selective Reproduction* (Oxford: OUP, forthcoming)

WILCOXON, K 'Statutory Remedies for Judicial Torts: The Need for Wrongful Birth Legislation' (Spring, 2001) *U of Cincinnati Law Rev* 1023

WIKLER, D 'Can We Learn from Eugenics?' (1999) 25 *JME* 183

WON, RH, CURRIER, RJ, LOREY, F and TOWNER, DR 'The Timing of Demise in Fetuses with Trisomy 21 and Trisomy 18' (2005) 25/7 *Prenat Diagn* 608

# Index

Abortion
  fetal anomaly after 24 weeks, 119–137
  medical profession, role of, 155–7
  prenatal screening and diagnosis (PND), 181–2
  rights-based, 153–5
  selective *see* Selective abortion
  United States
    Rights-based approach, 153–5
Abstinence, sexual, 20
Achondroplasia
  preimplantation genetic diagnosis (PGD), 314–15
Amniocentesis, 177
Any/particular distinction, 59–62
Aptitudes or abilities
  preimplantation genetic diagnosis (PGD), 285–8

Birth
  duty to avoid, possible 12
  harm and, 34–48
  wrongful, 26, 94–102

Children
  choosing whether to have, 12–14
Chorionic villus sampling, 21, 177
Consent to prenatal screening and diagnosis
  *see also* Informational duties
  aids not burdens, information that, 157–9
  autonomy, 157–9
  capacity, 145
  Down's syndrome, 146, 149–50
  generally, 144–5
  less serious or trivial matters, 152–3
  nature of screening or testing, 149–53
  NICE guidelines, 146
  Non-directive counselling, 147–8, 157
  offers of screening and testing, 145–9
  persuasion, 147
  purpose of screening or testing, 149–53
  rights, 151–3
  rights-based abortion, 153–7
  termination after, 148–9
  undue influence, 147
  voluntariness, 145–9

Contraception
  avoiding birth, 20
Cystic fibrosis, 31–2, 33, 37
  preimplantation genetic diagnosis (PGD), 225–8, 315–18

Deafness
  desire for deaf child, 41
  opportunity and, 309–13
  preimplantation genetic diagnosis (PGD), 300–304, 309–13
  selection for, 300–304, 309–13
'Designer babies', 247
Disability
  *see also* Disability ground of Abortion Act; Disabled child
  achondroplasia, 314–15
  assumptions about impairment, 50–54
  costs or difficulties or loss of benefits for parents, 46–7
  cystic fibrosis, 31–2, 33, 315–18
  deafness, 300–304, 309–13
  discrimination, 48–50
  Down's syndrome, 31–2, 33
  duty to avoid birth, possible 12
  effect, 26–2
  expressivist objection, 54–65
  flourishing, 28–9
  harmed condition model, 27
  impact of impairments, 27–8
  information on, 50–54
  interests of people with impairments, 48–65
  Lesch-Nyhan syndrome (LNS), 30
  Models of, 27–8, 48–50
  Nuffield Report, 17, 26
  selecting for, 297–319
    achondroplasia, 314–15
    cystic fibrosis, 315–18
    deafness, 300–304, 309–13
    Down's syndrome, 315–18
    harm, 297–300
    non–identity problem, 304–7
    non–person–affecting principles, 297–300
    person–affecting principles, 297–300

third–party assistance, 307–9
senses, loss of, 26–2
serious, difficulty of judging to be, 45
severity of condition
  cystic fibrosis, 31–2, 33
  Down's syndrome, 31–2, 33
  interests, whose, 32–4
  Lesch-Nyhan syndrome (LNS), 30
  life that someone may think is not worth living, 29–30
  life that someone will think is worth living, 30–32
  Tay-Sachs disease (TSD), 29, 32, 33
social model, 27, 28
Tay-Sachs disease (TSD), 29, 32, 33
understanding notion of, 11, 26–34
Disability ground of Abortion Act
*see also* Selective abortion
fetal anomaly after 24 weeks, 119–37
legal interests of parents, 89–94
serious handicap, 76–86
substantial risk, 73–6
wrongful birth, 94–102, 161
Disabled child
*see also* Disability
adaptation as family, 16
definition, 189–190
poverty, family, 17
preimplantation genetic diagnosis (PGD)
  avoidance of birth, 20–21
  testing, stage at which conducted, 20–21
prenatal screening and diagnosis (PND)
  avoidance of birth, 20
problems associated with, 17–18
quality of life, 17
selection practices
  factors influencing, 19
  positive duties in raising children, 15–20
  possibility of child, 14–15
Discrimination
disability, 48–50
European Convention on Human Rights, 116–24
sex selection, 320
Down's syndrome
  disability, 31–2, 33, 37
  preimplantation genetic diagnosis (PGD), 228–37, 315–18
  risk of, 172, 173–4
  screening, 146, 149–50, 172, 173, 177
  wrongful birth, 173–4
Duchenne muscular dystrophy, 221–3

Embryo
  gradualist account of moral status, 2, 21–3, 25, 38, 38, 45, 222
  legal status, 253–6
  moral status, 20–23, 253–6
  preimplantation genetic diagnosis (PGD) *see* Preimplantation genetic diagnosis (PGD)
  trivial uses of, fears of, 249–52
Eugenics
  context of decision–making, 67
  informational duties, 177
  meaning, 65–6
  preimplantation genetic diagnosis (PGD), 249–52
  reasons for selection, 66
  reproductive autonomy, 65–7
European Convention on Human Rights
  discrimination, 116–24
  life, right to, 103–8
  private and family life, right to respect for, 102–3, 332–45
  selective abortion
    Article 2, 103–8
    Article 3, 112–16
    Article 8, 102–3
    Article 14, 116–24
    discrimination, 116–24
    fetal rights or fetal value, 108–12
    generally, 102
    life, right to, 103–8
    private and family life, right to respect for, 102–3
    torture or inhuman or degrading treatment, 112–16
  sex selection, 330–345
  torture or inhuman or degrading treatment, 112–16

Fetal anomaly scan, 21
Fetus
  acquisition of interests, 23
  gradualist account of moral status, 2, 21–3, 25, 38, 44, 45, 47, 120
  moral status of embryo and fetus, 20–23
  personhood and, 54–6
  sentience, development of, 22–3

# Index

Flourishing
  disability, 28–9
  preimplantation genetic diagnosis (PGD), 264–70

Gradualist approach to embryo's and fetus' moral status
  embryo/fetus, 2, 21–3, 25, 38, 44, 45, 47, 222
  preimplantation genetic diagnosis (PGD), 248–9
  selective abortion, 120

Harm
  birth and, 34–48
  disability, selecting for, 297–300
  wrongful birth, 173
Harmed condition model, 27
Health, better
  preimplantation genetic diagnosis (PGD), 283–5
Human Fertilisation and Embryology Authority (HFEA); *see also* Preimplantation genetic diagnosis
  role in regulating preimplantation genetic diagnosis (PGD), 199–205
  role in establishing criteria for preimplantation genetic diagnosis (PGD), 197–9, 205–11
Human Genetics Commission (HGC); *see also* Preimplantation genetic diagnosis
  role in establishing criteria for preimplantation genetic diagnosis (PGD), 197–9, 205–11
Human rights *see* European Convention on Human Rights
Huntingtons' Chorea, 240

Impairments
  any/particular distinction, 59–62
  assumptions about, 50–54
  devaluing, 57–59
  impact of, 27–8
  interests of people with impairments, 48–65
  valuing those with, 57–9
*In vitro* fertilisation, 197
  preimplantation genetic diagnosis (PGD), 268–9

Informational duties
  *see also* Consent to prenatal screening and diagnosis
  abortion, 181–2
  abortion and rights–based approach
    medical profession, role of, 155–7
    right to abort for any reason, 153–5
    United States, 153–5
  disability, on, 50–54
  eugenics, 177
  generally, 143–4
  less serious or trivial matters, 152–3
  medical profession, role of, 155–7
  moral framework, 178–81
  nature of screening or testing, 149–53
  non-directive counselling, 147–8, 157
  prenatal screening and diagnosis, consent to
    aids not burdens, information that, 157–9
    autonomy, 157–9
    capacity, 145
    Down's syndrome, 146, 149–50
    generally, 144–15
    less serious or trivial matters, 152–3
    nature of screening or testing, 149–53
    NICE guidelines, 146
    Non-directive counselling, 147–8, 157
    offers of screening and testing, 145–9
    persuasion, 147
    purpose of screening or testing, 149–53
    rights, 151–3
    rights–based abortion, 153–7
    termination after, 148–19
    undue influence, 147
    voluntariness, 145–9
  purpose of screening or testing, 149–53
  reasons for exercising reproductive autonomy, 178–85
    abortion law, in, 181–2
    rights and, 151–3
    seriousness, 185–7
    wrongful birth, 144, 160–78, 182–5
Intelligence
  preimplantation genetic diagnosis (PGD), 280–83

Lesch-Nyhan disease, 30, 223

362  *Index*

Life, right to
  European Convention on Human
    Rights, 103–8

Non-person–affecting principles
  preimplantation genetic diagnosis
    (PGD), 202–3, 297–300
  reproductive autonomy, 38–48, 64–5
  selection practices, 38–48, 64–5
Nuchal translucency scan, 21, 177
Nurturing
  raising children, 13

PGD *see* Preimplantation genetic diagnosis
    (PGD)
PND *see* Prenatal screening and diagnosis
    (PND)
Poverty, family
  disabled child, 17
Preimplantation genetic diagnosis (PGD)
  achondroplasia, 314–15
  advantages, 243
  aesthetic/trivial features, selection for or
      against, 260–79
    central versus marginal features,
        261–4
    child's interests, 264–70
    embryo, claims of the, 270–74
    flourishing, 264–70
    impairments, interests of those with,
        275–7
    legalisation, 277–29
    meaning of serious/trivial distinction,
        260–61
    parents' interests and attitudes, 261–4
    professionals' role, 274–5
    treatment/enhancement continuum,
        261
  *in vitro* fertilisation, 269–70
  aptitudes or abilities, 285–8
  background, 199–205
  criteria, established by Human
      Fertilisation and Embryology
      Authority (HFEA) and Human
      Genetics Commission (HGC),
      205–11
    generally, 205–7
    PGD guidance, 209–11
    serious genetic condition, 208–9

    significant risk, 207–8, 212–13
  criteria for performance, 197
  cystic fibrosis, 225–8, 315–18
  deafness, 300–304, 309–3123
  'designer babies', 247
  developments, 1
  disability, selecting for, 297–319
    achondroplasia, 314–15
    cystic fibrosis, 315–18
    deafness, 300–304, 309–13
    Down's syndrome, 315–18
    harm, 297–300
    implications, 318–19
    non-identity problem, 304–7
    non-person–affecting principles,
        297–300
    parents' possible interests, 307–9
    person-affecting principles, 297–300
    third-party assistance, 307–9
  disabled child
    avoidance of birth, 20–21
    testing, 20–21
  Down's syndrome, 228–37, 315–18
  Duchenne muscular dystrophy, 221–3
  eugenics, 249–52
  future scope, 247–95
    aesthetic/trivial features, selection for
        or against, 260–79
    eugenics, 249–52
    interests at stake, 252–88
    legal status of embryo, 253–6
    moral status of embryo, 253–6
    reasons for choosing between
        possible lives, 252–88
    serious genetic anomalies, selecting
        against, 257–9
    subject of moral concern, 256–7
    trivial use of embryos, fears of,
        249–52
  gradualist approach to embryo's moral
      status, 2, 21–3, 25, 38, 44, 45,
      248–9
  health, better, 283–25
  health professionals' views
    generally, 211
    serious genetic condition, 213–43
    significant risk, 212–13
  Human Fertilisation and Embryology
      Authority (HFEA)

role in regulating preimplantation
     genetic diagnosis (PGD),
     199–205
role in establishing criteria for
     preimplantation genetic
     diagnosis (PGD), 197–9,
     205–11
Human Genetics Commission (HGC)
role in establishing criteria for
     preimplantation genetic
     diagnosis (PGD), 197–9,
     205–11
Huntingtons' Chorea, 240
impairments, interests of those with,
     255–7
*in vitro* fertilisation, 268–9
intelligence, 280–83
interests at stake, 252–88
interpretation of law, 197–246
legal context, 199–205
legal status of embryo, 253–6
Lesch-Nyhan disease, 223
less serious conditions, 225–37
licence, granted by Human Fertilisation
     and Embryology Authority
     (HFEA), 198, 200–201
likely degree of suffering, 220–37
methods, 197–8, 199
moral status of embryo, 253–6
negative selection, 247–8
non-person–affecting principles, 202–3,
     297–300
operation of law, 197–246
peer reviewers, 204
person-affecting principles, 297–300
PGD guidance, 209–11
positive selection, 248
prenatal screening and diagnosis (PND)
     and, 253
processes of, 270–74
professionals involved in, 204–5, 274–5
purpose, 197
reasons for choosing between possible
     lives, 252–88
regulation, 200
reproductive autonomy, 248
rights-based approach, 248
scientists' views
     aptitudes or abilities, 285–8
     generally, 211
     serious genetic condition, 213–43
     significant risk, 212–13

serious features, selection in favour of,
     279–88
health, better, 283–5
intelligence, 280–83
serious genetic condition, 208–9, 257–9
cystic fibrosis, 225–8
degeneration in progressive disorders,
     240–42
Down's syndrome, 228–37
Duchenne muscular dystrophy,
     221–2
family circumstances, 238–9
health professionals' views, 213–43
Huntingtons' Chorea, 240
intellectual impairment, extent of,
     237
Lesch-Nyhan disease, 223
less serious conditions, 225–37
likely degree of suffering, 220–37
Nuffield report, 224
persons seeking treatment of
     condition, view of, 214–20
reproductive experience of persons
     seeking treatment, 242–3
social support, availability of, 237–8
Tay-Sachs disease, 221, 224
therapy, availability of, 239
very serious conditions, 220–24
sex selection, 319–45
significant risk, 197, 207–8, 212–13
stages in, 199
subject of moral concern, 256–7
Tay-Sachs disease, 221–4
testing process, 20–21
tests that can be performed, 204
timing of screening or testing, 21
treatment/enhancement continuum,
     261
trivial features *see* aesthetic/trivial
     features, selection for or against
     *above*
trivial use of embryos, fears of, 249–52
uses, 297–349
very serious conditions, 220–24
Prenatal screening and diagnosis (PND)
     *see also* Informational duties
abortion, 181–12
developments, 1
disabled child
     avoidance of birth, 20
preimplantation genetic diagnosis
     (PGD) and, 253

364  *Index*

rights-based abortion, 153–5
   timing of test, 21
Private and family life, right to respect for
   European Convention on Human
      Rights, 102–3, 332–45
   sex selection, 332–45
Professionals
   abortion, role in, 155–7
   preimplantation genetic diagnosis
      (PGD), 204–5, 211–43, 274–5
Public policy
   wrongful birth, 189

Quality of life
   disabled child, 17

Reproductive autonomy
   choosing whether to have child, 12–14
   collective duty to reproduce, possible 13
   criticisms, 14
   defence of notion, 14–15
   eugenics, 65–7
   expressivist objection, 54–65
   freedom to avoid reproduction, 16
   full-blown autonomy, 13
   genetic connection, 12–13
   informational duties *see* Informational
      duties
   meaning, 13
   moral status of embryo and fetus, 20–23
   non-person–affecting principles, 38–48,
      64–65
   positive duties in raising children,
      15–20
   preimplantation genetic diagnosis
      (PGD), 248
   reasons to exercise, 182–5
   scope, 23–6
   selection practices
      abortion, 23
      any/particular distinction, 59–62
      birth and harm, 34–48
      choosing whether to have child,
         12–14
      collective duty to reproduce, possible
         13
      disability 26–34
         *see also* Disability
      eugenics, 65–7
      exercise, 12
      expressivist objection, 54–65
      full-blown autonomy, 13

genetic connection, 12–13
interests, 24–5
interweaving parents' and children's
   interests, 62–4
moral interests, 13–14
moral status of embryo and fetus,
   20–23
non-person–affecting principles,
   38–48, 64–5
nurturing experience, 13
opportunity, 64–6
person-affecting principles, 38–48
positive duties in raising children,
   15–20
possibility of disabled child, 14–15
quality of life, 17
rights, 23–4
scope of autonomy, 13
scope of reproductive autonomy,
   23–5
self-determination, 13–14, 25
self-expression, 14
trivial concerns, 25–6
self-determination, 13–14
self-expression, 14
United States, 182–5

Selection practices
   birth and harm, 34–48
   disabled child
      factors influencing, 19
      positive duties in raising children,
         15–20
      possibility, 14–15
   eugenics, 65–7
   expressivist objection, 54–65
   non-person–affecting principles, 38–48,
      64–5
   reproductive autonomy
      abortion, 23
      any/particular distinction, 59–62
      birth and harm, 34–48
      choosing whether to have child,
         12–14
      collective duty to reproduce, possible
         13
      disability 26–34
         *see also* Disability
      eugenics, 65–7
      exercise, 12
      expressivist objection, 54–65
      factors influencing decisions, 19

full-blown autonomy, 13
genetic connection, 12–13
interests, 24–5
moral interests, 13–14
moral status of embryo and fetus, 20–23
non-person–affecting principles, 38–48, 64–5
nurturing experience, 13
opportunity, 64–6
person-affecting principles, 38–48
positive duties in raising children, 15–20
possibility of disabled child, 14–15
quality of life, 17
rights, 23–4
risk averse individuals, 16
scope of autonomy, 13
scope of reproductive autonomy, 23–5
self-determination, 13–14, 25
trivial concerns, 25–6
self-expression
reproductive autonomy, 14
trivial concerns, 25–6
Selective abortion
Abortion Act, disability ground of
fetal anomaly after 24 weeks, 119–37
legal interests of parents, 89–94
serious handicap, 76–86
substantial risk, 73–6
discretion of doctors, 71–2
European Convention on Human Rights
Article 2, 103–8
Article 3, 112–16
Article 8, 102–3
Article 14, 116–24
discrimination, 116–24
fetal rights or fetal value, 108–12
generally, 102
life, right to, 103–8
private and family life, right to respect for, 102–3
torture or inhuman or degrading treatment, 112–16
fetal anomaly after 24 weeks, 119–37
burden on others, 135–6
fetus's interests, 124–34
gradualist approach to fetus's moral status, 2, 21–3, 25, 38, 44, 45, 47, 120

maternal interests, 120, 122–4
Nuffield Report, 119, 121
overall factors, 134–7
possible reasons for, 120–21
severity of handicap, 136–7
statistics, 119–20
suffering of the child, 134, 135
suffering of the mother, 134, 135
good faith judgment of doctors, 72
gradualist approach to fetus's moral status, 2, 21–3, 25, 38, 44, 45, 47, 120
Hansard guidance
serious handicap, 76–7
substantial risk, 73
interpretation of law, 71–141
law, 71–141
legal interests, parents'
disability ground of Abortion Act, 89–94
wrongful birth cases, 94–102
medical opinion, 72–3
moral interests of parents, 86–9
parents' moral interests, 86–9
RCOG guidelines
serious handicap, 77–86
substantial risk, 73–6
serious handicap
Hansard guidance, 76–7
live alone and be self-supporting, probability of being able to, 85–6
RCOG guidelines, 77–86
self-awareness and ability to communicate, probability of, 81–2
suffering that would be experienced, 82–3
treatment *in utero* or after birth, probability of effective, 78–81
substantial risk
Hansard guidance, 73
RCOG guidelines, 73–6
wrongful birth cases, 94–102
Self-determination
reproductive autonomy, 13–14, 25
Self-expression
reproductive autonomy, 14
Serious genetic condition
cystic fibrosis, 225–8
degeneration in progressive disorders, 240–42

Down's syndrome, 228–37
Duchenne muscular dystrophy, 221–2
intellectual impairment, extent of, 237
Lesch-Nyhan disease, 223
less serious conditions, 225–37
preimplantation genetic diagnosis (PGD), 208–9
  cystic fibrosis, 225–8
  degeneration in progressive disorders, 240–42
  Down's syndrome, 228–37
  Duchenne muscular dystrophy, 221–3
  family circumstances, 238–9
  health professionals' views, 213–43
  Huntingtons' Chorea, 240
  intellectual impairment, extent of, 237
  Lesch-Nyhan disease, 223
  less serious conditions, 225–37
  likely degree of suffering, 220–37
  person seeking treatment of condition, view of, 214–20
  reproductive experience of persons seeking treatment, 242–3
  social support, availability of, 237–8
  Tay-Sachs disease, 221, 224
  therapy, availability of, 239
  very serious conditions, 220–24
Tay-Sachs disease, 221, 224
very serious conditions, 220–24
Serious handicap
  Hansard guidance, 76–7
  live alone and be self-supporting, probability of being able to, 85–6
  RCOG guidelines, 77–86
  self-awareness and ability to communicate, probable degree of, 81–2
  suffering that would be experienced, 82–3
  treatment *in utero* or after birth, probability of effective, 78–81
  wrongful birth cases, 185–7
Sex selection
  children's interests, 321–6
  clinicians, views of, 326–7
  discrimination, 320
  embryo, claims of the, 323–6
  European Convention on Human Rights, 330–45

family balancing, 322
impairments, views of those with, 326–7
justification for legal prohibition, arguments regarding, 327–45
parents' interests, 321–6
preimplantation genetic diagnosis (PGD), 319–45
scientists', views of, 326–7
Significant risk
  preimplantation genetic diagnosis (PGD), 197, 207–8, 212–13
Social model of disability, 27, 28
Standard of care
  wrongful birth, 168–9, 169–78
Substantial risk
  Hansard guidance, 73
  RCOG guidelines, 73–6

Tay-Sachs disease, 29, 32, 33, 35, 36, 37, 221–4
Torture or inhuman or degrading treatment
  European Convention on Human Rights, 112–16
Trivial matters
  informational duties, 152–3
  selection practices, 25–6
  wrongful birth, 190

United States
  reproductive autonomy, 182–5
  wrongful birth, 161, 166–7, 174–5, 182–5

Warnock Report, 255–6
Wrongful birth, 26, 96–102
  basis of action, 166–9
  conscience of medical profession, 162–6
  degree of harm, 173
  disability ground of Abortion Act, 94–102, 161
  Down's syndrome, 173–4
  future scope of action, 187–92
  informational duties, 144, 160–78, 182–5
  mid-spectrum disabilities, 188
  public policy, 189
  reasons to exercise reproductive autonomy, 182–5
  reports, influence of, 189

risk of a given fetal condition, 172–8
scope of action, 187–92
seriousness, 185–7
source of duty to provide information, 160–62

standard of care, 168–9, 169–78
trivial matters, 190
United States, 161, 166–7, 174–5, 182–5